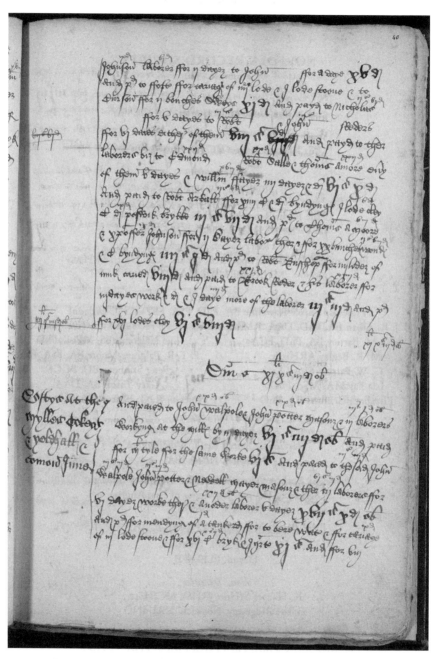

Frontispiece: A page from the chamberlain's account for 1539–40
(Norfolk Record Office, NCR, 18A/6, f. 40)

THE NORWICH
CHAMBERLAINS' ACCOUNTS
1539–40 to 1544–5

Edited by
Carole Rawcliffe

General Editor
Elizabeth Rutledge

Norfolk Record Society
Volume LXXXIII
2019

© The Norfolk Record Society, 2019

First published in 2019
by the Norfolk Record Society

ISBN 978-0-9957736-2-2

Typeset by Carnegie Book Production, Lancaster
Printed and bound by Short Run Press, Exeter

Dedicated to the memory of
Peter Martin

Contents

Maps, illustrations and plates

The author and publishers are grateful to Mr Brian Ayers and to the institutions listed above for permission to reproduce those images in which they hold copyright and to the Norfolk Museums Service for permission to use the painting of Norwich Market Cross by Thomas Hearne on the cover.

Acknowledgements

Work on this volume began eleven years ago, when, as the recipient of an AHRC Impact Award, I collaborated with Dr Christopher Bonfield on the production of a website on the history of the Norwich Blackfriars. My role on the project was to transcribe and edit extracts from relevant manuscripts, among which the chamberlains' accounts occupied pride of place. They were, indeed, so fascinating that I promptly submitted a proposal to the Norfolk Record Society for the publication of a scholarly edition, to appear at some unspecified future date. Inevitably, given the time that has elapsed since then, I have accumulated many debts, not least to the staff of the Norfolk Record Office, whose outstanding reputation for helpfulness and courtesy is richly deserved. The former county archivist, Dr John Alban, and his successor, Dr Gary Tuson, have offered generous support, as has Mr Tom Townsend, who dealt expertly and patiently with questions about the Norwich city records in his charge. His excellent catalogue of the chamberlains' rolls greatly facilitated my research. I am additionally indebted to Dr Tuson for permission to publish material from this remarkable archive. Thanks are also due to the staff of the British Library, the Institute of Historical Research, the National Archives, the Library of the Society of Antiquaries and the Warburg Institute in London, and of the University of East Anglia Library and the Heritage Centre at the Forum in Norwich.

I am grateful to the Centre of East Anglian Studies at UEA for a travel grant to cover some of my trips to London, and to the support staff of the School of History for their constant good humour in the face of technological incompetence. My early modern colleagues have guided a hesitant medievalist through the maze of Tudor history, offering valuable bibliographical advice and other useful suggestions. Dr Isla Fay kindly provided me with copies of her own transcripts of material from the chamberlains' accounts; Professor Matthew Woodcock advised me about music, drama and spectacle in sixteenth-century Norwich; Dr Stephen O'Connor helped to solve some knotty palaeographical problems; and Mr Brian Ayers responded with his customary alacrity to requests for information, books and images. Ms Cath D'Alton drew the maps. I owe a great deal to

Mr Alasdair Hawkyard for sharing with me his encyclopaedic knowledge of Tudor parliaments, to Dr Linda Clark for innumerable acts of kindness and to Ms Elizabeth Danbury, who far exceeded the demands of friendship by reading and commenting on an early draft of the Introduction. Especial thanks go to the series editor, Ms Elizabeth Rutledge, who has meticulously checked successive print-outs of the entire book, greatly improving both its layout and content. It has been a privilege to work with such a distinguished scholar and to benefit from her editorial expertise. Any lingering errors that have escaped her eagle eye are entirely my own.

This book is dedicated to the memory of my late partner, Peter Martin, who died in 2014, having been an unfailing source of support, reassurance and encouragement for the best part of thirty years. It could not, and would not, have been produced without him.

Carole Rawcliffe
Norwich 2019

Abbreviations

DCN	Dean and Chapter of Norwich
HoP, 1509-1558	S.T. Bindoff, ed., *History of Parliament: The Commons, 1509-1558* (3 vols, 1982)
INCO	T. Hawes, ed., *An Index to Norwich City Officers* (NRS, lii, 1986)
LPFD	Brewer, J.S., and others, *Calendar of Letters and Papers Foreign and Domestic for the Reign of Henry VIII* (21 vols, and 2 vols of *Addenda*, 1862-1932)
MFS	C. Rawcliffe, *Medicine for the Soul: The Life, Death and Resurrection of an English Medieval Hospital* (Stroud, 1999)
MN	C. Rawcliffe and R. Wilson, eds, *Medieval Norwich* (2004)
NA	*Norfolk Archaeology*
NCC	Norwich Consistory Court
NCR	Norwich City Records
NRO	Norfolk Record Office
NRS	Norfolk Record Society
ODNB	H.C.G. Matthew, ed., *The Oxford Dictionary of National Biography* (60 vols and index, Oxford, 2004)
RCN	W.H. Hudson and J.C. Tingey, eds, *Records of the City of Norwich* (2 vols, Norwich, 1906, 1910)
SLCN	J. Kirkpatrick, *The Streets and Lanes of the City of Norwich*, ed. W. Hudson (Norwich, 1889)
TNA	The National Archives, Kew
VCH	*The Victoria County History*

Introduction

From the character of the books it will readily be believed that this narrative is not related in a flowing story enlivened by Gibbon-like antitheses, but hinted rather than told in a succession of short and apparently disjointed entries, each of which records a throb of the city pulse [...] But these statements are not really disjointed, and those who know how to read these records aright may so put together the pieces of the puzzle as to obtain a series of pictures of English life in a provincial city.

J. Brigstocke Sheppard, 1883[1]

Norwich is notable for the profusion of its early sixteenth-century archives, which cast light on a wealth of topics, ranging from civic government, law, order and rebellion to charitable relief, public health, architecture and the impact of religious change. The chamberlains' accounts furnish a particularly vivid insight into the life of the city and its inhabitants, extending far beyond the basic issues of corporate income and expenditure which were their primary, but by no means sole, concern. The chamberlain of Tudor Bristol, whose role was very similar to that of his peers in Norwich, has been described as 'the manager of the corporation, its Chancellor of the Exchequer and Minister of Works'.[2] Indeed, the scope of his activities and

---

1 J. Brigstocke Sheppard, 'The Records of the City of Canterbury', *Historical Manuscripts Commission, IX, Part I* (1883), p. 131, with reference to the accounts of the city chamberlains, which survive in a 'fairly continuous series' from the late fourteenth century.

2 R.C. Latham, ed., *Bristol Charters 1509–1899* (Bristol Record Society, xii, 1947), p. 11. According to Betty Masters, the chamberlain of London was both 'the chief executive officer of the city' and 'the corporation's treasurer and banker': B.R. Masters, ed., *Chamber Accounts of the Sixteenth Century* (London Record Society, x, 1984), p. xxxiii; *eadem, The Chamberlain of the City of London 1237–1987* (1988), p. 1.

responsibilities, as initially defined by a royal charter of 1499, has prompted the observation that, generally speaking, the reputation of any English town or city could at this time 'be made or lost' in accordance with the capabilities of its chamberlains.[3]

Local antiquarians, such as John Kirkpatrick (d. 1728) and Francis Blomefield (d. 1752), have long recognised the importance of the Norwich chamberlains' accounts;[4] and a number of historians have more recently mined them for information about the late medieval and Tudor city.[5] A few short extracts from accounts spanning the years 1449 to 1545 were included by William Hudson and J.C. Tingey in the second volume of their *Records of the City of Norwich* (1910),[6] but none of these remarkable documents has yet been edited in its entirety. This omission may be partly because, on first reading, much of the detail that they contain can seem both repetitive and prosaic. Yet closer inspection soon reveals a very different picture. F.W. Brooks' contention that the rolls and paper books compiled by the chamberlains of York are in many respects 'the most rewarding of the civic records' reflects the value of such documents as an historical source.[7]

The six accounts presented in this volume add appreciably to our knowledge of urban topography and the nature of the built environment, while furnishing invaluable evidence about the upkeep and governance of what was then England's second largest city. Although it is now overshadowed by the traumatic events of Kett's Rebellion and its brutal aftermath,[8] the period that they cover was of particular moment in the history of Norwich, since it saw the acquisition of the Blackfriars complex by the city following the dissolution of monastic houses in the late 1530s.[9]

---

3 H.A. Cronne, ed., *Bristol Charters 1378–1499* (Bristol Record Society, xi, 1946), p. 12.

4 They are widely cited throughout *SLCN* and F. Blomefield, *An Essay towards a Topographical History of the County of Norfolk* (11 vols, 1805–10), iii and iv.

5 See, for example, A. King, 'The Merchant Class and Borough Finances of Late Medieval Norwich' (2 vols, Oxford University D.Phil. thesis, 1989), ii, chapters nine and ten; I. Faye, *Health and the City: Disease, Environment and the Government of Norwich, 1200–1575* (Woodbridge, 2015); and D. Galloway, ed., *Records of Early English Drama: Norwich 1540–1642* (Toronto, 1984).

6 *RCN*, ii, pp. 73–6.

7 F.W. Brooks, 'York – 1066 to Present Day', in A.L. Stacpoole, ed., *The Noble City of York* (York, 1972), p. 274. He describes the chamberlains, who were often owed money, as 'guardians of the city's overdraft'.

8 A. Wood, 'Kett's Rebellion', in *MN*, pp. 277–99.

9 For the significance of the Dissolution in the context of urban history, see R. Tittler, 'Reformation, Resources and Authority in English Towns: An Overview', in P. Collinson and J. Craig, eds, *The Reformation in English Towns 1500–1640* (Basingstoke, 1998), pp. 190–201.

While directing and financing its conversion into a unique public amenity that included a banqueting hall, communal granary, chapel, preaching yard, landing stathes and free school, the chamberlains had to contend with additional financial pressures occasioned by costly wars in France and a challenging combination of inflation, poor harvests and economic stagnation at home. The administrative demands involved led, in turn, to significant changes in the way that one of the chamberlains drew up his accounts. Since the traditional layout (which was medieval in origin) made it difficult to keep a close track of the cumulative cost and progress of so many ongoing projects, a more accessible, better-organised and clearer format was adopted. This pragmatic response in turn reflects the increasing bureaucratisation of urban government, so apparent during the later sixteenth century but already discernible in Norwich at this point.[10]

The civic background

According to estimates based upon the lay subsidy return of 1525, the population of Norwich then stood somewhere between 8,500 and 12,700, having perhaps been slightly higher at the start of the sixteenth century.[11] It continued to stagnate until the arrival of the Dutch and Walloon 'Strangers' later in the century, in part because of the frequent epidemics that affected most urban communities during the period. But whereas some English towns and cities were prosperous enough to attract new workers, Norwich, a cloth-producing centre, fell victim to a protracted slump in the international textile trade, which rapidly spread to other sectors. Steadily rising food prices and sporadic grain shortages compounded the problem. In November 1532, following one unusually bad harvest, the mayor informed Thomas Cromwell that he had never seen such 'povurte here that ys now & ydyllnese'. The price of wool was so high, he complained, 'that yt dekaye all the comodyte that be made theroff', resulting in wholesale unemployment and destitution.[12] Matters had hardly improved by the end of the decade,

---

10 P. Griffiths, 'Bodies and Souls in Norwich: Punishing Petty Crime, 1540–1700', in P. Griffiths and S. Devereaux, eds, *Penal Practice and Culture 1500–1900* (Basingstoke, 2003), pp. 89–90.

11 J. Pound, *Tudor and Stuart Norwich* (Chichester, 1988), p. 28, suggests a minimum population of 8,482, although he had previously favoured a more buoyant 12,726: 'The Social and Trade Structure of Norwich, 1525–1575', *Past & Present*, 34 (1966), pp. 49–69, on p. 50. King, 'Merchant Class and Borough Finances', i, pp. 24–7, opts for a figure of about 11,000 at this time, following a fall from 12,000 at the start of the century.

12 TNA, SP1/72, f. 17.

when the rulers of Norwich petitioned Henry VIII for possession of the recently dissolved Blackfriars' complex. Although due allowance should be made for special pleading, their reference to 'the verey vtter decaye of the sale of worstedis & sayes, as also of suche other thyngis as haue bene accustomed to be made within your gracis pouer citie' rings true.[13] The devastating plague of 1544–5 and the dearth that followed caused further dislocation, as poor people flocked to the city from the surrounding countryside, seeking relief.[14] It is hard to tell how far the dissolution of the city's monastic houses and threatened closure of three of its hospitals may have accelerated this recession and increased the incidence of poverty.[15] By February 1545 the situation had grown so alarming that the mayor commissioned a survey of the number of beggars resident in Norwich and the length of their stay within the walls.[16] Already, in 1543, in compliance with government legislation, the chamberlain had taken delivery of 184 tin badges to be worn by those with an official licence to seek alms in public, but these comparatively fortunate individuals were only the tip of a looming iceberg.[17] Initially undertaken on an experimental basis, the debasement of English coinage became a matter of fiscal policy from 1544 onward; the poor inevitably suffered most from the inflation and uncertainty that followed.[18]

In such testing times, when even slight fluctuations in the price of basic commodities had serious repercussions for its economy, Norwich was particularly vulnerable to the demands of the Crown, not just for money but for the men and supplies needed for defence at home and warfare abroad. It has long been recognized that Henry VIII tightened every available screw upon his subjects in order to finance the disastrous military campaigns of his last years;[19] and the impact of his policies is clearly apparent in the civic records. The provision of fully armed levies and ordnance was an expensive business, as the chamberlains' accounts reveal, and could place an intolerable

---

13 NCR, 8K/7 (b). At this time the assembly proposed to use the reserves of defunct religious guilds to combat 'the ruynous decaye off the same citie': NCR, 16D/2, f. 188ᵛ.

14 P. Slack, *The Impact of Plague in Tudor and Stuart England* (1989), pp. 127–8.

15 B. Ayers, 'Post-Medieval Archaeology in Norwich: A Review', *Post-Medieval Archaeology*, 25 (1991), pp. 1–23, on p. 3; R. Tittler, *The Reformation and the Towns in England: Politics and Political Culture c. 1540–1640* (Oxford, 1998), pp. 135–6; *MFS*, chapter seven.

16 *RCN*, ii, pp. cii, 172; NCR, 16A/5, p. 265.

17 See below, p. 205.

18 C.E. Challis, *The Tudor Coinage* (Manchester, 1978), pp. 81–105, 248–57. The chamberlain's account for 1544–5 contains references to losses through debased coinage, which had to be made good: below, p. 340.

19 F. Dietz, *English Public Finance 1485–1558* (Urbana, Illinois, 1920), pp. 144–58; J.J. Scarisbrick, *Henry VIII* (1968), p. 454.

strain on an already overstretched budget.[20] In May 1544 the mayor's court took the unprecedented step of cancelling the annual guild pageants because of the cost of sending men to France, supplying provisions for the royal army and supporting an already worrying number of 'pore people'.[21] Even more desperate measures followed four months later, when it was agreed 'upon various considerations' that the customary annual rate for cleaning the river would not be raised and that the mayor would not be fined for failing to undertake this important task.[22] The dredging of the Wensum and removal of accumulated waste were vital for commerce as well as health, and cannot have been abandoned lightly.[23] The paving and upkeep of the streets, which had previously been a source of great communal pride, also suffered. By the middle of the century the civic authorities reflected sadly upon the 'disworshipp' occasioned by their inability 'to maynteyne that thing which heretofore by ther predecessors have ben well maynteyned and lokyd unto'.[24] Efforts to remedy the 'fowle and fylthye' condition of the streets and clear the river, through the setting up of a special committee in 1552, drew specific attention to the longstanding 'wante of money' that had hitherto taken such a heavy toll upon the city's infrastructure.[25]

As Norwich's chief financial officers with specific responsibility for the maintenance of communal resources, the chamberlains who were elected during this difficult period faced daunting problems. In many respects, theirs was an experience shared by other chamberlains in other cities, as the London records confirm. In 1547 George Medley, who had served as

---

20 'Assessments' upon the residents for this purpose came to over £60 in 1542, £80 in 1544 and £50 in 1545 (below, pp. 124, 245, 302), while the production and transport of six guns for the royal army in France cost £46, less a rebate of £6 for unused metal (pp. 307, 322–3). When authorising these rates, the assembly stressed that poor people were not to be taxed (NCR, 16D/2, ff. 207, 211ᵛ), but the chamberlains still found it hard to meet their targets. Additionally, residents with goods worth over 20s had to contribute to the parliamentary subsidy of 1543, although the ceiling was raised to 100s in 1545: R. Hoyle, 'War and Public Finance', in D. MacCulloch, ed., *The Reign of Henry VIII: Politics, Policy and Piety* (1995), pp. 96–8.

21 NCR, 16A/5, p. 216. This measure was repeated in 1546 and 1547: NCR, 16D/2, ff. 213, 215.

22 NCR, 16D/2, f. 207ᵛ. This ruling was repeated in the following year (f. 211).

23 C. Rawcliffe, *Urban Bodies: Communal Health in Late Medieval English Towns and Cities* (Woodbridge, 2013), pp. 217–21.

24 *RCN*, ii, pp. 133–4. The walls were also in a state of 'gret decaye': Faye, *Health and the City*, pp. 22–3.

25 *RCN*, ii, p. 127; I. Fay, ed., 'The Norwich River and Street Accounts, 1557–61 and 1570–80', in E. Phillips and I. Fay, eds, *Health and Hygiene in Early-Modern Norwich* (NRS, lxxvii, 2013), p. 109.

chamberlain there since 1534, was excused further involvement in civic government for a lengthy period 'in recompense of the exceptional burden of his financial responsibilities during the past few years in connection with the new conduits, the provision of corn for the city, the setting forth of soldiers and other extraordinary burdens'.[26] It is hardly coincidental that the energetic and open-handed John Willis, who held office in Bristol between 1540 and 1548, subsidising many projects from his own purse, was hailed as 'the best chamberlain that ever was'.[27] The situation in Norwich was, however, compounded by specific local issues, including the long-term effects of the two devastating fires of 1507, which had destroyed at least 40 per cent of the city's housing stock. The process of clearing wasteland and rebuilding property continued throughout the sixteenth century, posing a major challenge as well as an opportunity for those in authority.[28]

Floods caused further destruction. In August 1542 torrential rain, eloquently described as 'the gret rage', damaged street surfaces, gutters and some of the city's many culverted streams, which became clogged with filth. Piles of muck and debris accumulated in public thoroughfares, adding to the mounting heaps of refuse (including a 'gret hylle' of manure next to the church of St Peter Mancroft) that had already begun to present a serious nuisance.[29] When repaving part of the market in the following year, the chamberlain, Robert Raynbald, reported that 'many gret holes' initially dug to provide sand for the masons had been filled by fly-tippers, causing extensive subsidence.[30] His programme of improvements none the less seemed inadequate, for in 1543–4 the sheriffs' court demanded that he should do more to clean up the castle ditches 'and other noyfull stretes in

---

26 Masters, ed., *Chamber Accounts*, p. xxxiv.

27 F.F. Fox, ed., *Adams's Chronicle of Bristol* (Bristol, 1910), p. 110; D.M. Livock, ed., *City Chamberlains' Accounts in the Sixteenth and Seventeenth Centuries* (Bristol Record Society, xxiv, 1966), p. xii.

28 Ayers, 'Post-Medieval Archaeology', p. 5; Tittler, *Reformation*, pp. 99–100; Fay, *Health and the City*, pp. 23, 78, 153. Recovery was discernible by 1547, in part because of tax concessions and communal investment. The assembly then announced that certain wards of the city, 'which wer beffor decayed [...] be at this present tyme (thankes be to God) well encresid, replenysshed & augmented': NCR, 16D/2, f. 220ᵛ.

29 Fay, 'Norwich River and Street Accounts', p. 108; *eadem, Health and the City*, pp. 156–7; below, pp. 140–1, 196, 191–3. In a city as hilly as Norwich, the effective disposal of rainwater posed constant difficulties: E. Rutledge, 'An Urban Environment: Norwich in the Fifteenth Century', *The Fifteenth Century*, 12 (2013), pp. 79–93, on p. 86.

30 See below, p. 193. Raynbald was himself guilty in this regard. While serving as chamberlain, he was fined 3s 4d by a local court for digging a pit 'jubardus [*dangerous*] for man and beste' near his home in Conesford: NCR, 5D/2.

the cite'.[31] Evidence that the market 'was growen greene dyuers tymes with grasse' in 1545 certainly suggests that the recession had tightened its grip, as does Raynbald's recourse to the strong-arm tactics of the ward constables in order to collect money for the third contingent of soldiers that had been mobilised within four years.[32]

Despite these vicissitudes, parts of Norwich still flourished, reflecting the uneven distribution of resources characteristic of all sixteenth-century English cities, and, indeed, the important distinction to be drawn between corporate and individual wealth.[33] The lay subsidy return of 1525 reveals that 60 per cent of its taxable assets were concentrated in the hands of just 6 per cent of the taxable population. Bearing in mind that 40 per cent of taxpayers reputedly earned 20s a year or less, and that at least a quarter of the inhabitants lacked the resources to make any contribution at all, the disparities between rich and poor must have seemed overwhelming.[34] Simmering below the surface, tensions between the civic elite, as personified by the twenty-four scarlet-robed aldermen, and those of the moderately affluent 'middling sort' were hardly new, but they, too, were further exacerbated by the added pressures described above. Attempts to raise a tax in 1542 towards the king's Scottish campaigns met with widespread resistance and allegations that the aldermen had rigged the assessment in order to avoid paying their share.[35]

Calumnies of this kind were particularly unsettling because participation in the higher levels of civic government brought with it an obligation to underwrite communal expenses and assist the less fortunate, or at least those who seemed deserving of support. During the grain shortage of 1545, for instance, the mayor personally donated 100 combs of wheat for 'the releeff of the pore people', while five of the aldermen provided a further fifty. Their less altruistic colleagues were ordered to follow suit at once or pay 30s to the chamberlain, who was responsible for the purchase, storage and distribution

---

31 See below, p. 254.

32 See below, pp. 312, 341.

33 King, 'Merchant Class and Borough Finances', i, p. 6. For the concrete expression of commercial success and political status by the ruling elite, see C. King, 'The Interpretation of Urban Buildings: Power, Meaning and Appropriation in Norwich Merchants' Houses, c. 1400–1660', *World Archaeology*, 41 (2009), pp. 471–88.

34 Pound, *Tudor and Stuart Norwich*, pp. 31–2. Norwich paid more into the royal coffers at this time than any other provincial city: W.G. Hoskins, 'Provincial Towns in the Early Sixteenth Century', *Transactions of the Royal Historical Society*, fifth series, 6 (1956), pp. 1–19, on p. 4.

35 NCR, 16A/5, pp. 37–43; and below, p. 168, where the chamberlains report a shortfall of about 10 per cent in the sums collected.

of subsidised grain supplies.[36] In general, however, a combination of public duty, religious faith and a less charitable fear of popular unrest ensured that assistance would generally be forthcoming in emergencies. In response to the crisis described above, Edmund Wood (d. 1548) left £100 in his will towards the cleaning of the streets, a further £20 for dredging the river, £40 to lay in stores of wheat or wool for emergencies, £40 for the education of youngsters from poor homes and £20 for 'healing poore diseased personnes'.[37] He may well have been inspired by the example of one of his predecessors, Robert Jannys (d. 1530), whose stained glass image presided over the new assembly chamber in the guildhall, its accompanying verses urging those below to leave behind an appropriate 'memoriall' in the form of good works devoted to civic improvement.[38]

Major projects, such as the construction of the massive market cross at the beginning of the century and the creation of a more imposing assembly chamber in 1532–4, relied heavily upon private funding.[39] A strong element of civic pride, intellectual commitment to the ideals of Christian humanism and even, perhaps, a hint of one-upmanship, prompted many individuals to dig deep into their pockets. Some, however, required more persuasion. As was the case regarding the purchase and conversion of the Blackfriars complex in the 1540s,[40] the aldermen and wealthier citizens were expected to offer voluntary contributions as an act of 'benevolence'. In practice, as subjects of Edward IV and Henry VII had previously discovered, the term masked a harsher element of compulsion. The eighteen prominent donors who furnished the chamberlains with over £19 in 1542–3 for the construction of utilities for the new banqueting hall evidently did so freely, although it is uncertain if all of the 235 individuals listed in Robert Raynbald's account for 1544–5 were quite so enthusiastic.[41] On 21 August 1545 the assembly decreed that any citizen who had hitherto withheld a donation towards 'the gret costes & charges' sustained at Blackfriars should be assessed and *ordered* to make an appropriate offering.[42] In this way, and in the face of

---

36 NCR, 16A/5, p. 293; below, pp. 243, 246, 270–1.

37 TNA, PROB 11/32/288.

38 Rawcliffe, *Urban Bodies*, p. 71.

39 B. Ayers, *Norwich: Archaeology of a Fine City* (Cirencester, 2009), pp. 142–3; Rawcliffe, *Urban Bodies*, pp. 358–9. The new assembly chamber reputedly owed its existence to 'the benevolence of the Aldermen, with the help of the Commons': G. Johnson, ed., 'Chronological Memoranda Touching the City of Norwich', *NA*, 1 (1847), pp. 140–66, on p. 144. Augustine Steward was certainly a major benefactor: Blomefield, *Norfolk*, iv, p. 228.

40 See below, p. 164.

41 See below, pp. 176–7, 303–6.

42 NCR, 16D/2, f. 211.

apparently insuperable economic problems, ambitious building schemes could be funded and new property bought, on the tried and tested principle that such investments would eventually pay for themselves. The success of these ventures depended in large part upon the organisational skills of the chamberlains, whose role in civic life had grown considerably over the previous century.

The office of chamberlain

The early history of Norwich's chamberlains is inextricably and sometimes confusingly linked to that of its treasurers. Although both were responsible for the management and upkeep of civic property until the mid-fifteenth century, the treasurers alone presented annual accounts for the receipts and expenses involved. The survival of Peter Flynt's accounts as treasurer for 1293–4 to 1304–5 (with gaps) points to the long history of this practice,[43] while the forty-one rolls still extant from between 1375 and 1436 provide valuable documentary evidence of the financial and administrative activities undertaken by his successors.[44] By contrast, only one chamberlains' account has come down to us from this period. It lists disbursements of £93 on the construction of the new guildhall between 1411 and 1413, which suggests that the chamberlains assumed control of major building works but otherwise adopted a purely supervisory or managerial role.[45] The apparent shortcomings of this system featured prominently among complaints levelled against the ruling elite by the wider community of enfranchised freemen in 1414, when previous treasurers stood charged not only with failing to render proper accounts but also with pocketing the substantial receipts that fell in after they had left office and for which they were still liable.[46] The recommendation that two chamberlains, elected annually by the leading citizens *and* commoners, should take control of any such revenues, making them freely available 'for the common profit and honour of the city' almost

---

43 NCR, 7A/1; *RCN*, ii, pp. 30–8.

44 NCR, 7A/2–26, 28–43.

45 NCR, 7A/27; R. Howlett, ed., 'A Fabric Roll of the Norwich Guildhall', *NA*, 15 (1904), pp. 164–89. The earlier history of their office is obscure. The Norwich custumal of *c.* 1300 notes that certain fines and forfeits were to be delivered by the bailiffs to the chamberlains, who would see that they were enrolled, account for them and ensure that they were put to communal use, but mentions no other responsibilities: *RCN*, i, pp. 183, 185.

46 *RCN*, i, pp. 73–4. A continuous run of treasurers' annual accounts survives from 1405 to 1414, disproving these allegations, although they may not have been audited in public, as was later the case: NCR, 7A/19–29.

certainly reflects a breakdown in established practice. So too does the further proposal that the treasurers should not make any payments or invest in new infrastructure without the approval of the chamberlains, who had evidently lost some of their authority.[47] The argument that 'good and certain governance' on their part would 'greatly avail and ease the commonality' was certainly not lost on Sir Thomas Erpingham, whose celebrated *Compositio*, or arbitration award, of 1415 served as the basis of civic government for the next four centuries and thus merits close examination.[48]

Among the many measures devised by Sir Thomas for the more equitable division of power between the elite and the community were provisions for the annual election, on 21 September, of the city's financial officers, who were henceforward to comprise two treasurers, four auditors to determine their account, two chamberlains and six advisers 'to be of counseil with the chamberleyns'. One chamberlain, one treasurer, two auditors and three counsellors were to be chosen by the sixty members of the newly constituted common council and the others by the twenty-four leading citizens (later known as aldermen). The latter alone were to select the common sergeant, whose task was to collect, and if necessary distrain for, the rents and other revenues that constituted the bulk of the treasurers' income. Together, these fifteen individuals would be answerable to a common assembly held between 29 September and 1 November at the end of their year in office, before which they would present a full statement of the current financial position, distinguishing sums that had still to be raised from 'redy money' already in hand. Significantly, the treasurers' personal liability for any outstanding sums charged to them at this time 'as debte be hem due' was underscored; they would have to answer to the assembly for every penny that remained unpaid or had not been allowed at the audit.[49]

The various provisions set out in the *Compositio* were further refined and developed over the next twenty years, as we can see from the oaths taken by the city's principal officers and recorded in its *Liber Albus*.[50] The treasurers

---

47 *RCN*, i, pp. 73–4.

48 *RCN*, ii, pp. 93–108. For the background to these events, see B.R. McRee, 'Peace-Making and its Limits in Medieval Norwich', *English Historical Review*, 109 (1994), pp. 831–66, on pp. 847–53.

49 *RCN*, i, p. 104.

50 Challenging the assumption of the Norfolk antiquary, Francis Blomefield, that these oaths dated from the reign of Henry VII or that of his son (*Norfolk*, iii, pp. 183–91), William Hudson and J.C. Tingey maintained that they could be no later than 1452 (*RCN*, i, p. cvi). The evidence below suggests that the oaths of the treasurers and chamberlains, at least, must have been drafted before 1445.

swore faithfully to account for everything laid to their charge and to exercise due oversight of civic property by conducting a full search of all such premises twice a quarter, accompanied by at least one of their counsellors or the town clerk and the common sergeant. Expenditure was to be recorded on a weekly basis at the guildhall every Saturday, while any outlay costing more than 40s had to be authorized in advance by the counsellors. Craftsmen and labourers employed on various projects were to be paid every week in cash rather than kind ('chaffar'), as had previously been the case.[51] The common sergeant, in turn, promised to levy any money due to the commonalty every quarter, delivering it to the treasurers within the next two months and promptly distraining or imprisoning defaulters who refused to pay. He was to be 'buxvm and obedient as well in worde and dede' to the mayor, the treasurers and their counsellors, reporting to them any suspicious persons likely to harm the city's interests and securing their approval before leasing any property or renegotiating any rents.[52] The chamberlains seem to have been temporarily side-lined, since neither of these two oaths refers to them; nor, unlike their fellows, were they required to make any formal commitment themselves. Before long, however, their status had risen dramatically, prompting a scribe to cross through the word 'treasurers' in the sergeant's oath and substitute that of 'chamberlains' above it.[53]

The circumstances leading to the emergence of the chamberlainship as a major civic office after this period of inactivity are tantalisingly obscure. Norwich's two treasurers discharged their duties regularly and uneventfully from 1415 until Michaelmas 1445, at which point the newly elected incumbents refused to serve, leaving the common sergeant, William Aubry, to step into the breach.[54] He rendered two full accounts, noting at the start of the second (1446–7) that there were 'neither treasurers nor chamberlains' to perform this task.[55] By Michaelmas 1447, William Oldbarly and Peter Laurence had been installed as chamberlains, but, since only the head of an account submitted in their joint names for the following year survives, it is impossible to tell what role, if any, the treasurers may still have played.[56] That Aubry retained some control over routine expenditure

---

51 NCR, 17B/3, rubricated no 184; *RCN*, i, p. 128.

52 NCR, 17B/3, rubricated no 184; *RCN*, i, pp. 128–9.

53 NCR, 17B/3, rubricated no 184.

54 NCR, 18A/1, f. 229.

55 NCR, 18A/1, f. 231. See *RCN*, ii, pp. 70–3, for extracts from Aubry's various accounts.

56 It constitutes the last entry in a volume of treasurers' accounts dated 1384 to 1448, being followed by three blank pages where the neat copy should have been made: NCR, 18A/1, f. 233.

during this transitional period is apparent from the fact that he remained answerable for all disbursements made over the years 1447–8 and 1448–9, although after a short overlap, between March and September 1449, the chamberlains assumed sole responsibility in this regard.[57]

Noting that the election of the city chamberlains and their six auditors was recorded annually in the assembly proceedings from 21 September 1452 onward without any further mention of the treasurers, Mary Grace conjectured that 'some change must have taken place' during the late 1440s to explain such a radical move.[58] The political climate of the city was clearly unsettled at this time, as the ruling elite sought to recover its prestige and reassert its authority in the face of lingering factionalism and unrest. Indeed, since the government of Norwich had been in royal hands for four years following 'the great insurrection' of 1443, the prospect of reaction and retrenchment hung constantly in the air.[59] In the event, none of the more conservative proposals set out by the mayor and aldermen in draft letters patent of 1447 was ever implemented, but it looks as if some less controversial attempts to streamline civic administration did bear fruit, notably regarding the role now undertaken by the two chamberlains.[60]

A hitherto unnoticed indenture tripartite drawn up between the chamberlains, the mayor and the commons in March 1449 (Appendix I) reveals that the chamberlains' financial commitments hardly differed from those of the treasurers before them, in so far that they remained accountable every year for whatever revenues and 'casueltes' might accrue to the community from within the city and its suburbs. Perhaps in response to earlier abuses, they had henceforward to seek written consent from the common council before approving any demand for money and pay all official wages promptly every six months in person. They were, none the less, granted use of their own seal for the authentication of documents

---

57 NCR, 17D/1, ff. iv˅–xiii˅. An exception occurred in 1497–8, when the common sergeant accounted alongside the two chamberlains and was, indeed, responsible for over £49 of the final deficit: NCR, 18A/4, ff. 18–20.

58 NCR, 16D/1, f. 17; M. Grace, 'The Chamberlains and Treasurers of the City of Norwich, 1293–1835', *NA*, 25 (1935), pp. 181–201, on p. 183.

59 C.D. Liddy, *Contesting the City: The Politics of Citizenship in English Towns 1250–1530* (Oxford, 2017), pp. 105–6. See also B.R. McRee, 'The Mayor's Body', in L.E. Mitchell, K.L. French and D.L. Biggs, eds, *The Ties that Bind: Essays in Medieval British History in Honor of Barbara Hanawalt* (Farnham, 2011), pp. 39–53; P. Maddern, 'Order and Disorder', in *MN*, pp. 198–200; and King, 'Merchant Class and Borough Finances', i, pp. 31–2.

60 *RCN*, i, pp. 119–22. King, 'Merchant Class and Borough Finances', ii, p. 289, refers to 'a tightening of supervision and personal accountability'.

and assured that the guidelines established in the *Compositio* of 1415 would otherwise remain in force.[61]

In one respect, however, the indenture of 1449 marked a significant development of the role that had previously been assumed by the treasurers. The chamberlains were charged with the preservation and custody of the civic archive, and thus assumed responsibility for Norwich's rapidly expanding store of official muniments, which had been gathered together from various places for storage in the guildhall as recently as 1440.[62] At the start of their term, they were to take delivery by formal indenture of 'all maner euydences, bokes and recordes' belonging to the city, while also keeping safe the accounts compiled by the assessors and collectors of whatever taxes and subsidies might be paid by the residents. They were, moreover, to ensure that copies of all documents issued under either the mayoral or the common seal, as well as acts and ordinances, were made and duly lodged in the archive, so that it remained up to date. To facilitate this task, they could demand the surrender of any written evidence presented before the city's judicial authorities, including the sheriffs, coroners and justices of the peace. The neglect and loss of such records, which were often treated as the personal property of individual officials, was a besetting problem in many late medieval towns and cities.[63] Given that further damage may have been sustained during the recent political upheavals, the need for greater security must have been apparent.

In an attempt to limit popular involvement in mayoral elections during the late 1440s, the rulers of Norwich had turned, as so often in the past, to the example of London.[64] Although their plans never came to fruition, it looks as if the capital furnished a more generally acceptable model with regard to the restructuring of the chamberlainship at this time.[65]

---

61 Significantly, a record of the assembly held on 21 September 1460 notes that the two chamberlains, their counsellors and the auditors of their account were elected '*secundum comsposicionem et ordinaciones ciuitatis*': NCR, 16D/1, f. 45ᵛ. The seal was made of silver by the goldsmith, John Elger, at a cost of 5s in 1449 and was still in use in 1552, when it was kept in the guildhall: NCR, 17D/1, f. ix; below, Appendix III.

62 Blomefield, *Norfolk*, iv, p. 228.

63 Even London had a serious problem on this score: R.R. Sharpe, ed., *Calendar of Letter-Books of the City of London: Letter-Book A* (1899), pp. ii–iv. See also E. Danbury, 'The Decoration and Illumination of Royal Charters in England, 1250–1509: An Introduction', in M. Jones and M. Vale, eds, *England and her Neighbours 1066–1453: Essays in Honour of Pierre Chaplais* (1989), pp. 157–8.

64 Liddy, *Contesting the City*, pp. 105–6.

65 Between April 1446 and the restoration of the city's liberties in December 1447 royal authority in Norwich had been exercised by Thomas Catworth, sometime mayor of

Since at least the late thirteenth century London's chamberlains had been responsible for custody of the city's records, some, such as Andrew Horn (d. 1328), making a major contribution to their reorganisation and preservation.[66] Admiration for, and emulation of, this system was certainly widespread. Indeed, the royal charter sanctioning changes to the government of Bristol in 1499 specified that the chamberlain's duties would be identical to those of his counterpart in London, including the safekeeping of 'all and all manner of charters, evidences, written obligations and muniments'.[67] According to an inventory of communal assets made by Robert Raynbald in 1552, some two years after his retirement (Appendix III), his successors still had oversight of an unspecified number of 'bookes of recordes, inrolments, accomptes an[d] suche other leke thynges' housed in the old council chamber of the guildhall. Volumes of royal and civic statutes lay nearer to hand in the new chamber, for ease of access during meetings, while 'evydences' relating to the newly-acquired Blackfriars were kept securely in 'an old chest bound with yron' in an upper room. The chamberlains themselves retained possession of a 'boxe' of twenty-two indentures confirming current leases of civic property, which Raynbald carefully itemised. Caroline Barron's suggestion that office holders with an interest in archives may have found such a post especially congenial, despite its many challenges, would certainly apply to him.[68]

By and large, because of what has been termed the inherent 'conservatism of urban administration amidst the political and religious vicissitudes of early modern England',[69] the basic responsibilities of Norwich's chamberlains changed very little from the 1450s until the nineteenth century. With a

---

London, who had strong local connections. It seems more than likely that he had a hand in these developments: L. Clark, ed., *History of Parliament: The Commons 1422–1461* (7 vols, Cambridge, 2019), iii, pp. 784–9.

66   In contrast to Norwich, the chamberlains of London were also charged with the task of protecting the goods of orphans: Masters, *Chamberlain of the City of London*, pp. 4–26; C. Barron, *London in the Later Middle Ages; Government and People 1200–1500* (Oxford, 2004), pp. 180–5. For similar arrangements at Exeter, see John Vowell, *alias* Hooker, *The Description of the Citie of Excester, III*, ed. W. J. Harte and others (Devon and Cornwall Record Society, xiv, 1919), pp. 814–15.

67   He was also to have a seal like that of the chamberlain of London (and presumably of Norwich): Cronne, ed., *Bristol Charters 1378–1499*, p. 176. By then, however, the common clerk of London had taken charge of the civic archive, no doubt because it was more practical to store records in his writing office, where they would most often be consulted.

68   Barron, *London in the Later Middle Ages*, p. 184.

69   R.B. Dobson, ed., *York City Chamberlains' Account Rolls 1396–1500* (Surtees Society, cxcii, 1978–9), p. xv.

few notable exceptions, the main items of income and expenditure and the sequence in which they were recorded in their accounts also remained surprisingly constant. Before turning to the documents themselves, it will be useful to examine in more detail the revenues accruing to the Tudor chamberlains and the ways in which they were spent. Such an exercise is greatly facilitated by the fact that, in common with their medieval predecessors, they followed a system of accountancy known as 'charge and discharge', which was designed to keep a precise record of receipts and disbursements (and thus to monitor the probity of the individuals concerned) rather than to determine profit and loss.[70] For this reason, even the smallest expenses, such as the cost of replacing the handles on the masons' tub, which came to one penny in 1544,[71] would be scrupulously recorded, as would every single sum for which the officers in question were answerable.

It is important to stress at this point that the chamberlains were not the only elected officers responsible for communal income and expenditure, although they alone have left a significant collection of account books and rolls to shed light upon their activities. We know far less about the work of their colleagues during the first half of the sixteenth century, which means that the city's total annual budget cannot now be reconstructed in its entirety because of the unfortunate loss of other vital evidence. In contrast to their counterparts in Newcastle-upon-Tyne and York, for example, the Norwich chamberlains were not routinely charged with the upkeep of the walls and dykes that formed the civic defences and therefore required constant maintenance.[72] Nor, despite their regular outlay on cutting back reeds and other growth from the river Wensum south of the city to make it navigable, did they always bear the annual cost of dredging and removing rubbish from its more polluted urban reaches, which fell to the mayor unless unusually complex operations were involved.[73] In his capacity as escheator

---

70 *MFS*, pp. 67, 278 note 15.

71 See below, p. 333.

72 C.M. Fraser, ed., *The Accounts of the Chamberlains of Newcastle upon Tyne 1508–1511* (Society of Antiquaries of Newcastle upon Tyne, records series, iii, 1987), p. xxiv and *passim*; Dobson, ed., *York City Chamberlains' Account Rolls*, pp. xxviii–ix. The cost of repairing the walls of Norwich was shared between the respective wards; the constables collected the revenues and accounted directly to the mayor: NCR, 17B/3, rubricated no 177; NCR, 16A/4, f. 29. In addition, individual aldermen sponsored work independently, as we can see from an account lodged by the executors of Richard Broun in the guildhall in 1543 itemising an outlay of over £28: NCR, 16A/5, p. 95.

73 Rawcliffe, *Urban Bodies*, pp. 217–21. Major campaigns for river cleaning, such as that conducted in 1532, generated numerous individual accounts, written up for the

of Norwich, the mayor was, moreover, personally answerable to the Crown for the revenues of any properties that fell into royal hands, while the sheriffs accounted for the annual fee farm at the Exchequer. Between them, the mayor and the sheriffs also took receipt of most of the fines and other judicial revenues raised in the city's various courts. In addition, the four clavors, or keepers of the chest where the city's reserves of cash were stored, accounted for all the money that passed through their hands each year, whether from the chamberlains or any other officials.[74] Some of it would have derived from payments made for entry to the freedom of Norwich and for the enrolment of apprentices, which had previously been assigned directly to the chamberlains but were by the 1530s collected (along with other miscellaneous sums) by a foreign receiver.[75] In practice, these arrangements proved to be fairly flexible,[76] although the underlying principle of separate responsibility remained strictly in force.

Income

A significant part of the chamberlains' income derived from shrewd investments in land, rents and property made by earlier generations of civic leaders.[77] The policy of enlarging this portfolio at every feasible opportunity continued, despite the challenging financial climate, in the period covered by this volume. Indeed, members of the ruling elite may well have felt a greater responsibility to build on the foundations laid by their predecessors in order to provide further safeguards against an uncertain future.

The city had obtained jurisdiction over the baileys of Norwich castle from the Crown in 1345 and with it the right to all the fixed rents due from

---

mayor by the common clerk: NCR, 16D/2, ff. 165ᵛ–6. Indeed, in 1541, receivers of the river were appointed to answer for the collection and expenditure of such revenues: 16D/2, f. 195ᵛ.

74 King, 'Merchant Class and Borough Finances', ii, chapter eight. The guild of St George, which was effectively synonymous with civic government, maintained a treasury from which money might be diverted for civic use, generally in the form of loans: M. Grace, ed., *Records of the Gild of St George in Norwich, 1389–1547* (NRS, ix, 1937), pp. 146, 149, 152; below, pp. 124, 180.

75 The clavors' accounts survive from 1550: NCR, 18D/13. Pound, *Tudor and Stuart Norwich*, pp. 99–100, tabulates their receipts and expenses from 1561 onward.

76 In 1542–3, for example, the chamberlains acknowledged receipt of several fines that should have gone to the sheriffs but had presumably been diverted to meet the extraordinary demands then being made on their budget: below, p. 177.

77 For an analysis of the chamberlains' income from rents between 1390 and 1536, see King 'Merchant Class and Borough Finances', ii, pp. 356–9.

tenements in the surrounding area.[78] These modest revenues, known as 'the castle fee', rarely ran to more than a pound or so, and were usually noted at the very start of the chamberlains' accounts after whatever sums might have been raised that year in landgable payments from a few designated properties. The landgable was an ancient type of ground rent levied by the authorities upon long-established burgage plots within the walls. In principle, these rents fell in annually, but it was uneconomic to collect them so often and years might elapse between attempts to do so.[79] A similar, but slightly more lucrative, income came from assize rents, which were also chargeable on ground or property, often because of some illicit encroachment on common land.[80] As we shall see below, it was notoriously difficult to keep track of such payments, although the chamberlains did their best in this regard, no sum being too small to escape their attention.

Far larger amounts of money accrued from the market stalls, shops, tenements and other holdings that had been acquired or built by the community over the years in the parish of Saint Peter Mancroft, in the commercial heart of Norwich. Recognizing that it could make substantial profits from the ownership of stalls where food and merchandise were sold, the city government staged what was effectively a compulsory purchase of the northern part of the market in the late fourteenth century. It then leased the stalls to individual traders at competitive rents, while prohibiting the sale of two dietary staples, fish and meat, elsewhere in the city.[81] This farsighted policy continued to bear dividends, not least because Tudor England was a nation of carnivores. In 1539–40, the year of the first account presented in this volume, the city's butchers occupied twenty-seven fixed stalls and five 'moveable' (temporary) ones, while butchers from the surrounding countryside sold their wares on Saturdays from a similar number of adjacent stalls. None then lacked tenants, as was also the case regarding the twenty stalls let to fishmongers. Two of the six stalls in the row consigned to rope-sellers ('the Ropery') were temporarily unlet, however, while some of the adjacent

---

78 E. Shepherd Popescu, *Norwich Castle: Excavations and Historical Survey, 1987–98, Part II: c. 1345 to Modern* (East Anglian Archaeology, 132, 2009), p. 543. During the late 1530s, some of these properties were 'brent by sodden fyer', while others lay vacant: NCR, 18A/5, ff. 12ᵛ–13.

79 E. Rutledge, 'Introduction', in M. Rodgers and M. Wallace, eds, *Norwich Landgable Assessment 1568–70* (NRS, lxiii, 1999), pp. 1–6.

80 Rutledge, 'Introduction', p. 12.

81 P. Dunn, 'Trade', in *MN*, p. 231; *RCN*, ii, pp. xxxv, 236–7; U. Priestley, *The Great Market: A Survey of Nine Hundred Years of Norwich Provision Market* (Norwich, 1987), pp. 8–11; King, 'Merchant Class and Borough Finances', ii, pp. 360–6.

wool shops lay vacant 'in the deffaute of ffermours' because of recession.[82] Even so, with a combined income of over £56, these various premises made a significant contribution to the city's coffers; and in 1542 the assembly saw fit to invest heavily in extending the butchery.[83]

Properties listed under the general heading of 'Houses and Tenements' were also largely concentrated in the market area, some having been recently 'new bilded' around the site of the common inn, just north of the guildhall, where construction work continued apace. The above-mentioned Robert Jannys presented three of his own tenements there to the city in 1519, the rents from which were earmarked for improvements in street cleaning.[84] A few other holdings lay in more scattered parts of Norwich, reflecting the piecemeal and often opportunistic nature of communal acquisitions. During the 1530s, for example, the chamberlains had extensively refurbished a row of thirteen derelict tenements near the river in Conesford, which now produced a useful 69s in rental income.[85]

Some of the chamberlains' other revenues came from farming out specific privileges, such as the right to collect tolls ('pety custom') paid on goods coming to market from outside the city, and permission to erect booths near the shire house in the south bailey of Norwich castle for the sale of food and drink to the public during the assizes.[86] The tenancy of two of the city's most valuable assets, its landing stathes and water mills, was also put out to tender, although responsibility for their upkeep remained with the chamberlains. The 'old' more northerly common stathe on the river Wensum in Conesford had been acquired by the city in January 1379 and the 'new' one just a few months later, at which point a ban was imposed upon the loading or unloading of merchandise anywhere else on the river so that tolls on shipping would be harder to evade. Since they could also demand compulsory payments for the use of the communal crane and warehouses, farmers were prepared to pay £15 a year to the chamberlains to rent the two stathes, while still turning a comfortable profit.[87] The three 'new' water mills built over the Wensum as it entered the city near Hell gate represented

---

82 There were thirteen wool shops in 1398–9, but only five are mentioned in 1539–40; the number of stalls in the Ropery had remained constant: *SLCN*, pp. 35–7.

83 NCR, 16D/2, f. 197; and below, pp. 126–31, 185–6.

84 NCR, 16D/2, f. 121.

85 Fay, *Health and the City*, p. 169.

86 Shepherd Popescu, *Norwich Castle*, p. 545; NCR, 16D/2, f. 182.

87 Dunn, 'Trade', pp. 228–9; M. Rodgers, *The River and Staithes of Tudor Norwich* (Norwich, 1996), pp. 34–5, 56–7; *RCN*, ii, pp. xxxv–vi, 233–6. The rent had, however, fallen by half since 1400: King, 'Merchant Class and Borough Finances', ii, pp. 375–7.

another major civic investment, begun at roughly the same time as the guildhall, but not fully operational until the 1430s because of difficulties in working the sluices.[88] They were leased by local millers, together with smaller mills in the adjacent suburb of Heigham, at a combined annual rent of £43. It was possible to charge so much because of a regulation obliging all the city's bakers to have their corn ground there, paying one toll ('the grynte') to the city and another to the miller.[89]

Along with a few small rents from tenants leasing towers, gardens and land beneath the walls, the chamberlains took delivery of an annual rental income of £8 bequeathed to the community by Robert Jannys in 1530 to pay the commercial tolls previously levied upon residents at the gates.[90] Two significant new items appeared for the first time in the chamberlains' account for the year 1539–40, each reflecting a historic concern on the part of the authorities to improve the urban environment, while also – in the long term, at least – generating additional revenue. In 1536 John Underwood, the suffragan bishop of Norwich and titular bishop of Chalcedon, agreed to lease a row of ten dilapidated tenements in Tombland to the people of Norwich for ninety-nine years at a peppercorn rent.[91] He was clearly acting at the behest of Alderman Augustine Steward (plate 2), who, prompted by 'goode will ffor the maynetenaunce of the citie', used his own funds in order to buy out two of the sitting tenants.[92] The chamberlains had to undertake comprehensive renovations, which initially ate into any potential profits, but these dwellings eventually earned almost £7 a year once the repairs were completed.[93] Steward went on to play a leading role in the acquisition of the Blackfriars complex in 1540, which, as we shall see below, cost so much money that it cannot have broken even for decades. Nevertheless, we should bear in mind that the purchase was not confined to the precinct on the south side of the river occupied by the Dominicans in 1538 and earmarked for civic use, but also included their original site 'over the water' to the north. This comprised a large walled garden containing an orchard, chapel and various other buildings in the parishes of St Clement and St Mary Incombusto,

---

88 Ayers, *Norwich*, p. 118. There had originally been four mills. For the controversies arising from their construction, forced demolition and subsequent rebuilding in the reign of Edward IV, see *RCN*, ii, 48–54; NCR, 9E/4–5; 17B/3, rubricated nos 66–91; McRee, 'The Mayor's Body', pp. 48–52.

89 In 1540 the rate was raised to 2*d* on each comb of wheat: NCR, 16D/2, f. 190.

90 TNA, PROB 11/24/3.

91 NCR, 16D/2, f. 179.

92 *RCN*, ii, pp. 122–3.

93 Fay, *Health and the City*, pp. xxv, 169–70.

along with a substantial tenement and its appurtenances in St Clement's, all of which could be rapidly converted into rental property.[94] From the very outset, the authorities sought to recoup some of their expenses by letting out any available garden space and whatever lodgings could attract a tenant 'ffor the best availe & profite of the comialtie'.[95] Between 1540 and 1545, annual receipts from Blackfriars rose from just over £4 to £14 as other parts of the site came onto the market following refurbishment.[96]

Despite the growing scale of their commitments, the mayor and aldermen seized the chance to consolidate their holdings and effect further improvements in the Tombland area in 1542–3 by acquiring a large, run-down tenement near the church of St Mary the Less for the bargain price of £13 6s 8d.[97] One year later they secured a four hundred years' lease of the church itself, which had been badly neglected by the dean and cathedral chapter and was by then redundant and in need of repair.[98] Extensive renovation made the property habitable, while adding considerably to the appeal of what had previously been an insalubrious part of the city.

The final source of income recorded in the accounts comprised a variety of miscellaneous payments known as 'foreign receipts', a catch-all title which included anything that did not fit easily under the previous headings. From the 1490s onward, the city employed a receiver to collect at least some of these revenues on the chamberlains' behalf, although it was not until 1515 that his annual election became a matter of record.[99] The post was occupied for several years by Robert Raynbald's father, Stephen, and from 1538 to 1547 by John Revell the elder, but unfortunately only one early and undated account survives to cast light upon their precise responsibilities or

---

94 NCR, 8K/7 (b). See also, M. Tillyard, 'The Acquisition by the Norwich Blackfriars of the Site for their Church c. 1310–1325', in U.M. Priestley, ed., *Men of Property: An Analysis of the Norwich Enrolled Deeds 1285–1311* (Norwich, 1983), pp. 5–11. The construction of a large, well-appointed new tenement south of the river 'at the two elms' with shops, warehouses and an imposing gateway bearing the city's arms proved to be a particularly shrewd investment: below, pp. 150–3, 286–90, 330–9.

95 NCR, 16D/2, f. 192.

96 See below, pp. 72, 299.

97 See below, p. 209; Fay, *Health and the City*, pp. xxv, 170.

98 See below, pp. 262–3. Some of the contents, such as the rood loft and choir desks, were sold off and parts were leased out to cover the costs: pp. 300, 302. Robert Tittler comments upon the general neglect of urban properties owned by ecclesiastical landlords at this time, as was clearly the case regarding the tenements acquired from the suffragan: 'For the "Re-Edification of Townes": The Rebuilding Statutes of Henry VIII', *Albion*, 22 (1990), pp. 591–605, on p. 597.

99 NCR, 16D/2, f. 107.

Plate 1. The cover of Robert Raynbald's account book, 1541–50
(Norfolk Record Office, NCR, 18A/7)

Plate 2. Alderman Augustine Steward (d. 1570)

Plate 3. The east end of the Norwich guildhall

The South Prospect of Black-friers Church in Norwich.

Ne fructus Quærant Nepotes
Eternitati dicunt.
THO: PETTVS Baronettus.

50

Plate 4 The common hall (former Blackfriars) from the south

the sums involved.[100] Other officers also contributed to the chamberlains' foreign receipts. On the infrequent occasions when landgable was collected throughout Norwich, they would take delivery of the proceeds from the collector. In 1539–40, for example, Richard Framyngham paid £10 13s 4d from the landgable to the chamberlains and a further 66s 8d to Augustine Steward to cover some of the latter's considerable expenses.[101] The farm of the communal 'mukbote', in which manure and refuse were conveyed downstream out of the city in return for a standard payment on every load,[102] was also noted at this point, as were any profits raised from the sale of surplus building materials and unwanted items of civic property. The bakers were collectively responsible for raising the above-mentioned 'gryntc', which netted between £5 and £10 a year, despite frequent mutterings on their part. Other receipts were far less predictable, but generally included whatever bequests wealthy residents might have left to the community, either in the form of hard cash or land that could be sold or rented out to fund specific projects. As in other English towns and cities of this period, freemen could avoid or postpone office holding by paying a substantial fine, or, in a few cases, donating property to the equivalent value; and these revenues, too, were generally listed among the foreign receipts.[103]

Last to feature were the payments made by previous chamberlains into the common chest in settlement of their accounts, sometimes, as we shall see, long after they had finally left office. In years when 'benevolences' or rates had been raised for specific purposes, such as the provision of subsidised grain, the arming of military levies or work on the Blackfriars' complex, the chamberlains would furnish appropriate details of the additional sums received at the end of their 'charge'. In order to meet the heavy financial demands that were being made upon them throughout the early 1540s, they became increasingly reliant upon supplementary payments of this kind. During the 1530s their net annual income (excluding arrears carried over from previous accounts) had fluctuated between a high of £218 in 1531–2 and a low of £172 in 1538–9, averaging just over £190 between these two dates.[104] Having reached the unprecedented figure of £343 in 1541–2, it rose further to £426 in 1543–4 and £444 in the following year, before returning to previous

---

100 Stephen served from at least 1512 (NCR, 7A/66), not 1515, as stated in *INCO*, pp. xvi, 129. For an undated account drawn up in his name, see NCR, 11G/1/1; and for Revell, *INCO*, p. 129.

101 See below, p. 74.

102 Rawcliffe, *Urban Bodies*, pp. 218, 220; Faye, *Health and the City*, pp. 148–9.

103 See below, pp. 32, 44.

104 NCR, 18A/5, *passim*; 18A/6, ff. 1–21.

levels once so many extraordinary calls upon the budget ceased.[105] How was all this money spent?

Expenditure

This part of the chamberlains' accounts began with a brief entry listing the modest assize rents paid to other landowners. By 1539 many of the recipients were recently suppressed monasteries or hospitals, such as St Giles's, Norwich, that would soon face dissolution. The last years of Henry VIII were a time of great anxiety and confusion so far as the city's surviving religious establishments were concerned. The process of dissolution, which had moved in fits and starts from the outset, was still far from complete, and in its later stages often owed more to accident than design.[106] As a religious conservative, whose views may have grated with a significant proportion of the more evangelically-minded civic elite, Henry had no quarrel with the theological principles that underscored the activities of chantries, hospitals, secular colleges and guilds. But in such a febrile environment they were falling prey, like the friaries before them, to acquisitive individuals and public bodies with a vested interest in their holdings. Alarmed by the scale of depredation and desperate for money, the king forced legislation through parliament in 1545 taking all such resources into his own hands. Meanwhile, the ruling elite continued to honour its obligations towards these various institutions, while carefully planning the best strategy for salvaging whatever assets might be put to communal use.[107]

Fees and wages, which came next, were, by contrast, traditionally 'the single heaviest regular charge' on any civic budget,[108] Norwich being no exception until building work started in earnest on the Blackfriars' complex in the 1540s. At around £80 per annum, these payments included the partial fees of two mayors, one succeeding the other at midsummer, three-quarters of the way though the chamberlains' accounting year, which ran from 29 September. The sheriffs, recorder, steward, town clerk, sword-bearer, sergeants at mace, sergeant of the market, beadle, any lawyers formally retained of counsel by the city and, of course, the chamberlains themselves, followed, some receiving supplementary payments for liveries (uniforms) as well as their fees. The most resplendent among them were undoubtedly the four city waits,

---

105 Net receipts fell to just below £218 in 1545–6, in line with greatly reduced outgoings of £207: NCR, 18A/7, ff. 196ᵛ, 122.

106 D. MacCulloch, *Thomas Cromwell: A Life* (2018), pp. 209–12.

107 *MFS*, chapter seven; below, p. 321 note 629.

108 Dobson, ed., *York City Chamberlains' Account Rolls*, p. xxxii.

or minstrels, who performed on public occasions wearing emblazoned liveries and heavy silver chains bearing the arms of Norwich.[109]

The upkeep of civic infrastructure, including street-paving, accounted for a significant share of the remaining expenses, varying from year to year according to need. The market stalls, guildhall, tenements, mills, stathes and other properties described above had to be kept clean, secure and in a good state of repair in order to attract reliable tenants. Damage to the fishmongers' stalls in the market, which were 'spoyled with thevys' in 1545, may furnish further evidence of recession, but expenditure on locks, bolts, bars, keys and other safeguards was invariably high.[110] It is interesting to note how much effort the chamberlains devoted to the removal of 'muck' from yards and privies, a continuous exercise that extended on a larger scale to the carting away of dung hills and rubbish from the city's streets, lanes and gates. The annual cleansing ('ffeyeng') and maintenance of the cockeys (culverted streams) that ran through various parts of Norwich into the Wensum, and of the cisterns and gratings that kept the river free of accumulated debris, was another priority, which, as already noted, could be hindered by lack of funds and bad weather. During the summer months the major operation known as 'cutting the river' was also undertaken by the chamberlains, who were responsible for overseeing the scything of reeds and sedge from the Conesford tower in the south east of the city all the way down to Surlingham on the Yare. Until Robert Raynbald reorganized the layout of the accounts, placing each type of expenditure under its own separate heading, these various routine charges tended to be undifferentiated and hard to disaggregate. It was, however, customary to record the outlay on any major building campaigns, such as the construction of new houses and other work at the common inn in 1539–40, which cost £30, as single, continuous entries.[111] Indeed, the practice of listing expenditure on labour and materials for these longer lasting projects on a weekly basis confirms that the requirement imposed upon the city's fifteenth-century treasurers to record their outgoings every Saturday was still being scrupulously observed.[112]

---

109 The chamberlains' accounts furnish most of our information about these musicians during the fifteenth and early sixteenth century: C.A. Jansssen, 'The Waytes of Norwich in Medieval and Renaissance Pageantry' (University of New Brunswick PhD thesis, 1977), pp. 24–65; G.A. Stephens, 'The Waits of the City of Norwich through Four Centuries to 1790', *NA*, 25 (1935), pp. 1–70.

110 See below, p. 309.

111 See below, pp. 83–7.

112 The chamberlains of Newcastle-upon-Tyne submitted their final accounts in a weekly

The chamberlains had also to make a number of occasional payments that fell into the broad category of 'minute expenses', among which were the salaries of priests serving the chantries of long-deceased citizens and less regular disbursements to visiting preachers, usually of a more evangelical persuasion. Outgoings sustained because of litigation, including a dispute with Sir John Shelton's widow over the liberties of the recently dissolved Carrow priory,[113] another with the residents of Cambridge over trading rights at the annual Stourbridge fair[114] and a third about the implementation of the will of the late town clerk, Leonard Spencer,[115] were regularly recorded. Roger Flynt's claim to jurisdiction in the suburb of Trowse Milgate, which dragged on for almost a decade in the court of augmentations, revived the city's epic battle with the former cathedral priory and prompted fierce resistance.[116]

Of particular interest to cultural and social historians are the lavish gifts of food, drink and expensive cloth designed to oil the wheels of patronage, most notably that of East Anglia's greatest magnate, Thomas Howard, third duke of Norfolk, and other members of his prolific family. One of his nieces, Ann Boleyn, had gone to the scaffold in 1536, and another, Catherine Howard, was executed in 1542, but, as the century's greatest survivor, Norfolk clung tenaciously to power and commanded the royal army during the Scottish and French campaigns of the 1540s.[117] His visits to the city were marked with precisely calibrated displays of deference, beginning with the payment of 2*d* as a reward to the nimble and sharp-eyed youth who climbed the tower of St Peter Mancroft in order to warn the aldermen of his approach.[118] Other recipients of civic largesse included royal heralds and bureaucrats employed in departments of state at Westminster, whose good will was vital for the pursuit of civic business, as well as potentially influential local men, such as Sir William Buttes, the King's physician.[119] Expert advice was often in demand, as from the duke of Norfolk's surveyor, who was consulted about the construction of the new kitchens at Blackfriars.[120]

---

format, in contrast to the practice in most other English towns: Fraser, ed., *Accounts of the Chamberlains of Newcastle upon Tyne*, pp. xii–iii.

113 See below, p. 163.

114 See below, pp. 206, 268.

115 See below, p. 205.

116 See below, pp. 265, 329.

117 D.M. Head, *The Ebbs and Flows of Fortune: The Life of Thomas Howard, Third Duke of Norfolk* (1995), chapter nine.

118 Perfume was also bought to fumigate the assembly chamber in his honour: see below, pp. 207, 326.

119 See below, p. 206.

120 See below, p. 156.

It is easy to see how the likes of John Eyer, a receiver in the court of augmentations, grew so prosperous, given that his 'favour' when pricing the lead at Blackfriars for the Crown cost the city £5, as well as the price of a gallon of claret and half a gallon of sherry.[121]

Evidence about festivities and entertainments, both elite and popular, may also be found among the 'minute expenses', not least in the form of rewards to visiting players, who delighted the mayor and leading citizens with their 'interludes'.[122] The erection and removal of a 'wrestlyng place' and of butts for displays of archery during the annual celebrations that had previously marked the mayor's riding to the Magdalen fair, just outside the city, were also supervised by the chamberlains. In 1539, three years after the feast of St Mary Magdalen had been declared 'abrogate and not halowed', the date of these celebrations changed from July to Whitsuntide, but the displays now staged within the walls grew more extravagant, reflecting what has been termed 'the reinvention of civic ritual' during a time of doctrinal upheaval.[123] Just as spectacular were the royal 'triumphs', such as those staged to celebrate the fall of Edinburgh and the (temporary) capture of Boulogne in 1544, when bonfires, music and processions were enlivened by the liberal provision of free beer.[124]

On these occasions, the mayor of England's second city had to cut an appropriate figure. Responsibility for the care, refurbishment and custody of civic regalia, including the sword that symbolised his authority and was carried solemnly before him on official occasions, also lay with the chamberlains.[125] The inventory of goods compiled by Robert Raynbald in 1552 (Appendix III) refers among other ceremonial items to four lavishly ornamented scabbards, two swords and two maces, one with 'armys of syluer and dobyll guylt wrought vpon crystall and set with stonys'.[126] The

---

121 See below, pp. 264, 267.

122 As Tittler observes, these payments were also 'a gesture of ingratiation' to the royal or aristocratic patron of the troupe: *Reformation*, p. 326.

123 M.C. McClendon, *The Quiet Reformation: Magistrates and the Emergence of Protestantism in Tudor Norwich* (Stanford, CA: 1999), pp. 96–100; NCR, 16D/2, f. 188ᵛ; A. Nelson, *The Medieval English Stage: Corpus Christi Pageants and Plays* (Chicago, 1974), pp. 127–8; Tittler, *Reformation*, pp. 318–19.

124 See below, p. 265. McClendon, *Quiet Reformation*, p. 107, suggests that the celebration of military successes (however transitory) proved less contentious than religious festivities, and was thus encouraged by the nervous authorities. She does not mention the civic investment in these victories, in terms of both money and men.

125 See below, p. 262.

126 One of these swords had been presented to the city by Henry IV, along with the charter of 1404: Blomefield, *Norfolk*, iii, p. 123; iv, p. 233.

contingents raised in Norwich to fight on Henry VIII's various campaigns also looked the part, being equipped at considerable expense by the chamberlains with armour, weapons and multicoloured liveries as specified by their exacting commander, the duke of Norfolk.[127] One of Raynbald's many duties during the military offensives of 1545 was to commission – and supervise the construction of gun carriages for – the six pieces of ordnance demanded by King Henry from the royal gunners who had armed his favourite warship, *The Mary Rose*.[128] It is in this section of the accounts that we can best appreciate the full extent of the chamberlains' activities.

The accounts and the audit

The practice of recording the annual income and expenditure of financial officers in both paper or parchment rolls *and* paper books was common in fifteenth- and early sixteenth-century English towns. The relationship between these two types of document varied, however, from place to place and over time. In Nottingham, for example, the chamberlains' rolls furnish a relatively concise Latin summary of the far more detailed 'particulars' contained in the small books kept by them in English throughout the year, sometimes in their own rather untidy handwriting and 'erratic orthography'.[129] The books compiled by the chamberlains of York from at least the 1440s likewise present a wealth of information not available in their rolls, which offered a more manageable synthesis for accounting purposes.[130] In sixteenth-century Faversham, on the other hand, the chamberlains' enrolled accounts were copied *verbatim* into a book for extra security, following 'dyuers vareaunces and inconvenyences' that had occurred because of poor record-keeping. Complaints that they had hitherto 'rested in billes and skroules some tyme in one mannes handes and kepyng and some tyme in another', and had thus often been unavailable, underscore the importance of the provisions made in the tripartite indenture of 1449, described above.[131]

---

127   See below, pp. 271–5.

128   See below, pp. 307, 322–3.

129   W.H. Stevenson, ed., *Records of the Borough of Nottingham, III, 1485–1547* (1885), pp. xiii–iv, 412–23. In Norwich, a very short abstract, sometimes of just a few lines, was often incorporated into the late fifteenth- and early sixteenth-century rolls, as, for example, NCR, 7A/54 (1493–4), 55 (1495–6), 70 (1518–19), 71 (1522–3). A similar practice was also adopted in some of the books, as in NCR 18A/2, ff. 29 (1470–71), 38 (1471–2), 52–3 (1472–3); 18A/3, ff. 35ᵛ–6 (1481–2); 18A/4, ff. 4ᵛ (1493–4), 8ᵛ (1494–5), 13 (1495–6).

130   Dobson, *York City Chamberlains' Account Rolls*, pp. xvi–vii.

131   D. Harrington and P. Hyde, eds, *The Early Town Books of Faversham c. 1251–1581* (Chippenham, 2008), pp. 98–9.

As we have seen, the treasurers of Norwich submitted enrolled accounts from the 1290s onward, if not before. Their only surviving book, a large volume of 283 folios (12″ x 16.5″), is neatly written in a series of trained hands. It contains lists of itemised receipts and expenses (comprising one brief entry per line) for each successive year between 1384 and 1447, with occasional omissions. Each individual sum received or spent appears in Roman numerals on the right-hand side of the page, but, despite the use of marginal headings to denote the major sources of income and principal outgoings ('stalls', 'mills', 'stathes' and so forth), no attempt has been made to calculate any totals or sub-totals, or to determine what the annual balances might be.[132] There is certainly nothing to suggest that the book was ever examined or annotated by the auditors, or that it was used to record the day to day *minutiae* of business omitted from the rolls. On the other hand, the clear, accessible format may well have served as a model for Robert Raynbald when he set out to improve the layout of the chamberlains' accounts a century later.

The chamberlains who held office in Norwich from the 1450s onward continued, like the treasurers before them, to produce books as well as enrolled accounts, probably in the 'cowntyng howse' assigned to them in the guildhall, where they kept a triple-locked chest bound in iron for storing cash and important documents.[133] In striking contrast to what had gone before, the three books that survive from the late fifteenth century seem rough and disorganised, having evidently been written in haste by scribes who left some entries blank, perhaps intending to complete them later.[134] Extensive deletions, revisions and marginal notes were made at the time of the audit, when the books would have been examined alongside the rolls. The latter, which are in general both neater and fuller, clearly represent a later stage in the accounting process.[135] Significantly, however, and no doubt reflecting their use as working documents, the late fifteenth-century books were not only smaller and more manageable (around 9″ x 12″), but they also adopted the same basic layout and sequence as the rolls, incorporating

---

132 NCR, 18A/1.

133 See below, p. 132.

134 NCR, 18A/2 (1470–90, with significant gaps; 231 folios); 3 (1479–88; 97 folios); 4 (1493–8; 31 folios, although rather larger at 12″ x 17″). Incomplete accounts for the years 1447–58 are now bound in NCR, 17D/1, The First Book of Apprenticeship Registers, ff. iv^v–xxxv.

135 Twenty-nine rolls survive from between 1457 and 1524 (NCR, 7A/44–72), along with three undated fragments from the sixteenth century (7A/73–5) and an abstract for the year 1512–13 (7A/76).

totals and sub-totals, along with a statement or summary of the estimated final balance for some years. Shortly after 1524, the date of the last surviving roll, it was apparently decided to rationalise what had become an unduly cumbersome system.[136] In order to avoid any further duplication of effort, the chamberlains henceforward kept only books; and by 1531, when the first surviving sixteenth-century account book begins, far greater care was being taken to produce a neat, orderly and comprehensive text.[137] These books were, moreover, almost entirely in English, a gradually emerging trend at the end of the previous century, but one that was now firmly established at the Norwich guildhall. It reflects the hands-on approach of the men who ran the city and were determined that nothing should escape their eagle-eyed attention, especially at the annual audit.

In theory, the chamberlains were expected to submit their accounts promptly at the end of the financial year (29 September) for scrutiny by the auditors and 'determination' before a group of senior officials, usually including the mayor, a few aldermen and the sheriffs. As far as we are aware, financial sanctions such as those employed in Nottingham during the early sixteenth century, threatening the two chamberlains with fines of 50s each should they fail to comply with a similar requirement, proved unnecessary.[138] So too did the practice adopted in York of demanding personal securities for the effective discharge of official responsibilities.[139] This was partly because the rulers of Norwich were prepared to compromise over deadlines, allowing ample time for the production of relevant material. Thus, for example, the account of James Marsham and Thomas Cook, the chamberlains for 1537–8, was not determined until early December 1540, just a few days before Cook and his new colleague, Thomas Beamond, submitted theirs for 1538–9.[140]

Most of the chamberlains' annual accounts either begin or end with the names of the four auditors (two aldermen and two commoners) whose task

---

136 A similar change was implemented in York: Dobson, *York City Chamberlains' Account Rolls*, p. xvii.

137 NCR, 18A/5.

138 The mayor faced a penalty of 100s, too, should he prove lax in enforcing this measure: Stevenson, ed., *Records of the Borough of Nottingham, III*, pp. 325–6. Considerable leeway had previously been allowed to accountants, which may explain why such heavy fines seemed necessary: *ibid.*, pp. 80–1.

139 A. Raine, ed., *York Civic Records, IV* (Yorkshire Archaeological Society, Records Series, cviii, 1945), pp. 45–6.

140 NCR, 18A/6, ff. 15–15ᵛ, 27ᵛ. An attempt by the assembly in November 1548 to recover all outstanding arrears by the following Easter specifically exempted the chamberlain and foreign receiver: NCR, 16D/2, f. 228.

was to ensure that all the various totals were correct, that every receipt and disbursement was adequately documented and that any allowances claimed by the accountants were fully justified.[141] In some instances, as in the years between 1531 and 1535, they would actually sign the accounts as further verification.[142] Adding up (and even worse subtracting) in unwieldy Roman numerals posed quite a challenge even to the most experienced auditor, who would use a board or cloth divided into squares known as 'chequers' for all but the most elementary calculations. Tokens denoting pounds (in tens, scores and hundreds), shillings and pence would be moved rapidly across the board from square to square as figures rose or fell, making it comparatively easy for the trained individual to read off a final figure or series of figures.[143] This system, which gave rise to the word 'exchequer', was widely employed throughout medieval and early modern England, albeit with varying levels of competence. The proposal, in 1501, that 'an auditour suche as is expert and lerned in the feate of audite after the fourme of th'exchequer' should be enlisted to tackle alleged abuses and negligence on the part of London's chamberlains suggests that the mayor and aldermen had limited confidence in the abilities of their own colleagues.[144]

Specialist advice seems never to have been required in Norwich. The margins of many of the chamberlains' account rolls and of their third surviving account book (1479–88) are, indeed, marked with the dots and lines that record the various stages of this procedure and reflect the skill of the auditors in mastering the necessary technique.[145] The actual formalities took place in the semi-public forum of the guildhall;[146] and it has been

---

141   The accounts of the chamberlains of Bristol were examined by six auditors from 1499 onward: Latham, ed., *Bristol Charters*, p. 8. York was beset by problems at this time. In 1536, eight auditors were appointed in response to 'sinyster enformacon' then circulating about the probity of the chamberlains. Suspicion persisted, and a team of four aldermen and five commoners was enlisted in 1540 to scrutinise their expenses, which included an unacceptably lavish outlay on 'dynners and drynkyns': Raine, ed., *York Civic Records IV*, pp. 15, 53.

142   NCR, 18A/5, ff. 14, 37, 64ᵛ, 84ᵛ, 102ᵛ. The practice resumed in 1551–2: NCR, 18A/8, ff. 20ᵛ, 39, 59ᵛ, 76ᵛ, 99, 125, 158, 181, 205, 230, 262, 279, 306, 338, 361ᵛ.

143   For an explanation of the procedures involved, see C. Johnson, ed. and trans., *Dialogus de scaccario: The Course of the Exchequer*, revised by F.E.L. Carter and D.E. Greenway (Oxford, 1983), pp. xxxv–vi; and D. Yaxley, *A Researcher's Glossary of Words Found in Historical Documents of East Anglia* (Dereham, 2003), p. 52.

144   Masters, *Chamberlain of the City of London*, p. 29.

145   As, for example, NCR, 7A/49, 52, 55, 58, 60, 61, 63, 65; 18A/3, ff. 82ᵛ, 83, 84, 87–92, 93ᵛ, 94, 95–5ᵛ, 96ᵛ, 97.

146   Large sums of money would customarily change hands 'vpon the chekyr in the cownsell chambyr': below, p. 329; and Appendix III.

suggested that the exuberant lozenge design in flush work on the east front should be read as a visual pun underscoring the fact that officialdom was here held to account (plate 3).[147] Preliminary meetings at which any potential problems might be ironed out were held in private, notably when a chamberlain died in office, as happened in 1531. On this occasion his successor spent 10s 8d on 'a soper at master mayeres & a dyner at the house of this accomptaunt', enabling the auditors to scrutinise all the available evidence in a less confrontational environment before the real examination began.[148]

Even under normal circumstances, the auditors required a daunting amount of supplementary documentation as they worked their way through each individual or 'particular' entry in the chamberlains' annual accounts. The loss of virtually all this material means that we are largely reliant upon passing references to such ephemeral items as the 'waster book' kept by Robert Raynbald to record his daily activities.[149] Extraordinary calls upon the budget generated a mass of additional paperwork. In 1496–7, for example, a separate book itemising expenses of £32 on the city's militia was presented at the audit; and forty years later John Florans referred to an outlay of £7 on dredging the river, 'as it appereth in a boke therof made off the particlere sommez shewed & allowed vpon this accompte'.[150] Artisans, such as the master carpenter, John Byrche, who worked under contract, would likewise submit a final 'byll of euery particler parcel' of their outgoings for approval.[151] Nobody was exempt from this process: even the mayor had to furnish his own book of particulars when claiming reimbursement for money spent on civic business.[152] Occasional survivals shed some light on the intense level of scrutiny involved. A detailed list of costs sustained in a campaign of river cleansing conducted in 1511–12 was accidentally preserved along with the chamberlains' account for this year, revealing that English was already being used in these subsidiary documents, and that they, too, had to be formally approved by the auditors, who pronounced a final

---

147 B. Ayers, 'Status, Power and Values: Archaeological Approaches to Understanding the Medieval Urban Community', in A. Falk, U. Müller and M. Schneider, eds, *Lübeck und der Hanseraum: Beiträge zu Archäologie und Kulturgeschichte* (Lübeck, 2014), pp. 227, 228.
148 NCR, 18A/5, f. 11.
149 See below, pp. 171, 272, 274. In this context a 'boke' would probably comprise no more than a quire or two of paper: below, p. 56.
150 NCR, 18A/4, ff. 16ᵛ–17; 18A/5, f. 150ᵛ.
151 See below, p. 151.
152 See below, p. 157.

'quietus' (acquittance) at the foot.[153] Raynbald's apologetic admission that it had not been possible 'to wright nor to remembyr' the various 'particlers' of his expenditure during the most dramatic phases of Kett's Rebellion, in the summer of 1549, confirms that supporting evidence was almost invariably required (Appendix II).

Certain 'last minute' expenses, such as the cost of writing up a clean copy of the account and of purchases of food and drink consumed at the audit,[154] could only be approved and recorded at the very end of the account, which often concluded with a list of unpaid debts charged upon (*unde super*) named individuals who still owed the chamberlains money. Many of the sums involved were assize rents, which rarely amounted to more than a few shillings each but could accumulate steadily over the years. Thus, for example, in 1522–3 Richard Leman was excused a backlog of 69s in assize rents due from thirty-eight different properties, each of which was carefully itemised on the back of his account roll.[155] A great deal of time and effort was spent on attempts to recover arrears of this kind, which posed a constant challenge to any landowner with extensive urban property. On the one hand, it was difficult to monitor changes of title whenever the freehold upon which a rent was charged changed hands, while on the other the cost of litigation made it economically unfeasible to distrain for such small debts on an individual basis.[156] Yet steps were clearly being taken to keep on top of the problem, as we can see from the inclusion of a new rental compiled on a parochial basis in the chamberlains' account for 1485–6, the total of which was actually corrected by the auditor.[157] The account submitted by John Florans in 1535–6 likewise included lists of all the individual payments due from the castle fee and from assize rents across the city, parish by parish. Capitalizing upon this initiative, in the following year he spent 16d on 'makyng off a newe boke ffor the office off the chamberleyn off all rentes & ffermes'.[158]

---

153 NCR, 7A/65, rot. 2.

154 Richard Framyngham was paid 40d for 'engrossing' the account until 1541–2, when his fee rose to 5s, although it is unclear what additional work he may have undertaken: see below pp. 89, 109, 167.

155 NCR, 7A/71.

156 *MFS*, pp. 96–7. During the early sixteenth century St Giles's Hospital, Norwich, recovered only a quarter of the assize rents due to it, having written off the remarkable sum of £384 in uncollected arrears during the 1460s.

157 NCR, 18A/3, ff. 79–82ᵛ.

158 NCR, 18A/5, ff. 105–17, 150ᵛ.

The burdens of office

Almost all civic offices made heavy demands upon the pockets, time and energy of those elected to them, which explains why the chamberlains' annual receipts usually included at least one or two substantial sums paid into the communal coffers by individuals who wished to avoid, or at least defer, the responsibilities involved.[159] Significantly, no exemptions from serving as chamberlain appear to have been sought during the 1530s or 1540s, even though the post was one of the most onerous on the roster.[160] It could prove financially crippling, as Thomas Grys discovered when, as 'treasurer or chamberlain' in the early 1440s, he borrowed large sums of money to cover certain official expenses and became personally liable as a result. Fifteen years later, by which time he was bankrupt and unemployed, the assembly granted him £10 in view of his poverty and the good service that he had given, but it made no attempt to mollify his creditors.[161] Grys was particularly unfortunate regarding the scale of his debts, but far from unusual in other respects.

The long-established principle of assigning personal responsibility for any unpaid arrears that had not been written off at the audit meant that each new chamberlain began his first term with a clean sheet, while his predecessor was obliged to raise any outstanding sums as best he could or settle the account himself.[162] Very rarely, and in marked contrast to the situation in York, did Norwich chamberlains record a *surplusagium*, or excess of expenditure over income, leaving them to subsidise civic expenses out of their own funds during their year in office (as Grys had apparently done) and attempt to recover the money later. They ended their account with an unspecified *surplusagium* in 1479–80 and another of just over £5 in 1482–3, but this state of affairs was highly unusual, and pales into insignificance when compared with the accumulated deficit of £507 facing the York chamberlains by 1486.[163] It was a minor miracle that

---

159 As, for example, NCR, 18A/6, ff. 35ᵛ–6.

160 In York, because of the 'great charges borne by the chamberlains in laying forth [...] great sums of money', at least six individuals sought exemption from holding this office between 1468 and 1521. The civic authorities exploited the situation by threatening those who lacked the necessary funds with election unless they paid a substantial fine: J.I. Kermode, 'Urban Decline? The Flight from Office in Late Medieval York', *Economic History Review*, new series, 35 (1982), pp. 179–98, on pp. 184, 186–8, 190, 195.

161 NCR, 16D/1, f. 31ᵛ; Grace, 'Chamberlains and Treasurers', pp. 196–7.

162 As noted above, this principle was enshrined in the *Compositio* of 1415.

163 NCR, 18A/3, ff. 22, 52ᵛ–3; Kermode, 'Urban Decline?', p. 187; Dobson, *York City Chamberlains' Account Rolls*, pp. xxv–vi, xxxi, xxxviii.

Robert Raynbald should exceed his budget by only £17 in 1544–5, given the extraordinary demands then being made upon civic finances.[164] He repaid himself promptly during the following year (under the separate heading of 'dettes payd A.D. 1546'), also retaining enough cash to cover a loan that he had previously advanced to buy wheat for the poor.[165]

The situation then returned to normal until the exceptional events and costly aftermath of Kett's Rebellion, which involved an additional outlay of over £212, largely spent on repairs and cleaning operations. Yet even here, Raynbald was able to recoup the £71 owing to him by September 1549 'of the reveneus of the cyte' and did not find himself out of pocket.[166] Indeed, on finally leaving office in 1550, he had accumulated £37 in arrears, which he paid off one year later by presenting the city with two tenements and an adjoining close in St Vedast's parish for the use of the newly acquired hospital of St Giles. Since the property was worth considerably more, he recovered the difference, noting the transaction diligently in his own hand at the end of his last account (see p. 34).[167] Others were understandably slower to honour their debts. Recognizing that it might prove difficult to raise such large amounts, the authorities were prepared to wait patiently for the final settlement of arrears, often in instalments.[168] Significantly, though, these obligations could remain in force for decades, even enduring beyond the grave. In 1541, twenty-five years after the death of Robert Barker, who had owed the community £29 from his time as chamberlain, his son and heir successfully petitioned for the debt to be halved, but still had to make good the rest in instalments of 66s 8d a year.[169] Authorities elsewhere were less forbearing: in an attempt to prevent such long delays the Winchester assembly then ruled that future chamberlains would have to settle their arrears within six months

---

164 See below, p. 342.

165 NCR, 18A/7, ff. 189, 198.

166 NCR, 18A/7, f. 314.

167 NCR, 18A/7, f. 344–4ᵛ; NCR, 4A/12, parish of St Vedast, deeds 54–5. In September 1551, Raynbald negotiated a twenty-one years' lease with the assembly, permitting him (and later his heirs) to farm all these holdings at an annual rent of 60s 'to the releif of the poore peopull of Goddes House': NCR, 16D/2, ff. 245ᵛ, 256ᵛ.

168 For example, it was not until 1524 that one of the two chamberlains who had accounted in 1497–8 delivered his share of the arrears (£17 10s 4d) at the guildhall and obtained his *quietus*. The common sergeant, who was answerable for the rest, then paid £22 9s 8d, but still owed £26 18s 9d: NCR, 18A/4, f. 20.

169 NCR, 16D/2, f. 193ᵛ. Barker was chamberlain in 1511–12: Grace, 'Chamberlains and Treasurers', p. 198. Only part of his (now anonymous) account survives, but it records a deficit of just over £29, as claimed: NCR, 17A/65; and below, pp. 99, 123.

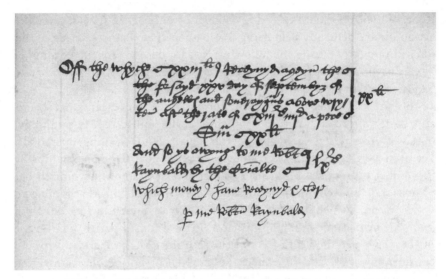

Robert Raynbald's signature at the end of his final account, 1549–50
(Norfolk Record Office, NCR, 18A/7, f. 344v)

of leaving office, 'apon payne of imprisonament, ther to remayne un till they have satisfied the same'.[170]

The expectation that chamberlains, like other leading civic officers, would have adequate time to devote to their duties further limited the number of potential candidates to those who could afford to delegate at least some of their own business affairs.[171] As the antiquary John Hooker, who served as chamberlain of Exeter in 1563, observed, 'his chardge is greate and in his office many thinges be required', notably that he should cultivate communal assets 'as a good husbande'.[172] In Norwich, the routine organisation and oversight of building work, repairs to infrastructure, street cleaning and the annual 'cutting' of the river could be timetabled well ahead, but special projects were harder to accommodate. In 1537, for example, John Florans was granted an additional fee of 40s for 'his laboures & peynes & diligens in vewyng & ouerlokyng the workmen' who had been engaged in a major

---

170 W.H.B. Bird, ed., *The Black Book of Winchester* (Winchester, 1925), p. 166.

171 In York, the chamberlains had to attend the mayor in the council chamber every day to collect fines and supervise disbursements. Since at least three of them held office concurrently, to spread the burden, penalties were imposed for absence: Dobson, *York City Chamberlains' Account Rolls*, pp. xxi, xxxviii.

172 He was also to be 'wyse and lerned and of great modestie and sobrietie': Hooker, *alias* Vowell, *Description of the Citie of Excester*, pp. 814–15.

campaign for cleansing and dredging the Wensum. He had spent over twenty-eight weeks ('x score dayez') directing their operations over the previous three years.[173] Emergencies, such as the opening of sluices and removal of the mill gates on 7 December 1538 to prevent flooding, were even less predictable and demanded immediate attention.[174]

Nor did peremptory orders from the Crown for the provision of fully equipped fighting men, 'well trymmed & ffurnysshed in euery behalff', whenever war threatened brook the slightest delay.[175] The remarkable speed with which the city's contingent was mobilised, armed and dispatched in September 1542 for service in Scotland and in June 1544 and August 1545 for France testifies to the smooth working of a complex administrative machine, in which 'master chamberlain' played a leading part.[176] The provision and safe storage of large quantities of grain for sale at subsidised prices during periods of dearth was even more important, at least from the standpoint of magistrates fearful of popular insurrection.[177] The task of policing fell largely to the ward constables, but the chamberlain might sometimes be required to admonish or discipline recalcitrant tenants or stallholders, such as butchers who traded in the wrong places.[178] The commitment to gaol of one angry citizen in April 1541 'for diuerz obprobrius words & mesdemenourz had & don' to Edmund Warden probably occurred while the latter was producing a survey of illicit encroachments at the behest of the mayor's court, although overt confrontations of this kind seem to have been rare.[179]

However modest the rent from civic properties, the authorities paid great attention to the negotiation of leases, frequently arranging a preliminary inspection of the site in question by one of the chamberlains, who would be consulted during any subsequent deliberations. Thus, for instance, successive chamberlains helped to implement a parliamentary act of 1535 for the compulsory seizure of land that had been devastated by the fires of 1507 and had lain unoccupied ever since, constituting both an eyesore and a demonstrable risk to health.[180] The acquisition of the Blackfriars' complex,

---

173 NCR, 18A/5, f. 153.

174 NCR, 16A/3, p. 140. The chamberlains were ordered to oversee these measures and presumably to ensure that the sluices and gates were functioning properly after the floods had abated.

175 NCR, 16A/4, f. 40ᵛ.

176 See below pp. 165–7, 271–5, 324–5.

177 See below, p. 48.

178 NCR, 16A/5, p. 190.

179 NCR, 16A/5, pp. 47, 54.

180 NCR, 16D/2, ff. 181–1ᵛ, 183–3ᵛ, 185–5ᵛ, 188; Tittler, 'For the "Re-Edification of Townes"', pp. 591–605; Rawcliffe, *Urban Bodies*, p. 173; Fay, *Health and the City*, pp. 153–6.

with its extensive gardens, in 1540, prompted another burst of activity, since the chamberlains were naturally expected to 'treate & declare ther myndes how & in what maner ffor the best availe & profite of the comialtie certen housez & groundes ther may be letten'. In March 1541, Edmund Warden not only had to advise on the tenancies offered to a group of leading citizens but also to inspect 'a certen noisaunce of water and muk made vnder the gret garden of the late Freres & to prouyde remedy theryn'.[181]

In theory, as we have seen, the chamberlains could enlist the help of a group of councillors or 'vewers', usually numbering four or six, who were elected along with them on 21 September each year in order to provide appropriate guidance, notably with regard to the evaluation of property.[182] In accordance with the strict principle of parity established in the *Compositio* of 1415, they comprised an equal number of aldermen (chosen by the aldermen) and commoners (chosen by the sixty), but not all seem to have pulled their weight. In May 1542 the new mayor, William Rogers, threatened to remove any elected officials who proved 'remysse & necligent'; and eighteen months later the assembly specifically criticised the six serving councillors (including Edmund Warden, the previous chamberlain) for their lack of 'diligence'. Henceforward, any of them who failed to discharge his obligations upon 'resonable request' would face a fine of 40d for each dereliction.[183] A man of Robert Raynbald's experience could, however, be relied upon to exercise his own judgement, as in March 1544, when he personally supervised the partition of common land in Coslany between five perspective tenants.[184]

Energy and stamina, as well as time, were at a premium. Unlike the mayor and some of the aldermen, the chamberlains rarely undertook official business in London, but their work was far from sedentary.[185] Besides making regular tours of civic property, supervising whatever building projects might be in hand and inspecting the river every summer, they had periodically to travel on 'outrydynges' around East Anglia. During the six years covered in this volume they rode to Hockering Park to examine oaks for timber and sailed to Yarmouth to buy paving tiles and other commodities. They spent six days in Cambridge contesting a claim to tolls payable at the Stourbridge fair and made repeated trips to the duke of Norfolk's residence at Kenninghall to discuss the city's contribution to the

---

181 NCR, 16D/2, ff. 192, 193ᵛ.
182 See, for instance, NCR, 16D/2, ff. 182ᵛ, 185ᵛ, 189, 192ᵛ, 196, 200, 204, 211ᵛ.
183 NCR, 16D/2, ff. 199, 205ᵛ.
184 NCR, 16D/2, f. 209.
185 Raynbald did, however, make two trips to London at a combined cost of 26s 8d in 1545–6 to attend the court of augmentations: NCR, 16A/5, p. 311.

war effort.[186] In the frantic summer of 1545, Robert Raynbald was obliged to chase after the duke as he dealt with a threatened coastal invasion, carrying with him what must have been a rapidly putrefying salmon as a gift from his fellow magistrates. He twice attended the royal audit at Bury St Edmunds – once to finalise negotiations over the ownership of the Blackfriars' complex and then with an armed guard for the delivery of the £152 demanded by the king in return for the lead roofing – and accompanied the city's contingent of soldiers on their way to embarkation at Ipswich.[187] Nor did Raynbald's many obligations end here. As recently-appointed bailiff of the manor of Barnham Hawkins, some ten miles west of Norwich, he was called upon to survey land and effect improvements there on behalf of the civic authorities, while also marshalling the defence and distributing *douceurs* in a protracted lawsuit brought against them by a neighbouring landowner.[188]

Notwithstanding this potentially hectic schedule, and the heavy financial and administrative commitments that went with it, a few public-spirited individuals were prepared not only to serve more than one term in office, but even to do so alone. In this respect, as we have seen, parallels may be found in early Tudor London and Bristol, whereas in York no cases of re-election to the chamberlainship are known between 1470 and 1530. Indeed, since they had 'to bere soch great chargez' because of the city's chronic debts, as many as six and never fewer than three chamberlains invariably worked together in York during this period.[189] The Norwich assembly first elected a single chamberlain in 1513, thereby setting aside the ruling made a century earlier that the aldermen and councillors should each choose their own nominee. The fact that William Bone was also to act as common sergeant (which would have greatly increased his workload) suggests that some crisis, such as plague, may then have prompted the rulers of Norwich to break with established precedent.[190] Yet the experiment clearly worked; and for the next twenty-four years single chamberlains, some of whom held office for several years in succession, became the rule rather than the exception. Both Richard

---

186 See below, pp. 133–4, 206 note 469, 267–8, 272.

187 See below, pp. 325–9, 340.

188 His accounts cover the years 1543–50: NCR, 24C/20/7, ff. 1–7. Confusingly, his adversary was named Chamberlain: NCR, 16A/5, p. 276; 24C/20/9.

189 Kermode, 'Urban Decline?', pp. 187, 190; Dobson, ed., *York Civic Chamberlains' Account Rolls*, p. xxxvii; A. Raine, ed., *York Civic Records, I* (Yorkshire Archaeological Society, Record Series, xcviii, 1939), p. 87.

190 Bone (or Roone in his accounts) was elected in late October 1513, almost a month after he should have begun his term in office: NCR, 16D/2, f. 101. Plague was then endemic: Rawcliffe, *Urban Bodies*, p. 372.

Leman (1518–27) and John Florans (1531–37) established significant records in this respect.[191]

Why a pair of chamberlains should have served in 1537–8 and again in 1538–9 after such a long gap is unclear, but the established pattern resumed at Michaelmas 1539, when Edmund Warden took office alone and this volume begins. Being then probably in his late thirties, Warden had, like most sixteenth-century chamberlains, already scaled the lower rungs of the civic hierarchy, first as a ward constable and then a member of the common council. He went on to progress steadily through the ranks, becoming a sheriff in 1544 and an alderman in 1555, while also sporadically acting as a surveyor, coroner and auditor.[192] For those with aldermanic aspirations, the chamberlainship clearly presented an important step in the *cursus honorum*, while others embraced the challenge of long-term service in a demanding but crucial post. Perhaps because of the additional pressures already generated by work on the Blackfriars complex, it was deemed expedient to elect two chamberlains when Warden stepped down in 1541. Neither William Morraunt nor William Hede, who served successively alongside Robert Raynbald, seem to have felt much lasting commitment to the task in hand. Morraunt, who died suddenly in 1543 just after becoming sheriff,[193] may indeed have regarded the post as a necessary stepping stone to higher office, while Hede apparently preferred (or was deemed better qualified for) less onerous duties as one of the city's four clavors.[194] In any event, Raynbald was more than capable of acting alone.

Robert Raynbald and his innovations

Even to the most casual observer, the contents of the two volumes of partially concurrent chamberlains' accounts now known as NCR, 18A/6 (1537–46)[195] and 18A/7 (1541–50) appear strikingly different. Although generally tidier and fuller than any of the earlier account books, 18A/6 is in most other respects identical in layout to its predecessors. In order to break up the content of increasingly long passages of continuous, unbroken text,

---

191 Grace 'Chamberlains and Treasurers', pp. 198–9.

192 *INCO*, p. 160. He died in 1576: NRO, NCC Reg. Cawston, f. 390–90ᵛ.

193 *INCO*, p. 108; NRO, NCC Reg. Hyll, ff. 181ᵛ–3; below, p. 263.

194 He was elected sheriff in 1547 and coroner in 1549 and died in 1553–4: *INCO*, p. 80; NRO, NCC Reg. Walpole, ff. 66–9ᵛ.

195 The last account in this volume, for 1545–6, was audited on 18 April 1547 (f. 234), which may explain why the dates on the binding and in W. Hudson and J.C. Tingey, *Revised Catalogue of the Records of the City of Norwich* (Norwich, 1898), p. 58, read '1537–1547'.

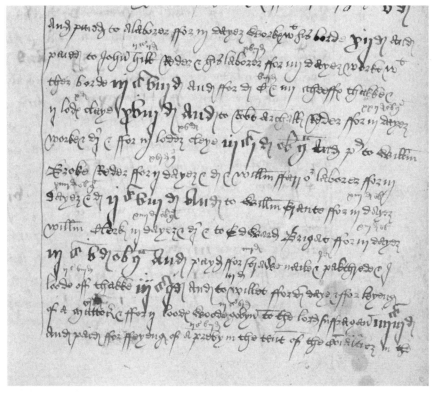

A detail of entries in the chamberlain's account for 1539–40
(NRO, NCR, 18A/6, f. 38)

sometimes running to several folios, the word or sum of money at the start or end of each new entry is marked in darker ink, making it easier to identify particular items. On the other hand, the practice of recording smaller, subsidiary payments (such as the cost of different types of nails or the wages of individual workmen) in cramped Roman numerals inserted between the lines may have proved useful, yet it resulted in multiple interlineations that can be confusing and hard to read (see above and frontispiece, p. ii).

By contrast, the accounts presented in 18A/7 comprise neatly itemised lists of individual receipts and expenses, each occupying a new line of text, in a layout roughly similar to that of the treasurers' account book described above. These entries are grouped into relatively short, coherent sections and, where appropriate, sub-sections, each clearly signed in the margin and each ending with a reckoning of the sums received or spent (see p. 40). In the case of major projects, such as the rebuilding of Blackfriars, an introductory

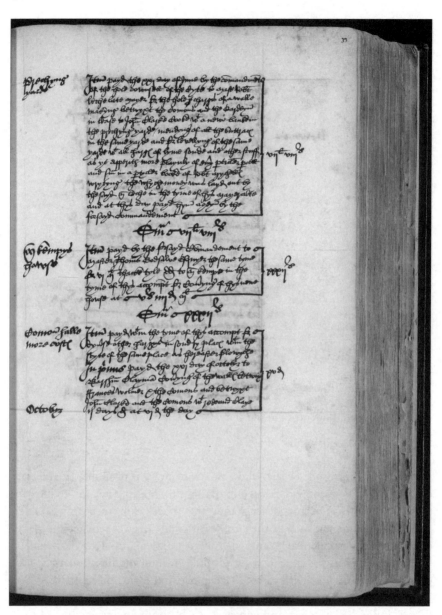

A page from the chamberlains' account for 1541–2
(NRO, NCR, 18A/7, f. 32)

passage lists the various works undertaken during the year, explains the sequence that follows and, in some instances, notes the provenance of the various materials used.[196] The approach is altogether more systematic: each market stall and tenement is carefully numbered or otherwise identified; the names of suppliers and workmen are almost invariably recorded; and care is taken to distinguish whatever commodities might have been donated or kept 'in store' from anything recently purchased. Any superfluous information, such as the *minutiae* of leases, is omitted; and, most notably, the long final section of the account listing unpaid rents and other modest sums (the '*unde super*') is reduced to a bare minimum. Most of the errors, omissions and corrections apparent in 18A/6 have been made good in 18A/7, which clearly draws upon a wide variety of other supplementary documentation of the sort that would have been presented at the audit or kept by the chamberlains for personal reference.

We are not told when, why or by whom it was decided to make these improvements, or to revise the accounts dating from 1541–2 to 1549–50 according to this new model, although circumstantial evidence provides convincing answers to each of these questions. Robert Raynbald, who acted as joint chamberlain from 1541 to 1543 and then alone until 1550, was clearly the driving force for change. The accounts presented in 18A/7 correspond exactly with his years in office, and the volume ends with an inventory of all the communal property, including important leases, that would have been in his care when he stepped down (Appendix III). The above-mentioned indenture tripartite of 1449 implied (but did not explicitly state) that, at the end of their period of service, chamberlains would have to answer for the safekeeping of all the muniments entrusted to them, and that some form of inventory would be required. Raynbald was, however, the first formally to incorporate such a document into his final account, thereby demonstrating the meticulous attention to detail and sense of personal responsibility that emerge so vividly from the material recorded in 18A/7.[197] The inventory (along with his signature on f. 344^v) certainly sets his personal stamp upon the account book, which he may well have envisaged as a fitting 'memoriall' to almost a decade of continuous and often stressful service (see p. 34).

Raynbald's background prepared him well for the rigours and responsibilities of civic office. He and his brother William joined the freedom together as mercers in 1524, when their father Stephen, a grocer who had previously

---

196 As, for example, below, pp. 211–12.

197 The practice became more common from 1553 onward, although these inventories are far less detailed than Raynbald's: NCR, 18A/8, ff. 38, 124–4^v, 125^v–6, 158^v–9, 181^v–2, 206–6^v, 231–1^v, 306^v–7^v, 362–3.

been foreign receiver, was serving as sheriff.[198] Since the latter had arrived in Norwich as an immigrant, possibly from the Low Countries, his rise through the ranks appears especially impressive.[199] William made greater use of these overseas connections, establishing himself as one of the wealthiest residents and leading ship owners of Ipswich, where he was elected three times as bailiff and at least once, in 1545, as MP.[200] But both brothers took full advantage of the Dissolution: William acquired part of the Ipswich Greyfriars, while Robert bought estates in Raynham and Watlington, together with the rectory and advowson of Ketteringham, following the suppression of Pentney priory.[201] These purchases, which cost him £129 in 1545, may well have been made with help from the above-mentioned John Eyer, whom he later named as one of his executors, in association with another staunch evangelical, the influential Norfolk knight, Sir Edward Warner.[202] With characteristic efficiency, he immediately produced 'a parfight extent and dragge of all the landes, pastures, medows and woodes' attached to the rectory. It was 'new wryten' by him in 1558 as a 'booke' of twenty-nine parchment folios (in the same format as NCR, 18A/7) to allow for subsequent acquisitions and exchanges and, no doubt, to assist Eyer and Warner in their eventual task.[203]

Raynbald's will, which he drew up in August 1559, as his sixtieth year approached, furnishes further evidence of his aptitude for business as well as his religious proclivities. Not only did he instruct his executors to compile 'a parfight inventorye' of all his goods immediately after his death (old habits clearly died hard), but he also urged them to ensure that each bequest was legally watertight by consulting a reliable lawyer. Such a step can hardly have been necessary, since, as he pointed out, 'I have taken good advisement in the making herof, pervsing yt many tymes, and haue wrytten euery word of the same with myn owne hand and subscribed my name vnder euery lesse of the same with my owne hand'.[204] It is easy to see why he showed so much

---

198 W. Rye, ed., *Calendar of the Freemen of Norwich from 1317 to 1603* (1888), p. 115.

199 He contributed to the alien subsidy of 1540 as a resident of Ber Street, where he had first served as a constable in 1506: NCR, 7 I/18; *INCO*, p. 129.

200 *HoP, 1509–1558*, iii, p. 190. At his death in 1556, William left bequests of over £2,200, as well as extensive property in Ipswich, to his wife and children, and £50 to his brother, whom he named as an executor: TNA, PROB 11/38/85.

201 *LPFD*, XX, part 2 (1545), no 266 (29).

202 For Eyer, see below p. 264 note 556; and for Sir Edward Warner (d. 1565) of Plumstead, *HoP, 1509–1558*, iii, pp. 550–1.

203 NRO, BOI 154/1.

204 NRO, NCC Reg. Goldingham, ff. 196ᵛ–8ᵛ. He was then fifty-nine years old, with a wife, Anne, and three children, to whom he left a total of £500 and extensive property. The will was proved on 18 January following.

interest in the way that his accounts were presented, even to the extent of revising them himself.[205]

Personal factors were not, however, the only reason prompting Raynbald to initiate change. The increasing length and complexity of the accounts submitted by the chamberlains during the 1540s made some form of rationalisation imperative. The section listing expenditure on the Blackfriars precinct in 1543–4 alone runs to ten densely written folios,[206] while that for the following year is over three times as long,[207] and thus more than *twice* the length of the entire account for 1537–8.[208] If, as Raynbald intended, these documents were to provide an official record that would be easy to consult, the content would need careful reorganisation and some judicious pruning.

Despite his desire to streamline the accounts by ruthlessly excising any unnecessary detail, Raynbald was himself prone to eloquent asides and revealing comments, which enliven an otherwise utilitarian text. We can, for example, sense his mounting disgust at the 'stynkyng fylth' removed in 1542 from the women's prison and from a 'wonderfull noysfull' gutter nearby (and appreciate why he should give 7*d* as a reward to the men who reluctantly worked there).[209] Constant importuning by stallholders' wives for tips and douceurs proved an irritant that occasionally got the better of him, as did the expectation that he would stand drinks for the palpably disreputable tenants of 'vytalling howses'.[210] He reports threats by the keelmen who had transported soldiers down river to Yarmouth in 1542 to throw his over-zealous assistant overboard on the return trip, forcing the terrified functionary to walk home; and disapprovingly identifies the unscrupulous tenants who 'ranne awaye' with their possessions, often at night, so that they could not be distrained for unpaid rent.[211] Not surprisingly, given his close personal involvement in the 'commocon' of 1549, he seized the opportunity to exculpate himself from any hint of collusion with 'tratour Kette and hys kytlynges'.[212] Although his account for 1548–9 falls outside the chronological range of this volume, the parts concerning official responses during the rebellion are presented in Appendix II, since they offer a compelling, if

---

205 See below, p. 57.
206 NCR, 18A/6, ff. 145ᵛ–54ᵛ: two folios numbered 145.
207 NCR, 18A/6, ff. 164ᵛ–97ᵛ: two folios numbered 168.
208 NCR, 18A/6, ff. 1–15ᵛ.
209 See below, pp. 132–3.
210 See below, p. 267.
211 See below, pp. 167, 239.
212 NCR, 18A/7, f. 310ᵛ.

carefully edited, report of events within the city that deserves to be better known.[213] Only Raynbald, one suspects, would have claimed among his expenses a bribe of 3s 4d offered to the rebels in the hope that he would not be frogmarched to their camp on Mousehold Heath and put on trial before the court of popular justice.

Having finally relinquished the chamberlainship in 1550, Raynbald purchased an exemption from further office holding at a cost of £30 in the following year. He clearly did not contemplate complete retirement, however, preferring to spend the last decade of his life in the less demanding post of clavor, rather than becoming an alderman, or even mayor.[214] Already by this date the newly acquired hospital of St Giles had begun to attract his attention; much of his time and expertise were henceforth devoted to its re-foundation and effective management as a civic institution for the destitute.[215] Despite his manifest rejection of the belief that salvation might be acquired through good works, he showed practical commitment to 'the comforte of the nedy pore', setting aside money in his will for the distribution of 'shirtes and smockes' among them.[216] A similar bequest to the assembly on behalf of 'the common welthe' of Norwich reflects his long involvement in schemes for the amelioration of urban life, of which the transformation of the Dominican friary was by far the greatest.

From Blackfriars to common hall

The impact of religious reform was soon felt in Norwich. In early May 1538, the monastic cathedral of Holy Trinity was the first in England to surrender to the Crown, thereby effecting a smooth and relatively painless transition from Benedictine community to secular college.[217] Rumours that the city's four mendicant houses would be next to face dissolution prompted the assembly to contemplate the bold step of acquiring the Dominican friary,

---

213 Sanitised extracts appear in F.W. Russell, *Kett's Rebellion in Norfolk* (1859), pp. 32, 34, 39, 67, 73–7, 82, 90, 98–9, 131–6, 139–40, 148, 154.

214 NCR, 16D/2, f. 245–5ᵛ; *INCO*, p. 129.

215 NCR, 16D/2, ff. 225, 246; 16C/2, ff. 239–9ᵛ, 245; 24A/23, Great Hospital account roll, 1549–50, m. 16ᵛ. See also *MFS*, chapters seven and eight. We may well have Raynbald to thank for the preservation of the hospital's medieval archive, as in 1551 he was one of the officials appointed by the assembly 'to vyewe, examyn and sorte oute all such evydences as apperteigne to the howse of the poore', making them readily accessible for consultation: 16D/2, f. 228ᵛ.

216 NRO, NCC Reg. Goldingham, f. 198ᵛ.

217 R. Houlbrooke, 'Refoundation and Reformation, 1538–1628', in I. Atherton and others, eds, *Norwich Cathedral: Church, City and Diocese, 1096–1996* (1996), pp. 507–8.

whose imposing church and central location, not far from the guildhall, already made it an ideal place for staging civic ceremonies (plate 4).[218] Before any overtures could be made to the king, however, it was essential to gain the approval of the duke of Norfolk, who was not only the house's most influential patron, but also the leader of the religiously conservative faction at court.[219] On 31 August 1538, the aldermen Augustine Steward and Edward Reed were despatched to Norfolk's palace at Kenninghall 'to haue hys graces will & pleasure iff the cominaltie shall make sute to the kynges grace to haue the graunte off the Blak Freres hous'.[220] The chamberlains equipped them with two gallons of spiced wine as a gift for the duke, followed by special messengers bearing 200 pears, six live swans and two cranes.[221]

Having succeeded in their mission, the civic authorities immediately embarked upon a campaign of intense political lobbying, in which Steward used his position as a prominent supporter of the government and one of Norwich's serving MPs to full advantage.[222] He was almost certainly the bearer of a letter dated 5 September to Thomas Cromwell, seeking his 'mediacion and godenes' in language guaranteed to elicit a favourable response. As he explained, the friary was 'scituate and stondeth in the mydde parte off the said citie to the great bewtifieng of the same'. It was, moreover, the place where 'I and my brethern and all our predecessours heretoffore, as well in causes touching the commaundement of the kynges highnes [...] as also ffor other causes consernyng the conseruacion off the comon welth of the same cite haue accustomably vsed to mete in comon counselles'. Ownership of such an important communal asset would consequently be far more than a simple matter of bricks and mortar, since it represented 'noon litill commodyte to the incresse off virtue and consueruacon of the comon welthe'.[223] The wording of this letter drew heavily upon the lexicon

---

218 For the early history and continuing topographical significance of the friary, see H. Sutermeister, *The Norwich Blackfriars* (Norwich, 1977).

219 As Head, *Ebbs and Flows*, pp. 273–6, reveals, Norfolk was himself a major beneficiary of the Dissolution. Since the prior of the Dominicans and his predecessor had asked in June 1537 for a ten-year lease made by them to William Morraunt to be entered in the civic records, it looks as if a change of ownership was already then under discussion: NCR, 16A/4, ff. 19ᵛ–20.

220 NCR, 16D/2, f. 185ᵛ.

221 NCR, 18A/6, f. 12ᵛ.

222 *HoP 1509–1558*, iii, pp. 383–5. When awarding Steward his expenses in May 1540, the mayor's court acknowledged that Blackfriars had been acquired through his 'gret labour, diligence, sute & meanes': NCR, 16D/2, f. 191ᵛ.

223 TNA, SP1/136, f. 73. In 1538–9 the chamberlains paid 20s to certain 'jentilmen vewing the Blak Freres ffor therr ffavours theryn', perhaps Cromwell's agents: NCR, 18A/6, f. 25ᵛ.

of civic humanism, reflecting a growing conviction on the part of men such as Steward and his fellow magistrates that an effective combination of 'preaching, teaching and charity' would enhance social stability, while simultaneously addressing the needs of the poor.[224] The Blackfriars' complex was envisaged from the outset as a place where these ideals might be translated into practice, as an expression of the physical and spiritual cohesion of the body politic.[225]

In May 1541, for example, the route of the annual procession held on Monday in Rogation Week was changed to end at the 'new hall', where a sermon could be delivered to the crowds in the open-air preaching yard.[226] Two years later the assembly agreed that the Corpus Christi procession, one of the highlights of the liturgical year, should begin and end there too.[227] The conversion of the chancel of the Dominicans' church into a chapel dedicated to St John enabled the authorities to celebrate these festivities in a suitably imposing civic context. It also greatly facilitated the reform of the craft guilds in 1543 'ffor the better perfectyng of some good and comely order [...] and ffor the better encrease of the comon welthe of this citie'.[228] Concerns about the lax observance of their respective feast days (in churches and chapels scattered throughout Norwich) and the neglect of commemorative masses for departed members could be met by a process of centralisation. Henceforward, feasts and masses were to be celebrated in the new hall and chapel, according to a strict roster and under the direction of a doctrinally acceptable priest, whose salary would be funded by the guildsmen themselves. Fees known as 'certens', which they paid 'ffor the mayntenance of dyuyne seruice to be had, celebrate and songe in the chapell of Saynt John' were collected by the chamberlain, who was also responsible for the building works involved.[229]

It was touch and go to have the chapel ready as planned for Easter Sunday 1543 and to stage the St George's day feast, the high point of the civic calendar, in the new banqueting-hall (the former nave). A dedicated team

---

224 A. Wood, *The 1549 Rebellion and the Making of Early Modern England* (Cambridge, 2007), pp. 30–40; W.R.D. Jones, *The Tudor Commonwealth 1529–1559* (1970), chapters two and three.

225 The acquisition of St Giles's hospital by the city from the Crown in 1547 marked a further development of this policy, which accorded closely with schemes then being pursued in the Low Countries: *MFS*, chapters seven and eight.

226 A new wainscot pulpit was built especially for the purpose: below, Appendix III.

227 NCR, 16A/4, f. 39ᵛ; 16A/5, p. 55; *RCN*, ii, p. 312.

228 *RCN*, ii, pp. 296–310, quotation on p. 297.

229 *RCN*, ii, pp. 297, 310–12; McClendon, *Quiet Reformation*, pp. 102–4; NCR, 18A/7, ff. 101ᵛ–2.

of craftsmen, labourers and cleaners had to work 'erly and late' to finish on schedule.[230] The installation of a perk (loft) and pair of organs acquired from the church of St George Tombland was only just completed in time for the Corpus Christi day service a few weeks later, in part because they 'did steke and whystyll' when first reassembled and had eventually to be repaired by an organ-maker from Ipswich.[231] This collective achievement is even more striking, given that the same men were also busy constructing or refurbishing all the various facilities, such as the bakery, buttery, cisterns, conduits, kitchens, larders, lavatories, pantry, poultry house, servery and wells, needed for staging feasts, ceremonies and civic entertainments. There was even a newly enclosed stretch of river for raising the swans that were consumed on grand occasions or presented to influential people as gifts.[232]

Well aware of their crucial role in 'balancing the interests of the rich against the anger of the poor', the rulers of Norwich had other, more inclusive plans for the future of the site.[233] A prominent element of their humanist agenda, and one that would certainly have appealed to Thomas Cromwell, was their promise to 'fynd a perpetuall free scole' at Blackfriars 'for the good erudicion & educacon of yought in lernyng & vertue'.[234] There were sound practical as well as pedagogic and doctrinal reasons for such a move, as the old episcopal grammar school had been destroyed in the fires of 1507, and the boys had since then been taught alongside the almoner's scholars in the cathedral. Although admirable in principle (especially to those with evangelical sympathies), the idea of a 'common school' funded jointly by the dean and chapter, who would pay the salaries of the master and other staff, and the city, which would provide the buildings, faced many obstacles. Having helped to clear their new premises of muck and rubbish and make it reasonably habitable, the master and scholars remained at Blackfriars for fewer than three years, moving first to the Green Yard near the cathedral and then, *via* St Giles's hospital, to permanent lodgings in the close.[235] It has been suggested that the city was anxious to put the

---

230 See below, pp. 222, 229.

231 See below, pp. 230–2, 285.

232 See below, p. 287.

233 Wood, 'Kett's Rebellion', p. 294.

234 NCR, 8K/7 (b). Cromwell had been closely involved in Cardinal Wolsey's educational schemes and rescued his school at Ipswich. Significantly, by 1540 it had moved from its original premises to the recently dissolved Blackfriars there: MacCulloch, *Thomas Cromwell*, pp. 112, 466–7, and for his general interest in education, p. 362. See also Jones, *Tudor Commonwealth*, chapter three.

235 *MFS*, pp. 201, 234; R. Harries, P. Cattermole and P. Mackintosh, *A History of Norwich School* (Norwich, 1991), pp. 25–9, 43–5.

schoolhouse to commercial use in order to pay off the money that it owed to King Henry, but, as the chamberlain's account for 1543–4 makes clear, the premises were requisitioned for one of the two granaries that were urgently needed to store the communal wheat supply.[236]

The frequency and severity of grain shortages, described above, made it highly desirable to stockpile supplies while prices were low, although such an exercise was difficult without an appropriate building. The Leadenhall market, where London's grain had been stored in secure, dry, well-ventilated conditions above ground since the fifteenth century, offered an ideal model, but would have been far too costly to emulate.[237] Suitable space could, however, be made available at Blackfriars, which had the added advantage of proximity to the river for easy access by boat. As we have seen, fear as well as philanthropy drove this agenda. In 1527, during one period of dearth, a local chronicler reported that 'there was so great a scarceness of Corn about Christmas that the Commons of the city were ready to rise upon the rich men'.[238] The situation between December 1543 and March 1544 seemed no better, prompting an outlay of at least £86 on wheat by Robert Raynbald, who ensured that neither the market nor the city's bakers lacked for subsidised supplies.[239] He stored the grain temporarily at the common stathe, in a nearby house that had recently been vacated by the anchoress of St Edward's and at Carrow priory, while pushing forward work at Blackfriars for the conversion of the schoolhouse and upper levels of the former infirmary into two spacious 'corn chambers'. Both were paved with tile purchased from the recently dissolved Greyfriars and Carrow priory, and where necessary re-glazed to keep out birds. A new gateway to accommodate the carts that transported the wheat uphill to the market was also constructed, as were broad, well-lit staircases allowing labourers to carry sacks up and down in safety.[240]

It is, none the less, uncertain how far the ruling elite anticipated the heavy costs and hard labour involved in their ambitious project, or the burden that would fall upon the shoulders of the chamberlains. As their accounts reveal, complaints voiced from at least 1538 by the Dominicans about the 'cold & smalle charyte' on which they had been obliged to subsist

---

236 Harries, Cattermole and Mackintosh, *History of Norwich School*, p. 26; below, pp. 279–83.
237 M.W. Samuel, 'The Fifteenth-Century Garner at Leadenhall, London', *Antiquaries Journal*, 69 (1989), pp. 119–53; Rawcliffe, *Urban Bodies*, pp. 282–3.
238 Johnson, 'Chronological Memoranda', p. 144.
239 See below, pp. 270–1.
240 See below, pp. 270, 275–6, 279–83.

clearly did not exaggerate. Without continuing support from the citizenry, it had proved impossible to maintain the fabric of their many buildings, while the 'brekyng of glasse wyndows with deffasynges off manye other thynges' committed by 'lygthe persons' of an evangelical persuasion had caused significant damage, enabling birds to nest in the priory church.[241] Fear that the opportunists who were already raiding the site for building materials would make off with the lead roofing and remaining glass led one of Cromwell's agents to post a guard on the premises in November of that year.[242] By the time that the city took formal delivery of the 'spoyled and sore dekayed' Blackfriars in June 1540 it was seriously dilapidated, with weeds sprouting upon the piles of refuse and rubble that lay everywhere.[243] In the following year alone, the chamberlain paid 26s for the removal of 188 'lodes' of muck and rubbish from the site; and before lessons could begin in the new school glass had to be replaced and yet more rubbish carted away.[244] The sudden collapse of part of the dormitory roof and the chapter house on Boxing Day 1541, perhaps because of earlier demolition work on the adjacent buttresses, caused further problems, not least for the carpenters who 'labored sore & in gret jeopardy havyng down the beamys & pryncy-palles' that remained.[245] Yet more 'dangeros clymyng' was required to stop up the holes in the steeple and the broken windows where birds entered the building, leaving dirt that soon became heavily encrusted.[246]

Setting aside the sum of £81 paid on 1 June 1540 for possession of the former friary,[247] the not inconsiderable expenses sustained in lobbying for the award[248] and the compensation of £152 demanded by King Henry for the lead roofing,[249] the city's outlay on its new common hall between 1540 and 1545 cannot have been less than £435.[250] An analysis of expenditure

---

241 TNA, SP1/137, f. 131.

242 *LPFD*, XIII, part 2 (1538), no 934.

243 *LPFD*, XV, no 831 (72); below p. 148.

244 See below, pp. 108–9, 122–3.

245 See below, pp. 153, 158, 220.

246 See below, p. 281.

247 *LPFD*, XV, no 831 (72); NCR, 8K/7 (b).

248 Augustine Steward recovered expenses of 66s 8d in 1539–40, £4 in 1540–1 and £20 in 1541–2, although he probably spent far more, as, for example, on paving tiles bought at his own cost from the Franciscan friary: below, pp. 74, 79, 123 note 192, 149.

249 See below, p. 340. Thomas Necton and Steward were bound over in personal sureties of 500 marks, underwritten by the assembly in May 1542, for the payment of this money: NCR, 16A/5, p. 311; 16D/2, f. 199ᵛ.

250 This total includes £9 for paving around the great garden north of the river in 1544–5: below, pp. 312–13. The entire project was effectively finished by 1544–5, and less than £15

sustained there in the accounting year 1542–3 alone reveals that the chamberlains then employed fourteen carpenters, thirteen masons, five tilers, two sawyers, two plumbers and two pinners, along with a glazier, a painter and an organ maker, on the transformation of the site. They were assisted by thirty-six labourers, some of whom worked regularly for the chamberlains, while others belonged to specialist teams assembled by the artisans themselves. In all, they were paid for a total of 1,839 days' labour, excluding tasks such as dismantling the great crucifix in the nave that took less than a day and piecework undertaken by contract for a pre-arranged fee.[251] The organisation involved seems all the more impressive, given that the chamberlains were also obliged to deploy many of these men elsewhere on a variety of other projects.

Men and materials

Even when no major building campaigns were in hand, the routine maintenance of civic property required the services of a substantial workforce, including carpenters, daubers, dyke-builders, glaziers, grinders, joiners, masons, miners (for demolition work), painters, pinners, plumbers, sawyers, scaffolders, smiths, thatchers and tilers, together with their apprentices and labourers. Carters and boatmen were needed to transport materials and to remove the debris that the builders left behind, while the suppliers of brick, clay, flint, glass, lime, nails and other ironwork, reed, sand, stone, straw, tiles and timber had to be commissioned and paid. One of the chamberlains' many responsibilities was to lay in equipment and material as cheaply as possible for future use, housing it safely or selling off anything surplus to requirements.

Getting supplies to the right place on time was a major logistical challenge, made easier by the creation of storage depots in appropriate locations. As had been the case when so many parish churches were being transformed in the later fifteenth century, parts of Norwich must have resembled building sites, with heaps of material lying ready for use all over the city.[252] In order to protect the public and deter theft, the London chamberlains were forbidden in 1479 from storing building supplies anywhere but the guildhall.[253]

---

was spent on the common hall in the following year: NCR, 18A/7, ff. 205ᵛ–10. Sutermeister, *Norwich Blackfriars*, p. 9, maintains that the rulers of Norwich 'got a good bargain', but does not consider the cost of repairs and rebuilding.

251 See below, pp. 211–33.

252 Rutledge 'An Urban Environment', pp. 91–2.

253 R.R. Sharpe, ed., *Calendar of Letter-Books of the City of London: Letter-Book L* (1912), p. 164.

No such restrictions obtained in Norwich. It made sense to keep bricks, boards and roof tiles in the chamber below the market cross, handy for work on the stalls and adjacent tenements,[254] while the cellars of the nearby guildhall and common inn proved equally useful in this respect. In 1541–2 the chamberlains purchased a battery of locks and keys to ensure that the great quantities of timber then being housed in the inn would be safe from thieves.[255] The newly acquired Blackfriars offered an ideal site for the storage of whatever large items might be needed in the Tombland area, while the common stathes in Conesford served a similar purpose regarding the city's riverside properties.

The recycling of materials from 'comon store' meant that some buildings must have been veritable palimpsests of cannibalised timber and stone. The use of 'old postes lyeng in the guyldhall vowlt some tyme, beyng […] of the old wrostlyng place at Magdalen' to make mangers in the stables at the common inn exemplifies a traditional emphasis upon the husbanding of resources and avoidance of waste.[256] From this perspective, it is easier to understand why the Dissolution was marked by such a ruthlessly unsentimental approach to buildings which, until recently, had dominated the physical and spiritual landscape of Norwich.[257] Hardly had the Blackfriars' complex passed into civic ownership, than twenty-six loads of roofing materials and thirty-six of timber, stone and tile were removed to the common inn, where new houses were being built.[258] 'Old tymbyr' from the roof of the monastic dormitory was likewise earmarked for extensions to the butchery in the market, while anything that seemed too rotten for reuse went to the glaziers for fuel.[259] At the same time, the Franciscan friary, which had been acquired by the duke of Norfolk, was systematically demolished, furnishing the chamberlains with forty-six loads of stone for street paving in 1542–3, as well as a ready supply of tiles, marble, 'great joists' for roofing and other materials for the conversion of the Blackfriars.[260] Three hundred great paving tiles for the granary came from Carrow priory in 1544, along with others excavated from

254 See below, pp. 192, 201, 203, 315, 333.

255 See below, p. 138.

256 See below, p. 310.

257 M. Howard, 'Recycling the Monastic Fabric: Beyond the Act of Dissolution', in D. Gaimster and R. Gilchrist, eds, *The Archaeology of Reformation 1480–1580* (Leeds, 2003), pp. 221–34.

258 See below, pp. 85–7.

259 See below, pp. 133, 137, 158.

260 See below, pp. 108, 136, 148–9, 153, 156, 194–7, 225, 255, 313, 320, 338. Stone was in such demand because East Anglia has no natural reserves for quarrying other than flint.

the cloisters there and bought as a job lot by the ever vigilant Raynbald, who rarely missed the opportunity to drive a bargain.[261]

The same craftsmen, labourers and suppliers were frequently employed by the chamberlains from one year to the next on different jobs across the city. Allowing for connexions of family and neighbourhood, this was no doubt because of their reliability, the high standard of their workmanship and the competitive pricing of the material on offer. An elite group of artisans was clearly valued for its expertise. Locks, keys, bolts and other items of hardware were supplied for much of this period by a smith known simply by his forename of 'Paschall' or 'Pascha', as was then a common practice where foreigners were concerned, perhaps because their surnames (in this case Wasshaw) were hard to pronounce. He lived near to hand in Conesford, an area popular with the 'aliens' who, like him, came to Norwich from overseas. Other immigrants, such as the mason, John Erne, settled in Ber Street, immediately to the west.[262] Erne and his team of labourers were in constant demand, as were his fellow masons, John Walpole and William and Robert Holland. The same carpenters, too, appear regularly throughout the accounts, headed by John Byrche and Nicholas Tutell, both of whom ran large and financially successful businesses.

Most of the men employed by the chamberlains received daily wages, which came to between $4d$ and $5d$ for a labourer and up to $7d$ or $8d$ for a master craftsman, especially if he were supervising a sizeable team of men or 'company', when the rate might rise as high as $10d$.[263] Those engaged in the building trade worked shorter hours in winter than summer, when it was lighter, and the weather improved. Set rather optimistically by parliamentary statute at twelve hours between March and September and nine for the rest of the year, with prescribed breaks for food, the working day of a sixteenth-century mason seems in practice to have been far less regimented.[264] Even so, regular purchases by the chamberlains of candles for artisans and labourers 'to worke by on evenings and mornynges' confirm that activity indoors began before dawn and continued well after dusk in

---

261 See below, pp. 281, 283.

262 Wasshaw, like Erne, paid 10s toward the 1540 subsidy on aliens: NCR, 7 I/18. By the time that he drew up his will, in 1555, he had acquired a tenement in the parish of St Mary the Less from the profits of his lucrative business: NRO, NCC Reg. Veysye, ff. 135ᵛ–7.

263 A few craftsmen, notably thatchers, who may have lived outside Norwich, were offered board as well as wages, but such arrangements were relatively uncommon: see below, pp. 77–8, 127, 129. See L.F. Salzman, *Building in England down to 1540: A Documentary History* (Oxford, 1967), chapter four, for general background.

264 D. Knoop and G.P. Jones, *The Mediaeval Mason* (Manchester, third edn, 1967), p. 105.

winter.[265] From time to time, skilled craftsmen contracted to work for the civic authorities 'a gret', in return for an agreed sum of money rather than a wage, as in 1543 when John Byrche undertook to make some of the seats and benches at the new hall for £11, payable in instalments.[266] Masons were often retained in this way for laying specific lengths of street paving, which they supplied themselves, along with sand and 'workmanshyppe'.[267] Women, such as the wife of one labourer who weeded the preaching yard in 1542 and the daughter of another who helped her father to empty a contaminated well shortly afterwards, were occasionally employed on an *ad hoc* basis at a lower rate of between 3*d* and 1*d* a day for menial tasks.[268] They do, however, appear as the suppliers of a wide variety of goods, ranging from the confections offered to visiting dignitaries to less predictable commodities, such as the large quantities of nails sold by Mistress Morraunt (the chamberlain's widowed mother), bricks by Mistress Trace and laths, lime and tile pins by Mistress Marsham, each of whom had taken over her late husband's business.[269]

Specialist equipment was shipped *via* Yarmouth from London, as in 1542–3, when three dozen customised shovels, reinforced with iron and steel, were acquired at a cost of 14*s* for work on the river; and 1544 when one of the aldermen purchased a Danish hopper for cleansing the wheat that had been stockpiled for poor relief.[270] Otherwise, the chamberlains bought or borrowed everything that they needed locally in Norwich or its immediate hinterland. In 1531 Pascha provided, at a cost of 12*d*, the iron letter 'N' used to brand ladders, barrows, pickaxes and shovels to denote civic ownership.[271] Even so, covetable items, such as pickaxes, could disappear (usually at night), as well as needing the regular repairs that are punctiliously recorded in the accounts. Some items, especially ropes, buckets and tall ladders, were borrowed for specific projects by the chamberlains, whose own stock appears to have been comparatively modest. This was a common practice, only deemed worthy of note when the owner had to be compensated because of

---

265 As, for example, below p. 137; and Salzman, *Building in England*, p. 62, and chapter three generally for working conditions.

266 See below, p. 216; and Salzman, *Building in England*, pp. 50–2.

267 See below, pp. 197, 255–6. The original contracts rarely survive; but see one of 1432 for the rebuilding of the old common stathe: *RCN*, ii, pp. 389–91.

268 See below, pp. 160, 192, 216.

269 See, for examples, below, pp. 135, 152, 187, 302.

270 See below, pp. 199, 271; and Appendix III.

271 NCR, 18A/5, f. 35ᵛ. It was still in use in 1550, along with a brand in shape of St George's cross: below, Appendix III.

damage ('hurte' or 'slytte') or excessive wear and tear. Ever ingenious, on one occasion, having paid compensation of 3s 4d for a broken ladder, the chamberlains used the two remaining halves to make new ones.[272]

Raynbald's accounts furnish a remarkable insight into the working conditions of the labourers and artisans whose daily experiences so rarely feature in the historical record, while reflecting his own attitudes as the employer of a large workforce. The perennial problem of the absentee workman who disappears midway through a project to finish another job elsewhere was a predictable source of irritation. The rival demands made on his carpenters' time proved to be 'a gret hynderans to the worke here', he complained when trying to complete a new tenement at the Blackfriars on schedule in 1544.[273] Even worse, were those whose clumsiness caused further setbacks. His exasperation with 'oon of the cookes' who managed to fracture a newly laid water pipe on the morning of the St George's day festivities is palpable;[274] and it clearly pained him to record the inevitable accidents (such as broken windows and damaged tools) that delayed the completion of these projects.

Eloquent on the shortcomings of those who failed to meet his exacting standards, Raynbald was, none the less, ready to praise men who worked hard, often in unpleasant or dangerous conditions, under his own watchful eye. He was even prepared to invest in the occasional (small) barrel of beer for those who endured 'extreme hote' weather or had to stay away from home overnight.[275] The masons who took 'moche paynes' cleaning a polluted well, up to the knees in 'vyle matter', earned his unstinting admiration.[276] So too did the carpenters who risked their necks when repairing the public pillory. 'Thowe yt do not appere outwardly that yt wold take suche tyme', he explained, 'yet no dowte yt was bothe paynfull and jepardos to make the same suer, abyll to bere any man'.[277] A sense of the increasing burden shouldered by civic employees of all stations as a result of wars abroad and famine at home emerges from the remarkable tribute paid by Raynbald to the labourer, Henry Woodruff, 'whose helpe the accomptant was fayne to haue'. Working constantly for sixty-five days between Midsummer and Michaelmas 1545, he coped with one emergency after another, running errands, assisting with the dispatch of guns and soldiers, tending the

---

272 See below, p. 203.
273 See below, p. 331.
274 See below, p. 229.
275 See below, pp. 204, 259.
276 See below, p. 336.
277 See below, p. 315.

granary, selling subsidised wheat in the market and, whenever a spare moment presented, weeding the area around the common hall. There was, indeed, 'much other turmoylyng to and fro', during which Woodruff was 'nevyr ydyll', and all for 4½*d* a day.[278] At a time when men of his class all too often prompted fear and suspicion, as well as overt contempt, it is rare to encounter an encomium of this kind.

---

278 See below, p. 339; and Appendix II for his loyal service during Kett's Rebellion.

Editorial method

The six chamberlains' accounts presented in this volume cover an unusually eventful period in the history of both the city of Norwich and the nation. They also document a major shift in the way that the chamberlains compiled and organised their accounts, which makes them especially interesting subjects for close analysis.[1] The accounts are to be found in two paper books: NRO, NCR, 18A/6 and 18A/7. The first, 18A/6 (1537–46), measures 9″ by 12.75″ and was rebound in the nineteenth century in nondescript cloth-covered boards with a suede spine. Its final account, for the year 1545–6, is written on paper of a slightly smaller size than the previous ones, with signs of progressively heavier damp staining on the bottom of successive folios.[2] It had long been customary to assign either the accountant or his scribe a quire or two of paper each year for a 'boke' in which a relatively neat copy of the relevant account would be written.[3] Eventually, a number of these 'bokes' would be gathered together into a composite leather-bound volume for storage in the civic archive in the guildhall. The account for 1545–6 seems likely to have been part of a separate volume covering the years 1545–51, the rest of which has now been lost, perhaps because of water damage, but on which Robert Raynbald clearly drew when compiling 18A/7.

Although it appears to have been rebound at roughly the same time as 18A/6, and now has identical nineteenth-century end papers, 18A/7 (1541–50) is otherwise strikingly different.[4] It is a little smaller, measuring 8.5″ by 12.25″. The tooled dark leather spine is Victorian, but the binder retained some of the manuscript waste (fragments of plainsong from a medieval service book) used for the original end papers and inner spine. He also preserved the expensive and finely decorated sixteenth-century leather

---

1 See above, pp. 38–41.

2 NCR, 18A/6, ff. 198–234.

3 See, for example, below pp. 162, 165.

4 I am most grateful to Nick Sellwood, chief conservation officer at the NRO, for examining these two volumes with me and for his expert opinion about the rebinding.

binding on the front and back covers (see plate 1). We cannot now tell if the previous chamberlains' account books were originally so handsome, but it is tempting to suggest that Raynbald may have wished to leave his mark on the outside as well as the inside of this testimony to nine years of dedicated service. The text of 18A/7 is written in the same neat, clear and uniform hand throughout, probably as a continuous exercise, with spacious, carefully ruled margins (p. 40). There are no significant revisions, marginalia, auditors' marks or other addenda associated with a working document. The inscription at the end of the final account in Raynbald's own hand (p. 34) is so similar in form to the writing in the rest of the text as to suggest that he may himself have been the scribe. Tellingly, the clean copy of the accounts which he compiled as bailiff of the city's manor of Barnham Hawkins (1543–50) *and* an extent of his own property in and around Ketteringham, 'new wryten' in 1558, are not only identical in layout to 18A/7 but are also in the very same hand.[5]

It is worth noting that the next volume of accounts (NCR, 18A/8), which covers the period 1551–67, adopts the layout devised by Raynbald and has a very similar leather cover, bearing the title 'the chamberlins acompte' embossed in contemporary lettering. The seventeen accounts were, however, produced by several different scribes and signed off by the auditors who inspected them. The binder, who inadvertently placed part of an inventory for 1557–8 before the end of the account for that year,[6] would have collected them together when there were enough individual 'bokes' to make a substantial volume.

Neither 18A/6 or 18A/7 was originally foliated. Arabic numbers were added much later in ink in a nineteenth-century hand, not always accurately, as some consecutive folios have the same number, while others remain blank. In the following text, blank folios are distinguished by the letter 'A' (as in 18A/6, ff. 54, 54A, 55) and duplicate folio numbers by an asterisk (as in 18A/7, ff. 71, 71*, 72). There is no folio numbered 133 in either 18A/6 or 18A/7 (which also lacks folios numbered 211 and 220). Close examination reveals that 18A/6 runs to 239 folios rather than 234 (the number of the last folio in the volume), and 18A/7 to 359 rather than 352.

This edition begins with two accounts (1539–40 and 1540–41) from 18A/6, illustrating what might be termed the 'traditional', rather cumbersome layout in use until Robert Raynbald decided to compile volume 18A/7 in

---

5 See above, pp. 37 note 188 and 42 note 203.

6 NCR, 18A/8, f. 124. A contemporary hand notes in the top margin that 'the leaves following ar not rightly placed by the bynder'.

a more accessible format. They are followed by four accounts from 18A/7 (1541–2, 1542–3, 1543–4 and 1544–5). Because 18A/6 covers the period 1537–1546, it is possible to make a detailed comparison between the two volumes, and to determine the full extent of Raynbald's many revisions. He was not simply improving and streamlining the layout, but also drawing upon other material (such as rentals and particulars of account now lost) in order to produce what he considered to be a more *accurate* as well as a more manageable text. The account for 1541–2 in 18A/7 (below, pp. 113–68), has been compared entry by entry with that in 18A/6, ff. 69–94ᵛ, each alteration, correction, excision and (occasional) extrapolation being referenced in the footnotes. In this way, we can better appreciate the meticulous care with which Raynbald approached his task. Footnotes to the accounts from 1542–3 onwards record only the more significant discrepancies between 18A/6 and 18A/7.

Where possible, every effort has been made to preserve a sense of the original orthography and layout, with some necessary modifications. In common with most sixteenth-century administrative and financial records, the chamberlains' accounts are heavily abbreviated and employ little punctuation. (One of Raynbald's most helpful innovations was to adopt a rudimentary form of paragraphing.) Contractions and suspensions have been silently extended, and minimal punctuation introduced in the interest of clarity. The capitalisation of proper nouns has been modernised. The thorn ('þ') has been rendered as 'th', but otherwise the original spelling has been retained, with the result that the letters 'g' and 'y', 'i' and 'j' and u' and 'v' are often interchangeable. Forenames and surnames appear in their original orthography, the only significant modification being the conversion of 'ff' into a capital 'F'. Abbreviated Christian names (such as *Rob't* for *Robert* and *Xofer* for *Christofer*) have been silently extended, except in the case of a labourer invariably known as Sander (Alexander) Clarke. Place names also take their sixteenth-century form; where appropriate the modern spelling appears in square brackets after the original version. Unless stated, all places are in Norfolk.

The title 'Mʳ', transcribed in the text as Master, was an honorific accorded to aldermen and other members of the ruling elite, while their wives and widows were customarily addressed as 'Mʳᵉˢ', or Mistress. These many individuals are identified as sometime office-holders in the index to this volume, but not in the footnotes unless some aspect of their affairs, such as the payment of a fine or debt, was of immediate concern to the chamberlains. T. Howes, *An Index to Norwich City Officers 1453–1836* (NRS, lii, 1986), furnishes further details of their official appointments. Members of the local gentry and aristocracy, senior clergy, visiting dignitaries and other figures from outside the ranks of the citizenry are identified on first appearance in the footnotes.

Latin words and phrases are italicised. Translations of those employed regularly by the chamberlains may be found in the glossary at the end of this volume, others are explained in footnotes as they appear. The glossary also provides a guide to English words and phrases no longer in common usage, or whose meaning has changed over the centuries, and identifies buildings and places that may now be hard to locate.

The chamberlains and their scribes followed a conventional system of dating based largely upon the saints' days and other religious festivals that still made up the ritual year despite the ongoing process of religious reformation ('St George' rather than '23 April'). A list of relevant saints' days and festivals and their place in the calendar appears after the glossary (pp. 401–3). When recording expenditure on long-running projects, the chamberlains usually listed their outgoings on a weekly basis, often calculated in terms of the major festivals: as in 'the xij^{te} weke after Myhelmes' (the twelfth week after Michaelmas, 29 September, when the accounting year began) or 'the weke byfore Crystmes'. Precise dates involving a moveable feast, such as the weeks before and after Easter and Whitsuntide, may be calculated with reference to the tables in C.R. Cheney, revised M. Jones, *Handbook of Dates for Students of British History* (Cambridge, 2000), pp. 155–235. From time to time, purchases of building material would be dated according to the day or week of the month ('xj^{te} Februarii', or 'iij^{de} weke of Aprelle'), which suggests that they may have been recorded separately from other outgoings.

Roman numerals

Officials throughout early sixteenth-century England used Roman numerals when compiling their accounts. Some recent editions of early modern and medieval records convert them into the more familiar Arabic numbers that we use today, but the original Roman numerals have been retained here. Their use conveys a better sense of the original, not least regarding the potential problems that the chamberlains and accountants would have faced when adding and subtracting without (or sometimes even with) access to a chequer board or abacus. They would also have conceived numbers and quantities very differently in a system that lacked a symbol for zero and frequently dealt in multiples of twenty. Thus, for example, m^{l} CCC iiij^{xx} bears no immediate resemblance to 1,380. These numbers can seem daunting, especially when they appear in a variety of combinations, but they follow simple rules:

Basic numbers: i or j = 1; v = 5; x = 10; C = 100; m^l = 1000

Numbers of equal value are always **added** together to provide a total: ij = 2 (1 + 1); xx = 20 (10 + 10); CC = 200 (100 + 100); m^l m^l = 2,000 (1,000 + 1,000)

When a larger number is followed by a smaller number the two are also **added** together: vj = 6 (5 + 1); xv = 15 (10 + 5); lx = 60 (50 + 10); lxxvij = 77 (50 + 10 + 10 + 5 + 1 + 1); Cxiij = 113 (100 + 10 + 1 + 1 + 1); m^l CCxviij = 1,218 (1,000 + 100 + 100 + 10 + 5 + 1 + 1 + 1)

When a smaller number is followed by a larger number the smaller is **subtracted** from the larger: ix = 9 (10 − 1); xix = 19 (10 + [10 − 1]); xl = 40 (50 − 10); xlix = 49 ([50 − 10] + [10 − 1]); xC = 90 (100 − 10)

When one number (usually 20, a score) appears *above* another the two are **multiplied** together: iiij^{xx} viij = 88 ([4 x 20] + 8); vj^{xx} = 120 (6 x 20); CC iiij^{xx} ix = 289 (200 + [4 x 20] + 9)

The Norwich chamberlains also employ the following to denote figures in the hundreds and thousands: CC *di'* = 250 (100 + 100 + *dimidia* or half 100); xv C = 1,500 (15 x 100); iiij m^l = 4,000 (4 x 1,000)

Currency

2 farthings (*qu', quartarium*) = 1 halfpenny (*ob', obolus*)
2 halfpennies = 1 penny (*d, denarius*)
12 pennies = 1 shilling (*s, solidus*)
20 shillings = 1 pound (*li, libra*) = 240*d*
This already long-established system remained in usage until 1971, when Britain adopted decimalisation.

  The mark, which was worth two-thirds of a pound (that is 13 shillings and 4 pence), was widely employed as a unit of currency in the early sixteenth century, its popularity serving to explain why so many of the receipts and payments recorded in the following pages are worth a mark (xiij*s* iiij*d*), half a mark (vj*d* viiij*d*) or a quarter of a mark (iij*s* iiij*d*).

Symbols and editorial conventions

Italic	editorial comment or elucidation outside the text
[*italic*]	editorial remarks within the text
[*at*] larg[*e*]	words or letters omitted in the manuscript which have been supplied
< >	words or numbers which have been deleted
* *	words which have been inserted
** **	words inserted within an insertion
/*italic*/	a marginal entry or annotation, brought into the text

Map 1 The parishes of late medieval and early sixteenth-century Norwich
© Cath D'Alton

Key to the parishes

1 All Saints Fyebridge
2 All Saints Timberhill
3 St Andrew
4 St Augustine
5 St Bartholomew
6 St Benedict
7 St Botolph
8 St Catherine
9 St Clement Conesford
10 St Clement Fyebridge
11 St Crowche
12 St Cuthbert
13 St Edmund
14 St Edward
15 St Etheldreda
16 St George Colegate
17 St George Tombland
18 St Giles
19 St Gregory
20 St Helen
21 St James
22 St John Maddermarket
23 St John Sepclchure
24 St John Timberhill
25 St Julian
26 St Lawrence

27 St Margaret Fyebridge
28 St Margaret Westwick
29 St Martin at Bale
30 St Martin at Oak
31 St Martin at Palace
32 St Mary Coslany
33 St Mary the Less
34 St Mary Unbrent
35 St Michael Coslany
36 St Michael at Plea
37 St Michael at Thorn
38 St Olave
39 St Paul
40 St Peter Hungate
41 St Peter Mancroft
42 St Peter Parmentergate
43 St Peter Southgate
44 St Saviour
45 SS Simon and Jude
46 St Stephen
47 St Swithin
48 St Vedast
49 St Christopher
50 St Margaret Newbridge
51 St Michael Conesford

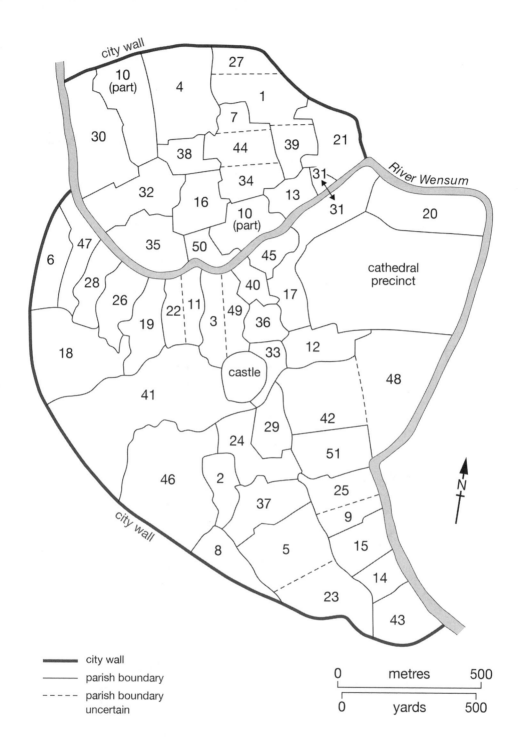

city wall

10 (part)

4

27

1

7

30

38

44

39

21

River Wensum

32

34

13

31

31

16

10 (part)

20

35

50

45

cathedral precinct

47

6

28

40

17

26

22 11

3 49

36

19

18

33

12

castle

48

41

29

42

24

51

46

2

37

25

9

8

5

15

23

14

43

N

city wall

parish boundary

parish boundary uncertain

0   metres   500

0   yards   500

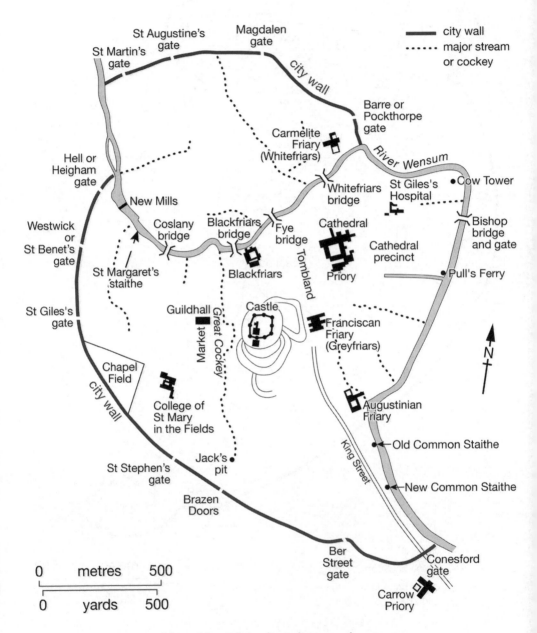

city wall
major stream or cockey

St Martin's gate
St Augustine's gate
Magdalen gate
city wall

Barre or Pockthorpe gate

River Wensum

Hell or Heigham gate

New Mills

Carmelite Friary (Whitefriars)

Whitefriars bridge

St Giles's Hospital

Cow Tower

Westwick or St Benet's gate

Coslany bridge

Blackfriars bridge

Fye bridge

Cathedral

Cathedral precinct

Bishop bridge and gate

St Margaret's staithe

Blackfriars

Tombland

Cathedral Priory

Pull's Ferry

St Giles's gate

Guildhall

Great Cockey

Castle

Market

Franciscan Friary (Greyfriars)

N

Chapel Field

College of St Mary in the Fields

city wall

Augustinian Friary

Old Common Staithe

King Street

New Common Staithe

St Stephen's gate

Jack's pit

Brazen Doors

Ber Street gate

Conesford gate

Carrow Priory

0   metres   500
0   yards   500

Map 2 Norwich in the early sixteenth century
© Cath D'Alton

THE ACCOUNTS OF
THE CHAMBERLAINS OF NORWICH,

1539–40 to 1544–45

[1539–40]

[*NCR, 18A/6, f. 28ᵛ*] Auditours   Austyn Styward, alderman
William Rogers, alderman
Stephen Reynbald
Thomas Cony

/*Civitatis Norwici*/ **The Accompte** off Edmond Wardon, chamberleyn off the citie off Norwiche, ffrom the ffest off Saynt Mighell th'archaungell in the xxxj yeere off the reign of King Henry the viij^(th) [*29 September 1539*] vnto the ffest off Saynt Mighell th'archaungell than next ffolowyng: that is to saye by oone hooll yeere

/*Arreragies*/ **Non** ffor it is the ffirst accompt off the seid accomptaunte
Summa nulla

/*Rente langable*/ **But** the seid accomptaunte chargeth hym selff & answerth off iijs, parcell off lxvs iiijd off rent langoll receyved withyn the tyme of this accompt ffor certen tenementes, late the priour & covent off Horsham Saynt Faith;[1] **Off** any thing receyued within the seid tyme off lxijs *iiijd* residue nothing here, ffor it is nat leuyable withyn the seid tyme
Summa iijs

/*Rent off the castill ffee*/ **But** the same chamberleyn answerth off xixs vjd *ob' qu'* off the rentes off the seid ffee, wher off the particler sommez apperen in the accompt of John Flouraunce, late chamberleyn, *terminat' anno regni regis Henrici viij xxviij ad ffestum Sancti Michaelis* [*29 September 1536*][2]
Summa **xixs vjd** *ob' qu'*

---

1 The Benedictine priory of Horsham St Faith, five miles north of Norwich, was dissolved in January 1537: *VCH Norfolk*, ii, p. 348.

2 'Ending at Michaelmas in the thirty-eighth year of the reign of King Henry VIII': see NCR, 18A/5, ff. 105–9.

[*f. 29*] /*Rente off assyse*/ And off viij *li* vijs xd *qu'*, wher off the particler sommes apperen in the seid accompt off the seid John Floraunce; And off ixd of rent assise off newe graunted to dyuers persons, as more playnly appereth in the accompte off Jamys Marssham & Thomas Cok, late chamberleyns, ended at Mighelmes *anno regni regis Henrici viij xxx* [*29 September 1538*];[3] And off xxd *qu'* of rent assise of new graunted, wher of the sommez particlerly apperen in the accompt of Thomas Cok & Thomas Bemond, late chamberleyns, ended at Mighelmes *anno regni regis Henrici viij xxxj* [*1539*][4]

Summa viij *li* xs iijd *ob'*

/*Ferme off the citie bochers*/ And off xliijs iiijd receyued withyn the tyme off this accompte off this accompte [*sic*] of John Hows & Richerd Barne, bochers, ffor an hole fferme off thre ffirst stallez in the market in the northende of th'est parte of the <iij ffirste> *said* stalles ayenst the yeldhalle porche; And off xvjs off Robert Tolye ffor a yere fferme off the ij next stalles towerd the southe; And off xxiiijs off Thomas Grene ffor a yeer fferme off ij next stalles towerd the south; And off xxiiijs off Richerd Deye ffor the yeere fferme off ij next stalles towerd the south; And off xvjs ffor a yere fferme off the next stalle towerd the southe receyued of Robert Seffrey; And off xvjs of Richerd Numan ffor the yere fferme of the next stalle towerd the south; And off xvjs off John [*f. 29ᵛ*] Barker ffor the yere fferme of the next stalle towerd the south; And off xs off Roger Baldry ffor the *yeere* fferme of the next stalle towerd the southe; And off ixs off the same Roger & Agnes Girdeler, widewe, ffor the yere fferme of the next stall towerd the southe deuyded bitwen them; And off xxxs ffor the yere fferme of the next stallys, beyng the last of the same est parte;[5] And off xxxvjs viijd off Andrewe Deye & John Fissher ffor the yeere fferme off the thre ffirste stalles of the other side of the seid bochery in the southende of the same; And off xvjs off Leonerd Rede ffor the yere fferme of the next stalle towerd the north of the same parte; And off xvjs of Robert Toly ffor the yere fferme of the next stalle towerd the northe; And off xijs off Robert Barbour ffor the fferme of the next stalle towerd the north; And off xiiijs off Henrye Harpour ffor the fferme of the next stall towerd the north; And off xiiijs of John Broun ffor the yere fferme of the next stall towerd the north; And off xxixs of William Cannerd ffor the yere fferme of the next stalles towerd the north; And off <xiiijs> xixs[6] off Jeffrey Rede ffor the fferme off the next stall towerd the north; And off xvjs off Henry Thornton ffor the yere fferme of the next stall towerd the north; And off xijs iiijd of John Clerk ffor the yere fferm of the next stall towerd the north; And off xls of Thomas Hobert ffor the yer fferm of the too laste stalles of the same west parte in the northende of the same; And off viijs off Andrewe Dey [*f. 30*] & Thomas Hoberd ffor a yeere fferme

3 NCR, 18A/6, f. 1ᵛ.

4 NCR, 18A/6, f. 16–16ᵛ.

5 In the previous year John Girdeler, Agnes' late husband, had farmed this stall, sharing the lease of the previous stall with Baldry: NCR, 18A/6, f. 16ᵛ.

6 This sum appears in the margin.

off a mouable stalle nere the yeldehall porche; And off viij*s* off Edmond Ferby ffor a yeere fferme of another mouable stall nere vnto the same; And off ij*s* off Robert Barbour ffor a quarter yer fferme of another mouable stalle nere vnto the same; And off iiij*s* off Robert Toly ffor a halff yere fferme of another mouable stall; And off ij*s* of Adam Kyng ffor the fferme of another mouable stall nere vnto the same by one quarter of a yere within the tyme of this accompt

Summa xxij *li* xiiij*s* iiij*d*

/*Ferme off the countre bochers*/ **Off** eny thing receyued ffor the fferme of the ffirst & ij^{de} stallez at the westende off the yeldhall within the tyme of this accompte nothing here in defaute off ffermers; **But** he answerth of xij*s* receyued off Thomas Toly ffor the yere fferme of the thirde stalle called the penticestalle at the westende of the seid yeldhall; **And** off xl*s* receuyed off Richard Vyncent ffor the yeere fferme of thre stalles next vnto the southside of the seid hall; **And** off xx*s* off [*blank*] Ket ffor the yere fferme of the ffirste stalle ffixed nere the seid hall in the northende of the same;[7] **And** off xvj*s* of Thomas Vyncent ffor the yer fferme of the ij^{de} stalle towerd the southe; **And** off xiiij*s* off Richard Newman ffor the yere fferme of the iij^{de} stall; [*f. 30*^{v}] **And** off xiiij*s* receyued off Peter Broun ffor the yere fferme off the iiij^{te} stalle towerd the south; **And** off xvj*s* of [*blank*] ffor the yere fferme of the vth stalle towerd the southe; **And** off xvj*s* of [*blank*] ffor the yere fferme off the vj^{th} stall; **And** off xiiij*s* off [*blank*] ffor the yer [*fferme*] of the vij^{th} stall towerd the south; **And** off xvj*s* off [*blank*] ffor the yere fferme of the viij^{th} stall towerd the south; **And** off xvj*s* off [*blank*] ffor the yere fferme of the ix^{th} stalle towerd the south; **And** of xiij*s* iiij*d* off [*blank*] ffor the yere fferme of the xth stalle towerd the southe; **And** of xiij*s* iiij*d* of [*blank*] ffor the yere fferme of the xj stalle towerd the south; **And** off xiij*s* iiij*d* off [*blank*] ffor the yere fferme of the xij^{th} stall towerd the south; **And** off xiij*s* iiij*d* of [*blank*] ffor the yeer fferme of the xiij stalle towerd the south; **And** off xiiij*s* of [*blank*] ffor the yere fferme of the xiiij stalle towerd the south; **And** off xiij*s* iiij*d* off [*blank*] ffor the yer fferme of the xv stalle towerd the south; **And** off xiij*s* iiij*d* of [*blank*] ffor the yere fferme of the xvj stalle towerd the south; **And** off xij*s* off [*blank*] ffor the yere fferme of the xvij stalle towerd the southe; **And** off xij*s* iiij*d* ffor the yeere [*fferme*] of the xviij stalle next towerd the southe; **And** off xij*s* iiij*d* off [*blank*] [*f. 31*] ffor the yeere fferme of the xix stalle towerd the south; **And** off xij*s* of [*blank*] ffor the yeere fferme of the xx stalle towerd the south; **And** off xij*s* off [*blank*] ffor the yer fferme off the xxj stalle towerd the south; **And** off xij*s* off [*blank*] ffor the yer fferme off xxij stalle towerd the south; **And** off xij*s* of [*blank*] ffor the yer fferme of the xxiij stalle towerd the south; **And** off xij*s* iiij*d* of [*blank*] ffor the yer fferme of the xxiiij stalle towerd the south; **And** of xij*s* off [*blank*] ffor the yer fferme of the xxv stall towerd the southe; **And** off xix*s* off [*blank*] ffor the yer fferme of the xxvj stall, beyng the laste in the south ende of the same stalles

Summa xx *li* xix*s*

---

7 Both Thomas and Nicholas Kett had leased stalls in the previous year: NCR, 18A/6, f. 17^{v}.

/*Roperye*/ **Off** eny fferme receyued withyn the tyme of this accompte ffor the ffirst & ij^{de} stalles in the southende off the same nothyng here in deffaute of ffermers *except iiijs;*[8] **But** he answere off vs receyued off Walter Feer ffor the yeer ffeerme off the iij^{de} stalle; **And** off vs off Thomas Crosse ffor the yeer [*fferme*] of the iiij^{te} stall; **And** off vs off Edmond Crokelyng ffor the yer fferme off the vth stalle; **And** off xs off the same Edmond ffor the yeer fferme off the vjth stalle ther, which is the last stalle in the northende off the same

***Summa* xxixs**

/*xxixs*/

[*f. 31*^v] /*Fisshe stalles, woolle shoppes*/ **And** off xiijs iiijd receyued off John Webster ffor the fferme of the ffirste stalle in the northende off the same stallez ffor the tyme off this accompte; **And** off viijs off Jerom Quasshe ffor the yeer fferme off the next stall towerd the south; **And** off viijs off Thomas Worlyngton ffor the yeer fferme of the next stall towerd the south; **Off** eny fferme receyued of the next stalle towerd the south ffor the ffirst quarter of the yeer within the tyme off this accompte nothing here in deffaute off ffermer; **But** he answer off ijs receyued off [*blank*] ffor the fferme off the seid stalle ffor the laste quarter off the yere within the seid tyme; **And** off xvjs of John Sewall ffor the yeere fferme of the ij next stalles; **And** off xvjs of Necholas Grene ffor the yer fferme off the ij next stalles; **And** off xvjs of Robert Norman ffor the yer *fferme* off ij next stalles towerd the south; **And** off viijs off Fraunces Skot ffor the yeere fferme of the next stalle; **And** off xvjs off Thomas Cok ffor the yeere fferme of ij next stalles; **And** off viijs off Edward Wardon ffor the yeer fferme off the next stall; **And** off viijs of [*blank*] ffor the yeer fferme off the next stalle; **And** off viijs off [*blank*] ffor the fferme off the next stalle; **And** off viijs off [*blank*] ffor the yeere fferme off the next stalle; **And** off viijs off [*blank*] ffor the yere fferme off the next stalle; **And** off xvjs off John Crowe ffor the yeere fferme of ij next stalles, whiche ben the laste of the same stalles in the southend therof; **And** off xiijs iiijd of John Larter ffor the yeer fferme off a tenement next the chircheyerd style of Saynt Peter, late in the fferme off John Nobill, with a chamber ouer the wolsshop ayenst the pultry market; [*f. 32*] **And** off xs off Herry Marlyng ffor the yeere fferme of a shopp, late in the fferme of John Florens; **And** off xxs off John Quassh ffor the yeere *fferme* of a tenement, late in the fferme of John White, ayenst the pultrye market; **And** off vjs viijd off John Halle ffor the yere fferme off a wolshop; **And** off vjs viijd off Robert Neve ffor the yere fferme off a wolle shop; **And** off vs of John Crossold ffor the yeer fferme of a wolshop; **And** off Henry Holden ffor the yeere fferme off a wolle shop ledyng vnto *the* wolshop parteyneng to the chauntery of John Cusyn: vs;[9] **And** off vs off William Hede ffor

---

8 This sum appears in the margin.

9 The chantry was established by Cusyn for two priests in the church of St Peter Mancroft in 1328, but later reduced to one: A. Watkin, ed., *Inventory of Church Goods temp. Edward III* (2 parts, NRS, xix, 1947–8), i, p. 3; ii, p. 151.

the yeer fferme of a voulte vnder the Bocherye; **Off** any fferme receyued within the tyme off this accompte ffor any other wolshoppes nothing here in the deffaute off ffermours

Summa xj *li* xjs

/*Ferme off housez and tenementes*/ **But** he aunswer of xxxs of Nicholas Barne ffor the yere fferme of a tenement called the Murage Loft with a shop in the sowthende[10] of the Roperye; **And** off xijs receyued of John Bedys ffor a yeere fferme off a tenement, late in the fferme off John Curat & after in the fferme of William Hede; **And** off xxs of Bryan Doraunt ffor the yer fferme off a tenement, late in fferme of John Dixe, with a fforge therunto belonging; **And** off xxiijs iiijd off Hugh Copland ffor a yere fferme of a tenement, late in the fferme off John Alen & Thomas Swanton; **And** of xviijs iiijd of Marke Heynes ffor the yere fferme off a tenement, late in fferme of John [*f. 32ᵛ*] Falke & of a chaumbber [*sic*] of newe bildild [*sic*] ouer th'entery on the north parte off the seid tenement, whiche chamber he holde by force of a graunte & leace therof to hym made ffor terme of yeeres by Thomas Cok & Thomas Bemond, late chamberleyns of the seid citie;[11] **Off** anye ffermeres within the tyme of this accompt of a tenement lieng in Ouer Newporte callid The Cage, *or of* a tenement lyeng vpon the Netherrowe, late in the fferme off John Dikenson, or of a tenement lyeng in Cutlerrowe next the castill diche, *late in fferme of Robert Evan*, or of a tenement in the seid Cutlerrowe, late in the fferme off John Rede, bower, vppon the other parte of the weye, nothing here ffor asmoche as the seid tenementes arn seuerally graunted to diuers persons & to ther heires ffor certen rentes yerly charged amonges the rentes off <assignez> assise, as in diuerse accomptes next before precedent more playnlye is conteyned;[12] **But** he answereth of xs viijd receyued within the tyme off this accompt of Adryan Johnson ffor the yer fferme off a tenement lyeng on th'est parte off *the gates of* the comon inne of *late* newbilded; **And** off xxvjs viijd of the same Adryan ffor the yeer fferm of the hede mese of the seid inne, also off *late* newbilded;[13] **And** also of xiiijs of John Sewall ffor the yere fferme of a tenement of the west corner of the seid hede mese, also of late newebuylded; **And** off xld of Thomas Necton, alderman, ffor the yeer fferme of a tenement lyeng ayenst th'estend of the chirche of Saynt Andrewe in Norwiche, late *graunted to* John Clerk, alderman, ffor the terme of lx yeeres begynnyng at Mighelmes *anno regni regis Henrici viij primo* [*29 September 1509*];[14] **And** of xld off Richard Framyngham ffor the yeer fferme

---

10 As stated in the previous account, it was in fact at the north end: NCR, 18A/6, f. 18ᵛ.

11 NCR, 18A/6, f. 19. Heynes was committed to prison and his wife to the stocks in June 1540 for rebuking the ward constable 'with dispiteffull wordes & shamefull wordes': NCR, 16A/5, p. 10.

12 NCR, 18A/6, f. 1ᵛ.

13 A new ten-year lease was confirmed by the assembly on 3 May 1536: NCR, 16D/2, f. 182.

14 NCR, 16D/2, f. 82.

of a scriptory on the southparte off the yeldhall; **And** off xvj*d* off Agnes Potter ffor the yeer fferme off a shop on the south side of the seid hall, late vsed ffor a scriptorye; **And** off vj*s* viij*d* off Nicholas Sywhat, alderman, [*f. 33*] ffor a yeere fferme off a parcell off comon *grounde* with a ffissheng, late in the fferme off Hugh Dodman; **And** off xxvj*s* viij*d* of Thomas Grewe, alderman, ffor the yeer *fferme* off Butter Hilles; **And** off xxvj*s* viij*d* off Johan Flyngant ffor th'yer fferme off the clothehalle; **Off** eny fferme receyued within the tyme off this accompt ffor an acre of lond, late Wauereyez, lyeng without Saynt Gyles yates, ner of a parcell of grounde lyeng ner Lord Dacres water, nor of the voide grounde lyeng at Tomlond, ner of eny tenementes sette vpon the comon grounde ner Saynt Austynsgates & Coslany gates, ner of the comon grounde next the walles in the Chapel Feldes crofte, ner of the crosse in the market, ner voulte vnder the yeldehalle nothing here ffor causes apparant in the accompte next precedent;[15] **But** he answerth of xij*d* receyued of the heires of Roger Applyard ffor a yer fferme off a dike without Westwykgates; **And** off xij*d* of Adryan Mace ffor the yere fferme of a parcell of a comon lane or comon grounde lyeng at Louelles stathee in the parisshe of Saynt Faste [*Vedast*], late graunted to hym & his assignes ffor the terme of xl yeres, the terme begynnnyng at Mighelmes in the xvij yer of the reign of Kyng Herry the viij^th [*29 September 1525*][16]

And off vs receyued of [*blank*] ffor a yere of the ffirste *tenement* of the tenementes with the killes in Conesford; **And** off vs off [*blank*] ffor the yer fferme of the ij^de tenement ther; **And** off vs of [*blank*] ffor the yer fferme of the iij^de tenement ther; **And** off vs off [*blank*] ffor the yeer fferme of the iiij^te tenement ther; **And** off vs off [*blank*] ffor the yer fferme of the vth tenement ther; **And** off vs off [*blank*] ffor the yeer fferme of the vj tenement ther; <**And** off vs of [*blank*] ffor the yeer [*f. 33^v*] fferme of the vj^te tenement ther;> **And** off vj*s* viij*d* off William Horn ffor the yer fferme off the vij^te tenement; **And** off xx*s* off William Pallyng ffor the yere fferme off the hede mese & yerdes therunto adioyneng;[17] **And** off ij*s* vj*d* of [*blank*] ffor the halff yere fferme of the viij^te tenement ther; **And** off ij*s* vj*d* off [*blank*] ffor halff yer fferme of the ix^th tenement ther; **And** off ij*s* vj*d* off [*blank*] ffor the halff yer fferme of the xth tenement ther; **And** off ij*s* vj*d* off [*blank*] ffor halff yere fferme of the xj^th tenement ther; **And** off ij*s* vj*d* off [*blank*] ffor halff yer fferme of the xij^th tenement ther

/lxixs vjd/[18]

---

15 The previous account explained that, for lack of tenants, these properties were 'in the handes off the comialtie': NCR, 18A/6, f. 19^v.

16 For Lovell's stathe, see *SLCN*, p. 4. The lease was confrmed on 21 September 1525: NCR, 16D/2, ff. 141^v–2.

17 The marginal letters 'b' and 'a' against the entries relating to Horn and Pallyng denote that they appear in the wrong order.

18 The correct sub-total should be 69*s* 2*d*.

Off eny fferme receyued of the xiij^th^ tenement, beyng the last of the same tenementes, or of eny *other* ffermez receyued withyn the tyme off this accompte off the seid tenementes nothing here in deffaute *off* ffermers; **But** he answerth of iiij*s* off too acres of londe fferme lyeng without Saynt Glesgatez, late Hemmynges

Summa xiiij *li* xviij*s* vj*d* /*cum iiij d plus*/[19]

/*Petye custome*/ **And** off cxiij*s* iiij*d* receyued off Robert Collard ffor the fferme off the petye custome ffor the tyme of this accompt

Summa cxiij*s* iiij*d*

/*Boothes*/ **And** off iiij*s* off Robert Broun ffor the fferme of boothes ayenst the shirehouse & castill gate ffor the seid tyme

Summa iiij*s*

/*Tenementes in the kynges handes*/ **And** off iiij*s* of Roger Leek ffor the yer fferme of a tenement in the parisshe of Saynt Benettes, late the priour of Bokenham;[20] **And** off v*s* of Richard Penyman, clerk, ffor the yere fferme of a tenement, late [*f. 34*] in the ffeerme of oone Stawn, cobbler, in the parisshe of Saynt Martyn atte the Palaysgate in Cowgatestrete; Off eny other fferme receyued within the tyme off this accompte ffor a tenement in the parisshe off Saynt Mighell atte the Plee, late in the fferme off Andrewe Thirkill, nothing here ffor it is decaied by casualtie of sodden ffyer; and it was late graunted to William Russell & to his heires fforeuer ffor j*d* of yerlye rent, which is yerly charged amonges the rent of assise

Summa ix*s*

/*The old & new stathes*/ **But** he answer off xv *li* receyued off William Pallyng ffor a yeer fferme of the seid stathes

Summa xv *li*

/*Ferme of the milles*/ **And** off xl *li* receyued of Stevyn Empson ffor a yer fferme of the milles of the seid citie; **And** off lxvj*s* viij*d* of the seid Stevyn ffor a yere fferme of Heigham milles withyn *& ffor* the tyme of this accompte

Summa xliij *li* vj*s* viij*d*

/*Yates & towers*/ **And** off viij *li* receyued of th'executours of Master Robert Jannys, alderman, off & ffor a certen annuytie or yerlye rent of late graunted to the comialtie ffor discharge of all maner tolles & customes to be taken at the gates of the seid citie;[21] **And** off xl*d* receyued of Thomas Grewe, alderman, ffor a yere fferme of a garden next & without the walles of the seid citie by Barre gates; **And** off xl*d* receyued of Walter Feere ffor a yeere [*f. 34^v^*] fferme of a tower next the ryver by Barregates; **And** off vj*d* off Hugh Boxfford ffor a yeer fferme off a tower next

---

19 'With 4*d* more'.

20 The Augustinian priory of Old Buckenham had been dissolved by February 1537: *VCH, Norfolk*, ii, p. 377.

21 For Jannys see above pp. 8, 18–19; and for his will TNA, PROB 11/24/3.

Fibriggates; **And** off xvj*d* off [*blank*] ffor a yere fferme off a tower callid the Brasen Doore ffor the tyme of this accompt

Summa viij *li* viijs vj*d*

/*Ferme off the scite of the late house or priory of Blak Freres & *gret* garden ther unto apparteyneng*/ **And** off xxixs j*d* of <William Alman ffor the fferme of a certen house, late new bylded on the south parte of the preching yerde, ffor iij quarters of a yere ended at Mighelmes in th'ende> *Richard Framyngham ffor certen ffermes receyued by hym off the seid housez & gardens within the tyme* of this accompte; **And** off vij*s* of William Moraunt ffor the fferme of a *litill* garden, parcell of the seid *gret* garden, ffor halff a yeer ended at <Mighelmes fforseid> *Halowmes after th'ende of this accompte*; **And** off *nihil per compotum*[22] of Henry Bakon ffor the fferme of a tenement & the chapell, with yerdes therunto apparteyneng, parcell of the seid gret garden, ffor [*blank*] ended at Mighelmes fforseid; **And** off *nihil per compotum* of John Birche & Thomas Wattes ffor fferme of another parcell off the seid garden ffor [*blank*] of a yere ended at Mighelmes fforseid

/*receptum per Framyngham*/[23]

And off xxs off John Quassh ffor another *parcell* of the seid garden ffor a quarter of a yeere ended at Mighelmes fforseid

And of *nihil per compotum* of John Baker ffor the fferme of another parcell of the same garden ffor [*blank*] of a yer ended at Mighelmes fforseid; **And** off *nihil per compotum* of Adrian Mace ffor the fferme of another parcell of the same garden ffor [*blank*] of a yer endid at Mighelmes fforseid

/*receptum per Framyngham*/

And of vs off William Marche ffor fferme of another parcell off the seid garden [*f. 35*] ffor halff <of> a yere endid at <Mighelmes fforseid> *Halowmes after th'ende of this accompt*; **And** off *nihil hic quia in proximo*[24] of Arnold Johnson ffor fferme of an osyer yarde, parcell of the seid garden, ffor [*blank*] of a yeere endid at Mighelmes fforseid; **And** off xiij*s* iiij*d* of John Baker ffor the fferme of a lane with an house bilded at the northende of the same, late parteyneng to the seid gret garden, ffor ij yeres <of a yere> endid at Mighelmes fforseid; **And** of vj*s* viij*d* receyued of William Alman ffor fferme of the prechingyerd ffor the yer endid at Crouchemes before th'ende of this accompte[25]

Summa iiij *li* xiij*d*

---

22 'Nothing by the account'.

23 'Received by [*Richard*] Framyngham'.

24 'Nothing here, as in the next account'. The osier ground is not, in fact, mentioned in the next account (below, pp. 97–8), but in that for 1541–2, when it had passed to William Marche (p. 121).

25 The last entry has been added in a smaller hand.

/Fermes off the houses late the suffragan busshop off Calcidonye/[26] **And** off vj*s* viij*d* off Robert Stephenson ffor the fferme of a tenement, ffirst of the seid tenementes, lyeng on the corner next Tumlond ffor a quarter of a yere endid at Mighelmes in th'ende of this accompt

/ij^de tenement/ **And** off iij*s* iiij*d* off John Suklyng ffor the fferme of the next tenement towerd the south ffor one quarter of the yere endid at Mighelmes fforseid

/iij^de tenement/ **And** off iij*s* iiij*d* of Thomas Mosse ffor the fferme of the next tenement ffor a quarter of a yer endid as is afforeseid

/iiij^te tenement/ **And** off eny fferme receyued off Thomas Bathcom ffor the fferme of the next tenement ffor oone quarter of a yere endid as is afforeseid

/v^te tenement/ **And** off eny *fferme* receyued of Syr Robert Lakenam ffor the fferme of the next tenement ffor a quarter off a yere endid as i̇s afforeseid

/vj^te tenement/ **And** of eny *fferme* receyued off Alys Punche ffor the fferme of the next tenement ffor a quarter off a yere endid at Mighelmes forseid

/vij^te tenement/ **And** off eny *fferme* receyued <off Moder Kedell> ffor fferme of the next tenement ffor a quarter off a yeer endid as is afforeseid nothing here, ffor the seid ffermers had ther dwellynges in the same vntill the seid ffest by graunte [*f. 35^v*] off the seyd busshop *except ij*s* receyued of Moder Kiddell by the handes of Master Stywerd*[27]

/viij^te tenement/ **Or** of eny thing receyued ffor the fferme of the next tenement lyeng vpon the corner nothing here in deffaute of a ffermour

/ix^te tenement/ **But** he answereth of <ij*s* iij*d*> *xxij*d** receyued of John West ffor the fferme off the next tenement towerd the west ffor a quarter of a yeer endid as is afforeseid

/x^te tenement/ **And** off xx*d* of Richerd Jermyn ffor the fferme of the next tenement ffor a quarter off a yer endid as is afforeseid
Summa* xviij*s* x*d

/Foren receptes/ **And** off xxij*s* receyued off Thomas Broun ffor the fferme of the mukboote, ouer & aboue xx*s* allowed to *the seid* Thomas ffor keping of the cokey ayenst the <cok> yate off Thomas Cod, alderman; **And** off vj *li* receyued of Master Fermour ffor the ij^de payement of xviij *li* due ffor the dette of Gregorye Cause;[28] **And** off vij *li* xviij*s* ix*d* receyued of John Revell, fforen receyuour, within

---

26 See above, p. 19.

27 Alderman Steward had bought out some of the tenants: see above, p. 19.

28 A marginal note reads 'ij payement'. The former mayor, Thomas Cause (d. 1509), had left money 'to the mayntenaunces off diuers comon charges of the comilatie', but it was only after protracted litigation against his son that the authorities secured a promise of

the tyme off this accompte; **And** off x *li* xiij*s* iiij*d* receyued of Richard Framyngham in partie of payment of diuers sommes off money by hym gadered of langoll rent, ouere & beside lxvj*s* viij*d* by hym payd to Austyn Stywerd, alderman, of the seid colleccon; **And** off xiij*s* iiij*d* receyued of John Gibbez ffor the iiij^te payement of lxvj*s* viij*d* gyffen to the comialtie ffor the purchase of a tenement callid The Cage;[29] **And** off xl *li* receyued within the tyme of this accompte of Jamys Marssham ffor the purchase of a closse with a tenement therunto annexed, which closse & tenement was late giffen to the comialtie by Robert Broun, mercer, in consideracon that the seid Robert shuld nat be elected nor chosen in to the state & degre of an alderman within the seid [*f. 36*] citie, but theroff clerly discharged fforeuer;[30] **And** of liij*s* iiij*d* receyued within the seid tyme of John Sutton & John Aldryche ffor ffynes gyffen by them to the comialtie ffor ther discharge of the office off constableship;[31] **And** off iiij*s* receyued of Syr John Doraunt ffor diuers rentes off dyuers tenementes parteyneng to the chauntery off Letyce Payn ffor iij yeres endid at Mighelmes *anno regni regis Henrici viij xxxj* [*29 September 1539*];[32] **And** off iiij *li* xiiij*s* receyued within the tyme of this accompte of the bakers of the citie of a newe grynte assigned to them by the comialtie at euery quarter of whete grynded at the mylles of the said citie, ouer & aboue suche sommez of money accostomed before to be paid to the ffermer of the seid milles by the said bakers at euery quarter of whete ther grynded, ffor a quarter of a yere <ffer> ended at Mighelmes in th'ende of this accompte;[33] **And** of ix*d* receyued within the tyme of this accompte ffor the fferme off dyuers fflesshe stallez on the market dayez *laten* by the daye; **And** of vj *li* <vj*s* viij*d*> *xiij*s* iiij*d** receyued of Wylliam Lee ffor the <thirde> *<ij^de>* *ffourte* *iiij *solucio** payment of the mese, late Master

£18 payable in three annual instalments: TNA, PROB 11/16/551; NCR, 16A/5, p. 6; 18A/6, ff. 12, 20^v. William Fermor (d. by 1559) of East Barsham, soon to be knighted, was then the sheriff of Norfolk and helped to broker this arrangement: Blomefield, *Norfolk*, vii, pp. 53–7; J. Baker, *The Men of Court 1440 to 1550: A Prosopography of the Inns of Court and Chancery and the Courts of Law* (2 vols, Selden Society, supplementary series, xviii, 2012), i, p. 665.

29 This civic property in the parish of St Peter Mancroft was badly decayed; and after an inspection by the chamberlain in May 1537 it was agreed that Gybbes might acquire the title for a token ground rent: NCR, 16D/2, f. 182–2^v.

30 Broun made over the property in the parishes of St Michael at Thorn and St Bartholomew on 21 September 1538, the decision to sell it being taken on 24 March following: NCR, 16D/2, ff. 186, 187, 190.

31 They were discharged in December 1539: NCR, 16A/4, f. 37^v.

32 Lettice Payne (d. 1317) founded two chantries in Norwich, in the churches of St Peter Mancroft and St Stephen, in 1313, but the endowments proved inadequate and they were assigned to a single chaplain before 1369: N. Tanner, *The Church in Late Medieval Norwich* (Toronto, 1984), p. 93; Watkin, ed., *Inventory of Church Goods*, i, p. 19; ii, p. 163. The property involved, along with that belonging to the chantry of John Cusyn (above, p. 68 note 9), was acquired for £100 by the city in 1549 after the dissolution of chantries: NCR, 16D/2, f. 228.

33 See above, pp. 19, 21.

Percyes, late sold hym;[34] **And** of xiij*s* iiij*d* receyued of the same William ffor an
annuall rent or annuytie of & ffor a certen tenement, parcell of the seid mese,
by hym to be payd to the comialtie duryng the natiurall lyff of Alys Scolehouse,
widowe;[35] [*f. 36*ᵛ] **And** of x*s* receyued of Thomas Barker, late fforen receyuour, by
the handes of Thomas Codde, alderman, in partie of payement of lxj*s* <vij> ix*d*
dependyng vpon hym off the arreragies of his accompt endid at Mighelmes *anno
regni regis Henrici viij xxix°* [*29 September 1537*]; **And** off iij*s* receyued ffor tyle &
selyng comyng off the late Blak Freres; **And** off xxix*s* iiij*d* ffor rede sold, which
be left of the rede prouyded ffor certen housez of newe edified within the comon
inne in the market; **And** off xvij*d* receyued off & ffor latthe sold of the godes of
the comialtie; **And** off iij*s* iiij*d* receyued ffor an olde cogge whele sold; **And** off
vj*s* viij*d* receyued ffor an olde chiste of the goodes of the comialtie; **And** off x
li receyued of Thomas Cok, late *chamberleyn*, ffor & in partie off payement
of xxj *li* xj*s* ij*d* *ob'* dependyng vpon the hedes of the seid Thomas Cok & Jamys
Marssham, chamberleyns, vpon the determynacon of ther accompt ended at
Mighelmes *anno regni regis Henrici viij xxx°* [*29 September 1538*];[36] **And** off xij*d*
receyued of the price of the toppes of certen <willoughes> *elmes* groweng vpon
the grounde of the comialtie in the parisshe of Saynt Peter of Hundgate

Summa lxxxxiiij *li* xj*d*

Summa totalis receptorum <onerata> CC liij *li* vij*s* *qu'*

[*f. 37*] /*Rente resolute*/ **Off** which the seid accomptaunte hath paied within the tyme
of this accompte in rent resolute, as yerly appereth in dyuers accomptes before: that
is to saye to Syr William Coppyng, prest of the chauntery of John Cosen: iiij *li*;
And to the heires of Roger Applyard: x*s*; **And** to the cathedrall chirche of the Holy
Trynytie of Norwich: xvij*s* iiij*d*; **And** to the late priory or manour of Carowe: vj*s*
viij*d*;[37] **And** to the same pryorye or manour ffor iiij busshelles of whete after the
price in the market of Norwiche: ij*s* iiij*d*; **And** to the maister of the hospitall of
Magdalen [*St Mary Magdalen, Sprowston*]: xij*d*;[38] **And** to the hospitall of Saynt
Gyle in Norwiche: xiij*s* iiij*d*; **And** to the manour of the late priory of Horsham

---

34 On 16 February 1535 Alan Percy (d. 1560), third son of the third earl of Northumberland
and sometime master of St John's College, Cambridge, 'of his godenes' gave the city his
messauge in the parish of St Martin Coslany to use as it saw fit. The property was sold in
August 1538 to Lee for £100, payable in annual instalments of £6 13*s* 4*d*, with the intention
of investing in tenements that would generate funds for cleansing the river and/or repairing
the walls: *ODNB*, xliii, pp. 676–7; NCR, 16A/4, ff. 4, 30. See also below, p. 90.

35 Alice was the widow of Alderman Henry Scolehouse, from whom Percy had acquired
the messuage: NCR, 16A/4, f. 4.

36 NCR, 18A/6, f. 15.

37 The Benedictine nunnery of Carrow, immediately to the south west of Norwich,
which was granted to Sir John Shelton in 1538: *VCH Norfolk*, ii, pp. 351–4.

38 This leper hospital, situated about a mile to the north of Norwich, lay in the patronage

Saynt Feith: x*s*; **And** to the late chapell of the Bek: iiij*s*;[39] **And** to the late abbey of Sibton: ij*s*;[40] **And** to the late priorye off Carrowe ffor Butter Hilles: x*s*; **And** to the late abbey off Langley: ij*s*;[41] **And** *to the late priory of Horsham ffor the suffragans housez and* to the maner of Heigham ffor londes late Master Hemmynges: \<viij*d*\> *\<stet\> stet*;[42] **And** to the same maner ffor fferme of Heigham milles, with the medewez & mersshez therunto belonging: lxvj*s* viij*d*; **And** to Syr John Doraunt, chauntery prest of Letice Payn: vj*s* viij*d*[43]

Summa xj *li* xiiij*s* viij*d*

/xj *li* xiiij*d* iiij*d* & iiij*d*/

/*Fees & wages*/ **And** also paid by the seid accomptaunt to Nicholas Sotherton, alderman, occupieng the office off mayraltie by iij quarters of a yer withyn the tyme of this accompte: \<thayral\> that is to saye ffrom Mighelmes in the begynnyng of the same accompt vnto Midsomer than next ffolowyng: xv *li*; **And** to Thomas Grewe, alderman, successour of the seid Nicholas, occupyeng the seid office by oone quarter of a yer residue of the seid tyme: that is to saye ffrom Midsomer fforseid vnto Mighelmes in th'ende of this accompte [*f. 37ᵛ*] nothing here ffor asmoche as v *li* due to hym ffor the seid last quarter off the yeer within the tyme off this accompte was payed to hym by the handes off John Trace, emonges other sommes of money giffen to the comialtie by the same John Trace ffor the office of sheriff after the deth off Thomas Waltere, late sheriff of the seid citie;[44] **And** to Jamys Marssham & *John Trace*, sheriffes off the said citie, in helpe towerd the ffee fferme: xxx *li*; **And** to \<Edmond Grey, esquyer,\> *Syr Nicholas Hare, knight*, recorder of the seid citie, ffor his ffee ffor the tyme off this accompte: C*s*;[45] **And** to John Corbet, gent',

---

of successive bishops of Norwich and was finally dissolved in 1547: C. Rawcliffe, *The Hospitals of Medieval Norwich* (Norwich, 1995), pp. 41–7.

39 The chapel or hospital of St Thomas the Martyr at Beck in Billingford, to the north west of Norwich: *VCH Norfolk*, ii, pp. 438–9.

40 The Cistercian abbey of Sibton in Suffolk which was dissolved in 1536: *VCH Suffolk*, ii, pp. 89–91.

41 The Premonstratensian abbey of Langley in Norfolk, which was dissolved in 1536: *VCH Norfolk*, ii, pp. 418–21.

42 The sum of 'viij*d*' appears in the margin. The land in question, which lay just outside St Giles's gate, was given to the city for use as a communal rubbish dump in 1537 by Alderman Robert Hemming in *lieu* of a fine for failing to attend the mayor's court: NCR, 16A/4, f. 19.

43 This entry has been added in a smaller hand and a note 'Syr John Doraunt vj*s* viij*d*' entered in the margin.

44 Trace was appointed sheriff on 3 May 1540 until the end of September following, and agreed to pay £20 (a marginal note has 20 marks) for the privilege: NCR, 16D/2, ff. 191ᵛ–2.

45 As one of the shire knights for Norfolk, Sir Nicholas Hare (d. 1559) was Speaker of the 1539 parliament, and thus a figure of considerable influence: *HoP, 1509–1558*, ii, pp. 296–7; *ODNB*, xxv, pp. 258–9; A. Hawkyard, *The House of Commons 1509–1558: Personnel, Procedure, Precedent and Change* (Oxford, 2016), pp. 107, 111.

<styward> *reteyned of counsell*, ffor his ffee ffor the seid tyme: xxvj*s* vij*d* ;[46] **And** to Henry Warde, gent', clerk of the mayer & comialtie, ffor his ffee: iiij *li* vj*s* viij*d*;[47] **And** to the kynges eschekir ffor dyuers londes & tenementes exchetid in to the kynges handes: xx*s* <vj*s* viij*d*> *non plus hoc anno**;[48] **And** to Antonye Pigot, gent', swordberer, ffor his ffee: lxvj*s* viij*d*; **And** to John Rede & Thomas Molle, seriauntes at the mace of the mayer, ffor ther wages: liij*s* iiij*d*; **And** to Robert Collard, seriaunt in the market, ffor his ffee: xxvj*s* viij*d*; **And** to the seid Robert ffor his lyuery: x*s*; **And** to the chamberleyn, nowe accomptaunt, ffor his ffee: iiij *li*; **And** to hym ffor his lyuerye: xiij*s* iiij*d*; **And** to the iiij waytes ffor ther wages & lyueryes: ix *li* vj*s* viij*d*; **And** to the bedell ffor his lyuerey: vj*s* viij*d*; **And** to Edmond Grey, esquyer, styward, ffor his ffee: xx*s*[49]

Summa **lxxix *li* xvj*s* viij*d***

/*lxxix li xvjs viijd*/

[*f. 38*] /*Costys off the houses in the market & stalles & other dyuers charges*/[50] **And** paied by the seid accomptaunt in October within the tyme of this accompte ffor j daye worke to John Howse, laborer, workyng ther: v*d*; **And** paied *iiij*s* iij*d** to Thomas Laurens & to Thomas Cok ffor v m^l & C latthe nayle & *j*d** vj*d* nayle & *xiiij*s* iiij*d** xxx C latthe pynnes ther expendid: xviij*s* viij*d*; **And** payed *xv*d** ffor C thakke & *ij*d** a quaier off paper & *xx*d** v lode cleye ffor the same worke: iij*s* j*d*; **And** payed to John Wright, carpenter, ffor mendyng off the stalles in the market: vj*d*; **And** payd *j*d** to a laborer makyng clean of the ledes *& tores* & *iiij*d** ffor strawe for [*illegible*]: v*d*; **And** paied to a laborer ffor iij dayez workes, with his borde: xij*d*; **And** paied *ij*s* ij*d** to John Hill, reder, & *xvij*d** his laborer ffor iiij dayez worke, with ther borde: iij*s* viij*d*; **And** *viij*d** for *di'* C & iiij cheeffes thakke & *x*d** ij lodes claye: xvij*d*; **And** *xxij*d* ob' qu'** to Robert Archall, reder, ffor ij dayez worke & *di'* & *xv*d** ffor iij lodez cleye: iij*s* j*d* ob' qu'; **And** payed *xvj*d* qu'** to William Broke, reder, ffor ij dayez & *di'* & *xiiij*d* ob' qu'** William Farrour, laborer, ffor iij dayez & *di'*: ij*s* viij*d*; **And** *xij*d* ob'** to William Grante ffor iij dayez, *xiiij*d*

---

46 The original figure has been altered by the scribe and for clarity 'xxvj*s* viij*d*' entered in the margin. For John Corbet (d. 1559) of Sprowston, see *HoP, 1509–1558*, i, pp. 698–9.

47 On 8 April 1539 the mayor and aldermen acknowledged a letter from Thomas Cromwell in support of Warde's appointment as clerk. They asked that their own candidate, Robert Watson (see below, Appendix II), might be preferred, as he was not a 'stranger' to them and would thus be better qualified, but clearly felt it unwise to pursue the point: TNA, SP1/150, f. 99. According to *HoP, 1509–1558*, iii, pp. 543–4, Henry Warde (d. 1556) of Kirby Bedon and Postwick was not elected clerk until 1542, but he had by then been in office for three years.

48 'No more this year'. The sum of 'xx*s*' appears in the margin.

49 This sum appears in the margin. For Edmund Grey (d. 1547) of Merton, see *HoP, 1509–1558*, ii, p. 252; Baker, *Men of Court*, i, p. 784.

50 The many interlineations that follow here and in the expenses section of the next account are not omissions. Individual payments, such as wages or the cost of specific items, were recorded in this way until Robert Raynbald set about streamlining the accounts.

ob' qu'* William Clerk iij dayez & *di'* & *xiijd ob'* to Edward Brigat ffor iij dayez: iijs vd ob' qu'; And payd *iiijd* ffor strawe, naile & *jd* pakthrede & *ijs viijd* j loode off thakke: iijs jd; And *iijd* to Willet ffor *di'* daye & *vjd* ffor leyeng of a mattok & *iijs vjd* ffor ij loodes woode govyn to the lord suffragan: iiijs iijd;[51] And paied *ijs viijd* ffor ffeyeng of a prevy in the tenement of the comialtiez in the [*f. 38ʳ*] fferme of Bryant Dorant: ijs viijd; & *xd* ffor caryeng off v lode off mukke & *iiijd* a dayes worke at the fforge & *iiijd* ffor makyng of a dore & *jd* the mendyng off a wey: xixd; And payer [*sic*] *xd* ffor a payer of chenys , ij stapelles & j lok ffor the comon bote & to Cotes & Thomas Broun & his laborer ffor j dayes workes aboute the *same:* xxjd

/*ljs xd ob'*/

And payd *ijs xd* to Willet ffor kepyng off xij cokeys ffor j quarter of a yere & *ijs viijd* ffor carieng awey of xvj lodez muke ffrom the comon inne & *ijd* j lode ffrom the market: vs;[52] And payd *xviijd* ffor iij comb' charcole *and ijd ffor* kepyng of the kokey in the parisshe off Saynt Symondes & *iiijd* ffor makyng off a barowe: ijs; And payd *viijd* at the commandement of master mayer ffor ffilling off a pitte in the market & *xljs* ffor CCC ffadomz rede ffor the comonz & *vjs viijd* ffor xx ffoote off latice ffor a wyndowu in the sembly chamber: xlviijs iiijd; And ffor a payer of gemowz ffor the same: vjd; And paid *iijs* ffor wages & bordez of John Couper, reder, & *iijs* William Hill, reder, & *iiijs* ij laborerz workynges [*sic*] vpon the comon housez by vj dayez: xs; And paid *xd* to Keteryngham ffor ij lodes cley to the same work, *vjd* carying awey of iij lode muk & *vjd ob'* ffor beryng off rede: xxijd ob'; And paid *iiijd* to a laborer ffor j dayes worke *to bete clay* & *ijd* ffor beryng of thak nayle & hemp: vjd; And paid *ijs iijd* to Barsham & his laborer ffor iij dayez worke daubyng ther & *vd* ffor splentes to the same worke: ijs viijd; And paid *vijs* ffor *di'* C ffadomz rede & *ijd* ffor vjd nayle ther expendyd: vijs ijd; And payd *vd* to a wright ffor j dayez worke ther, and payd *xijd* to John Couper, reder, & *xijd* William Hill, reder, & *xvjd* ij laborerz ffor ij dayez workes & *iiijd* ij C bynys: iiijs jd; And payd to Brook, reder, & his laborer ffor vij dayez workes ther vjs vd

/*iiij li viijs vjd ob'*/

/*Lord off Norff'*/ And paid ffor ij swannez vijs; j cranet ijs viijd; oone galon muskadele ijs; & a galon of Rynye xijd; sente to the [*f. 39*] duke off Norff' grace

And payed *viijs* in Candelmes terme within the tyme of this accompte ffor the steyng off certen procez oute of the kynges escheker ayenst dyuers of the justices off the peace within the citie & *iiijs iiijd* in Midsomer terme also: xijs iiijd

---

51 John Simpson, *alias* Salisbury (d. 1573), a well-connected former monk of Bury St Edmunds and prior of Horsham St Faith, became suffragan bishop of Thetford in 1536 and dean of Norwich in 1539: *ODNB*, l, pp. 710–11; MacCulloch, *Thomas Cromwell*, pp. 432–3.
52 The correct sum should be 5s 8d.

/Busshop of Norwich/[53] **And** payd ffor a galon of ipocras sent to the lord busshop off Norwiche: iiij*s*

And payed ffor diuers expences in Hillary terme: xviij*s* viij*d*; **And** payed to Master Styward towardes the purchase off the late Blakffreres at dyuers tymes: liiij *li*;[54] **And** payd at commandement off maister mayer to the gameplayers: viij*d*; & ffor a *dedimus potestatem* ffor Master Grewe, mayer: ix*s* iiij*d*

/lvj li xvijs viijd/

Summa lxiij *li* xviij*s* j*d*

/lxiij li xviijs jd/

/Costys at the comon stathe & Blakffreres & comon inne/ **And** paid *xiij*d** to Richard Broke, reder, & *xiij*d** John Gyles, reder, & *xviij*d** ther too laborers workyng ther in ther craftes by ij dayes at oone tyme: iij*s* viij*d*; **And** payd *iij*s* vj*d** ffor cariage off vij lodez rede ffrom the stathe to the market & *vj*d** ffor skeppes ffor *to* beere muk & *xij*d** ffor C & *di'* off brykke & *iij*s* iiij*d** v C off bryktyle: viij*s* <vij> iiij*d*; **And** payd *j*d** to Water Elye ffor mendyng off ij lokkes & *ij*d** j key & *ix*d** ffor a barowhele & a spendill & *iiij*d** makyng off a barre: xvj*d*; **And** payed [*f. 39ᵛ*] and paid [*sic*] *ij*s* vj*d** to Herry Carter ffor vj lodes cley & *x*d** caryieng of v lodes off muk: iij*s* iiij*d*; **And** payd *xviij*d** to John Couper & *xviij*d** William Hill, reders, & *iij*s** ther iij laborers ffor iij dayez worke another tyme: vj*s*; **And** paid *xvj*d** to Edmond Yonges ffor makyng off goter of lede ffor the new house in the market, *iiij*d** carying of v C bryk, *iiij*d*, j*d** ffor nailes, *vj*d** ij oken plankes ffor a pentyce: ij*s* vij*d*; **And** paid to Fader Priour[55] & Robert Curson ffor the ij newe roffez off the ij housez at the comon inne: lj*s*; **And** paid to John Graye ffor iiij*ˣˣ* ffadomz rede & to Totill, carpenter, ffor ij dayez worke: x*s* vd; **And** paid to Richard Brook, reder, & his compeny the ffirst weke in Lente ffor ther worke ther: xxvij*s* viij*d*; **And** paid *vj*d** to Herry Spark ffor ij lodes stone caryng, *<ix*d*> xiiij*d** to William Pecok, laborer, ffor iij dayez worke, *xij*d** to Roger Lawes ffor cariage off ij lodez ston &

53 William Rugge *alias* Repps (d. 1550), Benedictine abbot of St Benet Hulme, a staunch conservative and ally of the duke of Norfolk, became bishop of Norwich in 1536 and resigned in 1550: D. MacCulloch, 'A Reformation in the Balance: Power Struggles in the Diocese of Norwich, 1533–1553', in C. Rawcliffe, R. Virgoe and R. Wilson, eds, *Counties and Communities: Essays on East Anglian History Presented to Hassell Smith* (Norwich, 1996), pp. 103–4, 108–9.

54 Royal letters patent confirming the award in return for a payment of £81 made by Steward were issued on 1 June 1540: *LPFD*, XV, no 831 (72); on the following day he was assigned £40 towards this sum from the hanaper: NCR, 16A/5, p. 6; and on 10 June he obtained a receipt for £81 from the court of augmentations for the purchase of Blackfrairs: NCR, 8K/7 (b).

55 Doctor Thomas Briggs, the last prior of the Norwich Dominicans, who became rector of Bressingham and eventually chaplain to the Princess Mary: Blomefield, *Norfolk*, iv, pp. 217, 340.

xd ij lode sonde: iijs vjd; **And** paied to Richard Brook, reder, & his compeny the ijde weke off Lente & to ij masonz: xxvjs viijd; **And** payd *xiiijd* ffor C & iij quarters brykke ffor the masonz & *ijs iijd* to Foster ffor cariage of xvj loodez mukke & ij lodez of stoone: iijs vd

/vij li vijs xjd memorandum nota/

And paid *iijs vjd* to Newell Mayer, mason, & *ijs iijd* his laborer ffor vj dayes worke at the [*Black*] Freres: vs ixd; **And** payd to Broke, reder, & his compeny *vj reders in all* workyng ther another tyme & to oone oder laborer ffor vj dayes: xxxiijs ixd; **And** payed *ijs* [*for*] strawe, *xxjd ob'* prykwoondes & byndynges ix bunches & CCCC, & *iiijd* ffor nayle & *ijs* ffor xxiiij bonches to the seid worke: vijs jd ob'; **And** payd *ixd* to Christofer [*f. 40*] Johnson, laborer, ffor ij dayes, *vjd* to John [*blank*] ffor a daye: xvd; **And** payd to Foster ffor cariage of iiijor lode & j lode stoone & to Curson ffor ij bonches sweys: xjd; **And** payd *ijs vjd* to Nicholas [*blank*] ffor v dayes, *iijs* to Robert [*blank*] & *iijs* John [*blank*], reders, ffor vj daies, either of them: viijs <vjd> <ijd>;[56] **And** payd to ther laborers: *videlicet* *xxijd* to Edmond [*blank*], *xxd* Robert Salle & *xxijd* Thomas Amore, euery of them v dayes, & *xviijd* William Fayer iiij dayez & *di*': vjs xd; **And** paid *ijs vd* to Robert Arkall ffor xiiij C & *di*' byndynges, *vd* j lode cley, *ixd* C *di*' Poswik [*Postwick*] brykke: iijs vijd; **And** payd *viijd* to Thomas Amoore & *ixd* Christoffer Johnson ffor ij dayez labour ther & *ijs viijd* ffor xx bunches wondes & C byndynges: iiijs jd; **And** payed to Robert Busshop ffor iiij lodez of muk caried: viijd; **And** paid *xxjd* to Brook, reder, & *xiiijd* his laborer ffor iij dayes work & *di*' & *iiijd* j daye more of the laborer: iijs iijd; **And** payd ffor xvj lodes cley: vjs viijd

/iiij li ijs iiijd ob'/

***Summa* xj *li* xs iijd ob'**

/xj li xs iijd ob'/

/***Costys at the mylles, cokeys & yeldhall & comon inne*/** **And** paied *xixd ob'* to John Walpole & *xixd ob'* John Potter, masonz, & *iijs jd ob'* iij laborers workyng at the milles by iij dayez: vjs iiijd ob'; **And** paid ffor ml tyle ffor the same worke: vjs; **And** paied *iijs iijd* to the seid John Walpole, *iijs iijd* John Potter & *iijs iijd* Newell Mayer, masonz, & *vjs iijd* ther iij laborers ffor vj dayez worke ther & *xxijd ob'* anoder laborer v dayez: xvijs xd ob'; **And** payd *jd* ffor mendyng of a tankerd ffor to bere water & *ixd* ffor cariage of iij lode stoone & *xs ijd* ffor xvj C bryk & j quarter: xjs; **And** *viijd* ffor viij [*f. 40v*] baroughffull of house tyle & *iiijd* a barell ffor water: xijd; **And** paid *ijs ijd* to the seid Walpole & Potter & *ijs jd* iij laborerz ffor other ij dayez workes there: iiijs iijd; **And** payd ffor vj loodes sonde: ijs vjd; **And** paid ffor mendyng off a wyndouu in the counsell chamber: vjd; **And** payd ffor CCC & v score ffadoms rede, at xiiijs le C: liijs viijd; <**And** paid to John [*blank*] ffor [*blank*]

---

56 The deleted sum of 'viijs vjd' appears in the margin.

iiij*d* >*<stet>*;[57] **And** payd *xiiij*d** ffor caryeng of vij lodez of muk ffrom the fforge in the market & *ij*d** to William Filbek & *ij*d** William Smyth ffor *di'* dayez worke about the same: xviij*d*; **And** payd to Willet ffor kepyng the cokeys ffor the ij^{de} quarter: ij*s* x*d*; **And** to Herry Sparke ffor ij lodez muk caried: iiij*d*; **And** payd ffor CCC ffadoms rede & ffor stakkyng theroff & ffor other CCC ffadams & the stakkyng: iiij *li* xij*d*

/ix li ixs ijd/

And payed *viij*d** to Christoffer [*Johnson*] ffor a dayez worke, *vj*d** Robert Johnson j daye & *di'* & *ij*d** ffor castyng & caryeng sonde & *iiij*d** to Walter Elye ffor naylez & ffor mendyng of the raylez goyng to the counsell chamber: xx*d*; **And** payed *j*d** ffor an hengle ffor Hoberdes shoppe, *ij*d** caryeng off a lood off muk, *x*d* ob* ffor vij bunches off prykwoond & *xiiij*d** ffor caryage off vij loodes muk & *ij*s* vj*d** to John Tuysdayes son ffor ij loodes off stoon & the caryage: iiij*s* ix*d* ob'; **And** payed *ij*d** ffor nayles & *xij*d** to a carpenter & *viij*d** his laborer ffor ij dayez worke at the comon inne: xxij*d*; **And** paid *xx*d** ffor m^l m^l lathe nayle,[58] *iij*s* v C bryk & *vj*d** CCC tynned [*nails*]: vs ij*d*; **And** payed to John Gyles & Percy Ball, rederz, in partie of payement off the new redyng the new housez at the comon inne ffor CCC rede[59] *at viij*s* the C:* xxiiij*s*; **And** ffor lathe naile & thak: x*d*; **And** payd to the seid reders ffor leyeng *di'* C reede more: iiij*s*; **And** payd *xxij*d** ffor ix C byndynges & *di'* & *<viij*d*>** ij bunchez of [*f. 41*] sweyes, *xxij*d** ffor a lode off barlye strawe & *ij*d** ffor carieng off a lode off muke: ij*s* x*d*; **And** payed a laborer ffor digging off wrestlyngplace & diuers expences of settyng vppe the bothe rayles & conueyeng the tymber inne & oute & ffor teltes: vs ij*d* ob'; **And** payed ffor x lodes claye, ij lodes sonde, j lode stoone carying: vs iiij*d*

/lvjs viijd/

And payd *xvj*d** to Robert Davye ffor CC brikke & to Henry Sparke ffor <CC> systene [*sixteen*] hundred rede karyed ffrom the stathe to the comon inne: viij*s* x*d*; **And** to the seid Henry Sparke ffor viij lodes off muk caried: xvj*d*; **And** payd ffor brekyng vppe of the wrestlyng place & to Andrew Spencer ffor lettyng off gonnes whan master master [*sic*] mayer & master aldermen cam thether: xij*d*; **And** payed to Foster ffor cariage of iiij lodes muk & to Colson ffor mendyng of dores & plauncheres in the tenementes in Conesford & ffor cariag off v lodes muk: ij*s* iiij*d*; **And** payd to Willet ffor kepyng of xij cokeys ffor Midsomer quarter within the tyme off this accompte: ij*s* x*d*

/xvjs iiijd/

Summa xiij *li* ij*s* ij*d*

/xiij li ijs ijd/

---

57 The deleted sum of 'iiij*d*' appears in the margin.

58 The original figure has been altered by the scribe and for clarity 'ij m^l' entered in the margin.

59 A marginal note reads 'iij C *inqu*'.

/*Costes of the rever and cokeys & other charges*/ **And** payed *ij*s* to William Pallyng ffor boote hyer tyme of kyttyng the rever, *xij*d** ffor gryndyng of the sickill, *xiij*d** ffor iij orys & *v*d** ffor baste: iiijs vj*d*; **And** payd to Robert Geffreys ffor xiiij dayes workes, Nicholas Cook & Bartilmue Wymond ffor xiiij [*f. 41ᵛ*] dayes in kyttyng the rever, euery of them vj*d* le daye: xxjs; **And** ffor takyng off paynes with the sykkyll to Teyton: iiij*d*; **And** paid to Willet ffor kepyng off the cokeys ffor the last quarter: ijs x*d*; **And** paid to Walter Herryez ffor makyng clene off an house & ffor keping off the cokeye in the parisshe off Saynt Symond & caryeng awey off the muk: xiij*d*; **And** ffor mˡ mˡ mˡ lathe nayll ffor the comon inne: ijs vj*d*; **And** payd ffor mˡ CC pathen tyle ffor the new hall: xxiiijs

/<iij li xijs vijd>/

Summa lvjs iijd

/lvjs iijd/

/**Minute expences**/ /*Justices of assises*/ **And** paid ffor ij galons of ipocras viijs; ffor too galons off Gascoyne wyne xvj*d*; too dosen spycebrede ijs viij*d*; & ffor too pottes off waffers ijs⁶⁰ sent to the justyces off the assise

/*Syr Nicholas Hare*/ **And** payd *vijs vj*d** to Henry Oldeman ffor a pyke & *xvj*d** iij perches, which was [*sent*] to Syr Nicholas Hare, knight, atte commandement of master mayer: viijs x*d*; & ffor beryng off the premyssez & ffor makyng of the ipo[*c*]ras: vj*d*

/*Lord of Norff'*/ **And** paid ffor dyuers thinges prouyded ayenst my Lord of Norff' comyng: that is to saye *xvj*d** ffor ij galons of Gascoyn wynes, *vijs j*d** ffor ipocrast & ffor spyces to the same: viijs v*d*; & to Master Pykerell ffor ij synettes vjs viij*d*; & to Thomas Serston ffor ij synettes ixs; to Thomas Petyte ffor a synet iiijs; to Palmer ffor a synet iijs iiij*d*; to Bernerd ffor ij cranys ixs; ffor a potell off wyn & suger j *libr'* xiij*d*; to Master Sall ffor makyng the ipocras vj*d*; ffor spycebrede xij*d*; & ffor berers off the presentes x*d*

And ffor a potell of Gascoyn wyn at the yeldhall: viij*d*

/*Pursyvaunt*/ **And** paied to pursyvaunt at commandement off master mayer [*f. 42*] bryngyng certen thinges ffrom the kynges maiestie: vs

And payd at the commandement ffor seid *iiijs* ffor a synet & *xvj*d** ij galons Gascoyn wyn sent to Master Hoton: vs iiij*d*⁶¹

---

60 These confections would probably have been stamped with the arms of the city: A. Kumler, 'From Sacrament to Street Food', *Cabinet: A Quarterly of Art and Culture*, 58 (2016), pp. 63–71.

61 John Hutton, or more often Wotton (d. 1546), of North Tuddenham and Hockering, a protégé of Thomas Cromwell, was a justice of the peace for Norfolk from 1538 and a

/*Lord of Norff*/ **And** payd *viijd* ffor galon Gascoyn wyn, *iiijs* a galon off ipocras, *viijd* ffor spicebrede, *xijd* a potell of muskeadele off Gene, *vd* *di' libr'* suger & *vjd* ffor brede *& bere* expendid at the yelde[*hall*] at the ij^de comyng of my Lord off Norff': vijs iijd

/*iiij li vs vd*/

And payd ffor C *di'* xxij *libr'* off new yron ffor the chenys at the comon stathe, at jd qu' le *libr'*; xixs <qu'> ixd *ob'*; **And** ffor workyng off iiij^xx *libr'* of olde yron: iijs iiijd; **And** payd ffor mendyng of the scolys & chenys ther: xijd

/*xxiiijs jd ob'*/

/*Redditus resolutus*/ **And** ffor the xth of the late Blakffreres ffor the yere endid at Mighelmes in th'ende off this accompte: ixs;[62] **And** payd ffor the taske of ij acres off lond, late Hemmynges: viijd

/*ixs viijd*/

And payd to Master Sotherton ffor a rest of xls graunted to Master Sotherton toward his charges: xxxiiijs[63]

/*xxxiiijs*/

Summa vij *li* xiijs ijd *ob'*

/*vij li xiijs ijd ob' more in the last somme*/

/**Costes at the comon inne**/ /*The first weke*/ **And** payed *ijs ijd* to John Walpole, *ijs ijd* Thomas Dixson & *ijs ijd* John Wase, masonz, euery of them iiij dayez, & *xxiijd* to Robert Grene, mason, ffor iij dayez & *di'* workyng ther in the new bildeng of certen housez, at vjd *ob'* the daye euery of them: viijs vd; **And** payd *iiijs vjd ob'* to iij laborers, euery of them ffor iiij dayez, *xvd ob'* to one laborer ffor iij dayez *di'*, *xiijd ob'* to one laborer ffor iij dayez workyng, at iiijd *ob'* the daye: vjs xjd *ob'*; **And** payed *xxijd ob'* to William Grove, *xixd ob'* to Raff Cristmes, *xiijd* Adam Adamson & *xiijd* to [*f. 42^v*] [*John*] Crismes, carpenters, workyng in ther occupacon by x dayez & *di'* emonges them, at vjd *ob'* le daye: vs viijd <ob'>; **And** payed ffor m^l bryk: vjs; **And** to Herry Carter ffor caryage of xv loodez of [*blank*]: vs vd; & ffor ij chalder lyme ther expendid: iiijs viijd

/*ij^de weke*/ **And** payed *ijs vijd ob'* to John Walpole, *vs vd* Robert Grene, John Wase & *ijs xjd ob'* Thomas Dyxson, masonz, ffor workyng ther by xx *dayez di'* in all atwyxt *them*, at vjd *ob'* le day euery of them: xjs jd; **And** paid *ijs ob'* to

justice of gaol delivery at Norwich 1539–40: Baker, *Men of Court*, ii, pp. 1703–4; Blomefield, *Norfolk*, x, pp. 263–4.

62 This annual payment was made to the court of augmentations under the terms of the grant of the friary to the city: *LPFD*, XV, no 831 (72); Blomefield, *Norfolk*, iv, p. 339.

63 See NCR, 16A/5, p. 4.

John Willons, *ij*s ob'* Christoffer Stawn, *ij*s ob'* John Hall, *xxij*d ob'* Gregory Dores, *ij*s ob'* John Trewe and *ij*s iiij*d* Nicholas Malkyn, laborerz, workyng ther by xxij dayez in all atwyxt them, at iiij*d ob'* le daye euery off them: xij*s iiij*d ob'*; And paied *iij*s iij*d* to William Grove, *iij*s iij*d* Adam Adamson, *iij*s iij*d* Raff Crosse, *ij*s xj*d ob'* Symond Rose, *ij*s ij*d* John Crismes & *vj*d ob'* Thomas James, *carpenters*, workyng ther by xxviij dayez *& di'* in all atwyxt them, at vj*d ob'* le daye: xv*s* v*d*

/nota iij li xvj*s* j*d*/

/The iij*de* wekel And payed *xiiij*s* ffor m*l* m*l* m*l* latthe & *iij*s* ffor v C bryk ffor the same work: xvij*s*; And payd *xix*d ob'* to William Grove, *xix*d ob'* John Cristmes & *xix*d ob'* Raff Grosse, carpenterz, ffor ix dayez workez, euery of them iij dayez: iiij*s* x*d ob'*; And payed *xix*d ob'* to Robert Greene, *xix*d ob'* John Walpole, *xix*d ob'* John Wace, *xix*d ob'* Thomas Dixson & *xix*d ob'* Richard Dobilday, masonz, ffor xv dayez worke ther atwixt them: *videlicet* to euery of them ffor iij dayez: viij*s* j*d ob'*; And paid to iiij laborerz, euery of them ffor iij dayez: iiij*s* vj*d*; And payd to Nicholas Gamlyng ffor iij dayez work pynnyng the walles: xvj*d ob'*; And payd to Christoffer Stawn & Thomas Botyffaunt, laborers, ffor iij dayez euery off them: ij*s*; And payed to John [*f. 43*] Chapman ffor iij lodez brykke: viij*s* <x*d*> *vj*d*

/The iiij*te* wekel And paied to a laborer ffor ij dayes worke helpyng the workemen ther: viij*d*; And payd to Keteryngham ffor xj lode sonde ther occupyed: iiij*s* vij*d*; And ffor iij [*blank*]: iij*d*; And payd *ij*s ij*d* to Robert Greene, *ij*s viij*d ob'* John Walpole, *ij*s viij*d ob'* John Wase, *ij*s* Thomas Dixson & *ij*s viij*d ob'* Thomas [*blank*], masons, ffor xxiij dayes worke in all to geder: xij*s* iij*d ob'*; And payd to v laborers ffor xxiiij dayez atwixt them: viij*s* ij*d*; And payed to Gamlyng ffor iij dayez work pynnyng: xv*d*; And payd *ij*s v*d* to William Grove, *ij*s v*d* John Crystmes & *ij*s v*d* Raff Cristmes, carpenterz, ffor iiij dayes worke & *di'* euery of them: vij*s* iij*d*

/iiij li xvij*d*/

/The v*th* wekel And paid to Parcyvall, reder, ffor reffyn of the olde botery att the comon inne & ffor beryng oute of broken stuff at the Freres & in expences at the reyseng of the fflore off joystez: vij*d*; And payd ffor a lode off bryk & ffor leyeng vpp of tymber & borde: ij*s*; And paid to John Estowe at the makyng of the bargen with hym ffor the new parlour: iiij*d*; And to Edmond Egle ffor a chalder & a combe lyme & to Roger Lawes ffor iij lodez sond & ffor naylez: iiij*s* v*d*; And payd to Hugh Herryson ffor vj chalder & vj comb' lyme: xv*s* ix*d*; And paied *vj*d ob'* to John Walpole, *xiij*d* Robert Greene & *vj*d ob'* Robert Wase & *vj*d ob'* William Dixson, masons, ffor v dayez worke in all todeger: ij*s* viij*d ob'*; And payd to iiij laborerz ffor vj dayez worke & *di'* togeder: <ii>ij*s* iiij*d*; And payd *x*d* to William Grove, *xiij*d* John Crysmes & *<xiij*d> vj*d ob'* Rauff Crystmes, carpenterz, ffor iiij dayez worke & *di'* [*f. 43*ᵛ] to geder & *vj*d ob'* ffor a laborer a dayez worke & *di'*: ij*s*; And payed to Henry Sparke ffor cariage off vj loodez stoone & vj lodes off tyle ffrom the Blakffreres: iiij*s*; And payd ffor ij busshelles off collough hookes & hengilles ffor dores & ffor beryng inne off tymber to the Blake Freres: xij*d*; And payd to John Estowe in partie off payement of his bargen at too tymes: xl*s*; and ffor nayles: iiij*d* <*ob'*>

/iiij li xijs vjd/

/The vj^ie wekel And payd *iij*s* iij*d** to John Potter, *iij*s* iij*d** William Custe, *iij*s* iij*d** Roger Howman & *iij*s* iij*d** Thomas Rusbroke, masonz, ffor xxiiij dayes workes: *videlicet* euery of them vj dayez, at vj*d ob'* the day iche: xiij*s*; And payd *ij*s* iij*d** to Fox, *ij*s* iij*d** Johnson, *ij*s* iij*d** Malon & *ij*s* iij*d** Hynde, laborerz, to euery off them ffor vj dayez work, at iiij*d ob'* the daye: ix*s*; And paid *iij*s* iij*d** to William Grove, *iij*s* iij*d** John Crystmes & *iij*s* iij*d** Raff Crysmes, to euery of them vj dayez, at vj*d ob'* the daye: ix*s* ix*d*; And paid *ix*d** to William Pecok ffor j daye & *di'*, *xviij*d** to Nicholas Gardener, *xviij*d** Bartilmue Gillough & *xviij*d** John Alen ffor iiij dayez euery of them, & *iiij*d ob'** to John Barrett ffor a daye workes, laborerz, at iiij*d ob'* the daye: v*s* vij*d ob'*; And payd ffor a lode of sonde: v*d*

/The vij wekel And payd *ij*s* viij*d ob'** to William Grove ffor v dayes, *iij*s* iij*d** to John Crystmes & *iij*s* iij*d** Raff Crystmes ffor vj dayez either of them, carpenterz: ix*s* ij*d ob'*; And payd to Clemens & his man ffor vij dayez worke saweng: v*s* v*d*; And to Estow & Emson ffor xij brasez & xij barffreys: ij*s*; And payed to Birche ffor xij copull & j [*f. 44*] sparre: viij*s* iiij*d*; For iij fframe stodes: ij*s*; And payd to Spall ffor iiij [*blank*]: ij*s* viij*d*

/iiij li viijs vd/

/The viij^th wekel And payd *iij*s* iij*d** to William Grove, *iij*s* iij*d** John Cristmas & *iij*s* iij*d** Rauff Cristmes, carpenterz, ffor vj dayes: ix*s* ix*d*; And payd to Hugh Herryson ffor iiij chalder and iiij comb' lyme: viij*s* ij*d*; And payed to Georg Adamson ffor viij base stokkes, ix pillers & ij medilmotes: x*s*; And payd ffor ij lodez stoone caried ffrom the Freres: vj*d*; And payd *ij*s* viij*d ob'** to William Grosse & *ij*s* viij*d ob'** Rauff Cristmes, either of them ffor v dayez, & *ij*s* ij*d** to John Cristmes ffor iiij dayez off carpentercraft: vij*s* vij*d*; And paid ffor xj ffadoms off baste ffor the well: viij*d*; And payd to ij laborers ffor ij dayez labour either of of [*sic*] them & to other ij laborerz ffor j dayez labour either of them, at iiij*d ob'* the daye<s> euery of them: ij*s* iij*d*[64]

/The x & xj wekel And paid to William Grove, John Crismes & Rauff Crismes, wrightes, ffor vj dayez worke euery of them & to them ffor other xiiij dayez worke attwyxt them in all, at vj*d ob'* the daye a man: xvij*s* iiij*d*; And paied to Foster ffor [*f. 44^v*] cariage of xxvj lodes of the newe roff ffrom the new hall to the comon inne: vij*s*; And paid to Robert Hoode, William Warner & John Tuk, laborers, ffor v dayez euery of them, at iiij*d* <dayes> *ob' le [day]:* v*s* vij*d ob'*; And paied ffor nailez & [*blank*]: ij*s* iiij*d*; And payd ffor CC *di'* sixpeny nayle, CC *di'* fourepeny nayle: xix*d*

---

64 The original sum has been altered by the scribe and for clarity 'ij*s* iij*d*' entered in the margin and subsequently deleted.

ob'; And payd to a tyler & his laborer ffor j dayes worke at the late Blakffreres & j laborer ffor a nother daye: xiiij*d*

/iiij li xiiijs/

/*The xij^th weke, the xiij weke*/ And payd to Fraunces Covyll, tyler, ffor v dayes: iijs j*d ob'*; And *xiijd* to his laborer ffor iij dayes & *iiijd* to John Japle & *iiijd* John Hode, laborers, ffor other ij <other ij> dayez: xxj*d*; And payd *iiijd* ffor a barough whele & *xviijd* m^l m^l lathe nayle: xxij*d*; And payd to dyuers laborers: that is to saye *xxijd ob* to John Hughson ffor v dayez, *xviijd* to John Walton ffor iiij dayes, *xxijd ob* to John Doryng ffor v dayes, *xviijd* to John Tukke for iiij dayez, *xvd ob* to William [*blank*] ffor iij dayez *di'*, *xiijd ob* to William Warner for iij dayes, *vd* to other ij laborers ffor *di'* daye at the Freres, *ixd* to Robert Hoode ffor ij dayez, *ixd* to John Herryson ffor ij dayez workez ther: xjs j*d*; And payd ffor ix m^l tilepynnez: ijs iij*d*; And payd *xvjd* to William Grove ffor ij dayez *di'* & and [*sic*] *ijs ijd* to John Cristmes & *ijs ijd* Rauff Cristmes ffor iiij dayez workes either of them in carpenterz crafte: vs viij*d*; And payd *ijs ijd* to John Walpole & *xixd ob* John Jakys ffor vij dayez worke *togeder* in masonscraft: iijs ix*d ob'*; And paid *xviijd* to Baxster & *xviijd* Tolle, laborerz, ffor viij dayez work: iijs

[*f. 45*] /*The xiiij weke*/ And payd to William Woode, laborerz [*sic*], ffor iiij dayez work: xvij*d ob'*; And paid ffor m^l bryk: vjs; And payd *iijs jd ob* to Fraunces Covill & *ijs viijd ob* to John Fulkes, tylers, ffor v dayez work either of them: vs x*d*; And payd *xxijd ob* to Foxe, *xxijd ob* Doryng & <Doryng> *xxijd ob* Hughson, laborerz, ffor v dayez euery off them & *xjd* John Walton ffor ij dayez & *di'* there: vjs vj*d ob'*; And payed *ijs viijd ob* to Jakes & *ijs viijd ob* Dyxson, masonz, ffor v dayez work euery of them: vs vj*d*; And *xxijd ob* to Walton, *ixd* Brouster, *xxijd ob* Robert Fuller, *ijs vijd* Pecok & Ussher, laborers, ffor xviij dayez worke in all to geder: vjs xj*d*

/iiij li iiijs <iiijd> ixd nota vjd/

And payd *ijs iijd* to Fraunces Covill ffor ix m^l tyle pynnes & *iiijd* to a laborer ffor j dayez worke: ijs vij*d*; And paid John Estowe in ffull payement: xxiijs v*d*; And payd to Flowerdewe ffor m^l m^l m^l m^l house tyle: xxiiijs; And payd *ijd* to John Bedys ffor [*blank*] & *ixs iiijd* Hugh Herryson ffor iiij chalder lyme: ixs vj*d*; And payd ffor vij m^l lath naile: vs x*d*; And payd *viijd* to Edmond Yonges ffor makyng & leyeng inne of the webbes off leed & *viijd* to laborerz ffor j dayez worke ther: xvj*d*; And *ijd* to Abote ffor mendyng off a barough whele & *iiijs iiijd* to Herry Carter ffor caryeng of xiij lodes stoone & tymber ffrom the Freres to the comon inne: iiijs vj*d*; And payd to Estowe ffor chosyng of ij dormantes & [*blank*]: vj*d*; And paid to Foster ffor cariage off vj loodes off stone ffrom the Freres to the comon inne: ijs; And payed to a laborer ffor iij dayes workes: xiij*d ob'*; And ffor thak & strawe: iij*d*; And payd [*f. 45^v*] and payd [*sic*] to Jamys Marssham ffor xv chalders ij comb' *di'* [*lime*] expendyd at the comon inne *lxv comb'*, at the milles *xxxv comb'* & at the comon stathe *xxij comb' di':* xxxvs viij*d*; And payd *xvjd* to Fulkes, tyler, ffor ij dayez & *di'*, *xd* to

John Doryng ffor ij dayez & *vij*d* ob'* to Hynde ffor j dayez work & *di*': ijs ixd ob'; And payd to Grove in partie off payement ffor iiij baye wyndous: vs; And payd ffor a pece off baste ffor the masons & carpenterz: xijd; And payed ffor ij [*blank*]: xijd

/vj li vjd/

And payd *xiijd* to John Estowe & *xiijd* William Wynde, carpenters, ffor ij dayes worke either off them: ijs ijd; And payd *viijd, iiijd, viijd* to John Agas & Henry Spark ffor cariage ffor cariage [*sic*] off v loodes stoone ffrom the Freres to the comon inne: xxd; And payd to John Hoode, laborer, ffor the cariage off tymber & makyng a stage ffor a game: iiijd; And paid *iiijd* to Henry Sparke ffor cariage off a loode off stone & *xd* ffor ij loodes sande: xiiijd; And payd *iijd* ffor a lok & a keye to Westwykgates & *ijd* comon inne gate: vd; And paid *ijs* to William Wyndde, carpenter, ffor iiij dayez worke & *xijd* to a laborer ffor iij dayez worke: iijs; And payd *iiijd* ffor nayles, *iiijd* splentes & *ijd* strawe: xd; And payd *ijs ijd* to John Crysmes & *ijs ijd* Raff Crysmes, carpenterz, ffor iiij dayes worke either off them makyng a new stabill: iiijs iiijd; And payd *iiijd* to Pecok, laborer, ffor j dayez worke & *iijd* to Walton ffor beryng inne of tymber & *ijd* ffor candell ffor the wryghtes: ixd; And payd *iijs iijd* to John Estow, William Wynde, *iijs iijd* John Crysmes & Rauff Cristmes ffor xij dayes worke, euery off them iij dayez, [*f. 46*] in <Crist> wrightes crafte: vjs vjd; And payd *xiijd* to Cok ffor nayles & *iijd* ffor nayleng vp a fflewborde: xvjd; And payd to Fulkes, tyler, ffor vj dayez worke: ijs; And payd *vijd* ffor beryng vppe of tymber & lath & *vjd* ffor CCC lathe nayle: xiijd; And payd to Synger off Wenlyng [*Wendling*] ffor vij C *di*' house tyle: vs; And payd *ijs iijd* to Thomas Vpon & *xijd* William Pecok *laborers* ffor ix dayes workes to geder: iijs iijd; And payed *xviijd* to Thomas Palmer, mason, & *xiijd* his laborer ffor iij dayez worke: ijs vijd

/xxxvijs vd nota qu'l

Summa xxx li ijd

/xxxli ijd/

/*Costes at dyuers tenementes, comon stathe & the late Blak Frerys*/ And payed to a glasier ffor mendyng of the glasse wyndouz off the tenement in the fferme of John Larter: viijd; And payd to John Collerd, wright, ffor ij dayez worke ther & ffor naylez & sonde: xxjd; And payd *xxjd* to Hew Herryson ffor vj comb' lyme & *xxd* m^l m^l lathe nayle: iijs vd; And payd ffor evysborde & ffluebordes: xijd; And payd to Herry Barbour & Master Trace ffor lathe m^l *di*': xiijd; And payd to Osborn ffor m^l m^l m^l house tyle: xviijs; And payd to John Fulkes, tyler, & his ij laborers ffor iiij dayez workes vpon the seid tenement, at xvd le daye togeder: vs; And payd to John Prynce, laborer, ffor iij dayez worke & *di*': xvd ob'; And payd ffor iiij m^l tyle pynnes & *di*': xiijd ob'; And paid *iijd* ffor nailes ffor the plomer at the late Freres & to the plomer ffor shotyng off v C iij quarterz & ij *libr'* leed & leyeng theroff [*f. 46^v*] at the seid place & ffor ij *libr'* sowde: vijs vijd; And paid ffor my horse & Michelles to the audyte: xij*d*; **And** paid ffor a lok to the steple dore & to a carpenter ffor a dayez worke there: xj*d*; **And** payd ffor j lode cleye expendid at the tenementes late the suffraganz & to a carpenter ffor ij dayez work there: xviij*d*; **And** payd ffor hookes, hengilles & nayles: xij*d*; **And** paied to Tomson, wright, ffor makyng of ij dorez at the comon inne, ffor nailez & an hoke to the same doore: xv*d*; **And** payed ffor ij stoppes: ix*d*; **And** payd to the kynges playerz on Seynt Nicholas at the comandement of master mayer: x*s*;[65] **And** paid ffor a peyer off gemews ffor the chamber dore at the comon inne: viij*d*

/lviijs/

/*Blakffreres*/ **And** payd *iij*s* vj*d** to Thomas Elwar ffor vj dayes, *iij*s* iij*d** Robert Greene ffor vj dayez & *xviij*d** Thomas Palmer ffor iij dayes worke in masonscraft: viij*s* iij*d*; **And** payd to dyuers laborers: that is to saye *ij*s* iij*d** to John Hall ffor vj dayez, *xij*d** Thomas More ffor iij dayez, *ij*s** Robert Toke ffor vj dayez, *xx*d** Gregory Akyrs ffor v dayez: vj*s* xj*d*; **And** payd to William Wynde, carpenter, ffor j dayez worke: vj*d* ob*'*; & ffor iij *libr'* candell: iij*d* ob*' qu'*; **And** payd to William Wynde, wright, ffor j dayez work & *di'*: ix*d* ob*'*; **And** payd to Saunder, laborer, ffor j dayez worke & to William Clerk, laborer, ffor *di'* dayez worke: vj*d* ob*'*; **And** payd ffor iij *libr'* candell: iij*d* ob*' qu'*; **And** payd ffor nayle: ij*d*; **And** paid to a m*a*son & his laborer ffor j daye & *di'* off the mason & j dayez worke of the laborer: xiiij*d* ob*'*; **And** payd ffor a dore stalle & a lope to the chapell & a raile ffor the gother of vij ffote length: vij*s* vj*d*; **And** payd *j*d** ffor [*f. 47*] a snek, *iiij*d** beryng inne of tymber, *v*d** lathe nayle & *j*d** mendyng of pykes & hookes: xj*d*; **And** paid to a mason & his laborer ffor iiij dayez & *di'*: iij*s* xj*d*; **And** payd ffor xxij comb' lyme: vij*s* iiij*d*; **And** paid to a carpenter ffor ij dayez workes: xiij*d*; **And** payd to a mason & his laborer ffor iiij dayes work & *di'* & to a laborer ffor iij dayez worke: iiij*s* ix*d*; **And** payd *ij*s* j*d** ffor v lode sonde, *viij*d** ffor C brykke, *vij*d** ffor naylez, *xv*d** half a pece [*blank*], *v*d** iij *libr' di'* of [*blank*]: v*s* j*d*; **And** paid *vj*d** to a laborer ffor j dayes work & *di'*: vj*d*

/ls jd ob'/

Summa v *li* viijs jd ob*'*

/v li viijs jd ob'/

/*Costys off the cokeys*/ **And** paid to Foster & Spark ffor cariage of xiij lodes off <xiij loodes> muk ffrom the cokeys: ij*s* ij*d*; **And** payd ffor the ffeying of the sisternes in the parisshez off Saynt Martyns, Saynt Swithunez & Saynt Benettes: vij*s*; **And** payed to Spark & Foster ffor caryeng xxv lodez mukke ffrom the cokeys in Saynt Stevyns, Conesford, Fibrig & vj lodes ffrom diuers other cokys: v*s* ij*d*; **And** ffor cariage off ix

---

65 Galloway, ed., *Records of Early English Drama*, p. lxxxiv note 10, suggests that the group was 'probably the royal company of players of interludes, which began in the reign of Henry VII', and was usually assured of a liberal reception because of the royal name.

lodes ffrom ij cokeys: xviij*d*; And payd to Teyton ffor kepyng off the cokeys in Saynt Clementes & Saynt Martyns ffor the hooll yeere: xv*d*

Summa xvijs j*d* *ob'*

/*17s 1d*/

[*f. 47ᵛ*] /*Mynute expences*/ And payed ffor the accomptes in the kynges escheker <ffor> ffor Master Sywhat & Master Ferrour, late mayerz & escheterz within the sayd citie: lix*s* x*d*; And payd ffor v m^l thaktile gyffen to Fraunces Wulmer & Thomas Wulman towerd the reparaconz off certen housez in ther fferme, parcell off the late Freres: xxx*s*

/*v li vjs xjd*/

And paid to Syr John Doraunt, chauntery prest off Letyce Payn, ffor certen annuell *rent* yerly due to hym, beyng onpaid ffor iij yeres endid at Mighilmes *anno regni regis Henrici viij xxxj* [*29 September 1539*], vj*s* viij*d* by yeere: xx*s*[66]

Summa v *li* ixs x*d*

/*v li ixs xd*/

Summa totalis omnium solucionum & allocacionum CC xxxij *li* vj*s* j*d* *ob'*

/*CC xxxij li vjs jd ob'*/

And so he oweth xxj *li* x*d* *ob' qu'*

/*xxj li xd ob' qu'*/

Wheroff the seid accomptaunt axeth to be allowed of xl*d* payed by assignement of the auditerz to Richard Framyngham ffor engrosyng off this accompte; **And** of viij*s* giffen by the assignement afforeseid to the seid Framyngham ffor halff a lyuery; **And** of vj*s* viij*d* in expences of the auditers settyng vpon the determynacon off this accompte. **And** so the seid accomptaunt oweth xx *li* ij*s* x*d* *ob' qu'*

/*xx li ijs xd ob' qu'*/

And the seid accomptaunt [*f. 48*] answerth of xiij*s* iiij*d* receyued within the tyme of this accompte ffor the fferme off certen londes & tenementes in Berstrete, which Robert Broun late did giff to the comialtie ffor redempcon, exoneracon & discharge of certen offices leid vpon hym withyn the said citie, which londes & tenementes ben sold to the profite & commoditie of the comialtie to Jamys Marsham ffor a certen somme of money paid to the vse of the seid comialtie, as in the tytle off fforen receptes amonges other summes *beffore* more pleynly is conteyned.[67]

---

66 This sum appears in the margin.
67 See above, p. 74.

/Nota/ respectu quorundem reddituum assise & ffeodorum castri non comprehendorum
in hoc compotu quia satis annotantur in compotu proximo sequenti[68]

[f. 48ᵛ contains rough jottings in different hands, the latest dated 1544, regarding rents of
assise and rents from the castle fee that were on various occasions 'not charged' or respited,
along with a note of the dates of fourteen separate obligations entered by William Lee
on 8 June 1537 for the payment in the hanaper of 140 marks in annual instalments of
10 marks each.[69] The names of the chamberlains to whom the first six instalments were
delivered, ending with Robert Raynbald in 1543, are also recorded. Upside down, in
a different hand at the foot of the page, is the text of an agreement dated 4 February
(no year) whereby Thomas Morley[70] undertook to pay £50 to John Fellows, citizen and
alderman of London, in ten annual instalments of £5 each, over and above an immediate
payment of £10.]

---

68 'Note: the respite of certain rents of assize and of the castle fee not included in this
account because they are adequately noted in the account next following': see below,
pp. 109–10.

69 See above, p. 75 note 34.

70 Morley became an alderman in 1548: *INCO*, p. 108.

[*NCR, 18A/6, f. 50*]   Auditours   Augustus Styward, alderman
Ricardus Catlyn, alderman
Stephanus Reynbald
Thomas Conye

/*Ciuitas Norwici*/ **The Accompte** off Edmond Wardon, chamberleyn off the citie
off Norwiche ffrom the ffest off Saynt Mighell th'archaungell in the xxxij yere off
the reign of our soueraign lord Kyng Herry the viijth [*29 September 1540*] vnto the
ffest off Saynt Mighell th'archungell than next ffoloyng: that is to saye by oone holl
yeer

/*Arreragies*/ **And the seid** accomptaunt chargeth hym selff & doth aunswer of
xx *li* xiiijs ixd *ob' qu'* off the arrerages of his last accompte next precedent, as
in the ffoote or ende of the same accompte more playnly doth appere & xvij*d*
more[71]

Summa xx *li* xiiijs ix*d* *ob' qu'* & xvij*d*

/*Rent langable*/ **And** off iij*s*, parcell of lxv*s* iiij*d* of the seid rent receyued within
the tyme off this accompte ffor certen tenementes, late the priour & covent off
Horssham Saynt Feith; **Off** eny thing receyued within the seid tyme of lxij*s* iiij*d*
residue nothing here, ffor it [*is*] nat levyable within the seid tyme
Summa iij*s*

/*Rente off the castill ffee*/ **But** he answereth of xix*s* vj*d* *ob' qu'* off the seid rentes,
wheroff the particuler sommes apperen in the accompt off John Florence, late
chamberleyn, ended at Mighelmes in the xxviij of the reign of our seid soueraign
lord [*29 September 1536*]

/*Memorandum for Howman inter fforinsecos receptos hoc anno proxime propinquo*/[72]

Summa xix*s* vj*d* *ob' qu'*

/*Rent of assisse*/ **And** of viij *li* vij*s* x*d* *qu'* of the seid rentes, whereoff the
[*f. 50^v*] particler sommes apperen in the seid accompt off the seid John Florence endid
in the seid xxviij yer of Kyng Herry the viijth [*1536*];[73] **And** off ix*d* off rent off assise of
new graunted to dyuers persons, as *appereth* in the chamberleyns accompt endid
at Mighelmes in the xxx yeer of the reign off Kyng Herry viij [*29 September 1538*];
And off xx*d* *qu'* of rent assise off new graunted to dyuers persons, as in the accompt

---

71 '& xvij*d* more' has been inserted in another hand.
72 'For Howman [*see*] among the foreign receipts this year next following': below,
p. 99.
73 NCR, 18A/5, ff. 109^v–15.

off the chamberleyns endid at Mighelmes anno xxxj *regni regis predicti* [*29 September 1539*] more doth appere

/*Memorandum ffor Master Spencer oneratur proximo anno*/[74]

Summa viij *li* xs iij*d ob'*

/**Ferme off the citie bochers**/ And off xliij*s* iiij*d* receyued withyn the tyme of this accompte off John Hows & Richard Barn, bochers, ffor the hooll yeere fferme of thre ffirste stalles in the market in the northend of th'est parte of the seid stalles ayenst the yeldhall porche; And off xvj*s* off Robert Tolye ffor a yere fferme of the next stall towerd the southe; And off xxiiij*s* of Thomas Greene ffor the yere fferme of ij the next stalles towerd the south; And off xxiiij*s* off Richard Deye ffor the yeere fferme of the *ij* next stalles towerd the southe; And of xvj*s* of Richard Newman ffor the yeer fferme of the next stall;[75] And off xvj*s* off Robert Seffrey ffor the yer [*f. 51*] fferme off the next stalle towerd the south; And off xvj*s* of John Baker ffor the yere fferme of the next stalle towerd the southe; And off x*s* of Roger Baldrye ffor the fferme off the next stall towerd the south; And off ix*s* off the same *Roger &* Agnes Girdeler, widewe, ffor the yeere fferme off the next stalle towerd the south, deuyded bitwen them; And off xxx*s* off the same Agnes ffor the yeere fferme off the nexte stalles, beyng the laste off the same est parte; And off xxxvj*s* viij*d* off Andrew Deye & John Fissher ffor the yeere fferme off iij ffirste stalles of the other side of the seid bocherye in the southende off the same; And off xvj*s* of Leonard Rede ffor the yeere fferme of the next stalle towerd the northe off the same parte; And off xvj*s* ffor the yeer fferme of the next stall towerd the northe; And off xij*s* off Robert Barbour ffor the yeer fferme of the next stalle towerd the north; And off xiiij*s* off Henry Harpour ffor the yeere fferme of the next stalle towerd the northe; And off xiiij*s* of John Broun ffor the yeere fferme off the next stall towerd the north; And off xxix*s* off William Cannerd ffor the yer fferme off the next stalles [*sic*] towerd the north; And off xix*s* receyued of Geffrey Rede ffor the fferme of the next stalle towerd the northe; And off xvj*s* off Herry Thornton ffor the yere fferme off the next stalle towerd the northe; And off xij*s* iiij*d* of John Clerk ffor the yere fferme of the next stall towerd the north; And off xl*s* off Thomas [*f. 51ᵛ*] Heberd ffor the yeere fferme off the too laste stalles off the same west parte in the northend theroff

/xxj *li* xs iiij*d*/

And off viij*s* of Andrew Deye & Thomas Hoberd ffor the yere fferme off a mouable fflesshe stalle next vnto the yeldhall porche on the southe parte towerd the west; And of viij*s* of Thomas Ferby ffor the yere fferme of another mouabill stall ther towerd th'est; And of viij*s* of John Barbour ffor the yere fferme of a mouabill stall towerd th'est; And of viij*s* of Robert Tolye ffor for the yere fferme of a nother mouabill stall

---

74 'Master Spencer charged next year': see below, p. 113.

75 Marginal letters 'b' and 'a' against the entries relating to Newman and Seffrey denote that they appear in the wrong order.

ther towerd th'est; **And** of iiij*s* of [*blank*] ffor the halff fferme of a nother mouable fflesshe stalle ther towerd th'este

/*xxxvjs*/

Summa xxiij *li* vj*s* iiij*d*

[*f. 52*] /**Ferme off the countre bochers**/ **Off** eny thing receyued ffor the fferme of the ffirste stalle at the westende of the yeldhall ffor the tyme of this accompte nothing here in deffaute of ffermes, nor of eny fferme receyued ffor the ij^de stalle ther, nor the iij^de stalle ther, callid the pentyce stalle, ffor [*blank*] quarters of the yeere nothing, ffor the seid stalles wer in the new bildeng; **But** he answer of iiij*s* vj*d* of [*blank*] ffor the fferme of the seid ij^de stalle ffor ij quarterz of a yere ended at Mighelmes in th'ende of this accompte; **And** off vj*s* viij*d* [*blank*] ffor the fferme of the seid iij^de stalle ffor ij quarters of the yere ended at Mighelmes fforseid; **And** off xl*s* of Richard Vyncent ffor the yere fferme of thre stalles next vnto the southside of the seid hall; **And** off xx*s* of John Ket ffor the yere fferme of the firste stalle fixed next the seid yeldhall in the north ende of the same; **And** of xvj*s* off Thomas Kett ffor the yeere fferme of the ij^de stalle towerd the southe; **And** off xiiij*s* of Vyncent ffor the yere fferme off the iij^de stalle; **And** off xiiij*s* off Richard Newman ffor the yeere fferme of the iiij^te stalle; **And** of xvj*s* off [*blank*] ffor the yere fferme of the vth stalle; **And** of xvj*s* of [*blank*] ffor the yeer fferme of the vj^th stalle; **And** of xiiij*s* off [*blank*] ffor the yere fferme of the vij^th stalle; **And** of xvj*s* off [*blank*] [*f. 52ᵛ*] ffor the yere fferme of the viij^th stalle; **And** off xvj*s* off [*blank*] ffor the yeere fferme of the ix^th stalle; **And** off xiij*s* iiij*d* of [*blank*] ffor the yeer fferme of the x stall; **And** off xiij*s* iiij*d* off [*blank*] ffor the fferme off the xj stall; **And** off xiij*s* iiij*d* of [*blank*] ffor the yeer fferme off the xij^th stalle; **And** off xiij*s* iiij*d* off [*blank*] ffor the yeer fferm off the xiij^th stalle; **And** off xiiij*s* off [*blank*] ffor the yeer fferme off the xiiij stalle; **And** off xiij*s* iiij*d* of [*blank*] ffor the yeere fferme of the xv stalle; **And** off xiij*s* iiij*d* off [*blank*] ffor the yere fferme of the xvj stalle; **And** off xij*s* off [*blank*] ffor the yere fferme off the xvij stalle; **And** off xiij*s* iiij*d* of [*blank*] ffor the yeere fferme of the xviij stalle; **And** off xiij*s* iiij*d* off [*blank*] ffor the yeer fferme of the xix stalle; **And** off xij*s* off [*blank*] ffor the yer fferme of the xx stalle; **And** off xij*s* off [*blank*] ffor the yer fferme off the xxj stalle; **And** of xij*s* off Thomas [*blank*] ffor the yeer fferme of the xxij stalle; **And** off xij*s* of [*blank*] ffor the yeer fferme of the xxiij stalle; **And** of xiij*s* iiij*d* off [*blank*] ffor the yere fferme of the xxiiij stalle; **And** off xij*s* of [*blank*] Andrews ffor the yeer fferme off the [*f. 53*] xxv stalle; **And** of xix*s* off [*blank*] ffor the yeer fferme of the xxvj stalle, beyng the laste in the south ende of the same stalles

Summa xx *li* xviij*s* ij*d*

/**Roperye**/ **Off** eny fferme receyued withyn the tyme off this accompte ffor the ffirste & seconde stallez in the south ende off the same nothing here, ffor the ffirst is laten with the tenement of the comialtie callid the Murage Loft & the other stande sperd in defaute of a ffermer; **But** he answerth of v*s* receyued off Walter Feenne ffor the yere fferme of the iij^de stalle; **And** off v*s* off Thomas Crosse ffor the yere fferme off the iiij^te stalle; **And** of v*s* off [*blank*] ffor the yeere fferme off the vth stall; **And** off x*s* off [blank] ffor the yere fferme off the vjth stalle ther, which is the laste stalle in the north ende of the same

Summa xxvs

/*Fisshestalles & wolleshoppes*/ **And** off xiijs iiijd receyued off John Webster ffor the fferme off the ffirste stall in the northende of the same stalles ffor the tyme off this accompte; **And** of viijs off Jerom Quassh ffor the yer fferme of the next stall towerd the south; **And** off viijs off Thomas Worlyngton ffor the yere fferme of the next stalle; [*f. 53^v*] **And** of viijs off [blank] ffor the yere fferme off the next stalle; **And** off xvjs off John Sewall ffor the yeer fferme off the next stallez; **And** off xvjs of Nicholas Greene ffor the yeer fferme of the nexte stalle; **And** of xvjs off Robert Norman ffor the yeere fferme off the next stalles; **And** off viijs of <Edmond Wardon> *Fraunces Scot* ffor the yeere fferme of the next stalle; **And** off xvjs off Thomas Cok ffor the yeere fferme off the next stalles; **And** off viijs off Edmond Wardon ffor the yeere fferme off the nexte stalle; **And** off viijs off [blank] ffor the yeer fferme of the next stalle; **And** off viijs of [blank] ffor the yeere fferme of the next stall; **And** off viijs off [blank] ffor the yeere fferme of the next stalle; *And of viijs of [blank] ffor the yere fferme of the nexte stalle;^{76}* **And** off xvjs off John Crowe ffor the yeere fferme of the ij next stalles, which ben the last of the said stalles in the southende off the same; **And** of xiijs iiijd of John Larter ffor the yeere fferme off a tenement next the chirche style of Saynt Peter, with a chamber ouer the wolleshoppes ayenst the pultrye market, late in the fferme off John Nobill; **And** of xs off Herry Marlyng ffor the yeer fferme of a shoppe, late in the fferme off John Florence; **And** off xxs of John Quasshe ffor the yer fferme of a tenement, [*f. 54*] late in the fferme of John Whight, ayenst the pultry market; **And** off vjs viijd off John Halle ffor the yeer fferme off a wolle shoppe; **And** off vjs viijd off Robert Neve ffor the yer fferme of another wolle shopp; **And** of vs off John Crossold ffor the yeer fferme of another wolleshopp; **And** off vs of Herry Holden ffor the yere fferme of a wolleshop declynyng or lenyng to the wolle shop parteyneng to the chauntery of John Cosen; **And** off vs off William Hede ffor a <wolleshop> *voulte* vnder the bochery ffor tyme off this accompt; **Off** eny other fferme receyued within the tyme off this accompt ffor eny other wolleshoppes nothing here in defaute of ffermers

Summa xj *li* xvijs

/*Ferme off howses & tenementys*/ **But** he answerth off xxxs of [blank] Mayer ffor the fferme of a tenement callid the Murage Loft with a shopp in the south ende of the Roparey ffor the tyme of this accompte; **And** off xijs off John Bedys ffor the yeere fferme of a tenement, late in the fferme of William Hede & beffore in the fferme of John Curat; **And** off xxiijs iiijd off Hugh Copelond ffor the yeer fferme off a tenement, late in the fferme of John Aleyn & Thomas Swanton; **And** off [*f. 54^v*] xxs off Bryan Doraunt ffor the yeere [*fferme*] of a tenement with a fforge, late in the fferme of John Dixe; **And** of xviijs iiijd *of Marke Heynes* ffor the yere fferme of a tenement, late in the fferme of John Falke, and of a newe chamber of newe bilded on the north parte

---

76 The sum of 'viijs' appears in the margin.

of the seid tenement, which chamber the same Marke holdeth ffor terme of yeeres
bye graunte of the chamberleynz of the same citie;[77] **Off** eny fferme receyued within
the tyme of this accompte of a tenement lyeng in Ouer Newport callid The Cage,
or of a tenement lyeng on the Netherrowe, late in the fferme of John Dikenson, or
of a tenement lyeng in Cutlerrowe, next the castil diche, late in the fferme of Robert
Evan, or off a tenement on the other side of Cutlerrrow, late in the fferme of John
Rede, bower, nothing here, ffor that the same tenementes ben seuerallye graunted
to dyuers persons & to ther heires ffor euer by the comialtie ffor certen rentes yerly
charged amonges the rentes of assise, as in diuerse *accomptes* next beffore more
pleynly is conteyned; **But** he answerth off x*s* viij*d* receyued within the tyme of thys
accompte of Adrian Johnson ffor the yeere fferme of a tenement lyeng on th'est
parte of the south gate of the comon inne in the market, of late newe bilded; **And**
off xxvj*s* viij*d* of the same Adryan ffor the yeer fferme of the hede mese of the seid
comon inne, also of *late* new bilded; [*f. 54A*] **And** off xiiij*s* off John Sewall ffor the
yeer fferme of a tenement on the west corner of the seid hede mese, also of late new
bilded; **And** off xl*d* of Thomas Necton, alderman, ffor the yer fferme of a tenement
lyeng at th'estende of the chirche of Saynt Andrewe, late graunted to John Clerk,
alderman, & his assignes ffor terme of lx yeeres begynnyng at Mighelmes *anno regni*
regis Henrici viij primo [*29 September 1509*];[78] **And** off xl*d* off Richard Framyngham
ffor the yere fferme off a scriptorye on the south side of the yeldehall; **And** of xvj*d*
of Margaret Sancroft ffor the yer *fferme* of a shop vnder the south side of the seid
yeldhall, late vsed ffor a scriptory; **And** of vj*s* viij*d* of Nicholas Sywhat, alderman,
ffor the yere fferme of a certen parcell of comon grounde with a ffisshing, late in
the fferme of Hugh Dodman; **And** off xxvj*s* viij*d* off Thomas Grewe, alderman,
ffor the fferme off the hilles called Buttelerhilles ffor tyme of this accompte; **And**
off xxvj*s* viij*d* off Joone Flyngant ffor the fferme of the clothe halle; **Off** eny fferme
receyued within the tyme of this accompte ffor an acre of londe, late Wauereys, lyeng
without Saynt Gile gates, ner of a parcell of comon grounde lyeng nere Lorde Dacres
water, nor off the voide grounde lyeng at Tomlond, ner off eny tenementes sette on
the comon grounde nere Saynt Austyns gates & Coslany gates, nor of the comon
grounde lyeng next [*f. 54A*ᵛ] the walles of the citie in the Chapelffeld croftes,[79] nor
of the crosse in the market, nor voulte vnder the yeldhall, nothing here for diuers
causes apparaunt in the chamberleyns counte endid at Mighelmes in the xxxj yer of
the reign of our soueraign lord the kyng that now is [*29 September 1539*];[80] **But** he
answerth off xij*d*[81] receyued with[*in*] the tyme of this accompte *of the heires of
Roger Appilyerd* ffor the yere fferme off a dyke without Westwykgates; **And** of xij*d*

---

77 Marginal letters 'c', 'a' and 'b' against the entries for Copelond, Doraunt and Heynes
respectively denote that they appear in the wrong order.

78 NCR, 16D/2, f. 82. The tenement had been destroyed in the fire of 1507 and Clerk
agreed to rebuild it with a tile roof.

79 The word *'nota'* appears in the margin.

80 See above, p. 70 note 15.

81 This sum appears in the margin.

off Adrian *Mace* ffor fferme of a parcell of a lane or comon grounde lyeng in the parisshe off Saynt Faste [*Vedast*], late graunted to hym & his assignes ffor the terme of xl yeeres, the terme begynnyng at Mighelmes in the xvij yeere of the reign of Kyng Herry the viij^th [*29 September 1525*]

/xj li xijs iiijd with vijs *iiijd* ffor londes & ground ffolowyng/

And off vs of Richerd Sterkyn ffor the fferme *of the* the [*sic*] ffirst *of the* tenementes with the lyme killes in Conesford *in the south end of the same* ffor the tyme of this accompt; And of vs off Richerd Sterkyn ffor the yeer fferme of the ij^de tenement ther; And of vs off Elizabeth Stoorye ffor the yer fferme off the iij^de tenement; And off vs off Elizabeth Radclyffe ffor the yere fferme off the iiij^te tenement ther; And off vs off William Guylberte ffor the yeer fferme off the v tenement ther; And off vs off Agnes Lambert ffor the yeer fferm off the vj tenement ther; And of vjs viijd of William Horn ffor the yere fferme of the vij^th tenement ther; And off xvd ffor the fferme of the viij^th tenement ther ffor oone quarter; [*f. 55*] And off xxs off Agnes Pallyng ffor the yere fferme off the hede house & certen yerdes adiacent; And off vs off wydowe Richerdson ffor the yeer fferme of the ix tenement ther; And off vs of Thomas Purkyn ffor the yeer fferm of the x tenement ther; And of iijs ixd off Robert Dawes ffor the fferme off the xj tenement ther ffor <iijs ixd> iij quarterz of the yer;[82] And off iijs ixd off Nicholas Harden ffor the fferme of the xij tenement ther ffor iij quarters of the yeer;[83] And of vs receyued off John Fraunces ffor the *yere* fferme off the xiij tenement ther, whiche is the last of the seid tenementes in the northende of the same

/iiij li xjd/

And off vjs[84] off John Quasshe ffor the fferme of too acres off londes without Saynt Gylys gates, late Hemynges, ffor the tyme of this accompt; And off xvjd off Syr John Buxton, prest, ffor the fferme of a plotte off comon grounde in the parisshe of All Sayntes in Ber Strete on the southe parte of a comon well ther & lieth bitwen the tenement *late* of Cecily Wilton & the tenement of late [*sic*] Herry Bathcon, to hym graunted ffor terme off yeeres, this beyng the ffirste yere

Summa xv li xiijs iijd

/Petye custome/ And off cxiijs iiijd receyued of Robert Collerd ffor the fferme off the petye custome ffor the seid tyme

Summa cxiijs iiijd

[*f. 55ᵛ*] /Boothes/ And off iiijs off Robert Broun ffor the fferme off the boothes ayenst the shire hous & castil gate ffor the seid tyme

Summa iiijs

---

82 The period of the lease has been inserted in a blank space at the end of the line in a smaller hand.

83 The period of the lease has been inserted in a blank space in a smaller hand.

84 The original figure has been altered by the scribe and for clarity 'vjs' written in the margin.

/Tenementes in the kyndes [sic] handes/ And off iiijs off Roger Leek ffor the fferme
off a tenement in the parisshe off Saynt Benetes, late the priour off Bokenham [*Old
Buckenham*], ffor the tyme of this accompte; And of vs of Richerd Penyman, clerk,
ffor the fferme of a tenement, late in the fferme of oone Stawn, cobler, in the parisshe
of Saynt Martyn at the Palaysgate in Cowgate Strete; Off eny fferme receyued
withyn the sayd tyme ffor a tenement in the parisshe of Saynt Mighell at the Plee,
late in the fferme of Andrewe Thirkill, nothing heere, ffor it is decayd by casualtie of
soden ffyer & it was late graunted to Wylliam Russell & his heires fforeuer ffor jd off
yerly rent, which is charged amonges the rent off assise
Summa ixs

/The old & new stathez/ And off xv li receyued off Agnes Pallyng, widewe, ffor the
fferme of the same stathez ffor the tyme of this accompt
Summa xv li

/Ferme off the milles/ And of xl li receyued of Stevyn Empson ffor the fferme off
[*f. 56*] the milles off the citie ffor the tyme of this accompte; And off lxvjs viijd off
the seid Stevyn ffor the fferme off Heigham milles with certen medewes belonging
to the same ffor the seid tyme
Summa xliij li vjs viijd

/xliij li vjs viijd/

/Yatys & towres/ And off viij li receyued of th'executers off Master Robert Jannys,
alderman, off & ffor a certen annuytie or yerly rent off late graunted to the comialtie
ffor discharge of alle maner tolles & customes to be taken at the yates of the seid citie
& in the ffayers callid Trynytie ffayer & Pentecoste ffayer; And of xld off Thomas
Grewe, alderman, ffor the fferme of a garden next & without the walles of the said
citie by Barregates ffor the tyme of this accompt; And of xld receyued off Walter
Feere ffor the fferme of a tower next the rever by Barregates ffor the tyme of this
accompte; And of vjd off Hugh Boxfford ffor the ffor the [*sic*] fferme of a tower next
Fibriggates; And of xvjd off [*blank*] ffor the fferme of a tower callid the Brasen Doore
ffor tyme of this accompt
Summa viij li viijs vjd

/Ferme off the scite off the late house or priory off Blak Freres & garden/ And off
nihil hoc anno[85] off William Alman ffor the fferme of an house of late new bilded
on the southe parte of the late preching yerd [*f. 56ᵛ*] ffor the yere ended at Cristmes
next after th'ende of this accompt; And of [*blank*] of the same William ffor the
fferme off *a parcell of* the same preching yerd ffor the yere endid at [*blank*]
th'ende of this accompte; And off Thomas Wulman & Fraunces Wulmer [*blank*]
ffor the fferme of certen houses, to them graunted ffor terme off yeres, ffor the yere
ended at Mighelmes in th'ende off this accompt;[86] And off [*blank*] off John Clerk,

---

85 'Nothing this year'
86 See NCR, 16D/2, ff. 192–3ᵛ, 195, for the 'many communicacons had' over this and

cook, ffor the fferme of another parcell of the same preching yerd ffor [*blank*] endid at [*blank*] th'ende of this accompte

/*Nihil hoc anno*/

And of xiiij*s* off William Moraunt ffor the fferme of a parcell of the seid garden ffor a yer ended atte the *ffest of Halowmes after* th'ende of this accompt; And off xxvj*s* viij*d* off Herry Bakon ffor the fferme of a tenement & the chapell, with the yerdes therunto appointed, *parcell of the seid garden* ffor the yer ended at *Halowmes* after th'ende off this accompt; And off xiij*s* iiij*d* of John Birche & Thomas Wattes ffor another parcell off the seid garden ffor a yeer endid at Mighelmes in th'ende off this accompte; And off *iiij *li** [*of*] John Quassh ffor fferme of another parcell of the seid gret garden ffor oone yeer endid at Mighelmes in th'ende of this accompte;[87] And of vj*s* viij*d* of John Baker ffor fferme of another parcell of the seid garden ffor the yere endid at [*f. 57*] Mighelmes in th'ende of this accompte; And of x*s* off *Adrian Mace &* Edmond Woode, alderman, ffor the fferme off another parcell of the seid garden ffor the yeer ended at Mighelmes in th'ende of this accompte; And off x*s* off William Marche ffor the fferme of another parcell off the seid garden ffor the yer ended at Halowmes after th'ende off this accompte; And of xiij*s* iiij*d* off the same William ffor fferme of *an* oser grounde, parcell of the seid garden, ffor the yeer ended at Candelmes before th'ende off this accompte; And off vj*s* viij*d* off John Baker ffor the fferme of a lane with an house bilded on *the northe* th'ende of the same, late to the seid gret garden apparteyneng, ffor the yer ended atte Mighelmes in th'ende of this accompte

Summa ix *li* viij*d*

/***Ferme off the houses late the suffragan busshop off Caladony***/ And off xxvj*s* viij*d* off Robert Stevynson ffor the fferme off the ffirst tenement ther lyeng on the northe corner of the same tenementes ffor a yeer ended at Mighelmes in th'ende of this accompte; And off xiij*s* iiij*d* of John Suklyng *& Thomas Gogney* ffor the fferme of the ij^de tenement ther ffor a yeer endid at Halowmes after th'ende [*f. 57*] of this accompte; And off xiij*s* iiij*d* off Thomas Mosse ffor the fferme of the thirde tenement ther ffor the yer ended atte Mighelmes in th'ende off this accompte; And off xv*s* receyued off John Suklyngge ffor the fferme of the iiij^te tenement ther ffor iij quarters *of a yere* ended at Mighelmes in th'ende of this accompt; And off vij*s* vj*d* receyued of Syr Lakenham, prest, ffor the fferme off the vth tenement ther ffor iij quarters of *a yer* endid at Mighelmes in th'ende of this accompte; And off x*s* receyued off Moder Punche ffor the fferme of the vj^th tenement ther ffor a yeer endid at Halowmes after th'ende of this accompte; And off vij*s* vj*d* receyued of Moder Kyddell & Herry Deye ffor the fferme of the vij^th tenement ther ffor iij quarters *of the yer* endid at Mighelmes in th'ende of this accompte; And off xv*s*

some of the other new leases of property owned by the Domincans north and south of the river.

87 The note '*memorandum iiij quarters at Midsomer iiij li*' appears in the margin.

receyued off [*blank*] Ussher ffor the fferme of the viijth tenement ther ffor iij quarters *of a yeer* endid at Mighelmes in th'ende of this accompte; **And** off vjs <vjd> ixd⁸⁸ off John West & [*blank*] Cokkooe ffor the fferme off the ixth tenement ther ffor iij quarters of *a yere* endid at Mighelmes in th'end of this accompte; **And** of vjs viijd of Richard Jermyn & Moder Kyddell ffor the fferme off the xth tenement ther ffor the yeer ended at Halowmes after th'ende of this accompt; **And** of eny oder fferme receyued within the seid tyme of the seid housez nothing here, in deffaute of ffermers

Summa vj *li* xxjd

[*f. 58*] /**Foren receptys**/ **And** off xxs receyued of Thomas Broun ffor the fferme of the mukbote, ouer & aboue xxs allowed to the seid Thomas for kepyng of the cokey ayenst Master Coddes yate; **And** of iijs iiijd of [*blank*] Dewe *alias* Smyth ffor lisence to stoppe vp a lane *ducens a regia via in cimiterium ecclesiae Sancti Martini de Ballia*⁸⁹ & *to* annexe the same lane to his tenement ther; **And** of vjs viijd of [*blank*] Howman ffor a parcell of comon grounde vpon the castill ffee at th'est parte of his mese, somtyme [*blank*] Pye, coryer, after Salter, graunted to hym & his heires ffor euer ffor *qu'* of yerly rent; **And** of x *li* xviijd of the *comon* bakers of the seid citie ffor grynding at the milles of the same citie, ouer & aboue *suche* sommes of money as the same bakers doo paye to the ffermer of the sayde millez, ffor the tyme of this accompte;⁹⁰ **And** off vj *li* of Syr William Fermour, knyght, in full payemente off xviij *li* due to the comialtie ffor the dette of Gregory Cause;⁹¹ **And** off xls off Thomas Beere in partie off payement off v marces ffor ffyne gyven to the comialtie ffor a discharge of the office off constable & beryng the guyld off Saynt George;⁹² **And** off lxvjs viijd of John *Barker*, bruer, ffor the ffirste payement of x *li*, which he hath graunted to paye to the comialtie in ffull payement off all arrerages dependyng vpon Robert Barker, alderman, decessid, ffader to the same John, late chamberleyn, vpon the determinacon of his accompt;⁹³ **And** of xiijs iiijd of John Gibbes in ffull payement of v marces giffen to the comialtie ffor

---

88 The corrected figure appears in the margin.

89 'Leading from the king's highway into the cemetery of the church of St Martin at Bailey'.

90 The bakers' 'grynte' was raised to 2d on each quarter of corn ground on 5 March 1540, which no doubt explains why the amount was twice that received in 1539–40: NCR, 16D/2, f. 190.

91 The note 'iij payment' appears in the margin.

92 See NCR, 16A/4, f. 34^v. The cost of organising (and therefore subsidising) guild feasts could be prohibitive; and Robert Raynbald himself paid 40s in 1535 to be excused the obligation. There was unrest in Norwich at this time because junior bretheren were being required to shoulder the burden: King, 'Merchant Class and Borough Finances', ii, pp. 248, 355; *RCN*, ii, pp. 111–15; Grace, ed., *Records of the Guild of St. George*, pp. 18, 137, 155, 156.

93 Robert Barker ended his account as chamberlain in 1511–12 with arrears of £29 11s 1½d, which remained outstanding: NCR, 7A/65. At an assembly meeting on 11 March 1541 his

the purchase of a tenement called The Cage; **And** off xl*s* of Thomas Cok ffor a ffyne giffen to the comialtie ffor differryng the eleccon of th'office of shereff ffor oone yere[94]

Summa xxv *li* xj*s* vj*d*

Summa totalis receptorum onerata CC xvij *li* ij*s* x*d* & xvij*d*[95]

[*f. 58*ᵛ] /*Fees & wages*/[96] **Off** eny thyng payed by the seid accomptaunt to Master Thomas Grewe, alderman, occupieng the office of mayraltie by iij quarters off a yeer withyn the tyme off this accompte: that is to saye ffrom the ffest of Saynt Mighell in the begynnyng of the said accompt vntill the ffest off the Natyuytie of Saynt John Baptist than next ffolowyng, nothing here, ffor asmoche as the seid Master Grewe receyued of the goodes of the comialtie xv *li* by the handes of John Grace ffor his ffee ffor the seid iij quarters of a yeer; **But** the seid accomptaunt hath payd to Master Robert Leche, alderman, successour of the seid Master Grewe, occupieng the seid office by oone quarter of a yeer, residue of the seid tyme: that is to saye ffrom Midsomer to Mighelmes in th'ende of this accompte: v *li*; **And** to Master Thomas Cod & John Spencer, shreffes off the seid citie, in help towerdes the kynges ffee fferme: xxx *li*; **And** to Edmond Grey, esquyer, recorder off the seid citie, ffor his ffee ffor the tyme off this accompte: v *li*; <**And** to John Corbet, gent', styward, ffor his ffee ffor the seid tyme: *xxs*> *sequitur clare*[97] **And** to Henry Warde, gent', clerk of the mayer & comialtie, ffor his ffe: iiij *li* vj*s* viij*d*; <**And** to the kynges escheker ffor londes excheted in to the kynges handes: xxvj*s* iiij*d* *sicut plus hoc anno*> *sequitur clare* **And** to Antony Pigot, gent', sword berer, ffor his ffee: lxvj*s* viij*d*; **And** to John Rede & Thomas Molle, seriauntes at the mace of the mayer: liij*s* iiij*d* ffor ther wages; **And** to Robert Collerd, seriaunt in the market, ffor his wages: xxvj*s* viij*d*;[98] **And** to the same Robert ffor his lyuery: x*s*; **And** to the chamberleyn nowe accomptaunt ffor his ffee: iiij *li*; **And** to hym ffor hys lyuery: xiij*s* iiij*d*; **And** to the iiij waytes ffor ther wages & lyueryez: ix *li* vj*s* *viij*d**;[99] **And** to the bedell ffor his livery: vj*s* viij*d*; **And** to Master Corbet, stywerd, ffor his ffee: xx*s*; **And** to the kynges eschekyr ffor londes eschetid ffor Esterne terme: x*s*; **And** ffor Michelmes terme nothing here, ffor the accompaunt hath not paied it

Summa lxviij *li*

/<lxxix *li* xs viijd> lxviij *li*/

---

debt (along with an additional 40*s* due from him as an alderman) was commuted to £10, payable by his son and heir in three annual instalments: NCR, 16D/2, f. 193ᵛ.

94 He secured the postponement on 22 August 1541: NCR, 16D/2, f. 196.

95 This sum has been added in another hand, probably that of an auditor.

96 A capital letter 'B' in the margin here and an 'A' against the next set of entries, for 'rentes resolute', denote that they appear in the wrong order: see above, pp. 75–7.

97 'Follows clearly'.

98 This sum appears in the margin, crossed out.

99 This sum appears in the margin, crossed out.

[*f. 59*] /**Rentes Resolute**/ **Off** which the seid accomptauntes [*sic*] haue paied within the tyme of this accompt in rent resolute, as yerly appereth in diuers accomptes beffore: that is to saye to Syr William Coppyng, chauntery prest of John Cosyn: iiij *li*; **And** to the heires off Roger Applyerd, esquire: x*s*; **And** to the cathedrall chirch off the Holye Trynytie off Norwiche: xviij*s* iiij*d*; **And** to the late priorye or manour off Carowe: vj*s* viij*d*; **And** to the same priorye or manour ffor iiij busshelles off whete after the price in the market of Norwich: iij*s* iiij*d*; **And** to the maister of the hospitall of Magdalen [*St Mary Magdalen, Sprowston*]: xij*d*; **And** to the hospitall of Saynt Gyle in Norwiche: xiij*s* iiij*d*; **And** to the manour of the late priory off Horssham Saynt Feith: x*s*; **And** to the late chapell of the Bek [*Beck in Billingford*]: iiij*s*; **And** to the late abbey off Sibton: ij*s*; **And** to the manour or late priory off Carrowe ffor Butlershilles: x*s*; **And** to the late abbey of Langley: ij*s*; **And** *to the late priory of Horsham Saint Feithe ffor the suffragans house &* to the manour of Heigham ffor londes, late Robert Hemynges: viij*d*; **And** to the same manour ffor the fferme off Heigham milles, with the medewez & mersshez therto belonging: lxvj*s* viij*d*; **And** to Syr John Doraunt, chauntery prest of Letice Payn: vj*s* viij*d*; **And** payd ffor the tenth of the late Blak Frerys: ix*s*

Summa **xij** *li* **iij***s* **viij***d*

/*xij li iijs viijd*/

/*Costys atte the late Blak Frerys & off cokeys*/ **And** also payed by the seid accomptaunte within the tyme afforeseid *viij***d*** to John [*blank*] ffor ij dayez, *iij***d*** to William Wynde, carpenter, ffor *di'* day, *viij***d*** to John Elys ffor ij dayez & *xij***d*** to Geffrey Gaye, laborerz, workyng ther at one tyme & *j***d*** *qu'*** ffor [*f. 59*] j *libr'* candell ther expendid: ij*s* viij*d* *qu'*; **And** payd *xviij***d*** ffor lx dice hedid naile, *xvj***d*** a loke, iij keys & a plate, *vj***d*** j snek, *iiij***d*** j barre ffor the dore vnder the stepill vppon the southe side: iij*s* viij*d*; **And** payd *xj***d*** ffor a lok & iij keyez & j barre, *xiij***d*** *ob'*** ffor j borde & ij boltes of yron weyeng ix *libr'*, *v***d*** ffor a gemew & iij nayles & *vj***d*** a lok ffor the same dore: ij*s* xj*d* *ob'*; **And** payd *iij***d*** ffor iij prykkettes ffor the [*blank*], *x***d*** ffor a barre & *xj***d*** hokez & hengilles ffor a dore weyeng xiiij *libr'* of iron & *di'*: ij*s*; **And** payed ffor cariage off a lode off ffre ston: iiij*d*; **And** payd *iij***s*** vj***d*** to Hugh Herryson ffor xij comb' lyme & *v***s*** to John Clerk ffor m*l* *di'* C tyle: vij*s* vj*d*; **And** payd *x***d*** to Thomas Dixe, mason, & his laborer ffor j dayez worke & *iij***d*** ffor cariage off a loode ffre stoone: xij*d*; **And** payd *ij***d*** to John Elys ffor *di'* daye, *xij***d*** to Thomas Elware, ffre mason, ffor ij dayes & *ij***d*** to Gaye & *ij***d*** Pecok, laborerz, either of them ffor *di'* daye, & *iiij***d*** ffor a lok ffor a dore & *j***d*** *qu'*** j *libr'* candell: xxiij*d* *qu'*;[100] **And** payd to Foster & Lawes ffor caryage of lxx lodez muk ffrom the cokeys at dyuers tymes: xj*s* viij*d*; **And** payd to ij laborers ffor j dayes workes makyng a pytte in the kylleyerd ffor [*blank*]: ix*d*

/<*xxxvijs vijd*> *xxxvs vijd*/

---

100 The original figure has been altered by the scribe and for clarity 'xiij*d* *qu*' written in the margin.

And payed *xxj*d** ffor iiij sakkes off charcole ffor the counsell chamber & *ij*d** ffor an hengill [*f. 60*] ffor the tenement in the fferme off oone Larter: xxiij*d*

/*Mynute expences*/ **And** payd to [*Augustine*] Stywerd ffor money leide out by hym ffor the comonz ffor the seid late [*Black*] Freres: iiij *li*;[101] **And** payd to Snytall, smyth, ffor a grate of iron weyeng xvj *libr' di'* ffor the kokeye in Seynt Edmondes & ffor a lok ffor a wolleshopp: ij*s* v*d*; **And** payd *v*s** to Geywode ffor new glasse to the wyndouus of the tenementes late the suffragans & *iiij*d** repareng of diuers others thinges & ffor an hetche, *iiij*d** [*blank*]: v*s* viij*d*; **And** payd to Mastres Scolehous by the handes off Mastre Styward ffor Master Percye by the commandement of master meyer & his counsell by a wryting obligatory, wheryn the seid Master Percy, Master Ferrour, Master Sywhat & Master Stywerd stode bounde to her ffor the purchase of a mese which the same Percy gaff to the citie & after sold to Lee ffor C *li* sterling: lxvj*s* viij*d*;[102] **And** payd to Master Grewe, mayer, by the aduyce of the justices of the peaces & of the alderman in helpe towerd his charges of giftes & rewardes gyven tyme of his mayraltie: xl*s*; **And** payd *v*s** in expences of a man beryng a letter to my *lord* chauncellour[103] ffrom the mayer *& ffor bochers* concernyng killyng off calues[104] & *v*s** ffor his horse & *v*s** his labour: xv*s*; **And** payd ffor sendyng ffor a [*blank*]: xij*d*; **And** payd to Robert Dam ffor gatheryng the bakerz [*f. 60ᵛ*] halff pence ffor the [*blank*] yere: x*s*

/*xj li ij*s* viij*d*/

And payd *iij*d** ffor pak threde, *xvj*d** to Richard Snytall, smyth, ffor makyng off iron work xxxij *libr'*: xix*d*; **And** payd *xij*d** to Water Herryde, laborer, ffor iij dayez, *xij*d** to Key, smyth, ffor ij lokkes & iij keyez & *xij*d** to Snytall ffor the makyng off xxiiij *libr'* iron worke: iij*s*; **And** payd *ij*s* xj*d** to John Dowe & *ij*s* viij*d* *ob'** William Johnson, masonz, & *iij*s* ix*d** ther ij laborer [*sic*] ffor v dayez worke, euery off them: ix*s* iiij*d* *ob'*; **And** payd *iij*s* ix*d** to John Clerk, glasier, ffor ix dayez, *ij*s* x*d** to John Halybrede ffor viij dayez glasing the wyndous, *iij*s** to Richard Lathe ffor ix dayez & *ij*s* iiij*d** Thomas Monfford ffor vij [*days*] glasing the wyndous ther: xj*s* xj*d*; **And** payd *ij*s* viij*d** ffor viij *libr'* sowde ther expendid & *v*s* vij*d** ffor ther borde by the seid tyme: viij*s* iij*d*; **And** payed *xxij*d** to Snytall ffor workyng of xliiij *libr'* olde iron in barrez & *vij*d** xiiij *libr'* more & *ij*d** ffor a lytill keye & *ij*d** to a laborer ffor beryng off tyle: ij*s* ix*d*; **And** payd *iij*s* vj*d** to John Erne, *iij*s*

---

101 Payment of his considerable expenses was assigned on 3 May 1540: NCR, 16D/2, f. 191ᵛ.

102 See above, p. 75 note 34.

103 Thomas Audley, Lord Audley of Walden (d. 1544).

104 This entry presumably relates to the enforcement of parliamentary legislation regarding the slaughter of animals and sale of veal, mutton, beef and pork at fixed prices, which had been suspended in 1536 but was reintroduced in April 1540, much to the annoyance of English butchers. They secured its repeal in 1542 after vigorous lobbying: A. Luders and others, eds, *Statutes of the Realm* (1812–28), iii, 33 Henry VIII, c. 11 (pp. 844–5).

iij*d** William Johnson & *iijs iij*d** William Underwode, masonz, & *vjs ix*d** to iij laborers ffor vj dayez, euery of them: xvjs ix*d*; And paid *iijs iij*d** to John Carre, *iijs* Halybrede, *iijs* Thomas Man & *iijs* Richard Lathe, glasyers, ffor other vj dayez worke, euery of them, & *ijs iiij*d** ffor vij *libr'* sowde ther expendid: xiiijs vj*d*; And payd *ix*d* ob'** to the seid Kerre, *ix*d** Halybrede & *ix*d** Lathe ffor j dayez [*f. 61*] worke & *di'*, euery of them, & *xij*d** ffor [*blank*]: iijs iij*d* ob'; And payd *iijs* to a man ffor vj dayez workys mendyng the steple and *vs* ffor xxx [*blank*], *j*d** ffor whipcorde & *ij*d** ffor [*blank*]: viijs iij*d*

/iij li xixs ixd/

And payd *x*d** ffor viij *libr'* off [*blank*] & *xv*d** ffor werkyng of xxx *libr'* of [*blank*]: ijs j*d*; And payd *xxj*d** to Erne, *xix*d ob'** Johnsonz & *xix*d ob'** Underwode, masonz, & *iijs iiij*d ob'** to ther iij laborers ffor iij dayez worke, euery of them: viijs iiij*d ob'*; And payd *xix*d ob'** to the seid Erne ffor iij dayez & *ijs iiij*d** to the seid Johnsonz ffor iiij dayez & *iiijs j*d** to ij laborerz ffor v dayez worke & *di'*, euery of them: viijs ob'; And payd *viij*d** to Halybrede, glasier, & *iiij*d** an helper, workyng vpon the wyndouz of the steple, & *iij*d** ffor nayle & *iij*d** beryng of stolys in to the chapel: xviij*d*; And payd *iij*d** ffor conveyeng & *ij*d** cariage of certen stolys to the seid Freres & *j*d** ffor ij stapilles of iron: vj*d*; And payd *x*d** to the seid Erne ffor j dayez work *di'*, *xiij*d** to the seid Johnson ffor ij dayez, *xij*d** to Merssham ffor iij comb' lyme, *ix*d** to a laborer ffor ij dayez & *iiij*d ob'** to another ffor a dayez worke ther: iiijs ob'; And payd *v*d** to Snytall ffor ironworke & *iiij li** to Spratte ffor pathing tyle ffor the body of the late chirche & *xjs* ffor iiij chalder off lyme & a combe: iiij li xjs v*d*; And payd to Stevyn Johnson ffor ij stoles ffor the chapel: vjs viij*d*; And payd *iij*d** ffor [*f. 61ᵛ*] an hoke ffor a dore, *ijs vj*d** ffor vj loodes off sonde, & *iiij*d** ffor naylez ther expendid: iijs j*d*; And payd *xiiij*d** to Grove & *viij*d** his seruaunt, carpenters, ffor ij dayez worke, either of them: xxij*d*; And payd *iiij*d** for trymmyng of the tabernacle ffor the pixte & *xl*d** ffor the one halff of the caryage of the seid tyle ffrom Sprattes & *vj*d** to Snytall ffor [*blank*]: iiijs ij*d*; And payd *vj*d** for caryeng inne off the stolys [*and*] pulpite, *v*d** ffor a belrope & *xij*d** to Snytall ffor hokes & henglez, & *v*d** ffor ffetching of a botefull of thak & segges: ijs iiij*d*

/vj li xiiijs ob'/

/Bisshop of Norwich & Lady Hare/ And payd *vjs vj*d** ffor a present govyn to lord busshop of Norwiche in Lent by commandement off master mayer & his counsell & *vs ij*d** ffor a pyke goven to Ladye Hare at commandement forseid: xjs viij*d*[105]

And payd to Toppeffeld ffor the accompt of Master Pykerell, late mayer & escheter, & *quietus est* of the same: xxvijs v*d*; And payd at the commandement fforseid ffor

---

105 Catherine, daughter of Sir John Bassingbourne of Woodhall, Hertfordshire, and wife of Sir Nicholas Hare: *HoP, 1509–1558*, ii, pp. 296–7.

a platte made of the sa[nc]tuawy descripcon off the citie & ffor the sayntwarye by Boswell: viijs[106]

/Lord of Norff"/ **And** payd ffor dyuers thinges presentid & sent to lord duke off Norff' grace by commandement fforseid: that is *xijs* to Ponyet ffor ij pykes, *viijs* to Davye ffor x perches, *vjs viijd* to master mayer ffor ij cranes [f. 62] & *ijs viijd* to Stevyn Gesill ffor hym & his ij horse ij dayez & *xxd* to a man ffor hym & his horse goyng with the same: xxxjs

/Justices of assises/ **And** payd ffor dyuers thinges ordeyned ffor a present sent to the justices off assise: that is *vjs iijd* to Master Trace ffor grocery, *ijs viijd* ffor iiij galonz Gascoyn wyne, *viijd* ffor spyce brede, *ijs* ffor wafferz & *vjd* ffor makyng Ipocras & *vd* ffor laboures off the berers off the same: xijs vjd

And payd at the commandement fforseid ffor a rewarde goven to Master Fitz Hugh, clerk of the crown, ffor to haue his ffavour: xxs[107]

/v li xs vijd/

And payd to Willet ffor kepyng of certen cokeys at Crystmes ijs xd; **And** to hym at the Annunciacon of Our Blissed Ladye ffor the same cokeys iijs; **And** to hym ffor Midsomer quarter iijs; **And** to hym ffor Mighelmes quarter iijs; **And** payd to Agnes Pallyng ffor leyeng of vj C rede at the olde stathe yerd ijs

/xiijs xd/

And payd *iiijd* to Cook ffor j daye, *iiijd* to John Warde ffor j daye laboreng at the Freres, and *xiijd* to William Wynde, carpenter, ffor ij dayez, *iiijd, jd* ffor nayles and *xvijs* ffor m¹ m¹ m¹ brykke: xixs ijd; **And** payd *viijd* ffor hokes, hengles & *vjd* ij lateysis ffor the wyndouz of the tenementes late the suffragans: xiiijd; **And** payd *vjd* to a laborer ffor j daye & di' worke at the comon inne and *ijs viijd* ffor m¹ ffoure peny nayle & *xvjd* ffor caryeng of iiij loodes bryke: iiijs vjd; **And** payd [62ᵛ] *xijd* to Stevyn Johnson, laborer, ffor iij dayes & *iiijd* to Henry Spark ffor caryeng off a dormant & *iijd* to a mason ffor di' dayes worke: xixd; **And** payd *iijs iijd* to Andrewe Brown & *iijs iijd* to William Wynde, carpenters, ffor

---

106 The 'platte', now known as the Sanctuary Map, was produced in response to a demand by the government: Luders and others, eds, Statutes of the Realm, iii, 32 Henry VIII, c. 12 (pp. 756–8); SLCN, pp. 114–17. C. Barringer, 'The Changing Face of Norwich', in C. Rawcliffe and R. Wilson, eds, Norwich since 1550 (2004), pp. 3–5, mistakenly assumes that Thomas Boswell's subsequent corrections to the 'platte' (below, p. 162) were to the work of another artist, rather than his own.

107 Described as an 'assize clerk and versatile advocate', Thomas Fitzhugh was appointed in January 1541 as a justice of gaol delivery at Norwich: S. Gunn, Henry VII's New Men and the Making of Tudor England (Oxford, 2016), p. 169; LPFD, XVI, no 503 (49); Baker, Men of Court, i, pp. 678–9.

vj dayes worke, euery off them, & *xvj*d** to Master Rogers ffor a dormant & *ij*d**
to Jaye, laborer, ffor caryeng off sonde *di'* daye: viij*s*; And payd *ij*d** ffor mendyng
off ij ledders, *ij*d ob'** ffor ij *libr'* candell, *ij*d** ffor haye, *ij*s vj*d** to Keteryngham
ffor vj loodes sonde & *iiij*d** ffor an oken borde: iij*s* iiij*d ob'*; And payd *vj*d** ffor ij
hanses & *xvj*d** ffor lathe naile, lathe & candell: xxij*s*; And payd *ij*d** to a laborer
ffor *di'* daye, *j*d** ffor haye & *ij*s vj*d** ffor cariage off vj loode bryk & j lode stoone
& *v*d** ffor *di'* m¹ latthe nayle: iij*s* ij*d*; And payd *xv*s** to Grove ffor full payement
off & ffor iiij baye wyndouus & *ij*d ob'** ffor candell & *ij*d** ffor iiij [*blank*]: xv*s*
iiij*d ob'*

/lviijs ijd/

And payd *xij*s iiij*d** to iiij masonz & *iiij*s vj*d* <ob'>** iij laborers workyng ther ffor
vj dayes, euery if them, & *xxij*d ob'** to one other laborer ffor v dayez one weke:
xviij*s vij*d ob'*;[108] And payd the same weke *iij*s iij*d** to William Wynde & *iij*s
iij*d** to Andrew Broun, carpenterz, ffor vj dayez worke, euery of them: vj*s vj*d*;
And payed *xxj*d** to Stevyn Johnson ffor iij dayez, *ij*s** to Robert Mason ffor iiij
dayes & *xv*d** to Robert Bronde ffor iij dayes worke in masonscraft & *xvj*d ob'**
to William Wynde & *xvj*d ob'** Andrewe [*f. 63*] Broun, carpenterz, ffor ij dayez
worke & *di'*, either of them, & *iij*d** ffor stulpes, *j*d** hokes & hengilles: viij*s j*d*;
And payd *iij*s iiij*d ob'** to iij laborers for iij dayez, euery of them, & *ij*s ij*d** to
William Underwode, mason, ffor iiij dayez worke: v*s vj*d ob'*; And payd *xij*d** to
Thomas Hynde, laborer, ffor iij dayez worke & *ix*d** to John Keye ffor ij lokkes &
ij keyez: xxj*d*; And payd to iiij masons: that is to saye *iij*s vj*d** to Stevyn Johnson,
*iij*s iij*d** William Underwode, *iij*s** Thomas Mason & *ij*s vj*d** Robert Broun ffor
vj dayes worke, euery off them, & *ij*s iij*d** to Thomas Johnson, *ij*s iij*d** William
Safferey* & *ij*s iij*d** Roger Skerbergh, laborerz, ffor vj dayes, euery of them, &
*ij*d** to Walter Herryes ffor *di'* dayez worke: xix*s ij*d*; And and [*sic*] payd *xl*d**
ffor viij lodez sonde, *iiij*d** ij treyse to beere inne menour & *xiiij*d** to Richard
Snytall, smyth, ffor ij payer hookes & hengilles ffor the stabill doore at the comon
inne: iiij*s x*d*; And payd *ij*s x*d** ffo[r] v C brykke, *iiij*d** ffor a payer off trostilles
ffor a stapiller & *ij*d** ffor an hengill ffor a ffisshe shopp, *vij*d** ffor nayles & ffor
sowde & *iiij*d** mendyng of a gother in the tenement in the fferme of Thurston:
iiij*s iiij*d*

/iiij li viijs xd/

And payd *xviij*s viij*d** ffor vij C borde at ij*s viij*d* the C & *viij*s** ffor other CCC &
di' borde: xxvj*s viij*d*; And payd *xiiij*d** to Stevyn Johnson, *xij*d** Thomas Mason
& *x*d** William Smyth, masonz, ffor ij dayez worke, euery of them , *ij*d** to a
laborer ffor *di'* daye & *iiij*d ob'** to a laborer ffor j daye & *vij*d** ffor ij lodez of
tymber caried & *vj*d** ffor baste & *iiij*d** ffor a comb' lyme: v*s ob'*; [*63ᵛ*] And payed

---

108 The original figure has been altered by the scribe and for clarity 'xviij*s* vij*d ob'*' written
in the margin.

ijs xjd to Johnson, *ijs <xjd> vjd* Thomas Mason & *ijs jd <vjd>* William Smyth, masonz, ffor v dayez`worke, euery off them, *ijs vd* to William Safferey ffor vj dayez di', *ijs vijd ob'* to Georg Smyth ffor vij dayez, *xxijd ob'* to Thomas Lessey ffor v dayez & *ixd* to Georg Broke ffor ij dayez, laborers, <xiiijs vd> *xvs ijd*; And payd *ixs vjd* ffor iij lodes off brykke, *xvjd* ffor CC [blank], *xijd* ffor cariage of iij lodez off tyle & *xvd* ffor iij loodez sonde ther expendid: xiijs jd; And payd *xijd* to Snytall ffor a dosen ffanys ffor the chymney toppe, *viijd* ffor red oker & *vijd* blakke [blank]: ijs iijd; And payd *ijs vijd ob'* to Stevyn Johnson ffor iiij dayez di', *ijs vjd* Robert Mason & *ijs jd* Robert Broun, masonz, ffor v dayez, euery off them, *xxijd ob'* to Safferey & *xxijd ob'* Snell, laborers, ffor v dayez worke, euery of them: xs xjd ob';[109] And payd *vd* ffor latthe nayle & *ijd* [blank], *iijs* ffor CCCC di' & quarter brik, *ijd* ffor rosen & *iiijd* mendyng of the well: iiijs jd

/iij li xvijs iijd/

And payd *ijs iiijd* to Stevyn Johnson ffor iiij dayez, *iijs* to Thomas Mason & *ijs vjd* Robert Broun, masonz, *ijs iiijd* to Safferey & *ijs iiijd* Smyth, laborers, ffor vj dayez worke, euery of them, and *xxiijd* to a laborer ffor v dayez & *xvs* to Donston ffor v lodez [blank]: xxixs iijd; And payd *iijs xd* to Raff Cristmes & *iijs xd* John Cristmes, carpenterz, ffor vij dayes worke, either off them, [f. 64] in ij wekes & *ijs ixd* to William Grove, carpenter, ffor v dayez worke in the same wekes: xs vd; And payd *xviijs* ffor m^l m^l m^l latthe tyle, *xvijd* ffor CC di' bryk, *iijs vijd* xj C nayle, *viijd* CC di' nayle of iiijd le C, *xd* CC sixpeny nayle: xxiiijs vjd; And payd *xixd ob'* to John Crysmes ffor iij dayes, *xiijd* Raff Cristmes ffor ij dayez, carpenterz, and *vjd* to a carpenter ffor j dayez work & *xvd* ffor di' C off borde: iiijs vd *ob'*; And payd *iijs iijd* to the seid John & Rauff ffor iij dayes worke, either off them, & *iiijd* ffor cariage of [blank] & *ijd* to Cook, laborer, ffor di' dayez worke: iijs ixd; And paid *xvs* ffor m^l m^l m^l latthe, *vjd* to Thomas Jamys, carpenter, ffor j dayes worke & *ijd* ffor hangyng of a doore & *ixd* ffor m^l latthe nayle & *xiijd* to the seid Thomas ffor ij dayez work: xvijs vd; And payd *xxiijd* to William [blank], tyler, & *xvd ob'* to his laborer ffor iij dayes & di' worke, *xijs* ffor m^l m^l house tyle & *ijs* to Thomas Jamys ffor iiij dayes worke in carpenterscraft, *xvd* ffor iij lodez sonde & *xijs* ffor ij lode thaktile: xxxs vd ob'

/vj li iiijd/

And payd *iiijd* to a laborer ffor j daye worke, *viijd* to Robert Stevynson ffor makyng of ij steppez in the corner house & *xijd* to Estowe ffor the makyng of the cokstole: ijs; And payd *xiijd* to William [f. 64^v] [blank] ffor ij dayes worke, *ixd ob'* to Robert Rogerz, laborer, ffor other ij dayez & *xijd* to James Wright ffor other ij dayes worke, *iiijd* ffor nailes, *jd* hey ffor selyng: iijs iijd ob'; [And] *iiijd* [to] a couper ffor hopyng off tubbes, *xxd* ffor m^l m^l lathe naile, *iiijd* to Johnson, tyler,

---

109 The original figure has been altered by the scribe and for clarity 'xs xjd ob'' written in the margin.

ffor tylyng of [*blank*], and *xijd* ffor m^l m^l m^l m^l tyle pynnez: iijs iiijd; **And** payd *xxixs viijd* ffor xij chalder & vj comb' lyme, *xvd* to Jamyz Marssham ffor v C ffoure peny nayle, *xviijd* ffor iiij lode sonde, *vd* ffor a midiltre at the olde stathe & *vd* ffor a [*blank*] ffor the crane & *xijd* to Robert Tebold, laborer, ffor iij dayes worke: xxxiiijs iijd

/xlijs xd ob'/

And payd *vijs* to Thomas Jonson, tyler, ffor leyeng of vij m^l tyle & *vjd* to a nother tyler & his laborer ffor *di'* dayes worke & *ijs* to Thomas Johnson & master maier ffor CCC tyle, *vd* ffor a lode sonde, *vjd* ffor m^l m^l tyle pynnes, *iiijd* ffor threpenye naile: xs ixd; **And** payd ffor caryage off xiiij lodez muk: ijs iiijd; **And** payd *ijs* to Gogle ffor glaseng & mendyng off iij ffenestralles in the counsell chamber, *ijs* ffor wrightes & smythes work to the same: iiij<d>*s*; **And** payd *vjs viijd* to Master Sywhat ffor a leder of ffurre of xxxvj staves, *iijs ixd* to Henry Carter ffor ix lodes sonde & *vs* ffor cariage off xv lodes stone: xvs vd; **And** payd *iijs* to Henre Carter ffor cariage of xviij lodez muk ffrom the cokeye in Saynt Stevyns & *iiijd* to Richard Barne ffor reparacon of his shopp & *ijs* to Edmond Wyllet at the commandement of master meyer ffor his paynes taken in the busynes of the comialtiez & *xvjd* to Walter Herryez ffor kepyng the cokeye in the parisshe of Saynt Symondes & *vijs* to Jamys Marssham ffor ij chalder [*f. 65*] off lyme & *iiijd* to Herry Spark ffor ij lode muk & *xvjd* iiij lodez stoone caryeng: xvs iiijd

/xlvijs xd/

/*Rever*/ **And** payd *xijd* to Richard Bulware ffor grynding off the sykkyll, *iiijd* ffor v ffadomz baste & *xviijd* to Robert Jeffrey, *xviijd* John Lyng & *xviijd* Bartholomew Wymond ffor iij dayes worke, euery of them, kyttyng the rever the ffirste weke & *ijd* ffor a rope ffor the sikill, and *iijs* to Robert Tyton, *iijs* Robert Lyng & *iijs* Bartilmue ffor vj dayes worke, euery off them, on kyttyng the reuer the second weke, and *xxjd* to the seid Robert Geffrey, *xxjd* Robert Lyng & *xxjd* Bartilmue ffor iij dayez & *di'*, euery of them, the iij^{de} weke kyttyng the rever, and *xvjd* to Dousyng ffor bote hier by all the seid tyme: xxjs vijd

/*Wrestlyng place*/ **And** payd *xijd* to John Agas ffor carieng inne & oute of the bote tymber & rayles & *xijd* to a carpenter ffor settyng vppe & *viijd* takyng doun of the same & *ijs iiijd* to Master Homerston ffor the hauyng of vij telttes, *xiijd* to a laborer ffor iij dayez workes & *viijd* ffor beryng vppe of the raylles & tymber & *iiijd* ffor naylez, *ijd* lyne & *vjd* newe railez: vijs ixd

/xxixs iiijd/

/*Milles*/ **And** payed *xvd* to John [*blank*] ffor iij sparres & *iijs vjd* ffor vij cople off sparres & *vd* ffor oone sparre ffor the millez: vs ijd; **And** payed to John Tompson, carpenter, ffor xiiij dayes worke ther ffor wages & borde: vijs; **And** payed *xxijd* ffor iij dosen ffoote pale & *xld* to John Tomson, carpenter, ffor x dayes worke, *iijs viijd* to Jamys Tomson ffor xj dayez worke in carpenterscraft & *iijs ixd* to John

Graye, laborer, ffor xxij dayez worke & *di'* ther & **iiijd** ffor a sparre: xijs xjd; **And** paid **xiiijd** to John Salle, mason, ffor ij dayes worke, **ijs xjd** to Stevyn Johnson ffor v dayes, **ijs vjd** to John Dunston ffor v dayes, **xiijd** to Robert Hollond ffor ij dayez, **ijs vjd** to Robert Broun ffor v dayez & **xviijd** to Robert Mason ffor iij dayez: xjs viijd; **And** payed **xxijd ob'** to [*f. 65ᵛ*] William Safferey, laborer, ffor v dayes worke, **ixd** to Hyneryngham ffor ij dayez, **xxijd ob'** to Robert Brouster ffor v dayez, **ixd** to John Antony ffor ij dayez, **xvjd** to John Howez ffor iij dayez *di'* & **xiijd ob'** to Thomas Hauys ffor iij dayes: vijs viijd ob'; **And** payd **xxijd ob'** to John Tomson, carpenter, ffor iij dayez & *di'*, **xiijd** to Robert Marche ffor ij dayez, **vjd ob'** to John Estowe, **vjd ob'** Robert [*blank*], **vjd ob'** William Wynde, carpenterz, ffor j dayez workes, euery of them, & **xijs** to Flouredewe ffor iiij lodez off brykke: xvjs vijd; **And** payd **xxjd** to Stevyn Johnson, **xviijd** John Dunston & **xviijd** Robert Broun, masonz, and **xiijd ob'** to Safferey, **xiijd ob'** Brouster & **xiijd ob'** Ruste, laborerz, ffor iij dayez worke, euery off them, & **xld** ffor v C bryk: xjs vd ob'

/iiij li xijs vjd/

And payd **xvd** to Keteryngham ffor iij loodes sonde, **xvijd** ffor cariage of iij lodes stone ffrom the killes & **xvjd** iiij lodes stone & tyle & **vjd** j lode of lyme ffrom the kille: iiijs vijd; **And** payd **ijs vjd** to Walter Fere ffor vj lodez small stone, **iiijs** ffor xij comb' lyme, **xijs xd** to Hugh Herryson ffor v chalder lyme & *di'* & **xvjd** to Herry Carter ffor carieng of v lodez off mukke: xxs viijd; **And** **vjs iiijd** to master maier ffor ij lodes of bryk, **vjs** to Roger Lawes ffor cariage of [*blank*] loodes of stone to the mylles & **xld** ffor viij loodes sonde: [*blank*]

/Freres/ **And** payed **ijs iijd** to John Brouster, & **ijs iijd** Cook, laborers, ffor vj dayes worke, either of them, & **xxijd ob'** to Wymond ffor v dayez laboreng in oone weke: vjs iiijd ob'; **And** payd **xiijd ob'** to the seid Brouster for iij dayez & **ixd** to the seid Wymond ffor ij dayez in another weke and **xvd** to Abote, smyth, ffor makyng [*f. 66*] of [*blank*]: iijs jd ob'; **And** paied **xxs** to Keteryngham ffor carying off vij score & viij lodez of muk[110] & **vjs** to Roger Lawez ffor xl lodes muk ffrom the late Blak Freres: xxvjs; **And** paied **iijs vjd** to Fuller, mason, ffor vj dayes & **iijs iijd** Holland, mason, ffor other vj dayez, **vijd** Johnson, mason, ffor j dayez & **ijs jd** Dunston, mason, ffor iiij dayez, workyng ffor the comialtie at the late Greye Freres,[111] ffor stuff ther bought towerd the reparaconz don at the late Blak Freres: ixs vd; **And** payd **ijs vijd** to Clerk, laborer, ffor vj dayez, **ixd** to Grue

---

110 Keteryngham may have performed his task indifferently, for in May 1541 he was fined 10s by the sheriff's tourn for dumping the equivalent of ten cartloads of muck in the highway: NCR, 5A/1.

111 The house of the Norwich Greyfriars (Franciscans) was acquired by the duke of Norfolk in 1538 and systematically plundered for building materials: E. Rutledge, 'The Documentary Evidence', in P.A. Emery, ed., *Norwich Greyfriars: Pre-Conquest Town and Medieval Friary* (East Anglian Archaeology, 120, 2007), pp. 86–7; and above, p. 51.

ffor ij dayez, *xxij*d* ob'* to Herdyngham ffor v dayez, *xiij*d* ob'* to Wymond ffor iij dayez, *iiij*d* ob'* to Broun ffor a daye & *iiij*d* ob'* to Saffrey ffor j daye workyng at the seid late Freres: vij*s* j*d*; And payd *iij*s* ffor j lode bryk & *iiij*d* to Tebold ffor makyng of a [*blank*]: iij*s* iiij*d*; And payd *xj*d* to Saunder Clerke, laborer, ffor ij dayez worke pynnyng & *vj*d* to Preston ffor j daye & *di'* labour ther: xvij*d*; And payd *viij*d* ffor C bryk, *ij*d* ffor thak, *xij*d* to Garrerd ffor carieng awey off vj lodez muk, *xx*d* to Keteryngham ffor iiij lodez sonde & *ij*s j*d* ffor caryage of v lode stone: v*s* vij*d*; And payd *ij*s* to Edmond Yonges ffor iiij dayez worke mendyng the leed of the chirche ther & *iiij*d* to his man ffor helping hym & *vj*d* ffor C leede nayle: ij*s* x*d*; And payd *ij*s viij*d* to Walter Feere ffor viij comb' lyme & *v*s x*d* ffor vij lodes off broken ston, *viij*s ij*d* to Hew Herryson ffor iij chalderz & *di'* lyme & *xiiij*d* to Herry Sparke ffor the cariage of vij lodes [*f. 66ᵛ*] brykke to the seid late Freres: xvij*s* x*d*

/iiij li iijs/

And payd to Robert Damme ffor gatheryng off the halff pence of the comon bakers: v*s* /vs/

Summa totalis omnium solucionum & allocacionum C xlij *li* vs xj*d*

/C xlij li vs xjd/

And so he oweth lxxiiij *li* xvj*s* xj*d* and xvij*d* more

/lxxiiij li xvjs xjd & xvijd/

Wheroff the seid accomptaunt axeth to be allowed of xl*d* gyffen by the auditers to Richard Framyngham ffor engrosyng of this accomptaunt [*sic*]; And of viij*s* assigned by the seid auditers to the seid Framyngham ffor halff a lifferey, as in the accomptes precedent more at large doth appere; And of iiij*s* vj*d* in expences of the auditers sittyng vpon the determinacon off this accompt; And he oweth lxxiiij *li* xiij*d* and xvij*d* <*ob'*>

Wheroff the seid accomptaunt axeth ffurder to be allowed of diuers rentes assise aboue charged & nowe decaid, as vpon diuers consideracons declared to the seid auditers appereth: that is to saye of iiij*d* ffor the rent of a fforge in the parisshe of Saynt Clement, remoued ffor ij yeres ended at Mighelmes in the [*f. 67*] ende of this accompte, ij*d* by yere; And off viij*d* ffor the rent of a pale, late annexed to the mese late Blomffeldes in the parisshe of Saynt Martyns at the Paleys Gate, decaid ffor ij yeres endid as is afforeseid, iiij*d* by yeere; And of ij*s* ffor the rent of a fforge, late annexed to the mese late Tirrelles, ffor ij yeres & *cetera*, xij*d* by yere; And of iiij*d* ffor the fferme or rent of the tower in Conesford medewez, nowe stondyng voide ffor ij yeres as is afforeseid, ij*d* by yere; And off xxij*d* ffor the rent of certen housez, late the suffraganz, vpon the castill ffee, ffor oone yere endid at Michelmes in the xxxij yere of Kyng Henry the viijth [*29 September 1530*]

/vs ijd/

And also the same accomptaunt axeth to be respected off certen rentes beffore charged in the title of rentes of assise & castil ffe, ffor that diuers of the same rentes stonde sperd & other diuers of the same rentes the ffeez ben onknowen: that is to seye off ij*d* ffor the tenement off Roger Warde in the parisshe of Saynt Peter off Parmontergate vpon the castil ffee ffor ij yeres endid & *cetera*, j*d* by yere; **Off** iij*s* viij*d* ffor the rentes off Abraham Shalff & other diuers tenementes parteyneng [*to*] the Chapell in the Feldes ffor ij yeres & *cetera*, xxij*d* by yeere; **Off** ij*s* ij*d* of rent ffor certen tenementes, late Grycez, ffor ij yeres & *cetera*, xiij*d* by yere; **Off** iiij*s* ffor the rent of a parcell off ground, late Cecily Wiltonz, ffor ij yeres, ij*s* by yere;[112] **Off** viij*s* ffor the rent of a certen mese, somtyme Lytsters, ffor ij yeres & *cetera*, iiij*s* by yeere; **Off** iiij*d* ffor the rentes of a certen mese, late Welles, ffor ij yeres & *cetera*, ij*d* by yere; **And** of v*s* iiij*d* [*f. 67ᵛ*] <bryk to the seid late ffreres xv*s* x*d*>[113] ffor the rente of a mese, late Ondolffes, in the parisshe of Saynt Savyour ffor ij yeres & *cetera*, ij*s* viij*d* by yere; **And** of iiij*d* ffor the rent of the tenement, late Tyrryngtonz, in the parisshe of Saynt Austyn ffor ij yeres, ij*d* by yere

/*xxiiijs*/

And so the seid accomptaunt oweth byside the seid respectes lxxij *li* xj*s* xj*d* & xvij*d*

/*Wheroff vppon*/ Thomas Grewe, alderman, ffor the fferme of Butlershilles & a garden next Pokethorpe gates ffor ij yeres endid at Mighelmes in th'ende of this accompte: lx*s* /*it is paied by Master Rogers*/[114]

John Homerston, alderman, ffor ij yeres rent of his gardens, late Master [*blank*], endid as is afforseid: iij*d*

William Waller ffor rent of his garden, late Besfeldes, ffor ij yeres endid as is afforeseid: iiij*d*

Thomas Launceter ffor rent of diuers parcelles vpon the castill ffee ffor ij yeres & *cetera*: iiij*s* viij*d* /*it is paied into the hanaper x die Maii anno xxxiiij [1542]*/[115]

The tenauntes of diuers tenementes, late the duke off Suffolke, ffor ij yeres & *cetera*: xxxj*s* viij*d* /*soluti in hanaperio termino Mich' anno xxxiiij regni regis Henrici viij*/[116]

---

112 Marginal letters 'b' and 'a' denote that the entry relating to the rents of Abraham Shalff and others should appear after that for the ground formerly occupied by Cecily Wilton.

113 A marginal note refers the reader back to NCR, 18A/6, f. 66ᵛ, where this payment has been correctly entered.

114 Another marginal note reads '*anno xxxv regni regis Henrici viij* [1543–4]'.

115 Another marginal note reads '*Maij anno xxxiiij regni regis Henrici viij soluti hanaperio*'. On 5 May 1542 the mayor and aldermen agreed that, in return for a single payment of 20*s* to the use of the community, Launceter would in future be charged only 20*d* a year for his tenements in the castle fee because of fire damage. Their decision was confirmed by the assembly in November 1543: NCR, 16D/2, ff. 185ᵛ, 205.

116 'Paid into the hanaper in the Michaelmas term in the thirty-fourth year of the reign of Henry VIII'.

Hamond Lynsted, alderman, ffor rent of a garden in Coslany ffor ij yeres & *cetera*: xiiijs jd

Syr John Jermyn, knyght, ffor rentes of his tenement, late Loundes, ffor ij yeres & *cetera*: ijd

[*blank*] Petycer ffor the rent of the tenement, late Umffreys, ffor one yere endid as is afforeseid: vd

[*f. 68*] The heires off Roger Applyerd ffor fferme of a dyke without Westwikgates ffor ij yeres endyd as is afforeseid: ijs

[*blank*] Vssher ffor *di'* quarter fferme of an house, late the suffraganz, endyd & *cetera*: xvjd /*desparati*/[117]

Hugh Boxfford ffor the yere fferme of a tower at Fybriggatez endid & *cetera*: vjd

Fraunces Skot ffor the fferme of a ffysshe stall: iiijd

Thomas Samcroft ffor the fferme of a shop in the market, late a scyptory, ffor a yere endid as is afforeseid: xvjd /*desparati*/

Edmond Wodethorp ffor fferme off a tenement in Conesford: ixd /*desperati*/

/*v li xvijs xd*/

And vpon the seid accomptaunt of his clere dette by hym selff lxvj *li* xvs vjd

/*lxvj li xvs vjd*/

Wheroff the said accomptaunt haue paied to William Moraunt & Robert Reynbald, chamberleynz, xl *li*, which is charged in ther accompte ended at Michelmes *anno regni regis Henrici viij xxxiiij* [*29 September 1542*] in the title of fforen receptes;[118] & also to Robert Reynbald & William Hede xx *li*, which is charged in ther accompte endid at Mighelmes in the xxxv yeer of Kyng Herry the viij^te [*1543*] emonges other summes in the title of <*vnde*> fforen receptes;[119] & also to Robert Reynbald, chamberleyn, vj *li* *viijs iiijd*, whiche is charged in ther [*sic*] accompte at Mighelmes in the xxxvj yeer of the reign of Kyng Henry the viij^te ended [*1544*] in the title of fforen receptes, emonges other somes;[120] & xijs ffor the fferme of ij stalles charged in ther ffirste accompt vpon diuers consideracionz declared to Edward Rede, than maier, in Ester weke *anno xxxv predicto* [*1544*] & to the seid auditers, ffor that thei stode *voide*; vijs vjd ffor expences vpon the determacon of the seid accomptes vpon the consideracionz afforeseid allowed, ouer & beside iiij *li* xixs ixd ffor the *lxs* dette of Master Grew, ffor the *iiijs viijd* dettes of Launcetour

---

117 'Hopeless, written off'.

118 See below, pp. 123–4.

119 See below, p. 179.

120 See below, p. 243, where the figure recorded is £5 19s 8d.

tenementes, *xxxjs viij*d* of the duke of Suff', *xvj*d* Ussher, *xvj*d* Samcroft, *ix*d*
Wodethorp, also allowed [*f. 68ᵛ*] ffor causes & consideracionz in the title of *vnde
super* * mensioned*; soo the seid accomptaunt is cleere of any ffurder calling to a
receuyng off any other somme or sommes conteyned within the seid title of *vnde
super*, ffor asmoche as the seid maier, auditers & other his assistentes, the seid Ester
Monday, hath taken in to ther handes the said other somme & sommez conteyned
in the seid title of *vnde super* & therof discharged the seid accomptaunt, so that he
iustiffie the same to be yet oweng & iff nat he to be therof answerable & chargeable
at all tymez & *cetera*.[121]

---

121 This entry was added later in a different and smaller hand.

[*NCR, 18A/7, f. 1*]   1541

/*Ciuitas Norwici*/ The accompt of **Wylliam Morront and Robert Reynbald, chamberleyns of the cite of Norwiche,** ffrom the ffest of Seynt Mychaell th'arcangell in the xxxiij^ti yere of the reign of owur soueraign lord Henry the viij^te [*29 September 1541*], by the grace of God kyng of Inglond, France and Yrelond, defender of the ffaythe and in erthe next vnto Cryst supreme hede of the churche of Inglond and Yrelond,[122] vntyll the sayd ffest of Seynt Mychaell in the xxxiiij^ti yere of hys sayd reign [*1542*]: that ys to saye by oon hole yere

Receptes[123]

/*Arreragis*/ **In primis** the forsayd accomptantes do not answer nor charge them selvys of any dette for the arrerages of the last accompt, for as moche as thys ys the ffyrst accompt of the forsayd accomptantes: *nulla*
Summa nulla

/*Langoll rent*/ Item[124] they knowlege them selvys that they haue receyuyd of the baly of the manour or late pryory of Horsham Seynt Faythe for langoll rent of certen tenementes within the cite parteynyng to the sayd manour: iij*s*
Item of the baly of Heylesdon [*Hellesdon*] for langoll rent of a tenement in the paryshe of Seynt Symondes and Jude, late the duke of Suff', nowe the kynges magestees: ij*d*
Summa iijs ijd

[*f. 1ᵛ*] /*Castill ffee*/ Item receyuyd off dyuerse howses and growndes[125] stondyng vpon the ffee of the castill: xxj*s* ij*d* ob' qu'
Summa xxjs ijd ob' qu'

/*Rent assyse*/ Item receyuyd of rent of assyse gatherd of dyuerse howses and growndes within the cite, with viij*d* by yere of newe rent receyuyd of Master John Spencer:[126] viij *li* xs xj*d* ob'
Summa viij li xs xjd ob'

---

122 NCR, 18A/6, f. 69, omits Henry's titles, all of which were enacted in 1534, excepting that of king of Ireland, which followed in January 1542. See the section on Editorial Method, above, pp. 57–8, for the approach adopted in comparing the accounts presented in 18A/6 and 18A/7.

123 NCR, 18A/6, f. 69, has no such heading.

124 NCR, 18A/6, f. 69, does not itemise these rents.

125 NCR, 18A/6, f. 69, notes separately a rent of 20*d* paid by Thomas Launceter (see above, p. 110 note 115).

126 NCR, 18A/6, f. 69ᵛ, provides additional topographical detail about Spencer's holdings.

/*Ferme of the cite bochers*/ **Item** receyuyd of John Howse for the hole yere ferme of the ij fyrst stalles,[127] bothe in oon, in the northe ende of the est part of the sayd cite bochers: xxxjs iiijd; and of Robert Morrell for the iij^de stalle toward the southe: xijs – xliijs iiijd

Item of Thomas[128] Tolye for the hole yere ferme of the iiij^te and v^te stalles, bothe in oon: xvjs

Item of Thomas Grene for the hole yere ferme of the vj^te and vij^te stalles, bothe in oon: xxiiijs

Item of Rychard Dey th'elder[129] for the hole yere ferme of the viij^te and ix^te stalles, bothe in oon: xxiiijs

Item of Robert Sauerey for the tenth stalle: xvjs

Item of John Barker for the xj^te stalle: xvjs

Item of Rychard Newman for the xij^te stalle: xvjs

Item of Roger Baldry for the xiij^te stalle: xs

Item of the same Roger Baldry and of Agnes Guyrdler for the hole yere ferme of the xiiij stalle dyuydyd betwyxt them: ixs

[*f. 2*] **Item** of the same Agnes Guyrdler for the xv stalle, whyche is the last of the est part in the southe ende of the same rowe: xxxs

Item receyuyd of Andrewe Deye for the hole yere ferme of the fyrst stalle on the west part of the sayd bochery in the sowthe ende, with halff the second stalle dyvydyd betwyxt hym and John Fysher: xxs

Item[130] of the sayd John Fysher for the halff second stalle and for the hole iij^de stalle: xvjs viijd

Item of Gregory Pougeleon ffor the iiij^te stalle: xvjs

Item of Robert Toly ffor the v^te stalle: xvjs

Item of John[131] Barbowur for the vj^te stalle: xiijs iiijd

Item of Henry Harpowur for the vij^te stalle: xiiijs

Item of Thomas[132] Brown ffor the viij^te stalle: xiiijs

Item of Wylliam Cannard for the ix^te stalle: xxixs

Item of Jeffrey Reede for the x^te stalle: xixs

Item of Henry[133] Thornton for the xj^te stalle: xvjs

Item of Rychard Barne for the xij^te stalle: xiijs iiijd

Item of Thomas Hubbard for the xiij and xiiij stalles, bothe in oon, beyng the last of the sayd west part in the northe ende: xls

Summa xxj *li* xjs viijd

---

127 NCR, 18A/6, f. 69^v, does not number any of the permanent and moveable stalls rented by city butchers.

128 NCR, 18A/6, f. 69^v, has Robert, who farms only one stall for the same sum.

129 NCR, 18A/6, f. 69^v, does not refer to Dey as 'th'elder'.

130 NCR, 18A/6, f. 70, combines the two entries concerning Deye and Fysher.

131 NCR, 18A/6, f. 70, has Robert.

132 NCR, 18A/6, f. 70, has John.

133 NCR, 18A/6, f. 70, has Geoffrey.

/Movabyll stalles/[134] **Item** receyuyd of Thomas Hubbard for the hole yere ferme of the ffyrst stalle aboue the guyldhall dore: viijs

Item of Andrewe Dey for the second stalle: viijs

Item of Edmond Ferebye for the iij^d stalle: viijs

[*f. 2^v*] **Item** of Gregory Foxe for the iiij^te stalle: viijs

Item of John Barbowur for the v^te stalle, beyng the lowest on that rowe: viijs

Item receyuyd of Gregory Pougeleon for oon quarter ferme of a movabyll stalle set aboue the contry bochers: ijs[135]

Item of a strange bocher that hade a movabyll stalle ther the x day of Decembyr, on Crystmes evyn, Newe Yere evyn and the Saterday after Twelthe [*Night*]: viijd[136]

Summa xlijs viijd

/Contre bochers/ **Item** receyuyd of Rychard Newman[137] for ij days stondyng at the west ende of the guyldhalle vpon the stalle at the northe ende not couerd: iiijd

Item of Thomas Saye for halff a yere stondyng at the lesser stalle that ys couerd: vs; and of Thomas Savege for oon quarter ferme of the same stalle: ijs vjd – vijs vjd

Item of Thomas Boty and Richard Turner[138] for the hole yere ferme of the gretter stalle couerd: xiijs iiijd

Item of Rychard Vyncent for the hole yere ferme of iij stalles on the sowthe syde of the guyldhalle: xls

/Longrowe/ **Item** receyuyd of Jamys Kette for the hole yere ferme of the fyrst stalle at the northe ende of the Long Rowe ageynst the fyshemarket: xxs

Item of Adam Kyng for the fyrst halff yere ferme of the last stalle in the southe ende: viijs iiijd; and of Richard Dey[139] for the last halff yere: xs – xviijs iiijd

[*f. 3*] **Item** of xxiiij other men for the hole yere ferme of xxiiij stalles[140] betwixt the forsayd northe ende & southe ende on the same rowe, at xvjs euery oon of the xxiiij stalles: xix li iiijs

/iiij^or newe stalles/[141] **Item** receyuyd of iiij^or newe stalles made on the west part of the forsayd Longrowe: and fyrst of John Tewysday for halff yere ferme of the fyrst stalle at the northe ende: vjs

---

134 NCR, 18A/6, f. 70^v, combines the rents from moveable stalls with those from the city butchers in a single section.

135 NCR, 18A/6, f. 70^v, notes that this stall is 'nere the mese off William Hede vpon the ouerrowe'.

136 NCR, 18A/6, f. 70^v, does not furnish all these details.

137 NCR, 18A/6, f. 70^v, does not name Newman.

138 NCR, 18A/6, ff. 70^v–71, assigns no Christain names to Saye, Savege, Boty and Turner.

139 NCR, 18A/6, f. 71, omits any reference to Dey.

140 NCR, 18A/6, f. 71, furnishes a long list of stalls with twenty-four blank spaces where the names of the tenants should be.

141 NCR, 18A/6, f. 71, adds 'ffixed & oncouered'.

Item of Robert Castylden for oon quarter ferme of the second stalle toward the southe: ij*s*

Item of Thomas Savege for oon quarter ferme of the iij^de stalle: ij*s*

Item of strange[142] bochers stondyng in the iiij^te stalle at the southe ende dyuerse tymes: xx*d*

Summa **xxiiij** *li* **xvij***s* **ij***d*

/*Ropery*/ **Item** of the ffyrst stalle in the Ropery nothyng receyuyd within the tyme of thys accompt, for as moche as yt ys in lease with the Murage Loft: *nulla*

Item of Jamys Thyrkyll[143] for halff yere ferme of the second shoppe: ij*s*

Item of John Peke for the hole yere ferme of the iij^de shoppe: v*s*

Item of Robert Hynderson for the iiij^te shoppe: v*s*

Item of Walter Feer for the v^te shoppe: v*s*

Item of Robert Putcase[144] for the vj^te shoppe in the northe ende occupyed for a bochers shoppe: xv*s*

Summa **xxxij***s*

[*f. 3*ᵛ] /*Fyshshoppis*/ **Item** receyuyd of John Webster for the hole yere ferme of the ffyrst shoppe[145] in the northe ende: xiij*s* iiij*d*

Item of Jerome Qwashe for the second shoppe: viij*s*

Item of Thomas Worleton for the iij^de shoppe: viij*s*

Item of John Brodyshe for the iiij^te shoppe: x*s*

Item of John Sewell for the v^te & vj^te shoops in oon: xvj*s*

Item of Nycholas Grene for the vij^te & viij^te in oon: xvj*s*

Item of Robert Norman for the ix^te and x^te, bothe in oon: xvj*s*

Item of Frances Scotte for the xj^te shoppe: viij*s*

Item of Thomas Cocke for the xij^te & xiij in oon: xvj*s*

Item of Edmond Wardeyn for the xiiij shoppe: viij*s*

Item of Alyce Cobbe[146] for the xv shoppe: viij*s*

Item of Stephyn Guyssell for the xvj shoppe: viij*s*

Item of John Harryes for the xvij shoppe: viij*s*

Item of Robert Newman for the xviij shoppe: viij*s*

Item of John Crowe for the xix and xx^ti shopps, bothe in oon, in the southe ende: xvj*s*

Summa **viij** *li* **vij***s* **iiij***d*

---

142 NCR, 18A/6, f. 71, has 'diuers' rather than 'strange'.

143 NCR, 18A/6, f. 71, does not furnish a name.

144 NCR, 18A/6, f. 71, has Robert Putrasse, who farms both the fifth and sixth shops.

145 NCR, 18A/6, f. 71ᵛ–2, does not number the fish shops or wool shops, which are incorporated together in a single section, with a combined revenue of £12 7*s* 4*d*. The names of the tenants are, however, given in full.

146 NCR, 18A/6, f. 71ᵛ, describes her as a widow.

/*Wolshoppis*/ **Item** receyuyd of John Lartour for the hole yere ferme of a tenement next the churchestyle of Seynt Peter of Mancroft with certen <certen> chambyrs ouer, parcell of the wolshoppys: xiij*s* iiij*d*

Item of Henry Marlyng for the hole yere ferme of a shoppe vnder the forsayd chambers openyng in to the pultry market: x*s*

[*f. 4*] **Item** of John Qwashe for the tenement in the northe ende of the same rowe: xx*s*[147]

Item of Thomas Croshold[148] for the fyrst shoppe in the southe ende openyng toward the wolmarket: vj*s* viij*d*

Item of Kateryne Halle[149] for the second shoppe: vj*s* viij*d*

Item of Robert Neve for the iij^de shoppe: vj*s* viij*d*

Item of Stephyn Johnson for the iiij^te shoppe: iiij*s*

Item of Wylliam Parker for oon quarter ferme of the v^te shoppe: xij*d*; and for the rest of the yere no thyng for lacke of a fermer: xij*d*

Item of Richard Randolff for the hole yere ferme of a wolshoppe on the west part of a tenement bylongyng to the chantry of John Cosyn: vj*s* viij*d*

Item: of Wylliam Hede for the hole yere ferme of a vowlte vnder the southe ende of the ffyshopps and cite bochery, whyche is parcell of the forsayd wolshopps in euery accompt: v*s*

Summa iiij *li*

/*Tenementes and growndes*/ **Item** receyuyd of John Thurston for the hole yere fferme of a tenement in the Myddyll Rowe callyd the Murage Loft with the fyrst shoppe in the Ropery grauntyd to hym by lease: xxx*s*

Item of John Bedes for the fyrst halff yere ferme of a tenement on the southe corner of the same rowe: v*s*; and of Robert Mayhewe[150] ffor the last halff yere: vj*s* viij*d* – xj*s* viij*d*

[*f. 4*^v] /*Cobler Rowe*/ **Item** of Hewe Coplond for the hole yere ferme of the corner howse at the northe ende of Coblerrowe: xxiij*s* iiij*d*[151]

Item of Bryan Doront for the myddyll tenement with a forge on the same rowe: xx*s*

Item of Marke Heynes ffor the iij^de tenement on the same rowe with the newe buyldyng: xviij*s* iiij*d*[152]

---

147 NCR, 18A/6, f. 71^v, provides details of the previous farmers of the first three properties.

148 NCR, 18A/6, f. 72, does not mention Croshold, assigns two shops (the fourth and fifth) to Stephyn Johnson and lists the tenants of the others in a different order.

149 NCR, 18A/6, f. 72, has John Hall.

150 NCR, 18A/6, f. 72^v, has Mayer, and does not record what he paid.

151 NCR, 18A/6, f. 72^v, simply describes this property as 'a tenement', and, as in the case of the following two entries, names the previous farmer.

152 NCR, 18A/6, f. 72^v, refers to 'a chamber of new bilded on the northe parte off the same tenement'.

/*Comon inne*/[153] **Item** of Adryan Johnson for iij quarters ferme and ij monythys for ij parcelles of the comon inne, at xxxvijs iiijd by yere: xxxiijs[154]

Item of John Sewell for the hole yere ferme of a tenement at the west corner, beyng parcell of the sayd comon inne: xiiijs

Item of Master Nekton, alderman, for the hole yere ferme of a tenement in the paryshe of Seynt Andrewe, late in tenour of Master John Clarke, alderman: iijs iiijd[155]

Item of Richard Framyngam for a scryptory on the southe syde of the guyldhalle: iijs iiijd

Item of Margaret Sancroft for an other scryptory[156] ther within the vowlte dore: ijs

/*Pastures and landes*/[157] **Item** of Master Nycholas Sywhat, alderman, for the hole yere ferme of a certen grownde, water and ffyshynges above the newe mylles: vjs viijd

Item of Master Thomas Grewe, alderman, for the hole yere ferme of the Buttyr Hylles: xxvjs viijd

Item of John Qwashe for the hole yere iusment of the comon grownde vndyr the cyte walles in the Chappell of Feld croftes: xvjd

[f. 5] **Item** of Adryan Mace[158] for the ferme of a parcell of comon grownde vnder the college walle in the paryshe of Seynt Vedast: xijd

Item of John Qwashe for the fferme of ij acres of londe withowt Seynt Gyles gates, late Hemmynges: vjs

Item of Syr John Buxton for the ferme of a gardeyn in the paryshe of All Seyntes in Be[r]strete: xvjd

/*Clothe halle*/[159] **Item** of Jone Flyngant, wydowe, for the hole yere ferme of the clothe halle: xxvjs viijd

Summa xj *li* viijs viijd

---

153 NCR, 18A/6, f. 72ᵛ, has no separate sub-section for the 'comon inne', incorporating these entries under 'Cobler Rowe' and providing a detailed (but superfluous) list of tenements paying assize rent and thus not charged here.

154 NCR, 18A/6, ff. 72ᵛ–3, adds a lengthy note explaining that 'the seid Adryan hath a newe graunte of the seid hede mese & tenement, emonges other newe buyldynges [...] ffor the terme off v yeeres ffrom Mighelmes in the ende off this accompte ffor v merkes off fferme by yeer'. See NCR, 16A/5, p. 104, for the terms of the lease.

155 NCR, 18A/6, f. 73, records that this is the thirty-third year of a sixty-year lease.

156 NCR, 18A/6, f. 73, refers to 'a litll shopp [...] late vsed ffor a scriptorye'.

157 NCR, 18A/6, f. 73, has the Latin sub-heading 'transactions for terms of years', under which far longer entries furnish additional details about previous tenants and the number of years that have expired on current leases, as well as information about uncollected rents.

158 A manicule with an extended finger points to this entry, as a *nota bene* sign. NCR, 18A/6, f. 73ᵛ, has Isabel Mace, widow, noting that a forty-year lease was awarded to Adrian in 1525/6.

159 NCR, 18A/6, f. 73, incorporates this entry under 'transactions for terms of years'.

/*Tenementes in Conysford*/[160] **Item** receyuyd of Agnes Pallyng, wydowe, for the hole yere ferme of the hede place with a kylyarde in Southe Conysford ageynst the comon stathe: xx*s*

Item of Robert Teyton for ferme of the ffyrst tenement in the northe ende: v*s*

Item of John Frances for iij quarters ferme of the second tenement: iij*s* ix*d*; and for the other quarter nothyng for lacke of a fermer: iij*s* ix*d*

Item of Thomas Merser[161] for the iij^de tenement: v*s*

Item of Robert Elles for the iiij^te tenement: v*s*

Item of Thomas Purkyn for the v^te tenement: v*s*

Item of John Marshall for oon quarter ferme of the vj^te tenement: xv*d*; and than parcell of the same howse ffelle down; and after receyuyd off Widowe Rycheford for oon quarter ferme for the other ende of the same howse: xij*d* – ij*s* iij*d*

Item of Agnes Lambert for *di'* yere ferme of the vij^te tenement: ij*s* vj*d*; and for other halff yere nothyng for lacke of a fermer: ij*s* vj*d*

[*f. 5^a*] **Item** of Wylliam Horne for the ferme of the viij^te tenement with a parcell of grownde: vj*s* viij*d*

Item of Wylliam Guylbert for the ix^te tenement: v*s*

Item of Widowe Ratlyffe for the x^te tenement: v*s*

Item receyuyd for the stuff of John Camplyn,[162] who dyed in the xj^te tenement: x*d*; and of Thomas Rogers for the last halffe yere ferme of the same tenement: ij*s* vj*d* – iij*s* iiij*d*

Item of Richard Sterkyn for the xij^te tenement: v*s*

Item of Wylliam Vynt for the xiij tenement, beyng the last in the southe ende: v*s*

Summa iij *li* xviij*s* vj*d*

/*Pety custom*/ **Item** receyuyd of Robert Collard for the hole yere ferme of the pety custome: v *li* xiij*s* iiij*d*

Summa v *li* xiij*s* iiij*d*

/*Bothes*/ **Item** receyuyd of Robert Brown, jaylour of the castyll, ffor that non other persons but he and hys assygnes shall set any vytallyng bothes within the compas of the castyll dyche at any tyme of assyse and sessyons for thys yere: iiij*s*[163]

Summa iiij*s*

---

160 NCR, 18A/6, ff. 73^v–4, has no separate section for 'tenementes in Conysford', incorporating these entries under 'transactions for terms of years' and providing one combined total of £7 7*s* 2*d*.

161 NCR, 18A/6, f. 73^v, has John Marshall *and* Thomas Mercer.

162 NCR, 18A/6, f. 74, does not name Camplyn or note his death.

163 NCR, 18A/6, f. 74^v, does not record Brown's post or his exclusive right to set up booths.

/*Tenementes in the kynges hondes*/ **Item** receyuyd of Roger Leke for a tenement in the paryshe of Seynt Benet: iiij*s*; and of Thomas Hast for a tenement in Seynt Marten at Pales Gate in Cougate Strete: v*s* – ix*s*[164]

Summa ix*s*

[*f. 6*] /*Comon stathes*/ **Item** receyuyd of Agnes Pallyng, wydowe, for the hole yere ferme of the old and newe comon stathes with all customes therto bylongyng: xv *li*[165]

Summa xv *li*

/*Mylles*/ **Item** receyuyd of Stephyn Empson for the hole yere ferme of the newe mylles with all profyghtes and commodytees therto bylongyng: xl *li*

Item of hym for the hole yere ferme of Heyham [*Heighan*] mylles with certen medows, marshis, waters and ffyshynges therto belongyng: lxvj*s* viij*d*[166]

Summa xliij *li* vj*s* viij*d*

/*Gates and towers*/ **Item** receyuyd of Master William Rogers, alderman,[167] for a certen annuyte or yerely rent for the dyscharge of tolle and custom at all the gates of the cite and of ij ffayers cald Pencost and Trynyte fayers: viij *li*

Item of Walter Feer for ferme of a towur by the water syde next Pokethorpe gates: iij*s* iiij*d*

Item of Master Thomas Grewe, alderman, for ferme of a gardeyn vnder the cite walles from the sayd gates to the forsayd tower: iij*s* iiij*d*

Item of Hewe Boxford for ferme of a tower next Fybrygge gates: vj*d*

Item of Master Brown of Seynt Stephyns[168] for fferme of the Brasen Towur: xvj*d*

Summa viij *li* viij*s* vj*d*

/*Comon halle*/[169] **Item** receyuyd off William Almond for an annuall rent of the howses newe buyldyd ouer the gate[170] yerely payd at Crystmes: vj*s* viij*d*

---

164 NCR, 18A/6, f. 74ᵛ, refers to the previous year's account (above, p. 97) for an explanation as to why certain itemised rents have not been included here.

165 On 23 September 1542, the assembly declined a rival petition from Robert Hendry to lease the common staithes and granted Agnes a further six years' tenancy. Claims that she had been overcharging users of the staithes led, however, to an investigation and her replacement by John Styngate: NCR, 16D/2, ff. 196ᵛ, 197; Rodgers, *River and Staithes*, p. 56.

166 NCR, 18A/6, f. 75, refers only to meadows.

167 NCR, 18A/6, f. 75, has the executors of Robert Jannys.

168 NCR, 18A/6, f. 75, refers simply to Robert Broun.

169 NCR, 18A/6, f. 75ᵛ, has one composite section for the 'ferme off the late house or priorye of Blak ffreres & gret garden'. It was not until 15 January 1543 that the assembly voted to change the name formally to common hall: NCR, 16D/2, f. 201.

170 NCR, 18A/6, f. 75ᵛ, has 'an house of new bilded on the southe parte of the late prechingyerd'.

[*f. 6ᵛ*] **Item** of Thomas Wolman and Frances Wolmer for ij yeres ferme of the maltyng offyce ther & other growndes & howses adioynyng: vij *li* vj*s* viij*d*[171]

Item of John Clarke[172] for halff yere ferme of a gardeyn, nowe newly seuerd from the prechyng yarde and grauntyd hym by lease: vj*s* viij*d*

Item of Robert Foxe for iij quarters ferme of a tenement newe buyldyd, late the ankers howse: xxx*s*

/*Gret gardeyn*/[173] **Item** of Master Edmond Wood, alderman, for the hole yere ferme of parcell of the gret gardeyn: x*s*

Item of William Marche for oon hole yere fferme of an ayse yard, parcell of the same garden, endyd at Candylmes in the tyme of thys accompt: xiij*s* iiij*d*; and for halff yere ferme of an other parcell of the same gardeyn endyd at Owur Lady Annuncyacon: v*s*; and of hym for the last half yere ferme of bothe the forsayd growndes newly grauntyd to hym: xiij*s* iiij*d* for the terme of xx^ti yeres – xxxj*s* viij*d*

Item of Wylliam Morront ffor xj monethes fferme of an other parcell of the same gardeyn: xiij*s*[174]

Item of Henry Bacon for the yere ferme of ij howses and a pece of grownde, parcell of the same: xxvj*s* viij*d*

Item of John Byrche for the hole yere ferme of an other parcelle of the same gardeyn: xiij*s* iiij*d*

Item of John Qwashe for the yere ferme of an other parcelle of the same gardeyn: iiij *li*

[*f. 7*] **Item** of John Baker for the hole yere ferme of an other parcell of the same gardeyn: vj*s* viij*d*

Item of hym for the ferme of a lane with an howse on the northe ende of the same lane, whyche lane and howse dyd parteyne to the forsayd place, late cald the Blacke Fryers, and ys parcell of the sayd comon halle and gret gardeyn: vj*s* viij*d*[175]

Summa xviij *li* xviij*s*

/*Tenementes late lord suffrigantes*/ **Item** receyuyd of Robert Stephynson for the yere ferme of the fyrst tenement, beyng the corner howse ageynst Tomlond: xxvj*s* viij*d*

Item of Robert Gogney for the second tenement: xij*s* iiij*d*

Item of Thomas Mosse for the iij^de tenement: xij*s* iiij*d*

Item of John Sucklyng for half yere ferme of the iiij^te tenement: x*s*; for the iij^de quarter nothyng for lacke of a fermer; and of Rychard Coldon for the last quarter: v*s* – xv*s*[176]

---

171 See NCR, 16D/2, f. 195, for the terms of their new twenty-years' lease, which began at Michaelmas 1541, and f. 197, for the sealing of this lease.

172 NCR, 18A/6, f. 75ᵛ, describes Clarke as a cook. See NCR, 16D/2, f. 198ᵛ, for his lease, which was for twenty years, as from 25 March 1542.

173 See NCR, 16D/2, ff. 196, 197, for the sealing of these various leases.

174 Morront's lease, which was also for twenty years, should have begun at Michaelmas 1541: NCR, 16D/2, f. 195.

175 See NCR, 16D/2, f. 197.

176 NCR, 18A/6, f. 76, does not specify what each of them paid.

Item of Syr Robert Lakenam for the v^{te} tenement: xs

Item of Alyce Ponche, wydowe, for oon quarter ferme of the vj^{te} tenement: ijs vjd; and of John Sucklyng for viij monythis ferme of the same tenement: vjs – viijs vjd[177]

Item of Henry Dey for the vij^{te} tenement: xs

Item of John Vsher for oon quarter ferme of the viij^{te} tenement, beyng the corner howse next vnto Conysford: vs; and of Jeffrey Tybnam for viij monythis of the same: viijs iiijd – xiijs iiijd[178]

[f. 7ᵛ] **Item** of Richard Cocoo for the ix^{te} tenement: ixs

Item of Widowe Kedell for the tenth tenement, the last in the strete toward Seynt Mychaelles: vjs viijd

Summa vj li vs xd

/*Foren receptes*/ *In primis* receyuyd of Richard Wassoppe of one quarter fferme of an old mucke boote: vjs viijd; & of Edmond Brown for the rest of the yere for the same mucke bote: viijs <iiijd> – xiiijs viijd[179]

Item of the comon bakers of the cite for a newe grynte grauntid of euery comb' corn *ob*': x*li* vs x*d ob*'

/*Profyghtes of the comon halle*/[180] **Item** of Master Kempe, prest of the comon halle, for the offrynges of fraternytees of guyldes kept ther: lxviijs vd[181]

Item of Walter Halle, scolemaster of the gramer scole,[182] toward the glasyng of the scolehows wyndows: vs

Item of John Carre[183] for certeyn old glass that lay at the sayd comon halle: viijs

Item of the churche wardeyns of Seynt Peter of Mancroft for a stoppe of freston that stode at the west dore of the same halle, late the churche: vjs viijd[184]

Item of John Pylson for vj rowndelles of glasse that war gentylmens armys: xd

Item of Thomas Wolman for certen lede taken out of the same place by hym: vijs

Item of Wylliam Smythe for vj roff tyles caryed awaye by hym ther: vjd

[f. 8] **Item** of the shomakers and taylowurs toward the caryage away of mucke layd ther by them whan they kept ther guyldes in the same place: iiijd[185]

---

177 NCR, 18A/6, f. 76, does not specify what each of them paid.

178 NCR, 18A/6, f. 76, does not specify what each of them paid.

179 NCR, 18A/6, f. 77, does not specify what each of them paid.

180 NCR, 18A/6, f. 77, has no separate sub-section for 'profyghtes of the comon halle'.

181 NCR, 18A/6, f. 77, has 'in the chapell of Saynt John at the comon hall'. John Kempe was of a staunchly evangelical persuasion: McClendon, *Quiet Reformation*, pp. 82–3, 103, 131, 172, 200.

182 NCR, 18A/6, f. 77, refers simply to 'the scolemaister'.

183 NCR, 18A/6, f. 77, combines the two separate entries for Carre and Pylson (below) as one, and does not describe the glass.

184 NCR, 18A/6, f. 77, refers only to 'an haly water stope' and does not identify the purchasers.

185 NCR, 18A/6, f. 77ᵛ, conflates this payment with the next one from the schoolmaster.

Item of the forsayd scole master toward the caryen away of mucke layd ther by his scolers that came of makyng clene the scole: viij*d*

Item of Master Trase for j C brycke of comon store ther: viij*d*[186]

/*Redempcions*/[187] **Item** of John Cutler for parcell of xx markes govyn to the comialte for redempcon of all offyces: vj *li* xiij*s* iiij*d*[188]

Item of Thomas Brygges in party of payment of xx markes govyn to the comialte for the redempcion of all offyces in the cite: lxvj*s* viij*d*[189]

Item of Thomas Berre in full payment of an oblygacon govyn to the comialte for the dyscharge of constabyllshyppe & Seynt Georges guyld beryng: xxvj*s* viij*d*

Item of John Barkyr for the fyrst payment of lx*s* govyn to the comialte for the dyscharge of the shrevalte for iij yeres: xx*s*[190]

/*Dettes of accomptes*/[191] **Item** of the sayd John Barker for the second payment of x *li* for the arrerages of his fathers accompt, beyng chamberleyn: lxvj*s* viij*d*

Item of Edmond Wardeyn, late chamberleyn, in party of payment of the arrerages of his accompt: xx *li*[192]

Item of John Revell, fforen receyvour, for parcell of hys accompt: x *li*

[*f. 8ᵛ*] **Item** of Rychard Framyngham, collectour of the langoll rent, for parcell of hys accompt: iiij *li* vj*s* viij*d*

Item of Master Robert Leche, alderman, for parcell of the dette of Master Thomas Grewe, alderman, whyche he receyuyd of William Revys for a yere ferme of a gardeyn vnder the cite walles next Pokethorppe gates: v*s*[193]

Item receyuyd at the kynges awdyte kept at West Thorppe for a rent of xvj*s* by yere dewe to the comialte for certen tenementes, late the duke of Suff', for the arrerages of iij yeres endyd at Myhelmes *in anno Henrici viij xxxiij°* [*29 September 1541*]: xlviij*s*

Item of Wylliam Alee for an oblygacon dewe to the comialte at Owur *Lady* Day, the Annuncyacon, which was *in anno domini* 1541, parcell of C pownde for a mese late Master Alane Percyes: vj *li* xiij*s* iiij*d*

---

186 NCR, 18A/6, f. 77, specifies neither the purchaser nor the quantity of bricks.

187 NCR, 18A/6, f. 77, has no separate sub-section for 'redempcions'.

188 See NCR, 16D/2, f. 191ᵛ.

189 See NCR, 16D/2, f. 198–8ᵛ.

190 He claimed in August 1542, with some justice, gven the scale of his late father's financial obligations, to be 'sore endettid to dyuers persons & not off abilite to paye', as well as being 'sore charged with housholl': NCR, 16D/2, ff. 199ᵛ–200; above, p. 99.

191 NCR, 18A/6, f. 77, has no separate sub-section for 'dettes of accomptes'.

192 NCR, 18A/6, f. 77, records a total debt of £40, noting 'that xx *li*, parcell of this xl *li*, was paid oute of Seynt Georges boxe to Master *Styward* for expences don by hym ffor the citie & repayd to the boxe by Wardon, late chamberleyn, as parcell of his det & after paid out to Raynbald & Moraunt, chamberleynz'. The loan is documented in Grace, ed., *Records of the Gild of St George*, p. 146.

193 NCR, 18A/6, f. 78, simply reports a payment from Revys.

Item of the sayd William Alee for ij yeres ferme of a tenement adioynyng to the forsayd mese endyd at the ffest of the Puryfycacon of Owur Lady within the tyme of thys accompt: xxvj*s* viij*d*

/*Thynges sold*/[194] **Item** receyuyd for certen wood made of ij popylles in Master Awsten Stewardes closse in Seynt Vedastes: ij*s*
Item of Master Nycholas Sywhat, alderman, for an old mucke bote, late Andrewe Stubbys: vj*s* viij*d*
Item of Thomas Nycolles toward the makyng of certen stulpys and a barre in Cokey Lane, whyche war brokyn by hym afore: xij*d*

[*f. 9*] /*Other receptes*/[195] **Item** receyuyd out of Seynt Georges treasyry: xx *li*[196]
Item of Wylliam Whyttyll for settyng of marbyll stonys vnder the college walle[197] at Tomblond: vj*d*
Item of the sessement layd within the cyte for the sendyng of xl sowldyers in to Scotlond by the vertewe off my lord of Norff' letters: lx *li* xvj*s* *ob' qu'*[198]

Summa **C lvij** *li* **xviij***s* **ij***d qu'*

Summa totallis omnium receptorum **CCC xliij** *li* **xvj***s* **x***d ob'*

Wherof payd by the sayd accomptantes within the tyme of thys accompt for and in dyscharge of the forsayd receptes, as here after folowithe:

/*Rent resolute*/ **In primis** payd in rent resolute as yerely apperythe in other accomptes: that ys to saye to Syr Wylliam Coppyng, chantry prest of John Cosyn, for ferme of certen wolshopps, bochers shopps, with xv*s* iiij*d* by yere for rent of certen ffyshshopps: iiij *li*
Item to the heyers of Applyardes londes: x*s*
Item to the treasurer of the cathedrall churche of the Holy Trynyte in Norwyche: xviij*s* iiij*d*
Item to the late pryory of Carrowe for Butter Hylles and other rentes: xvj*s* viij*d*[199]

---

194 NCR, 18A/6, ff. 77ᵛ–8, has no separate sub-section for 'thynges sold'.

195 NCR, 18A/6, f. 78, has no separate sub-section for 'other receptes'.

196 See above, p. 123 note 192.

197 Since its refoundation as a secular college in 1538, the former monastic cathedral was often known simply as 'the college': Houlbrooke, 'Refoundation and Reformation', pp. 507–8.

198 On 21 September 1542 the assembly agreed that three parts of a tenth and fifteenth should be raised in every ward and suburb of the city to pay for the forty soldiers, any cash remaining to be spent on artillery: NCR, 16D/2, f. 200ᵛ. NCR, 18A/6, f. 78, itemises these contributions as follows: 'in Trouce ix*s*; in Southconesford xxxij*s* iij*d*; in Northconesford lij*s* ix*d*; in Berstrete iiij *li* iiij*s* vij*d ob'*; in Saynt Stevyns v *li ob'*; in Saynt Peters vj *li* xj*s* iij*d ob' qu'*; in Saynt Giles x*s* viij*d*; in Westwymer viij *li* x*s* v*d qu'*; in Midilwymer ix *li* vj*s* iij*d ob'*; in Estwymer and in Holmestrete v *li* xv*s* vij*d ob'*; Coslany viij *li* iiij*s* j*d ob'*; Colgate iij *li* xij*s* v*d qu'*; Fibrig iij *li* vj*s* ix*d*; Spitlond [*the fee of St Paul's hospital*] xv*s'*.

199 NCR, 18A/6, f. 78ᵛ, notes the 'other rents' in detail.

Item to the sayd place for iiij^{or} bushelles whete yerely payd by composycon,[200] which cost: iiijs viijd

Item to the hospytall of Magdaleyn [*St Mary Magdalen, Sprowston*]: xijd

[*f. 9*^v] **Item** to the late priory of Horsham Seynt Faythe: xs

Item[201] to the same manour for the tenementes late lord suffrygantes: iiijd

Item to the hospytall of Seynt Gyle: xiijs iiijd

Item to the chappell of the Becke [*Beck, Billingford*]: iiijs

Item to the late abbey of Sypton [*Sibton*]: ijs

Item to the late abbey of Langley: ijs

Item to the manour of Heyham [*Heigham*] for the lande late Hemmynges: iiijd

Item to the same manour for fferme of the mylles: lxvjs viijd

Item to the chantry of Lettys Payne: vjs viijd

Item to the kynges receyvour for the x^{te} of the comon halle: ixs[202]

Summa **xij** *li* **vs**

/Fees and wagis/ **In primis** payd to Master Robert Leche, alderman, beryng and occupyeng the offyce of mayer by the space of iij quarters of a yere within the tyme of thys accompt: xv *li*; and to Master William Rogers beryng the sayd *office* oon quarter of a yere: v *li* – xx *li*

Item to Master Felyx Puttocke and Master John Qwashe, shreves of the cite, for ther ffee: xxx *li*

Item to Master Edmond Greye, recorder, for his ffee: v *li*

Item to Master John Corbet,[203] steward, for hys ffee: xxs

Item to Master Sergeant Townysende,[204] reteynyd a cownsell with the cite, for halff yere ffee: xxs

Item: to Master Henry Warde,[205] town clarke of the cyte, ffor hys hole ffee: iiij *li* vjs viijd

[*f. 10*] **Item** payd in the kynges eschekyr for the proffers of Myhelmes *terme* in the begynnyng of thys accompt: xs; and for the proffers of Estern terme and Myhelmes terme in the ende of thys accompt: xxs – xxxs

Item to Anthony Pygot,[206] swordberer, for his wages: lxvjs viijd

Item to John Reed and Thomas Molle, sergeantes at the mace of master mayer, for ther hole yere wages, eyther of them xxvjs viijd – liijs iiijd

---

200 NCR, 18A/6, f. 78^v, has 'after the price in the market of Norwiche'.

201 A manicule with an extended finger points to this entry, as a *nota bene* sign.

202 NCR, 18A/6, f. 78^v, has 'the tenthe of the late blak ffreres'.

203 NCR, 18A/6, f. 79, describes both Grey and Corbet as esquires.

204 For Robert Townshend, a member of the Norfolk bench who was later knighted, see Baker, *Men of Court*, ii, p. 1544; C.E. Moreton, *The Townshends and their World: Gentry, Law, and Land in Norfolk c. 1450–1551* (Oxford, 1992), pp. 40–1; and below, p. 163. His town house in Norwich was, not surprisingly, a target of Kett's rebels: C.E. Moreton, 'Mid-Tudor Trespass: A Break-In at Norwich', *English Historical Review*, 108 (1993), pp. 387–98.

205 NCR, 18A/6, f. 79, describes him as a gentleman.

206 NCR, 18A/6, f. 79^v, describes him as a gentleman.

Item to Robert Collard, sergeant of the market, for hys hole wages: xxvj*s* viij*d*; and to hym ffor a lyuery: x*s* – xxxvj*s* viij*d*

Item: to Wylliam Morront and Robert Raynbald, chamberleyns, for theur ffee and lyuery: vj *li*

Item: to the iiij^{or} waightes for ther wages, euery of them xxvj*s* viij*d*; and for ther lyuerys, euery of them xx*s* – ix *li* vj*s* viij*d*

Item to the bellman[207] for hys wages: vj*s* viij*d*

Summa iiij^{xx} vj *li* vj*s* viij*d*

Costes and chargis don within the tyme of thys accompt vpon the bocheryes,[208] ffysh stalles, wolshopps, pultry market, guyldhalle and tenementes in the paryshe of Seynt Peter *of* Mancroft:

In primis payd the xxvij day of Octobyr to ij off Groves men[209] shoryng Guyrdlers shoppe & layeng in of newe grownselles ther, oon day worke: xiij*d*

Item for dyuerse sortes of nayle to close in ageyn the pannell with bourdes: ij*d*

Item[210] to Wylliam Johnson, mason, and hys laborer makyng a newe fowndacon vnder the sayd grownsylles and layeng of certen fylletes of lede ouer the porche & chappell of the guyldalle, oon day: xj*d*

[*f. 10^v*] **Item** to Master Marsham[211] for ij comb' lyme: viij*d*; for old bryckes: iij*d* – xj*d*

Item to Wylliam Morront for ffyfty pownde shette lede for the sayd ffyllettes, and part of that layd ovyr the porche at the cownsell howse dore: ij*s* j*d*

Item to Clement Appylby, plomer, for layeng of the same lede and for lede nayle: ij*d*

Item payd the iij^{de} day of Novembyr[212] to the sayd ij carpenters makyng shelvis in the wolshoppe on the west part of the chantry howse & layeng a newe planke without the stalle, oon day worke: xiij*d*

Item for okyn and ashyn astylles, for nayle, wood and berers for the sayd stalle and shelvis: ij*d*; and dyuerse sortes of nayles: iiij*d* – vj*d*

Item the iiij^{te} day to a laborer that made clene the same shoppe and the lane at Guyrdlers shoppe[213] & mendyng the florthis of bothe shopps: iiij*d* ob'

Item for mendyng the locke on the sayd woll shoppe dore & a newe key: ij*d*

Item for caryeng away of a lode mucke that came of those same howses to Sparke: ij*d*

---

207 NCR, 18A/6, f. 79^v, has 'the bedell, John Barre'.

208 On 23 March 1542 the assembly ruled that, with the advice of the mayor and others, the chamberlains were to 'ordeyn and prouyde' new stalls for the butchers: NCR, 16D/2, f. 197.

209 NCR, 18A/6, f. 80, simply refers to 'ij carpenters'.

210 NCR, 18A/6, f. 80–80^v, inserts here a sub-heading 'pultry market, wolle shoppes & guyldhall'.

211 NCR, 18A/6, f. 80, does not name Marsham or any of the other individuals mentioned in the rest of this sub-section.

212 NCR, 18A/6, f. 80, does not provide a date.

213 NCR, 18A/6, f. 80, records that he also cleansed the area round the market cross.

Item to Wyllliam Vynt in ernest of iij C fadam rede bought for reparacon of the bochery: j*d*[214]

/*The weke after Candylmes*/[215] **Item** payd to Richard Rysyng, reder, begynnyng to repare the bocheryes and ffyshopps for iiij days worke thys weke, at vj*d ob'* the day for hys wages and bourde: ij*s* ij*d*

Item to Wyllliam Bytson, reder, iiij days: ij*s* ij*d*

[*f. 11*] **Item** to John Chylde, reder, iiij days: ij*s* ij*d*

Item to John Trewe, Wyllliam Gardner and Edmond Kyng, ther laborers, euery of them iiij days, at iiij*d ob'* a day euery of them, with ther bourde: iiij*s* vj*d*

Item to Walter Tyte and Henry Wodroff, laborers, lodyng of rede at the stathe and caryeng of brokely out of the market,[216] yche of them iiij days: ij*s*

Item to Rychard Davy[217] for ij C lathe: xij*d*

Item to the masters of the reders for meseryng of suche rede as we bought of dyuerse men: iiij*d*

Item[218] for ij rakes to rake vp the brokyn rede: j*d*

Item for xxx ashyn byllettes to make leddyr stavys to such leddyrs as we borowd: iij*d*

Item for byrchyn bromys at ij tymes: ij*d*

/*The weke byfore Shroftyde*/ **Item** to the iij forsayd reders, euery of them iiij days, at vj*d ob'* the day euery of them: vj*s* vj*d*

Item to iiij of the forsayd laborers iiij days: vj*s*

/*The fyrst weke of Clene Lent*/ **Item** to the forsayd iij reders, euery of them ij days this weke: ij*s* iij*d*

Item to iiij laborers, euery of them ij days: iij*s*

Item to Rychard Grene, clay dresser, ij days: ix*d*

Item to Henry Holdyn[219] for ij C lathe: xij*d*

/*The second weke of Lent*/ **Item** to the forsayd iij reders, euery of them vj days, at iij*s* iij*d* euery of them: ix*s* ix*d*

Item to the forsayd v laborers, vj days euery of them, at ij*s* iij*d* euery of them: xj*s* iij*d*

Item for dyshes for the clay: j*d*

Item for j C byndynges bought by Damme: ij*d*[220]

---

214 NCR, 18A/6, f. 80, simply notes 'j*d* paid in ernest for rede'.
215 NCR, 18A/6, f. 80, has the the Latin sub-heading 'the week after Purification'.
216 NCR, 18A/6, f. 80ᵛ, furnishes none of this detail.
217 NCR. 18A/6, f. 80ᵛ, does not name Davy.
218 NCR. 18A/6, f. 80ᵛ, lists the last three entries in this sub-section in the next one, under the heading 'the weke before Shroftyde & the next weke'.
219 NCR, 18A/6, f. 80ᵛ, does not name Holdyn.
220 NCR, 18A/6, f. 81, lists this item under 'the iiijᵗᵉ weke [*of Lent*]'.

[*f. 11ᵛ*] /*The iij^de weke of Lent*/[221] **Item** payd to the forsayd iij reders for vj days worke thys weke, euery of them: ixs ixd

Item to the forsayd v laborers, vj days: xjs iijd

/*The iiij^te weke of Lent*/ **Item** to Rychard Rysyng and William Bytson, reders, eyther of them iij days: iijs iijd

Item to John Chyld, reder, ij days: xiijd

Item to iij laborers, euery of them iij days: iijs iiijd ob'

Item to John Chyldes laborer, ij days: ixd

Item to Henry Wodroff, laborer, makyng clene all the shoppys and market, v days: xxijd ob'

Item to Rychard *Rysyng* for broche wondes & byndynges: vs viijd: and to John Chylde: iijs vjd – ixs ijd

Item to Master Quashe for strawe: xvijd

Item to Henry Carter for clay, xiij lodes at vd: vs vd

Item to Henry Sparke[222] for caryeng away of mucke at dyuerse tymes, xlix lode at ijd: viijs ijd

/*Reede spent*/[223] **Item** to Wylliam Vynt for iij C rede at xiiijs: xlijs

Item to John Candler for j C rede: xiiijs iijd

Item to Pallyns wyff for ij C rede: xxviijs

Item to Reynold Grey for *di'* C rede to ffynyshe vp the worke: vijs

Item to Henry Sparke[224] for caryeng of the same vj C rede in to the market & *di'*: xiijs

/*Passyon weke*/[225] **Item** payd to a clayman mendyng the walles betwyxt the bochers & fyshmongers & dawbyng the peke ende of Redes shoppe, iiij days: xxd

Item for splentes and splent yarne: iiijd

[*f. 12*] /*Carpenters*/[226] **Item** payd to Nycholas Tuttell, carpenter, for xxj days worke at dyuerse tymes tendyng oonly to the reders, makyng newe all the fflewes at vj gabill endes, layeng of dyuerse newe sparrys, pecyng many sparrys, cradelyng the roffe of all the long howse betwyxt Guyrdlers shoppe and the Murage Loft, ffurryn all the sparrys ouer Sewelles shoppe, naylyng on of bourdes ouer the all the [*sic*] shoppys, as well bochery as ffyshmarket, ffrome Crows to Cannerdes, with many other leke thynges, at vjd ob' the day: xjs iiijd ob'

Item to Master Thetford[227] for ij newe sparrys: xijd

---

221 NCR, 18A/6, f. 80ᵛ, incorporates the second and third weeks of Lent into a single sub-section.

222 NCR, 18A/6, f. 81, does not name Quashe, Carter or Sparke.

223 NCR, 18A/6, f. 81, has no separate sub-section for these entries.

224 NCR, 18A/6, f. 81, also names Henry Carter.

225 NCR, 18A/6, f. 81, has no separate sub-section for these entries.

226 NCR, 18A/6, f. 81, has no separate sub-section for these entries, which are less detailed.

227 NCR, 18A/6, f. 80, does not name Thetford, but notes that the spars were purchased for 'Guyrdelers & Caunerdes shoppes'.

/Febuarii, Marche and Aprelle/[228] **Item** to the sayd carpenter for xxvj days worke more betwyxt tymes whan he dyd not tende to the reders and, after the reders war gon, reparyng euery shoppe of the cite bochers, mendyn ther wyndows, dores, stalles and shelvys within & without, at vj*d ob'* a day, with his bourde: xiiij*s* j*d*

Item to Bryan Doront, smythe, the ix*te* of Februarii for hookes, stapilles & other small yron worke, vj *libr'*: ix*d*

Item to Paschall the xiij day of the same monythe for hengilles, hookes, barrys, cappis, stapilles, sneckes, lachis & suche leke thynges, xj *libr'*: xvj*d*

Item to hym the last day of the same monythe for iiij *libr'* more of leke worke: vj*d*; the xiiij of Marche for a jemewe and ij gret stapilles for Cannardes shoppe: v*d*: a newe locke & key for Thorntons shoppe: iiij*d*; ij newe lockes for Grenys shoppe and Websters shoppe: x*d* – ij*s* j*d*

[*f. 12ᵛ*] **Item** to Henry Wodrof, laborer<s>, mendyng the florthes in the bochers shopps, ij days worke: ix*d*

/Maii & June/[229] **Item** payd to the forsayd carpenter for xviij days worke betwyxt tymes mendyng all the fyshshops, as dores, wyndows, shelvis & stalles, at vj*d ob'* [a] day: ix*s* ix*d*

Item to Pascall for dyuerse kyndes of yron worke xij *libr'*: xviij*d*

Item for claye iij lodes to Henry Carter: xv*d*

Item to Henry Wodroff, laborer, for vj days makyng the florthis in all the fyshmongers shoppis: ij*s* iij*d*

/Pultry market/ **Item** payd to John Byrche, carpenter, makyng newe stalles vyrownd the pultry market: and fyrst for vj days worke of iiij of hys men in the iij*de* weke of Lent, euery of them vj*d ob'* a day: xiij*s*

Item to Henry Carter[230] for caryeng of a lode of trustylles from the comon halle in to the market: iiij*d*

Item to John Smythe, mason, pathyng abought and vnder the same stalles & reysyng vp of the grownde in dyuerse places of the same market wher the grownde was sonke, iij days worke: xix*d ob'*

Item to hys laborer for the same iij days: xij*d ob'*

Item to Henry Sparke[231] for sonde a lode: v*d*

Item to hym for caryeng away of ij lodes of mucke & erthe that came from vnder the stalles: iiij*d*

Item to a laborer brekyng vp the old stalles, caryeng the old stuff to the comon inne, fechyn pathyn ston from thense and makyng clene the market whan they hade don, ij days: ix*d*

---

228 NCR, 18A/6, f. 81, has no separate sub-section for these entries.
229 NCR, 18A/6, f. 81ᵛ, has no separate sub-section for these entries.
230 NCR, 18A/6, f. 81ᵛ, does not name Carter.
231 NCR, 18A/6, f. 81ᵛ, does not name Sparke.

[*f. 13*] */iiij^{or} newe stalles/*[232] **Item** payd in Passyon weke to the forsayd John Byrche ffor vj days worke of iij of hys men makyng the iiij^{or} newe stalles for bochers on the west part of the Long Rowe, at vj*d ob'* a day euery of them: ixs ix*d*

Item to Henry Carter for caryeng of a lode of trustylles[233] in to the market: vj*d*

Item payd for vj ffurryn sparrys for bothyn tymbyr ffor the sayd stalles: ijs; to Paschall[234] for xviij yron hookes to put the crosse barrys vpon: ix*d*: and for xxj ffleshe hookes: xij*d* – iijs ix*d*

Item to a mason and hys laborer pathyng vnder and abought the same stalles, oon day: xj*d*

/Freshe water ffyshe stalles/ **Item** payd to the forsayd John Byrche the second weke after Estern for vj days worke of iij of hys men makyng iij rowes of newe stalles for the freshe water ffyshmongers: ixs ix*d*

Item to a mason and his man pathyng vnder and abought the same stalles, oon day: xj*d*

Item to Wylliam Morront[235] for vj^{xx} spekynges conteynyng xxx *libr'*, at j*d ob' libr'*, all whyche spekynges war occupyed abought all the forsayd stalles: iijs ix*d*

Item payd for mendyng of *an* yron spone that was borowd to make holys: ij*d*; byrchyn bromys: j*d* occupyed ther – iij*d*

/Wolshoppys/ **Item** payd the same weke[236] to Nycholas Tuttell, carpenter, mendyng dyuerse fawtes in the tenement in ferme to Master Qwashe,[237] ij days: xiij*d*

Item to Bryan Doront[238] for a lytyll ankyr of yron occupyed in the same tenement: iiij*d*

[*f. 13^{v}*] **Item** payd the vij^{te} day of June to the sayd carpenter makyng a newe stalle to one of the shoppe wyndows and a loope to oon of the chambyr wyndows in the same tenement, oon day worke: vj*d ob'*

Item to hym for iiij days worke in the weke after Relycke Sonday mendyng the wyndows & shelvys in an other wolshoppe for Wylliam Parker of Matyshale [*Mattishall*]: ijs ij*d*[239]

Item <day> for dyuerse yron worke ther: vj*d*

Item for clay a lode for the florthe of the same shoppe: v*d*; and to Wyllet for havyng of it in & makyng the florthe: iij*d* – viij*d*

---

232 NCR, 18A/6, f. 81ᵛ, has no separate sub-section for these entries.

233 NCR, 18A/6, f. 81ᵛ, notes that the trestles came from the common hall.

234 NCR, 18A/6, f. 81ᵛ, does not name Paschall, referring simply to the purchase of 'ironworke'.

235 NCR, 18A/6, f. 81ᵛ, does not name Morront.

236 NCR, 18A/6, f. 82, refers to the second week after Easter.

237 NCR, 18A/6, f. 82, refers at this point to work on a tenement 'in the fferme off Tythe aboute the synke & the wyndous', but in the third entry describes it as being leased by Qwashe.

238 NCR, 18A/6, f. 82, does not name Doront.

239 NCR, 18A/6, f. 82, does not mention Parker.

/Masons craft/[240] **Item** payd for masons craft thorowe owt all the bocherys, ffyshstalles, wolshopps and in a tenement ageynst the cross, in castyng of all the walles, gabylles and pannelles, with mendyng of many fawtes in them: and ffyrst payd to John Smythe, mason, for vj days worke in the second weke after Estern, at vj*d* *ob'* the day: ij*s* iij*d*

Item to Jamys Webster, his laborer, vj days: ij*s* iij*d*

Item to Henry Wodrof,[241] clayman, dressyng all the florethes in the tenement ageynst the cross, as well the chambyrs as by the grownde, vj days worke, at v*d* the day: ij*s* vj*d*

Item for clay iij lodes to Henry Carter: xv*d*

/The iij^{de} weke after Estern/ **Item** to the forsayd John Smythe, mason, v days: ij*s* viij*d* *ob'*

Item to Anthony Smythe, mason, v days: ij*s* viij*d* *ob'*

Item to Jamys Webster & Nycholas Voyse, ther laborers, v days yche of them: iij*s* ix*d*

[*f. 14*] **Item** to Nycholas Tuttell,[242] carpenter, mendyng dyuerse fawtes in the tenement ageynst the cross, ij days worke: xiij*d*

Item to Henry Wodroff, laborer, tendyng sometym to the masons & sometyme to the carpenters, fechyn all thynges to ther hondes, v days: xxij*d* *ob'*

/The iiij^{te} weke after Estern/ **Item** to the forsayd ij masons, eyther of them v days worke thys weke: v*s* v*d*

Item to ther ij laborers, v days: iij*s* ix*d*

Item to Henry Holden[243] for iij quarteres C brycke occupyed in the tenement in ferme of Master Qwashe: vj*d*; & for *di'* C for the toppe of the chymney ageynst the crosse: iiij*d*[244] – x*d*

/The v^{te} weke after Estern/ **Item** to the forsayd ij masons for iij days: iij*s* iij*d*

Item to ther ij laborers for the same iij days: ij*s* iij*d*

Item to Hewe Herryson for iiij chalder of lyme, lackyng oon comb', at ij*s* iiij*d*: ix*s*

Item to Henry Sparke[245] for sonde iij lode: xv*d*

Item to hym for caryen away ij lodes mucke that came of makyng clene the howses: iiij*d*

---

240 NCR, 18A/6, ff. 82–3, has no separate sub-section for these entries, which appear under 'wolshoppes'.

241 NCR, 18A/6, f. 82, does not name Wodrof.

242 NCR, 18A/6, f. 82, does not name Tuttell.

243 NCR, 18A/6, f. 82, does not name Holden, dates the purchase to the second week after Easter and describes the tenement as being 'in the fferme of Tytes'.

244 NCR, 18A/6, f. 82, dates this purchase to the fifth week after Easter.

245 NCR, 18A/6, f. 82, does not name either Herryson or Sparke.

/*Guyldhalle*/[246] **Item** payd to Henry Carter[247] for ij lodes clay layd at the guyldhall dore to mende the florthis in the prysons: x*d*; oon day worke of a laborer abought the sayd florthis: iiij*d ob'* – xiiij*d ob'*

Item to John Pylson, glasewright, mendyng all the glasse wyndows in the guyldhalle, viij days worke, at vj*d* the day: iiij*s*

Item for a sheffe of Burgony glass: xviij*d*

[*f. 14*ᵛ] **Item** payd for sowde j *libr'* j quarter: v*d*; to Paschall for xij yron barrys conteynyng v *libr'*: vij*d ob'* – xij*d ob'*

Item payd for newe mattes for the aldermens setes in the sembly chambyr: vj*d*

Item for takyn iij lockes of a chest bownde with yron stondyng in the chamberleyns cowntyng howse, for iij newe keys to them & settyng on: xvj*d*

/*Newe ffourmis*/[248] **Item** to John Byrche for iiij days worke of iij of hys men makyng iiij^or long fourmes in the myddes of the sembly chambyr, ij long fourmys vnder the walles, oon at the old cownsell howse dore, an other at the newe cownsell howse dore and a seate with a skewe within the cownsell howse dore, at vj*d ob'* a day euery of them: vj*s* vj*d*

Item to Henry Wodroff,[249] laborer, for iiij days makyng clene all the howsys and ledes in the guyldhalle and pullyng the wedes of The Cage and of all other tyled howses abought the guyldhalle: xviij*d*; and for caryeng away of iij lodes mucke that came of the same: vj*d* – ij*s*

Item the xx day of June to Paschall for a newe dobyll jemewe for the stockes without the guyldhall dore, with brades & naylyng on: ij*s* vj*d*

/*The weke in whiche Seynt Peter fell in*/[250] **Item** payd to iiij laborers, Wyllet, Halle, Wortes and Fuller, for oon day worke caryen the stynkyng fylth that came out of [*the*] synke in the womens pryson in to a pytte at the comon inne, iiij or v lodes in stondes: xx*d*

[*f. 15*] /*Dekays in the prysons*/[251] **Item** to Fuller[252] for oon day more helpyng to breke vp the gutter thorowe the prison in to the market to the syde of the cokey that com down from Master Catlyns, whyche was wonderffull noysfull: v*d*

Item to Wylliam Johnson, mason, brekyng & makyn ageyn the crown of the gutter thorowe out the prysons & in to the market to the sayd cokey, makyng & pathyng ageyn the synkes in bothe the prysons, mendyng of all the jakes and chymneys in the prysons and the fowndacon of a mayne walle in the menys prison & settyn fast the womens prison dore, v days: ij*s* viij*d ob'*

---

246   NCR, 18A/6, f. 82–2ᵛ, has no separate sub-section for these entries.
247   NCR, 18A/6, f. 82, does not name Carter.
248   NCR, 18A/6, f. 82ᵛ, has no separate sub-section for these entries.
249   NCR, 18A/6, f. 82ᵛ, does not name Wodroff.
250   NCR, 18A/6, f. 82ᵛ, has no separate sub-section for these entries.
251   NCR, 18A/6, f. 82ᵛ, has no separate sub-section for these entries.
252   NCR, 18A/6, f. 82ᵛ, does not name Fuller, or provide such eloquent detail.

Item to hys laborer the same v days: xxij*d ob'*

Item to Master Marsham[253] for lyme iiij comb': xiiij*d*

Item to Nycholas Tuttell, carpenter, makyng of synters for the vowtyng of the guttyr and cokey, ij newe frames for the synkes in the prisons, the iij^de frame for a grate of yron, a newe threshold for the womens pryson dore, newe feete for the stockes in bothe prysons and mendyng the plancher ouer the womens pryson, v days: ij*s* viij*d ob'*

Item to Henry Wodrof,[254] laborer, tendyng to the carpenter, fechyng of tymbyr from the comon halle, caryeng the stynkyng brycke that came of the synkes in to the comon inne yarde, makyng ageyn the florthis in the prysons and makyng clene the market, v days: xxij*d ob'*

Item to Flowerdewe of Hetherset[t] & Osbourn of Kyrby [*Bedon*] for brycke j m^l: vj*s* [*f. 15*^v] **Item** to Paschall for an yron grate for the synke in the womens pryson conteynyng xxv *libr' di'* and for an other lytyll grate for the menys pryson conteynyng iiij *libr'* at j*d ob'*: iij*s* viij*d*

Item gaff to the carpenter and other laborers bycause they grutchyd to worke in the yll savour ther: vij*d*[255]

Item gaff in leke reward to the mason: iiij*d*

Item to Henry Sparke[256] for caryeng away ij lodes of mucke & erthe whan all the worke was don: iiij*d*

Item to hym for sonde a lode: v*d*

Item to Paschall for mendyng the locke of the dore that gothe vp to the gret chambyr ovyr the sembly chambyr: iij*d*

Summa xx *li* xviij*s*

Memorandum that part of the tymbyr that made the trustylles to all the newe stalles in the merket war of old tymbyr that came of the dortowur roff of the comon hall that fell down; and all the rest *of* the tymbyr occupyed abought all the sayd stalles and other workes byfore expressyd, and all the plankes spent vpon all the sayd stalles and fourmes in the guydhalle war of comn store sawen and made of ten gret okes bought in Hokryn Parke [*Hockering Park*], whose chargis here after folowythe partyclerly *& cetera*:[257]

---

253 NCR, 18A/6, f. 82^v, does not name Marsham.

254 NCR, 18A/6, f. 82^v, does not name Wodrof or describe the uncongenial nature of his task.

255 NCR, 18A/6, f. 83, simply mentions a 'rewarde'. These men protested not only because the prison smelled foul, but because contaminated air was believed to spread pestilence: Rawcliffe, *Urban Bodies*, chapter three.

256 NCR, 18A/6, f. 83, does not name Sparke.

257 NCR, 18A/6, ff. 80–83, has no such memorandum.

/*Gret okes bought in Hokryng Parke*/[258] **In primis** payd the xvj day of Decembyr[259] to Master John Wutton, esquyer,[260] for x gret okes redy ffellyd in Hokryng Parke for comon store: xxx*s*

Item the same day to John Byrche, carpenter, for his days worke and horse hyer rydyng to Hokryng with the accomptantes to chose out the sayd trees ther: viij*d*

[*f. 16*] **Item** payd on the Fryday in Crystmes weke to the sayd Byrche rydyng thyther ageyn to hyer men to square and sawe the sayd tymbyr and to marke what lenghtes they shuld be cutte: viij*d*

Item payd the xij day of Januarii to Hancocke of Hokryng, carpenter, and hys man for ij days worke sawyng the sayd trees in to xxij stockes: ij*s* ij*d*

Item the same day to other ij carpenters for vij days worke hewyng and sqwaryng the sayd xxij stockes, at xiij*d* the day toguether: vij*s* vij*d*

Item payd at dyuerse tymes to the forsayd Hancoke and hys man for sawyng of xvij C planke & ix C bourde with ode mesyr at xiij*d* the C: xxviij*s* ij*d*

Item to Gryme of Hokryng and Greve of Honyngham [*Honingham*] for ther carte ware dyuerse tymes to drawe the stockes to the sawyn pytte: xvij*d*

Item payd to the sayd Gryme and Greve for caryeng home of all the sayd planke & bourde, with xij trustyll hedes that war sawyn of a toppe ende of oon of the sayd trees, at xj lodes at xviij*d* euery lode: xvj*s* vj*d*

Summa iiij *li* vij*s* ij*d*

/*Costes at iij tenementes in Coblerrowe*/[261] **In primis** payd to John Smythe and Thomas Rushebrooke, masons, makyng a newe vyce vp to Bryan Dorontes galery, mendyng the chymney, castyng all the walles and pannelles of the tenement and shud on the backe syde,[262] v days yche of them, at xiij*d* the *day* toguether: v*s* v*d*

[*f. 16*ᵛ] /*The iiij*ᵗᵉ *weke of Lent*/[263] **Item** to Andrewe Robynson and William Waget, ther laborers,[264] for the same v days worke, at ix*d* the day: iij*s* ix*d*

Item to Nycholas Tuttell, carpenter, cuttyng of steppys for the vyce, settyng newe stothis in the pannelles of the galery, mendyng the stayers vp to the chambyr, the wyndows and many other thynges in the same tenement, v days: ij*s* viij*d* ob'

/*Passyon wekel*/ **Item** to the forsayd ij masons fynyshyng vp the same howse and castyng all the gabyll ende with all the walles and pannelles of Hewe Coplondes tenement in leke maner, vj days: vj*s* vj*d*

---

258 NCR, 18A/6, f. 80–80ᵛ, incorporates all these eight entries in the previous section ('pultry market, wolle shoppes & guyldhall'), providing a combined total of £25 5*s* 2*d*.

259 NCR, 18A/6, f. 80, furnishes no date for this or any of the other entries in this section.

260 See above, p. 82 note 61.

261 NCR, 18A/6, ff. 83–4ᵛ, presents the sections on Cobbler Row and the Common Inn in reverse order.

262 NCR, 18A/6, f. 83ᵛ, does not mention the shed.

263 NCR, 18A/6, f. 83ᵛ, has no separate sub-section for these entries.

264 NCR, 18A/6, f. 83ᵛ, does not describe Robynson and Waget as labourers or distinguish between the wages paid to them and the two masons.

Item *to* the sayd *ij* laborers for the same vj days: iiij*s* vj*d*

Item to the forsayd carpenter naylyng of a gret clete of yron with forlockes vpon the ovyr sylle of the forsayd galery and ij newe ankers of yron in the ij endes of the same galery, settyng of newe stothis in the northe pannell of Coplondes howse, makyng a newe loope for the ovyr chambyr wyndowe, mendyng of the shoppe stalles and many other fawtes in that tenement, vj days: iij*s* iij*d*

Item to Bryan Doront for the forsayd clete & iij boltes with forlockes conteynyng xiiij *libr'*: xxj*d*

Item for the forsayd ij ankers with brodes & stapylles: xiiij*d*

/*Palme Sonday weke*/[265] Item to John Mason selyng Marke Heynis howse, mendyng his chymney and jakes & castyng all the howses within, iiij days worke: ij*s* ij*d*

Item for brycke j C to Henry Holden: viij*d*

[*f. 17*] Item to Thomas Rushbroke, mason, stagyng vpon the roff *of* the howse, makyng a newe toppe to the chymney & castyng all the walles and pannelles of the same tenement withowt, iiij days: ij*s* ij*d*

Item to ther ij laborers the same iiij days: iij*s*

Item to Henry Wodroff,[266] laborer, makyng clene all the sayd tenementes & strete vyrownd them and helpyng the masons, iiij days: xviij*d*

Item to the forsayd carpenter for oon day ther thys weke mendyng the wyndows and dores of Marke Heynys howse & makyng a newe jakes plank: vj*d ob'*

Item for heye myxt with morter for selynges: j*d*

Item to Bryan Doront[267] for a payer of hookes & hengylles for Marke Heynys shoppe dore: iiij*d*; an other payer with a snecke and a crome for Hewe Coplondes newe wyndowe: iiij*d*; and the ij^{de} payer for a newe wyndowe for his vowte: iij*d* – xj*d*

Item to Flowurdewe of Het[*h*]erset[*t*] for brycke for Marke Heynys chymney *di'* m^l: iij*s*

Item to Richard Pylson, glasewright, for ix foote of newe glass for Bryan Dorontes parlowur wyndowe: iij*s*

Item to Mastres Marsham for lyme iiij chalder: ix*s* iiij*d*

Item to Henry Wodroff for ij days more thys weke makyng clene dyuerse places of the market ageynst Estern, whyche war fowlyd with workmen: viij*d*

Item to Henry Sparke for caryeng away of iiij lodes of mucke and colder: viij*d*; and for sonde iiij lodes: xx*d* – ij*s* iiij*d*

[*f. 17^v*] /*Ester weke*/ Item payd to Anthony Smythe, tyler, removyng newe lathyng and tylyng of Bryan Dorontes galery, iij days worke: xix*d ob'*; and to Jamys Atkynsson,[268] his laborer, iij days: xiij*d ob'* – ij*s* ix*d*

---

265 NCR, 18A/6, f. 84, has no separate sub-section for these entries.
266 NCR, 18A/6, f. 84, does not name Wodroff here or in any of the following entries.
267 NCR, 18A/6, f. 84, does not name Doront or any of the other individuals mentioned in the rest of this sub-section.
268 NCR, 18A/6, f. 84, does not name Atkynsson.

Item to Nycholas Tuttell, carpenter, layeng newe sparrys vpon the forsayd galery, reysyng vp of Coplondes shudde, whyche lyethe betwyxt Dorontes shudde and Coplondes other shudde, to make them vnyforme, newe grownsellyng the same and layeng of newe sparrys ouer all the same shudde, iij days worke: xixd ob'

Item to Master Thetford[269] for v newe sparrys, besydes them that we hade of comon store: xxd

Item to Henry Wodroff, clayman, makyng ageyn the pannell of the same shudde & mendyng all the other pannelles in dyuerse places, iij days: xvd

Item for claye ij lode: xd; splentes and hempe: vd – xvd

Item to John Byrche[270] for j mˡ thacke tyle fechyd from the Gray Fryers: vs iiijd; and for caryage from thense: vjd – vs xd

Item to John Smythe, mason, fynyshyng all the forsayd workes, in smothyng, washyng and whytyng, iij days of hym & his laborer: ijs ixd

/The weke after Whyte Sonday/ **Item** to the forsayd tyler removyng, lathyng and newe layeng of all the shuddes <in the> /nullus/ [f. 18] on the backesyde of the sayd tenementes and Hewe Coplondes pentyse, vj days worke: iijs iijd

Item to Atkyns,[271] hys laborer, vj days: ijs iijd

Item to Osborn of Kyrby [Bedon] for thacke tyle j mˡ: vjs

Item to a laborer fechyng mˡ thacke tyle from the comon halle in a barrowe, oon day worke, with other worke: ob'

Item to Sander Clarke takyng down the same tyle at the comon halle: vd

Item to Stephyn Raynbald for tyle pynnys iiij mˡ: xd; and to Andrewe Qwashe ij mˡ: vjd – xvjd

Item to Herryson for ix comb' lyme: ijs viijd

Item to Henry Sparke for sonde a lode: vd

Item to Wylliam Morront for x corner tyles: viijd

Item to a laborer stoppyng vnder the evys of all the shuddes with clay & makyng clene the strete: ixd

Item for caryeng awaye of ij lodes of mucke and colder: iiijd; Item for an hengyll for Marke Heynys shoppe dore: ijd – vjd

Summa iiij *li* xiijs xd

/4 – 14 – 2/

/Comon inne/ *In primis* payd for glasyng of part of the wyndows in the chambyrs of the newe buyldyng at the comon inne with old glasse of comon store, beyng at the comon halle:

---

269 NCR, 18A/6, f. 84, does not name Master Thetford.
270 NCR, 18A/6, f. 84ᵛ, does not name Byrche.
271 NCR, 18A/6, f. 84ᵛ, does not name Atkyns or any of the other individuals mentioned in the rest of this section.

/*The weke byfore Seynt Andrewe*/[272] **And fyrst** payd to John Pylson, glasewright, for vj days worke thys weke, at vj*d* the day, bourdyng hym selff: ij*s*
Item for sowder j *libr'*: iiij*d*; rosen: j*d* – v*d*

[*f. 18*] /*The weke in whiche Seynt Andrewe fell in*/ **Item** to the forsayd glaser for v days this weke: ij*s* vj*d*
Item for sowde j *libr'*: iiij*d*
Item sadler nayle & tackes m¹ toguether: viij*d*
Item for ij *libr'* candyll to worke by on evenynges and mornynges: ij*d ob'*

/*The weke in whiche Owur Lady fell in*/[273] **Item** to the sayd Pylson for iiijᵒʳ days this weke: ij*s*
Item to a laborer that fechyd old rotten tymber and bourdes endes from the comon halle to the sayd comon inne for fewall for hym: ij*d*

/*The weke after Owur Lady*/ **Item** to the sayd glaser for vj days: ij*s*
Item for sadlers nayle & sprygge j m¹: viij*d*
Item sowde j *libr'*: iiij*d*
Item candyll ij *libr'*: ij*d ob'*

/*The weke byfore Crystmes*/ **Item** to the sayd Pylson for ij days that weke: xij*d*
Item to John Melton[274] for ledges of waynscote for the endes of all the wyndows that be glased: vj*d*
Item to Paschall for v loopys of yron: v*s*

/*The weke after Candylmes*/[275] **Item** to the sayd glaser for vj days this weke: ij*s*
Item for ij sheff of Burgony glasse to Wylliam Morront: ij*s*; sowde j *libr'*: iiij*d* – ij*s* iiij*d*

/*The weke byfore Shroftyde*/ **Item** payd to the sayd Pylson for vj days: ij*s*
Item for sadlers nayle *di'* m¹: iiij*d*
Item for ij *libr'* of sowde: viij*d*

                            Summa* xxx*s* iiij*d

For the whyche *summa* of xxx*s* iiij*d* ther was set vp in the same place vjˣˣ xv foote of glasse, besydes the reparacon of all the wyndows in the same place *& cetera*.[276]

---

272   NCR, 18A/6, f. 83, has one sub-section for 'the wekes before & after Seint Andrew'.
273   NCR, 18A/6, f. 83, has one sub-section for 'the wekes of Saint Nicholas, after Our Ladye & before Cristmes'. Unusually, here 'Owur Lady' refers to the feast of the Conception of the Blessed Virgin on 8 December, rather than the Annunciation on 25 March.
274   NCR, 18A/6, f. 83, does not name Melton or note that the ledges were made of wainscot.
275   NCR, 18A/6, f. 83, has one sub-sction for 'the wekes before Candelmes & Schroftyde'.
276   NCR, 18A/6, f. 83–3ᵛ, does not include this note.

[*f. 19*] /*Comon inne*/[277] **Item** more chargis at the sayd comon inne: and fyrst payd the ix day of Januarii to Paschall for a newe locke & keye to the dobyll dore in the gret howse wher all owur planke and tymbyr laye & for mendyng the locke of the other dore ageynst Normans: vij*d*

Item the xiiij day for an other newe locke & keye for the vyce dore vp to the chambyr of the same howse wher all owur bourde was layd: v*d*

Item on Shroft Monday to Henry Wodrof, laborer, ordryng vp of all owur bourde & planke that came from Hokryng with styckes: iiij*d ob'*

Item payd the xxiij day of June to Nycholas Tuttell, carpenter, newe reparyng and hangyng of the gret carte gate, iij days worke: xix*d ob'*

Item to Henry Wodrof, laborer, helpyng hym the same iij days: xiij*d ob'*

Item payd to Paschall for a newe bonde of yron, a gogeon and a vorell for the same gate, conteynyng xij *libr'*: xviij*d*

Item for mendyng the jemews of the same gate: vj*d*

Summa vj*s* j*d ob'*

/*Costes of the cokeys and market place*/ **In primis** couuenauntyd with Wyllet for castyng and kepyng clene of xviij seuerall cokeys[278] within the cite for xiij*s* iiij*d* the yere to be payd quarterly for euery <quarter> cokey, as hereafter folowythe: that is to saye for the cokey <for> by The iij Belles viij*d* a quarter,[279] The ij Nonnys iiij*d*,[280] Gardners iiij*d*, Master Catlyns ij*d*, Seynt Gregoryes j*d*, Seynt Lawrens j*d*, Seynt Sothons [*Swithin's*] ij*d*, Westwike gates j*d*, iij cokeys in Seynt Mychelles of Coslany j*d*, Seynt /*nullus*/ [*f. 19ᵛ*] Edmondes j*d*, Seynt Clementes in Fybrgge j*d*, Whyte Fryers brydge j*d*, Seynt Martens at the Palles Gate j*d*, Seynt Clementes in Conysford vj*d*, and Seynt Crowchys ij*d*, and Sent Andrews iiij*d*: *summa* iij*s* iiij*d* quarterly payd: xiij*s* iiij*d*

Item payd the fourte day of Novembyr[281] to Foster for caryeng of vj lodes mucke, whyche left was vpon hepys at dyuerse cokeys at Myhelmes last: xij*d*

Item on Crystmes evyn[282] to Roger Lawes for caryen of <x>xxviij lode from the cokey in Conysford, by a taly, wherof x lodes war vpon an hepe that was cast vp byfore Myhelmes: iiij*s* viij*d*

---

277 NCR, 18A/6, f. 83–3ᵛ, incorporates all the entries in this section in the previous one, providing a combined total of 36*s* 5½*d* and furnishing far less detail. The work was near completion by 23 March 1542, when the mayor was commissioned to inspect the finishing and letting of the common inn: NCR, 16D/2, f. 197.

278 NCR, 18A/6, f. 84ᵛ, lists only fourteen cockeys and, in common with other entries in this section, provides no breakdown of the payments made. See Fay, 'River and Street Accounts', p. 20; and M. Pelling, 'Health and Sanitation', in Rawcliffe and Wilson, eds, *Norwich since 1550*, pp. 126–31, for details about some of the cockeys named here.

279 The location remains unknown: Fay, 'River and Street Accounts', p. 108.

280 A tenement called 'The Signe of the Twoo Nonnes' was in Spurrier Row, now White Lion Street: Rodgers and Wallace, eds, *Norwich Landgable Assessment*, p. 64.

281 NCR, 18A/6, f. 84ᵛ, does not provide a date.

282 NCR, 18A/6, f. 84ᵛ, incorporates this entry in the following sub-section 'Crystmes' and refers to thirty-eight loads (here changed to twenty-eight).

/At Crystmes/ **Item** the last day of Decembyr to Robert Garrade for xviij lodes caryeng from all the rest of the cokeys that quarter and oon lode from the corner ageynst Mastres Osborns that came down with a rage: iijs ijd[283]

Item payd the x day of Marche to a mason that broke vp the cokey above the guyldhall dore & makyng it ageyn, oon day of hym & his man: xjd

Item to Wyllet makyng clene the same cokey: ijd

Item for a newe grate of yron set within the same cokey payd to Paschall: vjd

Item to John Byrche for oon day worke of oon of hys men framyng ij stulpys with a barre for Cokey Lane ende next Seynt Andrews & oon stulpe for the cokey in Conysford next Seynt Clementes; and framyng a rayle ouer the cokey ageynst Gardners: vjd ob'

[f. 19A] **Item** to a laborer to cary <the> the tymbyr to all the forsayd places & to make holys to the carpenters hande & to helpe hym in all thynges the same day: iiijd ob'

/At Estern/ **Item** payd to Foster for caryage of mucke from the cokeys in Seynt Gregoryes, Lawrens & Sothons iiij lodes: viijd; to Sparke for ij lodes from Master Catlyns: iiijd; to Roger Lawse for xiij lodes from Conysford cokey: ijs ijd; to Garrade for xxvj lodes from the rest of the cokeys: iiijs iiijd; to hym for iiij lodes out of the comon halle lane: viijd; to Sander Clarke for makyng clene of the same lane: ijd – viijs iiijd[284]

Item payd the day after Trynyte Sonday to Wyllet[285] for goyng in to the cokey ageynst Master Catlyns & castyng mucke out of the same, whiche was stoppid: iiijd

Item to Henry Sparke[286] for caryeng of ij lodes mucke from the same on Corpus Christi evyn: iiijd

Item to hym for caryeng of vij lodes out of the market the same day: xiiijd

/At Mydsomer/ **Item** to Foster for vj lodes from Seynt Gregoryes, Lawrens [*and*] at Sothons: xijd; to Roger Lawse for ix lodes in Conysford: xviijd; to Henry Sparke for ij lodes in the market: iiijd; to Garrade for xviij lodes from the rest of the cokeys iijs – vs xd

Item payd for reparacon of dekayes *of* certen cokeys, partly by occacon of a gret rage that fell the Fryday after Seynt Peter:[287] and fyrst to Nycholas Tuttell, carpenter, makyng a newe frame to the cokey in Seynt Lawrens, ij days worke: xiijd

---

283 NCR, 18A/6, f. 84ᵛ, provides none of this detail.

284 NCR, 18A/6, f. 85, notes a single payment to 'Foster, Henry Spark, Roger Lawes & Robert Garrerd ffor cariage off xlv lodes muk ffrom all the cokeys', as opposed to the fifty-one loads more fully itemised here, and does not name Clarke.

285 NCR, 18A/6, f. 85, does not name Wyllet.

286 NCR, 18A/6, f. 85, does not name Sparke.

287 NCR, 18A/6, f. 85, furnishes none of this detail.

[*f. 19A*[r] /*Dekayes of cokeys*/[288] **Item** to hym mendyng the frame of the cokey ageynst Master Catlyns & makyng a newe dore to the same, newe naylyng the grates of the cokeys in Seynt Crowches, ageynst Gardners and in Seynt Clementes of Fybrigge, ij days worke: xiij*d*

Item to Wylliam Johnson, mason, pathyng within the mowthe of the cokey by The iij Belles with bryke, makyng a newe crown to the arche of the same & stoppyng in the ij sydes of the grate, ij days: xiij*d*

Item to hym settyng vp the newe frame at Seynt Lawrens, makyng a newe crown to the arche ther, reysyng vp of all the pavement and settyng yt hyer *for* <&> water shoote, oon day: vj*d ob'*

Item to hym mendyng of holys that war gullid in at the cokeys in Seynt Andrews, Seynt Crowchys, ageynst Master Catlyns & Gardners, oon day: vj*d ob'*

Item to Yoxhale, hys laborer, the same iiij[or] days: xviij*d*

Item to Henry Wodrof,[289] laborer, for the same iiij days tendyng to the carpenter & mason, caryeng of tymbyr, brycke, ston and morter from the comon inne to all the forsayd places in a barrowe: xviij*d*

Item to Master Marsham[290] for ij comb' lyme: viij*d*

Item to Henry Holden[291] for iij C brycke: ij*s*

Item to Wyllet helpyng at the sayd cokeys to kepe the water from ther worke: ij*d*

Item to Grace for caryeng away of mucke and colder left at the cokey in Seynt Lawrens: ij*d*

Item to Paschall for a stapyll, an hespe & an hooke for the cokey dore ageynst Master Catlyns: iij*d*

[*f. 20*] **Item** to hym for gret nayles & stapylles for the grates of the forsayd cokeys: iiij*d*

/*Mucke caryed*/[292] **Item** payd for caryeng awaye of mucke that came down at the gret rage the Fryday after Seynt Peter and at dyuerse gret reynys that fell that tyme: and fyrst to Roger Lawse for vj lodes from Conysford: xij*d*

Item to Henry Sparke for ix lodes from The ij Nonnys: xviij*d*

Item to Foster for v lodes from Seynt Sothons and Seynt Lawrens: x*d*; to Henry Sparke for iiij[or] lodes out of the market ageynst the syse: viij*d* – xviij*d*

Item to Akyrs for swepyng of the market from Mydsomer tyll Lammes euery Satterday: viij*d*[293]

---

288 NCR, 18A/6, f. 85–5[v], has no separate sub-section for these entries.

289 NCR, 18A/6, f. 85, does not name Wodrof.

290 NCR, 18A/6, f. 85, does not name Marsham.

291 NCR, 18A/6, f. 85, does not name Holden.

292 NCR, 18A/6, f. 85[v], has no separate sub-section for these entries, which are less informative, notably about the 'gret reynys'.

293 NCR, 18A/6, f. 85[v], refers to 'sweping of the market dyuers tymes & caryage awey of the same ayenst the assise' and does not name Akyrs.

Item to Garrade for caryeng away of xliij lodes from the rest of all the cokeys, wherof xvj or xvij lodes lay in a hepe in the mydwaye at the cokey next The iij Belles, whyche hade lyen ther ij or iij yeres byfore & lettyd the passage of cartes: vij*s* ij*d*

/*Myhelmes*/ **Item** payd at Myhelmes to Foster for caryeng of vij lodes from Seynt Sothons, Lawrens, Seynt Gregorys and ageynst Master Catlyns: xiiij*d*

Item to Henry Sparke for vij lodes from The ij Nonnys, Gardners and from vnder the northe syde of the guyldhalle that came of the howsys ther: xiiij*d*

Item to Ketryngham for ij lodes from Seynt Martens at Pales Gate & Seynt Edmondes: iiij*d*

Item to Roger Laws for xj lodes from Conysford: xxij*d*

Item to Garrade for xiij lodes from the rest of all the cokeys in the cyte: ij*s* ij*d*

Item to hym for caryeng of xvj lodes mucke out of the market ageynst my lord off Norff' comyng: ij*s* viij*d*

[*f. 20ᵛ*] **Item** payd to Walter Harryes for the hole yere kepyng of the cokey in Seynt Symondes and caryeng awaye the fylthe of the same: xvj*d*

Item couuenauntyd at Lammes with Andrewe Robynson for swepyng and kepyng clene of the market place from Seynt Johns Lane to Coblerrowe and to carry awaye all the flythe of the same, he to haue xiij*s* iiij*d* by yere to be payd quarterly, wheurof payd hym for oon quarter endyd at Hallomes: iij*s* iiij*d*

Item payd for a lytyll frame with a grate for a cokey at the southe est ende of Seynt Clementes churche in Fybrygge gate: viij*d*

Summa iij *li* xviij*s* j*d*[294]

/*Ryver cuttyng*/ *In primis* payd for the charges of the cuttyng of the ryver from Surlyngham ffery vnto the towur in Conysford medows: and fyrst to John Bulward for gryndyng of the comon sheres: xij*d*[295]

Item for oon newe forlocke and a rubbe: ij*d*

Item for a newe bast, whyche seruyd ij cuttynges: xij*d*

/*Wytson weke*/ **Item** payd to Robert Teyton, cutter, iij days: xviij*d*

Item to Bartylmewe Wymond, rower, iij days: xviij*d*

Item to John Nonne, rower, iij days: xv*d*

Item for a bote and a man to rowe the accomptantes and other company to vewe the ryver and the worke by the commandment of master mayer: viij*d*

/*The weke after Trynyte Sonday*/[296] **Item** to the forsayd Teyton and Wymond for v days thys weke: v*s*

[*f. 21*] **Item** to John Nonne for v days: ij*s* j*d*

Item to Bulward for gryndyng the sheres ageyn: xij*d*

---

294 NCR, 18A/6, f. 85ᵛ, has 77*s* 11*d*, that is 2*d* less.

295 NCR, 18A/6, f. 86, furnishes none of these topographical details and does not name Bulward.

296 NCR, 18A/6, f. 86, combines this and the follwing sub-section as 'Corpus Christi weke & the next weke'.

/*The second weke after Trynyte*/ **Item** to Teyton and Wymond for vj days: vj*s*
Item to John Nonne for vj days: ij*s* vj*d*
Item payd for a bote and ij men to rowe the accomptantes and vj men of the assembly appoyntid to go se the ryver, who causyd the workmen to do more worke than was accustomyd to be don: x*d*

/*The iij^de weke after Trynyte*/[297] **Item** to the sayd Teyton and Wymond for v days: v*s*
Item to John Nonne for v days makyng an ende: ij*s* j*d*
Item gaff in reward to Teyton, cutter, bycause hys worke was praysed of the water men: ij*d*
Item to John Oldman[298] for his bote hyer for them, xix days: xix*d*

/*The second cuttyng at Bartylmewetyde*/ **Item** payd to John Bulward for gryndyng of the sheres ageyn & for ij newe forlockes: xiiij*d*
Item payd to the forsayd Teyton, cutter, and to Wymond and Robert Forse, rowers, ix days worke cuttyng the ryver ageyn, at xviij*d*: xiij*s* vj*d*
Item to Oldman for hys bote, ix days: ix*d*
Item to hym for a bourde that was stollen out of hys bote by nyght: iij*d*
Item payd for a bote and a man to rowe the accomptantes to vewe the ryver and ther worke: vj*d*

Summa xlix*s* vj*d*

[*f. 21^v*] **Costes** don within the tyme of thys accompt at the newe mylles in reparacon of the pales, brydges and newe removyng & tylyng of all the mylle howse & other thynges:

/***Mylles***/ ***In primis*** payd at Hallomes by the commandment of master mayer and hys brothern to John Estowe, carpenter, for the hole charge of a pale set by hym at the newe mylles from the <the> strete gate to the mylle damme, whyche pale was set ther in the tyme of Master Wardeyn, chamberleyn: xv*s*[299]

/***At Bartylmewe tyde***/[300] **Item** payd for removyng and newe layeng of all the tyle vpon the mylle howse: and fyrst to Wylliam Smythe, tyler, ffor viij days worke in all, at xij*d* the day for hys wages and bourde: viij*s*
Item to hym for the same viij days worke of John Antell and Wylliam Savery,[301] hys prentyses, Rychard Preston, George Cooke & Robert Mallard, hys laborers, euery of them v*d* a daye: xvj*s* viij*d*
Item to Garrarde Podyng, laborer, iiij days: xx*d*

---

297 NCR, 18A/6, f. 86, combines this and the follwing sub-section as 'Mydsomer weke'.
298 NCR, 18A/6, f. 86, does not name Oldman here or in the entry below.
299 NCR, 18A/6, f. 86, notes simply 'payd ffor a newe pale extendyng ffrom the gatehous vnto the mildame'.
300 NCR, 18A/6, f. 86–6^v, has no separate sub-section for these entries.
301 NCR, 18A/6, f. 86^v, describes Savery as a labourer.

Item to Wylliam Morront for iiij m^l gret <lathe> lathe nayle, iiij m^l *di'* at x*d* m^l: iij*s* ix*d*

Item to Osborn of Kyrby for vj m^l thacke tyle: xxxvj*s*

Item to Stephyn Raynbald, Thomas Albon and Andrewe Qwashe[302] for xxx m^l tyle pynnys: vj*s* iij*d*

Item for caryeng of j m^l tyle from the comon halle with a bote: vj*d*

Item to Master Marsham[303] for iij chalder *di'* of lyme: viij*s* ij*d*

Item to Henry Sparke[304] for sonde iiij lodes: xx*d*

Item gaff in rewarde amonges the tylers: iiij*d*

[*f. 22*] **Item** gaff in reward to the myllers servantes by cause they borowd leddyrs and caryed them home ageyn, made clene the mylle howse & holpe to onlade the tyle whan yt came inne: iiij*d*

Item payd to a laborer for oon day worke after the tylers hade don to make vp certen lyme that [*was*] left and caryed the sayd morter & tyle that [*was*] left to the comon inne: iiij*d ob'*

Item to a mason for iiij or v howurs worke to levell the mylle damme syde: ij*d*

/The weke byfore Myhelmes/[305] **Item** to Nycholas Tuttell, carpenter, makyng all the damme brydge newe & reparyng all the other brydges, v days worke: ij*s* viij*d ob'*

Item to hym for slytte of hys rope abought the tymber: ij*d*

Item to Henry Wodroff, laborer, the same v days: xxij*d ob'*

Item payd to Henry Sparke[306] for caryeng of a lode of gret tymbyr from the comon halle, whyche tymbyr was parcell of the same that was bought of Master Pyndern & left of the buyldyng of the buttry & pantry: vj*d*

Item to Wylliam Morront for viij*d* nayle j C: viij*d*

Item to Paschall for ij ankers off yron to hold the damme post and the beame toguether that bere the brydge, wayeng xxij *libr'* at j*d ob'*: ij*s* ix*d*

     Summa v *li* vij*s* vj*d ob'*

Memorandum that the rest of all other stuffe necessary for the sayd reparacions, as the rest of tyle, roff tyles, lathe, tymbyr and plankes, war all of comon store *& cetera*.[307]

/Comon stathes/ **Item** payd the xxiiij day of Januarii to John Ronhale, smythe,[308] for a plate of yron for the foote of the crane at the newe stathe: xiiij*d*; and to a carpenter and other ij men helpyng to take down the crane & trymmyng on the same plate: iiij*d* – xviij*d*

---

302 NCR, 18A/6, f. 86ᵛ, simply refers to 'dyuers persons'.

303 NCR, 18A/6, f. 86ᵛ, does not name Marsham.

304 NCR, 18A/6, f. 86ᵛ, does not name Sparke.

305 NCR, 18A/6, f. 86ᵛ, has no separate sub-section for these entries.

306 NCR, 18A/6, f. 86ᵛ, does not name Sparke or provide so much detail.

307 NCR, 18A/6, f. 86ᵛ, does not include this note.

308 NCR, 18A/6, f. 86ᵛ, furnishes neither a name nor a date.

[*f. 22ᵛ*] /*Passyon weke*/[309] **Item** payd to Wylliam Johnson, mason,[310] stoppyng in of a dore in the ston walle out of the old stathe yarde in to Seynt Clementes Lane, oon day worke: vj*d ob'*

Item to Nycholas Jube, his laborer, that same day: iiij*d ob'*

Item for ij comb' lyme & iiij barrowfull sonde: ix*d*

/*Mydsomer*/[311] **Item** to Nycholas Tuttell, carpenter, makyng of a newe *dore* for a corn chambyr in ferme of Barnard Vtber,[312] oon day worke: vj*d ob'*

Item to Paschall for a newe locke and keye & a stapyll for the same dore: v*d*

/*The weke after Seynt Peter*/ **Item**[313] to the forsayd carpenter makyng a parclosse with stothys at the southe tenement at the old comon stathe, a newe border for the harthe of the chymney in the northe tenement, ij newe wyndows ther and mendyng of all the steyers, planchers, wyndows & dores in bothe tenementes, vj days: iij*s* iij*d*

Item to Henry Wodroff, laborer, helpyng hym, fechyng of tymbyr and bourde from the comon inne & comon halle & makyng a newe florthe in the northe tenement, vj days: ij*s* iij*d*

Item to Wylliam Johnson, mason, makyng a newe harthe in the northe tenement, mendyng the fowndacon of the walles and chymneys in bothe tenementes, ij days of hym & his laborer: xxij*d*

Item for j comb' lyme & iij barrowfull sonde: <ix*d*> iiij*d*

Item to Robert Spalle[314] for ij waynscot bourdes for the wyndows and a pece of tymbyr for the border: x*d*

Item to hym for xj popyll bourdes: xxij*d*; and for an ashyn planke for the stayers: iij*d* – ij*s* j*d*

[*f. 23*] **Item** to Paschall for ij payer of hookes & hengylles for the ij newe wyndows: v*d*; oon hooke & oon hengyll for the dore in to the yarde warde: iiij*d*: a crome, a snecke & a lache for oon of the wyndows: j*d* – x*d*

Item a newe locke and key for the south tenement dore: v*d*

/*The weke after Relycke Sonday*/ **Item** to Henry Wodroff, clayman, lathyng & dawbyng the newe parclosse in the southe tenement & makyng a newe florthe in the same tenement & entry, vj days: ij*s* vj*d*

Item to Wylliam Morront[315] for j mˡ lathe nayle: ix*d*

Item lathe was of comon store, but payd for strawe: j*d*

---

309 NCR, 18A/6, f. 86*, has no separate sub-section for these entries.

310 NCR, 18A/6, f. 86*, does not name Johnson or his labourer.

311 NCR, 18A/6, f. 86*, has no separate sub-section for these entries.

312 Utber, an alien, was one of the richest corn merchants and commercial brewers then living in Norwich, where he eventually served as sheriff: NRO, NCC Reg. Corant, ff. 176ᵛ–80; NCR, 7 I/18; *INCO*, p. 157; and below, pp. 246, 270.

313 NCR, 18A/6, f. 86*, places this entry earlier in the section.

314 NCR, 18A/6, f. 86*, does not name Spalle.

315 NCR, 18A/6, f. 86*, does not name Morront.

Item for clay to Henry Carter[316] vj lodes: ij*s* vj*d*

/*Newe stathe*/[317] **Item** payd to Nycholas Tuttell, carpenter, the weke in whyche Mary Magdalen fell in, mendyng of dores, wyndows, planchers, stayers, mangers, rackes and many other thynges in the same place, iij days: xix*d ob'*
Item to a laborer helpyng hym, oon day: iiij*d ob'*

/*The weke in which Seynt Jamys fell in*/ **Item** to the forsayd carpenter for iiij days ther this weke abought the forsayd workes: ij*s* ij*d*
Item to Henry Wodroff,[318] laborer, fechyng of tymbyr and bourde from the comon halle & comon inne & helpyng hym the same iiij*or* days: xviij*d*

/*The weke after Seynt Jamys*/[319] **Item** to the sayd carpenter for vj days this weke: ij*s* iij*d*
Item to the sayd laborer vj days also: ij*s* iij*d*
Item to Spalle[320] for ij longe ashyn plankes: xij*d*
Item for ix other ashyn plankes of xij foote long: ij*s*
Item ij okyn crustes of the same lenght: x*d*
Item ij bunche of splentes to make rack stavis of: iiij*d*
Item to Wylliam Johnson,[321] mason, pynnyng the walles in the stabylles, warehowsys & chambers, vj days of hym & Yoxhale, hys laborer: v*s* vj*d*

[*f. 23*^v] /*The weke byfore Owur Lady Assumpcon*/[322] **Item** to the forsayd carpenter for iiij days: ij*s* ij*d*
Item to the forsayd mason pynnyng & rowcastyng the walles of the northe part of the gate, iiij days: ij*s* ij*d*
Item to the forsayd ij laborers iiij days: ij*s*
Item to Wylliam Horne[323] for hys bote caryeng of joystes and other tymbyr for the stabyll from the comon halle: iiij*d*
Item to Paschall for iij payer of small hookes and hengylles, with certen sneckes, cromys & lachis: xij*d ob'*
Item for iij payer more grettes conteynyng ix *libr'*: xiij*d ob'*
Item for a newe locke & key for Normans warhows dore on the southe part of the gate: v*d*

---

316 NCR, 18A/6, f. 86*, does not name Carter.
317 NCR, 18A/6, f. 86*, heads this sub-section 'Magdalen weke'.
318 NCR, 18A/6, f. 86^v*, does not name Wodroff.
319 NCR, 18A/6, f. 86–6^v*, has a single sub-section covering 'Seynt Jamys weke & the next weke'.
320 NCR, 18A/6, f. 86*, does not name Spalle.
321 NCR, 18A/6, f. 86–6^v*, names neither Johnson nor Yoxhale.
322 NCR, 18A/6, f. 86v*, has no separate sub-section for these entries.
323 NCR, 18A/6, f. 86^v*, does not name Horne.

/*The weke in whiche Owur [Lady] ffell in*/[324] **Item** to the sayd carpenter for v days this weke: ij*s* viij*d ob'*

Item to the sayd mason for v days: ij*s* viij*d ob'*

Item to the forsayd laborers the same v days: iij*s* <iij*d*> ix*d*

Item to Paschall for ij ankers of yron for the beame ouer the heye chambyr conteynyng xlj *libr'* at j*d ob'*: v*s* j*d*

/*The weke in whyche Seynt Bartylmewe ffell in*/[325] **Item** to the sayd carpenter for v days this weke: ij*s* viij*d ob'*

Item to the sayd mason pynnyng & castyng the walles on the innsyde of the place, v days: ij*s* viij*d ob'*

Item to John Erne,[326] mason, cryspyng the walles on the stretes syde, iiij days: ij*s* iiij*d*

Item to Yoxhale, laborer, v days & Nycholas Voyse, laborer, iiij days: iij*s* iiij*d ob'*

Item to Henry Wodroff makyng a newe florthe in the kechyn & mendyng the florthis in all the howsys in the same place, v days: xxij*d ob'*

/*The weke after Seynt Bartylmewe*/[327] **Item** to the forsayd carpenter for vj days this weke: iij*s* iij*d*

Item to John Erne, mason, ij days: xiiij*d*; and Wylliam Johnson vj days: iij*s* iij*d* – iiij*s* v*d*

Item to Nycholas <Voyse> *Yoxhale*, laborer, ij days: ix*d*

[*f. 24*] **Item** to Nycholas Voyse and Henry Wodrof, laborers, eyther of them vj days: iiij*s* vj*d*

Item to Paschall for iij payer of hookes and hengilles for iij newe wyndows conteynyng ix *libr' di'*: xiiij*d ob'*

Item for barrys, cappis, stapilles, cromis, sneckes and lachys iiij *libr'* at j*d ob'*: vj*d*

Item to Plattynges wyf for ij aldryng poles, whiche war splytte in to iiij rybbys for rackes of stabylles: vj*d*

Item for xxx byllettes to make racke stavys: iij*d*

Item to Pallyns wyf for halff C brycke: iiij*d*

/*The weke in which Owur Lady Natiuite fell in*/[328] **Item** to the forsayd carpenter and mason makyn an ende of all thynges in that place, iij days eyther of them thys weke: iij*s* iij*d*

Item to Teyton, laborer, iij days: xiij*d ob'*

Item to Henry Wodroff, laborer, makyng clene all the howses ther, iiij days: xviij*d*

Item to Henry Sparke for vj lode *of sonde* at dyuerse tymis: ij*s* vj*d*

---

324 NCR, 18A/6, f. 86ᵛ*, has no separate sub-section for these entries.

325 NCR, 18A/6, f. 86ᵛ*, has no separate sub-section for these entries.

326 NCR, 18A/6, f. 86ᵛ*, does not name Erne, or any of the other individuals mentioned in the rest of this section.

327 NCR, 18A/6, f. 86ᵛ*, has no separate sub-section for these entries.

328 NCR, 18A/6, f. 86ᵛ*, has no separate sub-section for these entries.

Item to Henry Carter for clay v lodes: ijs jd

Item to Master Marsham for lyme iiij chalder and a comb' at ijs iiijd the chalder: ixs vijd

Item to Paschall for iij newe lockes for dyuerse dores, with settyng on & mendyng of other lockes: xviijd

Item to hym for newe makyng of the gret swaype of yron for the carte gate: xvjd

Summa v li xixs ijd ob'

/5 – 19 – 8 ob'/

Memorandum that all other kynde of tymber and bourde, nayles, brycke and other thynges not here spokyn of war of comon store, whose chargis shalbe there of declaryd after in the tytyll of necessyrs bought for comon store & cetera.[329]

[f. 24ᵛ] /Tenementes in South Conysford/[330] Item payd for certen reparacions don within the tyme of thys accompt at the tenementes ageynst the comon stathe: and fyrst *payd* the fyrst day of Marche to Paschall for mendyng the locke of the dore of the tenement in ferme of Thomas Rogers: ijd

Item to hym for mendyng the hengylles of the dore wher John Frances dwellyth: ijd

Item for a newe locke and key for the tenement wher Wylliam Guylbert dwellyth: vd

/The weke in which Owur Lady Natiuite ffell in/[331] Item to Wylliam Johnson, mason, pynnyng and castyng the walle on the northe syde of the kyll yard gate, whyche was sore dekayd, oon day worke of hym and hys laborer: xjd

Summa xxd

/Tenementes late lord suffrigan/ Item payd the x day of Decembyr to John Carre, glassewright, for iij newe lyghtes for the parlowur wyndowe at the corner tenement next vnto Conysford, whyche war brokyn by a madde man: xviijd[332]

Item to hym for makyng of a lyght for the buttry wyndowe at the tenement wher John Suklyng dwellythe: vjd

Item to John Pylson, glassewright, for wourmanshyppe of a gret lyght for the buttry wyndowe at the tenement wher Henry Dey dwellythe, made of old glass of comon store lyeng at the comon halle, & settyng vp of the same: iijd[333]

Summa ijs iijd

---

329 NCR, 18A/6, f. 87, does not include this note.

330 On 23 March 1542 the assembly instructed the chamberlains and their counsel to 'order' these tenements, which, according to their report, were 'now in decaye': NCR, 16D/2, f. 197.

331 NCR, 18A/6, f. 87, has no separate sub-section for this entry and does not name Johnson.

332 NCR, 18A/6, f. 87, does not provide a name or date and furnishes none of this detail.

333 NCR, 18A/6, f. 87, does not name Pylson and furnishes less detail.

[*f. 25*] /*Gates & towurs*/ **Item** payd the vij^te day of Julii to Paschall for makyng of a newe spryng to the locke of Seynt Awstens gates, with takyng of and settyng on ageyn: vj*d*

Item to hym for a newe bolt with a jemewe for Sent Marteyns gates of Coslany: iiij*d*

Item to Ketryngham for ij lodes of gret gravell layd in a gret hole vnder the same gates: xij*d*[334]

Summa **xxij*d***

Costes and chargis hade and don within the tyme of thys accompt in the place late cald the Blacke Fryers, nowe cald the comon halle, whyche place was spoyled and sore dekayd and nowe newe reedyfyed and reparyd, as yt shall appere by the partyclers here after ffolowyng: and ffyrst for pathyng the churche nowe beyng the halle:[335]

/**Comon halle**/ *The weke after Seynt Faythe*/[336] **In primis** payd to John Erne, mason, begynnyng to pathe the halle, for v days worke thys weke, at vij*d* the day for hys wagis and bourde: ij*s* xj*d*

Item to Robert Hollond, mason, v days, at vj*d ob*': ij*s* viij*d ob*'

Item to Wylliam Johnson, mason, iiij days: ij*s* ij*d*

Item to Sander Clarke & Thomas Moone, laborers, havyng in lyme & sonde and makyng redy for the masons, yche of them vj days, at iiij*d ob*' the *day* eyther of them: iiij*s* vj*d*

Item to Thomas Brown and Thomas Bollyn, laborers, eyther of them iiij days: ij*s*

Item to Henry Wodroff, laborer, iij days: xiij*d ob*'

Item to Henry Vsher, laborer, ij days: ix*d*

Item to William Gardner, laborer, oon day: iiij*d ob*'

Item to Roger Laws for caryeng of x lodes of small pathyng tyle from the Grey Fryers; and to Henry Carter for vij lodes at ij*d* the lode: iiij*s* iij*d*

[*f. 25*^v] **Item** payd for packthrede for ther levell: ij*d*; bromis: *ob*'; iiij*d* nayle: j*d*; ij treyes to cary tyle: ij*d* – vj*d ob*'

/*The weke that Seynt Luke ffell in*/ **Item** to John Erne and William Johnson, masons, eyther of them iiij days: iiij*s* vj*d*

Item to Sander and Moone, laborers, iiij days: ij*s*

---

334 NCR, 18A/6, f. 87, does not name Ketryngham or mention the 'gret hole'.

335 NCR, 18A/6, ff. 87^v–8^v, does not include this preamble and reverses the order in which some 'mynute expenses' and the 'costes off the comon hall' appear.

336 NCR, 18A/6, ff. 88^v–92^v, itemises all expenditure on the Blackfriars' precinct in a single long section, with a combined total of £55 5*s* 11*d*. It is divided into just six sub-sections: 'pathing the body of the hall', 'the chapell', 'the newe tenement', 'chapter house', 'botery & pantery' and 'kechyn'; and no references are given in either the margins or the text to the dates or times when work took place. The layout below therefore represents a radical departure from established practice, making it immediately apparent on a weekly basis when, precisely where and by whom each specific project or task was undertaken, who supplied the materials and what each item cost.

Item to Thomas Barchom[337] for pathyn tyle j m^l: v*s* iiij*d*
Item to John Aldryche for j m^l *di'*: vj*s*

/*The weke that Sent Symond fell in*/ **Item** to John Erne and Robert Hollond, masons, eyther of them v days: v*s* vij*d ob'*
Item to Sander and Moone, laborers, v days: iij*s* ix*d*
Item to Thomas Bemond for pathyn tyle viij C *di'*: iiij*s*

/*The weke that Hollomes Day fell in*/ **Item** to John Erne for oon day: vij*d*
Item to Wylliam Johnson and Robert Hollond, iiij days eyther of them: iiij*s* iiij*d*
Item to Sander Clarke, laborer, ij days: ix*d*
Item to Thomas Moone & Henry Wodroff, iiij days eyther of them: iij*s*
Item to Robert Wace for iiij C pathyn tyle pekyd out in dyuerse places at the Grey Fryers to fynyshe vp the worke: xvj*d*
Item payd for candyll occupyed on evynynges and mornynges viij *libr'*: x*d*
Item to Herryson for lyme vj chalder: xiiij*s*
Item to Ketryngham for sonde v lode: xx*d*; and to Henry Carter for oon lode: v*d* – ij*s* j*d*
                                        Summa iiij *li* xvij*d ob'*

Memorandum that all the rest of the pathyn tyle occupyed in the sayd worke was bought at the Grey Fryers by Master Awsten Steward, alderman, & by hym payd for *& cetera*.[338]

[*f. 26*] /***Pathyng of the chappell***/ **Item** payd for pathyng of the chappell with newe pathyng tyle: and ffyrst payd at Yarmothe iiij m^l newe pathyng tyle anelyd of a meane scantlyng at xiiij*s* the m^l: lvj*s*
Item for ij m^l more of the same at xv*s* m^l: xxx*s*
Item for ffreyght of the same vj m^l from Yarmoth to Norwyche to the comon stathe: vj*s*; and for caryage from thense to the halle: ij*s* x*d* – viij*s* x*d*

/*The Imber Weke byfore Crystmes*/ **Item** payd to John Erne, mason, for settyng of the same, for vj days worke: iij*s* vj*d*
Item to Wylliam Johnson and Robert Hollond, masons, eyther of them vj days: vj*s* vj*d*
Item to Sander Clarke, Henry Wodroff, Thomas Moone, Robert Yoxhale and John Jube, labrorers,[339] euery of them vj days, at iiij*d ob'* the day: xj*s* iij*d*
Item for candyll viij *libr'*: x*d*; pakthrede: ij*d* – xij*d*
Item to Henry Sparke for sonde v lode: xx*d*
Item to Master Marsham and Herryson for lyme iij chalder *di'* at ij*s* iiij*d* the chalder: viij*s* ij*d*
                                        Summa vj *li* vj*s* xj*d*

---

337 NCR, 18A/6, f. 88^v, does not name Barchom or any of the other purveyors of building materials mentioned in this section.
338 NCR, 18A/6, f. 88^v, does not include this note.
339 NCR, 18A/6, f. 88^v, names none of these men or any of the other individuals mentioned in the rest of this section.

/A tenement ageynst the ij elmys/ **Item** payd ffor ffynyshyng of the tenement whyche is nowe the shoppe, and transposyng the vestry whyche ys nowe an halle, a buttry & a parlowur, and all the vowltes vnder nethe into warhowses, with moche charge in the same howses: and ffyrst payd the xij day of Novembyr to John Crystmes and Raphe Crystmes,[340] carpenters, for makyng of wyndows, dorestalles and loopys for the same howses, iiij days worke, at xiijd the day: iiijs iiijd

[*f. 26*ᵛ] **Item** payd for dyuerse sortes of nayles: xiijd

Item to Paschall for oon gret hengyll & ij newe hookes: viijd

Item ij smaller hengylles: vjd; for makyng of certen newe barrys, cappis, sneckes, cromys and lachys of an old pyxexe of owur own: iijd – ixd

Item for a locke and key for the dore in the southe ende of the dorter betwyxt the dorter & the tenement: viijd

/The weke after Hallomes/ **Item** to Wylliam Johnson and Robert Hollond,[341] masons, eyther of them vj days thys weke: vjs vjd

Item to Thomas Moone and Henry Wodroff, laborers, for the same vj days: iiijs vjd

Item for newe layeng of the comon pykexe: ijd; and a newe helve for the same: jd – iijd

Item for a ffurryn sparre for a barre for the shoppe wyndowe: iijd; for v C selyng nayle: vd – viijd

/The second weke after Hallomes/ **Item** to the forsayd ij masons ij days: ijs ijd

Item to Moone and Wodroff, laborers,[342] ij days: xviijd

Item payd to certen laborers makyng clene the waye to the water gate wher certen walles war ouerthrowne, coldryng out the brycke, rowe ston and pathyn ston, euery sort by them selff: that is to say to Yoxhale, Wymond, Browster and Avelen, euery of them vj days, at iiijd ob': ixs

/The iijᵈᵉ weke after Hallomes/ **Item** to John Erne,[343] mason, oon day: vijd; to Wylliam Johnson, mason, oon day: vjd ob' – xiijd ob'

Item to Moone and Wodrof, laborers, oon day: ixd

Item to Yoxhale and Sander, eyther of them vj days, and Henry Wodrof v days abought the forsayd coldryng of ston: vjs iiijd ob'

[*f. 27*] **Item** to Robert Wase for ij lodes of brycke at the Gray Fryers, with the whyche the lybrary wyndows war stoppid: ijs

Item to Roger Laws for caryage of them: vjd

Item to Henry Carter for ij lodes of clay for the florthe in the shoppe: xd

/The weke byfore Crystmes/ **Item** to John Byrche,[344] carpenter, for oon day worke of ij of hys men in the same tenement: xiijd

---

340 NCR, 18A/6, f. 89, simply refers to 'ij carpenterz'.

341 NCR, 18A/6, f. 89, names neither the masons nor their labourers.

342 NCR, 18A/6, f. 89, names neither Moone nor Wodroff.

343 NCR, 18A/6, f. 89, names none of the individuals mentioned in this sub-section.

344 NCR, 18A/6, f. 89, names only Byrche among the individuals mentioned in this and in the next two sub-sections.

Item to Paschall for hookes and hengylles x *libr'*: xv*d*

Item to Wylliam Morront for dyuerse sortes of nayle spent in fynyshyng & plancheryng of the same tenement: and ffyrst for vj*d* nayle ij C *di'*: xv*d*

Item iiij*d* nayle j m^l: ij*s* vj*d*; iij*d* nayle j m^l: xx*d*; ij*d* nayle *di'* m^l: viij*d*; lathe nayle for selyng j m^l: x*d*; Inglyshe nayles: j*d* – v*s* ix*d*

Item to John Carre, glasewright, for xlij foote of newe glasse set vp in the wyndows by the stretes sydes in the chambyrs ouer the shoppe at iiij*d* the foote: xiiij*s*

Item to Wylliam Johnson, mason, for iiij days ther in thys weke: ij*s* ij*d*; and to Wodrof, his laborer, the same iiij days: xviij*d* – ij*s* viij*d*

Item to Herryson for lyme spent in the sayd tenement syns Hallomes ij chalder: vij*s*

Item for sonde to Ketryngham vj lodes: ij*s*

Item for viij *libr'* candyll spent in that tyme: x*d*

/*The weke after Twelthe* [*Night*]/ Item to Wylliam Vyker, mynder, for vj days worke ovyr throwen of walles ther: ij*s* vj*d*

Item to Sander Clarke, laborer, brekyng of gret morter cloddes that came of certen buttraces ther that war betten down, ij days: ix*d*

Item for iiij fadam of bast for the walle: iiij*d*

Item for a newe pulley in the market: iij*d*

[*f. 27^v*] /*The second weke after Twelthe*/ Item to the forsayd Sander ffyeng of the welle and ij jakes and makyng clene the garden plote, to hym for vj days and Henry Wodroff v days: iiij*s* j*d ob'*

Item to John Howell, cowper, for ij newe stoppys for the welle, with j*d* worthe of nayles for the hoopis: ix*d*

Item to Paschall for xxiiij *libr'* of yron worke of hoopys and chenys for the same stoppys: iij*s*

/*The iij^de weke after Twelthe*/ Item to hym for yron worke for the forsayd pulley, with an hooke layd in the kechyn chymney to hange on an hake viij *libr'*: xij*d*

Item to hym for iij newe lockes and keys for the same tenement, with settyng on: xv*d*

Item to hym for xiij payer of hookes & hengilles & v barrys with cappis & stapilles conteynyng xxx *libr'*: ij*s* ix*d*

Item to John Byrche for ij days worke of oon of hys men makyng of wyndowe loopys and hangyng of them: xiij*d*

Item payd to hym for these parcelles of tymbyr and bourde folowyng, with wormanshype don in the same tenement in the monythe of Januarii, as it apperith by his byll of euery particler parcel: and ffyrst for ij stodes, an entertyse and an hanse at the vyce dore of the newe byldyd howse: viij*d*; a dore loope for the same dore: xviij*d*; xxvj foote of oken and popill bourde: x*d*; iij stoodes, an entertyse and an hanse for the partycon at the chymney ende: xij*d* – iiij*s*

Item a lytyll dore loope at the chymney ende: x*d*

[*f. 28*] Item oon stoode at the stayer hede: iij*d*; a dore loope to the same stode: xviij*d*; xv foote of bourde for the benchys: vj*d* – ij*s* iij*d*

Item a dore lope for the dore stalle next the howse late the vestry: xviij*d*; a loope for the buttry dore: xiiij*d*; a courbyll for the welle: iiij*d*; a jakes bourde: ij*d*; a bourde for the wyndowe in the chambyr late the vestry: j*d* – iij*s* iij*d*

Item to a dore loope at the stayers hede next the chymney bynethe: xviij*d*: xxxj foote of bourde for the partycon next the chymney: xiiij*d* – ij*s* viij*d*

Item for iiij days worke of a man: ij*s* ij*d*

Item for iiij *libr'* candyll spent syns Crystmes: v*d*

/*In the Clensyng Wekel*/ **Item** to John Pylson,[345] glasewright, for workmanshyppe of iiij^xx foote of glasse set vp in the same howses made of old glass of comon store, we fyndyng all stuff: and ffyrst to hym for xj days worke betwyxt tymes, at vj*d* a day: v*s* vj*d*

Item for ij *libr'* j quarter of sowde: ix*d*; lede j quarter C: xij*d*; sadlers nayle: ij C *di'*: ij*d* – xxiij*d*

Item to hym for settyng of the same: ij*d*

Summa vj *li* ij*s* v*d* *ob'*

/*The lybrary*/ **Item** payd for newe coueryng of the howse late the lybrary, nowe parcell of the forsayd tenement, with thacke tyle: and fyrst to John Asterby,[346] plomer, and hys man for oon day worke takyng down the lede that was on parcell of the same howse: xv*d*; and to ij laborers that toke down tyle of other old howsys xiiij m^l at v*d* m^l: v*s* x*d* – vij*s* j*d*

[*f. 28*ʳ] /*The Assencon Wekel*/ **Item** to an other laborer for ij days worke goyng of erandes for lyme, sonde, nayle, lathe, tyle pynnys, caryeng away the lede and the lede lathe that came of that howse: ix*d*

Item payd to Wylliam Smythe,[347] tyler, for newe lathyng and tylyng of all that same howse on bothe sydes, takyn by hym a gret: xxvj*s* viij*d*

Item to hym for takyng downe the lede lathe of the same howse, whiche was owur couuenaunt to do: iiij*d*

Item to Mastres Marsham, Henry Holden & other men ffor xxvj C lathe spent vpon the same howse: xiij*s* ij*d*

Item to Mastres Marsham for xvj m^l tyle pynnys: iij*s* iiij*d*

Item to John Byrche for xxv yardes of evys bourde, with the naylyng on: ij*s*

Item for iij C iiij*d* nayle for the evys bourdes for the lathe wher the sparrys war sappy: viij*d*

Item to Wylliam Morront for x m^l gret lathe nayle: viij*s* iiij*d*; and for ij m^l small lathe nayle: ij*s* iiij*d* – x*s* vij*d*

Item to Herryson for lyme xij comb': iij*s* vj*d*; to Feere for xj comb': iij*s* viij*d* – vij*s* ij*d*

345　NCR, 18A/6, f. 89ᵛ, does not name Pylson or explain that the glass came from the common store.

346　NCR, 18A/6, ff. 89ᵛ–90, does not name Asterby, but notes that he was paid 'by covenaunt agrette', namely a sum agreed in advance rather than by the day.

347　NCR, 18A/6, ff. 89ᵛ–90, names none of the individuals mentioned in this sub-section.

Item to Ketryngham for sonde ij lode: viij*d*

Item to a laborer that made clene the chambyr and yardes whan they hade don: iiij*d* ob'

Summa lxxij*s* ix*d* ob'

[*f. 29*] /***Chapter howse***/ /*The weke byfore Candylmes*/ **Item** payd for certen chargis for claryfyeng of the chapter howse, whyche fell down on Seynt Stephyns day within the tyme of thys accompt, and a gret part of the dorter roff: and ffyrst payd to Sander Clarke and Henry Wodroff,[348] laborers, caryen away the tymbyr, thacke tyle, brycke and ston, eyther of them vj days thys weke: iiij*s* vj*d*

Item for newe layeng of the comon pykexe: ij*d*

/*The weke in whiche Candylmes day fell in*/ **Item** to the forsayd Sander Clarke for iiij days: xviij*d*

Item to Henry Wodrof for v days: xxij*d* ob'

Item to Thomas Moone for ij days: ix*d*

/*The weke after Candylmes*/ **Item** to Sander Clarke, Thomas Mone and to Robert Yoxhale, laborers, euery of them vj days: vj*s* ix*d*

Item to Nycholas Tuttell, carpenter, shoryng the roff of the ij endes of the dorter that stode styll and onjoyntyng the tymbyr that was ffallen down, ij days worke: xiij*d*

/*The weke byfore Shroftyde*/ **Item** to the forsayd iij laborers, euery of them iij days thys weke makyng an ende, settyng up the tymbyr, brycke & ston in order: iij*s* iiij*d* ob'

Summa xx*s*

/***Buttry and pantry***/ /*The xj day Maii*/ **Item** payd for the chargis of the buyldyng of a newe buttry and pantry at the west ende of the halle: and fyrst payd to Master Pyndern, prest,[349] ffor xlij gret sparrys for joystes of the sayd buttry and pantry, whyche war parcell of the sparrys of the Grey Fryers chansell roff: xlij*s*

Item to hym for certen other brokyn tymbyr: iiij*s*

[*f. 29ᵛ*] /*The xij day Maii*/ **Item** to Henry Sparke[350] for caryeng of the same tymbyr to the comon halle at v lode: xx*d*

Item to iiij^or laborers that removyd them out of Master Pynderns howse in to the strete to lade them and onlade them ageyn, with other worke that day: xviij*d*

/*The xxvij day Maii*/ **Item** to John Byrche, carpenter, makyng of iij wyndows for the buttry and ij for the pantry, with yron grates all ffyve: vj*s*

---

348 NCR, 18A/6, f. 91, names neither Clarke or Wodroff or any of the other individuals mentioned in this section.

349 NCR, 18A/6, f. 91, does not refer to Pyndern as a priest or note where the wood came from.

350 NCR, 18A/6, f. 91, does not name Sparke.

Item to hym for workmanshyppe of ij dorestalles ffor the buttry and pantry inbowyd, iiij halff loopys to the same with batrons, all the sayd stuff beyng of comon store, but the hansys his own: xij*s* viij*d*

Item payd for gravyng of the ij hansys: xxij*d*

Item to hym for cuttyng of plankes & lyntelles for the dores & wyndows & for byllettes for the shelvys in those ij howsys: vj*d*

/*The iij*de* day of June*/ **Item** to Paschall for xiij*xx* xvij *libr'* of yron worke for the grates of the forsayd v wyndows at j*d* qu' *libr'*: xxviij*s* x*d*

Item for iiij*or* payer of hookes & hengilles for the sayd iiij*or* halff dores, conteynyng xxj *libr' di'* at j*d ob' libr'*: ij*s* vij*d ob'*

Item for ij newe lockes and keys for these same dores, with the settyng on: ij*s*

Item: for ij sneckes and lachys made with rynges: xij*d*

Item ij barrys with cappys and stapylles: iiij*d*

Item for ij C dyce hede nayle, tynnyd: v*s* iiij*d*

/*The vij day June*/ **Item** to John Byrche for x days worke of ij of hys men layeng the joystes ouer the sayd buttry and pantry and bourdyng the same redy to lay on the lede, at xiij*d* the day toguether: x*s* x*d*

[*f. 30*] **Item** to hym for v*xx* narrowe waynscotte bourdes for plancheryng of part of the sayd buttry: viij*s* iiij*d*

Item to Wylliam Morront[351] for xl brode waynscotte bourdes for the same purpose: v*s*

Item to Robert Raynbald for vj*xx* fayer and large waynscot bourdes, whyche dyd contayne v C ffoote & halff, wherwith the pantry ys oonly couerd and part of the buttry, at iiij*s* the C: xxij*s*

Item to John Byrche for j C dry bourde for the buttry and pantry dores: v*s*

/*Masons craft*/ **Item** payd for masons craft in the sayd buttry and pantry: and fyrst to Wylliam Johnson,[352] mason, for v days worke in the Assensyon Weke: ij*s* viij*d ob'*

Item to Robert Yoxhale and John Nonne, laborers, for the same v days: iij*s* ix*d*

Item to the sayd Johnson for vj days in the weke after the Assencon: iij*s* iij*d*

Item to John Erne, mason, for oon day: vij*d*

Item to hys laborer for the same day: iiij*d ob'*

Item to Robert Yoxhale, laborer, vj days: ij*s* iij*d*

Item to Sander Clarke, laborer, for v days ther thys weke and for iij days the last weke: ij*s*

/*Wytson Weke*/ **Item** to Wylliam Johnson, mason, iij days: xix*d ob'*

Item to Robert Yoxhale, his laborer, iij days: xiij*d ob'*

Item to Sander Clarke and Henry Wodrof, eyther of them oon day: ix*d*

---

351 NCR, 18A/6, f. 91*v*, does not name Morront or the other two purveyors of boards.

352 NCR, 18A/6, ff. 91*v*–2, does not name Johnson or any of the other individuals mentioned in the rest of this section.

/*Corpus Christi Weke*/ **Item** to Wylliam Johnson, mason, v days: ij*s* viij*d ob'*
Item to John Erne, mason, oon day: vij*d*
Item to Davy Scotte, his laborer, the same day: iiij*d ob'*
[*f. 30ᵛ*] **Item** to Robert Yoxhale, laborer, v days, to Sander Clarke ij days and Henry
Wodroff ij days: iij*s* iiij*d ob'*

/*The weke after Corpus Christi*/ **Item** to John Erne, mason, vj days: iij*s* vj*d*
Item to Wylliam Johnson, mason, vj days: iij*s* iij*d*
Item to Davy Scotte and Yoxhale, laborers, vj days: iiij*s* vj*d*
Item to Henry Wodroff makyng of the florthis in the sayd buttry and pantry, vj
days: ij*s* iij*d*

/*The xv of June*/ **Item** payd to Asterby, plomer, for meltyng and shotyng of xix C *di'*
xj *libr'* of lede at xij*d* C: xix*s* vij*d*
Item to hym for vij *libr'* lede, ouer & aboue owur own: iij*d*
Item to Robert Raynbald for a newe webbe of lede conteynyng ij C *di'* vij *libr'* at v*s*
C: xij*s* ix*d*
Item to Master Kempe for rowe lede ij C *di'*: x*s*
Item to Wylliam Morront for shet lede, whyche was cut for fyllettes to ffynyshe vp
the worke wythe, iij quarters iij *libr'*: iij*s* vij*d*
Item to the forsayd Asterby for vj days worke of hym and hys man coueryng the sayd
buttry and pantry, cuttyng of fyllettes and sowdryng the old lede that came of the
lybrary in dyuerse places, at vij*d* the day for hys *man* and viij*d* for hym selff: vij*s* vj*d*
Item to hym for sowder j *libr'*: iiij*d*

/*The xvij of June*/ **Item** to the baly of Normans[353] for caryage of all the lede to
Pokethorppe [*Pockthorpe*] and recaryage: xij*d*
Item to hym for clay for the florthys of the sayd buttry and pantry viij lodes: iij*s* iiij*d*
Item to hym for sonde xj lodes: iij*s* viij*d*
Item for newe layeng of the comon pykex: ij*d*
[*f. 31*] **Item** to Henry Sparke for ij lodes sonde: x*d*
Item to Nycholas Tuttell, carpenter, makyng of a wyndowe set above the ledes to
showe lyght to the vyce that gothe vp to the scolehowse & makyng of berers set in
the buttry to lay on vesselles with bere & ale, iij days worke: xix*d ob'*

/*The weke in whiche Mydsomer Day fell in*/ **Item** to John Erne, mason, in those
howses, oon day: vij*d*
Item to Davy Scotte, hys laborer, that same day: iiij*d ob'*
Item to Wylliam Johnson, mason, fynyshyng vp those ij howses, iij days thys weke:
xix*d ob'*
Item to Robert Yoxhale, hys laborer, iij days: xiij*d ob'*

---

353 Norman's or St Paul's hospital, a monastic foundation in the north of the city,
previously run by the Benedictine monks and then the dean and chapter of Norwich
cathedral: Rawcliffe, *Hospitals of Medieval Norwich*, chapter two.

/Lyme spent ther/ **Item** payd for lyme spent abought those ij howses: and ffyrst to Walter Feer for xiiij comb': iiijs viijd

Item to Harryson for ij chalder & v comb' *at* ijs iiijd: vjs ijd

Item to Master Marsham for iiij^{or} chalder at ijs iiijd: ixs iiijd

Summa xiiij *li* ixs xjd

Memorandum that all other thynges spent in thys buyldyng and byfore not spokyn of, as tymbyr for all the wyndowe stalles, dore stalles and lyntelles, for all them, and lyke wyse plankes for the nether scylys of all the wyndows, byllettes for shelvys, planke and bourde for shelvys, the rest of all the lede, all maner of nayle, with many other thynges, war of comon store *& cetera*.[354]

/A newe kechyn begon/ **Item** hereafter folowythe the charges payd within the tyme of thys accompt for the bgynnyng of a newe kechyn ther to be buyldyd: and fyrst payd to Robert Collard for hys labowur and horse hyer rydyng to Framyngham castyll [*Framlingham Castle, Suffolk*] to feche Master Gybbon,[355] master of my lorde of Norff' workes, to haue hys cownsell: xxd

[*f. 31ᵛ*] */The weke in whiche the Assumpcon of Owur Lady fell in/* **Item** gaff in reward to the sayd Master Gybbon for hys comyng hyther and for hys cownsell: xs

Item to dyuerse laborers betyng down the particions betwyxt the archys and the vowtynges and for claryfyeng of the grownde: and fyrst to Sander Clarke and John Ynglond,[356] eyther of them iiij days: iijs

Item to John Smythe and Mathewe Dabney, eyther of them iij days: ijs iijd

Item to Robert Garrade for caryeng a waye of colder xij lodes: ijs

/The weke in whiche Seynt Bartylmewe fell in/ **Item** to Sander and Inglond for ij days: xviijd

Item to Mathewe Dabney for iij days: xiijd ob'

Item to Thomas Elward, ffremason, workyng & makyng freston redy for geamys of the chymneys, v days that weke, at viijd the day: iijs iiijd

/The weke after Seynt Bartylmewe/ **Item** to the sayd Elward for iiij days *di'*: iijs

Item to Sander, laborer, ij days: ixd

Item to Thomas Wolman for certen freston bought of hym at the Grey Fryers viij lode: xxvjs viijd

Item to Henry Sparke for caryeng the same ffreston to the comon halle: iijs iiijd

---

354 NCR, 18A/6, f. 92, does not include this note.

355 NCR, 18A/6, f. 92, refers simply to 'a man & an horse ridyng for oone Master Guybon'. The latter was almost certainly Reginald Guybon (d. 1558) of Framlingham and Darsham: J. Corder, ed., *The Visitation of Suffolk 1561 Made by William Hervy* (2 parts, Harleian Society, new series, 2 and 3, 1981, 1984), ii, pp. 305–6.

356 NCR, 18A/6, f. 92–2ᵛ, names neither Clarke nor Ynglond, nor any of the other individuals mentioned in the rest of this section.

/*The weke in whiche Owur Lady Natiuite ffell in*/ **Item** to the forsayd Elward for iiij days: ij*s* viij*d*

Item to John Byrche, carpenter, for ij gret wyndows with myddylmotes for the sayd kechyn redy *made*, he ffyndyng all stuff: xx*s*

/*The weke after Owur Lady*/ **Item** to the sayd Elward for vj days and to Wylliam Thacker, ffremason, for vj days, at vij*d*: vij*s* vj*d*
Summa iiij *li* viij*s* ix*d ob'*

[*f. 32*] /***Prechyng yarde*/**[357] **Item** payd the xxj day of June by the commandment of the hole cownsell of the cyte to Master Robert Leche, late mayer, for the hole chargis of a walle makyng betwyxt the comons and the gardeyn in lease to John Clarke, cooke, with a newe bank in the prechyng yarde, mendyng of all the buttraces in the same yarde and for levellyng of the same yarde, with all charges of lyme, sonde and other stuff, as yt apperith more playnly of euery particler parcell and *summa* in a partycler booke of Robert Mychelles wrytyng,[358] the whyche money was layd out by the sayd Master Leche in the tyme of hys mayeralte and at thys day payd hym ageyn by the forsayd commandement: vij *li* viij*s*
Summa vij *li* viij*s*

/*Master Kempys howse*/[359] **Item** payd by the forsayd commandement to Master Thomas Godsalve, esquyer,[360] the same tyme for vj m¹ thacke tyle delyuerd to Master Kempe in the tyme of thys accompt for coueryng of hys newe howse at v*s* iiij*d* m¹: xxxij*s*
Summa xxxij*s*

/*Comon halle more costes*/[361] **Item** payd within the tyme of thys accompt for dyuerse other chargys in sondry places within the scyte of the same place, as hereafter folowythe:

/*Octobyr*/ **In primis** payd the xvj day of Octobyr to Barsham, clayman, coueryng of the walles betwix Frances Wolmer & the comons and betwyxt John Clarke and the comons with rede and claye, ij days *di'*, at vj*d* the day: xv*d*
[*f. 32ᵛ*] **Item** to John Edwardes, hys laborer,[362] ij days *di': xj*d*

---

357 NCR, 18A/6, f. 92, incorporates this section as a very brief entry under 'botery & pantery'.

358 Mychelles was one of the assessors appointed by the mayor in 1542 to raise money for cleaning the river, and may have acted as his assistant: NCR, 16A/5, p. 93.

359 NCR, 18A/6, f. 92ᵛ, incorporates this section as a very brief entry under 'kechyn'.

360 Thomas Godsalve the elder, registrar of the Norwich consistory court and formerly a monastic visitor, was father of [Sir] John Godsalve, MP for the city in 1539 and possibly 1542. He died in 1543 not 1542, as stated in *HoP, 1509–1558*, ii, pp. 221–2. See NRO, NCC Reg. Mingaye, ff. 275–86.

361 NCR, 18A/6, ff. 90–91, incorporates this entire section under 'the new tenement'.

362 NCR, 18A/6, ff. 90–91, does not name Edwardes or any of the other labourers mentioned in the rest of this section.

Item to John Page, laborer, to trete clay, ij days: ix*d*

Item to Henry Carter[363] for clay ij lodes: x*d*

Item ffor rede: vj*d*; thacke: vj*d*; strawe: j*d* – xiij*d*

/*Novembir*/ **Item** payd the iiij^te day to Wylliam Vyker, mynder,[364] for brekyng down the buttraces on the est syde of the chapter howse & levellyng the same walle: ij*s*

Item to hym the xj day brekyng of certeyn cantes vpon the walle[365] betwyxt the comons and Frances Wolmer and vpon the wall next the ryver and levellyng of them: xij*d*

Item to hym the xvij day for vndermynyng and ouerthrowyng of all the walles & buttraces betwyxt the dorter & the wall by the ryversyde: iiij*s*

Item the same day to John Carre, glasewright, for reparacon of all the wyndows in the scolehouse, late the fermery, fyndyng all stuff that went therto: vij*s*

Item the xviij day to Wylliam Vnderwood, tyler, for xij days worke reparyng the sayd fermery and the dorter, at vj*d ob'* day: vj*s* vj*d*

Item to Henry Grene, his laborer, xij days: iiij*s* vj*d*

Item to John Ellys, laborer, ix days: iij*s* iiij*d ob'*

Item to Walter Feere for lyme vj comb': ij*s*

Item to Ketryngham for sonde a lode: iiij*d*

Item to Osborn of Kyrby [*Bedon*] for ij m^l thacke tyle: xij*s*

Item tyle pynnys j m^l *di'*: iiij*d*; lathe nayle vij C: vij*d*; to Paschall for a locke for the store howse dore & settyng on: iiij*d* – xv*d*

[*f. 33*] /*Decembyr*/ **Item** payd the x day to the sayd Paschall for a newe locke and key for the dore in to the arches wher the kechyn shalbe byldyd: iiij*d*

Item the same day to Clement Appylby, plomer, for shotyng of iij C iij quarter viij *libr'* lede for a newe gutter at the west ende of the lybrary: iiij*s* v*d*

Item to hym for oon day worke of hym and a ladde makyng the same gutter: viij*d*

Item for caryage of the same lede to Pockthorpe to be shette & recaryage: iiij*d*; lede nayle: iij*d* – vij*d*

/*The weke after Hallomes*/ **Item** payd to Robert Yoxhale, Robert Browster and Bartylmewe Wymond, euery of them vj days, makyng clene the dorter,[366] gatheryng vp of tymbyr abought the yardes and howsys and bryngyng it in to the vowlte and caryeng of old rotten tymber[367] to the comon inne for fewall for the glaser: vj*s* ix*d*

---

363 NCR, 18A/6, ff. 90–91, does not name Carter or any of the other suppliers of materials mentioned in the rest of this section.

364 NCR, 18A/6, f. 90, records that he was retained 'by covenaunt in grette' rather than being paid a daily wage.

365 NCR, 18A/6, f. 90, refers to 'certen cynkes & the walles & botrasses'.

366 Work on the dorter was not completed until 23 March 1542, when the mayor and eight others were commissioned to inspect it: NCR, 16D/2, f. 197.

367 NCR, 18A/6, f. 90, does not note that the timber was recycled as fuel.

Item to Robert Brown, laborer, for v days that weke makyng clene & levellyng the cloyster: xxij*d ob'*

|The weke byfore Crystmes| **Item** to Wylliam Fayer, laborer, helpyng hym in the sayd cloyster, iij days: xiij*d ob'*

Item to John Erne, mason, pathyng the stepyll with pathyng tyle and the way that lede from the stepill to the cloyster with pathyn ston, iiij days: ij*s* iiij*d*

Item to Robert Hollond, mason, settyng in of a newe dore stalle at John Clarkes gardeyn by the stretes syde and fynyshyng of Sanders chambyr,[368] iiij days: ij*s* iiij*d*

Item to Yoxhale and Jube, laborers, iiij days: iij*s*

Item to Sander and Moone makyng clene of all the howses ageynst Crystmes, iiij days: iij*s*

[*f. 33ᵛ*] **Item** payd for bromys: j*d*; to Paschall for brasyng of the store howse dore key: ij*d* – iij*d*

Item candyll iiij *libr'*: v*d*; sonde iiij lodes: xvj*d* – xxj*d*

Item to Master Marsham for lyme ij chalder & a comb': v*s*

Item to John Aldryche for small pathyn tyle to ffynyshe vp the stepyll ij C *di'*: x*d*; to William Morront for iiij C: xvj*d*; to Master Steward for xxx gret tyles of Horsford makyng: xij*d* – iij*s* ij*d*

Item to John Byrche, carpenter, for ij days worke and an halff of ij of hys men that weke makyn a roff to the vyce at Sanders chambyr, withe fynyshyng many thynges in that chambyr, and cuttyng of thresholdes for all the dores of the stepyll and many other dores: ij*s* ix*d*

Item to hym for a gutter pece that convey the water out of the entry that lede from the stepyll in to the backyarde: iiij*d*

Item to hym for a newe dorestalle with a loope for John Clarkes gardeyn by the stretes syde: iiij*s*

Item to Paschall for a newe locke and key, a stapyll and a ryng for the same dore: xvj*d*

Item to hym for a newe locke & key for Sanders chambyr dore and a newe key for the locke on the northe dore in the hall: vij*d*

Item to Clement for candyll for the chappell all wynter iiij *libr'*: v*d*; to hym helpyng the prest to syng messe the hole yere: iiij*d*; gaff in reward amonges iiij laborers: iiij*d* – xiij*d*

[*f. 34*] *|The weke in whiche Twelth Day fell in|* **Item** payd to Sander Clarke for tylyng of the vyce that gothe vp to hys chambyr & fyeng the jakes that ys in that howse, ij days worke: ix*d*

Item to John Pylson,[369] glasewright, trymmyng vp of ij gret wyndows in the sayd Sanders chambyr with old glass of comon store, iiij days: ij*s*

---

368 It seems likely that Sander Clark was given accommodation in return for caretaking duties, as the site is known to have attracted thieves: see above, p. 49.

369 NCR, 18A/6, f. 90ᵛ, does not name Pylson, or note that the glass came from the common store.

Item to Paschall for workmanshype of xiiij yron barrys of comon store for the same wyndowe: iij*d*
Item for sowde j *libr'*: iiij*d*

/*The Clensyng Wekel* Item payd to Clement Appylby,[370] plomer, sowdryng the northe yle of the halle in dyuerse places, for a day and halff of hym and hys man: xviij*d*
Item to hym for sowde iij *libr' di'* at v*d libr'*: xvij*d ob'*

/*Rogacon wekel* Item payd to John Hast for carvyng of flagges in the castill dyche for the newe banke in the prechyng yerde: ij*d*; for caryeng thyther to a laborer: ij*d* – iiij*d*
Item to John Byrche, carpenter, for makyng a newe gate stalle and a loope with a clycke for the prechyng *yarde* with batrons, he fyndyng part of stuffe: v*s* vj*d*
Item to hym for *di'* C dry bourde for the same: ij*s* vj*d*
Item for gravyng of the hanse: vj*d*
Item to Paschall for dyce hede nayle *di'* C: xvj*d*
Item to hym for a payer of hookes and hengilles, with ij stapylles, ij barrys with cappis for the same gate conteynyng xv *libr' di'* at j*d ob' libr'*: xxiij*d*
Item for a payer of jemews for the clycke of the same gate with a rynge: xij*d*
Item for iij newe lockes with keyes, oon for that gate, oon for the gate betwyxt the prechyng yarde and the gardeyn, and the iij[de] for the gate out of the gardeyn in to the strete ageynst Seynt Peters: ij*s*

[*f. 34*[v]] /*Wytson Wekel* Item payd to John Goold,[371] carpenter, for makyng of a coffer to cover the hole in the roffe of the chappell wher the lampe dyd hange & ledyng of the same coffer, with nayles and layeng on: ix*d*
Item for bourde for the same coffer: iiij*d*
Item for leed redy shette iij[xx] xij *libr'*: ij*s*

/*Mydsomer wekel* Item to John Carre, glasewright, for newe makyng of ij panys of glasse in oon of the northe wyndows of the chappell, whiche was broke by the tylers whan the lybrary was tyled: ij*s*
Item to hym for mendyng of the west wyndows in the halle, whyche war brokyn in the tyme of buyldyng the buttry and pantry: iiij*d*

/*The weke after Lammes*/ Item payd to Sanders wyff for wedyng of the prechyng yarde, iij days worke: vj*d*

Summa vj *li* iij*s* ix*d*

Memorandum that certen tyle, lathe, brycke, stoune, old tymbyr, bourde and suche other leke thynges as war ther within the place war delyuerd to Master Kempe toward his charges of the buyldyng of hys howse by the consent of master mayer and hys brothern & owur cownsell.[372]

---

370 NCR, 18A/6, f. 90[v], does not name Appylby, but reports that he was 'soudyng diuers hooles on the lede', which was damaged.
371 NCR, 18A/6, f. 91, does not name Goold.
372 NCR, 18A/6, f. 92[v], does not include this note.

/Necessaryes bought/[373] **Item** payd for dyuerse necessuryers [*sic*] made & bought within the tyme of thys accompt mete for workemen to occupye, with other thynges nedefull to be hade in store, as bourde, lathe, brycke, tyle, all sortes of nayle, with suche other leke thynges bought at the best chepe at dyuers tymes:

/The xvij of Octobyr/ **And fyrst** payd to Bryan Doront, smythe, for makyng of a newe pykex of the old comon pykex, puttyng therto iij *libr'* of newe yron: vj*d*

[*f. 35*] */The vj*ᵗᵉ *of Februarii/* **Item** to Henry Holden for a newe barrowe: xij*d*
Item payd to Wylliam Morront for viij*d* nayle halff a m¹: ij*s* vj*d*; vj*d* nayle *di'* m¹: ij*s*; iiij*d* nayle j m¹ *di'*: iiij*s* ix*d*; iij*d* nayle j m¹: xx*d*; ij*d* nayle j m¹: xvj*d*; gret lathe nayle iij m¹: ij*s* vj*d*. *Summa*: xiij*s* ix*d*

*/The xj*ᵗᵉ *of Februarii/* **Item** payd to Chapman of Marlyngford [*Marlingford*] for a lode of okyn bourde conteynyng iiij C *di'* xv foote at ij*s* vj*d* C: xj*s* x*d*
Item the last day of Marche to Henry Marsham of Stratton Strawles[*s*] for xv C lathe: vj*s* viij*d*
Item for an ayle barrell for a water tubbe for the reders and masons: iiij*d*; to a cowper for sawyng & makyng the same with ij eeres: iij*d* – vij*d*

/The xxij of Aprelle/ **Item** to Osborn of Kyrby for thacke tyle to haue in store to amende fawtes with j m¹: vj*s*
Item the vj day of Maii to Thomas Flowurdewe of Het[*h*]erset[*t*] for brycke *di'* m¹: iij*s*
Item for a lytyll basket to take downe tyle with at the comon [*hall*] whan the lybrary was newe tyld: ij*d*

*/The xj*ᵗᵉ *of Maii/* **Item** to Wylliam Morront for more nayles: and ffyrst for xij*d* nayle j m¹: v*s*; vj*d* nayle j m¹: iiij*s*; iiij*d* nayle ij m¹: v*s*; iij*d* nayle j m¹ *di'*: ij*s* vj*d*; ij*d* nayle *di'* m¹: viij*d* – xvij*s* ij*d*
Item the same day to Jube of Bucknam Carleton [*Buckenham's manor in Carleton-Rode*] for lathe xij C: vj*s*
Item to Master Pyndern for j dossen furren sparrys: ij*s*
Item to Paschall for mendyng the barrowe spyndyll: j*d*

/The xij of Julii/ **Item** to Brygges of Bucknam Carleton for ten copyll of sawen sparrys: v*s*
Item to Flowerdewe for brycke *di'* m¹: iij*s*
Item for byrchyn bromys in the market: j*d*

[*f. 35*ᵛ] */The xxviij of Julii/* **Item** to Wylliam Morrront for more nayles: & fyrst for vj*d* nayle *di'* m¹: ij*s*; iiij*d* nayle *di'* m¹: xv*d*; iij*d* nayle *di'* m¹: x*d*; ij*d* nayle *di'* m¹: viij*d* – iiij*s* ix*d*

*/The iiij*ᵗᵉ *of Septembyr/* **Item** to hym for iiij*d* nayle *di'* m¹: xv*d*
Summa* iiij *li* ij*s* x*d

---

373 NCR, 18A/6, f. 87ᵛ, lists these items briefly under 'mynute expences' without noting either the date of purchase or the name of the purveyor.

/*Mynute expensys*/[374] **Item** payd for dyuerse mynute expensys within the tyme of thys accompt at sondry tymes as they chansed:

In primis payd for ij quayers of paper to make ij bookes for the receytes & paymentes of the accomptantes to kepe ther reknyng parfite: iiij*d*

/*The xxij day of Octobyr*/ **Item** payd to Robert Burgys[375] for fellyng of ij popylles in the hospytall closse in Sent Vedastes and makyng the toppis in to fagottes: ij*s*

/*Novembyr*/ **Item** payd to Neve[376] of Rynglond [*Ringland*] for iiij sackes of charcole layd in to the guyldhall for the cownsell chambyr at v*d* the sacke: xx*d*

/*Decembyr*/ **Item** payd on Seynt Stephyns day to the constabylles of Heyham [*Heigham*] for the kynges taske for ij acres londe without Seynt [*Giles*] gates, late Hemmynges: iiij*d*

/*Januarii*/ **Item** payd for helpe for the weyng of an old mucke boote that lay drownyd at Coslany brydge, whyche some tyme was Stubbys: iij*d*

/*Februarii*/ **Item** payd to Thomas Bosewell, paynter, for correctyng of a platte that was sent vp at thys terme for the establyshyng of the <seynt> seyntwary within the cyte accordyng to the statute: vj*s* viij*d*[377]

[*f. 36*] /*Marche*/ **Item** payd at Yarmothe for iij mastes for standerdes for the buyldyng at the comon halle: x*s*; for the ffreyght of them to Norwyche: ij*s*; for caryage from the comon stathe to the halle: vj*d* – xij*s* vj*d*

/*A present to the byshoppe of Norwyche*/ **Item** payd the xix day for ypocras a gallon: v*s* ij*d*; muscadell of Gene a gallon: ij*s*, sent to the byshoppe of Norwyche comyng thyther: vij*s* ij*d*

/*Aprelle*/ **Item** payd to the netterd for the sewte of a replevye ageynst the town of Laknam [*Lakenham*]: iiij*s* iiij*d*[378]
Item to Master Robert Ferrowur, alderman, for the redemyng of an *di'*C wight that longith to the comon stathe, the whyche he haue had in hys hondes syns the ston key was made ther: viij*d*

---

374 NCR, 18A/6 divides 'mynute expences' into two parts, the first (ff. 87ᵛ–8) ending with the entries listed below under 'Septembyr', while the second (ff. 92ᵛ–3ᵛ) lists all the subsequent disbursements. None of the entries are dated and most furnish far less detail than is provided here. Nor is any systematic attempt made to create sub-sections other than for gifts to the duke of Norfolk and the justices of assize.

375 NCR, 18A/6, f. 87ᵛ, does not name Burgys. The land in question belonged to the hospital of St Giles: *MFS*, pp. 95–6.

376 NCR, 18A/6, f. 87ᵛ, does not name Neve.

377 See above, pp. 103–4.

378 The city laid claim to common grazing land in the suburb of Lakenham, which had previously been a longstanding matter of contention with the cathedral monks: NCR, 9G/7; Liddy, *Contesting the City*, pp. 77–8.

/*May*/ **Item** payd in the Rogacon Weke for sedge to strowe abought the pulpet in the prechyng yarde at the comon halle the ij fyrst days: iiij*d*[379]

Item to a carpenter for newe stavyng of a ledder of Master Stewardes that was brokyn with the ffalle of the chapter howse ther: iiij*d*; and for xxx byllettes for the stavys of the same: iij*d* – vij*d*

/*Wytson Weke*/ **Item** payd for sedge to strowe the halle ther whan the prynces players playd an enterlude ther: ij*d*;[380] drynke for the players: ij*d*; to ij laborers that fechyd barrelles and tymbyr and made a scaffold for them: ij*d* – vj*d*

Item payd for an oblygacon makyng for John Barker, brewer, for the payment of lx*s* for iij yeres lyberte not to be chosen shreve: ij*d*[381]

[*f. 36*ᵛ] /*A present to the duke of Norff*/ **Item** payd to John Oldman for a gret pyeke cald a luse: x*s*; to Dewe of Beston [*Beeston*] for vj gret perchis: vj*s*; to a man that rode to Beston for them: viij*d*; in the market for ij gret elys: iij*s* iiij*d*, whiche present was govyn to hys grace on the Assencon evyn at Master Spencers place – xx*s*[382]

Item to ij men that holpe to bere the sayd ffyshe to Master Spencers to be in a redynes ther: ij*d*

/*The xxj day of June*/ **Item** payd to Master Robert Leche for a certen dette that he payd to Henry Sparke[383] for caryage that he dyd for the comons at the commandement of Master Nycholas Sutterton whan he was mayer: v*s*

/*A present *to* the justyces of assyse*/ **Item** payd for ipocras ij gallons x*s*; Gascoyn wyne ij gallons xvj*d*; ij pottes with waffers ij*s* iiij*d*; wafer cakes ij*s* iiij*d* – xvij*s*

Item to Master Trase[384] for iij yerdes of satten *reuersa*, whyche was govyn to my Lord Montagewe: xv*s*[385]

/*Rewardes Julii*/ **Item** gaff in reward the xxij day to Master Sergeant Townesend ffor his paynes, for that he was a cownsell with the cite agenst Master John Shelton, esquyer, at the comen halle for the varyans betwyxt the cite and my Lady Shelton for the lybertes of Carrowe: vij*s* vj*d*[386]

---

379 In May 1541 the assembly ruled that the annual civic procession on Rogation Monday would henceforth end at the Blackfrairs, where a sermon would be preached to the citizenry: NCR, 16A/4, f. 39ᵛ; 16A/5, p. 55.

380 The players who performed under the nominal patronage of Prince Edward (b. 1537): Galloway, ed., *Records of Early English Drama*, p. 363.

381 NCR, 18A/6, f. 88, simply refers to 'an obligacon ffor John Baker'. See above, p. 123.

382 NCR, 18A/6, f. 88, provides none of this detail.

383 NCR, 18A/6, f. 88, records a payment direct to Sparke.

384 NCR, 18A/6, f. 88, does not mention John Trase, who was then an auditor (see below, p. 168).

385 Sir Edward Montague, chief justice of the court of King's Bench: *ODNB*, xxxviii, pp. 699–700; Baker, *Men of Court*, ii, pp. 1130–32; *LPFD*, XVII, no 443 (40).

386 Sir John Shelton (d. 1539) had been awarded the site and buildings of Carrow priory by the crown in November 1538; and a dispute subsequently ensued with his widow concerning

Item gaff in reward to Seynt Stephyns lete for ther dylygens and paynes abought serchyng of doles in the heye waye betwyxt the Brasen Towur and the Stompyd Crosse: ijs[387]

[*f. 37*] /*Sent Jamys day*/ **Item** payd to a carpenter and a laborer settyng vp the bothe and wrostlyn place at the castyll diche and takyng down ageyn and for caryage and recaryage ffrom and to the guyldhalle: ijs iiijd
Item for the hyer of viij teltes, for trusse lyne, sedge for strewyng, drynke betwyxt tymis, nayles, <wesch> wetchyng ij nyghtes and suche other leke charges: vs iijd
Item to ij men that kept the bothe and style to kepe out the pepyll, for ther paynes and dyners that same day: xijd

/*August*/ **Item** payd for brede and drynke for master mayer and hys brothern syttyng an hole day in the cownsell howse abought the benevolens for the buyldyng of the howses at the comon halle: iiijd[388]

/*Septembyr*/ **Item** payd the xix day to Master Wylliam Toppysfeld of the exchekyr[389] for the costes of accompt and *quietus est* of Master Grewe, late mayer: xxvijs vd
Item payd to Master Henry Warde, town clarke, for the costes of the sewte and recouery of certen rentes of dyuerse howsys, late the duke of Suff' and the pryowur of Horsham Seynt Faythe: vj *li* xijs viijd[390]
Item payd at the kynges awdyte kept at Norwiche for the recorde of a decre grauntid out of the courte of agmenstacon, for the allowans of iijs by yere rent out of the late priory of Horsham Seynt Faythe, to Master Mylmay[391] for hys ffee: iijs iiijd; and to hys clarkes for the inrollment of the same: xxd – vs

[*f. 37ʳ*] /*Myhelmes*/ **Item** payd at the kynges awdyte kept at West Thorppe for the recorde of the same decre for the allowans of xvjs by yere rent for certen howsys in

the city's rights of jurisdiction over the site of the priory and its lands in Trowse. Both parties and their counsel met at Blackfrairs ('the newe hall') on 22 July 1542, but failed to reach an agreement: NCR, 16A/5, p. 117; W. Rye and E.A. Tillett, *An Account and Description of Carrow Abbey, Norwich* (Norwich, 1884), appendices V and VI. In March 1543, however, Lady Shelton (aunt of the late Anne Boleyn) agreed to compensate the city for encroachments near the walls by her servants: NCR, 16A/5, p. 140.
387 Stump Cross, a medieval cross at the junction of Magdalen Street and St Botolph Street where proclamations were made: *SLCN*, p. 83.
388 See above, p. 8.
389 For Toppesfield, see Baker, *Men of Court*, ii, p. 1540.
390 The case related to landgable due from property in what had been the fee of the prior of Horsham St Faith and from tenements in the parish of Saints Simon and Jude, which had formed part of an exchange between the king and Charles Brandon, duke of Suffolk, in 1538: Rutledge, 'Introduction', pp. 15, 18.
391 For the future Sir Walter Mildmay, then at the start of his meteoric carrer, see *ODNB*, xxxviii, pp. 119–26.

Norwiche, late the duke of Suff', to the awdytour ther for hys fee: iij*s* iiij*d*; & to the clarkes for the inrolment of yt: xx*d* – v*s*

Item payd ther for the makyng of a quytans for the dyscharge of the baly of Heylesdon [*Hellesdon*] for the receyte of lxiiij*s* for the arrerages of the aforsayd rent: iiij*d*

Item payd at the awdyte kept at Norwyche for a quytans for the tenth of the comon halle: viij*d*

Item to Robert Damme for gatheryng of *the* comon bakers grynt newe grauntyd: x*s*

Item payd to Master Kempe, prest of the comon halle, ffor hys hole yere wagys: vj *li* xiij*s* iiij*d*[392]

Item to Master Robert Leche, late mayer, for bankettes by hym made to men of honour and worshyppe whan they resorte to the cite,[393] grauntyd to euery mayer by acte of assembly: xl*s*

Item payd to Mastres Alyce Scolehowse, wydowe, ffor ij yeres annuyte for a mese in the paryshe of Seynt Mychaell of Coslany, late Master Percyes: xxvj*s* viij*d*

Item payd for iij quayers of paper occupyed in the cownsell howse, delyuerd to Rychard Framyngham at dyuerse tymes within the tyme of this accompt; and for a quayer and halff for a booke wherin thys accompt ys wryten: ix*d*

[*f. 38*] Item payd for the costes of the accomptant rydyng with Master Croke, alderman, to Westhorpe to the awdyte kept ther concernyng the forsayd decre, beyng forthe iij days in all, with hys horse hyer: v*s* vij*d*

Item gaffe in rewarde thys yere at dyuerse tymys by the dyscrecon of the accomptantes amonges the cite tenauntes and workemen, the bochers wyvis, bakers wyvys and in suche leke thynges as they sawe occacon, as yt appere more playnly in a byll delyuerd to the awdytours of euery particler parcell: iiij*s* x*d*

Summa xxv *li* v*s* iiij*d*

/*Fourty soldyers*/[394] Item payd for the chargys of ffourty soldyers sent in to Scotlond and delyuerd at Yarmothe the xxj day of Septembyr in the ende of thys accompt:

---

392 On 23 March 1542 the assembly agreed to provide Kempe with a 'resonabll stipende', to make up any shortfall in money paid to him for celebrating masses ('certeyns') for the city's various guilds: NCR, 16D/2, f. 197; above pp. 46, 122.

393 NCR, 18A/6, f. 92ᵛ, refers to 'rewardes goven by hym in tyme of his mayraltie to mynstrelles, game pleyers & suche other'.

394 NCR, 18A/6, f. 93–3ᵛ, incorporates the cost of 'sougers' as a sub-section under 'mynute expensys', noting that 'xviij bowemen, ffurnysshed with bowes & dagres, & xxij bilmen, ffurnysshed with swordes [*and*] dagers,' were sent 'to the dukes grace off Norffolk ayenst the Skottes'. For the background to this expedition, see Head, *Ebbs and Flows*, pp. 199–208; M.H. Merriman, *The Rough Wooings: Mary Queen of Scots 1542–1551* (East Linton, 2000), chapter three. The arrangements made between 3 and 9 September 1542 for the rapid mustering, selection, equipping and dispatch of enough men to satisfy the duke's demands are described in detail in NCR, 16A/5, pp. 109–16.

In primis payd for xxxvij Almayn ryvettes to dyuerse men, as yt appere by a byll of euery partycler person, at vijs vjd a pece: xiij *li* xvijs vjd

Item for chargys of dressyng of the sayd harnes with buckylles, nayles and lether, as yt apperyth partyclerly of euery parcell by the forsayd bylle: xxvijs iiijd

Item for xxij swordes and scaberdes and for scoryn and makyng clene of dyuerse of them, with some newe japys to them: xliiijs

Item for ffourty newe daggers: xls

Item for xxij bylles, with newe stavyng of xij *of* them: xxvs

Item for xviij newe ewen bowes: xxxvjs

Item to iiijᵒʳ seuerall men for iiijᵒʳ bowes of ther own, beyng soldyers: vijs iiijd

[*f. 38ᵛ*] **Item** payd for xij sheff of newe arrows with casses and guyrdylles bought at London by Master Edward Reede, alderman, with the caryage home: xxxiijs viijd

Item for oon sheffe and an halff bought here: iijs

Item payd for mendyng, fetheryng, hedyng, guyrdlyng and cassyng of xv sheffe *di'* gatherd vp here in the cyte: xixs vjd

Item payd for ffourty uyght cappys: viijs iiijd³⁹⁵

Item payd for the hole chargis of ffourty newe cotes made of canvas and lynyd with blanket, as yt appere partyclerly of euery parcell: vj *li* viijs vd

Item for makyng of xl cotes of whyte carsey of the kynges gyft: xxs

Item payd for ffourty payer of newe bootes: iiij *li*

Item for xx brasers & xx shotyng glovys: vjs viijd

Item ffor bowstrynges dystrybutyd amonges them: xvjd

Item ffor poyntes, v gross *di'* at xvjd: vijs iiijd

Item for laces ffor ffourty cotes: iiijd

Item to Master Lynsted, alderman, for hys costes & paynys rydyng ij tymes to Kenyngale [*Kenninghall*]³⁹⁶ to comon wyth my lord off Norff', his grace, concernyng the settyn forthe of the sayd fourty soldyers: xiijs iiijd

Item govyn in money amonges the soldyers at dyuerse tymes by commandement: xjs iiijd

Item for bere spent dyuerse tymes at the comon halle vpon them: iijs

Item to Pynchyn for hys paynis,³⁹⁷ costes and horse hyer rydyng to Yarmothe with letters: ijs ijd

[*f. 39*] **Item** payd for the costes of the forsayd soldyers sent to Yarmothe by water in a kele: and ffyrst for iij halff barrelles of bere: iiijs vjd; brede: ijs; butter: xvd; chese: xvjd – ixs jd

---

395 NCR, 18A/6, f. 93, has 'white' rather than 'nyght' caps.

396 NCR, 18A/6, f. 93ᵛ, does not record his destination, or the fact that he made two journeys. Hamond Lynsted's first visit on 3 September was to deliver a letter announcing that twenty-five men were ready to serve 'within oone ower warnyng', but the duke demanded twice as many. A compromise had been reached by 7 September, when Lynsted returned to Kenninghall to report that the authorities had 'chosen oute xl tallest & most apte & able men ffor the warres': NCR, 16A/5, pp. 112–13, 115–16.

397 NCR, 18A/6, f. 93ᵛ, refers to 'his labour sekyng botes'.

Item to Candler ffor the hyer of hys kele: vs vj*d*

Item for ther costes at Yarmothe, with oon nyght lodgyng byfore they war delyuerd: vij*s* iiij*d*

Item for the accomptantes costes ther ij days, with hys horse hyer: iij*s* iiij*d*; for Robert Damms costes goyng in the kele & comyng home on ffoote, beyng very ylle intretyd with them in the kele and leke to ben cast ovyr bourde: iij*s* iiij*d*[398] – vj*s* vij*d*

Item payd for the costes of the constabylles of Besttrete rydyng abought the contre sekyng of iiij*or* soldyers by cause they war sent for byfore the tyme appoynted: xx*d*

Item payd for newe naylyng, buklyng and letheryng of all the harneys that came home ageyn, with scoryng of the same and newe fetheryng and hedyng of the arrows that came home ageyn: xxiiij*s* ix*d*

Summa **xlij** *li* **xs vij***d*

Summa totallis omnium solucionum **CC lxxv** *li* **xij***s*[399] **viij***d ob'*

And so the forsayd accomptantes do owe lxviij *li* **iiij***s* **ij***d*

[*f. 39*᷎] **Wher of they** axe to be allowyd for these parcelles followyng:

In primis for the ingrossyng of thys accompt payd to Rychard Framyngham by the assygment of the awdytours: vs

Item for the expensys of the awdytours & others syttyng vpon the determynacon of this accompt: xs

Item they axe furder to be allowyd for dyuerse rentes aboue chargid and nowe dekayed,[400] for as moche as the ffees therof be vnknowen to the sayd accomptantes, as yt apperithe to the auditours by other accomptes afore made: xiij*s* iiij*d*

Item for halff a lyuery payd to Rychard Framyngham in the tyme of thys accompt grauntyd to hym by acte of assembly: vij*s*

Summa allocacionum **xxxvj***s* **iiij***d*

Summa totallis omnium solucionum et allocacionum **CC lxxvij** *li* **ixs** *ob'*

And so the forsayd accomptantes do owe lxvj *li* **vij***s* **x***d*

Wherof they axe to be respectyd vpon *vnde super* for certen rentes and fermys above chargid and not yet receyuyd, wherof the particlers do ffolowe:

And fyrst for rent of assyse of a tenement in the paryshe of Seynt Peter of Mancroft dewe by John Aleyn: x*s*

[*f. 40*] /*Respectes*/ **Item** of Robert Brown, jalyour, for the hole yere ferme of bothis set in castyll dyche in the tyme of sessyons and assyse chargyd in the tytyll of bothis: iiij*s*

---

398 NCR, 18A/6, f. 93᷎, simply notes that he attended to the soldiers.

399 The figure '13' has been written above in Arabic numerals in a contemporary hand.

400 NCR, 18A/6, ff. 93᷎–4, itemises each of these rents in considerable detail.

Item of Rychard Coldon for a quarter ferme of a tenement, late lord suffrigantes, whyche man ys gon & left nothyng for the accomptantes to dystreyn: v*s*

Item of Leonard Dales for the grynt of xxv comb' whete chargyd in the tytyll of bakers grynt amonges the fforen receytes: xij*d ob'*

Item for parcell of lx *li* xvj*s ob' qu'* taxyd for the settyng forthe of ffourty soldyers in to Scotlond, whyche the sayd accomptantes as yet haue not, nor in any wyse can, levey: vj *li* iij*s* ix*d ob' qu'*[401]

Summa respectorum vij *li* iij*s* x*d qu'*

Summa totallis omnium solucionum, allocacionum et respectorum CC iiij[xx] iiij *li* xij*s* x*d ob' qu'*

And so the forsayd accomptantes do knowlege them selvys clere detters to the comialte of the cyte afforsayd: lix *li* iij*s* xj*d ob' qu'*

Thys accompt was vewyd, examyned and determyned by the awdytors hereafter folowyng, the Monday the xiiij day of Maye in the xxxv yere of the reign of Kyng Henry the viij[te] [*1543*][402]

Edward Reed
Awsten Steward   aldermen

Thomas Moore
John Trase   comyners

---

401 Resistance may have been widespread: see, for example, NCR, 16A/5, pp. 122, 127–8.
402 NCR, 18A/6, f. 94[v], contains no record of such an examination, but lists the names of the auditors at the head of the account on f. 69.

/*Ciuitas Norwici*/ The accompt of Robert Raynbald and William Hede, chamberleyns of the cite of Norwiche, ffrom the ffest of Seynt Mychaell th'arcangell in the xxxiiij yere of the reign of owur soueraign lord Kyng Henry the viij^te [*29 September 1542*] vntyll the sayd fest of Seynt Mychaell in the xxxv yere of the reign of his sayd mageste [*1543*]: that ys to saye by oon hole yeere & *cetera*

Receptes

/*Arreragis*/ In primis the forsayd accomptantes do charge them selvys and answer for lix *li* iij*s* xj*d ob' qu'* of clere dette of the arreragis of the last accompt [*of*] Wylliam Morront and the forsayd Robert Raynbald, then chamberleyns; and answer for vij *li* iij*s* x*d qu'* of the arrerages of the sayd accompt, whyche as then was not by them levyed, as it apperith more at large in the ende of the same accompt: lxvj *li* vij*s* x*d*
                    Summa lxvj *li* vij*s* x*d*

/*Langoll rent*/ Item they knowlege them selvis that they haue receyuyd of the baly of the manour or late priory of Horsham Seynt Faythe for langoll rent of certen tenementes within the cite parteynyng to the sayd manour: iij*s*; and of the baly of Heylesdon [*Hellesdon*] for langoll rent of a tenement late the duke of Suff': ij*d* – iij*s* ij*d*
                    Summa iij*s* ij*d*

/*Castill ffee*/ Item receyuyd of dyuerse howses & growndes stondyng vpon the ffee of the castill: xxj*s* ij*d ob' qu'*
                    Summa xxj*s* ij*d ob' qu'*

[*f. 41ᵛ*] /*Rent assyse*/ Item receyuyd of rent of assyse of dyuers howsys and groundes within the cite, with vj*d* of newe rent of John Lynne;[403] and xij*d* of John Scarnyng:[404] viij *li* xij*s* v*d ob'*
Item[405]
                    Summa viij *li* xij*s* v*d ob'*

/*Cyte bochers*/ In primis receyuyd of John Howse for the hole yere ferme of the ij fyrst stalles, bothe in oon, in the northe end of the est part of the sayd cite bochers: xxxj*s* iiij*d*; and of Gr[*eg*]ory Fox for iij quarter ferme of the threde [*sic*] stalle toward the south: ix*s*; and of John Tolye for the iiij^te quarter of the same stalle: iij*s* – xliij*s* iiij*d*

---

403 NCR, 18A/6, f. 95ᵛ, notes this was for 'the easement of the archez off the citie walles next Hellegates'.
404 Despite the modest sum involved, considerable attention was paid to the negotiation and sealing of Scarnyng's lease: NCR, 16D/2, ff. 202ᵛ, 203, 204ᵛ.
405 The rest of the entry is blank.

Item of Thomas Toly for the hole yere ferme of the iiij^{te} and v^{te} stalles, bothe in oon: xvj$s$

Item of Thomas Grene for the vj^{te} & vij^{te} in oon: xxiiij$s$

Item of Richard Dey for the viij^{te} and ix^{te} in oon: xxiiij$s$

Item of Robert Savery for the x^{te} stalle: xvj$s$

Item of John Barker for the xj^{te} stalle: xvj$s$

Item of Rychard Newman for the xij^{te} stalle: xvj$s$

Item of Richard [*recte Roger*] Baldry for the xiij stalle: xs

Item of the sayd Roger and Agnes Guyrdler for the xiiij stalle dyvydyd betwyxt them: ix$s$

Item of the [*sayd*] Agnes for the xv stalle, which ys the last of the est part in the southe ende: xxx$s$

Item of Andrewe Dey for the fyrst stalle on the west part of the bochery in the southe ende, with half the second stall dyuydyd betwyxt hym & Fysher: xx$s$

[*f. 42*] **Item** of the sayd John Fysher for the other halff second stalle and for the hole iiij^{de} stalle: xvj$s$ viij$d$

Item of Gregory Pougeleon for the iiij^{te} stalle: xvj$s$

Item of Robert Toly for the v^{te} stalle: xvj$s$

Item of John Barbowur for the vj^{te} stalle: xiij$s$ iiij$d$

Item of Henry Harpowur for the vij^{te} stalle: xiiij$s$

Item of Thomas Broune for the viij^{te} stalle: xiiij$s$

Item of Agnes Cannard for the ix^{te} stalle: xxix$s$

Item of Jeffrey Reed for the x^{te} & xj^{te} stalles in oon: xxxv$s$

Item of Rychard Barne for the xij^{te} stalle: xiij$s$ iiij$d$

Item of Thomas Hubbard for the xiij and xiiij stalles, bothe in oon, beyng the last in the sayd west part in the northe ende: xl$s$

Summa xxj *li* xj$s$ viij$d$

/*Movabyll stalles*/[406] **Item** receyuyd of Andrewe Dey for oon quarter ferme of a movabyll stalle above the guyldhall dore endyd at Crystmes: ij$s$; and of John Saye for oon quarter ferme in the same place endyd at Myhelmes in the ende of thys accompt: ij$s$ – iiij$s$

Item of the sayd Saye stondyng with a bothe in the same place iiij^{or} market days byfore Mydsomer: viij$d$

Item of John Hanson for oon quarter ferme of the second movabyll stalle aboue the guyldhall dore endyd at Candylmes: ij$s$; and of other bochers stondyng in the same place v seuerall days within the tyme of thys accompt: xd – <xd> ij$s$ xd

Item of Edmond Ferebye for the hole yere of the iij^{de} stalle bynethe the guyldhall dore: vij$s$

[*f. 42^v*] **Item** of Gregory Foxe for the iiij^{te} stalle next: vij$s$

---

406 NCR, 18A/6, f. 96–6^v, combines the rents from moveable stalls with those from the city butchers in a single section.

Item of John Barbowur for the hole yere ferme of the v^te stalle, beyng the last on that rowe: viij*s*

Item of Henry Crashfeld stondyng with a movabyll stalle at the northe ende of the iiij^or newe stalles iiij^or seuerall days in harvest tyme: viij*d*

Summa xxxij*s* ij*d*

/*Contre bochers*/ *In primis* of any ferme receyuyd of any of the stalles at the west ende of the guyldhalle in the tyme of thys accompt nothyng by the yere for lacke of fermers; but receyuyd of dyuerse men stondyng ther by the day within the tyme of thys accompt, whos partycler namys do appere in my waster booke: vij*s* j*d*

Item receyuyd off Rychard and Walter Vyncent for the hole yere ferme of iij stalles on the southe syde of the guyldhalle: xl*s*

/*Long Rowe*/ **Item** receyuyd of Edward Rokysby for the hole yere ferme of the fyrst stalle at the northe ende: xx*s*

Item of Rychard Dey the yonger for the hole yere ferme of the last stalle at the southe ende: xx*s*

Item of xxiiij other men for the hole yere ferme of xxiiij stalles betwyxt the forsayd northe end and southe ende of the same rowe, at xvj*s* euery oon of them: xix *li* iiij*s*

/*iiij^or newe stalles*/[407] **Item** receyuyd of Thomas Pollard, Nycholas Holme, Edmond Toly and Wylliam Andrews stondyng in the iiij^or newe stalles dyuers days betwyxt Myhelmes and Crystmes: iij*s* iij*d*

[*f. 43*] **Item** receyuyd of John Wodcocke for iij quarters ferme of the fyrst stalle in the northe ende: ix*s*

Item of Edward Rokysby occupyeng the second stalle iij market days betwyxt Crystmes and Shroftyde: ix*d*; and of Nycholas Baxter for the last halff yere ferme of the same: vj*s* – vj*s* ix*d*

Item of Wylliam Andrews for oon quarter ferme of the ij^de stalle: iij*s*; of Edmond Toly for an other quarter ferme of the same stalle: iij*s*; and for the other quarter nothyng for lacke of a fermer: vj*s*

Item of Edward Rookysby for oon quarter ferme of the iiij^te stalle in the southe ende: iij*s*; and of Rychard Aleston for the last *di'*yere: vj*s* – ix*s*

Summa xxv *li* vs j*d*

/*Ropery*/ **Item** of the ffyrst shoppe in the Ropery nothyng, for <lacke of a> as moche as yt ys in lease with the Murage Loft; and for the second shoppe nothyng for lacke of a fermer; but receyuyd of John Peke for the hole yere ferme of the ij^de shoppe: v*s*

Item of Walter Feere for the iiij^te shoppe: v*s*

Item of Robert Hynderson for the v^te shoppe: v*s*

---

407 NCR, 18A/6, f. 97^v, treats the 'ferme of the litill rowe off stalles late of newe ffixed & couered' as a separate section, with receipts of 34*s*.

Item of Robert Putkase for iij quarter ferme of the vj^te shoppe, the last in the northe ende, nowe occupyed for a bochers stalle at xvs the yere: xjs iijd; and of Henry Carman for the last quarter of the same shoppe: iijs ixd – xvs

Summa xxxs

[*f. 43^v*] /*Fyshe shoppis*/[408] **Item** receyuyd of John Webster for the hole <yere> yere ferme of the fyrst stalle in the northe ende: xiijs iiijd

Item of Jerome Qwashe for the second shoppe: viijs

Item of Thomas Worleton for the iij^de shoppe: viijs

Item of John Brodyshe for the ffyrst halff yere of the iiij^te shoppe: vs; and for the last halff yere nothyng for lacke of a fermer: vs

Item of John Sewell for the v^te & vj^te shopps in oon: xvjs

Item of Nycholas Grene for the vij^te & viij^te in oon: xvjs

Item of Robert Norman for the ix^te & x^te, both in oon: xvjs

Item of Frances Scotte for the xj^te shoppe: viijs

Item of Master Cocke for the xij^te shoppe: viijs

Item of the sayd Master Cocke for the xij shoppe halff a yere: iiijs; for the iij^de quarter nothing for lacke of a fermer; and of Robert Newman for the last quarter: ijs – vjs

Item of Edmond Warden for the xiiij shoppe: viijs

Item of Alyce Cobbe for the xv shoppe: viijs

Item of Stephyn Guyssyll for the xvj shoppe: viijs

Item of John Harryes for the xvij shoppe: viijs

Item of Robert Newman for iij quarters and of Jane Chapman for oon quarter of the xviij stall: viijs

Item of John Crowe for the hole yere ferme of the xix and xx shopps, bothe in oon, and the last in the southe ende: xvjs

Summa viij *li* iiijd

[*f. 44*] /*Wolshoppis*/ **Item** receyuyd of John Lartour for the hole yere ferme of the tenement next the churche style of Seynt Peter with the chambyrs ouer, parcell of the wolshopps: xiijs iiijd

Item of Henry Marlyng for the hole yere ferme of a shoppe vnder the sayd chambyrs, openyng toward the pultry market: xs

Item of Master Quashe for the tenement in the northe ende of the same rowe next the fysh market: xxs

Item of Thomas Croshold for the yere ferme of the fyrst shoppe in the southe ende: vjs viijd

Item of William Patryke for the second shoppe: vjs viijd

Item for the iij^de shoppe for lacke of a fermer: *nullus*

Item of Stephyn Johnson for the iiij^te shoppe: iiijs

---

408 NCR, 18A/6, f. 98–8^v, is extremely confused here, because as well as listing receipts from woolshops in this section, the scribe mistakenly placed the first four entries in the wrong order, at the very end. The introduction of marginal letters 'A', 'B' and 'C' is designed to guide the puzzled reader.

Item of William Parker for the v^{te} shoppe: iiij*s*

Item of Henry Holden for the yere ferme of a shoppe on the west part of a tenement bylongyng to the chantry of John Cosyn grauntyd by lease: v*s*

Item of Wylliam Hede for a vowlte vnder the bochery: v*s*

Summa lxxiiij*s* viij*d*

/*Tenementes and groundes*/ Item receyuyd for ferme of certen tenementes and growndes bylongyng to the comialte lyeng in dyuers places: and fyrst receyuyd of John Thurston for the hole yere ferme of a tenement in the Myddyll Rowe cald the Murage Loft, with the fyrst shoppe in the Ropery grauntyd to hym by lease: xxx*s*

Item <of> of Robert Mayhewe and Henry Holden for the hole yere ferme of an other tenement at the southe corner of the same rowe ageynst the crosse in the market: xiij*s* iiij*d*

[*f. 44*^v] /*Cobler Rowe*/ Item receyuyd of Hewe Coplond for the hole yere ferme of the corner howse in the northe ende: xxiij*s* iiij*d*

Item of Bryan Doront for the myddyll tenement on the same rowe with a forge: xx*s*

Item of Marke Heynes for the ij^{de} tenement with the newe buyldyng: xviij*s* iiij*d*

/*Comon inne*/ Item of Adryan Johnson for the hole yere ferme of the hede place with the newe buyldyng: lxvj*s* viij*d*

Item of John Sewell for the hole yere ferme of a tenement parcell of the sayd comon inne on the west corner of the same: xiiij*s*

Item of Master Nekton, alderman, for the hole yere ferm of a tenement in the paryshe of Seynt Andrewe: iij*s* iiij*d*

Item of Richard Framyngham for a scryptory on the southe syde of the guyldhalle: iij*s* iiij*d*

Item of Margaret Sancroft for an other scryptory: ij*s*

/*Pasture and londes*/ Item of Master Nycholas Sywhat, alderman, for the ferme of a certen grounde, water & fyshynges above the newe mylles: vj*s* viij*d*[409]

Item of John Barbowur for the hole yere ferme of the Butter Hylles: xxvj*s* viij*d*

Item of Master Quashe for the iusment of the comon grounde vnder the cyte walles within Chappell of Feld croftes: xvj*d*

Item of hym for ij acres londe withowt Sent Gyles gates, late Hemmynges: vj*s*

Item[410] of Isbell Mace, wydowe, for a parcell of comon grounde in Seynt Vedastes: xij*d*

[*f. 45*] Item of Syr John Buxton for ferme of a garden in the paryshe of All Seyntes in Be[r]strete: xvj*d*

---

409 NCR, 18A/6, f. 99, records this entry at the foot of the page, a marginal 'A' denoting that the scribe accidentally omitted it from the main text.

410 A manicule with an extended finger points to this entry, as a *nota bene* sign.

/*Clothe halle*/ **Item** of Jone Flyngant, wydowe, for the fyrst *di'* yere ferme of the clothe halle: xiij*s* iiij*d*; and of Richard Flecher for the other *di'* yere: xx*s* – xxxiij*s* iiij*d*

Summa xiij *li* xs viij*d*

/*Tenementes in Conysford*/[411] **Item** receyuyd of John Styngate for the hole yere ferme of the hede place with a kylyarde in Southe Conysford ageynst the comon stathe: xx*s*

Item of Robert Teyton for ferme of the fyrst tenement in the northe ende of the same tenementes: v*s*

Item of John Frances for oon quarter ferme of the second tenement: xv*d*; and of Wydowe Syer for iij quarters ferme of the same tenement: iij*s* ix*d* – v*s*

Item of Nycholas Herden and John Marshall for the hole yere ferme of the iij^de tenement: v*s*

Item for the fyrst quarter ferme of the iiij^te tenement nothyng for lacke of a fermer; but receyuyd of Robert Dawes for the last iij quarters ferme: iij*s* ix*d*

Item of Thomas Purkyn for the v^te tenement: v*s*

Item of Wydowe Rycheford for the vj^te tenement: iiij*s*

Item of Agnes Lambert for the vij^te tenement: v*s*

Item of Wylliam Horne for the viij^te tenement with a parcell of the kylyarde: vj*s* viij*d*

Item of Wylliam Guylbert for the ix^te tenement: v*s*

Item of the executours of Elsabeth Ratlyffe for the fyrst half yere ferme of the x^te tenement: ij*s* vj*d*; for the iij^de quarter nothyng for lacke of a fermer; but receyuyd of John Noon for the iiij^te quarter in the same tenement: xv*d* – iij*s* ix*d*

[*f. 45*^v] **Item** for the fyrst halff yere of the xj^te tenement nothyng for lack of a fermer; but receyuyd of Elsabeth Story for the last halff yere: ij*s* vj*d*

Item of Rychard Starkyn for ij monythis of the xij^te tenement: ix*d*; and for the rest of the yere nothyng for lacke of a fermer: ix*d*

Item of the sayd Rychard Sterkyn for the hole yere ferme of the xiij tenement, the last: v*s*

Summa lxxvj*s* v*d*

/*Pety custom*/ **Item** receyuyd of Robert Collard for the hole yere fferme of the pety custome: v *li* xiij*s* iiij*d*

Summa v *li* xiij*s* iiij*d*

/*Bothes*/ **Item** receyuyd of Bryan Doront for the last half yere ferme of the grownde without the castyll gate to set bothes ther in the tyme of assyse and sessyons: ij*s* vj*d*; and the fyrst *di'* yere nothyng for lacke of a fermer: ij*s* vj*d*

Summa ij*s* vj*d*

---

411 NCR, 18A/6, ff. 99^v–100, incorporates all these entries, without any separate sub-heading, in the previous section.

/*Tenementes in the kynges hondes*/ **Item** receyuyd of Roger Leeke for a tenement in the paryshe of Seynt Benet: iiij*s*; and of Thomas Hast for an other in the paryshe of Seynt Marten at Pales Gate: v*s* – ix*s*

Summa ix*s*

/*Comon stathes*/ **Item** receyuyd of John Styngate for the hole yere ferme of the old & newe comon stathes: xv *li*

Summa xv *li*

[*f. 46*] /*Myllys*/ **Item** receyuyd of Stephyn Empson for the hole yere ferme of the newe mylles with all profyghtes and comodytees there bylongyng: xl *li*
Item of hym for the hole yere ferme of Heyham [*Heigham*] mylles with certen medews, marshys, waters and ffyshynges therto bylongyng: lxvj*s* viij*d*

Summa xliij *li* vj*s* viij*d*

/*Gates and towers*/ **Item** receyuyd of Master Wylliam Rogers, alderman,[412] for a certen annuyte or yerely rent for the dyscharge of tolle and custom at all the gates of the cite & of ij ffayers cald Pencost & Trynyte ffayers: viij *li*
Item of Walter Feer for ferme of a towur by the water syde next Pokethorpe gates: iij*s* iiij*d*
Item of Wylliam Bevys for ferme of a garden vnder the cite walles from the sayd gates to the forsayd towur: v*s*
Item of Hewe Boxford for ferme of a tower next Fybrygge gates: vj*d*
Item of Robert Brown for ferme of the Brasen Towur iij quarters: xij*d*; and for the other quarter nothyng for that the dores be kept opyn: xij*d*

Summa viij *li* ix*s* x*d*

/*Comon halle*/[413] *In primis* receyuyd of Wylliam Almond for an annuall rent or ferme of the howses newe buyldid ouer the gate yerely payd at Crystmes: vj*s* viij*d*
Item of Frances Wolmer for the fyrst halff yere ferme of suche howses as war in lease to hym thys yere: xxx*s* [*Item*] and of hym for the other di' yere awardyd by Master Edward Rede,[414] [*f. 46*ᵛ] Master Steward, Master Codde and Thomas Cony, wardysmen chosen betwyxt the sayd Frances Wolmer and Thomas Wolman: xxvj*s* viij*d*[415]
Item of John Clarke for the hole yere ferme of a gardeyn adioynyng vpon the prechyng yarde: xiij*s* iiij*d*
Item of Robert Foxe for the fyrst halff yere ferm of a tenement newe buyldyd ageynst the ij elmys: xx*s*; and for the other halff yere nothyng for lacke of a fermer: xx*s*

412 NCR, 18A/6, f. 100ᵛ, has the executors of Robert Jannys.
413 NCR, 18A/6, f. 101, refers to 'the late house or priory of Blak Freres'.
414 The scribe has here mistakenly written 'xxx*s*', repeating the previous entry.
415 For the readjustment of this rent by arbitration, see NCR, 16D/2, f. 202ᵛ.

/Gret garden/ **Item** of Master Edmond Wood, alderman, for the hole yere ferme of parcell of the gret gardeyn: x*s*

Item of Wylliam Marche for the yere ferme of ij parcelles of the same gardeyn: xxvj*s* viij*d*

Item of Wylliam Morront for the yere ferme of an other parcell of the same garden: xiiij*s*

Item of Henry Bakon for the ferme of ij howses and a pece of grownde, parcell of the same: xxvj*s* viij*d*

Item of John Byrche for the hole yere ferme of an other parcell of the same gardeyn: xiij*s* iiij*d*

Item of Master Quashe for the yere ferme of an other parcell of the same gardeyn: iiij *li*

Item of John Bakyr for an other parcell of the same: vj*s* viij*d*

Item of hym for ferme of a lane with an howse in the northe ende, whyche lane and howse ys parcell of the sayd comon halle & gardeyn: vj*s* viij*d*

Summa <x>xiiij *li* viij*d*

[*f. 47*] */Tenementes late lord suffrigan/* *In primis* receyuyd of Robert Stephynson for the yere ferme of the fyrst tenement, beyng the corner howse ageynst Tomlond: xxvj*s* viij*d*

Item of Robert Gogney for the second tenement: xiij*s* iiij*d*

Item of Thomas Mosse for the iij^de tenement: xiij*s* iiij*d*

Item of Thomas Callowe for the iiij^te tenement: xx*s*

Item of Richard Coldon for the fyrst quarter ferme of the v^te tenement: ij*s* vj*d*; and of Thomas Cuttyng for the second quarter of the same tenement: ij*s* vj*d*; and for the other half yere nothyng for lacke of a fermer: v*s*

Item of John Suklyng for the vj^te tenement: x*s*

Item of Henry Dey for the vij^te tenement: x*s*

Item of Jeffrey Tybnam for the viij^te tenement, beyng the corner howse next vnto Conysford: xx*s*

Item of Rychard Cocoo for iij quarters ferme of the ix^te tenement; and of Widowe Boys for the iiij^te quarter: ix*s*

Item of Wydowe Kyddell for the hole yere ferme of the x^te tenement, beyng the last: vj*s* viij*d*

Summa vj *li* xiiij*s*

/Foren receytes/ *In primis* receyuyd of dyuerse men of the benevolens goven toward the buyldyng of the newe howsys at the comon halle these sums of money ffolowyng:

And fyrst of Master Thomas Pykrell, alderman: xl*s*

Item of Master Robert Farrowur, alderman: xl*s*

Item of Master Awsten Steward, alderman: xl*s*

[*f. 47*^v] */Benevolens/* **Item** of Master Robert Leche, alderman: xl*s*

Item of Master Wylliam Rogers, alderman: xl*s*

Item of Master Robert Rugge, alderman: xxx*s*

Item of Master Edmond Wood, alderman: xxs
Item of Master Thomas Codde, alderman: xxs
Item of Master John Corbet, esquyer: xxs
Item of Master Lawse, alderman: xs
Item of Thomas Cony: xs
Item of Thomas Marsham: xs
Item of Wylliam Morront: xs
Item of John Cutler: xs
Item of Thomas Moore: xs
Item of Master Castylden, late deane of the cathedralle church of the Trynyte: xxs[416]
Item of Stephyn Raynbald: vjs viijd
Item of Wylliam Sandryngham: iijs iiijd

Summa xix *li* xs

/*Fynes for lacke of apparans*/ **Item** receyuyd of dyuers men for ffynes sessyd vpon them for lacke of apparans at a certen sessyons within the tyme of thys accompt, whose namys and ffynes partyclerly do appere here after:

And ffyrst receyuyd of Edmond Dowsyng: xxs
Item of Rychard Bray, sadler: iijs iiijd
Item of Wylliam Wylkyns, worsted weuer: iijs iiijd
Item of Rychard Bulward, smythe: iijs iiijd
[*f. 48*] **Item** of George Waffe *taylour*: iijs iiijd
Item of Roger Leeke, worsted weuer: iijs iiijd
Item of John Stockton, mercer: xxd
Item of John Bedes, smythe: iijs iiijd
Item of Thomas Grene, mason: iijs iiijd
Item of John Cutler, tanner, for a fyne sessid on hym for an vnlawfull bonde of a prentis: vijs vjd[417]

/*Redempcions*/ **Item** receyuyd of the executours of Adryan Mace toward the buyldyng of the comon halle, for that Seynt Georges brothern dyd not drynke at hys kepyng for, accourdyng to the custome: xxs[418]
Item of the executours of John Plattyng for the dyscharge of the same cause: vjs viijd
Item of Thomas Marsham for the dyscharge of beryng of Seynt Georges ffest: lxvjs viijd

---

416 William Castylden or Castleton (d. 1538) was the last Bendictine prior of Norwich and briefly the first dean of the newly constituted cathedral: J. Greatrex, *Biographical Register of the English Cathedral Priories of the Province of Canterbury c. 1066–1540* (Oxford, 1997), p. 491.
417 See NCR, 16A/5, pp. 126–7.
418 That is because the guild did not mark his exequies in the customary fashion: see NCR, 16A/5, p. 165.

Item of Master Harrydans, treasurer of Cryst Churche, for the dyscharge of the sayd ffest: xl*s*[419]

/*Dettes*/ **Item** receyuyd of Agnes Cannard, wydowe, for the dyscharge of a certen dette dewe to the comialte by Wylliam Cannard, late hyr husbond, for the ferme of a close in Seynt Bertylmews, with the place ther to adioynyng, late Master Browns & nowe sold to Jamys Marsham; and for the dyscharge of a certen *summa* of money grauntyd of benevolens toward the buyldyng of the comon halle by hyr sayd husbond: x*s*[420]

Item of John Barkyr, brewer, for the second /*nullus*/ [*f. 48ᵛ*] payment of lx*s* govyn to the comialte for the dyscharge of iij yeres not to be chosen shreve nor alderman: xx*s*

Item of hym for the last payment of x *li* govyn to the comialte for the dyscharge of the arrerages of hys fathers accompt for the office of the chamberleynshyppe of the sayd cite: lxvj*s* viij*d*

Item of Thomas Brygges for the second payment of xx^ti markes govyn to the comialte for the redempcon and dyscharge of all offyces within the cite: lxvj*s* viij*d*

Summa xvij li ixs ijd

/*Harneys sold*/[421] **Item** receyuyd of dyuerse men for ix harneys sold to them, whose partycler namys hereafter folowe:

In primis receyuyd of Master Thomas Pykrell, alderman, <for> for ij Almayn ryvettes full furnyshyd: xvj*s* iiij*d*

Item of Master Edward Reed, alderman, for oon harnes: vij*s* vj*d*

Item of Master Codde, alderman, for oon harneys: vij*s* vj*d*

Item of Master Davy, alderman, for oon harneys; viij*s* ij*d*

Item of Thomas Grey for oon harneys: viij*s*

Item of Robert Raynbald for oon harneys; vij*s* vj*d*

Item of Wylliam Buxton for oon harneys: viij*s* vj*d*

Item of John Querles for oon harneys: viij*s*

/*Bowes & arrowes*/[422] **Item** of John Bengemyn for a bowe: xx*d*

Item of John Crowe for a bowe: xviij*d*

[*f. 49*] **Item** receyuyd of John Reed, seruant with Master Edward Reed, mayer, for iij halff sheffe of arrowes: iij*s*; and for oon hole sheffe with a casse: ij*s* viij*d*, the whyche war sold to dyuerse men: v*s* viij*d*

Item to John Cotwyn the yonger for a arrowe casse with a guyrdyll: viij*d*

Item of the forsayd Master Rede for a bowe: xviij*d*

---

419 For Plattyng, Marsham and William Harrydans, see Grace, ed., *Records of the Gild of St George*, pp. 24, 150, 152. Harrydans, then a canon prebendary of Norwich cathedral, had formerly been a Benedictine monk there: Greatrex, *Biographical Register*, p. 517.

420 See NCR, 16A/5, p. 154.

421 NCR, 18A/6, ff. 102ᵛ–3, incorporates this section under 'foren receptes'.

422 NCR, 18A/6, f. 102ᵛ, lists these entries under the sub-section 'harneys sold'.

/Other thynges sold/ **Item** of the sayd Master Reede for ij sholvys shodde for water worke, parcell of iij dossen bought at London by Master Lynsted for the comons: x*d*

Item of Roger Bacheler, glasewright, for certen knottes of lede with a lytyll shrof of glasse that by [*sic*] left of glasyng of the comon inne: xvj*d*

Item of Edmond Wardeyn for xj fadam of rede that be left of the reparacon of the market: xvj*d*

Item of Master Awsten Steward, alderman, for parcell of an old roffe at the comon halle and iij or iiij other old peces & a newe lytyll popill plank: vj*s* viij*d*

Item of Master Morrant for viij C lathe lent hym whan he was chosen shreve of the comon store lyeng in the crosse of the market: iiij*s*

Item of hym for a lytyll ende of a planke: ij*d*

Summa **iiij** *li* **xvj***s* **x***d*

/Ryver money/[423] **Item** receyuyd of the constabylles within the cite,[424] by the consent of an assembly, certen sums of money gatherd by them for the reparacon of the ryver dewe in the xxxiiij yere of Kyng Henry the viij*te* [*1542–3*]:

In primis receyuyd of the constabylles of Southe Conysford: iiij*s* ij*d*

[*f. 49*ᵛ] **Item** of the constabylles of Northe Conysford: iij*s* viij*d*

Item of the constabylles of Be[r]strete: viij*s* iiij*d*

Item of the constabylles of Seynt Stephyn: xj*s* iij*d*

Item of the constabylles of Seynt Peter: xx*s*

Item of the constabylles of Seynt Gyles: ij*s* vj*d*

Item of the constabylles of West Wymer: xx*s*

Item of the constabylles of Middill Wymer: xxij*s* vj*d*

Item of the constabylles of Est Wymer: xviij*s* ix*d*

Item of the constabylles of Coslany: xix*s* ij*d*

Item of the constabylles of Colgate: vij*s* xj*d*

Item of the constabylles of Fybrygge: x*s* v*d*

Summa **vij** *li* **viij***s* **viij***d*

/Dettes of accomptes/[425] **Item** receyuyd of Edmond Warden for parcell of the arrerages of hys accompt of the chamberleynshyp: xx *li*[426]

Item of Stephyn Raynbald, surveyor of the obyte landes of Byshoppe Goldwell and Mastres Walters,[427] for parcell of hys accompt: xl*s*

423 NCR, 18A/6, f. 103, incorporates this section under 'foren receptes'.

424 Each of these constables collected from a sub-ward of the city: see *MN*, map 11, p. 167.

425 NCR, 18A/6, f. 103, incorporates this section under 'foren receptes'.

426 See above, p. 111.

427 Lands set aside by James Goldwell, bishop of Norwich (d. 1499), and Joan (d. 1502–3), widow of Henry Curteys and wife of alderman John Walters, for the celeberation of requiem masses: TNA, PROB/11/11/565; NRO, NCC Reg. Popy, ff. 428–9ᵛ.

/*Other dettes*/ **Item** of Mastres Agnes Sutterton, widowe, for the dette of Wylliam Alee, parcell of an C pownde for a mese, late Master Alane Percy, dewe to the comialte by oblygacon at the ffest of the Annuncyacon of Owur Lady in *anno domini* 1542: vj *li* xiijs iiijd

Item of Master Thomas Codde, alderman, for the fyrst halff yere ferme of the comon mucke bote: vs; and of Edward Aleyn for the other halff yere of the sayd old mucke mucke [*sic*] bote, whyche was sore decayed: vjs viijd – xjs viijd

[*f. 50*] **Item** of the sayd Master Codde for certen belles sold at Seynt Vedastes churche: xls[428]

Item of Master Wylliam Rogers, alderman, for the chargis of xx Flemynges kept prysoners in the guyldhall a long season in the tyme of thys accompt,[429] recouerd by hym at London: xiiij *li* ijs jd

Item receyuyd of the comon bakers of the cite for a newe grynt grauntyd of euery comb' corn *ob*': ix *li* iiijs[430]

/*Out of the treasury*/[431] **Item** receyuyd the xxij day of Marche within the tym of thys accompt out of Seynt Georges stocke: xx *li*

Item receyuyd the vj day of Aprelle folowyng out of the sayd treasury and of the forsayd stocke: xiij *li* xiijs iiijd

Summa iiij[xx] viij *li* viijs vd

/*Offrynges and certeyns of guyldes*/[432] **Item** receyuyd of Syr John Kempe, chapleyn of the comon halle, for the offrynges and certeyns of dyuers guyldes[433] kept ther in the tyme of this accompt, whyche partycler guyldes and sums do folowe:

In primis receyuyd of the offryng of *the* paryshe clarkes: iijs iiijd

Item of the shomakers offryng: vs vjd; & of them for a certen: iiijs iiijd – ixs xd

---

428 The parish church of St Vedast had been demolished by the dean and chapter in 1540 and its goods sold off: Blomefield, *Norfolk*, iv, pp. 105–6. On 8 September 1543 Codde's money was assigned by command of the mayor for street paving in Conesford: NCR, 16A/5, p. 179; below, p. 197.

429 On 10 March 1543 the Privy Council authorised a payment of £66 3s 9½d to the mayor of Norwich 'for so moche money disbursed by him and others for the bourding off certeyn Fleminges taken upon the see', that is as enemy aliens: TNA, PC2/1, f. 454.

430 There was considerable resistance to the increased rate and at least two bakers were imprisoned in November 1542 for refusing to pay: NCR, 16A/5, pp. 122–3.

431 These two loans were made 'toward the charges of ffynyssheng of the comon hall': Grace, ed., *Records of the Gild of St George*, p. 149. The guild may have been even more generous. According to Alderman William Clarke, who made copious notes on its history in 1731, it lent £210 6s 8d to the city in 1545, although no reference to this transaction apparently now survives: NCR, 8G/10, Clarke's notes no 1.

432 NCR, 18A/6, f. 103–3ᵛ, incorporates this section under 'foren receptes'.

433 See *RCN*, ii, pp. 310–12, for a list of the guild days and 'certeyns' (annual commemorative masses) of the city's twenty recognised guilds as fixed in 1543, along with their order of processing in civic ceremonies.

Item of the mercers offryng: x*s* xj*d*; and of them for a certen: v*s* – xv*s* xj*d*

Item of the smythis and masons offryng: ij*s* xj*d*; and for a certen: iiij*s* – vj*s* xj*d*

Item of the taylours offryng: v*s* x*d*; and of them for a certen: iiij*s* iiij*d* – x*s* ij*d*

Item of the bed weuers offryng: iij*s* viij*d*; and of them for a certen: iiij*s* – vij*s* viij*d*

[*f. 50ᵛ*] Item of the bochers offryng v*s* j*d*; and of them for a certen: iiij*s* – ix*s* j*d*

Item of the wullen wevers offryng: iiij*s*; and of them for a certen: iiij*s* – viij*s*

Item of the carpenters offryng: ij*s* vj*d*; and of them for a certen: iiij*s* – vj*s* vj*d*

Item of the ffyshmongers offryng oonly: iiij*s* ij*d*

Item of the reders offryng oonly: xx*d*

Item of the goldsmythis, sadlers, calendrers and dyers offryng oonly: ij*s* viij*d*

Item of them for a certeyn: iiij*s* iiij*d*

Item of the worsted wevers for a certen oonly: v*s*

Item of the inkepers offryng and bakers withe brewers: ij*s*; and a certen: iiij*s* iiij*d* – vj*s* iiij*d*

Item of the tanners for a certen oonly: iiij*s*

Item of the hatmakers for a certen oonly: v*s*

Summa v *li* x*s* vij*d*

Summa receptorum ciuitatis CC xlix *li* xx*d* qu'

Summa receptorum omnium forensecorum C xlij *li* xvij*s* viij*d*

Summa totallis omium receptorum CCC iiij*ˣˣ* xij *li* iiij*d* qu'

[*f. 51*] /*Wherof payd*/ by the sayd accomptantes within the tyme of thys accompt for and in dyscharge of the forsayd receytes, as here after folowithe:

/*Rent resolut*/ *In primis* payd in rent resolute as yerely appere in other accomptes, that ys to saye to Syr William Coppyng, chantry prest of John Cosyn, for ferme and rent of dyuerse thynges, as yt appere in the last accompt more at large: iiij *li*

Item to the heyers of Applyardes londes: x*s*

Item to the cathedrall churche of the Holy Trynyte in Norwyche for dyuerse rentes: xviij*s* iiij*d*

Item to the late pryory of Carrowe: xvj*s* viij*d*

Item to the *sayd* late pryory for iiij bushelles whete: ij*s* viij*d*

Item to the hospytall of [*St Mary*] Magdalen [*Sprowston*]: xij*d*

Item to *the* hospytall of Seynt Gyle: xiij*s* iiij*d*

Item to the late pryory of Horsham Seynt Faythe: x*s*

Item to the same late pryory for the tenementes late lord suffrygantes: iiij*d*⁴³⁴

Item to the chappell of the Becke [*Beck, Billingford*]: iiij*s*

Item to the late abbey of Sypton [*Sibton*]: ij*s*

Item to the late abbey of Langley: ij*s*

Item to the manour of Heyham [*Heigham*] for ij acres of londe, late Hemmynges: iiij*d*

---

434 A manicule with an extended finger points to this entry, as a *nota bene* sign.

Item to the same manour for Heyham mylles: lxvjs viijd
Item to the chantry prest of Lettys Payne: vjs viijd
Item to the kynges receyvour for the x^te of the comon halle: ixs
Summa xij *li* iiijs

/*Fees & wages*/ *In primis* payd to Master William Rogers, alderman, occupyeng the offyce of mayer iij quarters; and to Master Edward Rede beryng the sayd offyce oon quarter within the tyme of thys accompt: xx *li*

[*f. 51^v*] **Item** to Master Cocke and Master Davy, shreves, ffor ther holle yere ffee: xxx *li*

Item to Master Edmond Grey for hys ffee, recorder: v *li*

Item to Master John Corbet, steward, for hys ffee: xxs

Item to Master Sergeant Townesend, reteynyd of cownsell with the cite for hys ffee: xls

Item to Master Henry Warde, townclarke, for hys hole yere ffee: iiij *li* vjs viijd

Item payd in the kynges exchekyr for the proffers of Estern and Myhelmes termys: xxs

Item to Anthony Pygot, swordberer, for his hole yere wages: lxvjs viijd

Item to John Reed and Thomas Molle, sergeantes at the mace of master mayer, and to Robert Collard, sergeant of the market, for ther hole yere wages, euery of them xxvjs viijd – iiij *li*

Item the forsayd Robert Collard for a lyuery: xs

Item to Rychard Framyngham for a lyuery grauntyd to hym within the tyme of this accompt: xvjs

Item payd to Robert Raynbald and William Hede, chamberleyns, for the[*ir*] ffee and lyuerys: vj *li*

Item to iij of the iiij^or wayghtes for ther wages and lyuerys, euery of them <xxvjs viijd> /xlvjs viijd/: vij *li*

Item to the iiij^te wayght for halffe yere wages, who dyed after Estern: xiijs iiijd; and to the other newe wayght, who was amyttyd at Mydsomer, toward a lyuery: vjs viijd – xxs

[*f. 52*] **Item** to the sayd iiij^te wayght for hys quarter wages endyd at Myhelmes: vjs viijd

Item to the belman for hys wagys: vjs viijd

/*Annuytes*/ **Item** to Syr John Kempe, prest of the comon halle, ffor his annuyte grauntyd hym out of the same place: vj *li* xiijs iiijd[435]

Item to Mastres Alyce Scolehows, wydowe, for hyr annuytee out of a tenement in the paryshe of Seynt Mychaell of Coslany, late Master Alane Percys: xiijs iiijd[436]

Item to Robert Damme for gatheryng of the bakers grynt newe grauntyd: xs[437]

---

435 NCR, 18A/6, f. 116, this entry appears under 'mynute expences'.
436 NCR, 18A/6, f. 116, this entry appears under 'mynute expences'.
437 NCR, 18A/6, f. 116, this entry appears under 'mynute expences'.

Item to Clement, clarke of the comon halle, for his hole yere wages helpyng the prest ther: xvj*d*[438]

Item to Master Wylliam Rogers, late mayer, for bankettes by hym made to men of honour and worshyppe when they resorte to the cite, grauntyd to euery mayer: xl*s*

Summa iiij^{xx} xvj *li* x*s* viij*d*

Costes and chargis don within the tyme of thys accompt vpon the bocheryes, ffyshestalles, wolshopps, pultry market, guyldhalle and vpon other tenementes in the paryshe of Seynt Peter of Mancroft *& cetera*:

/Januarii/ **In primis** payd in the weke after Twelthe to Nycholas Tuttell, carpenter, for ij days worke at the Murage Loft, mendyng the shoppe wyndows & stalles: xiij*d*
Item to Paschall for ij gret stapylles: iiij*d*

/Marche/ **Item** payd the iij^{de} weke of Lent for ij days worke at the tenement in the pultry market in ferme of Master Qwashe, mendyng the plancher of the vowlte, the stayers and partycon in the shoppe: xiij*d*

/Aprelle/ **Item** payd the vj day of Aprelle to Roger Bacheler, glasewright, for scoryng and newe settyng of all the northe wyndowe at the Murage Loft withe certeyn newe glasse of hys own: xiiij*d*
[*f. 52ᵛ*] **Item** payd the xiiij day for a newe hengyll for Gregory Foxe shoppe dore in the cite bochery and for mendyng of the locke: iij*d*
Item for mendyng the locke on Frances Scottes shoppe dore in the ffysh market: j*d*

/Maye/ **Item** payd to Wylliam Johnson, mason, reysyng vp of the pavement on bothe sydes of the guyldhall within, whyche war sonke, layeng the marbylles currant & settyng the parclosse fast, ij days: xiij*d*
Item to hys laborer, Walter Colles, ij days: ix*d*
Item to Nycholas Tuttell, carpenter, makyng newe feet to the forsayd parclosse & layeng newe joystes vnder the forsayd pavement & mendyn the wyndows in Barnys shoppe in the bochery, iiij days worke: ij*s* ij*d*
Item to Henry Wodrof, laborer, that tentyd to the sayd carpenter and mason, fechyng tymber from the comon halle & other thynges nedefull, and tendyd to an other mason that dyd reparacion at the cokeys, as yt shall appere after ward amonges the cokeys, iiij days: xviij*d*

/June/ **Item** to the forsayd carpenter the second weke after Corpus Christi mendyng dyuers shoppis, stalles and wyndows in the bochery, vj days: ij*s* ij*d*
Item to the forsayd mason rowcastyng and smothyng all the walles and wyndows within the guyldhall, v days worke: ij*s* viij*d* ob'
Item to hys laborer, Walter Colles, v days: xxij*d* ob'
[*f. 53*] **Item** to Henry Wodrof, laborer, vj days that weke, tendyn and helpyng the sayd carpenter and havyng in thake tyle for coueryng of the iiij^{or} newe stalles ij*s* iij*d*

---

438 NCR, 18A/6, f. 154ᵛ, this entry appears under 'costes off the comon hall'.

/The iij^{de} weke after Corpus Christi/ **Item** to the forsayd mason makyng newe benchis in the guyldhall porche and new stayers vp to the chappell, vj days: iijs iijd
Item to Colles, his laborer, vj days: ijs iijd
Item to the forsayd carpenter newe plancheryng the tenement in the pultry market in ferme of Master Qwashe & mendyng many thynges in the same, vj days: iijs iijd
Item to Henry Wodrof, laborer, tendyng to hym and to the mason, vj days, & helpyng to drawe borde: ijs iijd

/The weke byfore Mydsomer Day/ **Item** payd to the forsayd mason rowcastyng and smothyng all the guyldhall porche & vyce vp to the sembly chambyr and fynyshyng all fawtes in the guyldhalle, iiij days thys weke: ijs ijd
Item to Colles, hys laborer, iiij days: xviijd
Item to Wortes, laborer, makyng clene the guyldhalle porche and steyers whan they hade don: ijd
Item to Master Marsham for lyme spent abought the forsayd worke xviij comb' at ijs iiijd the chalder: vs iijd
Item to Henry Sparke for sonde ij lodes: xd
Item to Flowerdewe of Het[h]erset[t] for brycke layd in the crosse of the market for comon store *di'* m¹, wherof part was spent vpon the benchys: iijs
Item payd that weke to Robert Rogers for ffyeng of the jakes in the tenement that Master Qwashe hathe: ijs
Item to hym for makyng the florthe in the vowlte of the same howse parfyght ageyn wher he beryed the <man> menur that came of the same jakes: iiijd
Item for a lode of marle for the same florthe: iiijd
[f. 53^v] **Item** to Wylliam Johnson, mason, and hys laborer, oon day makyng ageyn the pype of the jakes and pynnyng in the stayers in the same howse: xjd

/July/ **Item** payd the weke after Seynt Peter⁴³⁹ to Nycholas Tuttell, carpenter, makyng of a newe pentyse at Redes stall, bocher, oon day; and for ij days more mendyng the stockes in the womens prison, naylyng on of jemews on the shoppe stalles of the Murage Loft and dyvydyng Master Cockes shoppe in the fyshe market in to ij shoppys, with a newe partycon ther: xixd ob'

/The weke after Relycke Sonday/ **Item** to hym makyng a newe pentyse at Hubbardes stalle and Websters shoppe, and an other longe pentyse from Grenys stalle, the bocher, to Saveryes stalle, bocher, vj days: iijs <vjd> iiijd
Item to Paschall for hengylles, hookes, sneckes, cromys, lachys, barrys, cappys, stapylles and suche other leke thynges spent in the forsayd workes, ix *libr' di'* at jd *ob'* j *libr'*: xiiijd
Item for an hengyll for Normans shoppe dore: ijd *ob'*
Item a payer of jemews for the Murage Loft: viijd

---

439 The feast of St Peter *ad vincula* is on 1 August, which suggests that that this reference should be to the feast of Saints Peter *and* Paul on 29 June.

Item a payer of jemews for the stockes in the womens prison, with ij styropps and an hespe: ij*s*

Item for v spekynges occupyed abought the chekyr and parclose in the guyldhalle: iij*d*

Item for a newe key for Tolys shoppe & mendyng the locke & keye of Redes shoppe: iiij*d ob'*

[*f. 54*] /*Cownsell chambyr*/[440] **Item** payd the xxvj day of the same monythe for newe benchys couerd in the cownsell chambyr: and ffyrst payd to Mastres Catlyng for a fether bedde teke, whyche was cutte for bolsters mete *for* the sayd benchys: vij*s* iiij*d*; to John Clarke, cooke, for fethers, ij ston j *libr'* at iij*s* viij*d* ston: vij*s* vij*d*; to Raphe Ibottes for grene kendalle to covyr the sayd bolsters with, vij yardes at x*d* the yarde: v*s* x*d*; to Robert Fenne for cuttyng, gommyng, sowyng, fyllyng and naylyng on: xij*d*; payd for gum: ij*d*; for a rede skynne: iiij*d*; whyte hede nayle *di'* m¹: iiij*d* – *summa* xxij*s* viij*d*

Item payd to Wylliam Hed for an hooke bought by hym for oon of the bochers stalles: j*d*

Summa iij *li* xix*s* iiij*d ob'*

/*iiij*ᵒʳ *newe stalles couerd*/[441] **Item** payd to John Byrche, carpenter, for all the tymbyr worke for the coueryng <for the coueryng> of iiij newe stalles for bochers set vp on the west part of the Long Rowe at the southe ende: that ys to saye for iiij*ᵒʳ* grounsylles, iiij selys, xij postes, viij braces, xxviij copyll sparrys, lvj sparrys feete, iiij*ᵒʳ* sylles, iiij*ᵒʳ* balkes, viij roff bracys, xxij yardes of evys bourde, roffe trees, balffreys, ffynyalles and fflews, with all maner of workmanshyppe and reysyng: lxx*s*

Item for caryage of the tymbyr from Byrchys in to the market at ij lodes: x*d*

[*f. 54ᵛ*] **Item** to Robert Rogers, laborer, for oon day worke makyng holys and helpyng them: iiij*d ob'*

Item to Master Morront for iiij *libr'* spekynges spent ther: vj*d*

Item payd to William Smythe, tyler, for ij days worke tylyng the sayd stalles: xx*d*

Item to Robert Rogers, John Smythe and Wylliam Fox, laborers, euery of them ij days: ij*s* iij*d*

Item to Wylliam Fayer ther iij days pynnyng tyles: xij*d*

Item to Wylliam Hede for tyle pynnys iiij m¹: x*d*

Item lathe was of comon store, but payd to Master Morront for iij m¹ lathe nayle: ij*s* vj*d*

Item lyme iiij comb' to Master Marsham: xiiij*d*

Item sonde a lode to Sparke: v*d*

Item to Osborn of Kyrbye [*Bedon*] for thacke tyle v m¹ at vj*s* m¹: xxx*s*

Item to a poore man that went to Ashewell Thorppe [*Ashwellthorp*] for the tyler: ij*d*

Summa v *li* xj*s* viij*d ob'*

---

440 NCR, 18A/6, f. 106, incorporates this section under 'costes off the bochers stalles', etc.
441 NCR, 18A/6, ff. 105ᵛ–6, incorporates this section under 'costes off the bochers stalles', etc.

/Bochery agen/[442] **Item** payd in the weke after Seynt Bertylmewe to Henry Wodroff and Robert Rogers, laborers, yche of them iij days worke makyng of the florthis in dyuers shopps in the bochery: ijs iijd

Item to Henry Carter for vj lodes clay: ijs vjd

Summa **iiijs ixd**

Memorandum that certen tymbyr, moche bourde and nayle, with other thynges spent abought the forsayd reparacions and here not rehersed, war of the comon store, whose charges do appere amonges the necessaryes bought for comon store *& cetera*.

[*f. 55*] **Costes and chargis** don within the tyme of thys accompt vpon fynyshyng the halle parlowur, buttry, kechyn and other howses newe buyldyd at the comon inne, with pathyng of all the fyrst courte from the strete gate to the outward syde of the crosse stabyll bynethe the walle *& cetera*:

/The fyrst weke after Myhelmes/ **In primis** payd to Henry Wodroff, laborer, makyng of newe florthys with clay in all the forsayd newe howsys, v days worke this weke: xxijd *ob'*

Item to Nycholas Grene, couper, for a newe payle to cary water with to water the howsys and clay: iiijd

Item payd in the market to Brygges of Buknam Carleton [*Buckenham's manor in Carleton-Rode*] for x copyll of sawen sparrys for benchys and partycions to be made ther: vs xd

/The second weke after Myhelmes/ **Item** payd to Nycholas Tuttell, carpenter, makyn a partycon in the buttry and shelvys vyrounde the same howse, vj days: iijs iijd

Item to the forsayd Wodrof, laborer, helpyng the sayd carpenter & besy abought the forsayd florthys, vj days: ijs iijd

/The iijᵈᵉ weke after Myhelmes/ **Item** to the forsayd carpenter for ij days: xiijd

Item to the forsayd laborer ther ij days: ixd

Item to Roger Bacheler, glasewright, for vij foote of newe glasse set vp in the lytyll house next the parlowur: ijs iiijd

Item to hym for ij days worke that weke workyng of old glasse of comon store: xijd

Item to Wylliam Smythe for v payer hookes and hengylles, with certen lachis, sneckes and cromys xviij *libr'*: ijs iijd

Item for ij newe lockes and keys: xd

[*f. 55ᵛ*] */The iiijᵗᵉ weke after Myhelmes/* **Item** payd to the forsayd carpenter for iiij days that weke abought the benchys in the halle & a skrene at the ende of the same: ijs ijd

Item to the forsayd glaser workyng of old glasse for dyuers wyndows ther, v days: ijs vjd

Item for sowde j *libr' di'*: vjd; rosen: *ob' – vjd ob'*

---

442 NCR, 18A/6, f. 105ᵛ, incorporates this section under 'costes off the bochers stalles', etc.

Item sprygge *di'* m^l: iiij*d*

Item candyll spent on evenynges & mornynges syns Myhelmes iiij *libr':* v*d*

/*The* v^{te} *weke after Myhelmes*/ Item payd to Henry Carter for claye layd ther at dyuerse tymes for the florthes vj lode: ij*s* vj*d*

Item on Hallomes to Master Morront for a sheff of Burgony glasse occupyed the weke byfore: xviij*d*

Item to hym for nayle spent ther byfore and to be occupyed in that place oonly of all sortes: and ffyrst for vj*d* nayle *di'* m^l: ij*s*

Item iiij*d* nayle *di'* m^l: xv*d*; iij*d* nayle *di'* m^l: x*d*; ij*d* nayle j m^l: xvj*d* – ij*s* v*d*

Item to Nycholas Tuttell, carpenter, for ij days ther thys weke: xiij*d*

Item to Henry Sparke for caryeng of a lode of tymbyr and old bourde from the comon halle to the comon inne to be occupyed ther: iiij*d*

/*The* vj^{te} *weke after Myhelmes*/ Item to the forsayd carpenter for vj days: iij*s* iij*d*

Item to Henry Wodrof, laborer, vj days: ij*s* iij*d*

Item to Pallyns wyf for flekyn rede for selynges ij fadam: vj*d*

[*f. 56*] /*The* vij^{te} *weke after Myhelmes*/ Item payd to the forsayd carpenter for vj days this weke abought the benchys in the parlowur: iij*s* iij*d*

Item to Wylliam Johnson, mason, castyng of all the howsys within, vj days of hym & his laborer: v*s* vj*d*

Item to Henry Wodroff naylyng of lathe and rede vnder the joystes of all the howses to be selyd, vj days thys weke: ij*s* iij*d*

Item to Mastres Morront [*for*] lathe nayle for the sayd selynges j m^l: x*d*; ij*d* nayle j m^l: xvj*d* – ij*s* ij*d*

Item to Henry Sparke for sonde a lode: v*d*

/*The* viij^{te} *weke after Myhelmes*/ Item to the sayd carpenter for vj days this weke: iij*s* iij*d*

Item to the sayd mason abought the selynges for vj days of hym and Davy, his laborer: v*s* vj*d*

Item to the forsayd Wodroff for vj days: ij*s* iij*d*

Item to Henry Carter for more clay iiij lodes: xx*d*

Item for more fflekyn rede ij fadam: iiij*d*

Item for <ij> iiij *libr'* candyll syns Hallomes: v*d*

Item to Henry Holden for ij C lathe to fynyshe the selynges, for all the rest was of comon store: xij*d*

/*The* ix^{te} *weke after Myhelmes*/ Item to the forsayd carpenter for ij days: xiij*d*

Item to the forsayd mason for v days that weke: ij*s* viij*d ob'*

Item to Davy Scotte and Henry Wodroff, laborers, eyther of them v days: ij*s* ix*d*

Item to Henry Sparke for sonde ij lode: x*d*

Item to Thomas Barchom for small pathyng tyle for the entry of the halle iiij C *di'* at vij*d*: ij*s* vij*d*

Item to Basyngham for j C larger tyle: xij*d*

[*f. 56ᵛ*] /*The xᵗᵉ weke after Myhelmes*/ **Item** payd to Nycholas Tuttell, carpenter, for iiij days thys weke makyng of loopys for dores & wyndows: ij*s* ij*d*

Item to Henry Wodrof, laborer, stoppyng of all the holys betwyxt the sparrys of all the housys of the newe buyldyng, iiij days this weke: xviij*d*

Item for clay ij lode to Henry Carter: x*d*

Item to Adryan, fermer ther, for heye myxt with the morter for all the selynges: ij*d*; strawe to myxe with the claye: *ob'*; whypcord for the stringes of sneckes of dores: *ob'* – iij*d*

/*The xjᵗᵉ weke after Myhelmes*/ **Item** to the forsayd carpenter for iiij days: ij*s* ij*d*

Item to Wylliam Johnson, mason, ij days: xiij*d*

Item to Scotte & Wodroff, laborers, ij days: xviij*d*

Item for candyll to Master Cocke iiij *libr'*: v*d*

Item byrchyn bromys: j*d*; glovers shredes for syse for whytyng of the walles: j*d ob'* – ij*d ob'*

Item to Paschall for vj payer hookes & hengilles with sneckes, cromys & lachys xxiiij *libr'*: iij*s*

Item for vj rynges for dores: xij*d*; ij gret rynges for the halle and parlowur dores: vij*d* – xix*d*

Item for a locke & a stapyll for the halle dore: vj*d*

Item for a loope of yron for the est wyndowe in the halle, with settyng on: xij*d*

Item for yellowe okyr to culler the tymbyr worke in the halle & parlowur bycause yt was old tymbyr, whyche worke the mason dyd, x *libr'*: xv*d*

[*f. 57*] /*The xijᵗᵉ weke after Myhelmes*/ **Item** to the forsayd carpenter for v days this weke: ij*s* viij*d ob'*

Item to the forsayd mason for v days: ij*s* viij*d ob'*

Item to the forsayd ij laborers, v days: iij*s* ix*d*

Item for glovers shredes for syse for the cullers, with bere to grynde them wythe: ij*d ob'*

Item for ij *libr'* candyll to Master Cocke: ij*d ob'*

Item to Henry Holden for lathe j C for the partycon in the buttry: vj*d*; iiij*d* nayle *di'* m¹: xv*d* – xxj*d*

Item to Sparke for sonde a lode: v*d*

Item payd to Roger Bacheler, glasewright, for xlvij foote *di'* of newe glasse set vp in the est wyndow in the halle, and for xxvij foote *di'* in the parlowur, and for vij foote in ij lytyll wyndows on the west syde of the hall and parlowur: *summa* iiijˣˣ ij foote, at iij*d ob'* euery ffoote: xxiij*s* xj*d*

Item sprygge to set vp the sayd glasse *di'* m¹: iiij*d*

Item gaf in reward amonges the carpenters, masons and laborers to drynke ageynst Crystmes: vj*d*

Item payd thys weke to Master Marsham for lyme spent ther syns Myhelmes iij chalder & ij comb'; and to John Goldyng for ij chalder *di'* at ij*s* iiij*d*: xiij*s* v*d*

/*The second weke after Crystmes*/ **Item** payd to Wylliam Johnson, mason, begynnyng to pathe the fyrst courte from the strete gate to the vtter syde of the crosse howse bynethe the welle, v days thys weke: ij*s* viij*d ob'*

Item to Walter Colles and Gregory Akers, his laborers, v days, and Henry Wodroff iij days: iiij*s* v*d ob'*

Item to Nycholas Tuttell, carpenter, for iij days: xix*d ob'*

Item for packthrede for levellyng the pathyng: j*d*

[*f. 57*] **Item** to Henry Sparke for pathyng sonde iij lode: xv*d*

Item to hym for fechyng a lode of pathyn ston from the comon halle: iiij*d*

/*The iij^de weke after Crystmes*/ **Item** to the forsayd carpenter makyng trustylles for tabylles to be set fast in the grownde on bothe sydes the halle and parlowur, vj days: iij*s* iij*d*

Item for ij *libr'* candyll <candyll> spent thes ij wekes: ij*d ob'*

/*The iiij^te weke after Crystmes*/ **Item** to the forsayd carpenter makyng loopes for dores and wyndows for the chambyrs, vj days: iij*s* iij*d*

Item to the forsayd glasewryght for vij foote of newe glasse set vp in [*the*] buttry at iij*d ob'* foote: ij*s* j*d*

/*The v^te weke after Crystmes*/ **Item** to the sayd carpenter for iiij days this weke: ij*s* ij*d*

Item to the forsayd mason abought pathyn, j day: vj*d ob'*

Item to Gregory Acres, laborer, that day: iiij*d*

Item to Walter Colles, laborer, for v days that weke makyng the grownd redy with heynyng ageynst the comyng ageyn of the masons: xx*d*

Item to Henry Wodroff in that worke, iiij days: xviij*d*

Item to a begger, beyng a Flemyn, for one day ther set a worke by the commandment of Master Debyte: iij*d*

Item to Henry Sparke for pathyn sonde ij lode: x*d*

Item for ij *libr'* candyll: ij*d ob'*

/*The vj^te weke after Crystmes*/ **Item** to the sayd carpenter for v days this weke: ij*s* viij*d ob'*

Item to the sayd mason for iiij days *di':* ij*s* v*d*

Item to Grene, hys laborer, iiij days *di':* xviij*d*

Item to Walter Colles and Gregory Acres, eyther of them v days heynyng the grownde: iij*s* iiij*d*

[*f. 58*] **Item** to Henry Sparke for fechyng of a lode of pathyn ston ffrom the comon halle: iiij*d*

Item for pathyn sonde ij lode: x*d*

/*The vij^te weke, the fyrst of Clene Lent*/ **Item** to Nycholas Tuttell, carpenter, makyng loopys for dores and wyndows, vj days: iij*s* iij*d*

Item to Walter Colles and Gregrory Acres coldryng out ston & claryfyeng the voyde grounde on the est syde next Seynt Georges house and makyng it playne as it nowe lyethe, yche of them vj days: iiij*s*

Item to Wylliam Morront for sondry sortes of nayle fechynd of hym at dyuerse tymes syns Crystmes: and fyrst for vj*d* nayle *di'* m^l: ij*s*

Item iiij*d* nayle *di'* m^l: xv*d*; iij*d* nayle ij m^l: iij*s* iiij*d*; ij*d* nayle j m^l: xvj*d*; gret lathe nayle j m^l: x*d* – vj*s* ix*d*

Item to Paschall for vj payer hookes & hengilles, with certen cromys, sneckes & lachis, xxv *libr'* at j*d* ob': iij*s* j*d* ob'

Item for a locke with a key for the buttry dore: vj*d*

Item for vj rynges more for dores: xij*d*

/*The viij*^e *weke after Crystmes*/ **Item** payd to the forsayd carpenter hangyng dores and wyndows & makyng a frame for the washyng place in the kechyn, ij days: xiiij*d*

Item to Paschall for makyng of ij newe yrons of the iiij^{or} old yrons that laye in the chymneys of the halle and parlowur: iiij*d*; more to hym for other ij newe yrons for the other chymney made of his own yron: vij*d* – xj*d*

[*f. 58*^v] **Item** more to hym for sneckes, cromys & lachis ij *libr'*: iiij*d*

Item for a payer of jemews for a closet dore ther: iij*d*

Item to Wylliam Johnson, mason, fynyshyng vp the forsayd pathyng in the yarde, iij days: xix*d* ob'

Item to hym for ij days more makyng a place in the lytyll howse next the parlowur to washe in and layeng in of the forsayd iiij^{or} yrons in the chymneys and fynyshyng vp all thynges in these howses: xiij*d*

Item to Davy Scotte, his laborer, the same v days: xx*d*

Item to Gregory Acres for v days worke that weke brekyng down the walles betwyxt the lambe grounde[443] and the sayd comon inne to make them of a lyke heyght and levellyng the other syde next John Sewelles: xx*d*

Item to Henry Sparke for ij lode sonde for the pathyng: x*d*; & for fechyng of iij lodes of pathyn ston from the comon halle: <x>xij*d* – xxij*d*

/*The ix*^e *weke after Crystmes*/ **Item** to the forsayd Akers fynyshyng vp all the forsayd workes & makyng clene all the groundes in that place, ij days this weke: viij*d*

Item to Roger Bacheler, glasewright, for newe glasse sette up above the mydyll mote of the est wyndowe in the chambyr on the northe ende of the newe buyldyng and above the mydyll mote of the est wyndowe in the chambyr on the southe ende, xv foote in bothe wyndows: v*s*

Item for nayle to set yt vp with: j*d*

[*f. 59*] **Item** to Adryan Johnson for the slytte of hys well rope in the tyme of thys buyldyng, <ther> for makyng of morter ther for that place and for the reparacions in *o*ther places in the market & guyldhalle: iiij*d*

Summa xj *li* vj*s* x*d* ob'

---

443 The messuage known as The Lamb belonged to the guild of St George and the 'grounde' was paved in 1537: Grace, ed., *Records of the Gild of St George*, pp. 101–3, 105, 141.

Memorandum that all other thynges here byfore not rehersed, and most specyally bourde and tymbyr, war all of comon store, the chargis wherof shalbe declaryd here after *& cetera*.

/*Cokeys, stathes, systerns and stretes*/ **In primis** payd the iiij^te day of Novembyr to John Estowe, carpenter, for a pece of tymbyr that he sawed in ij aras peces, wherof the oon was nayled vpon the washyn stathe at Coslany brydge, with all chargis of workmanshyppe: iijs

/*Novembyr*/ **Item** with the other pece was made the steppys out of the kechyn in to the backhowse at the comon halle; and payd the xxiiij day to Robert Tooke & Walter Colles, laborers, fyeng the systern without Westwyke gates, iiij days: ijs viijd
Item payd the xxix day to Robert Foster for caryen of xv lode of mucke from Westweke gates that hade lyen of long tyme vnder the walles ther, whyche lettyd the passage of the pepyll: ijs vjd

/*Decembyr*/ **Item** the ix day to the sayd Foster for caryen of xiij lode mucke that came out of the sayd systern: ijs ijd
Item the xxiij day to young Ketryngham for caryeng of vij lodes mucke from dyuerse cokeys syns Myhelmes: xiiijd
[*f. 59^v*] **Item** to Robert Garrade for caryeng awaye of xxxij lodes from dyuers cokeys that quarter: vs iiijd

/*Februarii*/ **Item** the ix day to *a* laborer that made clene the comon halle lane, one day worke: iiijd
Item to Henry Sparke for caryeng of iiij lodes mucke out of the same lane: viijd
Item for a lode from the cokey ageynst Master Catlyns to Robert Rogers: ijd

/*Marche*/ **Item** payd at Owur Lady quarter to Foster for caryen of xiij lodes mucke syns Myhelmes from Conysford cokey in Seynt Clementes: ijs ijd
Item to hym for iiij^or lodes in that quarter from the cokeys in West Wymer: viijd
Item to Henry Carter for vj lode from Sporyrowe: xijd
Item to Robert Garrade for xxvj lodes from the rest of all the cokeys: iiijs iiijd

/*June*/ **Item** on Corpus Christi evyn for a lode caryeng from Gardners cokey: ijd; and for gren bowes to couer the same cokey on Corpus Christi day whan the processyon came bye: ijd – iiijd
Item payd the second day of June to Wylliam Johnson, mason, makyng a newe arche ouer the cokey in Seynt Clementes in Fybrygge, on day: vjd ob'
Item to hym for an other day mendyng the pavement abought the same cokey and the comon halle lane, whyche was broken with the stagyng at the buyldyng of the buttry and pantry the last yere: vjd ob'
[*f. 60*] **Item** to Walter Colles, his laborer, the same ij days: ixd
Item sonde was of comon store lyeng at the comon inne, but payd for lyme a comb': iiijd
Item payd to Nycholas Tuttell, carpenter, for oon day worke mendyng the frame of Fybrygge cokey and settyng vp of postes for the defense of cartes: vjd ob'

Item to Henry Wodroff, laborer, for oon day caryeng of bryke from the crosse in the market[444] to the forsayd cokey and tendyng to the carpenter: iiij*d ob'*

Item the xv day to John Smythe and an other man, laborers, makyng clene the systern in Seynt Sothons [*Swithin's*] next the ryver, ij days: xxij*d*

Item to the same ij men makyng clene the systern next the ryver at the est ende of Fybrygge keye, takyn agret: xviij*d*

/*The weke before Mydsomer*/ **Item** to a laborer that made clene the stretes vyrownde the comon halle place by the commandment of the vewers of the stretes: iiij*d*

Item for caryeng away of ij lodes mucke from thense: iiij*d*; and payd by the sayd commandment for makyng clene of the stretes ageynst certen comon howsys that stode sperde in dyuerse places of the cite: iiij*d*; and for caryeng of mucke from those places: v- xiij*d*

Item payd to John Walpole, mason, and his laborer for *di'* a day worke mendyng the cokey ageynst Gardners: vj*d*; and to Byrche for a pece of tymbyr for the cokey at Coslany churche: viij*d* – xiiij*d*

[*f. 60*ᵛ] **Item** payd to Nycholas Tuttell, carpenter, for vj days worke that weke mendyng many fawtes at dyuerse cokeys in the cite and makyng all a newe fframe at the forsayd cokey in Seynt Mychaelles & settyng of a gret post at the est corner of Hewe Coplondes howse in Coblerrowe to kepe of cartes and cuttyng of certen spurnys, plankes and other peces of tymbyr for sondry cokeys: iij*s* iij*d*

Item to Henry Wodroff, laborer, for the same vj days tendyng and helpyng the sayd carpenter: ij*s* iij*d*

Item to Paschall for mendyng the grate of the cokey at Seynt Mychaelles of Coslany and for ij newe stapylles for the same and for ij gret spekynges for the post at Coplondes corner: viij*d*

/*Mydsomer quarter*/ **Item** payd the weke after Mydsomer to Wylliam Johnson, mason, for ij days worke that weke settyng in the forsayd fframe at Seynt Mychaelles and pathyng ageyn abought it and mendyng the pavement at the foote of the Whyte Fryers brydge and at other cokeys wher reparacon was don by the forsayd carpenter: xiij*d*

Item to hys laborer, Walter Colles, ij days: ix*d*

Item to Ruddes wyf for caryeng of vj lodes mucke from Sporryrowe cokey this quarter: xij*d*

Item to yonge Ketryngham for caryeng of viij lode mucke from the systern at Fybrygge & for ij lodes from the cokeys in Seynt Marteyns: xx*d*

[*f. 60A*] **Item** to Henry Sparke for caryeng away of oon lode mucke that came of the wedyng of the grounde on the northe syde of the guyldhalle & of an other lode from Seynt Lawrens cokey: iiij*d*

Item[445] to Robert Garrade for caryeng of xlviij lode from the rest of all the cokeys in the cite: viij*s*

---

444   NCR, 18A/6, f. 108ᵛ, has 'caryeng of tyle ffrom the comon hall to the seid mason'.

445   NCR, 18A/6, f. 109, lists the next three entries under a separate sub-heading of 'Julye'.

Item payd the xxj day of Julij to a man that swept all the stretes vyrownd the comon halle place: iij*d*

Item for caryage of ij lodes mucke from thense: iiij*d*

/*Myhelmes quarter*/ **Item** payd at Myhelmes to Walter Harryes for hys hole yere wages kepyng clene and caryen awaye the fylthe from the cokey in Sent Symondes: xvj*d*

Item to Robert Tooke for castyng and kepyng clene of xiiij cokeys all the hole yere, payd quarterly ij*s* iiij*d*: ix*s* iiij*d*

Item to Edmond Orlowe for the hole yere kepyng & castyng the cokey in Conysford: ij*s*

Item to Robert Rogers for iij quarters of a yere kepyng clene and caryeng awaye the fylthe of ij cokeys above the guyldhall dore: <ij*s*> xviij*d*

Item to Andrewe Robynson for hys hole yere wages kepyng clene all the market place from Seynt Johns lane to Coblerrowe and caryeng the fylthe of the same awaye: xiij*s* iiij*d*

Item to Roger Lawse for caryeng of xj lodes mucke ffrom Conysford cokey at dyuerse tymes this yere and to Henry Sparke for iij lodes from Wymer warde this quarter: ij*s* iiij*d*

[*f. 60Aᵛ*] **Item** to Henry Carter for iiij lode caryeng thys quarter from the cokey in Sporryrowe: viij*d*

Item to Robert Garrade for xxxix lode from the rest of *all* the cokeys thys quarter: vj*s* vj*d*

Item to Sandyr Clarke, laborer, for swepyng and kepyng clene all the stretes vyrounde the comon halle and caryeng awaye the fylthe of the same betwyxt Lames and Myhelmes: xij*d*

Summa iiij *li* xiij*s* j*d*

Costes and charges don within the tyme of thys accompt vpon pathyng of certen stretes, lanes and growndes bylongyng to the comialte to pathe by reason of a certen acte made within the cite for pathyng of the stretes *& cetera*:[446]

/*Pathyng in the market place*/[447] *In primis* payd in the weke in whyche Seynt Nycholas ffell in to Wylliam Johnson, mason, pathyng abought the pyllery, whyche was not pathyd byfore, and reparyng of many gret holes in dyuerse places of the market, whyche war sonke by reason of mucke beryed in holys wher sonde was dygyd at the fyrst pathyng of the market,[448] iiij days worke thys weke: ij*s* ij*d*

---

446 According to assembly proceedings in June 1543, the act in question was passed in 1467 during the mayoralty of John Chittock. It provided for the laying of stone pavements to facilitate the drainage of water into the cockeys: NCR, 16D/2, f. 203ᵛ; *RCN*, ii, pp. 96–8.

447 NCR, 18A/6, ff. 109ᵛ–10, has no sub-section for paving the market place, but lists the last five entries under the sub-heading 'the weke after Our Lady Concepcon'.

448 The use of pits in market places for the temporary storage of rubbish and butchers' waste was common, although they were supposed to be emptied regularly: Rawcliffe, *Urban Bodies*, p. 152.

Item to Davy Scotte, laborer, iiij days and to John Bylowe, laborer, iij days: ij*s* iiij*d*

Item to the sayd mason for iiij days in the weke after Seynt Nycholas fynyshyng vp all thynges in the market place: ij*s* ij*d*

Item to Davy Scotte, laborer, iiij days: xvj*d*

[*f. 61*] **Item** to Henry Wodroff, laborer, iiij days: xviij*d*

Item to Henry Sparke for pathyn sonde vij lodes: ij*s* xj*d*

Item to hym for fechyn of pathyn ston from the comon halle v lodes: xx*d*; for fechyng of ij lodes of colder from the comon inne for heynyng: iiij*d*; and for *caryeng* of ij lode of mucke away whan all the workes war don: iiij*d* – ij*s* iiij*d*

/*Coblerrowe*/[449] **Item** payd for pathyn of the lane and the stretes vyrownd the comon howsys in Coblerrowe: and ffyrst payd in the iij^de weke after Corpus Christi day to John Erne, mason, for iiij days: ij*s* viij*d*

Item to Robert Hollond, mason, iiij days: ij*s* iiij*d*

Item to Sandyr Clarke, laborer, iiij days: xx*d*

Item to Robert Yoxhale and John Elles, iiij days: iij*s*

Item to John Elmam and John Erne, laborers, coldryng of pathyn *ston* at the comon halle and caryeng the same in to the strete to be redy to carry to the sayd worke, vj days, at ix*d* day: iiij*s* vj*d*

Item to John Erne and Henry Sparke for fechyn of xviij lodes of the same ston to the sayd worke: vj*s*

Item to Henry Sparke for sonde that weke vij lodes at v*d* the lode: ij*s* xj*d*

/*The weke byfore Mydsomer*/ **Item** to the sayd ij masons for vj days this weke fynyshyng vp all thynges ther: vij*s* vj*d*

Item to the forsayd iij laborers vj days: vij*s*

Item to the forsayd ij laborers at the comon halle vj days coldryng ston: iiij*s* vj*d*

Item for byrchyn bromys: j*d*

[*f. 61^v*] **Item** payd to John Erne and Henry Sparke for fechyng of xiij lodes of ston from thense: iiij*s* iiij*d*

Item to Henry Sparke for sonde this weke ix lodes: iij*s* ix*d*

Item to hym for caryeng a waye of iiij^or lodes mucke out of the lane byfore they beganne to pathe and iij lodes whan they hade don: xiiij*d*

/*Pathyng at Helle gates*/ **Item** payd that same weke to John Walpoole & Crystouer Edmondes, masons, pathyn at Helle gates and vnder the cyte walles as fare as the comon grounde gothe ther, at <xiij> *xiiij*d* the day to guether, eyther of *them* ij days: ij*s* iiij*d*

Item to Nycholas Voyse, Robert Palmer and John Barret, laborers, ij days: ij*s* iiij*d*

Item to John Walpole for vj lodes of pathyn ston: iij*s*; and to John Erne & yonge Ketryngham for fechyng of the same *ston* at the Gray Fryers: ij*s*; and to Henry Sparke for fechyng of ij lodes ston from the comon halle: viij*d* – v*s* viij*d*

Item to hym for sonde iij lodes: xv*d*

---

449   NCR, 18A/6, f. 110, employs the sub-heading 'the iij^de weke after Corpus Christi'.

/Wateryng place ther/[450] **Item** payd the weke after Mydsomer to the forsayd ij masons makyng of a fowndacon at the mowthe of the wateryng place next the newe mylles and pathyng bothe withowt the same & within a certen space to the ryver, ij days: ijs iiijd

Item to the forsayd iij laborers ij days: ijs iijd

Item to yong Ketryngham for caryeng of ij lodes of rowe ston for the fowndacon: viijd

[f. 62] **Item** to Nycholas Tuttell, carpenter, hewyng, sqwaryng and framyng of a long newe tre for a spurne at the waterynges mouthe ther and of an other pece for a post next vnto the pale ther, iij days worke, with layeng and settyng vp: xixd ob'

Item to yong Ketryngham caryeng of the sayd tymbyr from the comon inne: iijd

Item to hym for sonde ij lodes: xd

Item to John Erne for caryeng of iiij^{ior} lodes of ston ffrom the comon halle: xvjd

Item payd that weke to Henry Wodrof, John Elles and Robert Grene, laborers, coldryng of pathyn ston at the comon halle & caryeng of yt in to the strete redy to be caryed to the forsayd worke, euery of them v days, at iiijd ob' the day euery of them: vs vijd ob'

Item to Master Marsham for lyme for the fowndacon afforsayd iiij comb': xiiijd

/Pathyng at the newe mylles/[451] **Item** payd the weke after Seynt Peter to the forsayd ij masons pathyng ageynst all the groundes and yardes of the newe mylles, vj days: vijs

Item to the forsayd iij laborers, vj days: vjs ixd

Item to the forsayd iij laborers coldryng of ston at the comon halle, vj days: vjs ixd

Item to yonge Ketryngham for caryeng of xvj lodes ston from the comon halle this weke: vs iiijd

Item to John Walpoole for xvij lodes of ston from the Grey Fryers at xd the lode with caryage: xiiijs ijd

Item for sonde thys weke xvj lodes: vjs viijd

[f. 62ᵛ] */The weke after Relycke Sonday/* **Item** payd thys weke to the forsayd ij masons for vj days ffynyshyng vp all thynges ther: vijs

Item to the forsayd iij laborers, vj days: vjs ixd

Item to John Walpole for vj lodes of ston from the Gray Fryers with the caryage: vs

Item to yong Ketryngham for caryeng of vj lodes of ston from the comon halle: ijs

Item to hym for sonde x lodes: iiijs ijd

/Pathyng agenst the southe syde of Seynt Peters churche in the market/ **Item** payd the same weke to John Erne, mason, pathyng the comon grounde ageynst Seynt Peters churche, iij days di', at viijd the day: ijs iiijd

Item to Robert Hollond, mason, iij days di': ijs ob'

Item to Wylliam Johnson, mason, oon day: vijd

Item to Sander Clarke, laborer, iij days di', at vd: xvijd ob'

Item to Robert Yoxhale, laborer, iij days di': xvjd

---

450 NCR, 18A/6, f. 110–10ᵛ, employs the sub-heading 'the weke after midsomer'.
451 NCR, 18A/6, f. 110ᵛ, employs the sub-heading 'the weke after Saynt Peter'.

Item to Walter Colles, laborer, oon day: iiij*d ob'*

Item to Henry Wodrof, John Elles and Robert Grene, laborers, for oon day brekyng down a gret hylle that laye ther and caryeng away the menur in to a pytte that was dyggyd for sonde: xiij*d ob'*

Item to the sayd iij laborers for iiij days more that weke coldryng and caryeng of ston at the comon halle for the next pathyng: iiij*s* vj*d*

Item to John Erne for xviij lode of ston from the Grey Fryers with the caryage at x*d*: xv*s*

Item to John Aleyn for slytte of the rope at the comon welle for water to ramme with: j*d*

[*f. 63*] /*Pathyng agenst the duke of Suff' tenementes*/[452] **Item** payd in the weke in whyche Seynt Jamys ffell in for pathyng ageynst the lane and the southe ende of the tenementes late the duke of Suff': and fyrst to John Erne, mason, ij days: xvj*d*

Item to Robert Hollond, mason, ij days: xiiij*d*

Item to Sander Clarke, laborer, ij days: x*d*

Item to Robert Yoxhale, laborer, ij days: ix*d*

Item to John Erne for vij lodes of ston from the Grey Fryers with the caryage: v*s* x*d*

Item to hym for fechyng of iij lode ston *from* the comon halle: xij*d*

Item to Henry Wodrof, laborer, for ij days after all the forsayd places war pathyd vp & the sonde pyttes fyllyd vp with mucke, to levell the groundes and to gravell ouer them that no more mucke shuld be layd ther and to arme ageynst all the newe pathyng that war of the commons cost: ix*d*

Item to John Walpole, mason, pathyng aboute the stalles feete in the market place and above and abought the cokey in Seynt Sothons [*Swithin's*], ij days: xiij*d*

Item to hys laborer for the same ij days: ix*d*

Item to the sweper of the market that made clene abought *the* stalles and caryed away colder thense: ij*d*

Item to John Walpole for sonde and ston spent in these ij places: vij*d*; and *to* hym for a lode of ston govyn by master mayer to Horne the tanner toward the pathyng of the strete byfore hys howse: x*d*; and payd for packthrede spent at dyuerse tymes for levellyng: ij*d* – xix*d*

[*f. 63*v] /*Seynt Stephyns gates*/ **Item** payd in the weke after Seynt Peter for new settyng of the pavement from the vtterpart of the walles withowt Seynt Stephyns gates vnto the chanell on the insyde: and fyrst to Edmond Smythe, Robert Mason, Henry Hanse and Robert Brown, masons, euery of them oon day: ij*s* ij*d*

Item to John Trewe, Robert Ryket, Thomas Heynys and John Tompson, ther laborers: xviij*d*

Item to John Bynham, mason, a day *di'*: x*d*

Item to Andrewe Robynson, his laborer, that day *di'*: vij*d*

Item to Johnsons prentyse and hys laborer for oon day and halff: xvij*d*

---

452 NCR, 18A/6, f. III, employs the sub-heading 'Saynt Jamys weke'.

Item to Henry Sparke for sonde ij lode: x*d*

Item to hym for fechyng of a lode of ston from the comon halle: iiij*d*

Item to John Okes for tymbyr with workemanshype layd without the sayd gates to hold vp the banke, with a laborers worke to convey the water ther in to the dyche, in all chargis: ij*s* iiij*d*

Item to John Erne for ij lode of gret ston with the caryage from the Gray Fryers: ij*s*

/*Pathyng at Tomlond*/ **Item** payd in the weke in whyche Seynt Bartyllmewe ffell in to Master Robert Leche, alderman, for all costes of the pathyng of the comon grounde ayeynst the southe syde of Seynt Georges churche at Tomlond for ston, sond and workmanshyppe: xx*s*

/*Pathyng in Conysford*/ **Item** payd the v*te* day of Septembyr by the agrement of the hole cownsell in the cownsell /*nullus*/ [*f. 64*] howse that day to John Walpoole and his fellows for pathyng ageynst Master Byllyngfordes grounde in Seynt Peters of Conysford takyn by them agret: xxxiij*s* iiij*d*

Item payd to the sayd John Walpoole & his fellows by the commandement of the forsayd cownsell towarde the pathyng ageynst a poore womans howse cald Hemmyng ageynst the Fryer Awstens lane: vj*s* viij*d*

Item yt ys to be notyd that the forsayd xl*s* payd for the ij forsayd pavementes was receyuyd byfore by the accomptantes for certen belles sold by Master Codde at Seynt Vedastes churche: *nullus*

Item payd to Crystouer Emondes, mason, and his ffellows of xxviij yardes ageynst the ij lanys that lede from Seynt Martens at the Bayle downe to Seynt Vedastes next the Fryer Awstens lane at iij*d* the yarde, they fyndyng all maner of stuff and workemanshyppe: vij*s*

Summa xiiij li vijs vd

/*Ryvyr cuttyng*/ **In primis** payd in the weke byfore Mydsomer to Robert Tooke for gryndyng of the comon sheres: x*d*

Item for iij forlockes: iij*d*; for a bast roope: xij*d*; for a newe rubbe: j*d* – xvj*d*

Item for mendyng of oon of the comon orys: ij*d*

Item to Robert Teyton, cutter, for xvj days worke cuttyng of the ryver from Surlyngham ffery vnto the towur without Conysford gates: viij*s*

Item to Nycholas Marshall and Wylliam Bemond, rowers, for the same xvj days, at x*d* the day: xiij*s* iiij*d*

[*f. 64v*] **Item** payd for a bote and ij men to rowe the accomptantes with dyuerse other comyners assygnyd by assembly to Surlyngham ffery, as well to vewe the ryver as ther worke, with mete and drynke for all the company: iij*s* ij*d*

Item to Teyton for oon newe forlocke more and for packthrede to mende ther bast with all: ij*d*

Item gaf in reward to the forsayd iij workmen at ther levyng worke by cause they dyd ther partes well in the same worke: vj*d*

Item to John Oldman for xvj days hyer of hys bote for the sayd cutters: ij*s*

Summa xxixs vjd

Other costes and chargis[453] don within the tyme of thys accompt vpon the ryver within the cite betwyxt the newe mylles and the towur in Conysford medows:

/*The iiij^te day of Maye*/ **In primis** payd to yong Ponyet for hys bote and paynes rowyng Master Rogers, mayer, Master Cocke and Master Davy, shreves, with dyuerse other aldermen and comyners to vewe the ryver: iiij*d*

/*The second day of June*/ **Item** payd for the hyer of iij botes to rowe in Master Rede, than newe mayer, the ij forsayd shreves, with certen aldermen and xxj comyners, besydes the accomptantes and all the offycers: vj*d*
Item for a ferkyn of bere, spyce brede, manchettes, straweberyes, sugyr and wyne for a banket made at Newton Halle [*Trowse Newton*], with ij*s* payd to vj men that rowyd the sayd botes for ther days worke: vj*s* x*d*
[*f. 65*] **Item** payd at the ffery for the bote to fery ouer master mayer with the most part of the same company that came by londe: ij*d*

/*The xviij day of June*/ **Item** payd to ij men that rowyd master mayer with other company in Master Spencers barge to mete with my lord suffrigant at the ffery concernyng the *ryver* ther nere: iiij*d*

/*The xxiij day of June*/ **Item** to Teyton and Marshall rowyng master mayer and others in ij botes to vewe the ryver ageyn betwyxt the Whyte Fryers and Byshopps Gate: vj*d*

/*The weke byfore Mydsomer*/ **Item** payd to John Warde and other ij men with hym with dydalles byfore the mowthe of the systern at the est ende of Fybrygge keye, oon day: xviij*d*
Item to the fermer of the comon mucke bote for his bote and caryeng of the menur: viij*d*
Item to Thomas Mogges, Thomas Paterson and John Smythe with dydalles in Conysford a lytyll bynethe the Fryer Awstens, oon day worke: xviij*d*
Item to the same iij men with theur dydalles for oon other day above Coslany brydge: xviij*d*
Item to Wylliam Horne for his bote the same ij days: iiij*d*

---

453 NCR, 18A/6, ff. 111ᵛ–12, incorporates this section within the previous one ('costys of the rever'), listing the various entries under just four sub-headings: 'the weke beffore midsomer & after', 'the weke after Saynt Peter', 'Maij & June' and 'the weke before midsomer'. Some of the entries clearly relate to a lively debate in the mayor's court on 11 and 13 June 1543 as to how the river might best be dredged. One ambitious proposal, initially accepted, favoured the use of 'bordes & postes in maner of a sluse to stoppe inne the rever by the halff parte, contreyeng the water by the other halff, & so carye with cartes oute of the rever the grevell & suche like that shalbe taken in makyng the rever depper wher shalow places are'. The previous chamberlain, William Morraunt, and three others were, however, deputed to assess the viability of 'another conclusion theryn taken', while James Marsham (chamberlain in 1537–8), who advocated the more conventional use of 'dydalles & botes', was allocated 40*s* to 'approve his aduyce theryn gyven' and stage a trial run: NCR, 16A/5, pp. 167, 168.

Item to the forsayd iij men for the iij^de day, withe sholvis and barrows in the wateryng place next the newe mylles: xviijd

Item to Jamys Marsham for ij stoopys that he bought of Master Wood for the same vse: viijd

Item to Wylliam Hede for other ij stopys that he causyd Lambert to make: iiijd

/*The weke after Seynt Peter*/ **Item** payd to Master Lynsted, alderman, for ij dossen shode sholvis bought at London to be hade in redynes ageynst any worke shuld be don in the ryver: vijs iiijd

[*f. 65^v*] **Item** more to hym for oon other dossen sholvis shodde with stele: vjs; and for freight and all other chargis of them from London to Norwiche: xjd – vjs xjd

/*The weke after Relycke Sonday*/ **Item** payd to John Smythe, laborer, havyng out the damme that was made at the waterynges mouthe nexte Helle gates whan the masons had made an ende ther and scoryng all the sayd mouthe with a dydall and gravelyng the same & caryeng away the menur of the same, iij days: xvd

Summa xxxijs ijd

/*Newe mylles*/ **Item** payd the xix day of Decembyr within the tyme of thys accompt to John Byrche, carpenter, for a crosse pece of tymbyr for the ston at the londe mylle:[454] viijd; and to Stephyn Empson, fermer ther, for workemanshyppe of the same: iiijd – xijd

Item the xvij day of Marche to the sayd Byrche for an other pece for the myddyll mylle and to the myller for workmanshyppe: xijd

Summa ijs

/*Comon stathe*/ **Item** payd the xix day of Decembyr within the tyme of thys accompt for a newe locke and a key for a corn chambyr dore at the comon stathe and for mendyng of the locke of the carte gate by the stretes syde: vijd

/*The weke after Relycke Sonday*/ **Item** to Wylliam Johnson, mason, mendyng iij harthys and iij chymneys in the same place that war very sore dekayed, iij days worke: xixd ob'

[*f. 66*] **Item** to Walter Colles, his laborer, the same iij days: xiijd ob'

Item to Henry Carter for sonde a lode: vd

Item to Jamys Marsham for lyme iij comb': xijd

Item to Styngate for ij C wose brycke and to Dowsyn for j C red brycke: ijs

/*The weke after Seynt Jamys*/ **Item** to Nycholas Tuttell, carpenter, settyng vp of the iiij old postes with brasys and barrys at the ij washyng stathis ther and makyng oon new post to set on the banke next the medowe for the chene[455] and an other newe

---

454 During the sixteenth century there were three separate water mills at the new mills (Appendix III), that nearest the south bank of the Wensum being known as 'the londe mylle'.

455 The chain, which was raised and lowered by means of a capstan, spanned the Wensum at the New Common Staithe, thereby enabling the keeper to control the passage of boats in and out of the city and ensure that tolls were paid: Rodgers, *River and Staithes*, pp. 42, 47–8.

post set in the mydde ryver to hold vp the chene and hangyng of the sayd chene, iij days worke: xix*d ob'*

Item to Henry Wodrof, laborer, helpyng hym: xiij*d ob'*

Item to Paschall for a gret hooke for the post that stonde in the myddowe, a gret stapyll for the post in the mydde ryver, iiij^or ankers to hold the iiij^or postes at the ij stathis, with certen brodes, conteynyng all to guether xxiiij *libr' di'* at j*d ob' libr'*: iij*s* j*d*

Item to Walter Feer for an hempyng rope to <dw> drawe vp the chene with: viij*d*

Item to Bryan Doront, smythe, for a newe chene and a stapyll at the myddyll post in the ryver to hold vp the chene of the ryver: ij*s*

Item for iiij^or gret speckynges for the stathis: iij*d*

/*The weke byfore Myhelmes*/ **Item** to Stephyn Scryvener, glassewright, mendyng the wyndows in the kechyn and parlowur: xvj*d*

Item to Ryngold for an other newe locke and key for a corn chambyr dore ther: vj*d*

Summa xvij*s* iiij*d*

[*f. 66ᵛ*] /*Tenementes in South Conysford*/ **Item** payd the xiij day of Octobyr within the tyme of thys accompt to Paschall for a newe locke and a keye for the vij^te tenement ther: vj*d*

Item lost by the dethe of Elsabeth Ratleffe in the fyrst halffe yere ferme of the x^te tenemente: ij*d*

Summa viij*d*

/*Tenementes lord suffrigan*/[456] **Item** payd within the tyme of thys accompt for reparacions don vpon certen of the tenementes late lord suffrigan: and ffyrst payd the second day of Decembyr to Nycholas Tuttell, carpenter, makyng a newe hatche for the strete dore of the vij^te tenement, with other reparacions ther, ij days: xiij*d*

Item to Paschall for xliiij^ti dyce hede nayle for the same hatche, with a lache and a snecke: xij*d*

Item to Roger Bacheler, glasewright, for viij foote of newe glasse set vp in the same tenement: ij*s* viij*d*

/*The second weke of Lent*/ **Item** payd the forsayd carpenter newe plancheryng ouer the vowlte in the second tenement, iij days: xix*d ob'*

Item to Henry Wodrof, laborer, helpyng hym to shete bourde & to fetche yt from the comon inne the same iij days: xiij*d ob'*

/*The iij^de weke of Lent*/ **Item** to the sayd carpenter for other iij days thys weke fynyshyng vp the sayd plancher bothe in the parlowur, shoppe and buttry, with mendyng of the plancher on the chambyr & makyng a border for the chymney in the parlowur: xix*d ob'*

---

456 NCR, 18A/6, f. 112, lists the first eight entries in this section under 'the ij^de & iij^de weke in Lente'.

Item to Wylliam Johnson, mason, newe pathyng of the harthe and mendyng dyuerse fawtes in the same tenement, ij days of hym & his laborer: xxij*d*

[*f. 67*] Item to Henry Wodrof, laborer, tendyng to the carpenter, fechyng of brycke from the crosse in the market & fechyng morter from the comon halle, iij days: xiij*d ob'*

/*The weke after Mydsomer*/ Item payd to the forsayd carpenter makyng ij lattys dores of thynne bourde for the coueryng of the well at the viij^te tenement and of a newe border for the harthe in the vj^te tenement, ij days: xiij*d*

Item to Wylliam Johnson, mason, <mason> makyng a newe harthe & mendyng other fawtes in the vj^te tenement, oon day of hym & his laborer: xj*d*

/*The weke after Seynt Peter*/ Item to the sayd carpenter for hangyng of the forsayd dores ouer the welle & mendyng the shoppe wyndows, oon day: vj*d ob'*

Item to Paschall for ij payer hookes & hengylles: vij*d ob'*

Item to Wylliam Hede for ffyeng of the same welle, whiche he causyd to be don at Candylmes: xvj*d*

/*The fyrst day of Septembyr*/ Item to Roger Bacheler, glasewright, mendyng the wyndows in the iij^de tenement: iiij*d*

Item to Robert Osborn of Kyrby [*Bedon*] that same day for iij m^l thacke tyle layd in to those same tenementes to be in a redynes ther the next Marche: xviij*s*

Summa xxxiiij*s* xj*d*

/**Gates, towers and brydgis**/ Item payd within the tyme of thys accompt vpon reparacon of dyuerse thynges at towurs and brydges, as hereafter folowith: and fyrst the weke after Mydsomer Day to iiij^or laborers makyng of a cawusey withowt the Brasen Towur from the botom of the dycke levell with the waye, iij days worke, at xviij*d* the day to guether: iiij*s* vj*d*

[*f. 67^v*] Item to John Erne for his horse and carte caryeng of xx lode of menur from an hylle next Jackes pytte^457 to the sayd Brasen Towur for heynyng: xx*d*

/*The xxiiij day of Septembyr*/^458 Item payd to Stephyn Johnson and William Mayer for xxvj yardes of old freston redy wrowte, with halff a boltell, for coueryng of walles: xxv*s*

Item to Roger Davy, keleman, for caryeng of the sayd ston from Byshoppe gates to Coslany brydge: xij*d*; and to a laborer that holpe to lade yt and to vnlade yt: ij*d* – xiiij*d*

/*The weke byfore Myhelmes*/ Item to Thomas Ylward and William Thacker, ffremasons, newe scoryng of the same ston & makyng yt parfyght to be set, iij days worke: iij*s* vj*d*

---

457 Jack's pit was a large expanse of water, rather than a pit in the modern sense, which marked the source of the great cockey in the parish of All Saints, Ber Street: *SLCN*, pp. 13–17; Pelling, 'Health and Sanitation', pp. 13–17.

458 NCR, 18A/6, f. 113, dates none of the entries in this section.

Item to Newell Mayer, mason, settyng of the sayd ston vpon the walles abought the cryckes at Coslany brydge, ij days worke: xiiij*d*

Item to hys lab*o*rer for the same ij days: ix*d*

Item for ij comb' lyme & ij barrowfull of sonde bought at Smythis: ix*d*

Summa xxxviijs vjd

Dyuerse thynges bought[459] in the tyme of thys accompt at the best chepe as the tyme requeryd, to be hade in store in a redynes for reparacions and buyldynges, whiche thynges be not cowntyd byfore in the forsayd reparacions *& cetera*:

/Octobyr/[460] *In primis* payd the x^{te} day of thys monyth to John Howse of Yarmothe for a canspere of ffurre to make a shaft for the howse crome that long to the cyte, with frayght of the same: xj*d*

[*f. 68*] */Decembyr/* **Item** the xxiij day to Henry Marsham of Stratton [*Strawless*] for iiij C sawen pale, with rayles therto bylongyng: ix*s* viij*d*

/Januarii/ **Item** the v^{te} day to Neve of Rynglond [*Ringland*] for iiij^{or} sackes of charcole layd in the guyldhalle for fewall for the cownsell chambyr in cold wether: ij*s*

/Februarii/ **Item** the xxj day to Wylliam Morront for iij*d* nayle j m^l: xx*d*; the same day to Syr John Kempe for a ffurryn laddyr of xxiiij stavyz and an other of xj stavys: iij*s* – iiij*s* viij*d*

/Marche/ **Item** the last day to Brown of Wynfarthyn [*Winfarthing*] for a lode of okyn bourde conteynyng iiij C at iij*s* iiij*d*: xiij*s* iiij*d*

/Aprelle/ **Item** the xiiij day to Thomas Legwood of Sethyng [*Seething*] for a lode of joystes and bourde toguether: that is to saye, xij joystes and xij dry okyn bourdes of xij foote lenght and foote brode: vij*s* iiij*d*

/Maye/ **Item** the xix day to Bolton, servant with Syr John Shelton, knyght,[461] for a lode of lathe at v*d* ob': xiij*s* ix*d*

Item to Wylliam Morront for viij*d* nayle j C: vj*d*

/June/ **Item** to hym the second day for vj*d* nayle *di'* m^l: ij*s*

Item the ix day to Mathewe Barne of Wynfarthyng for a lode of bourde, wherof ther was ij C *di'* of oke and j C xx foote of ashe at ij*s* viij*d* C: ix*s* ix*d*

Item the xvj day to Jube of Bucknam Carleton [*Buckenham's manor in Carleton-Rode*] for xij copyll of sawen sparrys: viij*s*

---

459 NCR, 18A/6, f. 113–13^v, heads this section 'mynute expences'.

460 NCR, 18A/6, f. 113–13^v, lists all the purchases from October to May as a single sub-section.

461 Sir John (d. 1558), the son and heir of the late Sir John Shelton (see above, p. 163 note 386), was not knighted until 1547: *HoP, 1509–1558*, iii, p. 312. He is not mentioned in NCR, 18A/6, f. 113.

Item the xxiij day to John Gage of Moornyng Thorppe [*Morningthorpe*] for ix copyll of sparrys: vj*s*

Item the xxv day to Henry Holden for a newe barrowe with a whele: xij*d*

Item the last day to Wygmer of Tyttyshale [*Tittleshall*] for viij okyn stothis of x foote lenght: iiij*s*

[*f. 68*ᵛ] **Item** more to hym for xij stothys: iiij*s*; ij braces and v threshold peces: xvj*d* – vs iiij*d*

/*Juliï*/ **Item** the iiij*ᵗᵉ* day for newe layeng of *the comon* pykexe: iiij*d ob'*

Item the ix day to Wylliam Morront for nayle fechyd of hym the vj day of June last: and fyrst for iiij*d* nayle *di'* m¹: xv*d*; iiij*d* nayle *di'* m¹: x*d*; ij*d* nayle j m¹: xvj*d* – iiij*s* v*d*

Item more for nayle bought of hym thys present day: and ffyrst for viij*d* nayle j C: vj*d*

Item vj*d* nayle *di'* m¹: ij*s*; iiij*d* nayle *di'* m¹: xv*d* – iij*s* iiij*d*

Item iij*d* nayle *di'* m¹: x*d*; ij*d* nayle *di'* m¹: viij*d* – xvij*d*

Item the xiiij day to the forsayd Wygmer for ij lode of sqware tymbyr: that is to saye xij copyll joystes: x*s*

Item vj copyll stothys: iiij*s*; xij shorte peces for grownsylles and hede stalles for dores: ij*s* – vj*s*

/*Septembyr*/ **Item** payd the xxij day to Brown of Wynfarthyng for okyn bourde a lode conteynyng iiij C foote at ij*s* x*d* C: xj*s* vij*d*

Item the last day to John Sewell for a long espyn ladder, whyche was borowd to the comon halle by Edmond Wardeyn, chamberleyn, & ther broken, of the whyche was made ij ladders: iij*s* iiij*d*

Item to Flowrdewe of Het[*h*]erset[*t*] for j m¹ thacke tyle layd in the crosse of the market for comon store the weke after Wytsontyde: vj*s*

Item to hym for brycke a lode layd ther the vij day of August: iij*s*, whyche brycke & tyle be yet remaynyng ther; and payd to Wylliam Hede for ij C iij quarter brycke borowd of hym: xxij*d* – iiij*s* x*d*

Summa vj *li* xixs *ob'*

[*f. 69*] /*Chargys of iij popylles*/[462] **Item** as wher the master of the hospytall[463] gaf toward the buyldyng of the comon halle ij gret popylles growyng in Master Awsten Stewardes medowe in Seynt Vedastes paryshe, wherof the oon whan yt was ffellyd was hollowe and rotten a gret part, for the which he gaff an other, and so the accomptantes bought the sayd hollowe tre, for the whyche they payd hym: xx*d*

/*Ester weke*/ **Item** hereafter folowith the chargis of the sayd iij trees: and fyrst payd to John Cutler, carpenter, for hewyng and squaryng of oon of the same trees and cuttyng the same in iij stockes, taken agret: xviij*d*

---

462 NCR, 18A/6, ff. 113v–14, incorporates this section under 'mynute expences'.

463 Robert Codde, master of St Giles's Hospital and brother of Thomas Codde, alderman: *MFS*, p. 263.

Item to Henry Sparke for hys tryces and caryage of oon of those stockes to Barchcoms yarde to be sawen for dressers for the kechyn at the comon halle: viij*d*

/*The second weke after Estern*/ **Item** to the sayd carpenter hewyng, squaryng and cuttyng the other ij trees, vj days this weke: iij*s* iij*d*
Item to Peter Folo, sawer, helpyng hym iiij*or* days: xx*d*
Item to Henry Sparke caryeng an other blocke to Barcoms to be sawen: viij*d*; and to hym for the iij*de* blocke, beyng lesser: vj*d* – xiiij*d*
Item to John Stanfeld and John Mayes, sawers, ffor vj days worke thys weke, at xiij*d* the day: vj*s* vj*d*

/*The iij*de* weke after Estern*/ **Item** to the sayd Cutler and Peter Folo for iij days thys weke makyng an ende of hewyng, squaryng and cuttyng, at xj*d* *ob*'a day toguether: ij*s* x*d* *ob*'
Item to Henry Sparke for caryeng of v stockes more thys weke at ij lodes: xij*d*
Item payd for drynke for viij men, beyng in wages at the comon halle and ther an hole day with rolles & instruments, havyng them out of the medowe: iij*d*

[*f. 69*] /*The iiij*te* weke after Estern*/ **Item** to the forsayd Stanfeld and Mayes for vj days sawyng thys weke: vj*s* vj*d*
Item to Henry Sparke for caryeng of iiij lodes of stockes to the pytte thys weke: ij*s*

/*The v*te* weke after Estern*/ **Item** to the forsayd sawers for iiij days this weke: iiij*s* iiij*d*
Item to Henry Sparke for caryeng of iij lodes of plankes and bourde from the pytte to the comon halle the last weke & thys weke: xx*d*

/*The vj*te* weke after Estern*/ **Item** to the forsayd sawers makyng an ende of sawyng, iiij days thys weke: iiij*s* iiij*d*

Summa xxxix*s* iiij*d* *ob*'

/*Chargis of xij okes bought*/[464] **Item** payd to Master Harrydans, treasurer of Crystchurche, for xij okes stondyng in Ambryngale [*Arminghall*] wood at iij*s* iiij*d* the tre withowt the toppe: xl*s*
Item to Sendell of the same town, carpenter, for ffellyng, bryklyng and sawyng of them into xxv stockes, takyn by hym a gret: vj*s* viij*d*
Item to hym for for makyng way in the woode for the cartes to come to them & to helpe to lode them, iij days worke: xij*d*
Item to Robert Wace of E[*a*]rlham and Edmond Bowde for caryeng of <lode> xij lodes of them in to the comon inne yarde at xvj*d* a lode: xvj*s*
Item to Henry Sparke for caryeng of v lodes of them of the grettest at xx*d* the lode: viij*s* iiij*d*
Item to hym for hys takyll & tryces: xij*d*
[*f. 70*] **Item** payd for *di*'a barrell bere for the carters to drynke at ther comyng home and to fyll ther bottelles to the wood, the wether was so extreme hote: xij*d*

---

464 NCR, 18A/6, f. 114, incorporates this section under 'mynute expences'.

Item gaf to iiij^or seruantes of the caryars whan they hade don bycause they labored sore: iiij*d*

Summa iij *li* xiiij*s* iiij*d*

/*Other nessarys provydyd*/[465] **Item** payd within the tyme of thys accompt for other necessaryes provydyd for the vse of the comialte: and fyrst payd the xxix day of Januarii to Nycholas Tuttell, carpenter, hangyng vp of all the harnes in the guyldhalle, whyche was newe dressyd and storyd, and removyng and newe naylyng the iij armys at the est ende of the comon halle, oon day worke: vj*d ob'*
Item for longe nayles for the sayd besynes: iiij*d*

/*The vij^e day of Februarii*/[466] **Item** payd to Nycholas Isborn, goldsmythe, for xl tynne badges for poore pepyll: ij*s* viij*d*; and to Master Robert Leche, alderman, for iij^xx that he causyd to be made: iiij*s*
Item receyuyd of Master Robert Farrour, alderman, xxxix that he hade in kepyng; and ther was remaynyng in the guyldhalle xlv^ti: *summa* of all delyueryd in to the cownsell howse ix^xx iiij – vj*s* viij*d*

/*The xvj of June*/ **Item** payd to Master Rugge, alderman, for the newe statutes bought by hym at London: xvj*d*[467]
Item to hym for a copy of Master Leonard Spencers testament brought out of the byshoppe [*sic*] of Canterberyes regester: xvj*d*[468]
[*f. 70^v*] **Item** to a carpenter for oon day worke makyn of the newe shafft to the howse crome & mendyng the cokey ageynst Master Coddes: vj*d ob'*

/*The xxij day of August*/ **Item** payd <th> to John Cowper of Thorppe [*Thorpe St Andrew*], botewrite, ffor a newe mucke bote in all chargis: iiij *li* iij*s* iiij*d*

---

465 NCR, 18A/6, ff. 114–16^v, incorporates this section under 'mynute expences'.
466 These two entries clearly relate to proceedings in the mayor's court between 10 January and 3 February 1543, when (following an earlier scandal in 1541) the keepers of three of Norwich's former leper houses were found to have abused their position by issuing begging licences to workshy vagrants, in contravention of parliamentary statutes of 1531 and 1536: NCR, 16A/5, pp. 68–70, 130, 131; *MFS*, pp. 203–4. Significantly, just fifty certificates, with a seal bearing the legend 'citie of Norwiche impotent persons', had initially been distributed among the deserving poor in 1531, but, as fraudulent copies proliferated, tin badges seemed to offer a more viable and immediate means of identification: *RCN*, ii, pp. 161–2.
467 NCR, 18A/6, f. 114^v, notes that these unidentified statutes were dated 33 and 34 Henry VIII, namely the first two sessions of the 1542 Parliament.
468 Proceedings of an assembly held at Whitsuntide 1543 confirmed that, although Leonard Spencer (d. 1539), a former town clerk, had 'of his singuler zele, favour & goodmymde which he bare towerd this cite' left a silver gilt basin and ewer for 'garnyssheng' the mayor's house, his son would not surrender them: NCR, 16D/2, f. 203^v. Spencer's will, which constituted a vital item of evidence to be used in court, confirms this bequest, along with others of £20 to clean the river and £100 for the poor: TNA, PROB 11/26/282.

Item for a boxe to cary in certen charters to Cambrydge concernyng the lybertes of *the* cite: ij*d*[469]

Item payd ffor vij quayers of paper delyueryd to Richard Framyngham within the tyme of thys accompt for the cownsell chambyr: xiiij*d*

Item lost in the payment of iiij[or] lyght Frenche crownys payd vnto Master Wylliam Rogers for hys ffee of mayeralte, whyche crownys war receyuyd out of Seynt Georges treasury in the tyme of this accompt: vj*d*

Item payd to Master Trase, alderman, for vj bowes that he bought at London by the commandement of Master Rede, mayer: ix*s*

Item allowid a pore man, Henry Day, oon of the tenantes in the suffrigan howsys, for a pece of tymbyr that he layd in his gardeyn to hold vp the erthe: iiij*d*

Item allowid Robert Gogney, an other tenant ther, toward the reparacon of the hoopys & chenys of ij stoppis seruyng the well of iij tenementes: vj*d*

Item gaff in reward within the tyme of this accompt amonges the cite tenantes: ij*s* vj*d*

Summa v *li* viijs iiij*d*

[*f. 71*] **Presentes govyn**[470] to dyuerse persons within the tyme of thys accompt as hereafter folowith:

/*Master Doctour Buttes*/[471] *In primis* payd the morowe after Corpus Christi day to John Oldman for a gret pyeke: v*s*

Item to Cowper of Bastwycke [*Bastwick*] for an other pyeke and vj gret perchys: ij*s* iiij*d*

Item to Dowsyng for a gret rostyng ele: ij*s* viij*d*

Item to Edmond Pynchyn for hys costes and labowur caryeng the sayd present to Thornege [*Thornage*] to Master Buttes: xiij*d*; and for hys horse hyer to Thomas Davy: viij*d* – xxj*d*

/*Justyces of assyse*/ **Item** payd for a present govyn to the justyces of assyse: and fyrst for swete wyne ij gallons: ij*s* viij*d*

Item wyne sacke ij gallons: ij*s* viij*d*

Item ij pottes with waffers: iij*s* iiij*d*

---

469 On 8 September 1543, Robert Raynbald, as chamberlain, took delivery of charters of Richard II (1378) and Henry VI (1452) exempting citizens of Norwich from the payment of tolls throughout England (and therefore at the Stourbridge fair, staged annually outside Cambridge), for inspection by the mayor and bailiffs of Cambridge: NCR, 16A/5, p. 179. These charters were, in fact, confirmations of an earlier award by Edward II in 1305: *RCN*, i, p. 19; *Calendar of Charter Rolls, V, 1341–1417* (1916), p. 238; *Calendar of Charter Rolls, VI, 1427–1516* (1927), pp. 114–15. For the wider context of such disputes, see Liddy, *Contesting the City*, pp. 42–3.

470 NCR, 18A/6, f. 115–15[v], incorporates this section under 'mynute expences'.

471 [Sir] William Buttes (d. 1545) was physician to Henry VIII, and a leading advocate of the evangelical cause. He was born in Norwich, educated at Cambridge University and accumulated a substantial estate in Norfolk: *ODNB*, ix, pp. 278–9.

Item in waffer cakes v dossen: iijs iiijd

Item to Master Leche for an elle of fyne worsted govyn to my lord Montagewe: xvs

/My lord of Norff'/ **Item** payd to Notyngham of Hyklyng [*Hickling*] for a yong pyper crane: vs; and for caryage to Norwich: iiijd; to Edmond Wolcey for an other crane: vs – xs iiijd

Item to Osborn of Kyrby [*Bedon*] for vj fatte swannis: xviijs

Item for fechyng of them from Kyrby: iiijd

Item for kepyng of them vj days after: xijd

Item to Henry Sparke for ij C ffryers peers: iijs iiijd

Item for a closse mawnde to trusse them in: vjd

Item to Thomas Stephyns for hym selff and iij horses with <fed> peddes, ij days caryeng all the forsayd present to Kenynghale [*Kenninghall*]: vs

[*f. 71ʳ*] **Item** for the costes of Master Peter Rede and of Robert Collard to wayght vpon hym and ther horses to Kenyngale to present my lord of Norff' hys grace: iiijs

Item for the chamberleyns costes ij days rydyn to Langley, Okyll [*Acle*], Luddham [*Ludham*], Hyklyng and other townys for provysyon of the forsayd thynges: ijs

Item payd for parfume to make the cownsell chambyr swete ageynst my lord of Norff' comyng to the cite iij seuerall days: that ys to saye euery day a parfume panne made withe damaske water and clows: xijd; and for parfume candylles euery day: ijd – iijs vjd

Item for mendyng of the comon brushe: jd

Item to a laborer that made clene all the guylhalle ageynst hys comyng: ijd

Item to a man that wachyd hys fyrst comyng vpon Seynt Peters stepyll: jd

Item payd for a purpose pygge govyn to hys grace at hys fyrst comyng at Master Redes howse, than mayer: vijs vjd

Item for a man and an horse that caryed half that purpose to Kenyngale to my lady of Rychemond: xxd;[472] and an other man that caryed the other halff to Intwood [*Intwood Hall*] to my lady Gresham: iiijd[473] – ijs

Summa iiij *li* xvijs vijd

[*f. 71**] */Interludes/*[474] **Item** payd to the erle of Arnedelles players,[475] who playd on Myhelmes day in the begynnyng of this accompt an enterlude in the sembly chambyr of the guldhalle: vjs viijd, wherof was gatherd amonges the aldermen iiijs viijd, and so was payd by the accomptantes: ijs

---

472 Mary Howard (1519–59), daughter of the third duke of Norfolk, who married Henry VIII's illegitimate son, Henry Fitzroy (d. 1536), duke of Richmond, and lived as a widow with her father at Kenninghall: Head, *Ebbs and Flows*, pp. 132–3, 249–50.

473 Isabella, second wife of Sir Richard Gresham, sometime mayor of London and a prominent Norfolk landowner: *HoP, 1509–1558*, ii, pp. 248–50; *ODNB*, xxiii, pp. 760–4.

474 NCR, 18A/6, ff. 114ᵛ–16ᵛ, incorporates this section under 'mynute expences'.

475 The players of William Fitzalan, earl of Arundel (d. 1544): Galloway, ed., *Records of Early English Drama*, p. 357.

Item payd for parfume for the chambyr, whyche saverd sore: ij*d*;[476] and to a laborer that swept the chambyr and made a scafold vpon the fourmes ther: ij*d* – iiij*d*

/*Rewardes*/ **Item** gaf to Wylliam Walby for goyng to Sprowston to desyer Master Corbet to be here with master mayer on Wytson Wedynsday by viij of the clocke: ij*d*
Item gaf to oon of the justyces seruantes at the assyse tyme to commande Master Spencer to come to the ij justyces concernyng hys fathers wylle: viij*d*[477]
Item gaf in reward to a seruant of my lord of Sussex[478] who brought a bucke to master mayer and to hys brothern and comyners: iij*s* iiij*d*

/*Bankettes*/ **Item** payd the xvij day of Septembyr at Richard Flechers for the hole chargis of the sayd bucke etyng by master mayer with dyuerse of hys brothern and certen comyners, with other mete, brede, drynke and wyne, as yt apperithe by a byll of euery particler parcell, to the *summa* of: xxvj*s* ij*d*

/*Sewtes*/ **Item** payd the xix day of Maye to Master Warde, town clarke, for the costes of the sewte for the dyscharge of the homage of the comon halle: xxxv*s* viij*d*[479]
Item for the costes of the sewte of John Cutler and John Revell, foren receyvour, for certen money that they payd to Master Thomas Grewe[480] in the tyme of hys mayeralte: viij*s* x*d*

[*f. 71**] /*Taskes*/ **Item** payd the xx day of Decembyr to the constabilles of Heyham [*Heigham*] next Norwiche for the kynges taske for ij acres of lande withowt Seynt [*Giles*] gates, late Hemmynges: iiij*d*

/*Cowntes*/ **Item** payd the xix day of Maii to Master Toppysfeld of the eschekyr for the costes of the accompt and *quietus est* of Master Layer, late mayer: xxvij*s* v*d*
Item more to hym the xxvj day of Septembyr for the costes of the accompt and *quietus est* of Master Robert Leche, late mayer: xxvij*s* v*d*
Item at the kynges awdyte for a *quietus est* for the x*te* of the comon halle: viij*d*

---

476 NCR, 18A/6, f. 114ᵛ notes that the stench was caused 'by reason of a chymney in the prison wheroff the swote [soot] was brent'.

477 See above, p. 205 note 468.

478 Henry Radcliffe (d. 1557), Lord Fitzwalter and from 1542 second earl of Sussex, who had been married to Elizabeth Howard, half-sister to the duke of Norfolk, and played a prominent part in local politics: *ODNB*, xlv, p. 748.

479 Release of homage was finally granted by the Crown in 1549: NCR, 17B/3, rubricated no 108.

480 On 22 August 1541, the assembly found that, during his recent mayoralty, Thomas Grewe had illicitly retained various sums of money delivered to him for civic use. Despite its recommendation that those who had contributed should be reimbursed, he refused to comply, and on 23 March following declined the offer to make good his debts in annual instalments of £4. Finally, on 12 August 1543, William Rogers, then mayor, persuaded Grewe to repay £20 over the next 15 years and offered personal sureties for his compliance, lodged with Robert Raynbald: NCR, 16A/5, pp. 171–2; 16D/2, ff. 195ᵛ, 197; below, p. 243 note 512.

/*Wrytynges*/ **Item** payd the weke after Estern for ij wrytynges made by Rychard Stenyner to set vpon a boyes hede for pekyng and stelyng: j*d*

Item payd the fyrst day of June to Rychard Framyngham for a *dedimus potestatem* sent vp to London for Master Edward Rede, mayer: ix*s* iiij*d*

Item to hym the xxij day of Septembyr for makyng of a realese for Mastres Kateryne Manne for a tytyll that she claymed to haue in a parcell of the comon halle; and, for as moche as she wold not seale the sayd realese, the accomptant hath not payd hyr xl*s*, whyche was grauntyd hyr by the cownsell of the cite: viij*d*[481]

Item to hym for halff the chargis of xv oblygacions that Master Rogers sealyd to the comynalte for the dette of Master Grewe, alderman: xv*d*

Summa vij *li* iiij*s* iiij*d*

[*f. 72*] /*Purchase*/[482] **Item** payd to Wylliam Arnold of Cromer, gent',[483] for the hole purchase of a tenement in the paryshe of Seynt Mary Lytyll vpon the est corner of the churche yarde ther ageynst Tomlond: xiij *li* vj*s* viij*d*

Item to Master Watson for makyng of a dede wherby Master Awsten Steward, Master Codde and others toke state to the vse of the comialte: viij*d*

Item payd for the chargis of the <reasle> release of hys wyf byfore Master Edward Rede, mayer, and Master Rychard Lee, shreve: iiij*s*

Summa xiij *li* xj*s* iiij*d*

/*Tryvmphis*/[484] **Item** payd to Nycholas Tuttell, carpenter, for vj days worke framyng of xvj newe postes and viij copyll sparrys for a newe frame for the wrostlyng place ageynst Seynt Jamys day: iij*s* vj*d*

Item to vj laborers brekyng down of a butte in the castill dyche and framyng of a newe wrostlyng place, makyng of the butte newe at the est ende & cuttyng the hylles for the pepyll to sytte on, euery of them ij days, at iiij*d ob'* a day: iiij*s* vj*d*

---

481 Katherine Mann had lived as a recluse at the Norwich Blackfriars until the house's dissolution. On 23 May 1543, 'by the medyaconz of hir frindes & for a parfite quyetnez', she was offered 40*s* by the authorities 'for recompens & satisfaccon of suche title & interest & term' as she retained in her anchorhold, 'although in dede [she] haue but small colour therto': NCR, 16A/5, p. 155. The matter was finally settled in her favour in 1548, when she relinquished her title in return for an annuity of 20*s*. As a 'synglewoman' she was granted licence to remain in Norwich two years later, 'so long as she shall kepe her shoppe and be soole and vnmarryed': NCR, 16D/2, ff. 224ᵛ, 234. The best account to date of her remarkable intellectual, social and ecclesiastical circle may be found in M. Erler, *Women, Reading, and Piety in Late Medieval England* (Cambridge, 2002), pp. 100–6, although neither Erler or any of the other authors who discuss her career mentions this incident.

482 NCR, 18A/6, f. 116, incorporates this section under 'mynute expences'.

483 William Arnold (fl. 1553) owned a substantial estate in and around Cromer and Smallburgh: Blomefield, *Norfolk*, viii, pp. 103, 106; G.H. Dashwood, ed., *Visitation of Norfolk in the Year 1563* (2 vols, Norwich, 1878, 1895), ii, p. 309.

484 NCR, 18A/6, ff. 114ᵛ–15, incorporates this section under 'mynute expences', with the sub-heading 'wrestlyng place & Saynt Jamys daye'.

Item to the forsayd carpenter for ij days worke settyng the forsayd postes and rayles vp and makyng of a bothe: xiij*d*

Item for newe lyne: v*d*; pakthrede: j*d*; halff m^l bochers pryckes: ij*d* – viij*d*

Item for makyng of a tevell⁴⁸⁵ and for paper and lyne for the same tevell: vij*d*

Item for a botfull of sedge for strowyng of the bothe and game place: viij*d*

Item to ij men that wachyd the bothe ij nyghtes: viij*d*

[*f. 72*^v] /*Seynt Jamys day*/ **Item** payd for ryngyng of Seynt Peters gret belle to gyf knowlege to the aldermen and constabylles to be redy at an howur: iiij*d*

Item to iij men, wherof ij kept the gate of the game place and the iij^{de} kept the buttry: xij*d*; and for ther dyners and suppers that day: xij*d* – ij*s*

Item to Brownis man, jaylour, helpyng to bryng xij fourmys from the castyll yarde & to cary them home ageyn, whyche his master lent vs: ij*d*

Item to Master Homerston for the hyer of viij teltes for the coueryng of the bothe: ij*s* viij*d*

Item to Wylliam Hede for the losse that he hade in a rede bedde, whyche he lent to lyne the bothe and was ther sore torne: ij*s*

/*The next day*/ **Item** to the forsayd carpenter takyng downe of the sayd bothe and wroslyng place & markyng euery pece of tymbyr to be knowyn howe to set them vp yerely after, oon day worke: vj*d ob'*

Item to ij laborers helpyng ther the same day: ix*d*

Item to Henry Sparke for caryeng of all the tymbyr from the comon inne to the castyll dyche & for caryeng home ageyn to the guyldhall: viij*d*

Item payd for newe canvas for ij apuruns for the ij gyantes: ij*s* ij*d*; for peyntyng of them: xvj*d*; for peyntyng of Mary Gorgeyn: ij*s*; and to iij men that bare them: xij*d*, all which went the same day by commandment – vj*s* vj*d*

                    Summa **xxvij*s* iij*d* ob'**

[*f. 73*] /*Prysoners*/⁴⁸⁶ **Item** payd to Robert Barnard, jaylour, for the bourde of xx Flemynges that war sent from Yarmothe on Myhelmes evyn byfore thys accompt beganne for ij days bourde in hys tyme: iij*s* xj*d*

Item payd to Rychard Flecher, jaylour in the tyme of thys accompt, for the bourde of the sayd xx^{ti} Flemynges vij^{xx} iiij days, endyd the xix day of Februarii, at ij*s* j*d* euery day: xiiij *li* xvij*s* xj*d*

Item payd to Master Corbet for the chargis of a man and an horse to the kynges cownsell with letters concernyng the sayd xx^{ti} Flemynges kept here in pryson: xvj*s* ij*d*

Item payd for makyng clene of the pryson after ther delyuery, with caryeng away of ij lodes mucke: viij*d*

---

485 Nelson, *Medieval English Stage*, p. 128, states that the 'tevel' was a model of a devil. The context suggests a board, perhaps bearing such an image, used as a target at the archery butts or for some type of game.

486 NCR, 18A/6, f. 116–16^v, incorporates this section under 'mynute expences'.

Item payd the xx day of Januarii to iiij^or of the shreves offycers for ther costes and peynys caryen ix Scotes that came from Lynne [*King's Lynn*] to Norwyche to se them conveyed to Yarmothe: viij*s*; and for ther dyners and the Scotes byfore they went forthe: ij*s* – x*s*

Summa xvj *li* viij*s* viij*d*

Summa totallis omnium solucionum ciuitatis hoc anno CC xviij *li* iiij*s* iij*d*[487]

[*f. 73^v*] *Memorandum* that here after and last of all dothe folowe the cost and charge don in the tyme of thys accompt at the comon halle in buyldyng of these parcelles folowyng:[488]

In primis a newe kechyn out of the grownde, makyng of ij newe ovyns in the backhowse, with moche other worke and transposyng in the same howse

Item ffynyshyng of a wete larder with newe dores, wyndows, shelvys and many other thynges necessary to the same

Item ffynyshyng a dry larder or prevy kechyn in all thynges leke maner

Item pathyng of the courtes betwyxt all the sayd howses

Item makyng a newe welle out of the grownd with a condyte from thense to the boylyng offyce

Item ffynyshyng of a boylyng howse with ledes, systern and other thynges necessary for that howse

Item ffynyshyng of a dresser howse with all thynges necessary ther

Item makyng of a newe jakes out of the grownde in the backe courte with fense walles of ston vyrownd the same

Item conveyng awaye of *a* lane out of the strete in to all the forsayd offyces and scolehowse ther nere with fense walles of ston

Item ffynyshyng the buttry and pantry with shelvys, berers, brede hutchis and other thynges parteynyng to them

Item ffynyshyng the halle with castyng, smothyng & whytyng the walles and makyng rayles for hangyng vyrounde the same

Item makyng of x benchys with seates and backes with fourmys, trustylles and a sqware cubbard

Item makyng of a newe fowndacon and a mayne walle from the grownde vp in the arche betwen the halle and the stepyll

Item dyuerse necessaryes made and bought for the chappell

[*f. 74*] Item certen reparacions don vpon the tenement nere the ij elmys

Item certen reparacions don vpon the halle and chappell in the ledes

Item certen reparacions don vpon the buttraces in the prechyng yarde

---

487 NCR, 18A/6, f. 116^v, does not provide a separate total for expenditure at this point.

488 NCR, 18A/6, f. 116^v, does not provide an itemised list of work undertaken. This stage of the rebuilding campaign followed an initative by the assembly, on 11 August 1542, for the 'settyng ffor warde' of plans for 'the ffurnyssheng of certen housez off offices to be had at the new hall': NCR, 16D/2, f. 199^v.

Item pathyng of the courte betwyxt the strete gate and the halle

Item castyng Master Kempys newe howse in a culler

Item many other thynges don thys yere in dyuerse partes of the same place, whyche war to moche here to reherse, but more at large they shall appere

/*The* iij*de* *weke after Myhelmes*/[489] *In primis* payd to Nycholas Tuttell, carpenter, abought takyng down of the old rovys and planchers on the southe syde of the cloyster, wher of part was fallen down byfore, iij days: xix*d ob'*

Item to Henry Wodrof, laborer, the same iij days: xiij*d ob'*

Item payd the same weke at Yarmothe to old Mastres Byshoppe for ij dossen furryn sparrys for stagynges: v*s*

Item for freyght of them to Norwyche: iiij*d*

Item to Robert Foxe, fermer to the tenement agenst the ij elmys, for a barre, a stapyll and ij cappis for *the dore at* the ende of the dorter to be closse: iiij*d*

Summa viij*s* v*d*

/*The* iiij*te* *weke after Myhelmes*/ **Item** to the forsayd carpenter shoryng the planchour ouer the backhows wher the gabill was take down, takyng out the braces of the dormantes & conveyng other ij dormantes out of the same howse, oon day: vj*d ob'*

Item to certen laborers, some takyng downe the gabyll betwyxt the backhouse & the yarde, whiche ys nowe the kechyn, & some takyn down old chymneys in that place to haue brycke redy to buyld the kechyn: and fyrst to John Elles, v days: xxij*d ob'*

[*f. 74ʳ*] **Item** to John Sterlyng, Gregory Acres, Sander Clarke and Henry Wodrof, euery of them v days, at iiij*d ob'* a day euery man: vij*s* vj*d*

Item for ij *libr'* candyll this weke for evenynges *and* mornynges: ij*d ob'*

Summa x*s* j*d ob'*

/*The* v*te* *weke after Myhelmes*/ **Item** payd thys weke by the agrement of Master Rogers, mayer, and dyuerse other of his brothern to Frances Wolmer for a scaldyng lede, ij trows, a brayen stocke, with all the plankes vyrownd the backhowse ther: xxvj*s* viij*d*

/*Masons*/ **Item** to John Erne begynnyng the fowndacon of the kechyn, iiij days, at vij*d* the day: ij*s* iiij*d*

Item to Wylliam Johnson and Wylliam Hollond, yche of them iiij days, at vj*d ob'* a day: iiij*s* iiij*d*

Item to Thomas Ylward, fremason, begynnyng to set the jalmys of the chymneys, ij days: xiiij*d*

---

489 NCR, 18A/6, ff. 116ᵛ–21ᵛ, lists all expenses on the common hall in one single section, broken down into weekly sub-sections which contain far less detail, especially regarding the names of workmen and purveyors. Nor is any attempt made, as here, to indicate at a glance what was paid to specific types of craftsmen.

/*Laborers*/ **Item** to Sander Clarke, Robert Yoxhale, Davy Scotte, Gregory Acres and Henry Wodrof, euery [*of them*] iiij days, at iiij*d ob'* a day euery man: vij*s* vj*d*

/*Carpenters*/ **Item** to Nycholas Tuttell tendyng to the masons, ij days that weke: xiij*d*
Item to John Estowe and John Spyrlyng makyng a pentyse on the stretes syde all along the newe tenement ageynst the ij elmys & layeng of a planke byfore the stall of the shoppe, makyng ij pentyses on the garden syde, a newe courbyll to the welle and many other thynges ther, eyther of them iiij days: iiij*s* iiij*d*
[*f. 75*] **Item** to the sayd John Estowe for a newe dore stalle set at the chymneys ende in the kechyn goyn in to the backhowse: xx*d*

/*Tylers*/ **Item** to Robert Smythe tylyng of all the forsayd pentyses, iij days, at vj*d ob'* the day; and to Walter Colles, his laborer, iij days, at iiij*d ob'*: ij*s* ix*d*
Item to William Hede for ij m¹ tyle pynnys: v*d*
Item to Wylliam Morront for j m¹ lathe nayle: x*d*
Item to Henry Sparke for sonde spent in all the forsayd workes thys weke iiij lodes: xx*d*
Item for iiij *libr'* candyll thys weke: v*d*
                              Summa lv*s* ij*d*

/*The vj^te weke after Myhelmes*/ *Masons*/ **Item** to John Erne, mason, vj days: iij*s* vj*d*
Item to Robert Hollond, Wylliam Johnson and John Walpoole, euery of them vj days: ix*s* ix*d*
Item to Crystouer Stalam, apprentyse, vj days, at v*d ob'* the day: ij*s* ix*d*
Item to Thomas Ylward & Wylliam Thacker, fremasons, euery of them vj days: <vj*s* vj*d*> vij*s*

/*Laborers*/ **Item** to Yoxhale, Acres, Scotte, Jube, Wood, Clarke, laborers, euery of them vj days: xiij*s* vj*d*
Item to Henry *Sparke* for sonde this weke vj lodes: ij*s* vj*d*
Item to hym for caryeng away ij lodes mucke: iiij*d*

/*Carpenters*/ **Item** to John Byrche for makyng of the water gate next the sopehowse of the comon stuffe & for a loope to the same of his own stuffe: v*s* iiij*d*
Item for barrys, cappis and stapylles for the same gate with certen nayles made for the same: x*d*
Item for pack threde & nayles for the masons: iij*d*
[*f. 75ᵛ*] **Item** for iiij *libr'* candyll thys weke: v*d*
                              Summa xlvj*s* ij*d*

/*The vij^te weke after Myhelmes*/ **Item** to John Erne, mason, for vj days: iij*s* vj*d*
Item to Robert Hollond & John Walpole vj days and to Crystouer Stalam, prentyse, vj days and to Ylward, fremason, oon day: ix*s* x*d*

/*Laborers*/ **Item** to Yoxhale, Acres, Clarke, Jube, Wood & Elmam, laborers, euery of them vj days: xiij*s* vj*d*
Item to Henry Sparke for sonde vij lode: ij*s* xj*d*

Item for iiij *libr'* candyll thys weke: v*d*

Item to Smythe of Seynt Lawrens for iij stagyng hyrdylles: xij*d*

Item for a bast roppe for woldes: xij*d*

Item vpon an other agrement made by master mayer and hys brothern this weke with Frances Wolmer, for that we shuld haue parcell of his howse and close hym out, as it is nowe < closyd> closyd, ther was delyueryd to hym ageyn the lede with all the yron therto belongyng that we bought of hym the v^te weke after Myhelmes, and also payd hym in money: x*s*

Summa xlij*s* ij*d*

/The viij^te weke after Myhelmes/ **Item** to John Erne, mason, vj days: iij*s* vj*d*

Item to Hollond and Walpole vj days: vj*s* vj*d*

Item to Crystovyr Stalam vj days: ij*s* ix*d*

Item to Ylward, fremason, v days: ij*s* xj*d*

[*f. 76*] */Laborers/* **Item** to Yoxhale, Acres, Clarke, Jube, Elmam, Wood & Gladen, euery of them vj days: xv*s* ix*d*

Item to Henry Sparke for sonde vj lodes: ij*s* vj*d*

Item for candyll iiij *libr'* this weke: v*d*

Item to Master Davy, alderman, for a Spanyshe barre of yron conteynyng lviij *libr'* to make an ankyr for the chymney on the right honde of the kechyn dore: iij*s* viij*d*

Item to Paschall for workmanshyp of the same: xx*d*

Item to hym for oon newe hengyll for the kechyn dore, with ij newe hookes conteynyng vj *libr' di'*: x*d*

Item to Stanford of Heyham [*Heigham*] for j C thacke to be in a redynes agenst any sharpe *wether* shuld come to covyr <the workes> the workes with: xv*d*

Item to <to> John Ernys, carter, to feche it at the the [*sic*] newe mylles: iiij*d*

Item for eerys & hoopyng the water tubbys: ij*d*

Item for pecyng of the bell ropys and for a newe badryke for oon of the belles in the stepyll: iij*d*

Summa xlij*s* vj*d*

/The ix^te weke after Myhelmes/ **Item** to John Erne, mason, for v days: ij*s* xj*d*

Item to Robert Hollond & Walpole v days: v*s* v*d*

Item to Crystouer Stalam, apprentyse, v days: ij*s* iij*d ob'*

Item to Ylward, fremason, v days: ij*s* xj*d*

/Laborers/ **Item** to Sander Clarke & John Elmam v days: iij*s* ix*d*

Item to Yoxhale, Acres, Jube, Colles and Newell Wood, euery of them v days: viij*s* iiij*d*

Item to Henry Sparke for sonde iiij lodes: xx*d*

Item to Ketryngham for oon lode sonde: iiij*d*

Item for viij *libr'* candyll thys weke: x*d*

[*f. 76^v*] */Carpenters/* **Item** to John Byrche and all hys *men* takyng down the crucyffyxe: xij*d*; and to Richard Cotes for hys cownsell and helpe: iiij*d* – xvj*d*

Item spent in brede & drynke amonges the carpenters, masons, laborers & strangers, besyde abought the takyng down of the sayd crucyfyxe: iiij*d*

Item to Nycholas Tuttell, carpenter, for oon day ther this weke cuttyng of byllettes and helpyng down of the forsayd <cry> crucyfyxe: vj*d ob'*

Item for packthrede to bynde rede abought the ffreston pyllers in the kechyn to save *them* from the wether: j*d*

Summa xxxs ix*d*

/*The x*ᵗᵉ *weke after Myhelmes*/ **Item** to John Erne, mason, iiij days: ij*s* iiij*d*

Item to Hollond & John Walpoole iiij days: iiij*s* iiij*d*

Item to Crystouer Stalam, apprentyse, iiij days: xxij*d*

/*Laborers*/ **Item** to Sander Clarke & John Elmam iiij days: ij*s*

Item to Yoxhale, Acres, Jube, Colles and Henry Grene, euery of them iiij days: vj*s* viij*d*

Item to Henry Sparke for sonde iiij lodes: xx*d*

Item candyll iiij *libr'* this weke: v*d*

Item to Master Trase for j C lathe for the inclosyng of the newe chymneys with rede for the wether: vj*d*

Item payd this weke to Master Davy for an other Spanysh barre of yron conteynyng *di'* C ix *libr'* to make an other anker for the chymney next the boylyng howse: iiij*s*

Item to Paschall for workmanshyp of the same: xxij*d*

Item payd in the market for byrchyn bromys: j*d*

[*f. 77*] **Item** to Paschall for makyng of a newe pykex of ij peces yron that be left of the ij forsayd Spanyshe barrys, the whyche pykex was govyn to John Elmam in restytucon of a pykex of his that was stollen ther in a dyrke evenyng: iiij*d*

Item to Andrewe Qwashe for an other bast rope for woldes for stagynges at the gabyll in the halle: xij*d*

Summa xxviij*s*

/*The xj*ᵗᵉ *weke after Myhelmes*/ **Item** to John Walpole, mason, vj days: ij*s* iij*d*

Item to Robert Hollond ij days: xiij*d*

Item to Crystouer Stalam vj days: ij*s* ix*d*

/*Laborers*/ **Item** to John Elmam, laborer, vj days: ij*s* iij*d*

Item to Yoxhale, Acres, Jube, Grene, <and Colles> euery of them vj days, and to Colles ij days: viij*s* viij*d*

Item to Henry Sparke for sonde iiij lodes: xx*d*

Item to Nycholas Tuttell, carpenter, for ij days thys weke cuttyng of byllettes, leyng of thresholdes and shortnyng of dores & dore stalles: xiij*d*

Item to Robert Raynbald for ij newe stoppys redy made with hoopys and chenys of yron for the new welle: vj*s*

Summa xxvj*s* ix*d*

/*The xij*ᵗᵉ *weke after Myhelmes*/ **Item** to John Walpoole, mason, iiij days: ij*s* ij*d*

Item to Crystouer Stalam iiij days: xxij*d*

/*Laborers*/ **Item** to John Elmam and Gregory Acres v days: iij*s* ix*d*

Item to Robert Yoxhale v days, to Nycholas Jube and Henry Grene iiij days: iiij*s* iiij*d*

Item gaf in reward amonges the laborers: vij*d*

Item to Henry Sparke for sonde a lode: v*d*

Item for ij *libr'* candyll the last weke & ij *libr'* this weke: v*d*

[*f. 77*ª] **Item** to Clement, the clarke of the chappell, for iiij *libr'* candyll for the chappell all thys winter: v*d*

Item to Adryan Johnson for byllettes hade of hym to make cletes for stagynges: ij*d*

/*Lyme this quarter*/ **Item** payd to John Goldyng for lyme receyuyd from Byshoppe gates syns Myhelmes xj chalder *di'* at ij*s* iiij*d*: xxvj*s* x*d*

Item to Walter Fere for lyme receyuyd from Fybryggat viij chalder vj comb' at ij*s* iiij*d* the chalder: xx*s* v*d*

Item to Master Marsham for v chalder *di'* at ij*s* iiij*d*: xij*s* x*d*

/*Tymbyr worke*/ **Item** to John Byrche, carpenter, for a dore stalle for the kechyn and a lyntell for the same: iiij*s* viij*d*

Item for iij dresser [*howse*] wyndows: iiij*s* viij*d*

Item for a lyntell for the grettest wyndowe: xij*d*

Item for workmanshyppe of the mantyltrees for the iij chymneys in the kechyn, of the comon stuffe, and havyng vp of them: xx*d*

Item for the dore stalle, with a loope, betwyxt the scaldyng howse and the dresser [*howse*]: iij*s* iiij*d*

Item for the gret gate stalle in the entry, with an hanse, wherof part was of the comon *stuffe* and part of hys own stuffe, & for workmanshyppe: ij*s*

Item for a newe grownsyll for the dore betwyx the halle and the stapyll, and a lyntell: ij*s* iiij*d*

Item for trymmyng of the sayd grownsyll: xij*d*

Item for a courbyll for the newe welle: iij*s* iiij*d*

Item to Paschall for *yron* worke abought certen lockes and settyng on ageyn: v*d*

Summa iiij *li* xix*s* vij*d*

[*f. 78*] /*The fyrst weke after Crystmes*/ **Item** master mayer and dyuerse of his brothern dyd make couuenant with John Byrche the second day of Januarii for the makyng of x seates betwyxt the pyllers in the halle, with backes and dobyll benchys, and he to haue for them xj *li*; and gaf hym for a Godes peny this present day: iiij*d*

Item payd that weke for the hole charges & workmanshyppe of a newe stathe set vp at the water gate next Master Stewardes sope howse: xx*s*

Item to Paschall for xiiij spekynges for the same: ix*d*

Item to Andrewe Qwashe for a bast rope for the newe welle next the kechyn: xij*d*

Item to Robert Yoxhale and Nycholas Jube for fyeng of the newe welle to the water, iij days worke: ij*s*

Item to Sanders dowter [*daughter*] that holpe them the same iij days to empty ther stopps: iij*d*

Summa xxiiij*s* iiij*d*

/*The seconde weke after Crystmes*/ **Item** to John Erne, mason, fynyshyng vp the newe welle, pathyng of the courte wher the *well* ys & makyng a gutter from the welle in to the strete, v days ther thys weke: ij*s* xj*d*

Item to Robert Hollond, mason, v days: ij*s* viij*d ob'*

/*Laborers*/ **Item** to Sander Clarke & John Elmam v days: iij*s* ix*d*

Item to Robert Hoode iij days: xij*d*

Item for pakthrede and byrchyn bromys: ij*d*

Item for iiij *libr'* candyll these ij wekes: v*d*

Item to Henry Sparke for pathyn sonde ij lode and morter sonde oon lode: xv*d*

Summa xij*s* ij*d ob'*

[*f. 78ᵛ*] /*The iij*ᵈᵉ *weke after Crystmes*/ **Item** payd to Thomas Ylward and William Thacker, fremasons, hewyng and squaryng the baces of the fete of the pyllers in the halle to make them fytte for the carpenter to rayse the benchis, ij days: ij*s* iiij*d*

/*Laborers*/ **Item** to Sander Clarke, John Elmam & Henry Wodroff levellyng the cloyster,[490] vj days: vj*s* ix*d*

Item to Gregory Acres for vj days: ij*s*

Summa xj*s* j*d*

/*The iiij*ᵗᵉ *weke after Crystmes*/ **Item** payd thys weke to the forsayd iij laborers brekyng down the walles ouer the cloyster on the northe syde of the halle and levellyng all the long courte on the sayd northe syde of the halle to make the water to avoyde the sayd courte, vj days: vj*s* ix*d*

Item to Gregory Acres for the same vj days: ij*s*

Summa viij*s* ix*d*

/*The v*ᵗᵉ *weke after Crystmes*/ **Item** to John Erne, mason, smothyng all the newe gabyll betwyxt the halle and stapyll, iiij days thys weke: ij*s* iiij*d*

Item to Wylliam Johnson iiij days: ij*s* ij*d*

Item to Robert Hollond & John Walpole v days: v*s* v*d*

Item to Crystouer Stalam, apprentyse, v days: ij*s* iiij*d ob'*

Item to John Erne for oon day more brekyng of flynte redy for the blacke wall of the kechyn: vij*d*

/*Laborers*/ **Item** to Sander Clarke & John Elmam v days: iij*s* ix*d*

Item to Robert Yoxhale & Jube v days: iij*s* iiij*d*

Item to Gregory Acres iiij days: xvj*d*

Item to Henry Wodroff for oon day: iiij*d ob'*

[*f. 79*] **Item** payd to Acres for old clowtes to wash the newe gabyll in the halle & for byrchyn bromys: ij*d*

Item to Henry Sparke for sonde ij lodes: x*d*

Item for iiij *libr'* candyll spent these iij wekes past: v*d*

---

490 NCR, 18A/6, f. 118, notes that they were also 'makyng clene the housez'.

Item to Walter Feer for kylle ston for the blacke walle of the kechyn iij lodes: ij*s* vj*d*
Item to John Erne for fechyng of yt: xij*d*
Item to John Byrche in party of payment for the x benchys in the halle: xl*s*
Item more to hym by the commendment of the hole cownsell of the cite toward the fynyshyng of Master Kempys howse: xl*s*
Item to Thomas Goche for nayles fechyd by the masons for stagynges and steyes: ij*d*

Summa v *li* vj*s* viij*d*

/*The vj*^te *weke after Crystmes*/ **Item** to John Erne, mason, v days: ij*s* xj*d*
Item to Robert Hollond & John Walpoole v days: v*s* v*d*
Item to Crystouer Stalam, prentyse, v days: ij*s* iij*d* ob'

/*Laborers*/ **Item** to Sander Clarke for v days: xxij*d* ob'
Item to Robert Yoxhale, Nycholas Jube, Thomas Moone and Davy Scotte v days: vj*s* viij*d*
Item to Henry Sparke for sonde ij lodes: x*d*
Item payd for ij lytyll barrelles to cary water in for washyng of the newe gabyll: iiij*d*
Item to John Erne for v m^l wose brycke: xxvj*s* viij*d*
Item gaf to a man of Plompsted [*Plumstead*] to go to Blof[*i*]eld to send vs a man that made hyrdylles: j*d*

Summa xlvij*s* j*d*

[*f. 79*^v] /*The fyrst weke *of Lent*, the vij*^te *after Crystmes*/ **Item** to John Erne, mason, abought the blacke walle of the kechyn, vj days: iiij*s* vj*d*
Item to Wylliam Johnson, Robert Hollond and John Walpole, euery of them vj days: ix*s* ix*d*
Item to Crystouer Stalam, prentyse, vj days: ij*s* ix*d*

/*Laborers*/ **Item** to Sander Clarke pynnyng the blacke walle, vj days, at v*d* the day: ij*s* vj*d*
Item to Henry Wodrof & John Elmam vj days: iiij*s* vj*d*
Item to Robert Yoxhale, Davy Scotte, Nycholas Jube and Thomas Moone vj days: viij*s*
Item to Walter Feere for brekyng ston iij lodes: ij*s* vj*d*
Item to John Erne for caryeng of the same: xij*d*
Item to Henry Sparke for sonde vj lodes: ij*s* vj*d*
Item to Wylliam Morront for iij*d* & iiij*d* nayle delyueryd to Byrche byfore Crystmes for makyng of the loope of the water gate: ij*d*
Item to Paschall for a lytyll grate of yron that stonde byfore the gutter that ronne from the welle thorowe the kechyn: iiij*d*
Item for packthrede for the masons: j*d*
Item for nayles for stagyng: j*d*

Summa xxxvij*s* viij*d*

/*The viij*^te *weke after Crystmes*/ **Item** to John Erne, mason, v days: ij*s* xj*d*
Item to to [*sic*] Robert Hollond and Walpoole v days: v*s* v*d*

Item to Crystovyr Stalam v days: ij*s* iij*d ob'*
Item to Sander Clarke, pynner, v days: ij*s* j*d*

[*f. 80*] /*Laborers*/ Item to Walter Colles, pynner, v days: ij*s* j*d*
Item to John Elmam, Robert Yoxhale, Thomas Mone & Nycholas Jube <& Henry Wodroff> v days: vj*s* viij*d*
Item to Henry Wodroff ij days *di'*: xj*d ob'*
Item to Henry Sparke for sonde iiij lodes: xx*d*
Item to Walter Feere for brekyng ston ij lodes: ij*s* vj*d*
Item to John Erne for caryeng of the same: xij*d*
Summa xxvij*s* vij*d*

/*The ix*te *after weke* [*sic*] *Crystmes*/ Item payd the iij*de* Sonday of Lent to Sander Clarke for goyng to Blof[*i*]eld to hast home ij dossen hyrdilles that war spoken for ther: ij*d*
Item on the Monday next to John Jeffreys of Bloffeld for the sayd ij dossen hyrdylles: vj*s*
Item to Robert Harryes of the same town for bryngyng of them to the comon halle: xiiij*d*
Item to John Byrche in party of payment of the x benchys in the halle: xl*s*
Item to John Erne, mason, vj days: iij*s* vj*d*
Item to Robert Hollond & John Walpole vj days: vj*s* vj*d*
Item to Crystouer Stalam vj days: ij*s* ix*d*
Item to Wylliam Johnson, mason, iiij days: ij*s* ij*d*
Item to Sander Clarke & Walter Colles vj days: v*s*

/*Laborers*/ Item to Yoxhale, Moone <Elmam> & Jube vj days: vj*s*
Item to John Elmam vj days: ij*s* iij*d*
Item to Davy Scotte & Gregory Acres iiij days: ij*s* viij*d*
Item to Henry Wodroff iij days: xiij*d ob'*
Item to Henry Sparke for sonde v lode: ij*s* j*d*
[*f. 80*ᵛ] Item to Nycholas Tuttell, carpenter, for oon day this weke cuttyng the dormantes in the back howse & removyng the balke above the chymney: vj*d ob'*
Item for nayles for stagyng: j*d*
Summa iiij *li* ij*s*

/*The x*te *weke after Crystmes*/ Item payd for a newe pulley for the newe welle: iiij*d*
Item to Paschall for yron worke for the same: xv*d*
Item to Master Wardon for v C lede to make ij ledes for the scaldyng howse: xx*s*
Item to Asterby, plomer, for workyng of the sayd ledes, at xvj*d* C: vj*s* viij*d*
Item for caryage & recaryage of the same lede: vj*d*
Item for ij hoopys for the same to William Cowper: xx*d*
Item for lede nayle to Mother Curson: iiij*d*

/*Masons*/ Item to John Erne, mason, vj days: iij*s* vj*d*
Item to Johnson, Hollond & Walpoole vj days: ix*s* ix*d*
Item to Crystovyr Stalam vj days: ij*s* ix*d*

/*Laborers*/ **Item** to Sander Clarke & Henry Wodrof vj days: iiij*s* vj*d*

Item to John Elmam vj days: ij*s* iij*d*

Item to Yoxhale, Akers, Colles, Moone, Scotte & Jube, euery of them vj days: xij*s*

Item to Henry Sparke for sonde ix lode: iij*s* ix*d*

Item to Paschall for an anker of yron for the balke ouer the pastry howse that lye next the chymney conteynyng xiiij *libr*: xxj*d*

Item to hym for iij C brodes *for* the x benchis in the halle: iij*s*

[*f. 81*] /*Carpenters*/ **Item** payd to certen carpenters begynnyng to take downe part of the dorter roffe to frame yt for the kechyn roffe: and fyrst to John Byrche for v days, at x*d* day bycause he to*ke* charge of the worke: iiij*s* ij*d*

Item to Rychard Cootes for v days, at x*d* the day bycause he toke lyke charge of the sayd worke: iiij*s* ij*d*

Item to Wylliam Wynde, Andrewe Brown, Richard Cotes the yonger and Nycholas Tuttell, euery of them vj days, at vj*d ob'* a day: xiij*s*

Item to John Byrche the yonger and John Felbrygge, eyther of them v days: v*s* v*d*

Item to Thomas Wattes for iiij days: ij*s* ij*d*

Item payd to John Byrche the Satterday in this weke in party of payment of the x benchys in the halle: xl*s*

Item the same day to Master Kempe, the prest, for v rownde barrys of yron and certen yron roddes, with the whyche roddes & barrys war made the wyndows in the ij larders, which all toguether dyd conteyn iij*ˣˣ* xv *libr*: vj*s* iij*d*

Item payd for drynke on day thys weke for the carpenters, whyche labored sore & in gret jopardy havyng down the beamys & pryncypalles: iij*d*

Summa **vij** *li* **ixs vd**

/*The xj*ᵗᵉ *weke after Crystmes*/ **Item** payd on the Monday in the same weke to Master Pyndern, prest, for x copyll sawyn sparrys, iiij joystes, vj copyll stothis, viij sparrys endes of an ell long, ij plankes and a dore stalle inbowyd, all newe, whyche thynges dyd gret servyce in the forsayd buyldynges: xiij*s* iiij*d*

[*f. 81ᵛ*] **Item** to Paschall for xxxiiij hookes of yron layd in the walles abought the halle for the rayles of the hangynges, whyche conteynyd lviij *libr'* at j*d ob'*: vij*s* iij*d*

Item to hym for ij gret boltes of yron to anker in the joppe and the ij pryncypalles at the ende of the dorter next the lybrary, with brodes ther to: xiiij*d*

Item to hym for lenthyng out of v barrys of yron for oon of *the* wyndows for the wete larder: v*d*

Item to hym for cuttyng and makyng of xvj roddes fytte of a lenght for other iij wyndows for the sayd larder howsys, whiche yron was bought of Master Kempe, the prest, as yt appere byfore: iiij*d*

/*Masons*/ **Item** to John Erne, mason, vj days: ij*s* vj*d*

Item to Johnson, Hollond & Walpoole vj days: ix*s* ix*d*

Item to Crystovyr Stalam vj days: ij*s* ix*d*

Item packthrede for the masons: j*d*

Item to Henry Sparke for sonde vij lodes: ij*s* xj*d*

/*Carpenters*/ **Item** to John Byrche the elder for iiij days: iijs iiijd

Item to Richard Cotes the elder vj days: vs

Item to John Byrche the yonger, Richard Cotes the yonger, John Felbrygge, Andrewe Brown, Wylliam Wynde and Nycholas Tuttell, euery of them vj days, at vjd ob' day: xixs vjd

Item to Thomas Wattes iiij days: ijs ijd

Item to the forsayd John Byrche and Rychard Cotes for ther cranys and slytte of ther takyll and roppys, yche of them xijd: ijs

Item for ij lytyll barrelles more to carry in whytyng for the newe gabyll in the halle: iiijd

[*f. 82*] /*Laborers*/ **Item** payd to Clarke, Wodroff, Elmam, Acrelles, Colles, Yoxhale, Moone, Jube and Scotte vj days all, at iiijd ob' a day euery of them: xxs iiijd

Item gaf thys weke to Gregory Acres bycause he was hurte in the same worke: iiijd

Item to Paschall for newe layeng of the forsayd Acres pykexe and of the comon pykexe: ijd

Item to yonge Ketryngham and Henry Carter for x lodes claye for the florthis of the larders: iiijs ijd

Item for bromys in the market: jd

Item to John Byrche for a gutter pece that lye from the well to the kechyn dore: xvjd

Item for bourde abought the welle: xvjd

Item to hym for ij newe wyndows inbowd stondyng in the blacke walle in the kechyn: viijs

Item for ij lyntelles for ij gret wyndows ther: ijs iiijd

Item for the inbatyd wyndowe ouer the kechyn dore: iiijs; and for the wyndowe in the scaldyng howse made with barrys of yron: xvjd – vs iiijd

Item for the dore stalle for the wete larder: iijs

Item for the dore stalle out of the kechyn into the scaldyng howse: ijs viijd

Summa vj *li* ijs xd

/*The xij*^te *weke after Crystmes cald Dome Weke*/ **Item** to the forsayd John Byrche in party of payment of the x benchis in the halle: lxs

Item to Wylliam Morront for iiijd nayle *di'* m^l: xvd

Item for iijd nayle j m^l: xxd

[*f. 82*^v] **Item** to Master Gurney of Conysford for dry okyn bourde iij C *di'* xv foote at iijs iiijd C: xijs jd

Item to Wylliam Wynde for small pathyne *tyle* xij C *di'* at vjd C: vjs iiijd

Item for ashyn shydes to make hoke naylys: jd

/*Yron worke*/ **Item** to Paschall for iiij hookes layd with byllettes in the wete larder for the rayles to hang on mete conteynyng vij *libr' di'*: xjd

Item for layeng of the comon pykexe: jd

Item for yron grates for the wyndowe in the scaldyng howse conteynyng lvj *libr'* at jd ob': vijs

Item for an yron of owur own stuffe made *by* hym for the same wyndowe: iijd

/*Lyme*/ **Item** to Goldyng and Herryson for lyme receyuyd from them syns Crystmes xiij chalder at ij*s* iiij*d* the chalder: xxx*s* iiij*d*

Item to Walter Feere for lyme receyuyd from hym in the same tyme xij chalder: xxviij*s*

Item to Clement the sexten [*sexton*] makyng the chappell, the walles & the ymages clene agenst Ester, whyche war sore fowlyd: iiij*d*

Item spent in drynke on Good Fryday at nyght amonges the carpenters whan they reysed vp the beamys of the kechyn: ij*d*

Item payd on Ester evyn to the forsayd Master Gorney for iij C *di'* xxj foote more of corser bourde at ij*s* viij*d* C: ix*s* x*d*

[*f. 83*] /*Masons*/ **Item** to John Erne, mason, vj days: iij*s* vj*d*

Item to Johnson, Hollond and Walpole vj days: ix*s* ix*d*

Item to Crystovyr Stalam vj days: ij*s* ix*d*

Item to Henry Sparke for sonde iiij lodes: xx*d*

/*Carpenters*/ **Item** to John Byrche the elder ij days, at viij*d*: xvj*d*

Item to Richard Cotes the elder vj days, at viij*d*: iiij*s*

Item to John Byrche the yonger, Richard Cotes the yonger, Wylliam Brown, Andrewe Wynde, Nycholas Tuttell, John Felbrygge, euery of them vj days: xix*s* vj*d*

Item to Thomas Wattes ij days: xiij*d*

/*Laborers*/ **Item** to Clarke, Wodroff, Elmam, Acres, Colles, Yoxhale, Moone, Jube and Scotte vj days: xx*s* iij*d*

Item gaf by the commandement of master mayer and hys brothern amonges the masons, carpenters and laborers, xviij persons in all, for that they dyd worke erly and late this weke and also wrowght Mandy Thursday, Good Fryday and Ester evyn: iij*s*

Item to Master Kempe for a newe pyxt that he bought for the sakerment: viij*d*

Item to Clement the sexten *for washyng of* <of> the napery of the chappell and scoryng of the latten agenst Estern: iij*d*

Summa xj *li* vj*s*

/*The fyrst weke after Estern*/ **Item** payd to Thomas Flowerdewe of Het[*h*]erset[*t*] *for thacke tyle* <for> vj m^l for coueryng of the kechyn: xxxvj*s*

Item to the caryers that brought yt in: j*d*

Item to Henry Sparke for fechyng a gret ston morter, a gret okyn planke for the scaldyng howse & a coberd in the halle from the pallace: vj*d*[491]

[*f. 83^v*] **Item** to Wylliam Morront for vj*d* nayle *di'* m^l: ij*s*

Item to Paschall for a yron for the gretter newe ovyns mowthe conteynyng xxviij *libr'*: iij*s* vj*d*

Item to yong Ketryngham for sonde ij lode: viij*d*

Item to hym for claye ij lodes: x*d*

---

491 The palace of the bishop of Norwich to the north west of the cathedral.

/*Masons*/ **Item** to John Erne for iij days: xxj*d*

Item to Johnson, Hollond & Walpole iij days: iiij*s* x*d* *ob'*

Item to Crystovyr Stalam iij days: xvj*d* *ob'*

/*Carpenters*/ **Item** to Rychard Cotes the elder iij days: ij*s*

Item to Cotes and Byrche the yonger, to Brown, Wynde, Felbrygge <Felbryg> and Tuttell, euery of them iij days: ix*s* ix*d*

/*Laborers*/ **Item** to Wodroff, Elmam, Colles, Yoxhale, Scotte, Jube, Moone and Crowe iij days: ix*s*

Summa iij *li* xij*s* iiij*d*

/*The second weke after Ester*/ **Item** payd to Master Trase for ij *libr'* laten wyer for a lattyse for the scaldyng howse wyndowe: xij*d*

Item for whyte hede nayle *di'* m¹: iiij*d*

Item to Robert Fenne for makyng the same latyse: iiij*d*

Item to Arnold Johnson for v lattyses for the buttry and pantry wyndows: ij*s* j*d*

Item to hym for a basket with ij eerys: iij*d*

Item for byrchyn bromys & whypcord: ij*d*

Item to Flowerdewe for thacke tyle ij m¹: xij*s*

Item to hym for iiij*ˣˣ* gret pathyn tyles for the ovyns at iiij*s* ij*d* C: iij*s* iiij*d*

[*f. 84*] **Item** more to hym for brycke j m¹: vj*s*

Item to Master Trase, alderman, for lathe x C: v*s*

Item to Godfrey Harryson for iiij*ᵒʳ* gret latyse and ij lesser lattyses for the larder howses: ij*s* vij*d*

Item to yonge Ketryngham and Henry Carter for v lodes claye for the florthes of the dressers [*howse*]: ij*s* j*d*

Item to Henry Sparke for sonde v lodes: ij*s* j*d*

Item for pakthred for the masons: j*d*

/*Masons*/ **Item** to John Erne for vj days: iij*s* vj*d*

Item to Wylliam Johnson, Robert Hollond, John Walpole, Wylliam Jakes and Edmond Smythe, euery of them vj days, at vj*d* *ob'* day: xvj*s* iij*d*

Item to Crystouer Stalam, apprentyse, vj days: ij*s* ix*d*

Item to Wylliam Thacker, fremason, hewyng the pyllers at the survey [*howse*]: iij*d*

/*Carpenters*/ **Item** to Rychard Cotes th'elder vj days: iiij*s*

Item to Cotes and Byrche the yonger, Felbrige, Wynde, Brown and Tuttell vj days: xix*s* vj*d*

/*Yron worke*/ **Item** to Paschall for iiij ankers conteynyng iiij*ˣˣ* vj *libr'* to hold the walle plates and the beamys to guether of the kechyn at j*d* *ob'* *libr'*: x*s* ix*d*

Item for vj crampettes with brodes to hold the pryncypalles and the beamys to guether conteynyng xxvij *libr'*: iij*s* iiij*d*

Item for xxij fleshe hookes for the wete larder: xij*d*

Item for vj rynges for dores: xij*d*

Item for hookes, hengylles, barrys, cappis, sneckes, cromys & lachys lv *libr'* quarter at j*d* *ob'*: vj*s* xj*d*

Item for v C gret tenter hookes for the rayles in the halle at viij*d* C: iij*s* iiij*d*

[*f. 84ᵛ*] **Item** for layeng of the comon pykex & settyng of ij lockes of comon store vpon the dry larder howse and scaldyng howse dore: iiij*d*

/*Plomers*/ **Item** payd to Wylliam and John Asterby layeng of a gutter of lede by the chymney next the welle and makyng of a systern in the scaldyng howse and conveyeng of a condyte vnder the grownde from the welle to the forsayd systern, iiij days thys weke, at xiiij*d* a day toguether: iiij*s* viij*d*

Item to hym for sowde this weke xxij *libr'* quarter: vij*s* v*d*

Item for lede nayle j C: iiij*d*

Item to Master Wylliam Rogers, alderman, for viij C lede redy shette at v*s* the C for the sayd gutter, systern and condyte: xl*s*

/*Tymbyr worke*/ **Item** to John Byrche in full payment of xj *li* for the ten benchys in the halle: xl*s*

Item for vˣˣ iiij yardes of rayle in the halle for the hangynges, with settyng on of the tenter hookes & all workmanshyppe, takyn a gret: xvj*s*

Item for a dorestalle out of the buttry in to the chambyr ouer the vowtynges, an other dore stalle out of the kechyn in to the survey [*howse*] and for the iij^de dore stalle out of the kechyn court in to the backhowse courte at ij*s* viij*d* a pece: viij*s*

Item for an inbowyd dore stalle out of the southe syde of the halle in to the prechyng yarde: iiij*s*

Item for all the walle plates of all the kechyn on bothe sydes, with a pece tymbyr for the condyte: xiiij*s*

[*f. 85*] **Item** oon newe longe joppe for *the* kechyn roffe: xvj*d*

Item for ij shorter joppys ther: ij*s*

Item for viij newe pyrlynges at xvj*d* a pece: x*s* viij*d*

Item for iiij thycke braces: ij*s*

Item an entertyse pece to bere the sparrys betwyxt the ij pryncypalles at the syde chymney: xvj*d*

Item for xxvj yardes of evys bourde: ij*s* ij*d*

Item for the wyndowe next the survey [*howse*]: xx*d*

/*Laborers this weke*/ **Item** to Sander Clarke, Henry Wodrof, Nycholas Jube, John Elmam, Walter Colles, Robert Yoxhale, Davy Scotte, Thomas Mone, Nycholas Voyce, Walter Harryes, John Elles, Edmond Gladen *and* John Trewe, euery of them vj days, at iiij*d* *ob'* day: xxix*s* iij*d*

Item to John Crowe for iiij days *di'*: xx*d*

Item to Paschall for a newe locke and keye for the wete larder howse dore & for Inglyshe nayle: viij*d*

Summa xiiij *li* xvij*s* v*d*

/The iij^{de} weke after Estern/ **Item** payd to yong Ketryngham for clay for the florth of the backhowse and for the condyte iiij lodes: xx*d*

Item to Henry Sparke for sonde this weke x lodes: iiij*s* ij*d*

Item to Wylliam Wynde for xij thycke waynscot bourdes joynyd to guether by ij a pece, vj sengyll bourdes, iiij dobyll dores for gret coberdes, with iiij payer jemews with iiij rynges, whiche stuff was spent abought the brede hutchis in the pantry & newe herse in the chappell: ix*s*

Item to the forsayd plomers fynyshyng vp the condyte & makyng a long pype for Master Kempis house, iiij days: iiij*s* viij*d*

[*f. 85^a*] **Item** to hym for sowde ix *libr' di'* this weke: ij*s* ij*d*

Item for a pecke of grey salte to stoppe the pype of the condyte at the joyntes: ij*d ob'*

/Tylers/ **Item** payd to certen tylers for lathyng and tylyng the newe kechyn, the crepyll of the howse ouer the vowtynges, the pentys ouer the newe welle, the newe jakes howse & reparacon of all the backhowse: & ffyrst to Wylliam Smythe for v days: v*s*

Item to Anthony Smythe v days, at vij*d*: ij*s* xj*d*

/Laborers to them/ **Item** to Thomas Elward, Gregory Fayer, William Savery, Wylliam Sharvold & Wylliam Foxe, euery of them v days, at v*d* a day a man: x*s* v*d*

/Pynners/ **Item** to George Galt & John Browster v days: ij*s* ix*d*

Item to Robert Osborn of Kyrby [*Bedon*] for thacke tyle vj m^l and brycke j m^l *di'* at vj*s* m^l: xlv*s*

Item to hys man for ouer plus of tyle & brycke more than tale at dyuerse lodes: v*d*

Item for newe lyne for the tylers: j*d*

/Masons/ **Item** to John Erne for vj days: ij*s* vj*d*

Item to Wylliam Johnson, Robert Hollond, John Walpole, Wylliam Jakes, Edmond Smythe, Robert Hemmyng & John Dunston vj days: xxij*s* ix*d*

Item to Crystouer Stalam vj days: ij*s* ix*d*

/Carpenters/ **Item** to Richard Cotes th'elder vj days: iiij*s*

Item to Richard Cotes and John Byrche yonger, John Felbryge, Wylliam Wynde, Nycholas Tuttell and Andrewe Brown, euery of them vj days, at vj*d ob'* a day a man: xix*s* vj*d*

[*f. 86*] */Sawers/* **Item** to John Stanfeld and John Maye sawyng of sparrys, plankes, ledges, batorns and many other thynges of the comon store necessary for the sayd workes for the carpenters, vj days: vj*s* vj*d*

/Fremasons/ **Item** to Wylliam Thacker makyng iij steppys of marbyll at the dore out of the halle in to the prechyng yarde & fynyshyng of freston mete for certen of the benchys ther, ij days: xvj*d*

Item payd for the forsayd iij marbylles bought at the Gray Fryers of Master Seman: iiij*s*

/Laborers this weke/ **Item** to Sandyr Clarke, Henry Wodrof, John Elmam, Thomas Mone, Nycholas Jube, Robert Yoxhale, Walter Colles, Walter Harryes, John Fereby, Nycholas Voyce, John Trewe & Thomas Hynde, euery of them vj days, at iiij*d* *ob'* a day: xxvij*s*

Item to Wylliam Crowe, Edmond Gladyn and Thomas Lameroke, euery of them iiij days: iiij*s* vj*d*

Item to Gregory Acres & John Elles iij days: ij*s* iij*d*

Item to Wylliam Dale ij days, to Andrewe Robynson and John Symmys oon day: xviij*d*

Item to Flowerdewe of Heterset for brycke halff m¹: iij*s*

/Tymber worke/ **Item** to John Byrche for a dore stalle in the lane next the brydge for the scolers to go in to the scole in a longe entry ther: iij*s*

Item a dore stalle at the steyers feete of the scolehowse, an other dore stalle in the fense walle betwyxt the scolehowse entre: v*s* iiij*d*

[f. 86ᵛ] /Tymbyr/ **Item** for viij newe sparrys for the kechyn roffe: viij*s*

Item for gutter plankes for the same roffe: viij*d*

Item for xj yardes of rayle ouer the hyhe desse at the newe gabyll in the halle: xxij*d*

Item for x newe ffourmes of oke for x tabylles on the sydes of the halle at ij*s* iiij*d*: xxiij*s* iiij*d*

Item for a gret dore stalle out of the survey howse in to the kechyn courte: iij*s*

Item for a wyndowe stalle ouer the same dore: xvj*d*

Item for iij yardes of evys bourde for the pentyse ouer the welle & ij yardes for the chambyr ouer the survey howse: v*d*; a dore stalle for the jakes: xvj*d* – xxj*d*

/Yron worke/ **Item** to Thomas Lawrens for ij gret rynges for the scolehowse dore & the survey howse dore: viij*d*

Item to Paschall for vj small rynges: xij*d*

Item for ij gret dyce hede nayle for the rynges: ij*d*⁴⁹²

Item a rynge with a snecke for the prechard [*sic*] yarde dore next the gate: vj*d*

Item iiij hookes for the newe gabyll in the halle for the rayles conteynyng vij *libr'* j quarter: xj*d*

Item for hookes, hengylles, sneckes, cromes, lachis, barrys and cappys lxij *libr'* at j*d* *ob'*: vij*s* ix*d*

Item ffor the scolehowse gate a locke with ij keys and settyng on: x*d*

Item a locke & key for the survey howse dore: xij*d*

Item a locke for the bultyng howse: v*d*

Item ij plates of yron for the brynke of the fatte of the condyte by the welle: vj*d*

[f. 87] **Item** for lx dyce hede nayle for the batrons of the prechyng yarde dore: xviij*d*; a barre with cappys for the kechyn dore: ij*d*; for xl glasse barrys for the ij gret wyndows in the kechyn: xx*d* – iij*s* iiij*d*

---

492 NCR, 18A/6, f. 120, notes that they were to 'sette vnder the same rynges to knok at'.

Item for makyng of xviij glasse barrys of the comon stuff for the wyndowe in the pastry howse: viij*d*

Summa xij *li* xixs *ob'*

/*The iiij*ᵗᵉ *weke after Estern*/ Item payd to Arnold Johnson for oon gret lattyse for the backe howse wyndows, ij other for the gret wyndows in the kechyn on the lane syde, oon for the bultyng howse wyndowe and oon for the lytyll howse wyndowe for fowles next the servey: ij*s* j*d*

Item for candyll for the masons & plomer aboute the ovyns and condyte: j*d*

Item payd this weke to Wyllm [*sic*] Morront for dyuerse sortes of nayle: and fyrst for vj*d* j m': iiij*s*

Item iiij*d* nayle j m' *di'*: iij*s* ix*d*

Item iij*d* nayle j m': xx*d*

Item ij*d* nayle j m' *di'*: ij*s*

Item gret lathe nayle ij m': xx*d*

Item small lathe nayle x m': vij*s* vj*d*

Item small lathe nayle more j m': ix*d*

Item gret & small lathe nayle more *di'* m': v*d*

Item viij*d* nayle j C: viij*d*

Item xvj spekynges conteynyng iiij *libr'*: vj*d*

Item to hym for the losse of a French crown that was viij*d* to lyght, whyche was receyuyd amonges the benevolens money: iiij*d*

Item for gret tenter hookes for the halle *di'* C: iiij*d*

[*f. 87*ᵛ] /*Yron worke*/ Item to Paschall for an other yron for the lesser ovyns mouthe in the bakhowse conteynyng xxj *libr' di'*: ij*s* viij*d* *ob'*

Item for ij flat barrys of yron to bere vp the covys of the forsayd ovyns conteynyng xxxiiij *libr' di'*: iiij*s* iiij*d*

Item for ij gret stapylles for the barre of the dobell dore at the survey [*howse*], iiij cappis for the feete of the dresser [*howse*] wyndowe, with iiij stapylles & ij hespys: ix*d*

Item for hookes, hengylles, sneckes, cromis, lachis, stapylles, barrys and cappis xxj *libr'*: ij*s* vij*d* *ob'*

Item for a payer of jemews with iiij cappis, an hespe and a stapyll for the scaldyng howse wyndowe wher the pewter come inne: xij*d*

Item a locke and key for the kechyn dore: x*d*

Item an other for the pullery howse dore: vj*d*

Item an other for the dore in the fense walle in to the scolers entry: viij*d*

Item an other for the prechyng yarde dore in the halle, with stapylles to them all: xij*d*

Item for an other key to the sco*le*howse dore: iij*d*

/*Glasers craft*/ Item to John Gaywood for xxvij foote of newe glasse for oon of the gret wyndows in the kechyn; and to John Carre for xxvij foote *di'* for the other gret wyndowe at iiij*d* foote: xviij*s* ij*d*

Item to the sayd Carre for vj foote of newe glasse in the wyndow ouer the kechyn dore: ij*s*

Item to hym for xij foote *di'* of newe glass in the wyndowe in the backhowse: iiij*s* ij*d*

[*f. 88*] **Item** to hym for newe settyng of all the old glasse that was byfore in the same wyndowe: xij*d*

Item to hym for reparacon of oon pane in the est wyndowe of the northe yle in the halle that was broken all to peces: xij*d*

Item to hym for a newe pane of glasse in the est wyndowe in the chappell with a newe ymage of Seynt Kateryne: ij*s*

Item to hym for takyng down of vj panys in the halle wyndows & stoppyng them ageyn with nettes, oon day worke of ij men: xij*d*

Item to John Fytchet for vj nettes for the same: ix*d*

/*Fremasons*/ **Item** to Thomas Elward and Nycholas Cooke scoryng and fynyshyng vp the v pyllers in the kechyn that bere the mantyltrees, oon day worke: xvj*d*

/*Brycke*/ **Item** payd to Brytyff of Hetterset [*Hethersett*] for brycke m¹ *di'*: ix*s*
Item to Flowurdewe of the same town for *di'* m¹: ij*s*
Item to Osborn of Kyrby [*Bedon*] for *di'* m¹ with certen over: ij*s* ij*d*

/*Tylers*/ **Item** to Wylliam Smythe ffynyshyng vp all thynges ther, ij days thys weke: ij*s*
Item to John Anthony & John Fulkes ij days: ij*s* iiij*d*

/*Laborers to them*/ **Item** to Thomas Elward, Wylliam Sharvold, Wylliam Foxe, Gregory Fayer and Wylliam Saverey, euery of them ij days, at v*d* a day: iiij*s* ij*d*

/*Peynters*/ **Item** to Wylliam Motton for peyntyng and oylyng of all the tymbyr worke vyrownd Master Kempys newe buyldyng in a tymbyr culler, takyn a gret, fyndyng all stuff: xvj*s*
Item for xvj m¹ tyle pynnys at ij*d ob'* m¹: iij*s* iiij*d*
Item for xij C lathe to Master Trase: vj*s*

[*f. 88ᵛ*] /*Masons*/ **Item** to John Erne vj days: iij*s* vj*d*
Item to Wylliam Johnson, Robert Hollond, John Walpoole, Wylliam Jakes, Edmond Smythe and Robert Hemmyng, euery of them vj days: xix*s* vj*d*
Item to Crystouer Stalam vj days: ij*s* ix*d*
Item for Frenche packthred for the levellyng: ij*d*
Item to Henry Sparke for sonde vij lodes: ij*s* xj*d*
Item to yong Ketryngham for pathyn sonde ix lode: ij*s*

/*Carpenters*/ **Item** to Rychard Cotes th'elder vj days: iiij*s*
Item to Richard Cotes yonger, Wylliam Wynde, Andrewe Brown and Nycholas Tuttell, vj days: xiij*s*

/*Tymbyr*/ **Item** to Thomas Barchom for a newe coberd of waynscotte viij square stondyng in the halle: xv*s*
Item to John Byrche for a dorestalle out of the back howse in to the courte: ij*s* viij*d*

Item to hym for x yardes of gutter layd in the scolehowse entry: iijs iiijd

Item to hym for xvij sawen sparrys spent in the forsayd buyldynges at ixd copyll: vjs vd

Item in the market for ix copyll sawyn sparrys occupyed ther, also at ixd: vjs ixd

Item for ij long aldryng standerdes: viijd

Item for ashyn bourde dry iiij C di' & fyfty ffoote at iiijs C occupyed in the larders: xixs viijd

Item to John Byrche for ij longe fourmes with foote bankes for the hye bourde in the halle: vjs viijd

Item for vj trustylles for the same bourde: viijs

Item for a selyng bourde to fynyshe vp the brede hutchys to Wylliam Hede: iijd

[f. 89] Item to Wylliam Browster of Buxton for long mattes to lye vpon the benche at the hye bourde: ixd

/Laborers this weke/ Item to Sander Clarke pynnyng the newe walle in the prechyng yarde, the banke and all the buttraces, vj days, at vd day: ijs vjd

Item to Henry Wodroff, John Elmam, Nycholas Jube, Robert Yoxhale, Walter Harryes, Nycholas Voyse, John Trewe, Walter Colles, Robert Wright, Richard Grene, John Browster, Thomas Moone, euery of them vj days, at iiijd ob' a man: xxvijs

Item to Wylliam Dale and Thomas Lamerocke, eyther of them v days, at iiijd ob': iijs ixd

Item gaf in reward amonges some of the workmen who labored erly and late that weke to brynge all thynges to pase ageynst Seynt Georges ffest & for wachyng nelyng of the ovyns: ijs

Item for bromys to make clene all the howses and yardes ageynst Seynt Georges day: ijd

Summa xiij li xvs iijd

/The vte weke after Estern/ Item payd on the Sonday beyng Seynt Georgis evyn to Wylliam Johnson, Robert Hollond and Crystouer Stalam, masons, fynyshyng vp many thynges that lackyd, euery of them ijd: vjd

Item to Nycholas Tuttell, carpenter, that day: vjd

Item to Clark, Wodrof, Voyce and Colles, laborers, ther that day: viijd

/That weke/ Item to yong Ketryngham & Henry Sparke for *mucke* caryeng of vij lodes <of> thense that same day: xiiijd

Item for clay a lode that same day: vd

[f. 89ᵛ] Item payd to Wylliam Asterby on Seynt Georges day in the mornyng for newe sowdryng of a pece of the newe condyte, whiche was broke by oon of the cookes in makyng of an hole to set in a racke at the chymneys ende: iiijd

Item for sowde j libr' di': vjd

Item to Paschall for a grate of yron for the gutter in the courte next Master Kempis house: iiijd

Item payd that weke to Henry Wodrof, laborer, makyng clene all the lane from

Seynt Andrewes to the brydge, whych was very sore noyed with onlodyng of brycke, tyle & many other thynges ther syns Ester[493] & makyng of a florthe of clay in the scolers entry, iiij days: xviijd

Summa vs xjd

/*The vj*[te] *weke after Ester*/ Item to Henry Wodrof and John Elmam, laborers, caryeng of moche colder <ouer t> out of the backehowse & fynyshyng the florthe of that howse and makyng of a florthe of clay ouer all iij ovyns, iiij days: iijs

Item *to* yong Ketryngham for clay v lodes: ijs jd

Item payd for helpe to haue out the pulpet & fourmys in the prechyng yarde and havyng in ageyn on the Assenssyon day & caryeng home ageyn dyuers thynges byfore borowd: iiijd

Summa vs vd

[*f. 90*] /*The vij*[te] *weke after Estern*/[494] Item payd to the forsayd ij laborers makyng clene of all the courte betwyxt the northe yle of the halle and the cloyster and makyng all the grownde of the same currant to the synke, iiij days: iijs

Item for a basket with ij eerys to carry colder: iijd

Item to John Goldryng for lyme receyuyd from Byshope gate betwyxt Estern and Wytsontyde x chalder and halff at ijs iiijd the chalder: xxiiijs vjd

Item to Walter Feere for lyme receyuyd from Fybryge gate in the same tyme viij chalder & halff: xixs xd

Summa xlvijs vijd

/*The viij*[te] *weke after Estern*/ Item to Nycholas Tuttell, carpenter, for oon day worke preparyng to make a perke ouer the chappell dore to set on the organs ageynst Corpus Christi day: vjd ob'

Item to Sander Clarke & John Elmam, laborers, that same day fechyng of sparrys from Seynt Benettes & ffrom Seynt Clementes & makyng of holys for standerdes: ixd

Item the same day, beyng Trynyte evyn, to iiij[or] other laborers that holpe home the organs from Seynt George churche: viijd

Item to Thomas Barchom for takyng of them a sonder and settyng them vp ageyn: xijd

Item for whyte lethyr and glewe: jd

Item to the clarke of Seynt Stephyns for settyng of the pypys and tunyng of them: xijd

Item for brede and drynke for them all: iiijd

Item for a newe locke for the sayd organs: ijd

[*f. 90*ᵛ] Item payd on Trynyte evyn to Rychard Bate for a ffayer chest of waynscotte to set in the chappell to locke in the vestementes, chales & other necessaryes: xs

---

493 NCR, 18A/6, f. 121, notes that he carried away seven loads of muck.
494 NCR, 18A/6, f. 121, combines the sixth and seventh weeks after Easter in a single sub-section.

Item the same day in the merket for vj longe mattes to laye in the stolys of the chappell: xviijd

Summa xvjs ob'

/*The ix^te weke after Estern*/ Item payd more in the market on Corpus Christi evyn for other vj longe mattes and viij shorter mattes for the deskes in the chappell & for bromys: ijs jd

Item to John Byrche for ix copyll of sawen sparrys for the newe perke: vjs; and to John Estowe for vj copyll of grette sparris: vs – xjs

Item to John Byrche for ij standerdes: xijd

Item to Nycholas Tuttell, John Byrche yonger and Rychard Spyrlyn, carpenters, makyng the newe perke wher the organs do nowe stonde, euery of them iij days worke, at vjd ob'a man: iiijs xd ob'

Item to John Byrche th'elder for hym selff and ij of hys men more with hys crane and ropis havyng vp the organs on the same perke: xijd

Item to John Elmam, laborer, iij days and Sander Clarke oon day: xviijd

Item to Nycholas Tuttell, carpenter, for ij days more that weke abought makyng of a newe herse to stonde in the chappell: xiijd

Item to Henry Wodroff, laborer, for v days ther that weke: xxijd ob'

[f. 91] Item to Wylliam Morront for vjd nayle di' m^l: ijs

Item iiijd nayle j m^l: ijs vjd; iiijd nayle j m^l: xxd – iiijs ijd

Item payd at the comon stathe for iij ffurryn sparris for rayles in the chappell for hangynges: xijd

Item to a prest that sange masse on Corpus Christi day in the mornyng to consecrat an host for the pyxt ageynst processyon to be borne: iiijd

Item to other ij prestes that war decons that day: iiijd

Item payd for ij newe prykettes for the candyll styckes in the chappell: iiijd

Summa xxxijs vijd

/*The x^te weke after Estern*/ Item to Nycholas Tuttell, carpenter, fynyshyng vp the herse in the chappell, *ij days*: xiijd

Item to Wylliam Johnson, mason, workyng vp abought the ij newe ovyns in the backhowse & reysyng vp the gutter in the scolehowse entry to make yt more water shutte, iij days: xixd ob'

Item to Walter Collys, his laborer, iij days: xiijd ob'

Item to Henry Wodroff, laborer, ij days: ixd

Item to Henry Sparke for sonde a lode: vd

Summa vs

/*The xj^te weke after Estern*/[495] Item to Master Marsham for lyme receyuyd in to the place ffrom hym betwyxt Crystmes and thys present weke xxij chalder di' at ijs iiijd the chalder: lijs vjd

---

495 NCR, 18A/6, f. 121^v, combines the tenth and eleventh weeks after Easter in a single sub-section.

Item[496] to Robert Clarke, organ maker, for mendyng the organs, whyche dyd steke & whystyll: viij*d*

Summa liij*s* ij*d*

[*f. 91ᵛ*] /*The xijᵗᵉ weke after Ester*/[497] Item payd to Brytyff of Het[*h*]erset[*t*] for x m¹ brycke brought in at dyuers tymes syns Wytsontyde, whyche lye ther stylle at the ende of thys accompt redy ageynst the next somer at vj*s* m¹: lx*s*

Item to the carters for *di'* C more than tale: iij*d*

Item payd for the chargis of the clerkes that songe masse and evensong for the smythis and masons the Sonday byfore Mydsomer: xx*d*

Summa iij *li* xxiij*d*

/*The last quarter*/[498] Item payd for other chargis in the same place betwyxt Mydsomer and Myhelmes: and fyrst in the weke byfore Seynt Jamys to John Elles and Henry Wodroff, laborers, castyng the systern, late the dorter jakes, next the water gate, yche of them vj days, at ix*d* toguether: iiij*s* vj*d*

Item to Robert Grene in the same worke, ij days: ix*d*

Item the xxviij day of July to Master Flowurdewe of Heterset for *di'* m¹ brycke sent for to hym the weke byfore Seynt George: iij*s*

/*The weke byfore Owur Lady Assumpcon*/ Item to John Asterby, plomer, newe sowdryng and mendyng of the roff of the halle in dyuerse places, v days worke, at vij*d* the day: ij*s* xj*d*

Item to hys man for iiij days: xvj*d*

[*f. 92*] Item to Wylliam Hede for sowde xiiij *libr'*: iiij*s* viij*d*

/*The xxvij day of August*/ Item payd to Master Wylliam Rogers, alderman, for xxx m¹ bryke receyuyd ffrom Ambryngale [*Arminghall*] in the tyme of the forsayd buyldyng at v*s* iiij*d* the m¹: viij *li*

Item to Robert Norman for iiij*ᵒʳ* ryven ashyn sparrys, whyche war borowd of hym in the tyme of the sayd buyldyng: x*d*

Item payd to Master Kempe for ij newe napkyns by hym bought for the alter in the chappell: iiij*d*

Item for ij newe cruettes bought of Coplond: viij*d*

Item to Master Kempe for brede an [*sic*] wyne fownde by hym for strange prestes that resorted thyther in the tyme of thys accompt to syng masse: xx*d*

Item payd at Myhelmes in the ende of thys accompt to Master Awsten Steward, alderman, for j m¹ brycke payd for by hym to a man of Horsford in the tyme of the forsayd buyldyng: vj*s*

Summa ix *li* vj*s* viij*d*

---

496   NCR, 18A/6, f. 121ᵛ, dates this entry the thirteenth week after Easter.
497   NCR, 18A/6, f. 121ᵛ, dates all these entries the thirteenth week after Easter.
498   NCR, 18A/6, f. 121ᵛ, has 'other charges there', with no dates.

Summa totallis omnium solucionum communis aule C xxviij *li* iijs vij*d*

Summa totallis omnium solucionum ciuitatis predicte CC xviij *li* iiijs iij*d*

Summa totallis omnium solucionum hoc anno CCC xlvj *li* vijs x*d*

And so the forsayd accomptantes do owe xlv *li* xijs vj*d qu'*

[*f. 92ᵛ*] /*Wherof they axe*/ to be allowid for these parcelles folowyng:

In primis for the ingrossyng of thys accompt payd to Rychard Framyngham by the assygment of the awdytours appoyntyd: v*s*

Item for the expensys of the sayd awdytours and of others appoyntyd syttyng vpon the determynacon of thys accompt: x*s*

Item they axe furder to be allowyd for dyuers rentes above chargid and nowe dekayed, for as moche as the ffees therof be vnknowen to the sayd accomptantes, as yt apperith to the awdytours by other accomptes byfore made, wherin the partyclers do appere more at large: xiijs iiij*d*[499]

Item they axe to be allowyd for oon hole yere ferme of bothys in the castill diche endyd at Myhelmes *anno regni regis Henrici octavi* xxxiiij° [*1542*], dependyng vpon Robert Brown, jaylour, as in the tytyll of *vnde super* of the accompt of Wylliam Morront and Robert Raynbald, chamberleyns the sayd yere, ys conteynyd: iiijs;[500] for as moche as the sayd Brown haue <app> approvyd non vse of the sayd bothis at any tyme within the forsayd accompt: iiijs

Item for the grynt of xxv comb' whete dependyng vpon Leonard Dalys, baker, as in the sayd tytyll of *vnde super* is also declarid, and nowe the sayd Dalys [*is*] in poverte: xij*d ob'*

[*f. 93*] **Item** for oon quarter ferme of oon of the tenementes late lord suffrigan endyd at the fest of Seynt Mychaell in the forsayd yere: v*s*, dependyng vpon Richard Coldon, as in the tytyll of *vnde super* ys also conteynyd, the whyche Coldon ys gon and so the sayd ferme of v*s* ys with owt any recouery: v*s*

Item the*i* axe to be allowyd of iiij *li* ixs vd *ob' qu'*, beyng parcell of vj *li* iijs ixd *ob' qu'* dependyng vpon dyuerse pore men and other persons not levyabyll, as yt apperith to the awdytours, remaynyng not gatherd in dyuerse wardes of the sayde cite of a certen sesment taxid and set thorowout the sayd cite in the last accompt for the chargis of fourty soldyers sent in to Scotlond, as yt apperithe in the forsayd tytyll of *vnde super*, whyche iiij *li* ixs vd *ob' qu'* ys not in any wyse possybyll to be recouerd: iiij *li* ixs vd *ob' qu'*

Item for halff yere ferme of the old mucke bote endyd at Myhelmes in the ende of this accompt, above chargid in the tytyll of foren receptes, dependyng vpon Edward Aleyn, whyche Aleyn drownyd hym selff in Trowse ryver & so was not dystreynabyll: vjs viij*d*

---

499 See above, p. 167 note 400.

500 See above, p. 167.

Item for rent of a sygne set in the kynges hey waye ageynst the mese late Wylliam Norffolk cald The Whyte Horse, whyche sygne ys nowe pluckyd down, wherfor the rent ys not payabyll: j*d*

[*f. 93*ᵛ]   *Summa allocacionum* vj *li* xiiijs vij*d qu'*

Summa totallis omnium solucionum et allocacionum CCC liij *li* ijs v*d qu'*

And so the forsayd accomptantes do owe xxxviij *li* xvijs xj*d*

/*Respectes*/ **Wherof** they axe to be respectyd vpon *vnde* <*sp*> *super* for certen rentes and fermys above chargid and not yet receyuyd, wherof the particlers do ffolowe:

And fyrst for rent of a tenement in the paryshe of Seynt Mychaell at the Plee, late Master Pyndern, prest, nowe Henry Mynne, gent', parcell of the castyll ffee: j*d*
Item for rent of dyuerse tenementes & groundes in the paryshe of Seynt Marten at the Bayle, late Thomas Lancetour, parcell of the castill ffee: iiijs
Item for rent of a mese in the paryshe of Seynt Stephyn, late John Scotte, nowe John Pype, parcell of rent of assyse: ij*d*
Item for rent of a mese in the paryshe of Seynt Peter of Mancroft, late John Norman, nowe John Aleyn, parcell of rent of assyse: xs
Item for a quarter ferme of the ixᵗᵉ tenement, late <Wydo> lord suffrigan, indyd at Myhelmes, dewe by Wydowe Boyse: ijs iij*d*
Item for iij quarters ferme of the Brasyn Towur endyd at Mydsomer in the tyme of /
nullus/ [*f. 94*] thys accompt, dewe by Master Brown of Seynt Stephyns: xij*d*
    Summa respec' xvijs vj*d*

Summa totallis omnium solucionum, allocacionum et respectorum CCC liij *li* xixs
    xj*d qu'*

And so the forsayd accomptantes do knowlege them selvys clere detters to the comialte of the cite afforsayd: xxxviij *li* v*d*

Thys accompt was vewyd, examyned and determyned by the awdytours here after folowyng the Monday the xxvij day of Maii in the xxxvj yere of the reign of Kyng Henry the viijᵗᵉ [*1544*] *& cetera:*⁵⁰¹

Edward Rede
Edmond Woode   aldermen

John Qwashe
John Pettows   comyners

---

501 NCR, 18A/6, f. 123, contains no record of such an examination, but lists the names of the auditors at the head of the account on f. 95.

[NCR, 18A/7, *f. 95*]   1543

/*Ciuitas Norwici*/ The accompt of Robert Raynbald, chamberleyn of the cite of Norwyche, from the fest of Seynt Mychaell th'arcangell in the xxxv yere of the reign of owur soueraign lord Kyng Henry the viij^te [*29 September 1543*] vntill the sayd ffest of Seynt Mychaell in the xxxvj yere of his magestes reign [*1544*]: that is to saye by oon hole yere *& cetera*

Recepetes

/*Arreragis*/ *In primis* the sayd accomptant do charge hym selff and answer for xxxviij *li* vd of clere dette of the arreragis of the last accompt, the sayd Robert Raynbald and William Hede then chamberleyns; and he answer for xvijs vjd of the arrerages of the sayd accompt, whyche was not by them than levyed, as yt apperith more playnly in the ende of the same accompt: xxxviij *li* xvijs xjd
Summa xxxviij *li* xvijs xjd

/*Langoll rent*/ Item he knowlege hym selff that he haue receyuyd of the baly of the manour or late pryory of Horsham Seynt Faythe for langoll rent of certen tenementes within the cite parteynyng to the sayd manour: iijs; and of the baly of Heylesdon [*Hellesdon*] for langoll rent of a tenement late the duke of Suff': ijd – iijs ijd
Summa iijs ijd

[*f. 95^v*] /*Castill ffee*/ Item receyuyd of dyuerse howses & groundes stondyng vpon the castill ffee: xxjs ijd ob' qu'
Summa xxjs ijd ob' qu'

/*Rent assyse*/ Item receyuyd of rent of assyse off dyuerse howses and groundes within the cite, with vjd of newe rent recouerd: viij *li* xijs xjd ob'
Summa <xij *li*> viij *li* xijs xjd ob'

/*Cite bochers*/ *In primis* receyuyd of John Howse for the hole yere ferme of the ij fyrst stalles, bothe in oon, in the northe ende of the est part of the sayd cite bochers: xxxjs iiijd; and of Alyce Rede for the hole yere ferme of the iij^de stalle toward the southe: xijs – xliijs iiijd
Item of Thomas Toly for the hole yere ferme of the iiij^te and v^te stalles, bothe in oon: xvjs
Item of Thomas Grene for the vj^te and vij^te stalles, bothe in oon: xxiiijs
Item of Richard Dey th'elder for the viij^te and ix^te stalles, bothe in oon: xxiiijs
Item of Robert Savery and Wylliam Brown for the x^te stalle: xvjs
Item of John Barker for the xj^te stalle: xvjs
Item of Rychard Newman for the xij^te stalle: xvjs
Item of Roger Baldry for the xiij stalle: xs

Item of the sayd Roger and Agnes Guyrdler for the xiiij stall dyvydyd betwyxt them: ix*s*

[*f. 96*] **Item** of the same Agnes Guyrdler for the xv[th] stalle, whyche ys the last of the est part in the southe ende: xxx*s*

Item of Andrewe Dey for the fyrst stall on the west part of the sayd bochery in the southe ende of the same, with halff the second stalle dyvydyd betwyxt hym and John Fysher: xx*s*

Item of the sayd John Fysher for the other half second stalle & for the hole iij[de] stalle: xvj*s* viij*d*

Item of Gregory Pougeleon [*and*] of John Wodcoke for the iiij[te] stalle: xvj*s*

Item of Robert Tolye for the v[te] stalle: xvj*s*

Item of John Barbowur for the vj[te] stalle: xiij*s* iiij*d*

Item of Henry Harpowur for the vij[te] stalle: xiiij*s*

Item of Thomas Brown for the viij[te] stalle: xiiij*s*

Item of Agnes Cannard for the ix[te] stalle: xxix*s*

Item of Jeffrey Rede for the x[te] and xj[te] stalles, bothe in oon: xxxv*s*

Item of Richard Barne for the xij[te] stalle: xiij*s* iiij*d*

Item to [*sic*] Thomas Hubbard for the xiij and xiiij stalles, bothe in oon, beyng the *last* in the sayd west part in the northe ende: xl*s*

Summa xxj *li* xj*s* viij*d*

/*Movabyll stalles*/[502] **Item** receyuyd of John Saye for iij quarteres ferme of a movabyll stalle above the guyldhall dore endyd at Mydsomer: vj*s*; and for the last quarter nothyng for lacke of a fermer: vj*s*

Item of John Hanson for one quarter ferme /*nullus*/ [*f. 96*[v]] of an other stalle above the sayd guyldhall dore endyd at Crystmes: ij*s*; & for the rest of the yere nothyng for lacke of fermers: ij*s*

Item of Thomas Hubbard and other bochers stondyng in the same place by the day dyuerse market days: xx*d*

Item of Edmond Fereby for iij quarteres ferme of a movabyll stalle next the guyldhall dore downward endyd at Mydsomer: vj*s*; and for the last quarter nothyng for lacke of a fermer: vj*s*

Item of Gregory Foxe for the hole yere ferme of an other stalle ther next downward: viij*s*

Item of John Barbowur for the hole yere ferme of the iij[de] stalle ther downward: viij*s*

Item receyuyd of Robert Newman and of other bochers stondyng sondry tymes with a movabyll stalle at the northe ende of the iiij[or] newe stalles: iij*s* iij*d*

Summa xxxiiij*s* xj*d*

---

502 NCR, 18A/6, f. 125[v], combines the rents from moveable stalls with those from the city butchers in a single section.

/*Contre bochers*/ **In primis** receyuyd of Thomas Yemys for oon quarter ferme of the gretter stalle the west ende of the guyldhalle endyd at Crystmes: ij*s* vj*d*

Item for the other iij quarteres of the same stalle and for the lesser stalle nothyng by the yere for lacke of fermers; but receyuyd of dyuerse strange bochers that stode in those ij stalles dyuerse days within tyme of thys accompte: iij*s* iiij*d*

[*f. 97*] **Item** of Richard Vyncent and Walter, his sonne, for the hole yere ferme of iij stalles on the southe syde of the guyldhalle: xl*s*

/*Long Rowe*/ **Item** receyuyd of John Purkyn and Robert Plattyn for the hole yere ferme of the fyrst stalle at the north ende of the Long Rowe: xx*s*

Item of Richard Dey the yonger for the hole yere ferme of the last stalle on the same rowe in the southe ende: xx*s*

Item of xxiiij other men for the hole yere ferme of xxiiij stalles betwyxt the forsayd northe ende and southe ende at xvj*s* the stalle: xix *li* iiij*s*

/*iiij*^or^ *newe stalles*/[503] **Item** receyuyd of Nycholas Baxter for oon quarter ferme endyd at Crystmes for the fyrst stalle in the southe ende: iij*s*; for the next ij quarters nothyng for lacke of fermers; but receyuyd of William Andrews for the last quarter of the same stall: iij*s* – vj*s*

Item of strange bochers at the same stalle stondyng dyuers days in the vacacon tyme: xvj*d*

Item of Edmond Toly, Richard Adelston & Thomas Brown for the hole yere ferme of the other iij stalles at xij*s* euery of them: xxxvj*s*

Summa **xxv** *li* **xiij***s* **ij***d*

/*Ropery*/ **In primis** for the fyrst shoppe in the Ropery nothyng for that it is in lease with the Murage Loft; and for the second shoppe nothyng for lacke of a fermer; but receyuyd of John Peke for the hole yere ferme of the iij^de^ shoppe: v*s*

[*f. 97*^v^] **Item** of Walter Feer for the <vij> hole yere ferme of the iiij^te^ shoppe: v*s*

Item of Robert Hynderson for the v^te^ shoppe: v*s*

Item of Henry Carman for the fyrst half yere ferme of the vj^te^ shoppe, beyng the last in the northe ende, nowe occupyed for a bochers stalle: vij*s* vj*d*

Item of the sayd Henry Carman for the last halff yere ferme of the same shoppe: viij*s*

Summa **xxxs** **vj***d*

/*Fyshe shoppis*/ **In primis** receyuyd of John Webster for the hole yere ferme of the fyrst shoppe in the northe ende: xiij*s* iiij*d*

Item of Jerome Qwashe for the second shoppe: viij*s*

Item of Thomas Worleton for the iij^de^ shoppe: viij*s*

Item of Thomas Porter for the fyrst quarter ferme of the iiij^te^ shoppe: ij*s* vj*d*; for the second quarter nothyng for lacke of a fermer; but receyuyd of John Sewell for the last half yere: v*s* – vij*s* vj*d*

---

503 NCR, 18A/6, f. 126, treats the 'ferme of the litill rowe off stalles late of newe ffixed & couered' as a separate section, with receipts of 44*s* 4*d*.

Item of the sayd John Sewell for the fyrst halff yere of the v^te and vj^te shoppys, bothe in oon: viij*s*; and for the last halff yere nothyng for lacke of a fermer: viij*s*

Item of Nycholas Grene for the hole yere of the vij^te and [*viij^te*] stalles, bothe in oon: xvj*s*

Item of Robert Norman for the ix^te and the x^te shoppys, bothe in oon: xvj*s*

Item of Frances Scotte for the xj^te shoppe: viij*s*

Item of Master Cocke for the xij^te shoppe: viij*s*

[*f. 97A*] **Item** of Robert Newman for the xiij shoppe: viij*s*

Item of Master Warden for the xiiij shoppe: viij*s*

Item of Alyce Cobbe for the xv shoppe: viij*s*

Item of Stephyn Guyssell for the xvj shoppe: viij*s*

Item of John Harryes for iij quarters ferme of the xvij shoppe endyd at Mydsomer: vj*s*; and for the last quarter nothyng for lacke of a fermer: vj*s*

Item of Jone Chapman for the xviij shoppe: viij*s*

Item of John Crowe for the xix and xx shops, bothe in oon, beyng the last in the sowthe ende: xvj*s*

Summa vij *li* xiiij*s* x*d*

/ ***Wulshoppis*/**[504] ***In primis*** receyuyd of John Lartour for the hole yere ferme of a tenement next the churche style of Seynt Peter, with certen chambyrs ouer, parcell of the wolshoppys: xiij*s* iiij*d*

Item of Henry Marlyn for the yere ferme of a shoppe vnder the sayd chambyrs in the pultre market: x*s*

Item of Master Qwashe for the hole yere ferme of a tenement in the northe ende of the same rowe next vnto the fysh market: xx*s*

Item of Thomas Croshold for the yere ferme of the fyrst shoppe in the southe ende openyng toward the <p> wulmarket: vj*s* viij*d*

Item of Wylliam Partryke for the second shoppe: vj*s* viij*d*

Item for the iij^de shoppe for lacke of a fermer: *nullus*

Item of Stephyn Johnson for the iiij^te shoppe: iiij*s*

Item for the v^te shoppe, the last in the northe ende, for lacke of a fermer: *nullus*

[*f. 97A^v*] **Item** receyuyd of Henry Holden for the hole yere ferme of the vj^te shoppe, whyche ys adioynyng to the southe ende of hys mese: v*s*

Item of William Hede, *late* of the sayd Henry Holden, for the hole yere ferme of a vowlte vnder the southe ende of the cite bochery: v*s*

Summa iij *li* x*s* viij*d*

/***Tenementes and growndes*/ *In primis*** receyuyd of John Thurston for the hole yere ferme of a tenement in the Myddyll Rowe cald the Murage Loft, with the fyrst shoppe in the southe ende of the Ropery: xxx*s*

---

504 NCR, 18A/6, f. 127–7^v, combines rents from 'wolle shoppes & ffisshe shoppes' in a single section with no sub-headings.

Item of Wylliam Shalbery for iij quarters ferme endyd at Lammes of an other tenement at the southe corner of the same rowe: x*s*; and for the last quarter nothyng for lacke of a fermer: x*s*

/*Coblerrowe*/ Item of Hewe Coplond for the hole yere ferme of the northe corner tenement, with a lytyll corner shoppe and a vowlte vnder the smythy: xxiij*s* iiij*d*
Item of Bryan Doront for the myddyll tenement of the *same* rowe, with a smythis forge: xx*s*
Item of Marke Heynys for the iij^de tenement on the same rowe, with the newe buyldyng: <xx> viij*s* iiij*d*

/*Comon inne*/ Item of Adryan Johnson for the hole yere ferme of the hede mese of the comon inne, with parcell of the newe buyldyng: lxvj*s* viij*d*
Item of John Sewell for oon quarter ferme of a tenement, parcell of the sayd comon inne: iij*s* vj*d*
[*f. 98*] Item for the rest of the yere nothyng for lacke of a fermer, notwithstondyng yt was latten to oon Crystouer Dobbys, who after a lytyll tyme conveyd hys stuff awaye by nyght so that yt ys not knowen wher he ys becom & so ys not dystreynabyll: *nullus*
Item of Master Nekton, alderman, for the hole yere ferme of a tenement in the paryshe of Seynt Andrewe: iij*s* iiij*d*
Item of Richard Framyngham for a scryptory on the southe syde of the guyldhalle: iij*s* iiij*d*
Item of Margaret Sancroft for an other scryptory: ij*s*

/*Pastures and londes*/ Item of Master Nycholas Sywhat, alderman, for the ferme of a certen grownde, water & fyshynges above the newe mylles: vj*s* viij*d*
Item of John Barbowur for the hole yere ferme of the Butter Hylles: xxvj*s* viij*d*
Item of Master Qwashe for the iusment of the comon grounde vnder the cite walles, with the Chappell of Feld croftes: xvj*d*
Item of hym for the ferme of ij akers londe with out Seynt Gyles gates, late Hemmynges: v*s*
Item[505] of Ispell Mace, wydowe, of a parcell of comon grounde in Seynt Vedastes: xij*d*
Item of Syr John Buxton for ferme of a garden in the paryshe of All Seyntes in Be[r] strete: xvj*d*
Item of the myller of Cryngylford [*Cringleford*] for the last halffe yere easement of the crosse in the market to set in his meale sackes: xij*d*
Item of Rychard Flecher for the hole yere ferme of the clothe halle: xl*s*
                    Summa xiij *li* iij*s* vj*d*

---

505 A manicule with an extended finger points to this entry, as a *nota bene* sign.

[*f. 98ᵛ*] /*Tenementes in Conysford*/⁵⁰⁶ *In primis* receyuyd of John Styngate for the hole yere ferme of the hede place, with a kylyard, in Sowthe Conysford ageynst the comon stathe: xxs

Item of Robert Teyton for ferme of the fyrst tenement in the northe ende of the same tenementes: vs

Item of Wydowe Syer for iij quarteres ferme and of Widowe Frankyshe for oon quarter of the second tenement: vs

Item of Nycholas Hardyng for the iijᵈᵉ tenement: vs

Item of Robert Dawes for the iiijᵗᵉ tenement: vs

Item of Thomas Purkyn for the vᵗᵉ tenement: vs

Item of Widowe Rycheford for the vjᵗᵉ tenement: iiijs

Item of Agnes Lambert for the fyrst quarter ferme of the vijᵗᵉ tenement: xvd; and for the rest of the yere nothyng for lacke of a fermer: xvd

Item of Wylliam Horne for the viijᵗᵉ tenement, with parcell of the kylyard: vjs viijd

Item of William Guylbert for the ixᵗᵉ tenement: vs

Item of John Nonne for the fyrst half yere ferm of the tenth tenement: ijs vjd; for the iijᵈᵉ quarter nothyng for lacke of a fermer; but receyuyd of Jone Davy for the last quarter: xvd – iijs ixd

Item of Elsabethe Story for the xjᵗᵉ tenement: vs

Item of Thomas Damme for the fyrst quarter ferme of the xijᵗᵉ tenement: xvd; for the second quarter nothyng for lacke of a fermer; but of Widowe Haspy for the last halff yere: ijs vjd – iijs ixd

Item of Richard Starkyn for the xiij tenement, the last in the southe ende: vs

Summa iij *li* xixs vd

[*f. 98** – *pencil foliation*] /*Pety Custom*/ **Item** receyuyd of Robert Collard for the hole yere ferme of the pety custome: v *li* xiijs iiijd

Summa v *li* xiijs iiijd

/*Bothes*/ **Item** for the ferme of any bothes in the tyme of thys accompt set in the castyll dyche in the tyme of assyse or sessyons nothyng for lacke of ffermors: *nullus*

Summa nullus

/*Tenementes in the kynges hondes*/ **Item** receyuyd of Roger Leeke for a tenement in the paryshe of Seynt Benet: iiijs; and of Thomas Hast for an other tenement in Seynt Martens at Pales Gate in Cougate Strete: vs – ixs

Summa ixs

/*Comon stathis*/ **Item** receyuyd of John Styngate for the hole yere ferme of the old and newe comon stathis: xv *li*

Summa xv *li*

---

506 NCR, 18A/6, ff. 129ᵛ–30, incorporates all these entries, without any separate sub-heading, in the previous section.

/*Mylles*/ **Item** receyuyd of Stephyn Empson for the hole yere ferme of the newe mylles, with all profyghtes & commodytees thervnto bylongyng: xl *li*

Item of hym for the hole yere ferme of Heyham [*Heigham*] mylles, with certen medows, marshis, waters & fyshynges therto bylongyng: lxvj*s* viij*d*

Summa xliij *li* vj*s* viij*d*

/*Gates and towers*/ *In primis* receyuyd of Master William Rogers, alderman, for a certen annuyte or yerely rent for the dyscharge of a tolle and custome at all the gates of the cite and of ij ffayers callyd Pencost and Trynyte ffayers: viij *li*

[*f. 98*ᵛ] **Item** of Walter Feere for ferme of a tower by the water syde next Pokethorppe gates: iij*s* iiij*d*

Item of William Bevys for ferme of a gardeyn vnder the cite walles ther from the sayd gates down to the forsayd tower: v*s*

Item of Hewe Boxford for the hole yere ferme of a towur next Fybrygge gates: vj*d*

Summa viij *li* viijs x*d*[507]

/*Comon halle*/[508] *In primis* receyuyd of Wylliam Almond for an annuall rent or ferme of the howses newe buyldyd ouer the gate yerely payd at Crystmes: vj*s* viij*d*

Item of Frances Wolmer for the hole yere ferme of certeyn howsys cald the maltyng offyce, as they be nowe inclosed: xl*s*

Item of Syr Robert Shynkwyn, prest, for halff yere ferme endyd at Estern of a tenement adioynyng to the old kechyn: v*s*; and for the rest of the yere nothyng for lacke of ffermers: v*s*

Item of John Clarke for ferme of a garden, sometyme parcell of the prechyng yarde: xiij*s* iiij*d*

Item for the ffyrst quarter ferme of a tenement newe buyldyd, sometyme the ankers howse, nothyng for lacke of a fermour; but receyuyd of Thomas Pecke for the last iij quarters: xxx*s*

/*Gret gardeyn*/ **Item** receyuyd of Master Edmond Wood, alderman, for ferme of a parcell of the gret gardeyn: x*s*

Item of Wylliam Marche for ferme of other ij parcelles of the same gardeyn: xxvj*s* viij*d*

[*f. 99*] **Item** of Mastres Morront, wydowe, for ferme of an other parcell of the same gardeyn: xiiij*s*

Item of Henry Bacon for an other parcell of the same gardeyn, with a tenement and an howse, sometyme a chappell: xxvj*s* viij*d*

Item of John Byrche for an other parcell of the same gardeyn, with an howse therin: xiij*s* iiij*d*

Item of Master Qwashe for ferme of an other parcell of the same gardeyn: iiij *li*

---

507 NCR, 18A/6, f. 131, notes 'ffor the tower callid the Brasendoore nothing here, ffor it stande open on the daye tyme ffre & comon to euery person willing to *goo* & com to & ffrom the seyd citie by the same'.

508 NCR, 18A/6, f. 131, refers to 'the late howse or priorye of the Blak Freres'.

Item of John Baker for ferme of an other parcell of the same gardeyn: vjs viijd

Item of hym for ferme of a lane with an howse in the northe ende of the same lane, which is parcell of the sayd comon halle & gardeyn: vjs viijd

Summa xiij *li* xixs

/*Tenementes late lord suffrigan*/ *In primis* receyuyd of Robert Stephynson for the hole yere ferme of the fyrst tenement, beyng the corner howse ageynst Tomlond: xxvjs viijd

Item of Robert Gogney for the fyrst quarter ferme of the second tenement: iijs iiijd; for the second quarter nothyng for lacke of a fermer; and of Thomas Hewson for <lacke> the last halff yere: vjs viijd – <vjs viijd> xs

Item of Thomas [*Mosse*] for the iij^de tenement: xiijs iiijd

Item of Thomas Callowe for the fyrst quarter ferme of the iiij^te tenement: vs; for the second quarter nothyng for lacke of a fermer: vs

[*f. 99*^v] **Item** for the second quarter nothyng for lacke of a fermer; but receyuyd of Robert Gogney for the iij^de quarter: vs; and of John Cowper for the iiij^te quarter: vs – xs

Item of William Gravour for the fyrst quarter ferme of the v^te tenement: ijs vjd; for the second quarter nothyng for lacke of a fermer; of Robert Gogney for the iij^de quarter: ijs vjd; and of Thomas Hubbard for the iiij^te quarter: ijs vjd – vijs vjd

Item of John Suklyng for the fyrst quarter ferme of the vj^te tenement: ijs vjd; and of Thomas Callowe for the last iij quarteres: vijs vjd – xs

Item of Thomas Paterson [*for*] the vij^te tenement: xs

Item of Jeffrey Tybnam for the viij^te tenement: xxs

Item of Wydowe Boyse for the ix^te tenement: ixs

Item of Wydowe Kydall for the x^te tenement, the last in the strete that lede to Seynt Machell: vjs viijd

Summa vj *li* viijs ijd

/*Sent Maris churche*/^509 **Item** of Seynt Marys churche or of any parcell of the churche yarde nothyng within the tyme of thys accompt, for as moche as yt was not inclosed;^510 but receyuyd of Clement Belton for the fyrst halff yere ferme of a tenement at the est ende of the same churche, purchased the last yere of Master Arnold of Cromer: xs; and of hym for the iij^de quarter: ijs; and the other: iijs – xijs [*sic*]

[*f. 100*] **Rest** of that quarter he do clayme & withhold for ij stoppys that the accomptant toke from hym; but receyuyd of John Jowell for the last quarter: vs

Summa xvijs

/*Foren receptes*/ *In primis* receyuyd of Mastres Agnes Sutterton, wydow, for ij yeres ferme of a tenement in the paryshe of Seynt Mychaell of Coslany, late Master Alane Percy, indyd at the fest of the Puryfycacon of Owur Lady in the tyme of thys accompt: xxvjs viijd

---

509 NCR, 18A/6, f. 132^v, heads this section 'ferme off the tenement late Crankes'.

510 See below, pp. 262–3, 300.

Item of Thomas Endle and John Candler for the hole yere ferme of the comon mucke bote: xxvj*s* viij*d*

Summa liij*s* iiij*d*

/Dettes dewe to the comialte/[511] **In primis** receyuyd of Mastres Agnes Sutterton for the vj^te payment of an C *li* dewe by oblygacon at the fest of the Annuncyacon of Owur Lady, whiche was in *anno domini* 1543, for the purchase of a mese in the paryshe of Seynt Mychaell of Coslany, late Master Alane Percy: vj *li* xiij*s* iiij*d*

Item of John Sutterton for parcell of the arrerages of the accompt of John Florens, late chamberleyn: xvj*s* viij*d*

Item of Edmond Warden, late chamberlen, for the arrerages of hys accompt: v *li* xix*s* viij*d*

Item of Master Wylliam Rogers, alderman, for the fyrst payment of xx *li* dewe to the comialte ffor the dette of Master Thomas Grewe, alderman,[512] whyche he receyuyd [*from*] Master Trase, alderman: xxvj*s* viij*d*

Summa xiiij *li* xvj*s* <viij*d*> iiij*d*

[*f. 100^v*] */Redempcions/*[513] **Item** receyuyd of Thomas Bryggis for the iij^de payment of xx markes for the redempcon of <alderman> all offyces within the cite: lxvj*s* viij*d*

Item of John Barker, brewer, for the last payment of lx*s* govyn to the comialte for that he shuld not be chosen shreve nor alderman in iij yeres: xx*s*

/Fynes/ **Item** of Jeffrey Mychelles, baker, for a fyne of a trespase that he dyd concernyng his occupacon in the tyme that Master Leche was mayer: xx*s*

Summa v *li* vj*s* viij*d*

/Hamper/[514] **Item** receyuyd out of the hamper of the guyldhall toward the payment for iij C comb' whete bought by the accomptant for the realeffe of the pore pepyll of the cite: xxxix *li* xiij*s* iiij*d*[515]

Item receyuyd out of the sayd hamper toward the charge of fourty soldyers sent in to France with my lord of Norff' by vertu of the kynges magestes letters: v *li* vj*s* viij*d*

Summa xlv *li*

/Thynges sold/[516] **In primis** receyuyd of Master Trase, alderman, for ij tabylles that stode in the ffraytour at the comon halle, whyche howse ys nowe made a garner: xx*s*

Item of Alexander Mader for an other tabyll that stode in the same howse: x*s*

---

511 NCR, 18A/6, ff. 132^v–5^v, lists these entries under 'foren receptes' with no sub-heading.

512 See above, pp. 208–9. An itemised list of Grewe's debts to the community was drawn up by the assembly on 6 November 1543, amounting to over £32: NCR, 16D/2, f. 205^v.

513 NCR, 18A/6, f. 134–4^v, lists these entries under 'foren receptes' with no sub-heading.

514 NCR, 18A, f. 134^v, lists these entries under 'foren receptes' with no sub-heading.

515 For the scale of the crisis, during which wheat intended for shipment to London was requisitioned, see NCR, 16A/5, pp. 194, 197, 199, 200.

516 NCR, 18A/6, f. 134, lists this and the following section under 'foren receptes', with the sub-headings 'tables sold' and 'brykke, harnes & other thinges sold of the cytiez'.

Item of Thomas Pecke for an other tabyll: ix*s* viij*d*

Item of Thomas Sutterton for an other tabyll: vij*s* vj*d*

Item of Frances Wolmer for an other tabyll: viij*s*

[*f. 101*] **Item** of Master Robert Leche, alderman, for j m^l brycke sold to hym from the comon halle: vj*s* viij*d*

Item of Master Doctour Barret[517] for an other m^l bryke sold hym out of the same place: vj*s* viij*d*

Item of Master Cocke, alderman, for lx pales and iij rayles sold to hym from the comon inne: v*s* ix*d*

Item of Wylliam Pede, smythe, for a lytyll old brokyn chest bownde with yron that laye many a day in the guyldhalle: xvj*d*

Item of [*Thomas*] Crane, pynner, for a broken marbyll ston that laye vpon oon Prestons grave, hys wyvys husbond, in the churche yarde of Seynt Mary Lytyll: xij*d*

Summa iij li xvjs vijd

/*Harnes sold*/[518] **Item** receyuyd of Wylliam Pulley for an old sallet, parcell of old harneys that came out of Scotlond & receyuyd ageyn of Syr John Clere: xiiij*d*

Item of Thomas Alyson for a sallet: xiiij*d*

Item of John Surman for a sallet: xiiij*d*

Item of John Cranford for a sallet: xiiij*d*

Item of Wylliam Lockey for a sallet: xiiij*d*

Item of John Ward for a sallet: xiiij*d*

Item of Wylliam Brearton for a sallet: xvj*d*

Item of Wylliam Collard for a sallet: xij*d*

Item of Robert Marten for an old harnes: viij*s*

Item of iij seuerall men for iij old halberds, parcell of the sayd harnes: xviij*d*

[*f. 101*] **Item** receyuyd of Thomas Larewood for an old harnes withowt splentes: vij*s*

Item of Wylliam Pede, smyth, for v brokyn sallettes & other old peces of harneys: ij*s*

Summa xxvijs xd

/*Soldyers*/[519] **Item** receyuyd of the kynges gyft toward fourty cotes that war govyn to fourty soldyers: that ys to say for euery cote iiij*s*: viij *li*

Item more of the kynges gyft toward ther condyte money to Ypswyche [*Ipswich*], euery man xv*d*: l*s*

---

517 John Barret retained his post as divinity lecturer at Norwich cathedral priory after the Dissolution. He was a leading evangelical: McClendon, *Quiet Reformation*, pp. 68, 75–6, 131, 142, 163–4, 182.

518 As above, p. 243 note 516.

519 NCR, 18A/6, ff. 134v–5, lists this entry under 'foren receptes' with the sub-heading 'conduct money & ffor cotes of xl sougers'.

Item of Master Thomas Godsalve, esquyer,[520] toward the caryage of ther harneys to Ypswiche: iiij*s*

Item receyuyd of a sesment layd and gatherd within the cite for the dyscharge and settyng forthe of the forsayd ffourty soldyers: iiij^xx *li* viij*s* xj*d*[521]

Summa iiij^xx xj *li* ij*s* xj*d*

/*Bakers grynt*/[522] **Item** receyuyd of the comon bakers of the cite for a newe grynt grauntyd of euery comb' corne *ob*': viij *li* vij*s* iiij*d ob*'

Summa viij *li* vij*s* iiij*d ob*'

/*Offrynges and certens of guyldes*/[523] **Item** receyuyd of Syr John Kempe, prest of the comon halle, for the offrynges and certens of dyuerse guyldes kept ther within the tyme of this accompt: and fyrst of the paryshe clarkes offryng: ij*s* <vj*d*> vij*d*

Item of the mesers offryng: ix*s* xj*d*; and of them for a certeyn: <iiij*s* iiij*d*> v*s*

Item of the taylours offryng: iiij*s* ix*d*

[*f. 102*] **Item** of them for a certeyn: iiij*s* iiij*d*

Item of the schomakers offryng: ij*s* xj*d*; and of them for <an off> a certeyn: iiij*s* iiij*d*

Item of the masons and smythys offryng: ij*s* v*d*; and of them for a certeyn: iiij*s* iiij*d*

Item of the beddewevers offryng: ij*s* iij*d*; and of them for a certeyn: iiij*s* iiij*d*

Item of the wullen wevers, fullers and shermen offryng: ij*s* vij*d*; and for a certen: iiij*s* iiij*d* – vij*s* xj*d*

Item of the bochers offryng: ij*s* j*d*; and of them for a certeyn: iiij*s* iiij*d*

Item of the reders offryng: xxij*d*; and of them for a certeyn: iiij*s* iiij*d*

Item of the goldsmythes, sadlers, kalenders and dyers offryng: ij*s* ij*d*; and of them for a certeyn: iiij*s* iiij*d* – vij*s* vj*d*

Item of the carpenters offryng: ij*s* iiij*d*; and of them for a certen & benevolens: vij*s* viij*d*

/*Certens oonly*/ **Item** of the ffyshmongers for a certen: iiij*s* iiij*d*

Item of the worsted wevers for a certen: v*s*

Item of the tanners for a certeyn: iiij*s*

Item of the inkepers and typlers: v*s*

Item of the bakers, brewers and cowpers for a certeyn for ij yeres: xij*s* iiij*d*

Item of the hatmakers for a certen: v*s*

Item of the barbers certen ij yeres: vj*s* viij*d*

Item of the grocers for ij yeres certeyn: x*s*

Summa vij *li* ij*s* vj*d*

---

520 The younger son of Thomas Godsalve senior, who died in 1543: above, p. 157 note 360.

521 On 3 May 1544 the assembly agreed to levy a whole tenth and fifteenth throughout the city to meet the cost of sending forty soldiers 'prepared and ffurnysshed' to the king in France, 'the pooremen in enywise nat to be charged the same': NCR, 16D/2, f. 207.

522 NCR, 18A/6, f. 134^v, lists this entry under 'foren receptes' with no sub-heading.

523 NCR, 18A/6, f. 135–5^v, lists these entries under 'foren receptes' with no sub-heading.

[*f. 102ᵛ*] /***Whete sold**/*[524] ***In primis*** receyuyd for iij^{xx} comb' of Barnard Vtber whete sold in the market at v*s* the comb': xv *li*

Item wher ther was receyuyd iij comb' for jumeser,[525] ther was lost in the sale of the sayd lx comb' vij bushelles *di*'; and receyuyd of the ouer plus, beyng iiij^{or} bushelles and halff: v*s* viij*d*

Item receyuyd of dyuerse bakers for ffyfty comb' of the same whete at v*s* iiij*d* the comb': xiij *li* vj*s* viij*d*

Item receyuyd of Barnard Vtber for x comb' of hys own whete ageyn at v*s* the comb': l*s*

Item receyuyd for whete sold in the market betwyxt Wytsontyde and Myhelmes iij^{xx} xvj comb' at v*s* euery comb': xix *li*

Item more for xxx^{ti} comb' sold in the same tyme in the market at v*s* iiij*d* the comb': viij *li*

Item receyuyd of Master Doctour Manfeld[526] for iij comb': xv*s*

Item of the accomptant for a comb' delyuerd to my lady Shelton for rent dewe to Carrowe: v*s*

Item of John Manne for v comb': xxvj*s* viij*d*

Item of Thomas Cory for x comb': liij*s* iiij*d*

Summa lxiij *li* ij*s* iiij*d*

Memorandum that by reason of an hopper that tryed out moche tyters, tares & other wrecke and twyes meseryng by the *di*' bushell in the market and by shrynkyng with long kepyng ther was s[*l*]yt in at the last meseryng viij comb' and ij bushelles *& cetera.*[527]

Summa totallis omnium receptorum hoc anno CCCC lxiiij *li* xij*s* ixd ob' qu'

[*f. 103*] **Wherof payd** by the sayd accomptant within the tyme of thys accompt for and in dyscharge of the forsayd receptes, as hereafter folowithe:

---

524 NCR, 18A/6, f. 135ᵛ, lists these entries under 'foren receptes' as a sub-section headed 'receyued ffor whete'. For the escalating price of grain, see P. Bowden, 'Agricultural Prices, Farm Profits, and Rents', in J. Thirsk, ed., *The Agrarian History of England and Wales, IV, 1500–1640* (Cambridge, 1967), pp. 618–19 and table I, p. 818; C.J. Harrison, 'Grain Price Analysis and Harvest Qualities, 1465–1634', *Agricultural History Review*, 19 (1971), pp. 135–55.

525 The corresponding entry in NCR, 18A/6, f. 135ᵛ, refers to 'iij comb' of June mesure', namely the surplus when measured in June 1544.

526 Andrew Manfeld, doctor of physic, was involved in property transactions in Thwaite and Toft Monks in the 1520s and 1530s: J. Venn and J.A. Venn, *Alumni Cantabrigiensis I* (4 vols, 1922–7), iii, p. 133; NRO, BRA, 926/109; GIL 1/183–4.

527 Raynbald is here explaining that, through use of the hopper, which sifted out weeds, the apportionment of supplies into small quantities for sale in the market and natural shrinkage, eight combs and two bushels of the original supply have been lost. Commercial measures of grain usualy allowed for an element of 'spillage, wastage and loss': R.D. Connor, *The Weights and Measures of England* (1987), p. 157.

/*Rent resolute*/ **In primis** payd in rent resolute, as yerely appere in other accomptes: that is to say to Syr Wylliam Coppyng, chantry prest of John Cosyn, for ferme and rent of dyuers thynges, as yt appere in other accomptes: iiij *li*

Item to the heyer of Applyardes londes: x*s*

Item to the treasurer of the cathedrall churche of the Holy Trynyte in Norwyche for iij seuerall rentes, sometyme payd to iij seuerall offyces whan they war monkes: xviij*s* iiij*d*; and nowe of newe rent for the howse late purchased of Wylliam Arnold of Cromer: ij*s*; and for newe rent for the churche late cald Seynt Mary Lytyll: iiij*d* – xxj*s* viij*d*

Item to the late pryory of Carrowe: xvj*s* viij*d*

Item to the sayd *pryory* iiij bushelles whete that cost: v*s*

Item to the hospytall of [*St*] Mary Magdalen [*Sprowston*]: xij*d*

Item to the hospytall of Seynt Gyle: xiij*s* iiij*d*

Item to the late priory of Horsham Seynt Faythe: x*s* iiij*d*

Item to the chappell of the Becke [*Beck, Billingford*]: iiij*s*

Item to the late abbey of Sypton [*Sibton*]: ij*s*

Item to the late abbey of Langley: ij*s*

Item to the manour of Heyham [*Heigham*]: iiij*d*

Item to the same manour for the mylles ther: lxvj*s* viij*d*

Item to the chantry of Lettys Payne: vj*s* viij*d*

Item for the x^te of the comon halle: ix*s*

Summa* xij *li* viij*s* viij*d

[*f. 103^v*] /*Fees & wages*/ **In primis** payd to Master Edward Rede, alderman, occupyeng the offyce of mayer iij quarters, and to Master Henry Fuller, beryng the sayd offyce oon quarter within the tyme of thys accompt: xx *li*

Item to Master Thomas Marsham and Richard Lee, shreves of the cite, for ther ffee: xxx *li*

Item to Master Edmond Grey, recorder, for his ffee: v *li*

Item to Master Corbet, steward, for hys ffee: xxvj*s* viij*d*

Item to Master Sergeant Townesend, reteynyd a cownsell with the cite for hys ffee: xl*s*

Item to Master Gawdy,[528] reteyned a cownsell with the cite for halffe a yere ffee: xvj*s* viij*d*

Item to Master Catlyng,[529] reteynyd a cownsell with the cite for halff a yere ffee: xiij*s* iiij*d*

Item to Master Ward, townclarke, for hys ffee: iiij *li* vj*s* viij*d*

Item payd in the kynges eschekyr for the profers of Estern and Myhelmes termys: xx*s*

Item to Anthony Pygot, sword berer, for hys hole yere wagys: lxvj*s* viij*d*

---

528 For Thomas Gawdy (d. 1556) of Shotesham, see *HoP, 1509–1558*, iii, pp. 199–201; Baker, *Men of Court*, i, pp. 735–6.

529 For Richard Catlyn (d. 1556) of Honingham, see *HoP, 1509–1558*, i, pp. 593–4; Baker, *Men of Court*, i, p. 442.

Item to John Rede and Thomas Molle, sergeantes to master mayer, and to Robert Collard, sergeant of the market, for ther wages, euery of them xxvjs viijd: iiij *li*

Item to the forsayd Collard for a lyuery: xvjs

Item to Rychard Framyngham for a lyuery: xvjs

Item to Robert Raynbald, chamberleyn, for hys hole yere wages and lyuery: vj *li*

Item to the iiij[or] wayghtes for ther lyuerys: iiij *li*

[*f. 104*] **Item** to the sayd iiij[or] wayghtes for ther hole yere wages, euery of them xxvjs viijd: v *li* vjs viijd

Item to the bellman for hys wagys: vjs viijd

Item to Wylliam Corbet, newe water baly,[530] for hys hole yere wagys: xxs

/*Annuytees*/ **Item** payd to Syr John Kempe, prest of the comon halle, for his annuyte grauntyd hym out of the same place for terme of lyffe: vj *li* xiijs iiijd

Item to Mastres Alyce Scolehowse, widowe, for hyr annuyte out of a tenement in the paryshe of Seynt Mychaell of Coslany, late Master Percye: xiijs iiijd[531]

Item to Robert Damme for gatheryng of the bakers grynt: xs

Item to Clement, clarke of the common halle, for his hole yere wages newe grauntyd: iiijs

Item to Master Edward Rede, late mayer, for bankettes by hym made to men of honour & worshyppe when they resorte to the cyte, grauntyd to euery mayer: xls

Summa C *li* xvjs

Costes and chargis don within the tyme of thys accompt vpon the bocherys, ffyshe stalles, wulshopps, guyldhalle and vpon other tenementes in the paryshe of Seynt Peter of Mancroft *& cetera*:

/*The v[te] weke after Myhelmes*/ **In primis** payd to Nycholas Tuttell, carpenter, makyng a newe dore loope for the lane at the backe of Agnes Guyrdlers shoppe in the cyte bochery, and to Henry Wodroff, laborer, helpyng to drawe hys bourde with other worke in the sayd bochery *oon day*: xjd

[*f. 104[v]*] /*The vj[te] weke after Myhelmes*/ **Item** payd to the forsayd carpenter makyng a newe hatche for the guyldhall vowlte dore & fynyshyn vp the dore at Agnes Guyrdlers shoppe, ij days: xiijd

Item to the forsayd laborer the same ij days: ixd

Item for ij C iiijd nayle to Qwashe: viijd

Item for oon newe hengyll and hooke for the dore at Guyrdlers shoppe: iiijd

Item for a newe payer of hookes & hengylles for the hatche conteynyng vj *libr' di'* to Paschall: xd

---

530 Because of misdemeanours such as over-fishing and attempts by boat-owners to evade tolls, it was decided on 24 October 1543 to appoint a water bailiff, 'that suche enormyties shuld not be done': *RCN*, ii, pp. 124–5. On 1 May 1544 he was also charged with keeping order in the mayor's court: NCR, 16A/5, p. 213.

531 NCR, 18A/6, f. 158, this entry appears under 'mynute expences'.

Item to hym for a locke & ij keys for the newe hatche with settyng on: x*d*
Item for ij *libr'* candyll to worke bye: ij*d ob'*
Item payd to John Goose for vj dry okyn bordes for the sayd dore and hatche conteynyng iiij^{xx} foote at iiij*s*: ij*s* viij*d*

/*The fyrst weke after Crystmes*/ Item to Henry Wodrof makyng newe florthis in iij of the roppers shopps, oon day: iiij*d ob'*
Item for clay a lode to Henry Carter: v*d*

/*The iij*^{*de*} *weke after Crystmes*/ Item to the forsayd carpenter makyng newe shelvys in Thomas Crosholdes shoppe in the wolmerket & mendyng the wyndows in Roger Baldry & Gregory Pougeleon shopps in the bochery, ij days worke: xiij*d*
Item to Pede for certen yron worke: vj*d*
Item for mendyng the locke on Fyshers shoppe: j*d*

/*The iiij*^{*te*} *weke after Owur Lady*/ Item to Wylliam Johnson, mason, mendyng the buttrace on the est syde of the guyldhall porche, with other worke within, oon day of hym and hys laborer, Walter Colles: xj*d*
Item to William Pede for a newe locke & key for Alyce Rede shoppe dore, bocher: v*d*

[*f. 105*] /*The ix*^{*te*} *weke after Owur Lady*/ Item payd to the forsayd carpenter mendyng dyuers stalles in the bochery & fyshmongers, oon day: vj*d ob'*
Item to William Pede for a payer of jemews for an almery in Jeffrey Redes stalle, bocher: vj*d*
Item to hym for a newe heygoday for Grenis shoppe, fyshmonger: iij*d*

/*The iiij*^{*te*} *weke after Mydsomer*/ Item payd to the forsayd carpenter makyng iiij^{or} newe loopis for the shoppe wyndows of the corner howse in Coblerrowe, iiij days worke: ij*s* ij*d*
Item to Henry Wodrof, laborer, helpyng hym and goyng of erandes, beyng in the syse tyme, the same iiij days: xviij*d*
Item to Master Thetford for iiij^{or} sawen sparris for ledges for the same wyndows: xvj*d*
Item to Wylliam Pede for viij *libr'* of newe yron worke ouer & above the old yron worke: xvj*d*
Item to Mastres Morront for iiij*d* nayle *di'* m^l: xv*d*

/*The v*^{*te*} *weke after Mydsomer*/ Item iij*d* nayle *di'* m^l: x*d*
Item vj*d* nayle j C, all whyche nayle was spent vpon all the forsayd workes: vj*d*

/*The xij*^{*te*} *weke after Mydsomer*/ Item payd to Robert Rogers & to other iij laborers that made a pytte in the strete on the southe syde of Sent Peters churche & in the nyght fyed a jakes in the iij^{de} tenement in Coblerrowe & caryed the menur to the forsayd pytte,⁵³² with drynke & candyll: ij*s* viij*d*
Item for makyng clene the strete ageyn: <i>ij*d*

---

532 The work was undertaken at night to protect the inhabitants from the dangers reputedly posed by contaminated air: Rawcliffe, *Urban Bodies*, pp. 144–6.

[*f. 105ᵃ*] **Item** to Wylliam Johnson, mason, mendyng the walles of the sayd jakes & makyng all a newe pype vp to the chambyr, ij days: xiij*d*

Item to ij laborers fechyng ther morter and brycke from the comon inne, *ij days*: xviij*d*

Item to Harryson for ij comb' lyme: vij*d*

Item to Bryan Doront for an hengyll for Websters shoppe dore in the fyshemarket: iij*d*

Summa xxix*s* vj*d ob'*

Memorandum that all other thynges spent abought the forsayd reparacions here not rehersed war of the comon store, the paymentes wherof do appere <more> more at large amonges the necessaryes bought for comon store & *cetera*.

/*Comon inne*/ **Item** payd in the tyme of thys accompt for the ffynyshyng of certen howsys at the comon inne: and fyrst payd for layeng of a florthe of joystes thorowe out the long crosse howse and plancheryng the same, and makyng oon gret stabyll vnder that roffe with rackes and mangers on bothe sydes, with moche fynyshyng worke in that place:

/*The vjᵗᵉ weke after Myhelmes*/ And fyrst to Nycholas Tuttell, carpenter, begynnyng to laye the florthe of joystes, iiijᵒʳ days: ij*s* ij*d*

Item to Henry Wodrof, laborer, helpyng hym the same iiij days: xviij*d*

Item to Robert Rogers, laborer, helpyng ther oon day to feche joystes from the comon halle and popyll bourde: iiij*d ob'*

[*f. 106*] /*The viijᵗᵉ weke*[533] after Myhelmes*/ **Item** payd to the forsayd carpenter layeng vp the rest of the joystes, makyng a newe wyndowe for the stabyll & a threshold for the dore, vj days: iij*s* iij*d*

Item to Henry Wodroff vj days: ij*s* iij*d*

Item to John Elmam, laborer, ij days: ix*d*

Item to Wylliam Johnson, mason, removyng the stabyll dore & settyng the same in to the entry, stoppyng vp the old dore & settyng in the wyndowe, with moche other worke ther, vj days: iij*s* iij*d*

Item to Walter Colles, his laborer, vj *days*: ij*s* iij*d*

Item to Henry Sparke for sonde ij lode: x*d*

Item for *ij libr'* candyll for evynynges & mornynges: ij*d ob'*

/*The viijᵗᵉ weke after Myhelmes*/ **Item** to the forsayd carpenter begynnyng to plancher the sayd gret chambyr, vj days: iij*s* iij*d*

Item to Henry Wodrof, laborer, helpyng hym to shutte bourde vj days: ij*s* iij*d*

Item to Wylliam Johnson, mason, pynnyng in all the joystes endes, heynyng vp the walles in the entry & mendyng many rystes and craneys in the walles, iij days: xix*d ob'*

Item to Walter Colles, laborer, iij days: xiij*d ob'*

533　This should be the seventh week.

/*The ix^te weke after Myhelmes*/ **Item** payd to the forsayd carpenter ffynyshyng vp the forsayd plancher, v days: ijs viijd ob'

Item to the forsayd Henry Wodrof, laborer, the same v days: xxijd ob'

[*f. 106^v*] /*The x^te weke after Myhelmes*/ **Item** payd to the forsayd carpenter makyng of mangers and rackes on bothe sydes the gretter stabyll, iiij days thys weke: ijs ijd

Item to the forsayd laborer makyng holys in the grownde and walles, iiij days: xviijd

Item to Master Thetford for iiij copyll of sparris for rybbes for the rackes: ijs iiijd

Item to hym for a long ashyn standerd to cutte and ryve for racke stavys: viijd

Item for viij ashyn astyll & for iij^xx x byllettes: xjd

/*The xj^te weke after Myhelmes*/ **Item** to the forsayd carpenter fynyshyng vp the sayd stabyll in all thynges, vj days: iijs iijd

Item to Henry Wodrof, laborer, vj days: ijs ijd

Item to Sander Clarke, laborer, ij days: ixd

Item to Master Thetford for ij copyll more of small sparrys for steys: xiiijd

Item to Robert Hollond, mason, fynyshyng vp the walles above all the chambyrs & bynethe in bothe stabylles whan the carpenter had don, ij days worke of hym & his laborer: xxijd

Item to Henry Sparke for sonde a lode: vd

Item to Mastres Morront for nayle spent ther and in other places thys quarter: & fyrst for gret lathe nayle j m^l: xd; small lath nayle j m^l: ixd; ijd nayle j m^l: xvjd; iijd nayle j m^l: xxd; iiijd nayle j m^l: ijs vjd; vjd nayle *di'* m^l: ijs; viijd nayle ij C: xijd – xs jd

[*f. 107*] **Item** for candyll spent these iiij^or wekes *vj libr'*: vijd ob'

Item to Paschall for yron worke: iiijd

Item to Thomas Sutterton for iiijd nayle j m^l: ijs vjd

/*The fyrst weke after Crystmes*/ **Item** to Master Marsham for lyme <for lyme> spent in the forsayd workes this quarter xix comb' & to Harryson for iiij comb' at iiijd the comb': vijs viijd

Item to Nycholas Tuttell, carpenter, makyng a partycon in the tenement at the west corner of the comon inne for a dyvysyon betwyt the shoppe and the other howse, and an other particon betwyxt the shoppe and the buttry, iiij days: ijs ijd

Item to Henry Wodroff, laborer, iiij days: xviijd

Item to John Wright of Seynt Gyles for a newe joyst of xij foote long that was occupyed byfore Crystmes at the stabyll: xd

/*The second weke after Crystmes*/ **Item** to the sayd carpenter makyng ij newe lopys for the shoppe dore & buttry dore and shelvys vyrownd the shoppe and buttry, and mendyng all the shoppe wyndows, vj days: iijs iijd

Item to the forsayd laborer helpyng hym & lathyng betwyxt the stothis of the partycions the same vj days: ijs iijd

/*The iij^de weke after Crystmes*/ **Item** to the forsayd carpenter mendyng the stayers, parcloses in the chambyr, planchers and all the wyndows, iiij days: ijs ijd

Item to the forsayd laborer iiij days: xviijd

Item to Master Thetford for vij sparrys spent vpon the forsayd partycions: ijs iiijd

Item for a locke for the shoppe dore: vjd

[*f. 107ᵛ*] **Item** to Wylliam Pede for certen yron worke: viijd

/*The iiijᵗᵉ weke after Crystmes*/ **Item** to Wylliam Johnson, mason, makyng the forsayd partycions & mendyng many fautes in the same tenement, iiij days: ijs ijd

Item to hys laborer, Walter Colles, iiij days: xviijd

Item to Harryson for iiij comb' lyme: xvjd

Item to Henry Sparke for sonde a lode: vd

Item to Roger Bacheler, glasewright, newe settyng all the glasse in the chambyr wyndows with xij foote of newe glass: iiijs xd

Item for ij C small nayle to set yt vp: ijd

Item for iiijᵒʳ newe barrys for ij lyghtes: iiijd

/*The fyrst weke after Owur Lady*/ **Item** gaf to Adryan Johnson, fermer of the comon inne, toward a newe rope for his welle, for that we hade the vse of the same welle in the tyme of owur buyldyng ther and in other places of the market & guyldhalle whan reparacions war don any tyme these ij yeres past: xijd

/*The second weke after Mydsomer*/ **Item** payd to Wylliam Pede for vij new lockes & keys for vij dores in the same place: iijs vjd

Item for vij stapylles for the same lockes with a lytyll locke for the closet dore and other yron worke, as barrys & cappys: xvjd

Summa v *li* xxijd *ob'*

Memorandum that all the bourde spent vpon the planchers and plankes vpon the mangers in the gret crosse howse in the same place came of the popylles that war govyn out of Seynt Vedastes closse in the last accompt;[534] and all other bourde & other thynges here not rehersyd war of the comon store & *cetera*.

[*f. 108*] **Costes and chargis don** within the tyme of thys accompt vpon the comon cokeys, with kepyng of them clene, and vpon certen systerns, stathis, stretes ageynst the comon howsys and market place, with many chargis abought those thynges & *cetera*:

/*The xjᵗᵉ weke after Myhelmes*/ **In primis** payd to Robert Tooke, laborer, caryeng fylthe in a barrowe from the cokeys ageynst The iij Belles and ij Nonnys to a pytte made nere the oke at Tymbyr Hylle, iij days: xijd

Item to a poore man that made clene the strete ageynst Seynt Stephyns howses on the comon syde next the oke & caryed yt to the same pitte: iiijd

Item to other ij laborers fyllyng the sayd pitte with other mucke as was layd abought yt and levellyng the same, and ouer that gravelld it that no more fylthe shuld be layd ther: viijd

---

534 See above, pp. 203–4.

Item to Master Wood, alderman, for a lode of mucke that he causyd to be caryed from the ij cokeys in Seynt Clementes of Fybrygge: ij*d*

/*The xij*ᵗᵉ *weke after Myhelmes*/ Item payd this weke for the reparacon of a gret dekaye of a cokey in the myddes of Cokey Lane: and fyrst to John Erne, mason, newe pynnyng vp the fowndacon of the same cokey on bothe sydes a gret waye in lenght with in the grownde & makyng ageyn the crown of the same, iij days: xxj*d*
Item to Robert Hollond, mason, abought the same, also iij days: xix*d ob'*
Item to Sander Clarke & Robert Yoxhale, ther laborers, the same iij days: ij*s* iij*d*
[*f. 108*ᵛ] Item to John Elmam, laborer, fechyng bryke from Mallardes and other thynges to ther hondes the same iij days: xiij*d ob'*
Item to Master Marsham for lyme v comb': xx*d*
Item for sonde ij lode, the oon for morter and the other for pathyn the lane ageyn: x*d*
Item to Robert Mallard for iij C wose brycke: ij*s*
Item for ij *libr'* candyll to worke by in the grounde: ij*d ob'*

/*Crystmes weke*/ Item payd to Robert Tooke, laborer, makyng clene part of the cokey next Master Thomas Marshams corner, whyche brake down on Crystmes Day, that the water myght haue hyr course tyll it myght be made ageyn after Crystmes: ij*d*
Item payd to iij seuerall poore men that made clene the strete ageynst ij seuerall lanys in Conysford & agenst ij tenementes next the comon stathe that stode sperde & caryed away the filthe: iij*d*
Item to Robert Garrade for caryeng away of xlij lode mucke from dyuers cokeys this quarter: vij*s*

/*The weke after Crystmes*/ Item payd to Robert Tooke caryeng awaye a gret quantyte of mucke with his barrowe from the cokey in Conysford in to the kylyard ther next, iij days worke: xij*d*

/*The vij*ᵗᵉ *weke after Crystmes*/ Item to John Ern, mason, makyng the crown of the cokey ouer the foote of the Blacke Fryers brydge and a newe mowthe at the ryver syde, mendyng a gret part of the same /*nullus*/ [*f. 109*] walle that was dekayed, makyng a newe butment of freston to the fyrst arche and mendyng the pavement on all the brydge, makyng an other part of the crown of the cokey next vnto Master Thomas Marshams, whyche fell down on Crystmes Day, iiij days worke in all: ij*s* iiij*d*
Item to Robert Hollond, mason, helpyng hym the same iiij days: ij*s* ij*d*
Item to Sander Clarke and John Elmam, ther laborers, the same iiij days: iij*s*
Item brycke and ston war of comon store, but payd Harryson for lyme vij comb': ij*s* iiij*d*

/*The weke in which Owur Lady fell in*/ Item payd to Henry Carter for caryeng vj lodes mucke this quarter from The ij Nonnys cokey: xij*d*
Item to Henry Sparke for vij lodes from The iij Belles: xiiij*d*
Item to Roger Laws for v lodes from Conysford: x*d*
Item to Foster for v lodes from the newe mylles cokey & Seynt Lawrens: x*d*

Item to yong Ketryngham from Sent Marten and Seynt Edmondes cokeys iiij lodes: viijd

Item to Robert Garrade for xxvj lodes from the rest of all the cokeys in the cite: iiijs iiijd

/*At Mydsomer*/ **Item** to a poore woman that kept the strete clene byfore ij tenementes in Conysford: ijd

Item to Robert Garrade for caryeng of fourty lodes mucke from dyuerse cokeys this quarter: vjs viijd

/*Myhelmes*/ **Item** to Roger Laws for caryeng of iiij lodes from Conysford cokey; and to Rudde for vij lodes from The ij Nonnys cokey: xxijd

[*f. 109ᵛ*] **Item** to Robert Garrade for xlij lode from the rest of all the cokeys in the cite thys quarter: vijs

Item to Robert Tooke for hys hole yere wagys kepyng clene & castyng xvj seuerall cokeys: xiijs iiijd

Item to Robert Rogers for hys hole yere wages kepyng clene and caryeng away the fylthe of ij cokeys above the guyldhalle: ijs

Item to Walter Harryes for hys hole yere wagys kepyng the cokey in Seynt Symondes and caryeng away the fylthe of the same: xvjd

Item to Andrewe Robynson for hys hole yere wagys kepyng clene all the market place from Seynt Seynt [*sic*] Johns Lane to Coblerrowe ende & caryeng away the fylthe: xiijs iiijd

Item payd to John Warnys by the commandment of master mayer and the holle cownsell of the aldermen, for that by the commandment of certen inqwestes of the hedeburghs, lete & turne he reparyd Seynt Bartylmews lane, dyuerse ways in the castill dyche and other noyfull stretes in the cite: xxs[535]

Item more to hym by the sayd commandement for makyng a chanell in the lane that lede from Seynt Olaves churche to Seynt Martens at Oke[536] to convey the water out of Seynt Olaves strete to the cokey in Seynt Martens aforsayd: ijs

Item for a lode *of* sonde spent at the Blacke Fryers brydge payd to Henry Sparke: ‹xd› vd

[*f. 110*]　　　　　　　*Summa* v *li* viijs ixd ob'

Costes and chargis don within the tyme of thys accompt by the commandement of Master Edward Rede, mayer, and by the consent of the accomptantes cownsell vpon pathyng of certen stretes and growndes bylongyng to the comialte to pathe by vertu of an acte made within the cite for the same *& cetera*:[537]

535　NCR, 18A/6, f. 140ᵛ, does not refer to the role of the leets, and thus of residents, in effecting these sanitary improvements. For the importance of such evidence, see Rawcliffe, *Urban Bodies*, pp. 116–40.

536　Hore Lane, now St Martin's Lane: *SLCN*, p. 74.

537　See above, p. 193 note 446.

/The fyrst weke after Myhelmes/ **In primis** payd to Henry Wodroff and John Elmam, laborers, caryeng gravell from the newe pavement vnder Seynt Johns churche at Tymbyr Hylle down to the hollowe grownde ageynst the oke in the same paryshe, cald Swynemarket Hylle, to heyne the grownde to be pathyd, vj days: iiij*s* vj*d*

Item to Henry Carter for caryeng of viij lodes of colder from the comon halle: xvj*d*

/The second weke after Myhelmes/ **Item** to Henry Edryge, laborer, caryeng gravell from the churche walle to the sayd hollowe grownde and rammyng ther, iij days: xiij*d* ob'

/The iij^de weke after Myhelmes/ **Item** to Henry Wodroff caryeng colder out of the comon halle yardes, iij days: xiij*d* ob'

Item to Robert Garrade caryeng vj lodes to the sayd hollowe grownde: xij*d*

/The iiij^te weke after Myhelmes/ **Item** to John Erne for caryeng of xviij lodes of colder from the comon halle & xv lodes ffrom the Gray Fryers at ij*d* a lode: vs vj*d*

Item to Sandyr Clarke and Henry Wodroff spredyng the sayd colder & rammyng, iij days: ij*s* iiij*d*

Item to John Walpole and Crystouer Edmondes, masons, pathyng ayen the ende of the lane[538] that come *out* of the castyll dyche next John Howman /nullus/ [*f. 110^v*] to the chanell xvj yardes at iij*d* the yarde, thei fyndyng all stuff and workmanshyppe: iiij*s*

/The v^te weke after Myhelmes/ **Item** to Henry Edryde, laborer, caryeng out of colder at the comon halle, iiij days: xviij*d*

Item to John Elmam, ther with hym ij days: ix*d*

Item to John Erne for caryeng x lode from thense to the sayd hollowe waye: xx*d*

Item to Robert Garrade for vj lodes: xij*d*

Item to Henry Sparke for xviij lodes from the Gray Fryers at ij*d* ob' the lode: iij*s* ix*d*

Item to Sander Clarke & Walter Colles spredyng and rammyng the same, ij days: xviij*d*

/The vj^te weke after Myhelmes/ **Item** to Henry Sparke for caryeng x lodes from the Grey Fryers: ij*s* j*d*; to John Erne for xiij lodes from thense: ij*s* ij*d* – iiij*s* iij*d*

Item to Sander Clarke ij days ramyng: ix*d*

/The vij^te weke after Myhelmes/ **Item** to John Erne for caryeng of <ii>ij lodes from the ffryers: iiij*d*; & to Sparke for iij lodes: x*d* – xiiij*d*

Item more to the sayd John Erne, mason,[539] for pathyng all the strete ther on the syde next the oke ffrom Jamys Robertes corner down to Robert Brownys backe gate, whyche ys in lenght and brede xv^xx vj yardes, takyn by hym agret to set yt and

---

538 Golden Ball Lane: *SLCN*, p. 12.

539 Erne's activities did not always win approval. Some of the sand that he provided for this work may well have been excavated from a pit that he dug near Coslany gates, thereby threatening to undermine the city walls. On 8 November 1544 he was bound over in the substantial sum of £10 by the mayor's court to make good the damage: NCR, 16A/5, p. 253.

ramme yt, he fyndyng ston, sonde and workmanshyppe at iij*d* a yarde, the grownde beyng levellyd and rammyd to hys hondes: *summa* iij *li* xvj*s* viij*d*

[*f. 111*] /*The viij^te weke after Myhelmes*/ **Item** payd to Edmond Smythe, mason, pathyng all the lenght of the pytte[540] vnto the chanell in the forsayd paryshe of Seynt John at Tymbyr Hylle, takyn agret, he fyndyng all stuff & workemanshyppe: xij*s*

/*The vij^te weke after Crystmes*/ **Item** to John Doblyday, mason, pathyng ageynst the lane ende betwyxt the Fryer Awstens and Jamys Marshams place, and agenst the lane ende betwyxt Roger Lawse and John Hunt, xxx yardes at bothe lanys at iij*d* a yarde, he fyndyng all maner of stuff and workmanshyppe: vij*s* vj*d*

/*The viij^te weke after Crystmes*/ **Item** payd to John Erne for caryeng of iij lodes of pathyn ston from the comon halle to the strete next the oke in Be[r]strete, whyche ston master mayer gaf to John Bengemyn toward the pathyng agenst hys howsys ther: xij*d*
Item more to the sayd John Erne pathyn at the comon lane ende next Seynt Marten at Oke churche,[541] whyche conteynyd xxiiij yardes at iij*d* a yarde, he fyndyng all stuffe and workmanshyppe: vj*s*
Item more to hym pathyng ageynst the waterryng place in the same paryshe, whyche grownd conteynyd iiij^xx x yardes at iij*d* a yarde, he fyndyng all maner of stuff and workmanshyppe: xxij*s* vj*d*
Item to John Homerston, alderman, for the halff chargis for pathyng the lytyll lane that lede in to castyll dyche betwyxt his place and the tenement of Rychard Bengemyn of London, draper: v*s* vj*d*

Summa viij *li* viij*s* iiij*d*

[*f. 111^v*] **Costes and chargis** don within the tyme of thys accompt vpon the wynnyng, inclosyng and fensyng a certen yle out of the ryver in the paryshe of Sent Vedast nere vnto a place sometyme cald Rushmerstathe[542] *& cetera*:

/*The fyrst weke after Myhelmes*/ **In primis** payd to John Warnys, master workman, cuttyng the forsayd yle out of the ryver and hedgyng in the same and cuttyng a dyeke betwyxt the grownde that ys londyd <agen> ageynst the college walle and dydallyng the same rownde abought by Adryans oyseyarde, so that a kele or a bote may go rownde the forsayd yle, vj days worke this weke: iij*s*
Item to Raphe Sympson vj days: ij*s* vj*d*
Item to Roger Davy, laborer, vj days: ij*s* iij*d*
Item to Robert Force, laborer, vj days: ij*s* iij*d*

---

540 As in the case of Jack's pit (above, p. 201 note 457) this was not a 'pit' in the modern sense, but a water-source which supplied the local community: Pelling, 'Health and Sanitation', pp. 134–6.

541 See above, p. 254 note 536.

542 A landing stage in the river Wensum just south of the cathedral precint ('the college'), also known as Rushworth or Rushling stathe: *SLCN*, p. 6.

/*The second weke after Myhelmes*/ **Item** to the forsayd John Warnys vj days: iij*s*
Item to Raphe Sympson vj days: ij*s* vj*d*
Item to Davy and Force vj days: iiij*s* vj*d*

/*The iij^de weke after Myhelmes*/ **Item** to the forsayd Warnys v days: ij*s* vj*d*
Item to Raphe Sympson v days: ij*s* j*d*
Item to Roger Davy, Bartylmewe Wymond and John Elmam, euery of them v days: v*s* vij*d ob'*
Item for whypcord & packthrede for the nettes: j*d*

/*The iiij^te weke after Myhelmes*/ **Item** to the forsayd Warnys vj days: iij*s*
Item to Davy, Wymond and Elmam, euery of them vj days, at iiij*d ob'* a day: vj*s* ix*d*
Item for gryndyng of ther toolys and for a newe rubbe to whete ther toolys: iiij*d*

[*f. 112*] /*The v^te weke after Myhelmes*/ **Item** to the sayd Warnys for iiij days: ij*s*
Item to Davy and Wymond iiij days: iij*s*
Item to John Elmam ij days: ix*d*
Item to Bulward for mendyng *of* ij dydalles: iij*d*
Item for pakthred for nettes for ij dydalles: iij*d*
Item for knyttyng of the same ij nettes: iiij*d*
Item for whypcord for the same ij dydalles: j*d*

/*The vj^te weke after Myhelmes*/ **Item** to the forsayd Warnys for vj days: iij*s*
Item to Davy, Wymond & Elmam vj days: vj*s* ix*d*
Item to Thomas Enele, fermer of the comon mucke bote, for vj days worke of hym & hys bote dydallyng the ryver and dykes vyrownd the sayd yle, at viij*d* the day: iiij*s*
Item for whypcord & packthrede: j*d*

/*The vij^te weke after Myhelmes*/ **Item** to the forsayd Warnys makyng an ende ther and dydallyng the ryver all the lenght of the hospytall closse,[543] whyche was growen with sedge and almost londyd xxx^ti foote from the banke, and in leke maner from the fery[544] to the forsayd newe yle, vj days: iij*s*
Item to Roger Davy and Bertylmewe Wymond, eyther of them vj days: iiij*s* vj*d*
Item to the forsayd Roger Davy for his bote hyer xxxix days contynually occupyd ther: iij*s* iij*d*
Item to Thomas Enele for hys labowur and bote hyer, vj days thys weke: iiij*s*
[*f. 112^v*] **Item** to the forsayd Warnys for the slytte of hys toles and garlementes: iiij*d*

/*The iiij^te weke after Mydsomer*/ **Item** payd thys weke to the forsayd Warnys for mowyng down of reede, homlockes and other wrecke that was growen vp in the

---

543 The Hospital of St Giles owned various properties along the river in the parish of St Vedast, mostly leased out to tenants: *MFS*, pp. 95–6.
544 That is from the cathedral watergate, now known as Pull's Ferry and formerly as Sandling's Ferry: J. Campbell, *Historic Towns: Norwich* (1975), map 3.

sayd yle & spredyng of a gret <g> qwantyte of mener that was layd ther by mucke botes, and also dydallyng the ryver and crycke vyrounde the same yle bycause moche mener was fallen in by the sydes with onlodyng ther botes, vj days: iij*s*

Item to Henry Ferrowur, hys man, iiij days: xx*d*

Item to Bartylmes [*sic*] Wymond and Jamys Burgys for makyng of pyles & dryvyng of them the second weke after Myhelmes, whiche was forgotten byfore: ij*s* iij*d*

Summa iiij *li* ij*s* x*d* *ob'*

Memorandum that all thynges occupyed abought the hedgyng of the same yle, as pyles, stakes and wood, war of the gyft of John Mace & of the master of the hospytall [*Robert Codde*] of the stewynges of suche wood as grewe in ther growndes nere *& cetera*.

/*Ryver cuttyng*/ **Item** payd in the tyme of thys accompt for cuttyng of the ryver betwyxt Surlyngam fferry and the towur without Conysford gates: and fyrst to Robert Tooke for gryndyng of the comon sherys, with iij newe forlockes: xiij*d*

Item for vj fadam of newe baste with a newe rubbe and a whetston: viij*d*

[*f. 113*] **Item** to Robert Teyton, cutter, for xx days worke cuttyng the sayd ryver, at vj*d* a day: x*s*

Item to Wylliam Guylbert & Bartylmewe Wymond for the same xx days rowyng, at x*d*: xvj*s* viij*d*

Item to Andrewe Qwashe for vj fadam more of bast abought the mydworke: vj*d*

Item to John Dyxe for hym selff and his bote, with a crepar, oon day worke brekyng a gret bedde with wedes of halff a myle longe: vj*d*

Item to hym with his bote, ij days rowyng the accomptant to vewe ther worke: x*d*

Item spent the oon day in brede & drynke vpon the workmen & other company: vj*d*

Item to Hoodes wyf for hyr bote hyer the forsayd xx days: ij*s* ij*d*

Item gaf in reward amonges the workmen: iiij*d*

Summa xxxiij*s* iij*d*

Chargis of a newe crosse made and caryed to Hardley[545] and ther set vp in the place wher the shrevys of Norwyche yere*ly* do kepe a courte *& cetera*:

/*Hardley Crosse*/ **In primis** payd to Nycholas Tuttell, carpenter, makyng and framyng of a newe crosse to be set vp at Hardley, vj days worke: iij*s* iij*d*

Item to Nycholas Marry, gravour, inbostyng the hede of the same <crucyfyxe> crosse in ij partes with a crucyfyxe & the other ij partes with the cite armys, with a fynyall and other antycke worke, vij days worke, at vij*d* *ob'* the day: iiij*s* iiij*d* *ob'*

---

545 Hardley Cross was one of the pricincipal crosses (varying in number over the years from four to ten) marking the extensive boundaries of the city of Norwich. It stood some fifteen miles south-east of the city centre, at the point where the river Chet joins the Yare, denoting the limits of the city's jurisdiction over the Yare, along which goods were shipped to and from Great Yarmouth: *SLCN*, pp. 90–1; Rodgers, *River and Staithes*, p. 31.

[*f. 113ᵛ*] **Item** to Robert Hennoud, gravour, clensyng of the forsayd inbostyd worke, v days, at vj*d ob'*: ij*s* viij*d ob'*

/*The vᵗᵉ weke after Mydsomer*/ **Item** to the forsayd carpenter makyng a frame to be set in the grownde to mortes the crosse in & fynyshyng vp the crosse, iiij days: ij*s* ij*d*

Item to Rychard Steyner for castyng the sayd crosse in oyle & vernyshe, fyndyng all stuffe: xvj*d*

Item to Wylliam Pede for xvj spekynges: xij*d*

/*The xijᵗᵉ weke after Myhelmes*/ **Item** payd for bote hyer and ij men rowyng ij carpenters and ij laborers with the forsayd crosse, frame, plankes, hyrdylles and other thynges necessary for the reysyng of the sayd crosse: xvj*d*

Item to Nycholas Tuttell and John Byrche the yonger, carpenters, for oon day worke to Hardle to reyse vp the sayd crosse: xiij*d*

Item to Henry Wodrof and John Elmam, laborers, the same day: ix*d*

Item payd for the hyer of an horse for the accomptant to ryde with the shreves thyther to se the sayd crosse set vp: iiij*d*

Item gaf to Master Drakes man that rowyd the accomptant from Hardley flete⁵⁴⁶ to the place: ij*d*

Item gaf to the carpenters, laborers and rowers a ferkyn of small bere bycause they war forthe the more part of ij nyghtes: vj*d*

Summa xix*s*

[*f. 114*] *Memorandum* that the tymbyr wherof the forsayd crosse and frame <wr> war made of war parcell of xij okes that war bought in the last accompt at Ambryngale [*Arminghall*]; the chargis of hewyng and sqwaryng and sawyng shall appere amonges the mynute expenses *& cetera.*

/*Comon stathe*/ **Item** payd within the tyme of thys accompt for certen reparacions don at the newe comon stathe:

/*The iiijᵗᵉ weke after Myhelmes*/ **And fyrst** payd to Nycholas Tuttell, carpenter, newe plancheryng of a gret part of a corn chambyr ouer the halle, iij days: xix*d ob'*

Item to Henry Wodrof, laborer, helpyng hym to shotte bourde, to cary yt down from the comon inne & to stoppe with morter next the walles vyrownde the same chambyr, iij days: xiij*d ob'*

/*The vᵗᵉ weke after Myhelmes*/ **Item** to the sayd carpenter and laborer for other iij days this weke fynyshyng vp *the* sayd chambyr: ij*s* ix*d*; iiij*d* nayle *di'* m¹: xv*d* – iiij*s*

/*At Owur Ladys quarter*/ **Item** allowyd to John Styngate, fermer ther, for mendyng of other ij corn chambyrs: x*d*

Item payd that same tyme to Clement Appilbye, plomer, for newe castyng & sysyng

---

546 A broad dyke or waterway running from Hardley into the Yare. For Master Drake, see below, p. 263 note 551.

of ffyve C wyghtes clade in brasse & for <newe> newe rynges for dyuerse of them at xvj*d* C: vj*s* viij*d*[547]

Item to hym for oon newe quarter wight, that was lackyng ther: xx*d*

/*The fyrst weke after Owur Lady*/ **Item** to the forsayd carpenter for oon day mendyng the carte gate next the strete: vj*d* ob'

Item to Wylliam Pede, smythe, for certen newe yron worke, with plates and nayles for the sayd gate, with mendyng the locke: xiiij*d*

[*f. 114ᵛ*] **Item** more to hym for a newe coller for the sayd *gate*, a gret hooke, ij stapylles & a dossen gret nayles, all weyng xiiij *libr'*: xxj*d*

Item more to hym for a dossen brodes for the coller and a dossen dyce hede nayle for the jemews of the clycke gate: vj*d*

/*Tenementes ageynst the stathe*/ **Item** payd to Robert Hollond, mason, mendyng the ovyn within the sayd place and stoppyn in a dore and certen holys at the hede place next the kylyard, ij days worke in all: xiij*d*

Item to Bartylmewe Wymond, laborer, ij days: ix*d*

Item to Marsham for lyme ij comb' & sonde a lode: xiij*d*

Item to the forsayd carpenter makyng ij newe loopys for ij dores at the sayd hede place & layeng of ij newe thresholdes, ij days more: xiij*d*

Item to Wylliam Pede for ij payer of newe hengylles for the sayd dores conteynyng vij *libr'*: xj*d*

Item for a newe key to the tenement locke wher Elsabeth Story dwelle: iij*d*

Item to Styngate for the ij threshold peces and for brycke for the ovyn: vj*d*

Summa xxvs vj*d* ob'

/*Newe mylles*/ **Item** payd for certen costes don within the tyme of thys accompt at the newe milles:

/*The fyrst weke after Mydsomer*/ **And fyrst** to Nycholas Tuttell, carpenter, makyng a newe washyng stathe to be set in the ryver ther, iij days that weke: xix*d* ob'

[*f. 115*] **Item** to Henry Wodrof, laborer, helpyng hym the same iij days: xiij*d* ob'

/*The second weke after Mydsomer*/ **Item** to the sayd carpenter fynyshyng vp the sayd stathe & reysyng the same, mendyng the stayers in the servantes chambyr & the southe brydge, v days: ij*s* viij*d* ob'

Item more to hym for oon day makyng a payer of newe trustylles to bere the mylle ston at the northe mylle whan yt is hewen: vj*d* ob'

Item to the forsayd laborer helpyng hym ther, iiij days thys weke: xviij*d*

Item payd for iij speykynges for the sayd trustilles: iij*d*

---

547 Rodgers, *River and Staithes*, p. 47, suggests that these weights were needed to work the jib crane, but since they were 'sysed' (made to conform to the standard assize) they are more likely to have been used to weigh all merchandise passing through the staithe on which tolls other than cranage were paid.

Item to Henry Sparke for caryeng of the tymbyr of the newe stathe, trustylles & plankes for the southe brydge from the comon inne: iiij*d*

Item for a howur worke of a mason pynnyng in the forsayd newe stathe: j*d*

    Summa viij*s* ij*d*

Memorandum that the tymbyr wherof the stathe and trustylles war made was parcell of the xij okes that war bought in the last accompt at Ambryngale [*Arminghall*]; the chargis of hewyng and sawyng shall appere amonges the mynute expenses *& cetera.*

/*Gates & towers*/ **Item** payd for certen costes don within the tyme of thys accompt at dyuers gates within the cite:

/*The x*ᵗᵉ *weke after* <*Myhelmes*> *Crystmes*/ **And fyrst** payd to Nycholas Tuttell, carpenter, makyng a newe swayptre for Fybrigge gates, with moche other reparacon on the same gates, mendyng the frame of the parcolas, the clycke gate at Pokethorpe gates, with moche other worke at those gates, iiij days worke: ij*s* ij*d*

[*f. 115ᵛ*] **Item** to Henry Wodroff, laborer, helpyng hym the same iiijᵒʳ days: xviij*d*

Item to Master Thetford for a sawen sparre for the parcolas of Fybrige gates: iiij*d*

Item to Paschalle for mendyng a gret yron barre that ronne in the swayptre, for a newe vorrell for the ende of the swayptre, iiij woldes of yron, vj gret clynke nayles, *di'* C brodes, all whyche gere contaynyd toguether xl *libr'*: vj*s* viij*d*

Item for <hys> hys helpe & his man oon day: viij*d*

Item to hym for mendyng the lockes of Helle gates, with one newe keye ther: vj*d*

Item to hym for mendyng the locke of the clycke of Pokethorppe gates, a palme of yron for the gret barre, ij gret stapylles, certen brades and gret nayles, with hys helpe ther, almost a days worke: ij*s* viij*d*

Item payd ther in the strete for vj*d* nayles: j*d*

Item to Wylliam Johnson, mason, and Colles, hys laborer, for oon day worke mendyng dyuerse thynges at the sayd Pokethorp gates: xj*d*

/*The xij*ᵗᵉ *weke after Mydsomer*/ **Item** payd to Robert Toft, porter of Fybrige gates, for certen reparacions don ther by hym in the lodgyng ouer the gates: and fyrst for bourde, ledges, nayle & workmanshyp of a newe wyndowe loope in the chambyr: vij*d*

Item for clay, marle & workmanshyppe of /*nullus*/ [*f. 116*] the florthes ouer the gate, oon day worke of Dabney & the sayd Toftes: ij*s* iiij*d*

    Summa xviij*s* iiij*d*

/*ij lethyr harneys*/[548] **Item** payd for the chargis of ij lethyr harneys made by the commandment of Master Edward Rede, mayer, and his brothern, the aldermen: and fyrst payd the iij*ᵈᵉ* day of Maye in the cownsell chambyr to Stephyn Davy, tanner, for a gren nettes hyde & ij calvys skynnys: vj*s* viij*d*

---

548 NCR, 18A/6, ff. 154ᵛ–62, incorporates this and the following eleven sections in a single extremely long section entitled 'mynute expences', which appears at the very end of the account after expenditure on the common hall (ff. 145ᵛ–54ᵛ).

Item to Mastres Rede for iij elles of canvas for the insyde of the sayd ij harneys: xxj*d*

Item for shavyng of ij calvys skynnys: iij*d*

Item glewe: iiij*d*; buckylles: v*d*; nayle: ij*d*; lethyr for the buckylles: iij*d* – xiiij*d*

Item to Thomas Barchom the yonger makyng of ij harneys of the sayd stuffe: vs iiij*d*

Item to Thomas Boswell for castyng of them in a culler: iij*s*

Summa xviij*s* ij*d*

Costes and chargis for makyng of a newe scaberd for the sworde and of other thynges parteynyng to the same and to the swordberer *& cetera*:[549]

In primis payd to Master Awsten Steward, alderman, for blewe velvet bought by hym at London: xv*s*

Item to John Almond for makyng of a newe scaberd for the sworde and a garter, coueryng them with the sayd velvet, scoryng the sworde and trymmyng the hyltes: ij*s*

[*f. 116ᵛ*] **Item** to Peter Nelson for frendys for the hyltes: vj*d*

Item for fyne canvas for lynyng of the scaberd: ij*d ob'*

Item to Nycholas Isborn, goldsmythe, for newe makyng the old chape and a newe buckill & chape for the garter & guyldyng of them: ij*s* iiij*d*

Item to hym for syluer, ouer and above the syluer of the old chape: iij*s* ij*d*

Item payd for an elle of buckram, wherof was made a bagge to kepe in the hatte and a casse for the scaberd, with makyng: vij*d*

Item to Robert Hendry for the losse of a newe felt that he made, whiche wold not serve: vj*d*

Summa xxiiij*s* iij*d ob'*

/*Sent Maris churche*/ **Item** payd for the lease of the churche sometyme cald Lytyll Seynt Marys, with the churche yarde, the advyson of the same, with all other profyghtes therto bylongyng:[550] and fyrst payd to the deane and prebendes of the cathedrall churche of Norwyche for the purchase of a lease of CCCCC yeres, withowt impechement of wast, as yt apperythe more at large in the wrytynges made for the assuerans of the same to the comialte: xx *li*

Item to Balles, Master Corbettes clarke, for wrytyng the draughtes of the indentures and ingrossyng of the same: ij*s*; and to the brothern of the place for the seale: vj*s* viij*d* – viij*s* viij*d*

---

549 The ceremonial sword borne before the mayor was the physical symbol of his authority, and had therefore to be suitably impressive: Liddy, *Contesting the City*, pp. 38–9. Norwich boasted some striking regalia, which was entrusted to the care of the chamberlains: see Appendix III.

550 On 8 December 1543 the mayor and aldermen agreed to take on the lease of St Mary the Less from the dean and chapter, although matters were not finalised before the assembly until 21 September following: NCR, 16A/5, p. 190; 16D/2, f. 208; below, p. 302 note 615.

[*f. 117*] **Item** payd in ernest whan yt was fyrst bought: j*d*

Item payd to Master Drake and to Master Manuell, prebendes ther,[551] for the deskes stondyng in the qwere, which war reservyd at the fyrst bargayn: xv*s*

Item to John Gaywood, glasewright, for newe reparyng and mendyng all the wyndows in the churche & chansell, whyche war sore dekayd, he fyndyng all maner of stuff: iiij*s* viij*d*

Summa xxj *li* viij*s* v*d*

Dyuerse thynges bought in the tyme of thys accompt at the best chepe as the tyme requeryd, to be hade in store in a redynes for reparacions and buyldynges, whyche thynges be not cowntyd byfore in the forsayd reparacions & *cetera*:

/Novembyr/ **In primis** payd the x day to Robert Smythe, servant with Sir John Shelton, for a lode of goodly okyn bourde of xij foote lenght conteynyng iiij C *di'* at iij*s* iiij*d* C: xv*s*

Item the xiiij day to Robert Norman for <f> a bushell of charcole to make a fyer in the cownsell chambyr whan the newe shreve was chosen in the stede of Master Morront: iij*d*[552]

Item the xvij day to Neve of Rynglond [*Ringland*] for iiij^{or} sackes with charcole layd in the guyldhalle to haue a fyer whan they nede: ij*s*

/Januarii/ **Item** payd the v^{te} day to Chapman of Marlyngford [*Marlingford*] for a lode of dry bourde to fynyshe the workes at the comon inne conteynyng iij C: x*s*

/Februarii/ **Item** the ffyrst day to Neve ageyn for iiij^{or} sackes more of charcole: ij*s*

[*f. 117*^v] /Marche/ **Item** payd the xxvij day to John Styngate for iij heryng barrelles to packe in latten, brasse and shruff of metall gatherd abought the cite for the makyng of gonnys: xviij*d*

Item to Paschall for a vyce of yron fastid to a lytyll stole for the comon seale: iiij*s*

/Aprelle/ **Item** the xxij day to Thomas Barchom the yonger for a newe brede to gyve othys vpon made of waynsvotte & gravyn, with trymmyng in of the crucyfyx and glasse, and for the sayd crucyfyxe and glasse and for wrytyng of Seynt Johns Gospell,[553] in all chargis: ij*s* ij*d*

---

551 Edmund Drake and Henry Manuel, canons respectively of the fourth and third prebends of Norwich Cathedral: J.M. Horn, ed., *Fasti ecclesiae Anglicanae 1541–1857*, VII (1992), pp. 54, 55.

552 Morraunt died suddenly in office and Thomas Marsham was then elected: above, p. 38; NCR, 16/D2, ff. 199^v–200.

553 The paxbred, a tablet bearing a scared image, was customarily kissed by lay congregations during the celebration of mass as a substitute for reception of the Host, and testators in the mayor's court were required to take their oaths upon one: E. Duffy, *The Stripping of the Altars: Traditional Religion in England 1400–1580* (New Haven and London, 1992), p. 125.

Item payd for whyte paper delyueryd at dyuerse tymis thys yere to Rychard Framyngham viij quayers: xx*d*; & iiij quayers to the accomptant for the makyng of his bookes: viij*d* – ij*s* iiij*d*

Summa **xxxix*s* iij*d***

Presentes govyn to dyuerse persons within the tyme of this accompt as folowith:

/*My lord of Surrey*/[554] *In primis* payd in the market the xv day of Marche for a gret ffreshe salmon and a cravys to John Crowe: ix*s*
Item for a rostyng ele to Mastres Dowsyng: xviij*d*

/*Justices of assyse*/ **Item** payd to Syr Jamys Grene for ij pottes with waffers: ij*s* iiij*d*; to John Mannys wyff for spycebrede: xx*d*; wyne sacke ij gallons: ij*s* viij*d* – vij*s* viij*d*
Item to Master Leche for vj yardes of ffyne /*nullus*/ [*f. 118*] stamyn, wherof iij yardes was govyn to my lord Montagewe and other iij yardes to Master Felewe, clarke of the crown: xxiiij*s*[555]

/*The kynges surveyour*/ **Item** payd for a gallon of claret wyne and a pottell of wyne sacke sent to Seynt Leonardes to Master Eyer, surveyer to the kynges mageste,[556] for dyuerse consyderacions concernyng the comon halle and other thynges: ij*s*

/*Duke of Norff' bankettes*/ **Item** payd for malvesey, sacke and swete wyn, of euery of them a gallon, for a banket made in the ffeld without Seynt Stephyns gates on Ester Wedynsday for my lord of Norff' takyn musters ther iiij*s*; ij gallons of bere iiij*d*; manchettes iij*d*; spycebrede xvj*d*; appylles iij*d*; caraways & byskettes a boxe x*d* – vij*s*
Item for a ferkyn of bere dronke at the crosse in the market amonges the soldyers that war reteynyd whan they came home: ix*d*; and for brede for them: iiij*d* – xiij*d*
Item payd for the dyners and suppers of Robert Damme, Henry Wodroff and John Elmam, who caryed all the forsayd thynges & plate in to the feld and tendyd all that day vpon the forsayd besynes & soldyers: xij*d*

---

554 Henry Howard, earl of Surrey (d. 1546), son and heir of the third duke of Norfolk, who campaigned with his father in France: Head, *Ebbs and Flows*, pp. 211–13.

555 Felewe does not appear in Baker, *Men of Court*. He may have been the John Fallowes who received a grant of confiscated monastic property in Northamptonshire in 1540, at the same time as other royal officials, and who lived in the legal quarter of Holborn, near the courts at Westminster: *LPFD*, XVI, p. 96; XIX (part 2), p. 74.

556 Until the Dissolution, St Leonard's had been a dependent cell of Norwich cathedral priory overlooking the city on the east. It was then acquired by the above-mentioned earl of Surrey and turned into a mansion: Houlbrooke, 'Refoundation and Reformation', p. 526. John Eyer of Bury St Edmunds, 'a career civil servant in the court of augmentations of uncertain family origins', was the receiver of suppressed and surrendered monastic property in Norfolk and Suffolk, much of which he acquired for himself: W.C. Richardson, *History of the Court of Augmentations* (Baton Rouge, Louisiana, 1961), pp. 47–8, 50, 281; D. MacCulloch, *Suffolk and the Tudors* (Oxford, 1986), p. 74; *LPFD*, XIX (part 2), nos 166 (63), 340 (22); above, pp. 25, 42.

Item spent vpon Master Wardeyn, Thomas Redmond and Robert Mychelles, who by commandment went vpon the ryver to vewe certen thynges with the accomptant: iij*d*

[*f. 118ᵛ*] **Item** payd on Seynt Jamys evyn for drynke cald for by master mayer and his brothern in the cownsell chambyr: ij*d*

Item payd the vᵗᵉ day of August to Adryans wyf for master mayers dyner, Master Ward, Master Cocke, Thomas Cony, the accomptant, the swordberer, master mayers offycers & others who sat all that day in the sembly chambyr serchyng the treasure howse for wrytyng concernyng the lybertees of the cite & in especyall ageynst the sewte of Master Flynt: ij*s* x*d*⁵⁵⁷

Item payd the ix day of Septembyr for brede, bere, wyne and peers spent vpon master mayer & other the kynges commyssyoners syttyng at the comon halle for the kynges subsedy: ij*s* ix*d*

                Summa lix*s* iij*d*

/*Tryvmphis*/ **In primis** payd in the weke byfore Wytsontyde for a tryvmphe made for the vyctory hade at Edenburgh [*Edinburgh*] and Lethe [*Leith*] in Scotland:⁵⁵⁸ and fyrst for *di' C* astyll: ij*s* iiij*d*

/*Scotland*/ **Item** fourty fagottes of wood, of the which was made a fyer in the market place: xx*d*

Item to the iiijᵒʳ wayghtes playeng at Tomlond and at the crosse in the market in the tyme of processyon: xvj*d*

Item payd in the weke byfore Myhelmes for astyll *di' C*: ij*s* iiij*d*

[*f. 119*] /*Bullen*/ **Item** for fourty fagottes of wood, of the whiche wood and astyll was made a bonffyer in the market for the wynnyng of Bullen [*Boulogne*]: xviij*d*⁵⁵⁹

Item payd for *di' C* astyll for a ffyer made at Master Fullers gate, than mayer: xxij*d*

Item for wood for a ffyer made at Cryst Churche gate, ouer and above wood govyn: xx*d*

Item payd for iij barrelles of bere dronke at the forsayd iij ffryers [*sic*], with iij*s* in brede: xij*s*

Item to the iiijᵒʳ wayghtes playeng in dyuers places in the tyme of processyon: ij*s*

Item to Sucklynges iij laddes: xij*d*

---

557 Robert Flint (d. 1559) was an influential local lawyer with northern connections: *HoP*, *1509–1558*, ii, p. 154; Baker, *Men of Court*, i, p. 689. As leaseholder of the manor of Lakenham from the former cathedral priory, he claimed jurisdiction over land in Trowse Milgate, and thus came into direct conflict with the civic authorities. In 1544 he began a suit in the court of augmentations against them which dragged on until 1553: NCR, 9H/11, 12.

558 The mayor's court ordered a civic procession and bonfires in the streets on 28 May 1544: NCR, 16A/5, p. 218. For the Scottish campaign, which was led by the earl of Hertford, see Scarisbrick, *Henry VIII*, pp. 443–5; Merriman, *Rough Wooings*, chapter six.

559 Henry VIII entered Boulogne on 18 September 1544, but his triumph proved short-lived: Scarisbrick, *Henry VIII*, pp. 446–50.

/*Interludes*/ **Item** payd on the Sonday after Twelth Day to vj laborers that caryed xij long popill plankes from the comon inne to the comon halle to make a scaffold for an interlude to be playd ther by my lord of Sussex men: vj*d*[560]

Item to a carpenter that made the scaffold, with brede and drynke, as well for the players as for the laborers & carpenter: viij*d*

Item ther was govyn to the sayd players in reward x*s*, of the whyche was gatherd of master mayer and his brothern ij*s* x*d*, and so was payd by the accomptant: <vij*s* x*d*> vij*s* ij*d*

Summa xxxvj*s*

/*Rewardes*/ **Item** gaf to the prynces players the xviij day of Novembyr in reward bycause that master mayer hade no leyser to se them playe: iij*s* iiij*d*

[*f. 119ᵛ*] **Item** gaf to certen botewrightes that wrowght next Fybrygge keye for takyng vp of an aras pece of tymbyr that came from Sent Margarytes stathe,[561] with the makyng ageyn a crome that was broken in the takyng vp of yt: iiij*d*

Item gaf on Mydlent Sonday to Edmond Pynchyn, offycer, for hys peynys to *go* with the accomptant in to Be[r]strete to iij bochers that hade left ther stalles to fraye them, and so by that menys dyd get hys money: ij*d*

Item gaf amonges Mastres Suttertons chyldern whan the accomptant receyuyd xx nobylles of hyr for the dette of Wylliam a Lee for the purchase of the place in Seynt Mychaell of Coslany, late Master Alane Percyes: iiij*d*

Item gaf on Seynt Georges guyldday to a pursevant that brought certen letters and proclymacions ffrom the kyng: v*s*

Item gaf to Master Doctowur Kyng[562] prechyng at the comon halle on the Monday in the Rogacon weke: iij*s* iiij*d*

Item payd to Wylliam Walby for his horse hyer, paynes and costes rydyng to Marten [*Merton*][563] with a letter to master recorder from master mayer to requere hym to be here that weke for dyuerse wyghty cawses: xiiij*d*

Item gaf in reward to the sayd master recorder for hys peynys and for the costes of hys horses and men: x*s*

[*f. 120*] **Item** payd for the costes of a man and hys horse rydyng to Raynam [*Raynham Hall*] for Master Sergeant Townesend[564] to requere hym to come to the cite for certen wyghty cawses: xx*d*

---

560 The players of Henry Radcliffe, earl of Sussex: Galloway, ed., *Records of Early English Drama*, p. 370.

561 The churchwardens of St Margaret's subsequently undertook to repair the damaged stathe themselves: *SLCN*, p. 52.

562 Dr Henry King, who became a prebendary of Norwich cathedral in 1548, was an enthusiastic supporter of evangelical reform. Since even Matthew Parker considered one of his sermons too extreme, he proved to be a controversial figure: McClendon, *Quiet Reformation*, pp. 117, 134, 139, 172; Horn, *Fasti ecclesiae Anglicanae*, p. 59.

563 The country residence of the recorder, Edmund Grey, was at Merton, north of Thetford: *HoP, 1509–1558*, ii, p. 252.

564 See above, p. 125 note 204.

Item payd to an other man that rode the same day, beyng Relycke Sonday, to Marten [*Merton*] for master recorder for the same cawsys: xvj*d*

Item to the iij^de man sekyng for Master Rogers, beyng forthe ij days, whome he fownde at last at Waxham: ij*s* ij*d*

Item for the accomptantes horse hyer ij days rydyng ageyn for master recorder, whome he brought with hym to Norwyche: xij*d*

Item gaf in reward by the consent of the hole cownsell of the cyte to master recorder and Master Sergeant Townesend, eyther of them ij angelles in goold: xxxij*s*

Item payd to John Blome for the costes of master recorders iiij^or horses and men: ij*s*

Item gaf in reward the xxx day of August to a pursevant that brought the qwenys lettyrs[565] & a commyssyon for the subsedy: v*s*

Item payd for the costes of an horse and a man rydyng with the sayd letters & commyssyon to Syr Roger Towenesend[566] and other persons appoyntyd in the sayd commyssyon to appoynt what day thei shuld mete at Norwyche for the sayd subsedy: ij*s* viij*d*

[*f. 120^v*] **Item** gaf in rewarde to Master John Eyer, the kynges surveyour, for hys lawffull favour in the vewyng of the lede at the comon halle, xx crownys: v *li*

Item gaf to Asterby, plomer, for hys paynes & labowur meseryng the lede vpon the churche, chansell & ij yles, whyche was all to guether valued at xxxviij fother: xij*d*

Item gaf in reward in the tyme of thys accompt <to> amonges the bochers wyvys & other tenauntes wyvys, as to the myllers wyf, Mastres Qwashe and suche other that nevyr leve cravyng of the sayd accomptant; and also spent in the sayd tyme at suche tenauntes as kepe vytallyng howses, whyche thynges dyuerse of the tenauntes loke for of dewty, wherof the partyclers do appere more at large in a byll of euery parcell, whiche mownte to: iiij*s* vij*d*

/Postes and out rydynges/ **Item** payd in Mydlent weke for the hyer of ij horse for Master Davy, alderman, and Robert Collard to waight vpon hym to Yarmoth concernyng letters sent from the kynge: ij*s*

Item for shoyng of the sayd horses: v*d*

Item payd for the costes of the accomptant & hys horse hyer rydyng to Master Gonfeld of Gorleston[567] for certen oblygacions of John a Weltons and for to bye at Yarmothe pathyn tyle & other necessaryes for the comialte: ij*s* ij*d*

---

565 Queen Katherine Parr (d. 1548) was then acting as regent-general of England during Henry VIII's absence in France. The contents of these letters are not known, but probably related to the subsidy: S.E. James, *Kateryn Parr; The Making of a Queen* (Aldershot, 1999), chapter ten.

566 For Sir Roger Townshend (d. 1551) of Raynham, see *HoP, 1509–1558*, iii, pp. 470–1; Baker, *Men of Court*, ii, pp. 1545–6; Moreton, *The Townshends and their World*, pp. 27–38. The above-mentioned 'Master Sergeant Townesend' was his second son: see above, p. 125 note 204.

567 Possibly the John Gonnfeld who graduated from Cambridge in 511–12, although his identity remains uncertain: Venn and Venn, *Alumni Cantabrigiensis I*, ii, p. 231.

[*f. 121*] **Item** payd to Robert Collard rydyng the viij^te day of August to Waborn Hope [*Weybourne Hope*], for as moche as it was sayd that Frenchemen and Scottes war londyd vpon the cost, for his costes & horse hyer: xvj*d*

Item to John Crowes seruant rydyng the same day to Cromer for the same cawse: xvj*d*

Item the same day to Edmond Pynchyn rydyng to Sir Wylliam Paston^568 with lettyrs from Master Corbet for the same cawse: xvj*d*

Item to Wylliam Walby rydyng to Worste[*a*]d for the same cawse, for as moche as the fyrst tydynges came from thense: viij*d*

Summa ix *li* viij*s* iiij*d*

/*Sewtes*/ **In primis** payd on Corpus Christi evyn to Master Warde, town clarke, for the serche in the guyld halle in London for the mysorder of shrevys^569 dyuerse chargis and costes, as it apperith in a byll to the sum of: xxxij*s* viij*d*

Item left in gage with the mayer and hys brothern of Cambrydge for the tryall of owur lybertes whether the cytysens of Norwyche shall pay any custome or no: xx*s*^570

Item toward the costes of the accomptant, who rode to Cambrydge iij days byfore the fayer began & gaf attendans ther vj days byfore he cowd haue a dyrecte answer, rydyng bothe outwardes and homewardes by master recorder for that matter & other thynges: x*s*

[*f. 121^v*] **Item** payd to the town clarke of Cambrydge for recordyng owur sewte and of the sayd xx*s* left in th'andes of Thomas Bracy, water baly: xij*d*

Item payd to the ij shreves of the cyte for the levy of a fyne for the howse at Tomlond purchased of Master Arnold: vj*s* viij*d*

/*Comptes*/ **Item** payd in Ester weke to Master Wylliam Toppsffeld for the costes of the accompt & *quietus est* of Master William Rogers, late mayer and eschetour of the cite: xxvij*s* v*d*

/*Wrytynges*/ **Item** payd the xiij day of July for a *dedimus potestatem* for Master Henry Fuller, newe mayour: ix*s* iiij*d*

Item to the clarkes of the kynges awdyte for a quytans for the payment of the xth of the comon halle: viij*d*

Item to Master Watson for drawyng of certen indentures betwyxt the comialte &

---

568 Sir William Paston (d. 1554), a lawyer, JP and former courtier, lived at Oxnead and owned property at Cromer on the coast: *ODNB*, xlii, pp. 992–3; Baker, *Men of Court*, ii, pp. 1202–3.

569 NCR, 18A/6, f. 157^v, refers to 'mysorder of the shrevys to the mayer', which suggests that the search was for legal precedents that might be used to discipline the mutinous sheriff of Norwich, Thomas Marsham. On 9 April 1544 Marsham had become involved in a dispute with the mayor, Edward Rede, over a fee of 5*d* from a prisoner, which resulted in an unedifying brawl. He eventually capitulated on 17 June after further displays of intransigence, but by 12 July was engaged in another *fracas* with Rede: NCR, 16A/5, pp. 207, 210–11, 220, 228–9, 231–3, 239–40, 247, 260–1.

570 See above, p. 206.

Thomas Wolman and Frances Wolmer for a lease of certen howses within the scyte of the comon halle, and for drawyng of an indenture betwyxt the comialte and Frances Wolmer alone,[571] whyche draughtes nevyr toke place: xx*d*

/*Taskes*/ **Item** payd the fyrst day of Januarii to the constabylles of Heyham [*Heigham*] for the kynges taske of ij acres of londe without Seynt Gyles gates, late Hemmynges: iiij*d*

> **Summa** v *li* ixs ix*d*

[*f. 122*] **Other mynute** expenses with certen thynges forgotten in ther place *& cetera*:

In primis payd the vij^te weke after Myhelmes to John Elmam, laborer, for ij days worke at the oke ageynst Bulwardes in Be[*r*]stret armyng agyenst the newe pathyng that was made ther, levellyng the grene banke therto & gravellyng the same: ix*d*

Item payd for viij astylles to make standerdes & berers for shelvys that war made in a wolshoppe the iij^de weke after Crystmes: iij*d*

Item payd in the fyrst weke after Mydsomer to Nycholas Tuttell, carpenter, for hewyng and sqwaryng of ij trees with certen toppe endes to make a newe stathe at the newe mylles & a newe crosse to be set at Hardley, iij days: xix*d ob'*

Item to Henry Wodrof helpyng hym iij days: xiij*d ob'*

Item payd to Goose and hys ffellowe sawyng the sayd tymbyr mete for the sayd stathe and crosse, iiij days: iiij*s* iiij*d*

Item spent in drynke vpon ix or x shomakers jorneymen that holpe to remove the tymbyr in the comon inne yarde: ij*d*

Item to Wylliam Pede for mendyng the locke on the comon inne forgate: ij*d*

Item payd to Henry Wodrof for iij days worke in the v^te weke after Mydsomer makyng clene the guyldhall chambyrs & ledes and the stepyll at the comon halle, caryeng awaye moche dowes donge & fylthe: xiij*d ob'*

[*f. 122^v*] **Item** payd in the vij^te weke after Mydsomer to John Warnys for cuttyng of a dyeke out betwyxt the mayne ryver and the lesser ryver ronnyng at the backe of the howsys in Seynt Martens at Oke,[572] for v roddes at viij*d* the rodde, wherof was payd by Master Sywhat xvj*d*, and by the accomptant in the name of the comialte: ij*s*

Item to Andrewe Brown, carpenter, mendyng the cadge on the northe syde of the guyldhalle and for newe stavyng & trymmyng of the cooke stoole at Fybrygge keye, ij days: xiij*d*

Item to Andrewe Qwashe for nayles spent abought the cage: iij*d*

Item to Wylliam Pede for a gret yron vorell, a gret bolt with a pynne & a forlocke wyth certen brodes for the cookstole conteynyng x *libr'*: xv*d*

Item for a locke and certen stapylles to stay yt, that boyes breke yt not: vj*d*

> **Summa** xiiij*s* viij*d ob'*

---

571 See NCR, 16D/2, f. 205^v.

572 The drainage dyke was evidently dug across an island covered in pasture land situated immediately to the west of St Martin's parish, just above the new mills, dividing the river Wensum into 'main' and 'lesser' branches: see Campbell, *Historic Towns: Norwich*, map 3.

The costes and chargis of xviij^{xx} comb' whete bought *by* the accomptant betwixt Crystmes and Candylmes in the tyme of thys accompt for the ease of the poore inhabytans of the cyte *& cetera*:^{573}

In primis payd to Barnard Vtber for oon hundred comb' whete, full payd at vs: xxx *li*

Item to Wodroff of London for an hundred and fyfty comb', full payd: that ys to *say* viij^{xx} xviij comb' and ij bushelles at iiij*s* iiij*d* the comb', full payd: xxxix *li* xiij*s* iiij*d*^{574}

[*f. 123*] **Item** payd to George Durbar of Colchester & to Roger Porter of Re[e]pham Market for xx comb' whete, full payd at iiij*s* the comb': iiij *li*

Item to Raphe Ybottes and dyuers other persons for xxx comb' whete, full payd at vs the comb': vij *li* xs

Item payd in the market for iij comb' whete to make vp <xx> xviij^{xx} score comb', bare meser: xvs

Item payd for meseryng of the whete bought of Wodrof of London; for chambyr rome of the same at the comon stathe, at the ankers howse in Seynt Edwardes and at Carrowe tyll suche tyme as chambyr rome was provydyd at the comon halle; and for removyng and caryeng the same to the comon halle: xixs iiij*d*

Item payd for caryage of iij^{xx} comb' of Barnardes whete from the comon stathe in to the market and v^{xx} vj comb' of whete from the comon halle at dyuers tymes; and for the dayly steryng of the same whete, bycause it lay so thycke, tyll the chambyrs myght be redy to lye more at large; & onys in *a* fetnyght to fanne yt; and euery monythe to ronne yt thorowe an hopper, with the hyer <with the> of xij teltes to covyr yt from the dust of the work men pathyng the same chambyr; a mannys labour euery Wedynsday & Satterday from Wytsontyde tyll Myhelmes sellyng part of the same in the market, with byeng of bromys dyuers tymis /nullus/ [*f. 123^v*] and suche leke charges from Crystmes in the begynnyng tyll Myhelmes in the endyng: lxvs iij*d*

Item payd for ij oblygacions makynge betwyxt Barnard Vtber and the accomptant for the delyuery of an C *comb'* whete on his behalff and for the payment of the same on the accomptantes behalff, with a godes peny govyn hym: ix*d*

Item for makyng of ij newe eerys for the <Item> accomptantes bushell, whiche was broken ther: viij*d*

Summa iiij^{xx} vj *li* iiij*s* iiij*d*

573 He was acting on the orders of the mayor's court: NCR, 16A/4, f. 43^v.

574 This wheat may have been requisitioned as it was about to leave Norwich. On 19 January 1544 half a cargo belonging to George Walden of London was commandeered for civic use by the mayor, and on 9 February 200 combs belonging to other 'men of London' were detained at the common stathe: NCR, 16A/5, pp. 194, 197. See also pp. 199–200 for attempts by the aldermen to estimate how much grain remained in the city and what might be provided for poor relief.

Memorandum that here ys to be notyd that the hole chargis of xviij^{xx} comb' whete bought by the accomptant, bare meser, from the fyrst day to the last in all charges dyd cost iiij^{xx} vj *li* iiij*s* iiij*d*. And he hathe chargid hym self in the tytyll of whete sold, amonges the foren receytes, all losse of meser allowid, lxiij *li* ij*s* iiij*d*; and hathe left lyeng at the comon halle to the vse of the comialte v score comb' whete, bare meser, at v*s* the comb': *summa* <x> xxv *li*. *Summa* of the money receyuyd and of the whete remaynyng: iiij^{xx} viij *li* ij*s* iiij*d*. And so <the> he haue cleryd to the vse of the comialte and all charges borne xxxviij*s*, the whyche the sayd accomptant hathe imployed as here after folowith *& cetera*:

In primis payd for ij bare sholvys to stere & remove the sayd whete with: iiij*d*
Item for a newe ffanne: x*d*
Item for a stryke & a collrake with a long staffe to drawe the whete a brode: iij*d*
Item for a Danske hopper made with wyer bought at London by Master Trase: xiij*s* iiij*d*
Item for caryage of the same from London: xvj*d*
Item for viij newe sackes: vj*s* viij*d*
[*f. 124*] **Item** for nayles for mendyng the sayd hopper: j*d*
Item awardyd to the accomptant by the consent of the hole cownsell of the cite at the assembly holden on Seynt Mathews day for hys <pli> paynes abought the forsayd whete all the rest of the clere profyght of the sayd whete, whyche ys: xv*s* ij*d*[575]

Summa xxxviij*s*

/*Fourty soldyers*/ **Item** payd for the chargis of ffourty soldyers sent in to France with my lord of Norff' & delyuerd at Ypswyche [*Ipswich*] the ix day of June in the tyme of thys accompt:[576]

In primis payd to lx men reteynyd for soldyers, euery of them iiij*d*, wherof xx^{ti} of the worst war syftyd out: xx*s*
Item payd for the brekefastes of the fourty that war fully<d> amyttyd the same *day* that they musterd byfore my lord of Norff' his grace: vj*s* viij*d*
Item payd for brede and drynke for them and the others that war reteynyd dyuerse days before & after whan they musterd, with rewardes govyn to dyuerse of them whan they lettyd ther tyme, as yt appere more at large in the waster booke, with drynke dyuerse tymes for the aldermen: v*s* vij*d*

---

575 The assembly in question, held on 21 September 1544, awarded Raynbald just ii*s* in expenses, but it was then assumed that he had bought only 300 combs of wheat: NCR, 16D/2, f. 208.

576 On 3 April 1544, Henry VIII ordered the mayor to supply forty 'able footmen', eight of whom were to be fully-equipped archers and the rest 'well harneysed' billmen, along with as many mounted combatants as possible, to serve under the duke of Norfolk: NCR, 15A/5, p. 203. For the latter's less than distinguished role as commander of this campaign, see Head, *Ebbs and Flows*, pp. 211–15.

Item for the costes of the accomptant rydyng to Kenyngale [*Kenninghall*] to cownsell with Master Holdyche[577] and Master Knyvet, the capteyn,[578] of dyuerse matters, beyng forthe ij days, with his horse hyer: ijs iiijd

Item to my lord his graces secretory for a copy of the instruccions: iijs iiijd

[*f. 124ᵛ*] **Item** to dyuerse armerers & laborers, whose partyculer namys and days workes do appere in the sayd waster booke,[579] for newe letheryng, naylyng and buklyng fourty Alman ryvettes, with scoryng of the most part of the same & lynyng of fourty sallettes & fourty gorgettes with canvas: xxjs iiijd[580]

Item to dyuerse men for harneys nayle, bukkylles, lethyr, canvas, threde, rape oyle, brenne, wax, glewe and dyuerse other thynges occupyed abought the sayd harneys, whiche particler parcelles & mennys namys do appere more at large in my sayd waster booke: xxixs vijd

Item to Peter Freman for a payer of newe splentes to furnyshe oon of the comon harneys that lacke splentes, and to dyuerse other men for the exchange of other splentes that war very ylle: iijs xd

Item payd at London and to dyuerse men of the cite for xxxvj skulles, ouer and above iiijᵒʳ that war receyuyd of dyuerse men with iiijᵒʳ harneys: xxxvjs

Item for the exchange of ij skulles and for cariage home of the skulles from London: xijd

Item to dyuerse men for xxxij gorgettes, ouer and above viijᵗᵉ that war receyuyd with dyuerse harneys bought at sondry prices, as yt appere more at large in the forsayd waster booke: xxvjs ijd

Item for ffourty swordes at ijs: iiij *li*

Item for ffourty daggers: xls

Item for ij sworde guyrdylles for Alexander Gouerley and Lawrens Dugrell: viijd

[*f. 125*] **Item** for the exchange for ij swordes for them: ijs

Item gaf toward ther blewe cappys bycause they cost aboue the pryce of the other: ijd

Item payd for fourty blewe cappys to put in ther skulles at vijd euery cappe: xxiijs iiijd[581]

---

577 Robert Holdyche (d. c. 1562), Norfolk's receiver general and steward, and a prominent figure in the county: Head, *Ebbs and Flows*, pp. 232, 260–1.

578 The 'hotheaded, conceited and clever' Sir Edmund Knyvet (d. 1551) of Buckenham Castle was Norfolk's nephew, although their relations were often fraught. Neither *HoP, 1509–1558*, ii, pp. 482–3, nor R. Virgoe, 'The Earlier Knyvetts: The Rise of a Norfolk Gentry Family', *NA*, 41 (1990–93), pp. 249–78, on pp. 270–1, mentions Sir Edmund's service in France.

579 NCR, 18A/6, f. 160ᵛ, refers to 'a scedule here shewed', making no mention of a 'waster booke'.

580 For a description of the type of armour customarily worn by local levies, see P. Millican, ed., *The Musters Returns for Divers Hundreds in the County of Norfolk, 1569, 1572, 1574 and 1577, II* (NRS, vi, 1936), pp. xiii–xiv.

581 The caps were made, at Norfolk's command and to his design, by William Taillour of London: NCR, 16A/5, p. 205.

Item payd at London for fourty hattes, blewe and rede, to were ouer ther skulles at viij*d* a hatte: xxvj*s* viij*d*

Item to Thomas Guele toward a blewe cappe, who was reteynyd in stede of an other man that was put out after the cappis war govyn: iiij*d*

Item for the exchange of the other mannys sworde: iiij*d*

Item for a dagger for the sayd Guele by cause the other man wold not delyuer his dagger: xij*d*

Item to Mast toward an other dagger, for that he hade broken hys fyrst dagger: iiij*d*

Item payd for a drome for Peter Freman, who was foreman of the company: x*s*

Item for ix bowes for viij archers, for that oon was broke in the feld at the muster, at ij*s* viij*d*: xxiiij*s*

Item to Butfeld for layeng of v of the sayd bowes & mendyng of them all at dyuers tymis: ij*s* iiij*d*

Item for bowstrynges at dyuerse musters: x*d*

Item to euery archer whan he receyuyd his bowe j*d* for strynges; and at his goyng forthe ij*d*: ij*s*

Item to John Gardner for viij bowe cassis: v*s* iiij*d*

Item for viij shotyng glovys & viij brasers: iiij*s*

Item to Alen and Welles for vj sheffe arrows at ij*s* viij*d* the sheffe: xvj*s*

Item to John Guyle for vj cassis for them: ij*s* iiij*d*

[*f. 125ᵛ*] Item at London for ij sheffe arrows with cassis: v*s* viij*d*

Item to Rycherd Flecher for viij guyrdylles: xiiij*d*

Item payd to Mastres Morront for ij grosse of thredyn poyntes that she causyd to be made: ij*s* vj*d*

Item more to hyr for vj dossen armyn poyntes: xv*d*

Item <to> to John Okes for xiiij dossen at iij*d* dossen: iij*s* vj*d*

Item gaf to euery soldyer to bye poyntes for hys hose *and* doblet j*d*: <j*d*> iij*s* iiij*d*

Item payd for xxxj newe bylles at xv*d*: xxxviij*s* ix*d*

Item payd to Master Awsten Steward, alderman, for ij armyn cotes of canvas made jerkyn facon with brest plates sperde on the shulders, whyche he causid to be made for Gouerley & Dugrell: vj*s* viij*d*

Item for xxxviij more of the same cotes in all charges of canvas, lynyng and makyng at ij*s* x*d* *ob'* euery cote, oon with an other: v *li* ix*s* iiij*d*

Item for fourty payer of hose of rede and blewe clothe <clothe> with martyngales stytchid with rede and blewe threde and lynyd with rede and blewe clothe at vj*s* *ob'* euery payer,[582] oon with an other, savyng vij*d* lesse in the holle som of them, whose partycler costes of <must> owt sydes, lynyng, canvas, makyng and caryage of the clothe from London appere more at large in the forsayd waster booke: xij *li* xiij*d*

---

582 The design and colour were likewise specified in detail by Norfolk in a list of instructions sent to the mayor and aldermen in April 1544: NCR, 16A/5, p. 205.

Item for fourty doblettes of blacke fustyan with Ytalyon wastes at iij*s* iiij*d* euery doblet, oon with an other;[583] and iiij*d* ouer in the hole som in all charges, with lynyng & makyng: vj *li* xiij*s* viij*d*

[*f. 126*] Item payd for ffourty blewe cotes gardyd with rede clothe at vj*s* vij*d* euery cote, oon with an other,[584] in all charges of clothe & makyng: xiij *li* iij*s* iiij*d*

Item for the costes of Master Hamond Lynsted, alderman, and hys man rydyng to Buknam [*Buckenham Castle*] to knowe of Syr Edmond Knyvet what day the soldyers shuld set forward: xiij*d*

Item payd to the ffourty soldyers for ther condyte money to Ypswyche, euery of them ij*s* vj*d*: v *li*[585]

Item gaff to euery of them in hys purse at Ypswyche whan they toke shyppyng v*s*: x *li*

Item for the charges of the sayd fourty soldyers at Ypswiche oon day *di'* byfore they toke shyppyng at vj*d* the day, euery of them: xxx*s*

Item payd at Ypswiche for the hyer of an howse to laye in ther gere tyll it was shypid; and for changyng of a skulle, for mendyng iiij^{or} harneys, with other expenses by the waye, as yt appere by Master Lynstedes byll, with the costes of hym and hys man in all chargys: xviij*s*

Item to Henry Sparke for hym selff and his carte to Ypswyche with ther caryage: xx*s*

Item for the hyer of ij teltes to trusse in ther clothis and for coueryng the carte, with ij*d* for strawe for savegard of the harneys: ix*d*

Item to Master Awsten Steward, alderman, & to dyuerse other men for xij Almayn ryvettes full furnyshyd <e> in euery condycon at x*s* a pece: vj *li*

Item to dyuerse other men for ten Almayn ryvettes not parfyght, some lackyng sallettes /*nullus*/ [*f. 126*^v] and all they lackyng gorgettes, abatyng them for euery sallet xx*d* and for euery gorget xij*d*, and so payd for those ten harneys: iiij *li* vij*d*

Item ther was delyuerd forthe amonges the sayd soldyers xiiij Almayn ryvettes of the comon store that came out of Scotlond, whose chargis of scoryng & lethryng ys declaryd byfore in the fyrst part of the reknyng. But payd for reparyng of vj old harneys that war beleft in the guyldhall after the soldyers war gon, whyche war parcell of those that came out of Scotlond: that ys to say in scoryn, letheryn, naylyng and buklyn, with certen newe rybbys, newe syse peces, newe shulder peces, newe elbowe peces & oon payer of newe splentes, with nayles, buckylles and lethyr, in all charges, whose particler parcelles appere in the sayd waster booke, of the whiche sayd vj harneys ther was delyuerd ageyn to iiij^{or} seuerall men iiij^{or} of the same harnes

---

583 As also specified by Norfolk: NCR, 16A/5, p. 205.

584 At Norfolk's insistence, these coats were to be 'after suche facion as all ffotemens [*infantry*] be made at London': NCR, 16A/5, p. 205.

585 As also specified by Norfolk: NCR, 16A/5, p. 205.

in stede of ther harnes that went in to France, to make vp the nombyr of fourty; and the other ij war sold as yt appere amonges the receytes in the tytyll of harneys sold: xijs iijd

Item lost by the payment of certen ylle money that the sayd accomptant hade amonges other money out of the hamper of /nullus/ [f. 127] the guyldhalle toward the settyng forthe of the forsayd soldyers: vijd

> *Summa* iiijˣˣ ix *li* xjs xd

Memorandum that hereafter and last of all dothe folowe the cost and charge don within the tyme of thys accompt at the comon halle in makyng and transposyng of these parcelles folowyng & cetera:[586]

In primis fensyng out Frances Wolmer from the comialte with ston walles

Item makyng a newe carte gate to come to the corn chambyrs

Item transposyng certen howses makyng them corn chambers

Item makyng vij newe tabylles for the halle of popyll plankes and xxx newe trustylles of oke for x tabylles

Item inclossyng a grownde with ston walles to kepe in sygnettes

Item heynyng the ston walles betwyxt the sope howse and the comialte and coueryng all the forsayd newe walles

Item makyng a newe carte gate out of the strete next the ij elmys in to the est part of the same place and levellyng of all that courte from the strete syde down to the ryver

Item buyldyng a newe howse out of the grownde ouer the sayd gate & so forthe to the est ende of the lybrary, transposyng the sayd lybrary in to an halle, a buttry and a very fayer parlowur

Item a newe kechyn with an ovyn and a vowlte vnder the same with a welle ther in and iij newe chymneys in those howses

Item transposyng all the vowltes, makyng them warehowses

Item makyng a storehowse ther to laye in necessaryes

Item many other thynges don thys yere in dyuerse partes of the same place, whyche ar to moche here to reherse, but more at large they appere & cetera.

[f. 127ᵛ] /The vᵗᵉ weke after Myhelmes/ **In primis** payd on Hallomes evyn for iiij *libr'* candill delyueryd to Clement for the chappell all this wynter: vd

Item to Paschall for a newe key and mendyng a locke at Syr Robert Shynkwyns chambyr: iiijd

/The viijᵗᵉ weke after Myhelmes/ **Item** to Wylliam Johnson, mason, stoppyng in of dores & wyndows to closse out Frances Wolmer ffrom the comialte, iij days: xixd ob'

Item to Water Colles, his laborer, iij days: xiijd ob'

Item to John Elmam, laborer, ij days bycause the stuff laye far off: ixd

---

586 NCR, 18A/6, f. 145ᵛ, does not provide an itemised list of work undertaken.

/*The ix^{te} weke after Myhelmes*/ **Item** to John Byrche, carpenter, for a newe carte gate stalle set betwyxt the commons & Frances Wolmer, with ij halff loopys for the same, with trymmyng the yron worke on & hangyng them: xx*s*

Item to the forsayd mason settyng in the sayd gate & closyng out Frances Wolmer, v days: ij*s* viij*d ob'*

Item to John Erne, hys master, helpyng to set the forsayd gate, oon day: vij*d*

Item to Walter Colles, laborer, v days: xxij*d ob'*

Item to John Elmam, laborer, v days and to Sander Clarke oon day: ij*s* iij*d*

Item to Paschall for collers, cappys, pynnys, a gret stapyll, with other yron worke: ij*s* iij*d*

Item payd for a sawen sparre to make a long stondyng barre to close in the ij loopys: iiij*d*

Item to John Byrche for a dore stalle with a lope set next the scolehowse vyce for Shynkwyn to go to hys chambyr by the scolers lane: ij*s* iiij*d*

[*f. 128*] **Item** to Paschall for a payer of hookes & hengilles for the same, with a locke & ij keys & a stapyll: xvij*d*

/*The x^{te} weke after Myhelmes*/ **Item** to Wylliam Johnson, mason, stoppyng out of dores & wyndows on the old kechyn syde, *iij* days: xix*d ob'*

Item to Colles, his laborer, the same iij days: xiij*d ob'*

Item to Sandyr Clarke & John Elmam, laboreres, makyng way for the mason & brekyng down old walles for stuff, iiij days this weke: ij*s*

/*The xj^{te} weke after Myhelmes*/ **Item** to the forsayd mason makyng parfyght a chambyr with the wyndows and chymney betwyxt the dorter and the fermery halle, whyche was very sore spoyled, vj days ther this weke: ij*s* iij*d*

Item to Colles, his laborer, the same vj days: ij*s* iij*d*

Item to John Byrche for a newe mantyll tre for the chymney in the same chambyr: x*d*

Item to Sandyr Clarke and John Elmam, laborers, abought brekyng of walles, vj days: iiij*s* vj*d*

/*The xij^{te} weke after Myhelmes*/ **Item** to the forsayd mason fynyshyng vp the forsayd chambyr, v days: ij*s* viij*d ob'*

Item to Colles, his laborer, v days: xxij*d ob'*

Item to John Byrche for a dore stalle set betwyxt that chambyr & the fermery: xx*d*

Item to John Elmam, laborer, helpyng the mason & makyng clene the howses, the halle and chappell ageynst Crystmes, ij days: ix*d*

Item for bromys thys quarter: j*d ob'*

Item to Henry Sparke for sonde occupyed in that place syns Myhelmes vij lodes at v*d*: ij*s* xj*d*

[*f. 128^v*] **Item** to Master Marsham for lyme spent in the same place syns Myhelmes xxxvj comb': xij*s*

Item for candyll for the workemen on mornynges and evynynges syns Myhelmes viij *libr'*: x*d*

/*The fyrst weke after Crystmes*/ **Item** payd to Wylliam Johnson, mason, selyng and rowcastyng of the porche vnder Master Kempis chambyr, oon day of hym & his laborer: xj*d*

Item to Mastres Morront for lathe nayle j m¹ *di*': xv*d*

Item for viij*d* nayle, wherof part was spent abought the carte gates j C: vj*d*

Item payd for lathe ij C: xij*d*; & heere: j*d* – xiij*d*

/*The second weke after Crystmes*/ **Item** to John Byrche, carpenter, the yonger, for v days worke and John Wattes, carpenter, for iiij days makyng vij newe wyndows for the vowt vnder the southe ende of the dorter and ij wyndows for the vowlt vnder the lybrary, all made of the comon stuffe: iiij*s* x*d ob*'

Item to Master Thetford for vj sawen sparrys for pyllers for the same wyndows: ij*s*

Item to John Erne, mason, settyng in the same wyndows & rowcastyng the forsayd vowltes, vj days, at vij*d* the day: iij*s* vj*d*

Item to Wylliam Johnson, mason, abought the same worke vj days and Robert Hollond, mason, iiij days: v*s* v*d*

Item to Sander Clarke and Walter Colles, laborers, vj days and John Elmam ij days: v*s* iij*d*

<**Item** candyll that weke iiij *libr*': v*d*> /*This come after ward*/

[*f. 129*] **Item** to Bertylmewe Wymond & John Elmam, laborers, caryeng of clay in to the howses that war the lybrary, makyng newe florthes ther, vj days: iiij*s* vj*d*

/*The iij*ᵈᵉ *weke after Crystmes*/ **Item** to the forsayd iij masons, euery of them iiij days this weke, styll abought the forsayd wyndows & vowltes, at xx*d* the day all toguether: vj*s* viij*d*

Item to Clarke, Colles & Elmam, laborers, iiij days: iiij*s* vj*d*

Item to Henry Wodrof helpyng ther, ij days: ix*d*

/*The iiij*ᵗᵉ *weke after Crystmes*/ **Item** to John Erne, mason, pathyng of the newe storehowse, closyng in a wyndowe ther, settyng in *ij* dorestalles in the same howse & a wyndowe, with moche fynyshyng worke in the same, vj days: iij*s* vj*d*

Item to Robert Hollond the same vj days: iij*s* iij*d*

Item to Clarke & Yoxhale, laborers, vj days: iiij*s* vj*d*

Item to Henry Wodroff and John Elmam, laborers, makyng of florthes, vj days: iiij*s* vj*d*

Item to Henry Carter for clay vij lodes: ij*s* xj*d*

Item to Bartylmewe Wymond, laborer, brekyn down an alter in the gret vowlt cald Thomas Beckettes chappell,[587] caryeng out the stuff of the same, with moche other worke ther, vj days: ij*s* iij*d*

---

587 The cult of St Thomas Becket, which 'represented the triumph of the Western Church over a king of England', incurred the animosity of evangelicals: D. MacCulloch, *Thomas Cranmer* (1996), pp. 227–8. For the chapel, see C. Green, 'Becket's Chapel, Norwich', *NA*, 33 (1965), pp. 298–309.

Item to Robert Spalle for a dore stalle for the newe storehowse on the cloyster syde: ijs iiijd

Item to Nycholas Tuttell, carpenter, makyng an other dore stalle for that same howse, a wyndowe stalle, ij dore loopys with lyntelles, steppys & dyuers other thynges, vj days: iijs iijd

Item for ij lockes for the same dores to Pede: xvjd

[*f. 129ᵛ*] **Item** to the sayd Pede for yron worke for these ij dores & a newe barrowe spyndylle: xiijd

/*The vᵗᵉ weke after Crystmes*/ **Item** payd to Nycholas Tuttell, carpenter, makyng a newe wyndowe with vij lyghtes for the parlour, late parcell of the lybrary,[588] with moche tendyng that weke to the masons, v days worke: ijs viijd ob'

Item to John Byrche <for> for a pece of tymbyr for the nether scyle of the forsayd wyndowe: viijd

Item for a sparre to lye on the walle in the nether part of the same wyndowe and a long lyntell for the same wyndowe and iij peces for steppys of the vowlte dore: ijs iiijd

Item to hym for a gret dore stalle set in the wall on the northe syde in to the vowlte: iiijs iiijd

Item to John Erne, mason, settyng in the forsayd vowlte dore & makyng the stayers, v days: ijs xjd

Item to Wylliam Johnson, mason, v days & Robert Hollond iiij days settyng in the forsayd wyndow in the parlowur, with moche ffynyshyng worke: iiijs xd ob'

Item to Sander Clarke, Henry Wodroff & John Elmam, laborers, v days and to Walter Colles iiij days: vijs jd ob'

Item to Wylliam Pede for a payer of hengilles for the gret old dore betwen the ij vowltes: xiijd

Item a locke for the same dore: xiiijd

Item to Henry Sparke for sonde spent ther these v wekes past x lodes: iiijs ijd

[*f. 130*] **Item** for x *libr'* candyll spent ther in that tyme: xijd <qu'> ob'

/*The vjᵗᵉ weke after Crystmes*/ **Item** payd to the forsayd carpenter makyng a payer of loopys for the vowlte dore on the north syde & hangyng them and other dores, iiij days: ijs ijd

Item to John Erne, mason, ij days, Robert Hollond ij days and Wylliam Johnson iiij days fynyshyn vp all the vowltes, chambyrs & other workes in that tenement: iiijs vd

Item to Sander Clarke, laborer, ij days, Walter Colles ij days, John Elmam iij days & Henry Wodroff vj days: iiijs xd ob'

Item payd that weke for ij *libr'* candyll & bromys jd: iijd ob'

Item to Wylliam Pede for ij payer hookes and hengylles for the vowlt dores conteynyng viij *libr'*, an yron barre with a stapyll & an hespe layd in the walle for the

---

588 NCR, 18A/6, f. 146, reports the use 'of olde stuffe of the store of the comialtie ffor the chamber on th'estende of the librarye'.

closyng of the oon half dore conteynyng x *libr'*, a newe locke with a key and a plate for the same dore xij*d* – iij*s* iij*d*

Item to the sexten of Seynt Andrews mendyn the frame of oon of the belles in the stepyll & for newe hangyng the same belle: iiij*d*

/*The vij*^te *weke after Crystmes*/ **Item** to the forsayd carpenter *plancheryng* of a chambyr betwyxt the dorter and the fermery to make yt a corn chambyr, vj days: iij*s* iij*d*

Item to Henry Wodrof, laborer, helpyng hym to shot bourde & layeng joystes in the grownd & fyllyng betwyxt them with colder, vj days: ij*s* iij*d*

Item for iij lattys for iij wyndows ther: xix*d*

[*f. 130*^v] **Item** to Mastres Morront for iij*d* nayle j m^l: xx*d*
and for iiij*d* nayle *di'* m^l: xv*d*

Item to Wylliam Pede for a newe locke, a key & a stapyll for the newe dore in the same chambyr: vj*d*

Item to Robert Hollond, mason, mendyng certen fawtes in a corn chambyr within Frances Wollmers romythe, whiche Master Balle hyer, ij days: xiij*d*

Item to John Elmam, hys laborer, ij days: ix*d*

Item to John Erne, mason, fynyshyng vp the newe store howse that was begon the iiij^te weke after Crystmes, ij days: xiiij*d*

Item to Sander, hys laborer, ij days: ix*d*

Item to Wylliam Spratte for ij C *di'* of small pathyn tyle to fynyshe vp the same howse: ij*s* vj*d*. All the rest spent in the same howse was of the comon store, whyche was cowntyd in the last accompt: ij*s* vj*d*

/*The viij*^te *weke after Crystmes*/ **Item** to the forsayd carpenter fynyshyng vp the forsayd corn chambyr & mendyng certen fawtes in the chambyr within Frances Wolmers romyth that Master Balle hyer, ij days: xiij*d*

Item to Henry Wodrof with hym ij days: ix*d*

Item more to hym for other ij days makyng clene the forsayd chambyrs and all the howses ageynst the ij elmys: ix*d*

Item to Robert <E> Hollond, mason, pynnyng in the walles vyrownd the sayd chambyrs /nullus/ [*f. 131*] whan the carpenter hade don & layeng the long yron in the wall for speryng of the vowlte dores vnder the lybrary, ij days: xiij*d*

Item to Elmam, his laborer, the same ij days: ix*d*

Item for plaster of palleys for the sayd yron: j*d*

/*The x*^te *weke after Crystmes*/ **Item** payd to Wylliam Johnson, mason, settyng a newe dore stalle in the newe corn chambyr, late the scolehows, sometyme the ffrayter, and stoppyng in the old dore at the vyce & mendyn the pavement in dyuers places, vj days: iij*s* iij*d*

Item to Colles, his laborer, vj days: ij*s* iij*d*

Item to John Byrche for the same dore stalle: ij*s* iiij*d*

Item to hym for a loope for the same: ij*s* iiij*d*

Item to Wylliam Pede for a payer of hookes and hengylles for the same, a locke, a key, a stapill and a ryng, all for the same dore: xv*d*

Item payd that weke to Gregory Akers and John Elmam, laborers, swepyng the roff and walles of all the forsayd gret chambyr & fechyng home of small pathyn tyle with barrows from dyuerse places of the cite wher yt was bought for the pathyng of the same howse wher the tabilles stode, yche of them vj days: iiij*s* vj*d*

Item payd in the market for bromys: j*d*

Item to Master Palmer of Seynt Gregoryes for small pathyn tyle ij C: ij*s*; to John Bronde for viij C at x*d* C: vj*s* viij*d*; and to Plattynges wyf for vij C iij quarter at ix*d* C: v*s* x*d* – xiiij*s* vj*d*

Item bought that weke of John Basyngham a /*nullus*/ [*f. 131*ᵛ] gret quuantyte [*sic*] of pathyn tyle of all sortes, wherof the sums shall appere hereafter, and gaff hym in ernest at the byeng of them: j*d*

Item payd to Arnold, basket maker, for xlij lattys set in xlij lyghtes of the wyndows in the forsayd gret chambyr, late the scolehows: vij*s*

/*The xj*ᵗᵉ *weke after Crystmes*/ **Item** to Wylliam Johnson, mason, settyng in a dorestalle out of the cloyster at the steyers fete of the forsayd chambyrs, with mendyng of the arche ther that was dekayed, and also begynnyng to pathe wher the tabylles stode in the forsayd gret chambyr, late the scolehows, vj days: iij*s* iij*d*

Item to Robert Hollond, mason, castyng the walles wher the tabylles & benchis stode, iiij days that weke; and to John Ern for ij days: iij*s* iiij*d*

Item to Walter Colles, laborer, vj days: ij*s* iij*d*

Item to Bartylmewe Wymond iiij days: xviij*d*

Item to Sandyr Clarke ij days: ix*d*

Item to Henry Wodrof and John Elmam, laborers, helpyng out coldyr & muke that laye a foote depe vnder the setes of the sayd tabylles and benchis, vj days: iiij*s* vj*d*

Item to Robert Browster, laborer, helpyng ther that weke, ij days: xiij*d* *ob'*

Item for packthrede and bromys: ij*d*

Item to Thomas Culley for vij C small pathyn tyle, to John Cubyt for iiij C and to old Barchom for ij C *di'* at xij*d* the C: xiij*s* vj*d*

[*f. 132*] **Item** to John Bronde for ij C *di'* at x*d* C: ij*s* j*d*

Item to Master Grenewod for v C at xiiij*d* C: v*s* x*d*

Item to John Basyngham for v C at xvj*d* C: vj*s* viij*d*

Item to Henry Sparke for caryeng of iij lodes marle from Fybrygge gates, whyche myxt among the lyme for the pathyng: xij*d*

Item to Nycholas Tuttell, carpenter, makyng loopys for wyndows & dores & hangyng them, makyng a border for the chymney in the fermery and certen steppys, vj days this weke: iij*s* iij*d*

Item payd for a sawen sparre for the sayd border: iiij*d*

Item for vj rynges for dores: xv*d*

Item for ij payer hookes & hengylles for the ij dores at the stayers ffeete: xv*d*

Item for ij lockes with keys & stapylles for those ij dores, with ij*d* in Inglyshe nayle: xiiij*d*

/*The xij^te weke after Crystmes*/ **Item** to John Byrche for a dore stalle that stonde in the entry at the steyers feete out to the courte next the maltyng offyce, an other that stonde at the stayers hede in to the fermery, nowe made a corn chambyr: vs iiijd

Item this weke to Wylliam Johnson and Robert Hollond, masons, pathyng the sayd fermery chambyr with gret pathyn tyle so far as owur gret tyle wold reche & trymyng the wyndows with brycke and tymbyr, v days: v vd

Item to the sayd carpenter makyng ij wyndowe stalles set at the west ende of the sayd howse to feche in lyght & trymmyng the tymbyr mete for the wyndows, v days: ijs viijd ob'

[*f. 132^v*] **Item** to John Byrche for vj peces of newe tymbyr for the forsayd wyndows: ijs

Item payd that weke to my Lady Shelton for iij C gret pathyn tyle lyeng at Carrowe [*priory*]: xvs

Item to old Barchom for iij C di': xvijs vjd

Item to John Basyngham for vj C: xxxs

Item to Henry *Sparke* for caryeng of the iij C tyle from Carrowe: viijd; & a lode from Barchom: iijd – xjd

/*Laborers this weke*/ **Item** to Bartylmewe Wymond, Walter Colles, Henry Wodroff, John Elmam, euery of them v days: vijs vjd

Item to Browster helpyng ij days: ixd

Item payd for oon day worke more that weke of all the sayd masons, carpenters & laborers iiij [*sic*] occupied with ladders, sparrys, roppys and other ordynaunces for stoppyng in of certen holys in the chappell and stepyll wyndows wher dowes came inne & dyd moche dysplesyr: iijs jd ob'

Item to Roger Bacheler & Abraham Panworth, glasewrightes, tendyn ther an hole afternon and for ther glasse: xijd

Item gaf in reward amonge part of those workemen for ther paynes & dangeros clymyng & for brede & drynke that day: xd

Item to Henry Sparke for sonde spent in that place these vj wekes past vij lode: iijs xjd

Item to John Byrche for the dore stalle and loope that stonde at the steyers feete vp to the corn chambyrs in to the cloyster warde: iiijs viijd

[*f. 134*][589] /*The weke in which Owur Lady fell in, beyng Mydlent weke*/ **Item** payd thys weke bothe for gret pathyn tyle and smalle to fynysh vp the ij forsayd chambyrs: and fyrst to Wylliam Spratte for ij C smalle tyle, lackyng x tyles: xxijd

Item to Master Cocke, alderman, for iiij C di': iiijs vjd

Item to Wylliam Browderer of Yarmothe for vj C: vjs

Item to the sayd Broderer for ij C di' of gret tyle: xs

Item to oon Grose of the same town for ij C di' of gret tyle at iiijs iiijd C: xs xd

Item to the porters ther for caryeng of all the sayd tyle to the kele: vjd

Item to John Candler for freyght to Norwyche: xxd

---

589 There is no folio numbered 133.

Item for freyght therof from the stathe to the comon halle: vj*d*

Item to Nycholas *Tuttell* for makyng iij wyndowe stalles,[590] with other worke that weke, v days: ij*s* viij*d ob'*

Item to Wylliam Johnson, mason, settyng in the dore stalle at the stayers feete next the maltyn offyce & a <dore stalle> wyndowe stalle in to the cloyster to feche in lyght to the stayers & layeng of steyes in the walles ther, with moche worke in that corner, v days: ij*s* viij*d ob'*

Item to Robert Hollond, mason, helpyng hym ther <v days> iij days: xix*d ob'*

Item to Walter Colles, John Elmam and Henry Wodrof, laborers, euery of them v days: v*s* vij*d ob'*

Item to Pede for vij payer hookes & hengylles spent at the tenement ageynst the ij elmys: xviij*d*

[*f. 134*ᵛ] **Item** for cromys, sneckes & lachys iiij *libr'*: viij*d*

Item Inglyshe nayle for hengylles j C: iij*d*

/*The fyrst weke after Owur Lady*/ **Item** payd to the forsayd carpenter makyng a stage above vpon the stapyll to take down the crosse and fane to be mendyd & makyng rayles at the stayers goyng vp to the corn chambyrs, iij days worke this weke: xix*d ob'*

Item to Master Thetford for iij sparrys for the rayles: xij*d*

Item to Wylliam Johnson, mason, settyng in iiij°ʳ wyndows abought the plancher that ys ouer all the steyers that go vp to the corn chambyrs to feche in lyght, mendyng the steyers that go vp to the sayd plancher, stoppyng in a dore betwen the old kechyn & the sayd chambyr & fynyshyn all the tresans at the steyers hede, vj days: ij*s* iiij*d*

Item to Colles, his laborer, vj days: ij*s* iij*d*

Item to Wylliam Pede, smythe, takyng down the crosse on the stepyll, newe makyng the same and the fane & settyng vp ageyn: vj*s*

Item for a latten plate for deys for the fane: iiij*d*

Item for xxiiij brades: iij*d*

Item to hym for vj payer more of small hookes & hengylles spent at the tenement next the ij elmys, conteynyng x *libr' di'*: xvj*d*

Item to Mastres Morront for nayle fechyd of hyr at dyuers tymys in this quarter & occupyed abought the forsayd reparacions: and fyrst for iiij*d* nayle j mˡ *di'*: ij*s* ix*d*

[*f. 135*] **Item** iij*d* nayle j mˡ: xx*d*; vj*d* nayle j C: v*d* – ij*s* j*d*

Item to Henry Wodrof and John Elmam, laborers, takyng down the stage on the stepyll whan the smythe & carpenter hade don & makyng clene the stepyll from the toppe to the grownde & all the ledes abought the stepyll, chappell & churche, whyche war sore foulyd with dowes donge, and caryeng away moche mucke, with moche other worke in the same place, vj days: iiij*s* vj*d*

Item payd that weke for bromys: j*d*

---

590 NCR, 18A/6, f. 149, reports that two windows were 'sette in the westende of the late ffermery & one in the south side ouer the steyres hede'.

Item to John Carre, glaser, for newe makyng all the clarystoryes in the wyndows in the newe corn chambyr, late the fermery, to kepe out dowes, for his glasse & workmanshyppe: iijs viijd

/*The second weke after Owur Lady*/ **Item** to Arnold for xxvj shorte lattyses for the wyndows in the same chambyr at ijd a pece: iiijs iiijd

Item for iiij^or long lattyses & oon gret lattyse: xxijd

Item for wyer to fasten the lattyses to the wyndows payd to Master Trase *j *libr'**: vjd

Item to Pede for a locke & key and a stapyll for the same chambyr dore: viijd

Item to my Lady Shelton for the pathyn tyle of an yle of the cloyster at Carrowe bought of hyr at aventur as yt laye: xiijs iiijd

Item to Henry Sparke for caryage of the sayd tyle to the comon halle at iij lodes: ijs

Item to Henry Wodrof & John Elmam, laborers, brekyng vp the forsayd pavement, scoryng the tyle & caryeng it out to the carte, ij days worke: xviijd

[*f. 135^v*] **Of** the whiche yle we hade <we hade> iiij C di' of hole tyles of the grettest scantlyng, certen tyles of dyuerse scantlyns & a cart lode of broke tyles and freston; and payd to John Basyngham for pathyn tyle of a meane skantlyn ij C: iijs iiijd

Item to Wylliam Johnson & Robert Hollond, masons, fynyshyng vp the chambyr that was the fermery with gret tyle & the gret howse that was the freyter with small tyle, yche of them v days: vs vd

Item to John Ern, mason, helpyng them iiij days to make an ende byfore Estern: ijs iiijd

Item to Walter Colles & Robert Yoxale, laborers, v days, to Sander Clarke & Bartylmewe Wymond iiij days, to Henry Wodrof & John Elmam iiij days, makyng clene the chambyrs & all other howses in the place after the masons & removyng the whete & spredyng the same: ixs ixd

Item to Nycholas Tuttell and John Byrche the yonger begynnyng to make tabylles for the halle of dry poplyn plankes sawen in the last accompt, iiij days worke of eyther of them: iiijs iiijd

Item payd thys weke to Harryson & Goldyng for lyme spent in that place syns Crystmes iiij^xx ix comb' at iiijd euery comb': <xxx> xxixs viijd

Item to Henry Sparke for sonde spent ther these iij wekes past iiij lodes: xxd

Item gaf amonges the workmen ageynst Estern that wrowght ther all thys yere: xijd

[*f. 136*] **Item** payd thys weke to John Byrche th'elder for xxx newe trustylles of oke to serve for ten newe tabylles in the body of the halle: xxxs

Item to Leonard Yonges for a newe slevyd syrples for Clement, the clarke of the halle: iijs iiijd

Item to Feers wyf for ij newe ropys for the belles in the stepyll conteynyng xij *libr'* [*hemp*]: xviijd

Item to Paschall for a snecke with a ryng for the clycke gate in the prechyng yarde: iiijd

/*The iij^de weke after Owur Lady, beyng Ester weke*/ **Item** payd to the forsayd carpenters for iij days worke abought the forsayd tabylles: iijs iijd

Item to John Carre, glaser, mendyng the wyndow at the steyers hede betwen the corn chambyrs: vj*d*

/*The iiij^te weke after Owur Lady*/ **Item** to the forsayd ij carpenters fynyshyng vp vij tabylles of popyll for the halle, makyng ij newe fourmys for the chappell & mendyng the deskes ther, iij days worke: iij*s* iij*d*

Item to Wylliam Johnson, mason, pynnyng vp all the buttraces, walles & banke in the prechyng yarde, whych war dekayed the last wynter with the gret frost, & the newe porche at the halle dore, iij days worke of hym & Colles, his laborer: ij*s* ix*d*

Item to Sandyr pynnyng after hym oon day: v*d*

Item to Henry Wodroff makyng clene all the howses and yardes ageynst Seynt Georges guyld day, iiij days worke: xviij*d*

Item to John Byrche for a newe porche reysed ouer the halle dore in to the prechyng yarde, with ij seates and screnys, in all chargys: xxvj*s* viij*d*

[*f. 136ᵛ*] **Item** more to hym for vj newe joystes, with certen bourde & workman-shyppe, ouer the wall of the southe yle next Master Kempys howse, to be couerd with lede: iiij*s*

/*The v^te weke after Owur Lady*/ **Item** payd for lede spent vpon the sayd porche and <yle> walle of the sayd southe yle: and fyrst to Master Wylliam Rogers, alderman, for iij webbys of lede redy shotte conteynyng iij C j quarter xiiij *libr'* at v*s* C: xvj*s* x*d*

Item to Master Rugge, alderman, for oon gret webbe conteynyng ij C j quarter xiiij *libr'* at v*s* C: xj*s* xj*d*

Item to Wylliam Sandryngam for v C rawe lede at iiij*s* iiij*d* the C; and to the accomptant for j C ij *libr'* rawe lede at iiij*s* iiij*d*: xxvj*s*

Item to Clement Appylby, plomer, shotyng the forsayd lede, with j C xxiij *libr'* of old lede of comon store: *summa* vij C xxv *libr'* at xij*d* C: vij*s* iij*d*

Item more to the sayd plomer for ouer plus of hys own lede redy shotte *di'* C ij *libr'*: iij*s*

Item more to hym for iiij^or days worke about the sayd porche and walle, at viij*d* the day: ij*s* viij*d*

Item for sowde iiij *libr' di'*: xviij*d*; rosen: *ob'*; lede nayle ij C: xij*d*; viij*d* nayle j C: vj*d*; sadlers nayle for the batylment: j*d*; and iiij*d* nayle *di'* mˡ: xv*d* – iiij*s* iiij*d* *ob'*

Item to Wylliam Pede for xxiiij longe brodes for the battylment and the screne: vj*d*

Item for caryeng of the lede to the plomers and recaryeng from thense: viij*d*

Item payd that weke for bromys: j*d* *ob'*

[*f. 137*] **Item** to Wylliam Johnson, mason, closyng vp betwyxt the pyllers of the glase wyndows after the porche was fynyshyd, castyng the walles vnder nethe, selyng the entry at the dore in to the gardeyn next Seynt Peters & newe castyng the walles at the backe of Master Kempys howse after the plomer hade don ther, iiij days worke: ij*s* ij*d*

Item to Colles, his laborer, the same iiij days: xviij*d*

Item to Henry Wodrof, laborer, tendyng iiij days to the plomer and oon day makyng clene the gutters & ledes ouer Master Kempys howse and all the yardes ther abought: xxxij*d* *ob'*

/The vj^te weke after Owur Lady/ **Item** to the forsayd mason coueryng of all the tabylles of the clarystoryes of the southe yle with morter and thacke tyle to make the water to shote from the glasse, ij days of hym & hys man: xxij*d*

Item to Henry Wodrof, clayman, makyng a pannell betwyxt Frances Wolmer & the chamber ouer the newe backhowse, iiij days: xx*d*

Item to Bartylmewe Wymond seruyng hym: xviij*d*

Item to the sayd Henry fynyshyng vp the same pannell alone & makyng clene the chambyrs on bothe sydes, oon day: v*d*

/The vij^te weke after Owur Lady/ **Item** to the sayd Henry and John Elmam coldryng brycke & ston out of an arche that felle down the last wynter in the southe corner of the chapter howse, ij days: xviij*d*

Item for ij days more to the sayd Henry pullyng vp nettylles & wrecke within the growndes ther: ix*d*

[f. 137ᵛ] /The viij^te weke after Owur Lady/ **Item** to the sayd Henry caryeng out a gret hepe of coldyr that lay in the cloyster yarde that was cast out of the scolehows wyndows whan the tabylles war removyd, iiij days worke: xviij*d*

Item payd this weke, beyng the Assencon weke, to Master Marsham for xxij comb' lyme receyuyd from hym to the comon halle syns Crystmes: vij*s* iiij*d*

/The ix^te weke after Owur Lady/ **Item** payd this weke to the forsayd Henry Wodrof, laborer, spredyng and levellyng colder in the closse courte next the malt hows <vij> *vj* days: ij*s* iij*d*

/The x^te weke after Owur Lady/ **Item** more to hym this weke abought the forsayd courte, ij days: ix*d*

Item payd this weke to Edmond Arnold of Ypswyche *[Ipswich]*, organ makyr, for takyn a sonder the organs in the chappell & newe reparyng them, whyche war very sore dekayed: vj*s* viij*d*

/The xj^te weke after Owur Lady/ **Item** to Master Kempe for washyng of the alter clothis & awbys ageynst Corpus Christi day: iiij*d*

Item for scoryng of the latten & mendyng of the lampe, with xx^ti fadam of lyne for the sayd lampe and hangyng vp: xj*d*

Item for v^xx *libr'* lede made in a weyght to hange in a coffer in the roffe *of the chappell* for the sayd lampe: iiij*s*

Item to Asterby for castyng the same weyght holdyng styll the just weyght: xiiij*d*

Item for a stapyll & nayles for the same: iij*d*

Item to John Goold for makyng the coffer & trymmyng on the lampe & wight: iiij*d*

Item to ij prestes that war decon & subdeacon: iiij*d*

[f. 138] **Item** to an other prest that sange masse in the mornyng to consecrate the sakerment: iiij*d*

/*The xij*ᵗᵉ *weke after Owur Lady*/ **Item** to Grene, cowper, for settyng a newe botome in to oon of the stoppys at the kechyn welle: ij*d*

Item for ij newe yron hoopys to Pede: vj*d*

Item to John Erne and Robert Hollond, masons, makyng a partycon walle with a dorestall in yt in the gret vowlt at the tenement ageynst the ij elmys, eyther of them iij days: iij*s* iiij*d ob'*

Item to the sayd Robert for oon day more rowecastyng and fynyshyng the sayd walle: vj*d ob'*

Item to Robert Yoxhale, laborer, iij days: xiij*d ob'*

Item to Sander Clarke, laborer, vj days: ij*s* iij*d*

Item to Henry Wodrof, laborer, levellyng the sayd vowltes & makyng florthis of clay in the same & fechyng the *clay* out of the strete: xxij*d ob'*

Item to Henry Sparke for sonde iij lode: xv*d*; & for fechyng ij lodes marle from Byshopps gates kylle to myxt with the lyme: viij*d* – xxiij*d*

Item to Henry Carter for iij lodes of clay: xv*d*

Item to John Byrche for the dore stalle set in the partycon walle: iij*s* iiij*d*

/*The weke in whiche Mydsomer fell in*/ **Item** to Nycholas Tuttell, carpenter, makyng a gret loope for the sayd dore stalle, ij loopys for wyndows in the howse within the partycon and cuttyng byllettes to be layd in the walles for shelvys, iiij days worke: ij*s* ij*d*

Item to Master Thetford for iiij°ʳ newe sparris to cutt for byllettes for the sayd warehowse: xvj*d*

[*f. 138ᵛ*] **Item** to John Erne, mason, layeng in of the sayd byllettes & smothe castyng all the sayd howse, ij days: xiiij*d*

Item to Sandyr Clarke, laborer, ij days: ix*d*

Item to Henry Wodrof helpyng the sayd carpenter and mason, iij days: xiij*d ob'*

Item to Wylliam Pede for a payer of hookes & hengilles conteynyng viij *libr'*, a newe locke & a stapyll for the sayd dore, with settyng on of them: xx*d*

/*The vj*ᵗᵉ *weke after Mydsomer*/ **Item** payd for transposyng of all the howses in the forsayd tenement ageynst the ij elmys and begynnyng to buyld a newe howse out of the grownde with a carte gate: and fyrst payd for an ayle barrell to make a newe water tubbe: v*d*

Item for cuttyng the sayd barrell & for hoopys and eerys: iij*d*; for dyshys: j*d* – iiij*d*

Item for mendyng of a payle: j*d*

Item payd to Nycholas Tuttell and John Byrche the yonger, carpenters, shoryng the old howse, removyng the steyers, partycions & planchers, with moche other turmoylyng, to make waye for the masons begynnyng the fowndacions, vj days: vj*s* vj*d*

Item to John Erne and Robert Hollond, masons, begynnyng the fowndacon of a gret mayne walle in the vowlte & speryng vp at the ende of the strete next the carte gate, vj days: vj*s* ix*d*

Item to Sandyr & Yoxhale, laborers, vj days: iiij*s* vj*d*

Item to Henry Wodroff & John Elmam caryeng awaye old tymbyr, iiij days *di'*: ij*s* iiij*d ob'* [*f. 138A*] /*The vij^te weke after Mydsomer*/ **Item** to the forsayd ij carpenters takyng downe the rest of the howses to the grownde & makyng certen dore stalles, v days this weke: vs vd

Item to Wylliam Johnson and Robert Hollond, masons, bryngyng vp the forsayd mayne walle & returnyng the same toward the northe & settyng in the vowlt dore, yche of them v days: vs vd

Item to John Erne, mason, begynnyng the newe chymney in the gret chambyr, bryngyng that vp in the est gabyll of the lybrary, v days: ijs xjd

Item to Sandyr Clarke, Robert Yoxhale, Richard Wysbyche, Bartylmewe Wymond & John Elmam, laborers, euery of them v days: ixs iiijd ob'

Item to Henry Wodrof helpyng to fyll vp the gret hole wher the carte gate shalbe, iiij days: xviijd

Item to Wylliam Pede for a pece of a barre of yron *layd* from <f> the backe of the forsayd chymney to the brest of the same conteynyng viij *libr'*: xijd

Item payd that weke to John Warnys castyng of a mote next the ryver to kepe yn sygnettes, wher some tyme was the ffryers jakes, ij days of hym and his man: ijs; and to other ij laborers that holpe a waye the menur that came out ther the same ij days: xviijd – iijs vjd

/*The viij^te weke after Mydsomer*/ **Item** to the forsayd ij carpenters makyng newe wyndowe stalles for the kechyn, a mantyll tre for the chymney in the parlowur & cuttyng old joystes to couer the vowlte in the kechyn, eyther of them vj days: vjs vjd

[*f. 138A^v*] **Item** to Wylliam Pede for v yron barrys for the kechyn wyndowe by the stretes syde conteynyng xxiiij *libr' di'*: iijs jd

Item to John Erne, Wylliam Johnson & Robert Hollond, masons, rysyng vp with the forsayd workes, vj days: xs

Item to Wodroff, Elmam, Wymond, Yoxhale and Wysbyche, laborers, vj days euery of them: xjs iijd

Item to Sandyr Clarke pynnyng the blackes walles [*sic*], vj days thys weke: ijs vjd

Item to Walter Feere for brekyn ston ij lode: xxd

Item to Henry Sparke for fechyng the same: vjd

Item to hym for sond syns Mydsomer xij lodes: vs

/*The ix^te weke after Mydsomer*/ **Item** to the forsayd ij carpenters hewyng & sqwaryng of viij trees with certen toppe endes lyeng at the comon inne, whyche war bought at Ambryngale [*Arminghall*] in the last accompte, vj days: vjs vjd

Item to John Stanfeld and hys man sawyng parcell of them, vj days this weke: vjs vjd

Item to Nycholas *Marry*, gravyr, drawyng & inbostyn the cite armys vpon the dormant that lyeth ouer the newe carte gate, ij days worke: xvd

Item to Robert Hennoud, joynour, for other ij days clensyng the same: xiiijd

Item to the forsayd iij masons bryngyng vp the forsayd mayne walle, the ij returnyd blacke walles, the jeamys of the carte gate and makyng all thynges to ther hyght & levell for the joystes, vj days euery of them: xs

Item to Sandyr, Yoxhale & Colles vj days: vj*s* ix*d*

[*f. 139*] **Item** to Elmam, Wodroff & Wymond and Wysbyche, laborers, euery of them vj days: ix*s*

/*The x*^{te} *weke after Mydsomer*/ **Item** payd to the forsayd ij carpenters styll hewyng & sqwaryng of tymbyr for the sayd newe howse *vj* days: vj*s* vj*d*

Item to the forsayd ij sawers vj days: vj*s* vj*d*

Item to the forsayd Erne and Hollond, masons, begynnyng the chymney & ovyn in the kechyn, vj days: vj*s* ix*d*

Item to Sandyr & Clarke [*sic*], ther laborers, vj days: iiij*s* vj*d*

Item to Wodroff, Wysbyche and Elmam caryeng of coldyr to fyll vp the grownd at the carte gate for cartes to come inne, vj days: vj*s* ix*d*

Item to Pede for ij yron hookes layd in the kechyn chymney conteynyng x *libr'*, and an yron grate for the vowlt wyndowe next the carte gate conteynyng xiiij *libr'*: iij*s*

/*The xj*^{te} *weke after Mydsomer*/ **Item** to the forsayd ij carpenters makyng an ende *of* hewyng, inbowyng the dormant ouer the cart gate, makyng the threshold & stulpys of the sayd gate, a frame for the forsayd yron grate, postes and steppys for the vowlt dore, with moche other besynes that weke, v days eyther of them: v*s* v*d*

Item to the forsayd ij sawers ij days: ij*s* ij*d*

Item to John Erne and Robert Hollond, masons, makyng a fense walle out of the grownde from the northe ende of the dortour to the water gate to fense in the mote ther, v days: v*s* vij*d* ob'

Item to Sandyr & Yoxhale, laborers, v days: iij*s* ix*d*

Item to Wodrof *&* Elmam sometyme helpyng them and sometyme the carpenters, v days: iij*s* ix*d*

Item to Thomas Trase *v days*, John Knotte *iiij*, John Woodes *iiij*, Wylliam Kyrby *ij* and John Mylles *one day*, laborers, /*nullus*/ [*f. 139*^{v}] caryeng colder in barrows out of the forsayd grownd inclosyd to levell the courte next the carte gate, xvj days worke of a man amonges them: vj*s*

Item to Henry Sparke for caryeng of iiij^{or} lodes of sawen tymbyr from the comon inne to the sayd comon halle for the sayd newe howse: xvj*d*

/*The xij*^{te} *weke after Mydsomer*/ **Item** payd to the forsayd ij carpenters begynnyng to laye forthe the newe howse to frame, v days: v*s* v*d*

Item to the forsayd ij sawers iij days that weke: iij*s* iij*d*

Item to John Erne and Robert Hollond, masons, fynyshyng vp the forsayd fense walle next the newe mote & heynyng of all the walles betwen the comons & the sope howse, vj days: vj*s* ix*d*

Item to Sandyr *vj*, Yoxhale *vj*, Woodrof *v* & Elmam *v*, laborers, ij of them vj days & the other ij v days: viij*s* iij*d*

Item to Robert Wace for thacke a lode to couer the forsayd *walle* wythe: ij*s* vj*d*

Item to John Styngate for xx fadam rede: iij*s* iiij*d*

Item for fechyng the same [*from*] the stathe in a bote: iiij*d*

/The xiij weke after Mydsomer, the last & next byfore Myhelmes/ **Item** to Nycholas Tuttell & John Byrche, the forsayd carpenters, framyng of the newe howse, eyther of them vj days: vj*s* vj*d*

Item for ashyn astyll & byllettes for hooke nayles for the carpenters: ij*d*

Item to John Barsham, clayman, coueryng the forsayd newe walles, vj days of hym and of Hanys & Kyrby, hys laborers: vij*s* vj*d*

[*f. 140*] **Item** to Master Quashe ffor strawe for the claye: vj*d*

Item to Henry Carter for claye vj lodes: ij*s* vj*d*

Item to Styngate for iiij^or^ fadam more of rede: viij*d*

Item to Henry Wodrof and John Elmam, laborers, helpyng the carpenters & claymen, with moche other turmoylyng that weke, vj days: iiij*s* vj*d*

/Bryckel/ **Item** payd thys weke to Brytyff of Het[*h*]erset[*t*] for vj m^l^ brycke receyuyd from hym syns Mydsomer for the gates, dores, wyndows & chymneys; < vj m^l^ > and from Seman of Wyndam [*Wymondham*] for v m^l^ at vj*s* m^l^: lxvj*s*

/Tymbyr and bourde for the loopys of the carte gate/ **Item** payd to John Byrche for iiij^or^ long peces dry [*stothis*], vj onchis sqware, for the sydes of the loopys and ij peces for the ovyr and nether partes: iiij*s*

Item for x dry stothis for ledgys for the same: iij*s* iiij*d*

Item for vj dry sparrys for the batrons: ij*s*

Item for dry bourde iij quarters of an C: iij*s*

/Yron worke/ **Item** to Wylliam Pede for ij gret vorelles, ij collers, ij coytes and ij ponchys conteynyng xxiij *libr' di':* ij*s* xj*d*

Item for xxx brades: ij*d*; vj*d* nayle ij C: x*d*; viij*d* nayle j C: vj*d* – xviij*d*

Item dyce hede nayle of xij*d* bore *di'* C; and an other *di'* C of viij*d* bore, tynnyd: vj*s*

Item for a payer of jemews and a ryng for the coueryng of the vowlt wyndowe in the strete next the gate with the grate: xij*d*

Item for layeng of the comon pykexe: ij*d*

Item payd to Harryson and Goldyng for lyme receyuyd ffrom them syns Ester in to this place xvj chalder at ij*s* viij*d* the chalder: xlij*s* viij*d*

[*f. 140^v^*] **Item** to Henry Sparke for sonde spent ther in these v wekes last past xv lodes: vj*s* iij*d*

/Tymbyr and bourde/ **Item** to Leonard Sutterton for xvj joystes for the sayd newe howse of xix foote lenght, viij onchys brode & vj onchys thycke: xvj*s*

Item more to hym for iij lode of okyn bourde occupyed ther in planchers, pentyses, dore loopes, wyndows & in suche leke thynges xij C iij quarteres at ij*s* x*d* C: xxxvj*s* j*d*

Item more to hym for hart lathe a lode: xiiij*s*

Item to hym for xxiiij copyll of sawen sparrys of xvj foote lenght at vij*d* coppyll: xiiij*s*

Item to hym for vj copyll of stothis for pyllers of wyndows at vij*d* the copyll: iij*s* vj*d*

Item to Robert Lyncon of Tasburgh for a lode of ashyn bourde conteynyng iiij C iij quarteres at ij*s* vj*d* C: xj*s* x*d*

Item to Robert Osborn of Kyrby [*Bedon*] for v m¹ thack tyle layd ther redy for the coueryng of the newe howse at vjs m¹: xxxs

Item payd for brede & drynke for the caryars that browght home the tymbyr, bourde and lathe from Shelton: vjd

Summa solucionum communis awle: lxiiij *li* xvijs ijd ob'

Memorandum that the rest of the tymbyr for the newe howse was all of the trees bought in the last accompt at Ambryngale [*Arminghall*]; and all other stuff here not rehersyd, as moche old tymbyr, more bryke, ston & other thynges war of the comon store *& cetera*.

[*f. 141*] *Summa totallis omnium solucionum hoc anno* CCCC xxxj *li* ixs xjd

And so the forsayd accomptant do owe xxxiij *li* ijs xd ob' qu'

Wherof he axythe to be allowyd for these parcelles folowyng:

In primis for the ingrossyng of thys accompt payd to Rychard Framyngham by the assygment of the awdytours: vs

Item payd for the expenses of the awdytors & of others appoyntyd syttyng vpon the determynacon of thys accompt: xs

Item he axe furder to be allowyd for dyuers rentes above chargid & nowe dekayd, for as moche as the ffees therof be vnknowen to the sayd accomptant, as yt apperith to the awdytours by other accomptes byfore made, wherof the partyclers appere at large: xiijs iiijd

Item for rent of a sygne set in the kynges heye waye ageynst the mese, late Wylliam Norffolke, cald The Whyte Horse, whyche sygne ys nowe plucke down, and that notwithstondyng ys still charged in the tytyll of rent of assyse: jd

Item for iij quarteres ferme of the Brasen Towur endyd at Mydsomer in the last accompt dependyng vpon Robert Brown, mercer, as in the tytyll of *vnde super* do appere more at large;[591] & nowe, for as moche as the sayd Robert Brown ys not dystreynabyll and vtterly do denye /*nullus*/ [*f. 141*ᵛ] ffor the payment therof xijd, by cause he was put from the sayd towur without any warnyng of the sayd accomptant: xijd

Item for oon quarter ferme of a bochers stalle dewe by Gregory Pougeleon, chargid in the tytyll of the cyte bochers, for as moche as the sayd Pougeleon was hangyd with in the tyme of thys accompt: iiijs[592]

Item for certen dettes of dyuerse poore men and of other persons not levyabyll, as yt apperythe to the awdytours, parcell of iiijˣˣ *li* viijs xjd remaynyng not gatherd in dyuers wardes of the cyte of a certeyn sesment taxyd and set for the charges of ffourty soldyers sent in to France within the tyme of thys accompt, whyche ys chargyd above in the tytyll of soldyers amonges the fforen receptes: vij *li* vs

---

591 See above, p. 234.

592 NCR, 18A/6, f. 162ᵛ, notes that he was 'atteynt of ffelony [...] & sufferd ffor the same by reason wherof he had no goodes to distreyne'.

Item payd to John Rede and Thomas Molle, offycers to master mayer, for ther paynes goyng for the constabylles that war gatherers of the forsayd sesment and for other partycler persons that war detters to the comialte to make answer byfore master mayer and the awdytours for ther sayd dettes: xij*d*

Item for rest of oon quarter ferme of a /nullus/ [*f. 142*] ffyshestalle endyd at Mydsomer, dewe by John Harryes, who ranne away & caryed the key with hym & was not dystreynabyll, whiche ys chargid in the tytyll of ffysh stalles: iiij*d*

Item for rest of oon quarter ferme of a bochers stalle endyd at Crystmes dewe by Robert Savery, who ys an impotent and a very poore man and not dystreynabyll, which ys chargid in the tytyll of cite bochers: viij*d*

Summa allocacionum ix *li* v*d*

Summa totallis omnium solucionum et allocacionum CCCC xl *li* xs iiij*d*

And so the forsayd accomptant do owe xxiiij *li* ij*s* v*d ob' qu'*

Wherof he axe to be respectyd vpon *vnde super* for certen rentes and fermys above chargyd and not yet receyuyd, wherof the partyclers do ffolowe:

/*Respectes*/ *In primis* ffor rent of a tenement in the paryshe of Seynt Mychaell at the Plee, late Master Pyndern, prest, nowe Henry Mynne, gent', parcell of the castill ffee chargid in the ffoote of the last accompt in the tytyll of respectes: j*d*; and for an other peny for rent of the same tenement dewe in the ende of thys accompt, whyche ij*d* he vtterly denye to paye: ij*d*

[*f. 142ᵛ*] Item for rent of assyse of a mese in the paryshe of Seynt Swythyn, late John Clementes, nowe Stephyn Empson, not yet levyed: *qu'*

Item for oon quarter ferme of a tenement in the paryshe of Seynt Mary Lytyll endyd at Myhelmes, chargid in the tytyll of suffrigan tenementes, dewe by Wydowe Boyse: ij*s* iiij*d*

Item for oon quarter ferme of a tenement ageynst the comon stathe indyd at Myhelmes, dewe by Nycholas Hardyng: xv*d*

Item for parcell of a quarter ferme of an other tenement ther, dewe by Wylliam Guylbert: xj*d*

Item for oon quarter ferme of a fyshe shoppe endyd at Myhelmes, dewe by Robert Newman, ffyshmonger: ij*s*

Item for the last payment of lx*s*, dewe by oblygacon at Myhelmes by John Barker, brewer, for a fyne govyn to the comialte for that he shuld not be chosen shreve nor alderman for iij yeres, chargid in the tytyll of redempcions: xx*s*

Summa debitorum xxvj*s* vij*d qu'*

Summa totallis omnium solucionum, allocacionum et respectorum CCCC xlj *li*
xvj*s* xj*d qu'*

And so the sayd accomptant do knowlege hym selff clere detour to the comialte **xxij** *li* xv*s* x*d ob'*

[*f. 143*] *Memorandum* that the sayd accomptant hathe in hys custody lyeng at the comon halle to the vse of the comialte ffyve score comb' whete bare [*mesyr*] at vs the comb': xxv *li*

Summa xxv *li*

Thys accompt was vewyd, examyned and determyned by the awdytours here after folowyng vpon the Monday the ffyrst of June in the xxxvij yere of the reign of Kyng Henry the viij^te [*1545*] & cetera.[593]

Awsten Steward
Edmond Wood   aldermen

Thomas Cocke[594]
Thomas Cony   comyners

---

593 NCR, 18A/6, f. 163ᵛ, contains no record of such an examination, but lists the names of the auditors at the head of the account on f. 124.

594 Cocke was appointed auditor on 31 September 1544 as a replacement for James Marsham, who died suddenly in office, perhaps of plague, which was then endemic: NCR, 16D/2, f. 208.

[1544–45]

/*Ciuitas Norwici*/ The accompt of Robert Raynbald, chamberleyn of the cyte of Norwyche from the ffest of Seynt Mychaell th'arcangell in the xxxvj yere of the reign of owur soueraign lord Kyng Henry the viij^te [*29 September 1544*] vntyll the sayd ffest of Seynt Mychaell in the xxxvij yere of his magestes reign [*1545*]: that ys to say by oon hole yere *& cetera*

Receptes

/*Arreragis*/ *In primis* the sayd accomptant do charge hym selff and answer for xxij *li* xvs x*d ob'* of clere dette of the arreragys of the last accompt [*of*] the sayd Robert Raynbald, then chamberleyn. And he answer for xxvj*s* vij*d qu'* of the arrerages of the sayd accompt, whyche was not then by hym levyed, as yt appere more at large in the ende of the same accompt: xxiiij *li* ij*s* v*d ob' qu'*

Summa **xxiiij li ij*s* v*d ob' qu'***

/*Whete sold*/[595] **Item** he knowlege hym selff that he haue receyuyd of the poore inhabytans of the cite for iiij score xvij comb' and a bushell whete sold in the market at v*s* iiij*d* the comb', whyche whete was parcell of v^{xx} comb', bare mesyr, remaynyng at the last accompt, for the *summa* of xxv *li* and ys parcell of the arrerages of the sayd accompt: xxv *li* xviij*s* viij*d*

Summa **xxv li xviij*s* viij*d***

[*f. 144^v*] *Memorandum* that ther was wastyd of the forsayd v^{xx} comb' whete in the hole yere kepyng with that whyche dyd set in the mesyr in the market ij comb' & iij bushelles.

/*Langoll rent*/ **Item** receyuyd of the baly of the manour or late priory of Horsham Seynt Faythe for langoll rent of certen tenementes within the cite parteynyng to the sayd manour: iij*s*; and of the baly of Heylesden [*Hellesden*] for langoll rent of a tenement late the duke of Suff': ij*d* – iiij*s* ij*d*
Item [*blank*]

Summa **iiij*s* ij*d***

/*Castyll ffee*/ **Item** receyuyd of dyuerse howses and growndes stondynge vpon the castyll ffee: xxj*s* ij*d ob' qu'*

Summa **xxj*s* ij*d ob' qu'***

---

595 NCR, 18A/6, f. 164, combines this section under arrearages, whch are 3*s* 4¼*d* higher because of the inclusion of certain uncollected assize rents. Wheat prices remained high in 1544–5, and the demand for subsidised supplies continued: see above, p. 246 note 524.

/*Rent assyse*/ **Item** receyuyd for rent of assyse of dyuers houses and growndes within the cite, with x*s* of newe rent for the comon grownde betwen the ij ryvers in the paryshe of Seynt Marten at Oke,[596] nowe thys yere recouerd: ix *li* ij*s* xj*d* ob'

Summa ix *li* ij*s* xj*d* ob'

/*Cyte bochers*/ **Item** receyuyd of John Howse for the hole yere fferme of the ij fyrst stalles, bothe in oon, in the northe ende of the est part of the sayde cyte bochers: xxxj*s* iiij*d*; and of Alys Reed for the iij^de stalle toward the southe: xij*s* – xliij*s* iiij*d*

Item of Thomas Toly for the iiij^te & v^te stalles: xvj*s*

Item of Thomas Grene for the vj & vij^te stalles: xxiiij*s*

Item of Richard Dey for the viij^te & ix^te stalles: xxiiij*s*

[*f. 145*] **Item** of John Hylle for the hole yere of the x^te stalle: xvj*s*

Item of John Barkyr for the xj^te stalle: xvj*s*

Item of Rychard Dey th'[*y*]onger for the xij^te stalle: xvj*s*

Item of Roger Baldry for the xiij stalle: x*s*

Item of the sayd Roger & Andrewe Dey for the xiiij stalle dyvydyd betwyxt them: ix*s*

Item of the same Andrewe for the xv stalle, whyche ys the last of the est part of the south ende: xxx*s*

Item of Wylliam Aleyn for the fyrst stalle on the west part in the southe ende, with halff the second stalle dyvydyd betwyxt hym and John Fysher: xx*s*; and of the sayd Fysher for the other halff, with the hole iij^d stalle: xvj*s* viij*d* – xxxvj*s* viij*d*

Item of John Wodcocke for the iiij^te stalle: xvj*s*

Item of Edmond Toly for the v^te stalle: xvj*s*

Item of John Barbowur for the vj^te stalle: xij*s* iiij*d*

Item of Henry Harpowur for the vij^te stalle: xiiij*s*

Item of Thomas Brown for the viij^te stalle: xiiij*s*

Item of Agnes Cannard for the fyrst *di'* yere of the ix^te stalle: xiiij*s* vj*d*; & of Thomas Brown the yonger for the last *di'* yere: xv*s* – xxix*s* vj*d*

Item of Jeffrey Reed for the x^te & xj^te stalles: xxxv*s*

Item of Richard Barne for the xij^te stalle: xiij*s* iiij*d*

Item of Thomas Hubbard for the xiij & xiiij stalles, the last in the northe ende: xl*s*

Summa xxj *li* xij*s* ij*d*

[*f. 145^v*] /*Movabyll stalles*/[597] **Item** receyuyd of Gregory Foxe for the hole yere ferme of a movabyll stall bynethe the guyldhalle: vij*s*

Item of John Barbowur for the second stalle: vij*s*

Item of Henry Carman for the fyrst *di'* yere of the iij^de stalle downward: iiij*s*; for the iij^de quarter nothyng for lacke of a fermer; but of John Wodcocke for the last quarter: ij*s* – vj*s*

---

596 See above, p. 269. NCR, 18A/6, f. 164^v, lists the names of the six tenants.
597 NCR, 18A/6, ff. 165^v–6, combines the rents from moveable stalls with those from city butchers in a single section.

Item for any movabyll stalles set above the guyldhalle dore this yere nothyng for lacke of fermers; but *receyuyd of* dyuers men stondyng in the same rowe dyuerse days thys yere: ijs ijd

Item of John Fysher for the last *di'* yere ferme of a movabyll stalle at the northe ende of the iiij⁰ʳ newe stalles: iiijs

Summa **xxviijs ijd**

/**Contry bochers**/ *In primis* receyuyd of Thomas Toly for the fyrst quarter ferme of the gretter stalle at the west ende of the guyldhalle: iijs iiijd; for the next *di'* yere nothyng for lacke <for lacke> of a fermer; but receyuyd of Thomas Randolff for the last quarter: iijs iiijd – vjs viijd

Item for the other stalles at the sayd west ende nothyng by the yere for lacke of fermers; but receyuyd of certen strange bochers stondyng ther dyuers days thys yere: ijs iiijd

Item of Thomas & Walter Vyncent for the iij stalles on the southe syde of the guyldhalle: xls

[*f. 146*] /**Long rowe**/⁵⁹⁸ Item receyuyd of Robert Plattyng for the fyrst quarter ferme of the fyrst stalle at the northe ende of the Long Rowe: vs; for the second quarter nothyng for lacke of a fermer; and of John Tewysday the yonger for the last halff yere: xs – xvs

Item of Richard Dey the yonger and of William Brown for the hole yere ferme of the last stall of the same in the southe ende: xxs

Item of xxiiij^ti other men for xxiiij stalles betwyxt the forsayd northe ende & southe ende at xvjs euery stalle: xix *li* iiijs

/iiij⁰ʳ *newe stalles*/⁵⁹⁹ Item of Nycholas Andrews for the hole yere ferme of the fyrst stalle in the southe ende: xijs

Item of Edmond Toly for the second stalle: xijs

Item of Thomas Brown for the fyrst quarter of the iijᵈ stalle: iijs; for the next *di'* yere nothyng for lacke of a fermer; and of John Hylle for the last quarter: iijs – vjs

Item of Thomas Barkyr for iij quarteres ferme of the iiijᵗᵉ stalle: ixs; and for the last quarter nothyng for that the sayd Barker ranne away byfore Myhelmes to Bullen [*Boulogne*] and so was not dystreynabyll: ixs

Summa **xxv *li* vijs**

/**Ropery**/ Item for the fyrst shoppe in the Ropery in the southe ende nothyng for that it is in lease with the Murage Loft; and for the /*nullus*/ [*f. 146ᵛ*] second shoppe nothyng for lacke of a fermer; but receyuyd of John Peke for the iijᵈᵉ shoppe: vs

Item of Walter Feer for the iiijᵗᵉ shoppe: vs

Item of Robert Hynderson for the vᵗᵉ shoppe: vs

---

598 NCR, 18A/6, f. 166, incorporates these entries without any sub-heading under 'countre bochers'.

599 NCR, 18A/6, f. 166ᵛ, presents these entries as a separate section.

Item of Henry Carman for iij quarters ferme of the vj^{te} shoppe, the last in the northe ende, nowe occupyed for a bochers stalle: xij$s$; and of Gregory Foxe for vj wekes in the laste quarter: ij$s$ – xiiij$s$

Item [*blank*]

Summa xxix$s$

/*Fyshopps*/ **Item** receyuyd of John Webster for the hole yere ferme of the fyrst shoppe in the northe ende: xiij$s$ iiij$d$

Item of Jerome Qwashe for the second shoppe: viij$s$

Item of Thomas Worlton for the iij^{de} shoppe: viij$s$

Item of John Sewell for the iiij^{te} shoppe: xs

Item for the v^{te} and vj^{te} shoppis, both in oon, nothyng for lacke of a fermer: *nullus*

Item of Nycholas Grene for the vij & viij^{te}: xvj$s$

Item of Robert Norman for the ix^{te} and x<j>^{te} shopps: xvj$s$

Item of Frances Scotte for the xj^{te} shoppe: viij$s$

Item of Master Cocke, alderman, for the xij shoppe: viij$s$

Item of the xiij shoppe for lacke of a fermer: *nullus*

Item of Master Warden for the xiiij shoppe: viij$s$

Item of Alyce Cobbe for the xv shoppe: viij$s$

Item of Stephyn Gostlyn for the xvj shoppe: viij$s$

Item for the xvij shoppe for lacke of a fermer: *nullus*

Item for the xviij shoppe for *the* fyrst *di'* yere *nullus* [*f. 147*] ffor lacke of a fermer; but receyuyd of John Crowe for the last *di'* yere of the same shoppe: iiij$s$

Item of the sayd John Crowe for the hole yere ferme of the xix & xx stalles, bothe in oon, the last in the southe ende: xvj$s$

Summa vj li xj$s$ iiij$d$

/*Wulshoppis*/[600] **Item** receyuyd of John Lartor for the hole yere ferme of a tenement next the churche style of Seynt Peter with the chambyrs ouer the wolshopps: xiij$s$ iiij$d$

Item of Henry Marlyn for a shoppe vnder the forsayd chambyrs openyng toward to [*sic*] pultry market: xs

Item of Master Qwashe for a tenement in the north ende of the same rowe next the fyshmarket: xx$s$

Item of Thomas Croshold for the fyrst shoppe in the southe ende openyng in to the wolmarket: vj$s$ viij$d$

Item of Wylliam Patryke for the second shoppe: vj$s$ viij$d$

Item of Robert Kyndersley for the iij^{de} shoppe: vj$s$ viij$d$

Item of Stephyn Johnson for the iiij^{te} shoppe: iiij$s$

Item for the v^{te} shoppe for lacke of a fermer: *nullus*

---

600 NCR, 18A/6, ff. 167–8, combines the rents from 'ffisshe stalles & wolle shoppes' in a single section with no sub-headings. Half way through the section four lines relating to the Ropery appear by mistake and have been deleted.

Item of Henry Holden for the vj^{te} shoppe, whiche ys adioynyng to the southe ende of hys mese on the other syde: vs

Item of hym for a vowlte vnder the southe ende of the cite bochery: vs

Summa <xj li xvijs viijd> iij li xvijs iiijd

/Tenementes and groundes/[601] Item receyuyd of John Thurston for the hole yere ferme of a tenement in the Myddill /nullus/ [f. 147^v] Rowe cald The Murage Loft, with the fyrst shoppe in the southe ende of the Ropery: xxxs

Item for the fyrst halff yere ferme of an other tenement at the southe corner of the same rowe nothyng for lacke of a fermer; but receyuyd of Henry Jepson for the last di' yere of the same tenement: vjs viijd

/Coblerrowe/ Item of Hewe Coplond for ferme of the north corner howse with a lytyll corner shoppe and a vowlte vnder the smythis shoppe: xxiijs iiijd

Item of Bryan Doront for the mydill tenement on the same rowe: xxs

Item of Marke Heynes for the iij^{de} tenement on the same rowe with the newe buyldyng: xviijs iiijd

/Comon inne/ Item of Adryan Johnson for the hole yere ferme of the hede place of the comon inne, with parcell of the newe buyldyng: lxvjs viijd

Item of John Sewell for the yere ferme of a tenement on the west corner, parcell of the forsayd comon inne: xvjs

Item of Master Nekton, alderman, for ferme of a tenement in the paryshe of Seynt Andrewe: iijs iiijd

Item of Wydowe Potter for the hole yere ferme of a scryptory on the southe syde of the guyldhalle, late in the ferme of Richard Framyngham: ijs

Item of Jane Chapman for the last di' yere ferme of an other scryptory ther: xijd; & for the other di' yere nothyng: xijd

[f. 148] /Pastures and landes/ Item receyuyd of Master Nycholas Sywhat, alderman, for ferme of a certen grounde, water *&* fyshynges above the newe mylles: vjs viijd

Item of John Barbowur for ferme of Butter Hylles: xxvjs viijd

Item of Master Qwashe for the iusment of the comon grounde vnder the cite walles in the Chappellfeld croftes: xvjd

Item of hym for ij acres of grounde without Seynt Gyles gates, late Hemmynges: vs

Item[602] of Isbell Mace for a pece of comon grounde in Seynt Vedastes vnder the college walle: xijd

Item of Syr John Buxton, prest, for a garden in the paryshe of All Seyntes in Be[r] strete: xvjd

---

601 NCR, 18A/6, ff. 168–9, has no sub-headings in this section, which also incorporates entries relating to tenements in Conesford, treated below as a separate section.
602 A maniculae with an extended finger points to this entry, as a *nota bene* sign.

Item of the myller of Cryngylford [*Cringleford*] for the hole yere easement of the crosse in the market to set in his mele sackes ageynst the market day: ij*s*

Item of Rycherd Flecher for the clothe halle: xl*s*

Summa xiij *li* xj*s* iiij*d*

/*Tenementes in Conysford*/ **Item** receyuyd of John Styngate for the fyrst *di'* yere ferme of the hede place with the kylyard in Southe Conysford: x*s*

Item of Robert Teyton for *di'* yere ferme of the ffyrst tenement in the northe ende: ij*s* vj*d*

Item of Wydowe Frankyshe for the second tenement: ij*s* vj*d*

Item for the iij^de tenement for lacke of a fermer: *nullus*

Item of Robert Dawes for the iiij^te tenement: ij*s* vj*d*

Item of Thomas Purkyn for the v^te tenement: ij*s* vj*d*

Item for the vj^te tenement for lacke of a fermer: *nullus*

[*f. 148^v*] **Item** for the vij^te tenement for lacke of a fermer: *nullus*

Item of Wylliam Horne for halff yere ferme of the viij^te tenement: iij*s* iiij*d*

Item of Wylliam Guylbert for the ix^te tenement: ij*s* vj*d*

Item of Jone Davy for the x^te tenement: ij*s* vj*d*

Item for the xj^te tenement for lacke of a fermer: *nullus*

Item for the xij^te tenement for lacke of a fermer: *nullus*

Item of Rychard Sterkyn for the fyrst *di'* yere of the xiij tenement, the last in the southe ende: ij*s* vj*d*

Item of John Bronde for the last half yere fferme of the forsayd hede place, kylyard & tenementes grauntyd to hym by lease: xxxiij*s* iiij*d*

Summa lxiiij*s* ij*d*

/*Pety Custom*/ **Item** receyuyd of Robert Collard for the hole yere fferme of the pety custome: v *li* xiij*s* iiij*d*

Summa v *li* xiij*s* iiij*d*

/*Bothes*/ **Item** for the ferme of any bothes within the tyme of thys accompt set in the castyll diche in the tyme of assyse or sessyons nothyng for lacke of fermors: *nullus*

Summa nullus

/*Tenementes in the kynges hondes*/ **Item** receyuyd of Roger Leke for the hole yere ferme of a tenement in the paryshe of Sent Benet: iiij*s*; and of Thomas Hast for an other in Sent Martens at Pales Gate: v*s* – ix*s*

Summa ix*s*

[*f. 149*] /*Comon stathes*/ **Item** receyuyd of John Styngate for the hole yere fferme of the old and newe comon stathes: xv *li*

Summa xv *li*

/*Mylles*/ **Item** receyuyd of Stephyn Empson for the hole yere ferme of the newe mylles with all profygtes and comodytes thervnto bylongyng: xl *li*

Item of hym for the hole yere ferme of Heyham [*Heigham*] mylles with certen medows, marshis, waters & ffyshynges therto bylongyng: lxvjs viijd

Summa xliii *li* vjs viijd

/*Gates and towers*/ Item receyuyd of Master William Rogers, alderman, for a certen annuyte or yerely rent for the dyscharge of tolle and custome at the gates of the cite, and of ij fayers cald Pencost and Trynyte ffayers: viij *li*

Item of Walter Feer for ferme of a towur by the water syde next Pokethorppe gates: iijs iiijd

Item of Wylliam Bevys for ferme of a garden vnder the cyte walles ther from the sayd gates down to the forsayd tower: vs

Item of Hewe Boxford for the hole yere ferme of a towur next Fybrygge gates: vjd

Summa viij *li* viijs xd

/*Comon halle*/[603] *In primis* receyuyd of Wydowe Almonde for an annuall rent or ferme of the howses newe buyldyd ouer the gate yerely payd at Crystmes: vjs viijd

[*f. 149ᵛ*] Item of Frances Wolmer for the hole yere ferme of certen howses cald the maltyng offyce as they be nowe inclossed: xls

Item for ferme of a tenement nere the old kechyn, late in ferme to Syr Robert Shynkwyn, nothyng for lacke of a fermer: *nullus*

Item of John Clarke for a gardeyn sometyme parcell of the prechyng yarde: xiijs iiijd

Item of Thomas Pecke for the fyrst half yere ferme of a tenement newe buyldyd sometym the ankers howse: xxs; and of hym for the last halff yere ferme of the same: xxxiijs iiijd – liijs iiijd

/*Gret garden*/ Item receyuyd of Master Edmond Wood, alderman, for ferme of parcell of the gret gardeyn: xs

Item of Wylliam Marche for ferme of other ij parcelles of the same gardeyn: xxvjs viijd

Item of Mastres Morront, wydowe, for ferme of an other parcell of the same gardeyn: xiiijs

Item of Henry Bakon for ferme of an other parcell of the same gardeyn with a tenement & an howse, sometyme a chappell: xxvjs viijd

Item of John Byrche for an other parcell of the same gardeyn with a workehowse therin: xiijs iiijd

Item of Master Qwashe for an other parcell of the same gret gardeyn: iiij *li*

Item of John Bakyr for an other parcell of the same gret gardeyn: vjs viijd

[*f. 150*] Item of the sayd John Baker for ferme of a lane with an howse in the northe ende, whyche ys parcell of the sayd comon halle & gardeyn: vjs viijd

Summa xiiij *li* xvijs iiijd

603 NCR, 18A/6, f. 170, refers to 'the late howse or priory of Blak Freres'.

/Tenementes late lord suffrigan/ **Item** receyuyd of Robert Stephynson for the hole yere ferme of the fyrst tenement, beyng the corner howse next Tomlond: xxvj*s* viij*d*
Item of Thomas Hewson for the second tenement: xiij*s* iiij*d*
Item of Thomas Mosse for the iij^de tenement: xiij*s* iiij*d*
Item for the iiij^te tenement, beyng the hede place, for lacke of a fermer: *nullus*
Item for the fyrst quarter ferme of the v^te tenement nothyng for lacke of a fermer; but receyuyd of Syr Jamys Mathewson for the second quarter: ij*s* vj*d*; and of Awsten Cobbe for the last *di'* yere: v*s* – vij*s* vj*d*
Item of Thomas Callowe for the vj^te tenement: x*s*
Item for the fyrst *di'* yere of the vij^te tenement nothyng for lacke of a fermer; but receyuyd of William Farewell for the last half yere: v*s*
Item of Jeffrey Tybnam for the viij^te tenement: xx*s*
Item of Wydowe Boyse for iij quarteres ferme of the ix^te tenement: vj*s* ix*d*; and for the last quarter nothyng for lacke of a fermer: vj*s* ix*d*
Item of Wydowe Kyddall for the hole yere ferme of the x^te tenement, beyng the last in the strete that lede toward Seynt Mychaell at the Plee: vj*s* viij*d*

Summa v *li* ix*s* iij*d*

[*f. 150^v*] */Seynt Maryes churche/*[604] **Item** receyuyd of Wylliam Waller for halff yere ferme of Seynt Maryes churche endyd at Myhelmes grauntyd to hym for xx yeres, whose lease began at the Annuncyacon of Owur Lady last past: vj*s* viij*d*[605]
Item of John Derne for half yere ferme of the west ende of the churcheyarde, as yt is nowe newly inclosed with ston walles, grauntyd to hym by lease, whyche began at the sayd ffest: iij*s* iiij*d*
Item of John Jowell for the hole yere ferme of all the south & est partes of the sayd churche yarde, as it is nowe newly inclosed, with the tenement ther to annexid, late purchased of Arnold: xxvj*s* viij*d*

Summa xxxvj*s* viij*d*

/Foren receptes, alias foren ffermes/ **Item** receyuyd of Mastres Agnes Sutterton, wydowe, for the hole yere ferme of a tenement in the paryshe of Seynt Mychaell of Coslany endyd at Candylmes, late Master Alane Percy: xiij*s* iiij*d*
Item of Rychard Harman for iij quarteres ferme & of Richard Walpoole for the last quarter ferme of the comon mucke boate: <xl*s*> xxvj*s* viij*d*

Summa xl*s*

/Dettes dewe to the comialte/[606] **Item** receyuyd of Mastres Agnes Sutterton, widowe, for the vij^te payment of an C *li* dewe by oblygacon at the fest of the Annuncyacon of Owur Lady, whyche was in *anno domini* 1544, for the purchase of a mese in the paryshe of Seynt Mychaell of Coslany, late Master Percys: vj *li* xiij*s* iiij*d*

---

604 NCR, 18A/6, f. 171^v, adds 'fferme off the tenement late Crankes'.
605 The lease was sealed on 21 August 1545: NCR, 16D/2, f. 211^v.
606 NCR, 18A/6, f. 172–2^v, incorporates this section under 'fforen receptes' with no sub-heading.

[*f. 151*] **Item** of the sayd Mastres Sutterton for the viij^te payment of the forsayd purchase dewe at the forsayd ffest within the tyme of thys accompt: vj *li* xiij*s* iiij*d*

Item of Master William Rogers, alderman, for the second payment of xx *li* dewe by oblygacon for the dette of Master Thomas Grewe, alderman: xxvj*s* viij*d*

Item of John Revell the xxviij day of August ffor parcell of his accompt of the foren receyte: v *li*

Item of John Awelton for parcell of the bequest of Master Gardner, late alderman: xxvj*s* viij*d*[607]

Item of Thomas Brygges for the last payment of xx^ti markes govyn to the comialte for the dyscharge of all offyces within the cite: lxvj*s* viij*d*

Summa **xxiiij** *li* **vj***s* **viij***d*

/*Redempcions*/[608] **Item** receyuyd of Master Richard Catlyng, alderman, for the redempcon and dyscharge of the offyce of mayeralte all his lyffe: xx *li*[609]

Item receyuyd the xxiiij day of August of Master John Aldryche, alderman, for the lyberte not to be chose shreve of vj eleccions next folowyng: xx *li*[610]

Item of Wylliam Hede for the lyberte not to be chosen shreve at the next eleccon: xl*s*[611]

/*Hamper*/ **Item** receyuyd the xxiiij day of July out of the hamper of the guyldhall toward the payment of the lede of the comon halle: xxxiij *li* x*s*[612]

/*Bakers grynt*/ **Item** receyuyd of the comon bakers for a newe grynt grauntyd of euery comb' *ob*': vij *li* iiij*d ob*'

Summa **iiij**^xx *li* **x***s* **iiij***d ob*'

[*f. 151*^v] /*Other fforen receptes*/[613] **Item** receyuyd of John Reed, netterd, toward the reparacon of the ffences of the comon closse with owt Seynt Stephyns gates: xx*s*[614]

Item of Jeffrey Reed, bocher, toward the transposyng of his shoppe in the cite bochery a syde of lambe left at the accomptantes howse on Ester evyn, whyche was worthe at that day: xij*d*

---

607 Robert Gardener (d. 1508), three times mayor of Norwich, made many generous bequests for civic improvements: NRO, NCC Reg. Spyltymber, ff. 93^v–4^v; Rawcliffe, *Urban Bodies*, pp. 358–9. For Awelton, a tailor, see NCC Reg. Hyll, ff. 240–1.

608 NCR, 18A/6, f. 172–2^v, incorporates this section under 'fforen receptes' with no sub-heading.

609 See NCR, 16A/5, pp. 256, 290. He was exempted on 21 August 1545: NCR, 16D/2, f. 211^v.

610 He was exempted on 17 July 1545: NCR, 16D/2, f. 211.

611 He was exempted on 21 August 1545: NCR, 16D/2, f. 211^v.

612 See above, pp. 25, 37, 49.

613 NCR, 18A/6, f. 172–2^v, incorporates this section under 'fforen receptes' with no sub-heading.

614 Reed was appointed on 13 August 1544 under sureties that he would repair these fences, and rendered an account on 11 February following: NCR, 16A/4, ff. 44^v, 49; 16A/5, pp. 237, 274.

Item of John Gybbys for a popyll that grewe on the comon grownde in Butter Hylles, which he fellyd whan he made his dyke & caryed awaye with out the knowlege of the accomptant: viijd

/Thynges sold/ Item receyuyd of John Thyrkyll, shomaker, for vij old ffourmes that stode in Seynt Marys churche: vijs

Item of Thomas Farrowur for the font that stode in the same curche, with a lytyll marbyll ston that laye ther bye: vjs viijd

Item of Master Felyx Puttocke, alderman, for j C thacke tyle of the comon store: viijd

Item of the churche wardeyns of Sent George at Tomlond for the roodloft and the deskes of the qwere in Seynt Maryes churche: xxxs[615]

Item of Thomas Barchom for the alter and an old tabernacle in the same churche: iijs iiijd

Item of Mastres Trase for j C di' of brycke of the comon store at the comon halle: xijd

Summa iij li xs iiijd

/Soldyers/[616] Item receyuyd of the kynges gyft for the condyte money of fourty soldyers to Ypswiche [Ipswich]: ls

[f. 152] Item receyuyd more at Ypswiche of the kynges gyft for vj days wages of the sayd fourty soldyers: that ys to saye for euery man iijs: vj li

Item receyuyd of a sesment layd and gatherd within the cite for the dyscharge and settyng forthe of the forsayd fourty soldyers: lli vs xd[617]

Summa lviij li xvs xd

/Offrynges & certens of guyldes/[618] In primis receyuyd of the offryng of the paryshe clarkes: iiijs

Item of the mesers offryng: ixs viijd; and of them for a certeyn: vs – xiiijs viijd

Item of the taylours offryng: iijs ixd; and of them for a certeyn: iiijs iiijd – viijs jd

Item of the shomakers offryng: iiijs iiijd; and of them for a certeyn: iiijs iiijd – viijs viijd

Item of the masons & smythis offryng: iijs iijd; and for a certeyn: iiijs iiijd – vijs vijd

Item of the bedweuers offryng: xxd; and of them for a certeyn: iiijs iiijd – vjs

---

615 In accordance with the terms of a parliamentary statute of 1545, authorising the union of churches worth £6 a year or less with adjacent wealthier ones, St Mary the Less was merged with St George Tombland: Luders and others, eds, *Statutes of the Realm*, iii, 37 Henry VIII, c. 21 (pp. 1013–14).

616 NCR, 18A/6, f. 172ᵛ, incorporates this section under 'fforen receptes' with no sub-heading.

617 On 21 August 1545 the assembly agreed to levy a rate of either a half or an eighth of the customary tax on moveables, at the discretion of the mayor and aldermen, to pay for the soldiers, 'the poremen in eny wyse nat to be charged to the same': NCR, 16D/2, f. 211ᵛ.

618 NCR, 18A/6, ff. 172ᵛ–3, incorporates this section under 'fforen receptes' with no sub-heading.

Item of the wullen weuers, shermen and ffullers offryng: iijs iiijd; and of them for a certeyn: iiijs iiijd – vijs viijd

Item of the bochers offryng: iijs ijd; and of them for a certeyn: iiijs iiijd – vijs vjd

Item of the claymen & reders offryng: xxd; and of them for a certeyn: iiijs iiijd – vjs

[f. 152ᵛ] **Item** of the prestes offryng oonly: vs xjd

/Certens only/ **Item** of the goldsmythis, sadlers, dyers and calendrers for a certeyn: iiijs iiijd

Item of the ffyshmongers for a certeyn: iiijs iiijd

Item of the carpenters for a certeyn: iiijs iiijd

Item of the worsted weuers for a certeyn: vs

Item of the tanners for a certeyn: iiijs

Item of the inkepers & typlers for a certeyn: vs

Item of the bakers, brewers & cowpers: vjs viijd

Item of the hatmakers for a certen: vs

Item of the barbowurs for a certeyn: iijs iiijd

Item of the grocers for a certeyn: xs

Summa vj *li* viijs jd

/Benevolens/[619] **Item** receyuyd within the tyme of thys accompt of certen aldermen, comyners and forens inhabytantes within the cite of ther benevolens toward the purchase of the comon halle, the payment of the lede and other buyldynges in the same place, these sums of money here after folowyng:[620]

In primis receyuyd of the gyft of Master Awsten Steward & Master Doctour Codman, executours of the last wyll and testament of Master Roger Cullam, gentylman: iiij *li*[621]

Item of Master Peter Reed, executor of the testament & last wylle of Master Edward Reed, late alderman of this cite: xls[622]

---

619 NCR, 18A/6, ff. 173–4ᵛ, incorporates this section under 'fforen receptes', with a sub-heading 'benevolence'. The payments made by specific individuals are there recorded between the lines over their names, but no reference is made to their crafts or trades; and no total is provided.

620 On 21 August 1545 the assembly authorised the mayor to require citizens who had hitherto refused to contribute toward 'the gret costes & charges' of acquiring Blackfrairs to do so: NCR, 16D/2, f. 211ᵛ. It is unclear if this list includes such people, or was compiled previously, although the appearance of the fishmonger, Jerome Quashe, suggests a degree of coercion. He had been imprisoned in December 1542 for refusing to contribute towards the cost of the Scottish campaign and behaving 'obstynatly & presumptuously in the open court'. In view of his continuing defiance, he was pronounced 'a quareller & disturber of the pease and of moche yll behauiour', but he remained unrepentant: NCR, 16A/5, pp. 127–8.

621 Roger Colham died in 1530, having left money for his burial, the erection of a tomb and the support of a chantry for the next seven years in the Dominican friary, Norwich: NRO, DCN 69/2, ff. 72–3ᵛ.

622 Edward Reed died in 1544: TNA, PROB 11/30/434; *HoP, 1509–1558*, iii, pp. 184–6.

[*f. 153*] /*Benevolens*/ Master Henry Fuller, alderman: xx*s*

Rychard Catlyng, alderman: x*s*
John Homerston, alderman: xx*s*
Felyx Puttocke, alderman: xx*s*
Thomas Cocke, alderman: xx*s*
Henry Crooke, alderman: xiij*s* iiij*d*
Rychard Davy, alderman: xx*s*
Master Nycholas Sywhat, alderman: xx*s*
Master Thomas Bawbyr, alderman: iij*s* iiij*d*
Hamond Lynsted, alderman: vj*s* viij*d*
Thomas Grenewood, alderman: x*s*
Mastres Trase, wydowe: xv*s*
Mastres Marsham, wydowe: v*s*
Edmond Warden: x*s*

Master Henry Warde, town clarke: xiij*s* iiij*d*
John Cutler, tanner: vj*s* viij*d*
Thomas Grey, mercer: vj*s* viij*d*
Wylliam Hede, capper: vj*s* viij*d*
Robert Brown of Seynt Stephyns: vj*s* viij*d*
Rychard Cocke, worsted weuer: vj*s* viij*d*
Rychard Flecher, sadler: iij*s* iiij*d*
John Bengemyn, draper: v*s*
Robert Garrade, worsted weuer: v*s*
Leonard Yonges, mercer: iij*s* iiij*d*
Rychard <Flecher> Bray, sadler: iij*s* iiij*d*
John Blome, draper: xx*d*

[*f. 153ᵛ*] /*Benevolens*/ John Pype, baker: xx*d*

John Davy, calenderer: iij*s* iiij*d*
Rychard Rudde, mercer: iij*s* iiij*d*
Henry Bacon, grocer: x*s*
Peter Webster, brewer: iij*s* iiij*d*
John Carre, baker: iij*s* iiij*d*
Andrewe Qwashe, grocer: iij*s* iiij*d*
Robert Norman, fyshemonger: x*s*
John Bungay, worsted weuer: viij*s*
George Walden, grocer: ij*s*
Wylliam Waller, mercer: v*s*
John Erne, mason: v*s*
Thomas Johnson, rapheman: iij*s* iiij*d*
Edmond Senyors, worsted weuer: iij*s* iiij*d*

Robert Floode, scryvener: iij*s* iiij*d*
Robert Mychelles, scryvener: iij*s* iiij*d*
Alexander Mather: vj*s* viij*d*
John Aleyn, tanner: xx*d*
Symon Crabbe, worsted weuer: xx*d*
Thomas Hogeons, sadler: iij*s* iiij*d*
Andrewe Deye, bocher: iij*s* iiij*d*
Edward Robynson, taylour: iij*s* iiij*d*
Thomas Swanton, shomaker: iij*s* iiij*d*
John Cubyte, worsted weuer: iij*s* iiij*d*
Robert Palmer, mercer: v*s*
Wylliam Farrowur, draper: v*s*

[*f. 154*] /*Benevolens*/ Thomas Hubbard, bocher: xx*d*

Wylliam Butfeld, bower: xx*d*
Robert Hennoud, joynour: iij*s* iiij*d*
John Walby the elder: ij*s* iiij*d*
Stephyn Johnson, mason: v*s*
Jamys Lynne, worsted weuer: v*s*
Wylliam Lynne, tanner: viij*s*
John Crosse, worsted weuer: ij*s*
Edmond Woode, barbowur: iij*s* iiij*d*
Jeffrey Mychelles, baker: iij*s* iiij*d*
Henry Harpowur, bocher: iij*s* iiij*d*

John Cocke, worsted weuer: v*s*
Thomas Morley, dyer: v*s*
John Atkyns, notary: x*s*
Thomas Moore, draper: viij*s*
Robert Homphrey, sherman: ij*s*
Thomas Norgate, worsted weuer: iij*s* iiij*d*
John Barker, worsted weuer: iij*s* iiij*d*
John Swayne, baker: iij*s* iiij*d*
Thomas Thetford, draper: v*s*
John Knyght, brewer: v*s*

Master John Spencer, gent': xs
John Sadler, grocer: iiijs
Henry Vmphrey, draper: ijs viijd

Syr Wylliam Sallet, parson of Seynt
John of Madermarket: iijs iiijd
John Manne: vs

[f. 154ᵛ] /Benevolens/ John Quashe, ffyshmonger: vs

Mastres Grene, widowe: viijs
John Bakyr, gent': ijs
Syr Wylliam Tompson, prest: iijs iiijd
Syr Robert Cokson, parson of Seynt
Clementes in Fybryge: vjs viijd
Mastres Jannys, wydowe: vs
John Bronde, lyme brenner: vs
Thomas Kynge, grocer: iijs iiijd
John Danyell, worsted weuer: iijs iiijd
Henry Atmere, lernyd man: iijs iiijd
Robert Bettes, dyer: vs
Thomas Ylward, fremason, and
Wydowe Mase toguether: vs

John Mase, brewer: ijs
Barnard Vtber, brewer: xs
Mastres Cecyly Suffeld: xijd
Syr Henry Fayer, prest: ijs
Thomas Wolman, grocer: vs
Edmond Dowsyng, ffysherman: xs
Master Codde, master of the hospytall:
xs
Thomas Blocke, worsted weuer: iijs iiijd
Robert Abell, worsted weuer: iijs iiijd
Thomas Wade, husbondman: ijs viijd
John Derne, vyntner: ijs viijd
Raphe Marsham, grocer: iiijs

[f. 155] /Benevolens/ Thomas Asketyll, gent': xijd

Thomas Barchom, joynour: xijd
John Bedes, smythe: ijs
John Walpoole, mason: iijs iiijd
Rychard Sucklyng, bakyr: vjs viijd
John Baker, grocer: vs
Thomas Lynne, tanner: vs
Rychard Bulward, smythe: iijs iiijd
John Wryght, carpenter: iijs iiijd
Roger Leeke, worsted weuer: iijs iiijd
Thomas Pyktowe, mason: xxd
Robert Goye, fyshmonger: xxd
John Crykmay, baker: iijs iiijd
Wylliam Hylle, calendrer: iijs iiijd
Nycholas Aleyn, tanner: xijd

Wylliam Mabbys, worsted weuer: xijd
George Harryson, cowper: xijd
Robert Mallard, mercer: ijs
Robert Watson, scryvener: iijs iiijd
Wylliam Spratte, vyntner: xxd
Thomas Wygge, worsted weuer: vs
John Crowe, ffyshmonger: iijs iiijd
Thomas Lawrens, mercer: iijs iiijd
Wylliam Guylbert, grocer: iijs iiijd
Nycholas Grene, fyshmonger: vs
Henry Colffer, brewer: vs
Robert Lyng, parchement maker: vjs
viijd
Thomas Palmer, inkeper: vjs viijd

[f. 155ᵛ] /Benevolens/ John Pettys, taylour: vjs viijd

John Thyrkyll, worsted weuer: ijs
Thomas Beere, goldsmythe: viijs
John Sutton, mercer: iijs iiijd
Thomas Querles, grocer: iijs iiijd
Thomas Sutterton, grocer: iijs iiijd
Wylliam Lyon, hosyer: ijs
George Wasse, taylour: ijs
Wylliam Stede, inkeper: ijs
John Reede, mercer: ijs

Robert Barnard, inkeper: ijs
John Raye, tanner: iijs iiijd
Wylliam Laryson, draper: iijs iiijd
Wylliam Wylkyns, worsted weuer: iijs
iiijd
Crystouer Some, bed weuer: xijd
Rychard Olyff, grocer: xijd
Thomas Goche, grocer: viijd
Robert Welles, fflecher: ijs viijd

Vyncent Tesmond, glovyr: xvj*d*
Robert Kynges, tanner: iij*s* iiij*d*
Robert Foxe, shomaker: xx*d*
Thomas Bevys, worsted weuer: xx*d*
John Howse, bocher: iij*s* iiij*d*

Robert Ysode, tanner: xx*d*
Thomas Culley, grocer: xx*d*
Rychard Bate, grocer: iij*s* iiij*d*
Jerome Quashe, ffyshmonger: xx*d*

[*f. 156*] /*Benevolens*/ Robert Martens, taylour: xx*d*

Thomas Parker, haberdasher: iij*s* iiij*d*
Wylliam Chant, worsted weuer: xx*d*
Thomas Larewood, worsted weuer: xx*d*
Thomas Grene, bocher: iij*s* iiij*d*
Nycholas Manne, taylour: xx*d*
Thomas Crane, pynner: xx*d*
Robert Mayhewe, shomaker: iij*s* iiij*d*
John Lynne, tanner: xx*d*
Robert Wagster, worsted weuer: xx*d*
John Pye, shomaker: iij*s* iiij*d*
John Revell the yonger: xx*d*
Master Currant, notary: xx*d*
Wylliam Lytylwood, pynner: iij*s* iiij*d*
Wylliam Sandryngham, pewterer: xx*d*
Thomas Barne, mercer: xx*d*

John Barker, brewer: iij*s* iiij*d*
Thomas Brygges, wolman: vj*s* viij*d*
Thomas Whalley, grocer: xij*d*
Crystouer Grape, weuer: xij*d*
John Thurston, shomaker: xij*d*
Robert Hendry, mercer: ij*s*
Henry Shypdam, coryer: v*s*
Wylliam Kylham, shomaker: xvj*d*
John Porter, barbowur: xvj*d*
John Browderer, brewer: xvj*d*
Wylliam Morley, dyer: v*s*
Henry Grenewood, taylour: xij*d*
Robert Hynderson, taylour: ij*s*
George Drury, capper: ij*s*

[*f. 156ᵛ*] /*Benevolens*/ Cornelys Peterson, haberdasher: xij*d*

Henry Sparke, caryar: ij*s*
Wylliam Swere, shomaker: xij*d*
Thomas Wattes, carpenter: xij*d*
John Goold, carpenter: xij*d*
Robert Saburn, wevyr: xij*d*
Wylliam Deynes, worsted weuer: ij*s*
Syr Henry Cawse, prest: ij*s*
Henry Albon, barbowur: xij*d*
Mastres Morront, wydowe: iiij*s*
John Hudson, worsted weuer: xij*d*
George Wylson, taylour: xij*d*
Jeffrey Reed, bocher: v*s*
Master Bryan Taylour: viij*s*
John Paterson, dyer: ij*s*

Wylliam Belle, mason: xvj*d*
Wylliam Emondes, worsted weuer: viij*d*
Robert Stalworthy, whelewright: ij*s*
Wylliam Myles, cowper: xij*d*
John Morley, dyer: xij*d*
John Ducker, sadler: ij*s*
Thomas Welles: xx*d*
Thomas Goodlam, taylour: xx*d*
Symon Newton, goldfyner: xx*d*
Mathewe Watson, taylour: xx*d*
John Potter, mason: xx*d*
Rychard Snytall, smythe: xx*d*
John Almond, armerer: xij*d*

[*f. 157*] /*Benevolens*/ Wylliam Cowper, cowper: xij*d*

John Rycheman, taylour: xij*d*
Thomas Nycolles, haberdasher: ij*s*
Frances Wolmer, grocer: ij*s*
Edmond Wolsey, mercer: xx*d*

Thomas Barker, worsted weuer: xvj*d*
John Pykovyr, worsted weuer: iij*s* iiij*d*
Robart Raynbald, grocer: iij*s*

Summa l *li* xv*s* iiij*d*

/Brasse and latten/[623] **Item** receyuyd of John and Robert Owyn of London, gonners,[624] for ix C j *libr'* of course metall, whyche was the rest of xviij C xiiij *libr'* of metall delyuerd to them to make gonnys for the cite at xvs C: vj *li* xvs vj*d ob'*

Summa vj *li* xvs vj*d ob'*

Summa totallis omnium receptorum CCCC lxvij *li* xijs iij*d*[625]

Wherof payd by the sayd accomptant within the tyme of thys accompt for and in dyscharge of the forsayd receptes as here after folowithe:

*/Rent resolute/ **In primis** payd in rent resolute as yerely it appere in other accomptes: that is to say to Syr Wylliam Coppyng, chantry prest of John Cosyn, for ferme and rent of dyuers thynges, as yt appere in other accomptes: iiij *li*

[*f. 157ᵛ*] **Item** to the heyer of Applyardes londes: xs

Item to the cathedrall churche of the Holy Trynyte in Norwiche for dyuers rentes: xxjs viijd

Item to the late pryory of Carrowe: xvjs viijd

Item to the sayd place iiij bushelles whete that cost in the market: vjs iiijd

Item to the hospytall of [*St*] Mary Magdalen [*Sprowston*]: xijd

Item to the hospytall of Seynt Gyle: xiijs iiijd

Item to the late pryory of Horsham Sent Faythe: xs iiijd

Item to *the* chappell of the Becke [*Beck, Billingford*]: iiijs

Item to the late abbey of Sypton [*Sibton*]: ijs

Item to the late abbey of Langley: ijs

Item to the manour of Heyham [*Heigham*] next Norwiche: iiijd

Item to the same manour for the mylles ther: lxvjs viijd

Item to the chantry of Lettyce Payne: vjs viijd

Item at the kynges awdyte for the xᵗᵉ of the comon halle: ixs

Summa xij *li* xs

/Fees and wagis/ **Item** payd to Master Henry Fuller, alderman, beryng the offyce of mayer iij quarteres of a yere; and to Master Robert Rug, alderman, beryng the sayd offyce oon quarter within the tyme of this accompt: xx *li*

---

623 NCR, 18A/6, f. 174ᵛ, has the heading 'gonnes'.

624 The mayor and aldermen clearly intended to purchase the best ordnance available or were perhaps ordered to employ the services of the Owen brothers, who made guns for the king. Some of their work still survives, including three guns salvaged from the wreck of Henry VIII's great warship *The Mary Rose*, one bearing an inscription which proclaims their English birth: A. Hildred, '"Brass" Guns', in *eadem*, ed., *Weapons of Warre: The Armaments of The Mary Rose* (The Archaeology of the Mary Rose, 3, Portsmouth, 2011), pp. 22, 29, 47–9, 59–63, 92–3. C. Ffoulkes, *The Gun-Founders of England* (Cambridge, 1937), p. 49, mistakenly assumes that Robert was dead by 1540.

625 NCR, 18A/6, f. 195, records total receipts of £467 14s 7¼d.

Item to Edmond Wardeyn & Robert Merlyn, shreves, <shreves> of the cite for ther ffee: xxx *li*

Item to Master Grey, recorder, for hys ffee: v *li*

Item to Master Corbet, steward, for hys ffee: xxvj*s* viij*d*

[*f. 158*] Item to Master Gawdy, reteynyd a cownsell: xxxiij*s* iiij*d*

Item to Master Catlyng, reteynyd a cownsell: xxvj*s* viij*d*

Item to Master Warde, townclarke, for hys ffee: iiij *li* vj*s* viij*d*

Item payd in the kynges eschekyr for the proffers of Estern and Myhelmes termes: xx*s*

Item to Anthony Pygot, sword berer, for his wages: lxvj*s* viij*d*

Item to John Rede and Thomas Molle, sergeantes at the mace of master mayer, and to Robert Collard, sergeant of the market, for ther wages: iiij *li*

Item to the forsayd Collard for a lyuery: xvj*s*

Item to <the> Rychard Framyngham for a lyuery: xvj*s*

Item to Robert Raynbald, <f> the accomptant, for his hole yere wages and lyuery: vj *li*

Item to the iiij*or* wayghtes for ther wages, euery of them xxvj*s* viij*d*; and to them, euery of them, xx*s* for ther lyuerys: ix *li* vj*s* viij*d*

Item to the bellman for hys wagys: vj*s* viij*d*

Item to the water baly for hys wages: xx*s*

/*Annuytees*/ Item to Syr John Kempe, prest of the comon halle, for hys annuyte: vj *li* xiij*s* iiij*d*

Item to Clement, clarke ther, for his wages: iiij*s*

Item to Mastres Alyce Scolehowse, wydowe, for hyr annuyte out of a tenement in Seynt Mychaelles of Coslany, late Master Percys: xiij*s* iiij*d*[626]

Item to Robert Damme for gatheryng of the bakers grynt newe grauntyd: x*s*

Item to Master Henry Fuller, late mayer, for his annuyte grantyd to euery mayer: xl*s*

[*f. 158^v*]   **Summa C *li* vj*s***

Costes and charges done within the tyme of thys accompt vpon the bocherys, ffyshstalles, wolshopps, guyldhalle and vpon other tenementes in the paryshe of Seynt Peter of Mancroft *& cetera*:

/*The iij^{de} weke after Myhelmes*/ **In primis** payd to John Fulkes, tyler, newe poyntyng all the Long Rowe of the contry bochery, v days, at <ij*s*> vj*d ob'* the day; & to John Elles, laborer, v days, at iiij*d ob'* a day: iiij*s* vij*d*

/*The iiij^{te} weke after Myhelmes*/ Item to the sayd Fulkes newe poyntyng the Ropery & the cyte bochery adioynyng to them, iiij days of hym & his sayd man: iij*s* viij*d*

Item to Robert Osborn for thacke tyle j m^l: vj*s*

Item for lathe j C: vj*d*; lathe nayle to Mastres Morront *di'* m^l: v*d* – xj*d*

/*The v^{te} weke after Myhelmes*/ Item to Henry Sparke for sonde a lode: v*d*

---

626 NCR, 18A/6, f. 195^v, this entry appears under 'mynute expences'.

Item to Henry*son* for lyme vj comb': ij*s*

Item payd to the sweper of the market makyng clene the market after the tylers oon day: iiij*d* ob'

Item to Sparke caryeng away colder v lodes: x*d*

/*The fyrst weke after Crystmes*/ Item to Wylliam Pede for a newe gret stock locke platyd ouer with plate for burnyng, with a newe key for the womans prison dore, with certen forlockes, a plate for the locke hole and settyng on of the same: v*s* viij*d*

Item for newe stelyng of the ponche for the jaylour to stryke of yrons withe: ij*d*

[*f. 159*] /*The iiij*ie* weke after Crystmes*/ Item payd to Nycholas Tuttell, carpenter, mendyng the planchers & a bay windowe at a tenement in Coblerrowe wher Mark Heynis dwell, oon day: vj*d* ob'

/*The vj*ie* weke after Crystmes*/ Item to the forsayd Pede for mendyng ij lockes in the fyshmarket & other ij at the scryptoryes on the southe syde of the guyldhalle: ix*d*

/*The xij*ie* weke weke* [*sic*] *after Crystmes*/ Item payd to Nycholas Tuttell & John Byrche the yonger, carpenters, mendyng & reparyng dyuers of the ffyshmongers shopps that war spoyled with thevys in Lent, yche of them iiij days: iiij*s* iiij*d*

Item to the forsayd Pede for hookes, hengylles, barrys, cappys & mendyng dyuers lockes: xxij*d*

Item payd to Styngate for j C popyll bourde to make plancheryng ouer the sayd shoppys: ij*s* viij*d*

Item all other bourde was of comon store, but payd to Mastres Morront [*for*] iij*d* nayle *di'* m^l: x*d*

Item iiij*d* nayle *di'* m^l: xv*d*; vj*d* nayle ij C: x*d*; viij*d* nayle j C: vj*d* – ij*s* vij*d*

Item for Inglyshe nayles: j*d*

/*Cyte bochery*/ Item that same weke to Wylliam Grove, carpenter, brekyng vp Thomas Grenys shoppe & reysyng the same hyer, transposyng all the wyndows, dores & other thynges in the same howse, vj days this weke: ij*s* iij*d*

Item to Henry Wodrof, laborer, helpyng hym ther, iiij days this weke: xviij*d*

Item all bourde & tymbyr war of comon store, savyng payd to the sayd Grove for ij newe plankes occupyed ther: vj*d*

[*f. 159*^v] Item payd to Pede for certen newe yron worke, with mendyng part of the old: vij*d*

/*The weke in which Owur Lady fell in*/ Item to the forsayd Tutell & Byrche fynyshyn vp the fyshmongers shopps, transposyng Reedes shoppe & Thomas Tolys in the cite bochery, v days: v*s* v*d*

Item to Goose for ij C popyll bourde spent ther: iiij*s* viij*d*

Item to the forsayd Grove fynyshyng vp Grenys shoppe, ij days worke: xij*d*

Item to Wylliam Johnson, mason, & his laborer mendyng the walles & pannelles of dyuerse [*sic*] in the forsayd shopps, ij days worke: xxij*d*

Item lyme ij comb' & sonde a lode: xij*d*

Item to Holdyn for brycke j C: viij*d*

Item to Henry Wodroff & John Elmam, laborers, tendyng to the carpenters & caryeng vij or viij lodes of colder in to Grenys shoppe to heyne the florthe & mendyng dyuerse florthis in the cite bochery, eyther of them v days: iij*s* ix*d*

Item to Henry Carter for clay iiij lodes: xx*d*

Item to Pede for certen newe yron worke, mendyng moche old yron worke & lockes: xiiij*d*

Item for a newe locke & key for a wolshoppe in ferme of Stephyn Johnson: vj*d*

/*The fyrst weke after Owur Lady*/ **Item** to the forsayd ij laborers fynyshyng vp the florthis & makyng clene the shopps ageynst Estern, ij days: xviij*d*

Item to Henry Carter for ij lode clay more: x*d*

Item to Thomas Grene for nayles bought by hym for Grove the carpenter: ix*d*

[*f. 160*] /*The second weke after Mydsomer*/ **Item** payd for oon newe hengyll for a wyndowe in the cite bochery in ferme of Roger Baldry: iij*d*

Item to Henry Wodrof, laborer, makyng newe florthis in all the Ropery shoppis & mendyng dyuerse fawtes in the Murage Loft, vj days: ij*s* iij*d*

Item to Henry Carter for ij lode claye: x*d*

Summa iiij *li* xij*s* iiij*d*

/*Comon inne*/ **Item** payd in the tyme of thys accompt for makyng of a newe stabyll in the est ende of the crosse howse at the comon inne:

/*The fyrst weke after Owur Lady*/ **And fyrst** payd to Nycholas Tuttell & John Byrche, carpenters, makyng mangers & rackes on bothe sydes of the same howse, iiij days: iiij*s* iiij*d*

Item all the postes that war set in the grownde for mangers war old postes lyeng in the guyldhall vowlt some tyme, beyng the postes of the old wrostlyng place at Magdalen, but payd for iiij copyll sparrys for rackes & steyes: ij*s* viij*d*

Item all other tymbyr for the mangers and plankes war of comon store, but payd for iiij^xx byllettes for racke stavys: viij*d*

Item to Mastres Morront for ij C vj*d* nayle: x*d*

Item to Henry Wodrof & John Elmam helpyng the carpenters, fechyng tymbyr & plankes to ther hondes, makyng holis for the postes & moche other worke, ij days of them: xviij*d*

[*f. 160*^*v*] **Item** to Wylliam Johnson, mason, & his laborer oon day pynnyng the mangers & steyes: xj*d*

Item for lyme a comb' to Harryson: iiij*d*

/*The xj^je weke after Owur Lady*/ **Item** payd for plankyng of the same stabyll: & fyrst to Leonard Sutterton for a lode of plankes conteynyng ij C foote & a quarter at iiij*s* viij*d* C: x*s* vj*d*

Item to hym for an other lode conteynyng ij C vij foote: ix*s* vij*d*

Item to hym for ij lode of joystes conteynyng xviij copill: xij*s*

/*The weke in whiche Mydsomer Day fell in*/ **Item** payd to Nycholas Tuttell, carpenter, layeng the sayd joystes & plankes on bothe sydes of the same stabyll, v days worke: ij*s* viij*d* ob'

Item to Henry Wodrof, laborer, helpyng hym the same v days & stoppyng vnder the mangers with claye & to Robert Rogers, laborer, oon day helpyng them: ij*s* iij*d*

Item to Henry Carter for clay a lode: v*d*

Item to Mastres Morront for viij*d* nayle ij C: xij*d*

Summa xlix*s* viij*d* ob'

Costes and chargis don within the tyme of this accompt in kepyng clene the cokeys, systerns, stathis, stretes and market place *& cetera*:

/*Cokeys*/ *In primis* payd to Robert Tooke for his hole yere wages castyng & kepyng clene xvj seuerall cokeys within the cite: xiij*s* iiij*d*

Item to Andrewe Robynson for his hole yere wages kepyng clene all the market place from Seynt Johns Lane to Coblerrowe ende & caryeng away the fylthe of the same: xiij*s* iiij*d*

[*f. 161*] **Item** to Robert Rogers for hys hole yere wages kepyng clene & caryeng awaye the fylthe of ij cokeys in the market above the guyldhalle: ij*s*

Item to Walter Harryes for his hole yere wages kepyng clene & caryeng awaye the fylthe of the cokey in Seynt Symondes: xvj*d*

Item payd to Robert Garrades man for caryeng a waye of xxxij lodes mucke from dyuers cokeys betwyxt Myhelmes & Crystmes within the tyme of thys accompt: v*s* iiij*d*

Item to Ruddes wyf for iiij*or* lodes of mucke that she causyd to be caryed from the cokey ageynst The ij Nonnys in this quarter: viij*d*

Item to Ketryngham for vj lodes this quarter from iij cokeys in Seynt Edmondes & Seynt Martens: xij*d*

/*The iij*de* weke after Crystmes*/ **Item** payd to Barsham, porter of Westwyk gates, for caryeng away a gret qwantyte of dry fylthe that lay vnder the syde walles without the sayd gates that came of makyng clene the way & cokey ther: xij*d*

Item to the sayd Barsham & Water Eryng for makyng clene the <systern> *cokey* ther & caryeng away *a gret mowtayn of* the fylthe of the same, takyn a gret: ij*s* viij*d*

Item to Garrades man for caryeng of xlix lodes of mucke from dyuers cokeys betwyxt Crystmes and Estern: vij*s* ij*d*

Item to Ruddes wyf for iiij*or* lodes that quarter ffrom the cokey ageynst The ij Nonnys: viij*d*

[*f. 161ᵛ*] **Item** to Robert Rogers for makyng clene the cyte bochery and Ropery, whyche war sore noyed with fylthe in the tyme of Lent: iiij*d*

/*Mydsomer*/ **Item** payd to Garrades man for caryeng of liij lodes of mucke from all the cokeys syns Estern: vij*s* x*d*

Item to John Barsham and other ij laborers fyeng the systern withowt Westwyke gates, castyng out above j C lodes of mucke, to ij of them for vij days worke & to the iij^{de} man for iiij days: *summa* xviij days of a man, at v*d* the day: vij*s* vj*d*

Item to John Styngate, fermer of the comon stathe, toward the makyng clene of the comon stathe yarde, whyche was very noyffull: xij*d*

Item payd for a newe barrowe delyueryd to John Barsham, porter of Westwyke gates, to kepe clene the sayd gates and cokey ther: xij*d*

/Myhelmes/ **Item** to Garrades man for caryeng of xliiij^{ti} lodes mucke from dyuerse cokeys syns Mydsomer: vij*s* iiij*d*

Item to Ruddes wyf for viij lodes that she causyd to be caryed syns Ester from the cokey ageynst The ij Nonnys: xvj*d*

Item to Ketryngham for xiij lodes from the iij cokeys in Seynt Martens at Pales Gate and Seynt Edmondes syns Crystmes: ij*s* ij*d*

Item to Roger Lawes for caryeng of xiiij lodes mucke from the cokey in Conysford in the all the [*sic*] tyme of thys accompt: ij*s* iiij*d*

Item to Andrewe Robynson for wedyng of */nullus/* [*f. 162*] the market place in dyuers places, whyche was growen grene dyuers tymes with grasse: viij*d*

Summa iiij *li* ij*s*

Costes and charges done within the tyme of thys accompt by the commandement of the hole cownsell of the cite vpon pathyng of ij stretes vnder the west & southe sydes of the gret gardeyn of the comialte, parcell of the comon halle *& cetera*:

/The iij^{de} weke after Crystmes/ **In primis** payd to Henry Wodrof and John Elmam, laborers, coldryng out of pathyn ston at the comon halle to be spent at the forsayd worke, vj days: iiij*s* vj*d*

/The iiij^{te} weke after Crystmes/ **Item** to the sayd ij laborers brekyng down old walles at the comon halle & coldryng of pathyn ston, eyther of them vj days: <v> iiij*s* vj*d*

Item to John Erne for xij lode of sonde spent at the forsayd worke these ij wekes: iiij*s*

Item to hym for caryeng of xxiiij lodes of ston from the comon halle at iij*d* a lode: vj*s*

/The v^{te} weke after Crystmes/ **Item** to the forsayd ij laborers coldryng ston at the comon halle, vj days: iiij*s* vj*d*

/The vj^{te} weke after Crystmes/ **Item** to them also thys weke coldryng ston ther, eyther of them v days: iij*s* ix*d*

Item to John Erne for xij lode of sonde spent ther these ij wekes past: iiij*s* iiij*d*

Item to hym for caryeng of xix lodes ston these ij wekes from the comon halle: iiij*s* ix*d*

/The vij^{te} weke after Crystmes/ **Item** to the forsayd ij laborers coldryng ston at the comon inne, comon halle and */nullus/* [*f. 162^v*] in Seynt Marye churche yarde, vj days: iiij*s* vj*d*

Item to John Erne for caryeng of ix lodes ston from the comon halle, iiij lodes from the comon inne & ij lodes from Seynt Marys churche: iij*s* ix*d*

/*The viij^te weke after Crystmes*/ **Item** to the forsayd ij laborers coldryng ston styll at the forsayd places, v days: iij*s* ix*d*
Item to John Erne for caryeng of xx lodes of pathyn ston thys weke: v*s*
Item to hym for sonde spent ther these ij wekes past ix lode: iij*s*
Item to Mastres Bakon for a remnant of ston that beleft the pathyng on hyr husbondes syde: iiij*d*

/*The ix^te weke after Crystmes*/ **Item** payd to Henry Wodroff coldryng of ston at the comon halle, iiij days thys weke: xviiij*d*
Item to John Erne for pathyng of all the west syde & levellyng the grownde & fyndyng all maner of workmanshyppe, and the accomptant layeng all maner of stuff by hym, at j*d* euery yarde, on whyche syde was xxiiij^xx yardes just: *summa* xl*s*

/*The x^e weke after Crystmes*/ **Item** to the sayd Erne for sonde spent ther these ij wekes past xj lode: iij*s* viij*d*
Item to hym for caryeng of vj lodes of gret ston ffrom the comon halle for the chanell on the southe syde of the sayd gret gardeyn: xviij*d*

/*The xj^te weke after Crystmes*/ **Item** to John Basyngham for xx^ti lodes of gret pathyn ston bought of hym at the Graye Fryers at vj*d* euery lode: x*s*

[*f. 163*] /*The xij^te weke after Crystmes*/ **Item** to John Elmam, laborer, coldryng of ston at the comon halle, vj days: ij*s* iij*d*
Item to John Erne for caryeng of xx^ti lode of pathyn ston from the Grey Fryers: v*s*

/*The weke in which Owur Lady fell in*/ **Item** to hym for caryeng of viij lodes of ston ffrom the comon halle these ij wekes past: ij*s*
Item to hym for sonde spent ther these iij wekes past xvj lodes: v*s* iiij*d*

/*The fyrst weke after Owur Lady*/ **Item** payd to hym for takyng vp of all the old pathyng on the southe syde of the sayd grete gardeyn, levellyng the grownde & newe settyng the same ageyn, iiij C iiij^xx yardes, at j*d* euery yarde, he fyndyng all workmanshyppe: xlvj*s* viij*d*
Item to hym for sonde this weke iij lodes: xij*d*
Item gaf in reward amonges the poore laborers: vj*d*

/*The x^e weke after Owur Lady*/ **Item** payd to the forsayd John Erne for caryeng awaye of lvj lodes of menur that beleft on the west syde of the sayd gret gardeyn whan yt was pathyd, at j*d ob'* euery lode: vij*s*
Item to a laborer for oon day worke whan he hade don to pare vp all the menur clene and to swepe & make clene all the sayd lane: iiij*d*
Item to Garrades man for caryeng a way oon lode mucke after all was made clene: ij*d*

Summa ix *li* iij*s* vij*d*

/*Ryver cuttyng*/ **Item** payd for cuttyng of the ryver within the tyme of thys accompt: and fyrst for gryndyn of the sheres and for certen forlockes: xiij*d*

[*f. 163ᵛ*] /*Wytsontyde*/ **Item** for vj fadam of newe bast, with a newe rubbe and a whetston: viij*d*

Item for mendyng of oon of the comon oores: ij*d*

Item to Robert Teyton, cutter, for xxj days worke, at vj*d* the day, cuttyng the ryver: x*s* vj*d*

Item to Wylliam Guylbert & Bartylmewe Wymonde, rowers, for the same xxj days, at x*d*: xvij*s* vj*d*

Item for vj fadam of bast more to Master Cocke abought the mydworke: vj*d*

Item to Wylliam Vynt for hys bote hyer the same xxj days: ij*s* iiij*d*

Item payd for a bote hyer & iij men rowyng Master Lee and Master Davy and others[627] by the appoyntment of master mayer to vewe the ryver: xiiij*d*

Item to Edmond Yong and John Grace for ther paynes & bote hyer rowyng Master Rugge, mayer, Master Steward, Master Fuller, Master Wood and others vpon the ryver within the cite to vewe the fawtes therof & from thense to Newton: xvj*d*

/*The second cuttyng*/ **Item** payd in the weke after Lammes to the forsayd iij men for newe cuttyng & ransakyng at Wyklyngham [*Wicklingham*] flattes & other sholdes wher the wrecke was growen vp ageyn, vj days: viij*s*

Item for newe gryndyng of the sheres: viij*d*

Item to <to> Wylliam Vynt for hys bote hyer the same vj days: vj*d*

Summa xliiij*s* v*d*

[*f. 164*] /*Comon stathes*/ **Item** payd within the tyme of thys accompt for certen reparacions don at the old and newe comon stathes: and fyrst to Wylliam Pede for an hespe of yron for the myddyll tre of the carte gate of the old comon stathe & ij stapylles: vj*d*

Item for settyng on of the same yron worke and for mendyng the locke of the halle dore at the stathe & a newe key for the same dore: viij*d*

/*The iiijᵗᵉ weke after Crystmes*/ **Item** to Nycholas Tuttell, carpenter, for oon day worke mendyng the fframe that drawe vp the cheane tyll a newe may be made, whyche sodenly dekayd: vj*d* ob'

/*The xijᵗᵉ weke after Crystmes*/ **Item** to the forsayd Nycholas and to John Byrche the yonger makyng a newe fframe or capstayn to wynde vp the cheane, ij days worke: ij*s* ij*d*

Item to Wylliam Grove for a gret ende of tymbyr for the capsteyn & an other pece layd in the grounde wherin the capsteyn ys fframyd: xvj*d*

Item to Wylliam Johnson, mason, & his laborer for oon day makyng the pavement ageyn abought the sayd capsteyn & mendyng the pavement in dyuers places of the same howse: xj*d*

---

627 NCR, 18A/6, f. 181, reports that the party incuded the chamberlain and that it travelled as far as Surlingham.

Item for lyme a comb' to Marsham: iiij*d*

Item to Henry Holden for ij C brycke: xx*d*

Item to Henry Wodroff, laborer, fechyng of tymbyr from Grovys & from the comon halle & brycke out of the market, and dyggyng sonde in the kylyarde & brekyng the grownde wher ther capstayn stonde, ij days worke: ix*d*

/Tenementes agenst the comon stathe/ **Item** payd for a newe locke & keye for the v^te tenement */nullus/* [*f. 164^v*] next the kylyard, with certen sneckes, lachis and cromys for ij dores ther & vsettyng on: viij*d*

Summa ixs vjd ob'

/Newe mylles/ **Item** payd in the tyme of thys accompt to Nycholas Tuttell, carpenter, layeng of ij newe plankes at the southe brydge of the newe mylles, whyche sodenly dekayed & myschevyd an horse, with stoppyn of certen holys at the other brydge, oon day: vj*d ob'*

Summa vjd ob'

/Gates and towers/ **Item** payd to Wylliam Pede for mendyng the locke on the clycke of Seynt Gyles gates: ij*d*

Item to hym for a newe hespe and a pynne for the locke of Conysford gates: vj*d*

Summa viijd

/Pyllery/ **Item** payd in the tyme of thys accompt to John Byrche the yonger & Nycholas Tuttell, carpenters, mendyng the pyllery, ij days worke: ij*s* ij*d*

Summa ijs ijd

Nota that the tymbyr, plankes, bourde & nayle occupyed at the newe mylles war all of the comon store & leke maner the myddyll tre and all other thynges occupyd at the pyllery; and, thowe yt do not appere outwardly that yt wold take suche tyme for the reparacon therof, yet no dowte yt was bothe paynfull and jepardos to make the same suer, abyll to bere any man *& cetera*.

/Tenementes late lord suffrygantes/ **Item** payd in the tyme of thys accompt for certen reparacions don vpon the tenementes late lord suffrygantes:

In primis payd for a bast rope for the welle of the iiij^te tenement: xvj*d*

[*f. 165*] */The weke in which Myhelmes day ffell in/* **Item** for a newe stoppe: iiij*d*; for mendyng the chenys & naylyng on the hoopys: ij*d*; whiche tenement stode sperde & the sayd well was occupyd by the tylers and workemen ther: vj*d*

Item for lyne for the tylers ledders: ij*d*

Item to Wylliam Smythe, tyler, newe poyntyng all the howses bylongyng to the fyrst tenement next Tomlond & newe removyng a gutter and a shudde on the backsyde & newe lathyng & layeng ageyn the sayd gutter & shudde, v days worke, at viij*d* the day: iij*s* iiij*d*

Item to John Thurston and Thomas Hubbard, his laborers, the same v days, at x*d*: iiij*s* ij*d*

Item to Henry Sparke for sonde layd ther iij lodes: xv*d*

/*The second weke after Myhelmes*/ **Item** to the forsayd tyler removyng the tyle of all the howses of the second & iij^{de} tenementes, newe lathyng & cownter lathyng & layeng the same ageyn, vj days thys weke: iiijs

Item to John Anthony, tyler, his apprentys, for vj days, at vj*d* the day: iijs

Item to the forsayd ij laborers vj days: vs

Item to Wylliam Savery, laborer, ij days: x*d*

Item to John Byrche for xxv^{ti} newe sparrys ffeete at j*d ob'* a pece: iijs j*d ob'*

Item for xxix yardes of evys bourde: ijs v*d*

Item for ij newe sparrys and v small stothis for ffurrynges of sparrys and for wyndbemys ther lackyng: xxiij*d*

[*f. 165^a*] /*The iij^{de} weke after Myhelmes*/ **Item** to the forsayd Wylliam Smythe, tyler, aboute styll the howses of the ij^{de} & iij^{de} tenementes, v days: iijs iiij*d*

Item to John Anthony, his apprentys, v days: ijs vj*d*

Item to the forsayd ij laborers v days: iiijs ij*d*

Item to John Byrche for ij newe sparrys: x*d*

Item to Robert Stephynson toward a newe stoppe for the welle of the fyrst tenement: iiij*d*

/*The iiij^{te} weke after Myhelmes*/ **Item** payd to the forsayd tyler removyng parcell of the gret tenement & hye howse so far as Thomas Mosse chambyrs go, with newe lathyng & layeng the same ageyn & mendyng all the pentyses on the stretes syde from that place to the corner next Tomlond, vj days that weke: iiijs

Item to John Anthony, his apprentyse, vj days: iijs

Item to the forsayd ij laborers vj days: vs

Item to Henry Sparke for sonde a lode: v*d*

Item to Wylliam Johnson, mason, mendyng all the gabylles from the fyrst tenement to the place wher they left worke, iij days of hym & his man: ijs ix*d*

/*The v^{te} weke after Myhelmes*/ **Item** to the forsayd mason & Colles, his laborer, mendyng the pavementes of the kechyns and harthis in the iij fyrst tenementes, iiij days: iijs viij*d*

Item to Robert Osborn of Kyrby [*Bedon*] for vij m^l thacke tyle occupyed ther ouer & above iij m^l layd in ther and accomptyd in the last accompt: xlijs

Item to Robert Seman of Wyndam [*Wymondham*] for a lode of well brent brycke for the gabylles: iijs

Item to Mastres Morront for gret lathe nayle viij m^l at x*d* the m^l: vjs viij*d*

[*f. 166*] **Item** for cownter nayle *di'* m^l: iiij*d ob'*

Item ij*d* nayle for the sappy sparrys iij m^l *di'*: iiijs viij*d*

Item iiij*d* nayle *di'* m^l: xv*d*; and vj*d* nayle j C: v*d*; spent aboute the evys bourde & sparris fete – xx*d*

Item to Robert Kyrby, laborer, makyng clene all the chambyrs so far as the tylers hade wrowght and all the yardes and strete, iiij days worke: xvij*d*

Item to Henry Sparke for caryeng awaye xiiij lodes of colder and mucke: ijs iiij*d*

Item to Edmond Wood, barbowur, for ten m^l tyle pynnys spent in the same worke: ij*s* vj*d*

/*The vj^{te} weke after Myhelmes*/ Item to Henry Wodrof and John Elmam stoppyng all the holys vnder the evys betwyxt the sparres of all the howses that war at this tyme reparid, eyther of them vj days: iiij*s* vj*d*
Item to Henry Carter for clay iiij lode: xx*d*
Item for strawe: ij*d*; byrchyn bromys: j*d* – iij*d*
Item to Leonard Sutterton for a lode of lathe, wherof xxij C was spent ther: xiiij*s*

/*The vij^{te} weke after Owur Lady*/ Item payd to John Erne and Wylliam Johnson, masons, makyng a newe ovyn in the tenement next Tomlond, removyng the wyndowe in the buttry, whiche was made gretter to feche in more lyght, newe castyng all the sayd buttry, stoppyng vp a dore in the vowlte, makyng a newe pavement in the yardes of the fyrst & seconde tenementes to convey the water in to the strete, whiche byfore sanke in to the howses to ther dystruccon, ij days worke of them bothe: ij*s* iij*d*
[*f. 166^v*] Item to the sayd ij masons newe lathyng & castyng dyuerse pannelles in the corner tenement ageynst the Grey Fryers & in the next tenement toward Tomlond, brekyng vp a gutter that lede the water from those ij tenementes, which was stoppd, and made yt ageyn & mendyng the pavementes within those ij tenementes, ij days worke: ij*s* iij*d*
Item to Sander Clarke, Robert Yoxhale, John Elmam and Henry Wodrof, laborers, iiij days: vj*s*
Item to Seman of Wyndam for j lode bryke ffor the ovyn & pavementes: ij*s*
Item to Paschall for an yron for the cove of the ovyn conteynyng v *libr' di'*: viij*d*
Item to hym for a grate of yron for the gutter at Tybnams & for mendyng the locke of the vj^{te} tenement dore: vj*d*
Item to Henry Holden for j C lathe for the pannelles at Tybnams: vj*d*
Item to Herryson for lyme spent ther in all the forsayd workes xxxj comb': x*s* iiij*d*
Item to Henry Sparke for sond for the masons ij lode: x*d*; and for fechyng ij lode of pathyn ston from the comon halle: viij*d* – xviij*d*
Item for caryeng awaye iiij lodes mucke that came of makyng clene the howses: viij*d*
Item to Wodroff & Elmam for oon day more makyng clene the howses & yardes: ix*d*
                    Summa viij *li* xiiij*s* vij*d*

[*f. 167*] Costes and chargis don within the tyme of thys accompt in makyng of newe walles vyrownd Seynt Marys churche & inclosyng the growndes to seuer all tenementes and reparyng the tenement vpon the est corner, lately purchased of Master Arnold of Cromer *& cetera*:

/*The fyrst weke after Myhelmes*/ In primis payd to Thomas Paterson and Wylliam Kyrby, laborers, brekyng down the walles abought the bankes in the churche yarde & caryeng the ston in to the churche to kepe dry ageynst the masons come to worke, v days: ij*s* ix*d*

/*The second weke after Myhelmes*/ **Item** to John Erne and Robert Hollond, masons, makyng a blacke walle from the tenement late purchased of Arnold vnto the churche yarde gate & so returnyd to the churche porche, eyther of them vj days: vjs ixd

Item to Sander Clarke & Robert Yoxhale, ther laborers, the same vj days: iiijs vjd

/*The iij*de *weke after Myhelmes*/ **Item** to the forsayd ij masons styll abought the sayd walles, v days: vs vijd ob'

Item to Robert Yoxhale and Wylliam Kyrby, laborers, the same v days: iiijs ixd

Item to Sander Clarke pynnyng the forsayd blacke walle the same v days: ijs jd

Item to Henry Wodrof and John Elmam, the comon laborers, sometyme helpyng the sayd masons, sometyme the tylers at the suffrigan howsys & sometyme the carpenters at the comon <inne> halle & havyng inne bryke and tyle, yche of them v days: iiijs ixd

[*f. 167*] /*The iiij*te *weke after Myhelmes*/ **Item** to the forsayd ij masons fynyshyng the sayd blacke walle & returnyd walle, coueryng the same with thacke *tyle* and roffys, vj days: vjs ixd

Item to the forsayd ij laborers vj days: iiijs vjd

Item to Sander Clarke pynnyng vj days: ijs vjd

Item to Henry Holden for a newe barrowe to be occupyed ther and in other places: xijd

/*The v*te *weke after Myhelmes*/ **Item** to the forsayd ij masons makyng an other walle at the est ende of the sayd churche, coueryng the same with thacke tyle, iiij days: iiijs vjd

Item to the forsayd ij laborers iiij days: iijs

Item to Sander Clarke pynnyng iiij days: xxd

Item to Henry Sparke for sonde spent ther these iij wekes abought those walles xj lode: iiijs vijd

Item to hym for caryeng of xvj lodes ston from the comon *jake* to the same worke: vs iiijd

Item to John Byrche for a dore stalle with an hanse set in the newe walle at the est ende of the churche yarde: iijs

Item to Seman of Wyndam [*Wymondham*] for brycke a lode for powdryng of the blacke walles and for the tabylles of the same: iijs

Item to Robert Osborn of Kyrby [*Bedon*] for thacke tyle for coueryng of the same walles j mˡ: vjs

Item more to hym for roffe tyles j C: vjs viijd

/*The tenement ther next*/ /*The vj*te *weke after Myhelmes*/ **Item** payd the <same> *sext* weke to Wylliam <Johnson> *Vnderwod*, mason, mendyng the chymneys, harthis and jakes within the tenement at the est /*nullus*/ [*f. 168*] ende, with newe castyng all the walles, with moche reparacon in the same tenement, vj days: iijs iijd

Item to Walter <Colles> *Harryes*, his laborer, vj days: ijs iijd

Item to ij laborers that ffyed the synke & jakes in the vowlte in the nyght tyme & beryed the fylthe of the same in a pytte made on Tomlond: xij*d*[628]

Item for candyll that nyght & that weke ij *libr':* ij*d ob'*

/*The vij^te weke after Myhelmes*/ Item to the forsayd Vnderwood and Harryes ffynyshyng vp the tenement & makyng a partycon walle on the northe syde of the church betwyxt John Dern & that tenement, iiij days: iij*s* viij*d*

Item to Henry Sparke for sonde ij lode: x*d*

Item to Nycholas Tuttell & John Byrche, carpenters, makyng a partycon in the shoppe of the forsayd tenement for a buttry & newe lopis for the strete wyndowe in the parlowur & bourdes for the graven worke in the same wyndowe & for the wyndows in the chambyrs, a loope for the buttry dore, mendyng all the planchers, with moche bochyng in the same tenement, vj days: vj*s* vj*d*

Item to Wylliam Pede for hookes, hengylles, sneckes, cromys, lachis and other yron worke: xxij*d*

Item to Henry Wodrof & John Elmam coueryng the walle on the northe syde, makyng clene the howses & growndes, caryeng home the stagyng tymbyr, hyrdylles and barrelles to the comon halle, ij days: xviij*d*

[*f. 168^v*] Item clay for the walle a lode: v*d*

Item rede and strawe for the same: ij*d*

Item payd to Harryson and Goldyng for lyme spent abought the forsayd walles & tenement viij chalder and vj comb' at ij*s* viij*d*: xxiij*s* iiij*d*

/*The viij^te weke after Myhelmes*/ Item to John Byrche, carpenter, fynyshyng vp all the forsayd besynes within the tenement, makyng a newe pentyse ouer the dore & wyndowe in to the gardeyn and a newe loope for the dore set in the newe walle at the est ende, vj days: ij*s* iiij*d*

Item to Pede for yron worke for that dore: ix*d*

/*The ix^te weke after Myhelmes*/ Item to Stephyn Scryvener takyng down all the glasse in the same tenement, newe scoryng and settyng ageyn the most part in newe lede, with puttyng to moche newe glasse: vj*s* x*d*

Item more to hym for a xj foote of newe glasse set up in iiij corners of ij baye wyndows in the chambyrs and oon gret lyght: iij*s* viij*d*

Item for *di'* m^l small nayle for the same: iiij*d*

Item to Pede for xx barrys of yron for the gret wyndowe in the parlowur: x*d*

/*The iij^de weke after Owur Lady*/ Item payd to Wylliam Waller for a day worke of ij carpenters that he set a worke to take downe the bell frame in the stepyll: xiij*d*

Item for caryage of the same tymber to the comon halle by Laws carte: iiij*d*

/*The iiij^te weke after Owur Lady*/ Item to John Erne and Wylliam Johnson, /*nullus*/ [*f. 169*] masons, begynnyng to make an other blacke walle ffrom the place *<wher>*

---

628 See above, p. 249 note 532, and Fay, *Health and the City*, p. 170.

nowe John Derne to the churche gate, with a returne walle to the churche porche, settyn ij dore stalles in the same walle, iiij days: iiij*s* vj*d*

Item to Robert Yoxhale, John Elmam & Henry Wodroff, laborers, the same iiij days: iiij*s* vj*d*

Item to Sander Clarke pynnyng iiij days: xx*d*

/*The v*ᵗᵉ *weke after Owur Lady*/ **Item** to the forsayd ij masons styll abought the sayd blacke wall & returne walle, v days: v*s* vij*d ob*'

Item to the forsayd iij laborers v days: v*s* vij*d ob*'

Item to Sandyr Clarke pynnyng v days: ij*s* j*d*

/*The vj*ᵗᵉ *weke after Owur Lady*/ **Item** to the forsayd ij masons fynyshyng vp the forsayd blacke walle & returne wall, coueryng them with thacke tyle and roffys, vj days: vj*s* ix*d*

Item to the forsayd iij laborers vj days: vj*s* ix*d*

Item to Sander Clarke pynnyng ij days: x*d*

Item to hym laboryng iiij days: xviij*d*

Item to Master Leche for brycke for powderyng of the walles a lode: iij*s* iiij*d*

Item to Henry Sparke for fechyng of the same: vj*d*

Item to hym for caryeng of v lodes mucke from vnder the walle at the est ende, whiche cam of makyng clene the tenement, strete and growndes at the last reparacon: x*d*

Item to hym for fechyng of v lode of ston from the comon halle in this tyme: xx*d*

Item to hym for fechyng of v lode of blacke hede ston from the Grey Fryers: xx*d*

Item to hym for sonde ix lode: iij*s* ix*d*

[*f. 169*ᵛ] **Item** to John Basyngham for v lode of blacke hede ston at the Grey Fryers: v*s*

Item to Thomas Mosse for an hepe of ston lyeng in hys gardeyn ther at honde: vj*d*

Item to Robert Stephyn for an hepe of ston lyeng in his garden ther at honde: xij*d*

Item to Seman of Wyndam for *di*' mˡ brycke for the tabylles of the same walles: iij*s*

Item to Robert Osborn of Kyrby for j mˡ <bryke> *tyle* for the coueryng of the same walles: vj*s*

Item to hym for j C roffys for the same: vj*s* viij*d*

Item to John Byrche for ij gret dorestalles with hansys set in the same walle: vj*s* viij*d*

Item to Nycholas Tuttell & John Byrche, carpenters, makyng ij half loopys for the grette dore stall that lede in to the churche & for oon other gret loope for the dorestalle next John Dernes, with hangyng of them, iij days: iij*s* iij*d*

Item to Paschall for iij payer of hookes & hengylles, with ij flatte barrys, cappys & stapylles xxviij *libr*' & Englyshe nayle: ij*d* – iij*s* viij*d*

Item to hym for yron worke for the leuer of the oon halff dore & for a strong locke & keye for the other *di*'dore & for ij rynges for the ij dores: ij*s* ij*d*

/*The ffyrst weke after Mydsomer*/ **Item** payd to John Erne & Wylliam Johnson, masons, makyng a fense wall on the northe syde of the churche betwyxt the stepyll ende & the starre grownde,[629] coueryng the sayd walles with tyle & roves & pathyng the entry next the porche, iiij days: iiijs vjd

[*f. 170*] **Item** to Robert Yoxhale and Sandyr Clarke, ther laborers, the same iiij days and to John Elmam and Henry Wodrof, laborers, caryeng ageyn the stagyng, tymbyr, hyrdylles & barrelles to the comon halle & levellyng the grownde within, iiij days: vjs

Item to John Byrche for a pece of tymbyr to laye byfore the porche dore whan it was pathyd: iiijd

Item to Harryson and Goldyng for lyme spent ther syns Owur Lady Day ix chalder *di*: xxvs iiijd

Item to Henry Sparke for sonde ther this weke a lode: vd

Item to hym for caryeng of ij lode colder that cam of makyng clene the strete & churche yarde: iiijd

Summa xiij *li* xjs ijd

Memorandum that moche ston more than here in ys declaryd that went to the makyng of all the sayd walles, moche tymbyr, bourde & nayle spent abowght the reparacon of the tenement, dore lopys & pentyses <wall> war all of the comon store *& cetera.*

/*Comon closse*/ **Item** payd in the tyme of thys accompt for the reparacon of the dyekes abowght the comon closse without Seynt Stephyns gates these chargys folowyng:

In primis payd to John Warnys of Dreyton [*Drayton*], *alias* Abbottes, with Richard, hys son, in ernest that they shall newe cast the dyeke & bucke the fense & laye lawer wher need requere, at jd a rode, euery rode conteynyng xxj foote, the accomptant layeng lawer by them: ijd

/*The fyrst weke after Candylmes*/ **Item** payd in the market for lawer ageynst the next weke j m¹ *di*: xviijd

[*f. 170ᵛ*] **Item** payd to the forsayd Warnys & his sonne ffor dyekyng & workyng of vˣˣ rodes: viijs iiijd

Item to Robert Quentrell & John, his sonne, ffor dyekyng & workyng in leke maner vˣˣ xiiij rodes at the forsayd pryce: ixs vjd

Item payd for more lawer vij C: vijd

Item to the forsayd Qwentrell & his sonne scoryng, buckyng & hedgyng small plottes by the day, vj days, at xd the day: vs

Summa xxvs jd[630]

---

629 The Star was a tenement in Tombland then belonging to the guild of St George: Grace, ed., *Records of the Gild of St George*, pp. 21, 146, 156. In June 1548 Raynbald and others made a search for evidence that would enable the city to acquire it after the dissolution of the guild: NCR, 16D/2, f. 225ᵛ.

630 NCR, 18A/6, f. 185ᵛ, has a total of 24s 3d.

Chargis of vj newe gonnys of brasse cald faconettes made in the tyme of thys accompt, with all ther necessaryes, as well for ther newe metall & castyng the old as for byndyng with yron, stockyng, whelyng, exyltreyng, lymers, shoyng, chenys, with all other thynges to them bylongyng, as folowyth *& cetera*:

/*Gonnes*/[631] *In primis* ther was delyueryd by th'andes of Master Awsten Steward, alderman, to Robert and John Owen, gonmakers to the kynges mageste, certen metall of the comialte to the *summa* of xviij C xiiij *libr'*, wherof they spent vpon the sayd gonnes but ix C xiij *libr'* and put therto of ther own ffyne metalle xvj C xxvj *libr'*, for the whyche *payd* for euery C xxiiijs: xix *li* ixs vd

Item the hole *summa* of the metalle was xxv C xxxix *libr'*, wherof was wastyd iiij C just; & so the vj peces conteynyd xxj C xxxix *libr'*, for the whyche payd for castyng and makyng for euery C xs: x *li* xiijs iijd

[*f. 171*] **Item** for vj stockes of elme at vjs a pece: xxxvjs

Item for the yron worke of the sayd vj stockes, as well plates, boltes, forlockes, shetylles, ryvetes, lynpyns, chenys, stapylles and nayles, as all other thynges parteynyng to the same, weyng in all iiij C xxxix *libr'* at ijd *ob' libr'*: v *li* xvijd *ob'*

Item for vj payer of whelys at vjs: xxxvjs

Item for vj extylltrees: vjs

Item for vj payer of lymers at xxd: xs

Item for vj ropys for the same lymers: vd

/*Master Steward*/ **Item** payd to Master Awsten Steward for certen costes layd out by hym: and fyrst for ffreyght of the metalle to London, with the charges of takyn out of the shyppe & howse romythe: vs

Item for caryage of the sayd metalle to Salesbery Place[632] & for recaryage to the gonners: ijs

Item for caryage of the gonnys to the shyppe whan they war ffynyshyd: xvjd

Item for warfage and cranage at London: ijs

Item for vj *libr'* of gon powder to shote them ther: ijs vjd

Item for a ladyll and a sponge, with dyggyng of vj yron stonys out of the grownde after they war shette, wyche war govyn with them: ixd

Item for <Yarmothe> *London* ffreyght for the sayd vj gonnys, with all ther artyllery, conteynyng iij tonnes *di'*: ixs

Item for cranage at Yarmothe: xiijd

Item for Yarmothe ffreyght at Norwiche: ijs iijd

---

631 NCR, 18A/6, ff. 191ᵛ–2ᵛ, incorporates this section under 'mynute expences'.

632 Salisbury Place, to the south of Fleet Street and within a short distance of the Thames, was used for the storage of metal for ordnance, being also the site of the foundry of the celebrated Italian gun-makers, the Arcani. The Owens were based north of the Tower, at the royal foundry in Houndsditch: Ffoukes, *Gun-Founders of England*, pp. 43–50; Hildred, '"Brass" Guns', pp. 22, 29.

[*f. 171ᵛ*] /*Th'accomptant*/ **Item** payd by the accomptant these parcelles: fyrst for cranage at the comon stathe: vj*d*

Item to Wylliam Pede for makyng a newe hede to a bolt that was brokyn & for vj newe forlokes that war lost by the waye: iiij*d*

Item to Henry Sparke for oon of his horse to draw them from the stathe to the guyldhalle ende: vj*d*

Item for an other horse to drawe them out of the market to the comon halle: ij*d*

Item to Nycholas Marry makyng a mowld of ffreston: xvj*d*; and for a clave to set yt in: iiij*d*; xij *libr'* lede for pyllettes: vj*d* – ij*s* ij*d*

/*The weke after Mydsomer*/ **Item** to Thomas Pate for ij horses to cary ij of them withowt Westwyke gates & home: iiij*d*

Item for a rolle of matche to shote them: j*d*

Item to Thomas Warlowe for shotyng of them byfore my lord of Norff' his grace: viij*d*

/*The second weke after Mydsomer*/ **Item** payd to Rychard Snytall for strakes, nayles and shoyng the vj payer whelys takyn by hym agret of Master Rugge, mayer: iij *li* xx*d*

Item to hym for viij hoopys of yron for the navys of iiij payer of the same whelys, with certen bondes wher the wheles war crackyd: iiij*s* viij*d*

Item to hym more in reward by the consent of master mayer and others, for that he complayned to be a loser by the forsayd bargayn: ij*s*

Item to hys men for fechyng them from the comon halle & havyng home ageyn: viij*d*

[*f. 172*] **Item** to Stalworthy, whelewright, for ij newe ffellows for ij seuerall whelys: xvj*d*; and for oon newe extyltre for oon of the gonnys, with trymyng on the same vpon the stocke: xx*d* – iij*s*

Item more to hym for makyng of xxᵗⁱ beddes on ij payer of wheles for dolages: xij*d*

Item to John Ronhale for xxᵗⁱ dolages & xl clynke nayles & viij hoopys for the sayd ij payer whelys, wayeng all toguether xxv *libr'* at ij*d libr'*: iiij*s* ij*d*

/*The iijᵈᵉ weke after Mydsomer*/ **Item** payd at London for gon powder a ferkyn conteynyng lxx *libr'* at v*d libr'*: xxix*s* ij*d*; for the fferkyn: vj*d* – xxix*s* viij*d*

Item to John Agas for caryage home of the same: ij*s*

Item to Snytall for clowtyng of ij extyltrees, with a newe lynpyn & ij forlockes: xij*d*

Item payd for ij horses & ij men to drawe the forsayd vj gonnys from the comon halle to the comon stathe, ther to be delyueryd to Yarmothe by vertewe of the kynges lettyrs: viij*d*⁶³³

Item to a man that holpe them out of the comon halle: ij*d*

Item for lede to make more pyllettes in store byfore the delyuery of the mowld xiiij *libr'*: vij*d*

Summa xlvj *li* xiiij*s* v*d* ob'

---

633 The six guns arrived at Yarmouth on 31 July 1545: NCR, 16A/5, p. 288.

/Fourty soldyers/[634] **Item** payd for the chargys of ffourty soldyers sent to Bulleyn [*Boulogne*] in the tyme of this accompt by vertu of the kynges letters and delyuerd at Ypswiche [*Ipswich*] the xiij day of August:[635]

In primis payd to l<x>iiij men reteyned for soldyers, euery of them iiij*d*: xvij*s*

[*f. 172*] **Item** payd for ffourty payer of hose for fourty men that war chosen out of the sayd liiij men: that ys to saye for xxxij payer at iij*s* v*d* euery payer, and for viij payer made with martyngalys at iij*s* vij*d* euery payer: vj *li* xviij*s*

Item for ffourty doblettes of whyte fustyan at iij*s* iiij*d*, with lynyng and makyng euery oon: vj *li* xiij*s* iiij*d*

Item for xxij uyght [*white*] cappis for the byllmen at iij*d* euery cappe, and for xviij Scottyshe cappis <at> for the archers at vij*d* euery cappe: xvj*s*

Item for xviij skulles for xviij archers at xj*d*: xvj*s* vj*d*

Item for xviij bowes at ij*s* viij*d* a bowe: xlviij*s*

Item for xviij brasers & shotyng glovys: vj*s*

Item for bowstrynges, euery of them j*d*: xviij*d*

Item for xx^ti sheffe of arrows sent for to Yarmoth at ij*s* iij*d* euery sheffe: xlv*s*

Item for xij arowe cassys that came with them: vij*s*

Item for the costes of an horse & a man rydyng for them to Yarmothe, with the caryage home: ij*s* vij*d*

Item for viij cassys made here at home: v*s* <viij*d*> viij*d*

Item for xx^ti guyrdylles to Master Flecher: iij*s* iiij*d*

Item to a flecher for trymmyng of them in ther cassys and guyrdylles: x*d*

Item payd for ffourtye swordes & fourty daggers: vj *li*

Item to Master Awsten Steward, alderman, for xxij newe Almayn ryvettes, full furnyshyd with splentes, gorgettes & sallettes at xij*s* a pece: xiij *li* iiij*s*

Item for xxij newe bylles at xvj*d*: xxix*s* iiij*d*

[*f. 173*] */Soldyers/* **Item** payd for ij grosse of armyn poyntes: ij*s* vj*d*

Item to Nycholas Grene for a drome: ij*s*

Item gaf to euery soldyer for hys brekefast the same day they dyd set forward to Ypswyche ij*d*: vj*s* viij*d*

Item gaf to euery soldyer at the cite gates for his condyte money to Ypswiche xv*d*: l*s*

Item gaf to euery soldyer at Ypswiche for oon day costes byfore thei war receyuyd in to the kynges wages vj*d*: xx*s*

---

634 NCR, 18A/6, ff. 192^v–4, incorporates this section under 'mynute expences'.

635 No doubt drawing upon the previous year's experience, this contingent was assembled and equipped at remarkable speed. On 31 July 1545 the duke of Norfolk ordered a general muster at Chapel Field the following day, at which eighteen archers and twenty-two billmen were selected, with orders to be ready at an hour's notice 'on pain of death'. On 2 August, however, Norfolk informed the mayor of his 'suer knowlege that the Frenche navy is at this present betwen the narrowe sees, in somoche that I dare not aduenture to embarke suche souldiours as shuld goo oute of your citie vntill suche tyme as I shall receyue ffurther aduertisement'. The men finally left Norwich, fully armed, on 8 August, arriving at Ipswich two days later: NCR, 16A/5, pp. 288–90.

Item payd ther by the commandment of my lord of Norff' to euery soldyer for vj days wages iijs: vj *li*

Item gaf to euery soldyer for goyng a foote iij myles to the shyppe ijd: vjs viijd

/*Other costes at Norwyche*/ **Item** payd for *di'* barrell bere & certen brede spent vpon them in the guyldhalle the fyrst day that they musterd & for a ferkyn the last day: iijs ixd

Item for the costes of Master Thomas Marsham, alderman, & his man rydyng to Kenyngale [*Kenninghall*] to comon with the dukes grace concernyng the settyng forthe of them: iiijs iiijd

Item to armerer for mendyng the harneys, with the chargys of lethyr, buckylles & nayles: iiijs jd

Item to ij laborers that fechyd the harneys from Master Stewardes to the guyldhalle & dyd harneys the soldyers: viijd; and to the iij^d laborer that contynually for vj days tendyd to the soldyers, went of erantes & holpe the armerer: ijs xjd

Item to Henry Sparke for his carte & horse & ij men caryeng ther harneys and artyllery to Ypswiche: xvs; for the hyer of ij teltes to couer them: viijd; ffor strawe: jd – xvs ixd

Item for mendyng of the drome: iiijd

[*f. 173*^v^] /*More chargis at Ypswiche*/ **Item** for the hyer of an howse at Ypswiche to laye in ther harneys & other artyllery: viijd

Item to an offycer that brought vs to ij lodgynges that was appoyntyd wher the soldyers shuld lye: iiijd

Item to the maryners that caryed the fourty soldyers in ther neckes [*on their shoulders*] to the boote & rowyd them to the shyppe: viijd

Item for mendyng the harneys at Ypswiche whiche was dekayed in buckylles & lether: ijs xjd

Item for the hyer of iij horses v days at xvd the day: vjs iijd; and to John West, appoyntyd to ryde with Master Flecher & the accomptant to kepe ther horses & to wayte on them: xxd – vijs xjd

Item for all the costes of horse & men v days, with shoyng of horses, mendyng of sadylles and the costes of Madde Jamys to Ypswyche & ther: xxvjs xjd

/*More charges at Norwyche forgotten*/ **Item** for newe trymmyng of the accomptantes sheffe of arrowes, whiche was frayed in the tyme of the musters, with certen arrows lost: xd

Item to euery soldyer for poyntes for his hose jd: iijs iiijd

Item to Peter Freman for callyng the solders to guether the same day they set forward to Ypswiche with his drome: ijd

Item to Raphe Nytyngale the day byfore: ijd

Item to the sexten of Seynt Peters that wachyd [*for*] my lord of Norff' comyng to the cyte on Seynt Peters stepyll: jd

         Summa **lvj** *li* **xviijs jd**

[*f. 174*] **Mynute expensys** as vpon presentes, bankettes, rewardes, outrydynges, sewtes, wrytynges and suche other leke expensys *& cetera*:[636]

/*Duke of Norff'*/ ***In primis*** payd for a present send to the duke of Norff' his grace to Kenyngale [*Kenninghall*] the xxix day of Novembyr within the tyme of thys accompt: and ffyrst to Robert Osborn of Kyrby [*Bedon*] for vj *fatte* swannys: xxiiijs
Item to Thomas Palmer for ij cranys: xijs viijd
Item for ij C gret qwynces bought of sondry persons at dyuerse pryces: vijs vijd
Item for a gret closse mawnde to trusse them in: vjd
Item to John Crowe for a man & iij horses to cary the sayd present to Kenyngale: vs
Item ffor the costes of the accomptant & Robert Collard, appoyntyd to ryde with hym, in all charges, with ther horse hyer, ij days: iiijs iijd

/*Duches of Rychemond*/[637] **Item** payd for a present govyn to my lady of Rychemond at Carrowe the xix day of Januarii: and fyrst payd for ij pottes with ffyne wafers: iijs iiijd
Item for ij gallons of fyne ipocras: xiijs
Item to John Mannys wyf for fyne spyce brede made with swete water & suger: ijs viijd

/*Duke of Norff' ageyn*/ **Item** payd for other ij gallons of ypocras, ij pottes with wafers and spycebrede provyded ageynst the xxviij day of <Marche> Januarii to sytte vpon the benevolens: xixs[638]
Item for an ownce of parfume <to> brent in the cownsell chambyr to heyer the howse: vjd
Item for a parfume panne with clows, damask water & other ingredyens: xijd
[*f. 174ᵛ*] **Item** the dukes grace beyng seke of the flyxe came not at *the* forsayd day appoyntyd, wherfor by the cownsell of Master Holdyche ij fflagons of syluer fyllyd with the sayd ypocras, whiche dyd hold a gallon *di'*, was sent to Kenyngale by John Goffys, servant, who hade for hys paynis and hys horse hyer & costes: ijs
Item payd for a gallon *di'* of ypocras more made ageynst his comyng the viijᵗᵉ day of Februarii, at whyche day all the forsayd ger was presentyd: ixs ixd
Item for an other parfume panne, with other parfumes to make the cownsell chambyr swete: xviijd
Item to a man that swept the guyldhall chambers, ledes and stayers ageynst hys comyng: ijd
Item to a man waytyng hys comyng of Seynt Peters stepyll: jd; and for brede & drynke for master mayer & his brothern waytyng at the guyldhalle for his graces comyng: ijd – iijd

/*An other present to his grace*/ **Item** payd in the market on Mydsomer evyn for a

---

636 NCR, 18A/6, ff. 191–6, places 'mynute expences' (including the outlay on guns and soldiers) after expenditure on the common hall (ff. 185ᵛ–91).
637 See above, p. 207 note 472.
638 Orders were issued by the mayor on 25 January 1545 for appropriate preparations to be made for the duke's arrival: NCR, 16A/5, p. 264.

ffreshe salmon: ij*s* viij*d*; and for the hyer of ij horses & the costes of the accomptant & a man rydyng with hym to Waborn Hope [*Weybourne Hope*], Sheryngham [*Sheringham*] and Baconsthorppe [*Baconsthorpe*] caryeng the sayd salmon to the dukes grace and to knowe his plesyr concernyng the comyssyon for the antycypacon: iij*s* ij*d* – v*s* x*d*[639]

/An other present to his grace/ **Item** payd for an other present govyn to hys grace comyng to the cite the last day of June syttyng vpon the comyssyon for the iij^de */nullus/* [*f. 175*] payment of the subsedy cald the antycypacon: and fyrst for ij gallons of ffyne ypocras: xiij*s*

Item for ij pottes of ffyne waffers: iij*s* viij*d*
Item for ffyne spyce brede to John Mannys wyff: ij*s* iiij*d*
Item to Mastres Morront for a jolle of freshe sturgeon and a ronde: xiij*s* iiij*d*

/Justices of assyse/ **Item** for a present govyn to the justices of assyse the viij^te day of Julii: and fyrst to Mastres Trase for ij elles of ffyne worsted: xxvj*s* viij*d*
Item ffyne spyce brede: ij*s* viij*d*
Item claret wyne ij gallons: ij*s* viij*d*

/Bankettes/ **Item** payd the ffyrst day of Julii for manchettes *j*d*, spycebrede *iij*d*, old apples *iiij*d*, claret wyne *viij*d*, secke *iiij*d* and bere *xvj*d* for Syr Roger Townysend, Syr Wylliam Paston, master mayer and the other comyssyoners syttyng all that day at the comon halle vpon the valuacon of the antycypacon: iij*s*[640]
                      Summa ix *li* iiij*d*

/Rewardes/[641] **Item** gaf in reward to a pursevant that broute a proclymacon vnder the kynges seale the viij^te day of Octobyr to put Frenchemen at lyberte to dwell peseably with in thys realme thowe thei be no denysens, notwithstondyng any other proclymacions byfore made to the contrary: v*s*[642]
Item gaf in reward the ix day of Januarii to a pursevant that brought a proclymacon to gyf all men lyberte to set forth shyppis of warre: v*s*
Item gaf in reward the xj day of Januarii to my lord of Sussex players[643] bycause master mayer */nullus/* [*f. 175^v*] and hys brothern war at no leyser to se them playe, and also the comon halle at that tyme occupyed with the kynges greyne: v*s*

---

639 Desperate to raise money for the war effort, in June 1545 the government sought to 'anticipate' the payment of a parliamentary subsidy due in the following February by asking wealthier tax payers to contribute seven months in advance and thus avoid a potentially higher rate of assessment: R. Schofield, *Taxation under the Early Tudors 1485–1547* (Oxford, 2004), pp. 133–4.
640 For the undated commission, see *LPFD*, XX (part 1), no 623, p. 326.
641 NCR, 18A/6, ff. 194^v–5, incorporates this section under 'mynute expences'.
642 The original proclamation ordering all non-denizen French to leave England was issued on 19 July 1544: P.L. Hughes and J.F. Larkin, eds, *Tudor Royal Proclamations: Volume 1, The Early Tudors (1485–1553)* (New Haven and London, 1964), no 234.
643 See above, p. 266 note 560.

Item gaff in reward the last day of Marche to a servant of Syr Richard Suthwelles[644] that brought a letter concernyng the payment of the benevolens: ij*s*

Item gaf in reward the viij*te* day of Aprelle to an other man that brought <a> letters from the kynges cowncell for oon George Chylde to be sett vpon the pyllery: xx*d*[645]

Item gaf in reward the xxviij day of Aprelle to a pursevant that brought letters concernyng merchantes ventrers for suche iniuryes as any of them haue susteynyd of the emperours subiectes: v*s*[646]

Item gaff in reward the xxj day of June to a pursevant that brought the kynges commyssyon for the iij*de* payment of the subsedy callyd the antycypacon: iij*s* iiij*d*; and to Robert Colllarde [*sic*] for his paynes, costes & horse hyer rydyng with hym to Kenyngale with the sayd commyssyon to knowe my lordes plesyr ther in: ij*s* viij*d* – vj*s*

Item gaff in reward the xxviij day of August to a copyll of the kynges menstrelles who went all the contry ovyr to men of worchyppe: iij*s* iiij*d*

/*Enterludes*/ **Item** gaf in reward to my lord prynces players[647] playeng an interlude vpon the Assencon Day in Master Castyldens place byfore master mayer & his brothern and certen comyners: vj*s* viij*d*

Summa xxxix*s* viij*d*

[*f. 176*] /*Outrydynges*/[648] **Item** payd ij horse hyer & costes of the accomptant and a man with hym rydyng the xxix day of Januarii to Kenyngale [*Kenninghall*] to my lordes grace with the subsedy bookes, bryngyng answer ageyn concernyng the benevolens than to be grauntyd to the kynges mageste, beyng forthe ij days, in all chargis: v*s* iiij*d*

Item payd for the costes of a man & horse & his paynis rydyng to Syr Jamys Bullen[649] with lettyrs [*and*] bryngyng ageyn a certyfycat concernyng one Thyrkyll of Lynne [*King's Lynn*] for money makyng: xx*d*

Item to Thomas Brown, jaylour of the castyll, for that he toke charge to carry Ryxe of Der[*eh*]am, the promoter,[650] to Thetford assyse: iij*s* iiij*d*

---

644 Sir Richard Southwell (d. 1564) of Wood Rising in Norfolk was then treasurer of the king's wars and one of the commissioners on the 'anticipation' sitting in Norwich: see *ODBN*, li, pp. 707–9; *HoP, 1509–1558*, iii, pp. 352–4.

645 Chylde, *alias* Wethers, was pilloried for six hours on 2 May 1545 by the justices of the peace, on the charge of 'inventyng off ffalse brutes' or rumours: NCR, 16A/5, p. 277.

646 NCR, 18A/6, f. 195, refers to 'wronges don by the Duchemen'.

647 See above, p. 163 note 380.

648 NCR, 18A/6, ff. 195–6, incorporates this section under 'mynute expences'.

649 Sir James Boleyn (d. 1561) of Blickling was then clerk of the peace in Norfolk and Suffolk: *HoP, 1509–1558*, i, p. 456.

650 NCR, 18A/6, f. 195, adds '& a troublous person'. Ryxe was an informer with dubious credentials: see NCR, 16A/5, pp. 270–2.

Item payd the second day of June to Bryan Doront for his paynes rydyng in post that nyght to Thetford with the kynges letters, ouer & above xx*d* that my lord of Norff' gaf hym: xij*d*

Item to John West rydyng in post iij tymes to Syr John Heydon[651] and to *Syr* Wylliam Paston with my lord of Norff' lettyrs concernyng the settyng forthe of the soldyers in the contry: v*s*

Item for the costes & horse of the accomptant rydyng to Bery [*Bury St Edmunds*] to paye the xth of the comon halle, and to conclude a full bargayn with Master Heyer[652] for the tenement in Seynt Clementes of Fybrygge on the southe est corner of the gret gardeyn and <takyy> takyng a draught of the dede out of hys patent,[653] beyng forthe iij days, in all chargis: iiij*s* vij*d*

[*f. 176*^v] /*Sewtys*/ **Item** payd the xxij day of Aprelle in the opyn courte in the cownsell chambyr vpon the chekyr byfore Master Henry Fuller, mayer, & his brothern the aldermen ther present xx angelles in goold for an ende to be made with Master Flyntes sewte, at viij*s* the angell: viij *li*[654]

/*Wrytynges*/ **Item** payd for makyng of *a* wrytyng that was sette vpon George Chyldes hede, who was set vpon the pyllery by vertu of letters that came from the kynges cownsell the viij^{te} day of Aprelle: ij*d*

Item for halff the chargys of seale & wrytynges of Wylliam Wallers lease for Seynt Marys churche: ij*s*[655]

Item for ij oblygacions, makyng the oon for the sayd Waller & the other for John Awelton: viij*d*

Item for halff chargis of seale & wrytynges of John Brondes lease for the hede place and xiij tenementes with the kylyarde in South Conysford: iij*s*[656]

Item for a *dedymus potestatem* for Master Rugge, newe mayer: ix*s* iiij*d*

Item to the clarkes of the kynges awdyte kept at Bery for a quytans for the payment of the xth of the comon halle, with the serche for the tenement in Seynt Clementes: xij*d*

Summa ix *li* xvij*s* <iiij*d*> j*d*

---

651 Sir John Heydon (d. 1551) of Baconsthorpe, was then, like Sir William Paston, a JP and member of the commission to raise the 'anticipation': Baker, *Men of Court*, i, pp. 866–7.

652 See above, p. 264 note 556.

653 See NCR, 8K/7 (b); and *LPFD*, XV, no 83 (72), for the letters patent.

654 The minutes of the mayor's court for 27 April 1545, NCR, 18A/6, f. 195^v, note that the money was paid to Master Corbet 'incontynently to be emploid & expended in & about the vrgent causes ffor the citie'. On 16 April 1545 the same court had authorised John Corbet and William Rugge to attempt to settle Flynt's suit against them and pay him whatever legal expenses seemed reasonable: NCR, 16A/5, pp. 275, 276.

655 The lease was sealed on 21 August 1545: NCR, 16D/2, f. 211^v.

656 The lease, for twenty years, was sealed on 9 May 1544: NCR, 16D/2, ff. 208^v–9.

/Other mynute expenses/[657] **Item** payd for a quayer of paper delyueryd to Framyngham in the tyme of this accompt; and for ij quayers for the accomptant for the makyng of hys bookes: ix*d*

[*f. 177*] **Item** for a dobyll butte *of* lethyr, whyche was seasyd by oon Ryxe of Der[*eh*] am, a promoter, the xxv day of Februarii, not to be lawffull: ij*s*[658]

Item for horsemete for master recorders <horse mete> vj horse, beyng here in the cite iij days whan master mayer tooke hys charge: vj*s* vj*d*

Item to Neve of Rynglond [*Ringland*] for charcole for all the wynter in the tyme of thys accompt for the cownsell chambyr iiij sackes: ij*s*

Summa xj*s* iij*d*

Memorandum that here after and last of all do folowe the cost and charge don within the tyme of thys accompt at the comon halle in ffynyshyng vp of the tenement ageynst the ij elmys that was begonne the last yere, makyng of a newe vestry, newe castyng the chappell, with trymmyng of many other thynges in the same place;[659] also the payment of all the lede of the place to the kynges mageste and the kepyng of certeyn greyne lyeng ther all this yere *& cetera*:

Comon halle

/The fyrst weke after Myhelmes/ **In primis** payd to Nycholas Tuttell and John Byrche, carpenters, knyllyng the rof of the newe howse, whyche was begonne in the ende of the last accompt, v days this weke: v*s* v*d*

Item for vj ashyn astylles to make hooknyales: ij*d*

/The second weke after Myhelmes/ **Item** to the sayd ij carpenters makyng the pannelles of the sayd newe howse, vj days: vj*s* vj*d*

Item to John Goose and his man, sawers, for vj days worke sawyng sparrys feete, evys bourde, ledgys for dores, batrons for the newe carte gate & suche other thynges: vj*s* vj*d*

[*f. 177*]ᵛ] **Item** to Henry Wodrof and John Elmam, comon laborers, sometyme helpyng the sayd carpenters, sometyme the masons at Seynt Marys churche, sometyme the tylers at the suffrygantes tenementes to haue in tyle & brycke, vj days: iiij*s* vj*d*

*/The iij*ᵈᵉ *weke after Myhelmes/* **Item** to the forsayd ij carpenters fynyshyng the pannelles & reysyng them, v days: v*s* v*d*

---

657 NCR, 18A/6, ff. 195ᵛ–6, incorporates this section under 'mynute expences'.

658 NCR, 18A/6, f. 195ᵛ, explains that the 'dobble butte of tanned letther' had been confiscated because it was inadequately tanned. For the case, see NCR, 16A/5, p. 270.

659 NCR, 18A/6, f. 191, adds the note: 'quantite of stone occupied there & moche olde tymber of the comon store comyng of the transposing of the bildynges, olde roffes had doun & bell fframe of Saynt Maryes chirche'.

Item to John Byrche the eldyr for vj pryncypall sparrys for the newe roffe ther: vj*s* vj*d*[660]

/*The iiij^{te} weke after Myhelmes*/ **Item** to the forsayd ij carpenters reysyng the roffe of the sayd newe howse, naylyng on sparrys fete, evys bourde & makyng of a wyndowe to be set in the peke wall at the est ende of the same howse, vj days: v*s*

Item to Henry Wodrof and John Elmam, laborers, helpyng them to rayse & takyng down the peke in the old howse, vj days: iiij*s* vj*d*

/*The v^{te} weke after Myhelmes*/ **Item** here ys to be notyd that the ij forsayd carpenters in the iiij^{or} wekes byfore war many tymes at the suffrygantes howses, settyng vp newe sparrys, naylyng on sparrys fete and evys bourde, with moche besynes for <ther> the tylers ther, whyche was <whyche> a gret hynderans to the worke here. And also payd to them for iiij days this weke makyng a pentyse with brase & pendon ouer the steyers that go vp to the gret parlowur and removyng the parclose in the same howse to make it largyer: iiij*s* iiij*d*

[*f. 178*] **Item** to Wylliam Smythe, tyler, for lathyng and tylyng of the same howse, iiij days: ij*s* viij*d*

Item to Thomas Hubbard & John Thurston, his laborers, the same iiij days: iij*s* iiij*d*

Item to Henry Sparke for sonde a lode: v*d*

Item to the sayd tyler for vij m^l tyle pynnys: xxj*d*

Item to Mastres Morront for v m^l lathe nayle: iiij*s* ij*d*

/*The vj^{te} weke after Myhelmes*/ **Item** to the forsayd ij carpenters fynyshyng vp the carte gates, whyche war bygon byfore Myhelmes, and hangyng them vp, with moche other worke that weke, vj days: vj*s* vj*d*

Item to John Erne and Robert Hollond, masons, ffynyshyng vp the chymneys in the kechyn and chambyr ouer the kechyn, vj days: vj*s* ix*d*

Item to Sandyr Clarke & Robert Yoxhale, ther laborers, the same vj days: iiij*s* vj*d*

/*The vij^{te} weke after Myhelmes*/ **Item** to the sayd ij masons & ij laborers makyng a peke wall at the est *ende* of the sayd newe howse & goyng forward with the chymney in the gret parlowur, vj days: xj*s* ij*d*

Item to Henry Wodrof & John Elmam, laborers, lathyng betwyxt the stothis of the newe howse, makyng clene the vowlte, kechyn & other howses, caryeng out moche ston & colder, iiij days: iij*s*

Item payd that weke to Brygges of Buknam Carleton [*Buckenham's manor in Carleton-Rode*] for xij copyll sparrys for partycions: vj*s*

/*The viij^{te} weke after Myhelmes*/ **Item** to Nycholas Tuttell, carpenter, settyng vp sparrys ageynst the newe chymney & makyng a gutter & joynyng bothe howsys toguether, vj days: iij*s* iij*d*

---

660 The letter 'b' appears against this figure and 'a' against the one of 5*s* immediately below, as they have evidently been entered in the wrong order and should be transposed.

[*f. 178ᵛ*] **Item** to Wylliam Smythe, tyler, tylyng vp the newe howse all the lenght of the gutter by the newe chymney & the old howse ageynst the chymney, closyng bothe howses to guether & tylyng the pentys ouer the parlowur dore, ij days: xvj*d*

Item to John Thurston, his laborer, ij days: x*d*

Item to John Anthony, his prentyse, makyng Master Stewardes howse parfyght ageyn, whiche was sore brokyn with makyng of the peke, & mendyng the pentyse in the strete & other fawtes, iiij days: ij*s*

Item to Thomas Hubbard, his laborer, iiij days: xx*d*

Item to Clement Appylby, plomer, for a newe webbe of lede for the gutter conteynyng ij C *di'* xiiij *libr'* at vj*s* C: xv*s* ix*d*

Item to hym for layeng the same gutter: iiij*d*

Item for lede nayle for the same gutter: ij*d*

Item to John Erne, Robert Hollond & Wylliam Johnson, masons, fynyshyng vp the chymney in the gret parlowur, with the toppys of all the chymneys newe made, castyng them within & makyng the arches at ther backes with thacke shordes, vj days: x*s*

Item to Sander, <clo> Colles & Yoxhale, ther laborers, the same vj days: vj*s* ix*d*

Item to Henry Wodrof & John Elmam brekyng down a gret hurdas in the gret vowlt and caryeng out the menur the same vj days: iiij*s* vj*d*

Item for packe threde to bynde rede abought the toppys of the chymneys to save them: ij*d*

Item to Master Leche for bryke j m^l: vj*s* viij*d*

Item to Osborn of Kyrby [*Bedon*] for *di'* m^l bryke: ij*s*

[*f. 179*] /*The ix^{te} weke after Myhelmes*/ **Item** payd to the forsayd ij carpenters, Tuttell and Byrche, makyng tymbyr worke for the vyce that goth out of the parlowur in to the newe buyldyng and layeng a florthe of joystes thorowe out all the entry out of the kechyn in to the yarde, makyng iij dore stalles & loopys for them, a wyndowe for the buttry, with many other thynges, vj days: vj*s* vj*d*

Item to Wylliam Pede for ix *libr'* of yron worke: xiiij*d*

Item to the forsayd iij masons pathyng the gret parlowur with gret pathyng tyle that was bought at Yarmothe in the last accompt, makyng the harth of the chymney ther, makyng a stewe in the chambyr ouer the shoppe, bryngyng vp a vyce out of the parlowur in to the newe buyldyng, with moche other ffynyshyng worke, vj days: x*s*

Item to Sander, Yoxhale, Colles, Wodroff and John Elmam, laborers, the same vj days: xj*s* iij*d*

Item to Wylliam Smythe, tyler, closyng in the newe howse on the northe syde of the newe chymney out of the parlowur, oon day: viij*d*

Item to John Thurston, his laborer, that day: v*d*

Item to Basyngham for gret pathyn tyle to ffynyshe vp the gret parlowur j C *di'*: viij*s*

Item here ys to be notyd that all the thacke tyle, bryke and lathe spent in the forsayd worke syns Myhelmes not spokyn of war of the comon store provydyd in the last accompt; but nowe payd to Seman of Wyndam [*Wymondham*] for j m^l brycke to ffynyshe vp the toppys of the chymneys: vj*s* [*f. 179ᵛ*] **Item** to Henry Sparke for caryeng of ij lodes bryke ffrom the crosse in the market to fynyshe vp the worke & other ij lodes from Master Lechys: xvj*d*

/*The xᵗᵉ weke after Myhelmes*/ **Item** to John Byrche th'elder for a gret pece of tymber for a lyntell of oon of the wyndows in the newe parlour: xij*d*

Item for iij stothes for a dore stalle: x*d*

Item to hym for a dore stalle set in the walle next the pond yarde in the last accompt: ij*s* iiij*d*

Item to the forsayd ij carpenters makyng a new wyndowe with vj lyghtes for the gret parlowur, plancheryng halff the newe chambyr & provydyng steppys, lyntelles & other thynges for the masons, v days worke thys weke: v*s* v*d*

Item to Leonard Sutterton for iiij stothys for pyllers for the forsayd wyndowe: xiiij*d*

Item to the forsayd iij masons pathyn the kechyn & the harthe in the same, the entry in to the yarde, with dyuers steppis ther, selyng the same entry, makyng an ovyn in the kechyn & rowcastyng the same kechyn, settyng in the wyndowe in the parlowur & an other in the buttry, rowcastyng the chambyrs, with moche fynyshing worke that weke, v days: viij*s* iiij*d*

Item to the forsayd v laborers v days: ix*s* iiij*d ob'*

Item to John Bengemyn for a fayer wyndowe with viij lyghtes set in [*the*] halle: iiij*s*

Item rede okyr for the chymneys: j*d*

[*f. 180*] /*The xjᵗᵉ weke after Myhelmes*/ **Item** to the forsayd ij carpenters shortyng the forsayd wyndowe bought of Bengemyn & makyng an other wyndowe to be set in the halle with v lyghtes, transposyng the parclosse in the halle & the dore in the same & the dore in the parclosse of the parlowur & shortyng the dore stalle in the vowlt next the welle, with moche other ffynyshyng worke thys weke, v days: v*s* v*d*

Item to the forsayd iij masons makyng the steyers in to the vowlte next the welle, settyng a dore stalle betwyxt the vowlt and the arche vnder the strete, rowcastyng all the vowlt & arche, the gate howse & all the walles of the sope howse place that war sore brokyn with the newe buyldyng, smothyng all the walles in the gret parlowur & newe chambyr, with moche other fynyshyng worke, v days: viij*s* iiij*d*

Item to the forsayd v laborers the same v days: ix*s* iiij*d ob'*

Item for ij newe eerys for the masons tubbe: j*d*

/*The xijᵗᵉ weke after Myhelmes, the last & next byfore Crystmes*/ **Item** payd to the forsayd ij carpenters makyng a pentyse with brasys & pendons ouer the kechyn dore & vowlt dore, with moche other fynyshyng worke that weke, vj days: vj*s* vj*d*

Item to Leonard Sutterton for iiij sawen sparrys for the sayd pentys: xvj*d*

Item to hym for ij square stothys for ij postes for the partycon in the halle: x*d*

Item to the forsayd iij masons makyng fowndacions in the lytyll courte on the northe syde of the chappell for a newe vestry to be made ther with blacke walles, and selyng the gret parlowur, with other howses in the same tenement, vj days: x*s*

[*f. 180ᵛ*] **Item** to the forsayd v laborers vj days: xj*s* iiij*d*

Item to John Ern for caryeng of ij lodes of brekyng ston ffrom Feers kylle: viij*d*

Item to Walter Feere for the same ston spent vpon the blacke walles of the newe vestry: xx*d*

Item to Thomas Albon for xj C dry lathe for the selyng in the parlowur, entry, stewe, wyndows & other places at vij*d* C: vj*s* v*d*

Item to Mastres Morront for vj m¹ selyng nayle: iiij*s* vj*d*

Item for fyne heye to myxe with morter for the selynges: iij*d*

Item payd to Sadler for candyll occupyed amonges the workemen on evynynges & mornynges syns Hallomes xxviij *libr'* at j*d* qu' *libr'*: ij*s* xj*d*

Item for byrchyn bromys & other bromys: j*d* ob'

Item to Henry Sparke for sonde occupyed in the same place syns Myhelmes xxij lodes at v*d*: ix*s* ij*d*

/*The weke in which Crystmes Day fell*/ **Item** payd to the forsayd iij masons settyng in ij wyndowes in the halle, with castyng that howse and vyce in to the courte warde, ij days: iij*s* iiij*d*

Item to the forsayd ij carpenters makyng dore loopys & provydyng lyntelles ij days: ij*s* ij*d*

Item to the forsayd v laborers ij days: iij*s* ix*d*

Item gaf in reward ageynst Crystmes amonges the workmen & laborers who wrowght ther contynually from Lammes in the last accompt tyll this present Crystmes: xiiij*d*

Item to John Goose for j C dry poplyn bourde to fynyshe vp the plancher ouer the kechyn: ij*s*

[*f. 181*] /*The fyrst weke after Crystmes*/ <Th> **Item** payd to the forsayd Nycholas Tuttell and John Byrche, carpenters, makyng steppis and other worke for the newe steyers out of the gret vowlt into the lytyll courte next the chappell, and a pentys with brase & pendon ouer the sayd vowlte dore & plancheryng vp the rest of the chambyr ouer the kechyn, with other workes tendyng to the masons, v days: v*s* v*d*

Item to John Ern, Wylliam Johnson & Robert Hollond, masons, makyng the newe stayers out of the gret vowlt, settyng a newe dorestalle aloft & stoppyng the old dore wher the hordas was, levellyng the courte & pathyng the same, v days: viij*s* iiij*d*

Item to the forsayd v laborers v days: ix*s* iiij*d* ob'

Item to John Byrche th'elder for the dorestalle for the forsayd vowlt dore: ij*s* viij*d*

Item for vij peces of tymbyr for steppys ther: ij*s* iiij*d*

Item more to hym for viij peces of viij onchis sqware for steppys ther also: ij*s* viij*d*

Item to Henry Sparke for pathyn sonde a lode: v*d*

Item to Andrewe Qwashe for ij blacke plates that war occupyed to the newe stewe: vj*d*

Item to Mastres Morront for dyuers sortes of nayles fechyd of hyr at sondry tymes syns Myhelmes spent at this sayd newe buyldyng and at the tenement at the est ende of Seynt Marys churche abowght the planchers, partycions, pentyses and suche leke thynges: and fyrst for viij*d* nayle iij C: xviij*d*; vj*d* nayle *di'* m¹: ij*s*; iiij*d* nayle j m¹: ij*s* vj*d*; iij*d* nayle *di'* m¹: x*d* – vj*s* x*d* [*f. 181ᵛ*] **Item** to Thomas Pecke for dyuerse sortes of nayle fechyd of hym syns Myhelmes at sondry tymes as they nedyd: & fyrst for vj*d* nayle j C: v*d*

Item iiij*d* nayle ij mˡ: v*s*; iij*d* nayle j mˡ: xx*d*; ij*d* nayle j mˡ: xvj*d*; gret lathe nayle j mˡ: x*d*; small lathe nayle ij mˡ: xviij*d* – x*s* iiij*d*

/*The second weke after Crystmes*/ **Item** payd to Goldyng and Harryson for lyme receyuyd from them in to the comon halle place for all workes don ther syns Myhelmes xxj chalder vj comb' at ij*s* viij*d* euery chalder: lviij*s*

Item to Wylliam Pede for iij payer hookes & hengelles for dores, with certen small yron worke, xvj *libr' di'*: ij*s* j*d*

Item for iij payer jemews for vyce dores: xxij*d*

Item for layeng of the comon and of ij laborers pykexys that war sore worn & slytyn ther: vj*d*

Item to Leonard Sutterton for iij sparrys that war occupyed for the rayles of the newe stayers that go down to the gret vowlt: xij*d*

Item more to hym for viij copyll sparrys receyuyd ffrom Shelton at Hallomes, whyche war occupyed aboughe the newe howse: v*s* iiij*d*

Item to Clement, clarke of the chappell, for iiij *libr'* candyll for the chappell all wynter: v*d*

Item to Henry Wodrof, laborer, makyng clene the cloyster & fechyng in menur out of the grownde that was the chapter howse to fyll vp the corner ther nere to make yt levell with the rest, iiij days: xviij*d*

Item for candyll spent ther these iij wekes viij *libr'*: x*d*

Item for whypcord for lachis of dores: *ob'*

[*f. 182*] /*The second weke after Owur Lady, beyng Ester weke*/ **Item** payd to John Stanford, sawer, for a rowe oke lyeng at his dore in Seynt Gyles: ij*s* x*d*

Item for caryeng the same to the comon inne: iiij*d*

Item to Nycholas Tuttell & John Byrche, carpenters, hewyng & sqwaryng the same tre & other ij gret trees, beyng the rest & last of xij okes that war bought at Ambryngale [*Arminghall*] in the xxxvᵗᵉ yere of kyng Henry the viijᵗᵉ [*1543–4*], iij days worke: iij*s* iij*d*⁶⁶¹

Item to the forsayd Stanford & his man brekyng the same ij trees in to sqware tymbyr for plankes, pyllers, corner pyllers, guyrdyns, myddylmotes for ij gret baye wyndows for the newe howse next the ij elmys; and for walplates & a dorestalle for the newe vestry in the chappell, iij days: iij*s* iij*d*

Item to Henry Wodrof & John Elmam, laborers, mendyng the florthis in the kechyn & other howses agenst Sent Georges guylde & sometyme helpyng the carpenters and sawers, iij days: ij*s* iij*d*

/*The iij*ᵈᵉ* weke after Owur Lady*/ **Item** to the forsayd ij carpenters makyng a frame for a dresser set at the west ende of the halle next the northe dore & a loope for the

---

661 See above, pp. 204–5.

same, with trymmyng of plankes & lyntelles for the same, makyng a courbyll layd in the botom of the [*well*] next the kechyn & a payer of loopis for the vowlt dore on the southe of the tenement next the ij elmys, iiij days worke: iiij*s* iiij*d*

Item to Pede for a newe locke & keye for the sayd vowlt dore: x*d*; & for ij payer of hookes & hengylles for the same dores: vj*d* – xvj*d*

Item to Henry Sparke for caryeng of a lode /*nullus*/ [*f. 182*ᵛ] of the forsayd newe sawen tymbyr from the comon inne to the comon halle: vj*d*

Item to John Erne & Wylliam Johnson, masons, settyng in the forsayd dresser, layeng the courbyll in the welle, workyng vpon the same to the old worke & closyng the chapter howse dore, vj days: vj*s* ix*d*

Item to Sander Clarke & Yoxhale, ther laborers, iiij*s* vj*d*

Item to Henry Wodrof & John Elmam brekyng the hole wher the dresser stond, drawyng the well, makyng yt deper & drawyng out moche vyle matter, with moche other worke, vj days: iiij*s* vj*d*

Item for a newe bast for the welle: xvj*d*

Item for ij C wose brycke to laye vpon the corbyll: xvj*d*

Item for brome fagottes to dry the workmen whan they came out of the welle: ij*d*

Item gaf to John Ern for his payn, ouer & above hys wages, for oon day workyng in the welle, with part of the nyght, stondyng contynually to the knees in the water: viij*d*; and to Wylliam Johnson, beyng in the well with hym: iiij*d* – xij*d*

Item to Henry Wodrof, who was oon hole day in the welle conveyeng out the mudde: iiij*d*

Item to John Elmam that drewe out the water & fylthe contynually, ij days: ij*d*

Item to other ij laborers that toke moche paynes abought that besynes: ij*d*

Item for byrchyn bromys & other bromys to make clene all the howses agenst the guyld: j*d ob'*

[*f. 183*] **Item** to Paschall for a payer of jemews, a barre & a stapyll, all tynnyd, for the loope of the newe dresser on the out syde, an hespe with ij eeys on the in syde: xviij*d*

Item for mendyng the locke on the scaldyng howse dore: ij*d*

/*The iiij*ᵗᵉ *weke after Owur Lady*/ **Item** to the forsayd ij carpenters makyng tymbyr rackes for the kechyn & begynnyng to make a fayer baye wyndowe, with pyllers & myddylmote inbowd, set on the stretes syde next the ij elmys, *iiij days*: iiij*s* iiij*d*

Item to a man with a sythe that mowyd down all the nettylles, dockes & wrecke in the yardes ther: ij*d*

Item for mendyng the locke on Thomas Peckes vowlt dore: ij*d*; and for a newe botom for oon of the stoppys of the kechyn welle: ij*d* – iiij*d*

/*The v*ᵗᵉ *& vj*ᵗᵉ *wekes after Owur Lady*/ **Item** to the forsayd ij carpenters fynyshyng vp the sayd baye wyndowe & settyng vp; and makyng a dore stalle inbowyd for the newe vestry, viij days these ij wekes: viij*s* viij*d*

Item for byrchyn bromys to make clene the stretes & lane ageynst ageynst [*sic*] the gaudays: j*d*

/*The vij^te weke after Owur Lady*/ **Item** to Master Doctowur Kyng[662] prechyng at the comon halle Monday & Tewisday this weke: vjs viijd

Item to the forsayd ij carpenters makyng a roffe for the newe vestry, copyll bownd with wyndbemys, & a loope for the dore made with dyce hede nayle and batrons, v days: vs vd

Item to Paschall for a payer of hookes and hengylles for the same dore conteynyng xij *libr'*: xviijd

Item for *di'* C dyce hede nayle of ij scantlyns: ijs

Item for Inglyshe nayle for the same dore: ijd

[*f. 183^v*] **Item** to Wylliam Pede for iiij sockettes of yron for the leuers of the ij levys of the carte gate next the ij elmys & ij gret barrys, with certen cappys & stapylles, conteynyng xxiiij *libr'* at ijd *libr'*: iiijs

Item for a long barre of yron with a stapyll & a cappe for a leuer of the oon leffe of the southe dore of Thomas Peckes vowlt: viijd

Item to Leonard Sutterton for x copyll of sparrys for the rof and wyndebemys of the newe vestry at viijd the copyll: vjs viijd

Item to John Aleyn for a iiij^or square wyndowe with lockyd barrys of yron for the sayd vestry: vjs viijd

/*The viij^te weke after Owur Lady*/ **Item** payd to John Ern and Wylliam Johnson, masons, settyng in the vestry dore, making vp the gabyll of the same vestry, selyng the same vestry within, pathyng the same & rowcastyng all the same, vj days worke of eyther of them: vjs ixd

Item to Sander, Yoxhale, Wodrof & Elmam, laborers, euery of them vj days: ixs

Item to Jamys Leche for small pathyn tyle for the sayd vestry iiij C & to Wylliam Spratte for iij C *di'* at xijd C: vijs vjd

Item for ij *libr'* here for selyng: ijd

Item to Wylliam Smythe, tyler, for lathyng & tylyng the sayd vestry, takyn agret: xxd

Item for iij m^l tyle pynnys: ixd

Item to Mastres Morront for lathe nayle for tylyng & selyng within iij m^l: ijs vjd

Item to Osborn for ij m^l thacke tyle: xijs

[*f. 184*] **Item** ther was spent vpon the same howse and vpon the selyng within vij C lathe, wherof iiij C was of comon store beleft at the reparacon of the suffrigantes howses at Hallomes, & so payd for iij C more: xviijd

Item to Paschall for a rynge with a sneck & a lache for the vestry dore: viijd; and for a locke, a key, a stapyll & a plate for the locke hole of the same dore, with the settyng on: xxd – ijs iiijd

Item to Robert Seman of Wyndam [*Wymondham*] for j m^l good brycke for the coueryng of the gabyll of the vestry & for settyng of wyndows & dores: vjs

Item payd that weke to the forsayd ij carpenters, beyng in hande with an other fayer bay wyndowe with pyllers & myddylmote inbowed, to be sette on the chambyr

---

662 See above, p. 266 note 562.

ouer the kechyn on insyde at the newe tenement next the ij elmes, with other worke tendyng to the masons, vj days worke: vjs vjd

/The ix^te weke after Owur Lady/ Item to the sayd ij carpenters fynyshyng vp the sayd wyndowe & reysyng the same, iij days: iijs iijd

Item to the forsayd ij masons rowcastyng vyrond all the comon halle chapell, iij days: iijs iiijd

Item to Sander, Yoxhale & Wodrof, laborers, iij days: iijs iiijd ob'

/The x^te weke after Owur Lady/ Item to Herryson, cowper, for ij newe stoppys for the kechyn welle: viijd; to Paschall for oon newe yron hoope, for mendyng of an other, for iij newe eerys, di'C Inglyshe nayle & settyng on: xiijd – xxjd

Item payd for mendyng of the water tubbe: ijd ob'

Item to John Byrche for a newe dore stalle set in the entry next the vestry with*in* Thomas Pecke: ijs iiijd

[f. 184^v] Item to the forsayd ij carpenters makyng an alter, dobyll bourdyd, with coffers all along the newe vestry to laye ther vestmentes, bookes & other necessaryes & makyng ij long lectorns for the ij sydes of the chappell ageynst the prest guyld, v days: vs vd

Item to the forsayd ij masons makyng a newe buttrase in the lytyll courte at the tenement next the ij elmys, settyng a dore stalle in a wall in the entry that lede vp to the halle in the same courte and rowcastyng all the walles in the sayd entry, v days: vs viijd ob'

Item to Sander & Yoxhale, ther laborers, v days: iijs ixd

Item to Henry Wodrof, laborer, makyng clene all the yardes, chappell & howses ageynst Corpus Christi day & helpyng the masons the same v days: xxijd ob'

Item payd for scoryng of the lampe, candyllstyckes and other latten ageynst Corpus Christi day: vjd

Item for washyng the lynyn ageysnt the same day: iijd

/The xj^te weke after Owur Lady/ Item to Nycholas Tuttell, carpenter, makyng a lectorn for the mydquere for rectorwryes, an other to stonde at the hye alter ende & the iij^de for the organs, mendyng the feet of the gret candylstyckes, makyng foote bankes for ij trustylles in the halle to serue for the ij endes of the hygh tabyll and many <other> other thynges ageynst that day, vj days: iijs iijd

Item to John Jowell for ij fayer lectorn hedes that came out of the Grey Fryers: iijs iiijd

Item to Wylliam Johnson, mason, settyng a dore stalle in to the newe stabyll at the tenement next the ij elmys, stoppyng vp an other dore ther in the same howse, makyng vp a walle all the brede /nullus/ [f. 185] of that howse to the hyght of the grownde of the stabyll, whervpon ys set a partycon betwyxt the sayd stabyll and the heye howse, with other fynyshyng worke in the same howse, vj days: iijs iijd

Item to Sander & Wodroff, laborers, vj days: iiijs vjd

Item Inglyshe nayle for the carpenters: ijd

/*The xij^{te} weke after Owur Lady*/ **Item** payd to Leonard Sutterton for a lode of joystes and sparrys toguether for the partycon & plancher of the sayd stabyll conteynyng x copyll at vij*d* the copyll: vs x*d*

Item to the forsayd carpenter makyng a particon in the sayd stabyll with stothis & bourdyd, a racke, a manger, a payer of steyers out of the stabyll in to the heye howse; & plankyd the sayd stabyll; and makyng an old dore fytte for the stabyll, vj days: iij*s* iij*d*

Item to Paschall for yron worke for the sayd dore: xvij*d*

Item to John Byrche for an aras pece of tymbyr conteynyng iiij yardes, whiche was cut in to iij steppys for the stayers that go out of the stabyll in to the heye howse: xvj*d*; and for a long slender sparre for the racke: iiij*d* – xx*d*

Item for xx byllettes for racke stavys: ij*d*

Item for a popyll planke for the manger: iij*d*

Item for j quarter C popyll bourde for the newe awlter in the vestry: viij*d*

Item for a wyde dore stalle for the stabylle: <v>ij*s* viij*d*

Item to John Erne & Wylliam Johnson, masons, smothyng the vestry & all the comon halle chappell & pathyng half the stabyll with ston and ffynyshyng all thynges in that place for this yere, vj days: vj*s* ix*d*

[*f. 185^v*] **Item** to Sander, Yoxhale & Wodroff, laborers, vj days: vj*s* ix*d*

/*The weke in whiche Mydsomer Day fell in*/ **Item** payd to Mastres Morront for nayle fechyd of hyr at dyuerse tymes syns Owur Lady Day: and fyrst for vj*d* nayle iiij C: xx*d*; iiij*d* nayle j m^l: ij*s* vj*d*; iij*d* nayle j m^l: xx*d*; ij*d* nayle di' m^l: viij*d*; lathe nayle di' m^l: v*d* – vj*s* xj*d*

Item to Harryson and Goldyng for lyme spent in the same place in all workes syns Ester lxxiiij comb' at iiij*d* euery comb': xxiiij*s* viij*d*

Item to Henry Sparke spent ther in the same tyme for sonde vij lodes at v*d*: ij*s* iiij*d*

/*Betwen Mydsomer & Myhelmes*/ **Item** payd to Henry Wodrof, laborer, workyng at the comon halle lxv days in thys quarter, beyng all ways redy at the accomptantes handes to go on erandes and in the other tymis workyng at the comon halle: that is to say my lord of Norff' comyng dyuers tymes in that quarter to the cite, the justyces of assyse, receyvyng home of the newe gonnys, the shotyng of them without Westwyke gates, the shoyng of them, the conveyng of them to Yarmothe, the settyng forthe of fourty soldyers, with many suche leke thynges, whose helpe the accomptant was fayne to haue; and other whyles kepyng the whete in the same place and ij days in a weke makyng sale therof in the market; and in the rest of all other tymes kepyng the groundes clene, whiche dyuers tymes thys somer war ovyr growen with wyldernes, and brekyng down of old walles and levellyng the growndes, wyth [*f. 186*] moche other turmoylyng to and fro, and nevyr ydyll, at iiij*d* ob' euery day: xxiiij*s* iiij*d* ob'

And payd in that tyme for newe layeng of the comon pykexe: ij*d*

/*At Myhelmes*/ **Item** payd to Master Kempe, prest of the comon halle, for dyuers thynges layd out by hym this yere: and fyrst for wyne & waxe for strangers that daly resorte & syng masse in the chappell: ij*s*

Item for washyng of iij awbys & certen napkyns: iiij*d*

Item for iij newe guyrdylles for vestmentes iij*d*

Item for threde and pynnys: j*d*

Item to the clarke & sexten of Seynt Andrews for ther helpe at the prestes guylde: vj*d*

Item to ij prestes that war deacon & subdeacon on Corpus Christi day: viij*d*

   Summa solucionum communis awle **xxxvj** *li* **ixs vijd ob'**

/*Leed*/[663] **Item** payd at Bery [*Bury St Edmunds*] the xv day of August in the tyme of thys accompt to Master John Eyer, receyvour to the kynges mageste for the leed of the churche chansell, stepyll and ij yles of the comon halle, surveyd and valewed in the last accompt at xxxviij fudder after iiij *li* euery fudder: C lij *li*

Item for the hyer of iij horses for the accomptant and for other ij men appoyntyd to ryde with hym for savegarde of the sayd money, beyng forthe iij days, at xvj*d* a day: iiij*s*

Item to Robert Barnard, jaylour, rydyng with the sayd accomptant, appoyntyd by master mayer and the cownsell of the cite, for his paynes: ij*s* iiij*d*

[*f. 186*v] **Item** to John West rydyng with them, by the sayd appoyntment, to kepe ther horses: xvj*d*

Item for the costes of them iij and of ther horses: ix*s* x*d*

Item to a man that fechyd Master Fullers horse at Kyrby [*Bedon*] and caryed hym ageyn: ij*d*

Item lost in iij very bare Frenche crownis that war payd to the sayd Master Eyer: ij*s*

Item lost in xxx*s* of dandy prattes & Dylvyn grotes sold to John Bengemyn for xxiij*s* iiij*d*: vj*s* viij*d*

Item lost in the sale of a very ylle sowderd crown sold at Styrbrydge fayer [*Stourbridge fair*]: xvj*d*

Item lost in xiiij*s* of clyppyd money & broke Inglyshe coyne, whyche was sold ther by the ownce at iij*s* xj*d* the ownce: ij*s* iij*d*

   Summa **C liij** *li* **xs xjd**

 Summa totallis omnium solucionum hoc anno **CCCC lxxiij** *li* **xiijs ijd ob'**[664]

And so ys owyng to the sayd accomptant for the paymentes by hym payd thys yere, ovyr and above the receytes by hym receyvyd: vj *li* xj*d ob'*

Item the sayd accomptant do axe to be allowyd for these parcelles folowyng:

---

663 NCR, 18A/6, ff. 190v–91, incorporates this section under 'comon hall', with the sub-heading 'money paid ffor the leede & other charges to the same'.

664 NCR, 18A/6, f. 196, records an outlay of £473 15s 6½d.

In primis ffor the ingrossyng of thys accompt payd to Rychard Framyngham by the assygment of the awdytours: v*s*; and for the expensis of the sayd awdytours & others appoyntyd, syttyng vpon the determynacon of thys accompt: xij*s* – xvij*s*[665]

[*f. 187*] /**Allowances**/ **Item** he axe furder to be allowyd for dyuerse rentes aboue chargyd and nowe dekayed, for as moche as the ffees therof be vnknowen to the sayd accomptant, as yt apperith to the awdytours by other accomptes byfore made: xiij*s* iiij*d*

Item for rent of a sygne in the kynges hey waye agenst the mese late Wylliam Norff' cald The White Horse, whyche sygne is nowe plucke down & that notwithstondyng is still chargid in the rent of assyse: j*d*

Item for rest of quarter ferme of a tenement in Conysford agenst the comon stathe, endyd at Myhelmes *anno regni regis Henrici octavi* xxxvj° [*29 September 1544*], dependyng vpon Nycholas Hardyng, as in the tytyll of *vnde super* in the last accompt yt dothe appere:[666] iiij*d*, whyche can not be levyed: iiij*d*

Item for rest of quarter ferme of a fyshe shoppe, endyd at the sayd ffest, dependyng vpon Robert Newman in the sayd tytyll of *vnde super*, which Newman ys very poore & not dystreynabyll: xvj*d*

Item he axe to be allowyd for certen dettes of dyuerse poore men & other persons not levyabyll, parcell of l *li* vs x*d*, remaynyng not gatherd in dyuers wardes of the cite of a certen sesment taxid for the chargis of xl soldyers sent to Bullen [*Boulogne*] & delyueryd at Ypswiche [*Ipswich*] the xiij day of August, whiche l *li* vs x*d* is chargid above in the tytyll of soldyers amonges the foren receytes; and the sayd dettes not levyabyll do appere more at large in a byll of euery particler parcell delyuerd to the awdytours: xxxij*s* iiij*d*

[*f. 187*] **Item** for a reward govyn to John Rede & Thomas Molle, offycers to master mayer, for ther peynes dyuers tymes goyng for the constabylles & other men concernyng the sayd soldyers money; and for the wardens & festmakers of certen companyes concernyng ther offrynges & certens; and for dyuerse men concernyng the benevolens of the comon halle: xvj*d*

    Summa allocacionum lxv*s* vij*d*

Summa totallis omnium solucionum et allocacionum CCCC lxxvj *li* xviij*s* ix*d ob'*

And so the comialte do owe to the forsayd accomptant: ix *li* vj*s* vj*d ob'*

Item de [*sic*] axe furder to be respectyd vpon *vnde super* for certen rentes and fermys above chargid and not yet receyuyd, wherof the partyclers do folowe:

In primis for parcell of a rent of a tenement in the paryshe of Seynt *Mychaell* at Plee, late Master Pynderne, prest, nowe Henry Mynne, gent', parcell of the castyll ffee by hym denyed: ij*d*, whiche ys chargid in the ffoote of the last accompt in the

---

665 NCR, 18A/6, f. 197, adds '& ffor other gret labours & paynes taken by the accomptaunt & considered by the auditers'.

666 See above, p. 291.

tytyll of *vnde super*; and for an other j*d* for rent of the same tenement dewe in the ende of thys accompt, whiche ys aboue chargid in the tytyll of the castyll ffee, whyche forsayd iij*d* he vtterly do denye to paye: iij*d*

Item for rent of a tenement, late Master Thomas Aldryche, alderman, nowe John Myllycent of Yarmoth, in the paryshe of Seynt Mychaell at Plee /*nullus*/ [*f. 188*] aboue chargid in the tytyll of rent of assyse not yet levyed: iiij*d*; and for rent of a certen grounde adioynyng to the sayd tenement, late Wylliam Russell, alderman: j*d* – v*d*

Item for oon quarter ferme of a tenement in the paryshe of Seynt George at Tomlond, late lord suffrigantes, indyd at Myhelmes in the ende of thys accompt, dewe by Awsten Cobbe: ij*s* vj*d*

Item for the hole yere rent or annuyte dewe to the comialte for the discharge of tolle & custome of all the gates of the cite by the executours of Master Robert Jannys, alderman, above chargid in the tytyll of gates and towurs, withholden for certen cawses well knowen to the awdytours and also to the hole cownsell of the cyte: viij *li*[667]

Summa debitorum viij *li* iij*s* ij*d*

Summa totallis omnium solucionum, allocacionum & respectorum CCCC iiij[xx] v *li* xxiij*d ob'*

And so the comialte do owe clere to the forsayd accomptant xvij *li* ix*s* viij*d ob'*

Thys accompt was vewyd, examyned & determyned by the audytours hereafter folowyng vpon the Tewysday the xxv[te] of Maye in the xxxviij yere of the reign of Kyng Henry the viij[te] [*1546*] *& cetera.*[668]

Awsten Steward
Edmond Wood   aldermen

Robert Brown
Robert Watson   comyners

---

667 The matter is not noted in the proceedings of the assembly or of the mayor's court for 1544–5.

668 NCR, 18A/6, f. 197[v], contains no record of such an examination, but lists the names of the auditors at the head of the account on f. 164.

Appendix I

Indenture tripartite defining the duties of the chamberlains, 1449

[*NCR, 15F/7*]

In Dei nomine, Amen: This indenture tripartite maketh [*inserted:* mencion] that be holl consent & assent of a comone counsell holden in the guyldehalle in the cite of Norwich vppon the Friday in the ffest of Seynt Benet [*inserted in a later hand*: 21ˢᵗ day] in the moneth of March in the tyme of William Asshwell, maire of the said cite, it is ordeyned, graunted and estabelisshed, as in the boke of actis signed with the lettre C clerely is comprehended,[1] that th'office of chaumberleyns yerely chosen in and for the same cite of Norwich shall be from this day forward to receyue & kepe, in the name of the comone of the same cite, of the iiij clauers of the said cite be indenture tripartite all maner euydences, bokes and recordes that longe to the cite at this day, of which indenture tripartite on parte shall remayne toward the maire for the yere beyng, the ijᵉ parte toward the said chaumberleyns, & the iijᵉ parte shall abide with the clauers, as is aforesaid. And also the said chaumberleyns shall receyue & kepe in the forme aforesaid all sommes of money that groweth dayly or shall growe vnto the comone aforesaid, aswell of the arrerages of accownte of all accowntantes that arn & shall be for to accounte vnto the said comone, as in any other forme: that is, to wite, of all enrollementz of apprentizes, intres of whatsoeuer citezeins, of all maner fynes, amercymentz, issues, legaces and all & singuler other casueltes qwhatsoeuer & in what maner wise partenyng or owe to partene vnto the said comone. And also the said chaumberleyns shall receyue & kepe in like forme all rolles indented to be made betwixt the assessours & colyonres [*collectors*] that shall be assigned be the comone counsell of the saide cite to assesse & gadere in any warde or wardes in & for the same cite for any taske, tallage or subsidie from the day of the date herof there to be assessed & gadered: that is, to wite, in this forme that the

---

1 The book in question is most likely to have been the *Liber Albus* (NCR, 17B/3), which contains a loose paper folio inscribed with the words 'C libro albo' in a sixteenth-century hand (I am most grateful to Tom Townsend for this information). The oaths of other civic officers were entered in it (rubricated no 184), but there is no evidence of any deliberations regarding the chamberlainship.

said assessours shall be beholden to delyuer vnto the said chaumberleyns the parte of there indenture forth with after the said assessours haue assessed & indented with the said colyonres; and the said colyonres shall be beholden to delyuer there parte of the same indenture vnto the forsaid chaumberleyns assone as thei haue gadered any soche taske, tallage or subsidie. And also the said chaumberleyns shall receyue a copy of all maner writinges which shall passe vnder the comone seall & vnder the seall of th'office of mairalte; and the said copyes to be entred of recorde be ouersighte of the said chaumberleyns, and than soche writinges so enseled to be deliuered; and that all actes & ordenaunces made & to be made be the semble for gouernaunce & encres of the cite be entired of record be ouersight of the said chaumberleyns. And also the said chaumberleyns & eche of them shall haue be vertu and exercise of there office auctorite frely with oute interupcion to aske in euery comon counsell as them or either of them semeth expedient for the comone all recordes that arn & shall be presented, aswell aforn meyre, shirreves and coroners, as aforn justice of the pes in the cite, for the yere or tyme being, and exercise and execucion of all & singuler other articles reherced beforn longyng to th'office of chaumberleyns. And of all sommes of money receyued in the forme aforesaid the said chaumberleyns joyntely ne seuerally shall not be compelled to paye no parcell therof with oute assent of a comone counsell and a warant directe to the said chaumberleyns enseled in a comone counsell vnder the signet of the maire for the tyme beyng and the seal of iiij most sufficiant comoners beyng in the same comone counsell. And also the said chaumberleyns of all & singuler sommes of money in the forme aforesaid receyued & payed shall accownte therof onys in the yere accordyng to th'ordenaunce of the cite. And also the said chaumberleyns shall haue a seall apropred to there office to ensele seche writinges as longeth to there office: that is, to wite, copyes of fredom graunted vnto citezeins vnder [*interlineated*: the maires seall of office or of shrreves with the chaumberleyns seall on the bakside therof] and acquitances of receytz of paymentz and of legaces and of all & singuler other thinges that cometh or parteneth to there office. And that all singuler officeres, of what degre or condicion that thei or any of them be, shall from this day forward be payed alonly be the said chaumberleyns or be on of them of soche rewarde, wages or salerye as is, or shall be, dewe vnto them or to any of them at the halfe yere and non rather, and be non other whatsoeuer officer. And ferthermore it is graunted, ordeyned & estabelisshed that the said chaumberleyns and either of them shall exercise and execute all & singuler other grauntes, constitucions and ordenaunces partenyng to there office, as is comprehended & specified in a certen composicion made in the ij⁵ yere of the regne of Kyng Henry the v^te on Seynt Valentynes day [*14 February 1415*].² In recorde and witnesse of all & singuler premisses to th'one parte of this indenture tripartite remaynyng toward the said chaumberleyns the seall of th'office of the mairalte of the said cite is sette; and to the ij⁵ parte of the said indenture tripartite toward the mair that is & shall be after in the cite also remaynyng the seall of th'office of

---

2 *RCN*, i, p. 104.

chaumberleyns is sette; and also the thridde parte of the said indenture tripartite abidyng vnder the kepyng of the iiij clauers of the said cite for the yere beyng with the seall of the offices of the mairalte and chaumberleyns is mad myghti. Dat', inacted and delyuered in a comown counsell the place and day beforn rehereced in the xxvij^ti yere of the regne of Kyng Herry the sixte [*1448–9*].

Appendix II

Robert Raynbald's expenses
during Kett's Rebellion, 1549

[*NCR, 18A/7, f. 301*^{*v*}] **Other** mynute expenses hade & payd betwyxt Mydsomer & Mighelmes in the tyme of thys accompt of, for and by reason of a commocon steryd & reysed of the comon pepyll of Norff' and Norwiche and inkennelld vpon Mushold Hethe [*Mousehold Heath*] and in Thorpe Wood & in the place cald Leonardes [*the former priory of St Leonard*] therunto adioyning *& cetera*:[1]

/*July*/ **In primis** the ix day of July to Edmond Pynchyn for his costes rydyng to London in post and from thense to Wynsore [*Windsor*] to the kynges cownsell with letters concernyng the rysyng of the sayd pepyll: xl*s*[2]

Item to John Revell the yonger for an horse, sadyll & brydyll for the sayd Pynchyn: vij*s*

Item payd to an other man for his paynis, costes and horse hyer rydyng with letters for the same cause to Sir Roger Townesend: v*s* ii ij*d*[3]

Item to the iiij^{de} man for leke causes rydyng with lettyrs to Syr Wyllyam Paston knyght: ij*s*[4]

Item for drynke in the cownsell chambyr the ix^{te} and x^{te} days of July: vij*d*

Item to dyuerse persons ronnyng of erandes in those days sondry wayes & tymes: vj*d*

Item gaf in reward the xiij day of July to Pursevant Grove who brought a commyssyon to Master Watson vnder the gret seale of Inglond for refourmacon of dyuers thynges: xl*s*[5]

---

1 For background to the rebellion, see D. MacCulloch, 'Kett's Rebellion in Context', *Past & Present*, 84 (1979), pp. 36–59; Wood, 'Kett's Rebellion', pp. 277–99; and *idem*, *The 1549 Rebellions*, chapter one.

2 On 1 July Protector Somerset had summoned the leading gentry of Norfolk and other counties to Windsor to discuss measures for the suppression of uprisings in the West Country. There was, therefore, a lack of local leadership when Kett's contingent of Norfolk rebels arrived at Bowthorpe, just outside Norwich, on 9 July: Wood, *The 1549 Rebellions*, p. 50.

3 See above, p. 267 note 566.

4 See above, p. 268 note 568.

5 The commission, announced by Protector Somerset on 8 July, was to continue previous

Item to Pynchyns wyff for brede & drynke in the cownsell *chambyr* that <the> day & for candyll lyght above & bynethe, the cownsell syttyng all that day & nyght tyll after mydnyght: xviij*d*

[*f. 302*] **Item** for a man & ij horses to brynge the forsayd pursevant to Attylburghe the xiiij day at nyght: iiij*s*[6]

Item the same day to Longe Lawrens for a payer shoos by commandment of the cownsell: xij*d*

Item payd in that monythe for mendyng the locke on Coslany gates and a newe keye ther: xij*d*

Item to Master Sywhat for mendyng of ij lockes on Seynt Awstens gates & ij newe keys ther: xvj*d*

Item to Grene for leke chargis at Conysford gates and ij newe keys ther: xvj*d*

Item to John Ely for mendyng the locke on the Brasen Tower and a newe key ther: viij*d*

Item for certen newe keys & mendyng lockes and yron worke at other sondry gates: ij*s* vij*d*

Item gaf in reward on Mary Magdalen evyn to Master Yorke harrold at armes, viij peces of good [*sic*] cald soueraigns by commandement of the cownsell: iiij *li*[7]

Item payd to ij men that made that nyght after vj^{xx} pyllettes of gonshotte: xvj*d*

Item for mete & drynke for them that nyght: viij*d*

Item for wood, astyll and candyll: xij*d*

Item for ij C xiiij *libr'* lede at vs C: xs viij*d*

Item for a bundell of large brown paper dyvydyd amonges all the gonners that nyght: ij*s*

Item for xv *libr'* of matchis dyvydyd amonges all the sayd gonners at viij*d*: xs

Item to Lambert for iij stavys to make ladylles and sponges for the gonnys: vj*d*

[*f. 302^v*] **Item** to Lowthe for xiiij bolles hade that nyght to Bysshops gates to carye erthe to rampere the gates: xxj*d*

Item for iiij^{or} newe sholvys that war lost ther: ij*s*

Item to Raphe Marsham for ij sholvys & to Master Grey for oon sholve that war borowd that nyght: xviij*d*

---

inquiries into the illicit enclosure of common land, one of the principal grievances of rebels throughout the country: Russell, *Kett's Rebellion*, pp. 25–6; Wood, *The 1549 Rebellions*, p. 50. For the 'redoubtable' Robert Watson (d. by 1559) and his subsequent involvement with the rebels, see MacCulloch, *Thomas Cranmer*, pp. 433–4, 456; *HoP, 1509-1558*, iii, pp. 560–1.

6 In late June a crowd had destroyed enclosures at Attleborough, some sixteen miles to the south west of Norwich: Wood, *The 1549 Rebellions*, p. 60.

7 Bartholomew Butler (d. 1566), York herald at arms, was sent by Protector Somerset to negotiate with the rebels, who declined to accept the offer of a royal pardon that he made to them on 21 July and were duly denounced by him as traitors. These dramatic events prompted the mayor and aldermen to place the city on a defensive footing and close the gates: Wood, *The 1549 Rebellions*, pp. 64–5. For Butler, see W.H. Godfrey and A. Wagner, *The College of Arms, Queen Victoria Street* (1963), p. 302.

Item to Surman for iij newe shoos set vpon the accomptantes horse that nyght at mydnyght: ix*d*

Item to Butfeld wyffe for ij dossen bowstrynges for the bowes in the guyldhalle: viij*d*

Item to ij men that caryed a pece of ordynaunce to the old comon stathe yarde: viij*d*

Item to dyuers men for plates, nayles, stavis & lambys skynnis for ladylles & sponges and for makyng of them to dyuers men: iij*s* vj*d*

Item for caryage of Sir Wylliam Pastons ij gret gonnys from the comon stathe to the castyll: xvj*d*

Item to Andrewe Qwashe for ij plates with certen nayles delyuered to Thomas Warlowe & for other ij plates & nayles delyuered to Robert Stephynson for makyng of ladylles for gonnys: ij*s*

Item for ij gret coynes for the forsayd gonnys: viij*d*

Item for a bondell of small brown paper sent to the castyll & comon stathe to shote certen yron gonnys that came from <Ga> Caster [*Caister*] Halle [*near Great Yarmouth*]: xij*d*

Item for matche sent thyther ij *libr'*: xvj*d*

Item for drynke for the gonners ther: iiij*d*

Item for lynpyns for dyuers gonnys: iiij*d*

[*f. 303*] **Item** to a man of the country for his too hand staffe to make a sponge for the gon at the old comon stathe: ij*d*

Item for drynke for the ij brothern of the Applyardes who wachyd that place that nyght: ij*d*

Item for drynke for Master Thomas Godsalve & a gret company of others that kept Sir Wylliam Pastons gret peces that nyght in the castyll yarde: vj*d*

Item to Brays man & an other man that waytyd vpon the accomptant all that nyght, caryeng of gon powder, sholvys, bolles, stavys and other the forsayd thynges to the places wher they war occupyed: viij*d*

/*Magdalen Day*/ **Item** here ys to be notyd vpon the next day, beyng Mary Magdalen day,[8] the accomptantes servyce don the nyght byfore & specyally for makyng of the gon shote was bewrayd by John Fyshman to traytour Ket, so that he sent to my howse abought the nombyr of iiij*xx* men, of whiche nombyr Robert Ysod, tanner, John Barker, bocher, Echard, myller of Laknam [*Lakenham*], and oon Pryowur of Heyham [*Heigham*] war cheffe mesengers, whiche persons with ther ffellows caryed the accomptant to the guyldhalle and ther tooke awaye oon hole barrell with gon powder & a remnant of an other barrell that beleft the nyght byfore and certen *yron* pyllettes & lede pyllettes that seruyd for the yron slyng and certen morres pyekes that lay ouer the sembly chambyr & compellyd the accomptant to pay for lyne and a mawnde to cary the sayd pelffer: vj*d*

[*f. 303ᵛ*] **Item** they cam ageyn to the accomptantes howse and tooke from thense vj*xx* pyllettes of lede that war made the nyght byfore and also they toke from hym in corn powdur & serpentyn powder of hys own goodes to the sum of vj *li* & ode money; &

---

8 That is 22 July, when the city fell to the rebels.

besydes that compellyd hym to paye for a newe ferkyn to put in the gon shotte: v*d*; & for lyne to trusse and carry ther pelfer wythe: iij*d* – viij*d*

Item the next day, beyng the xxiij of July, a gret sorte of the same company with others to the nombyr of an C persons at the lest came ageyn to the accomptantes howse & toke awaye of his own goodes these parcelles folowyng: ij bowes, iij sheffe of arrowes with casses & gyrdylles, iiij Alman halberdes, ij blacke bylles, certen clubbys and stavys, ij Almayn ryvettes, as fayer as any war in Norwiche, and a jacke of fustyan, and caryed the accomptant away with them to Mushold to haue hym to the tre[9] for makyng of the forsayd gonshotte; and by the way he intretyd them so that they caryed hym to Norwiche bothe, where he gaf them for remyssyon for goyng to the tree: iij*s* iiij*d*

/*Lord markques*/ **Item** payd in the tyme of my lord marqwes beyng in the cyte[10] for stavys, plates, skynnis, nayles, bolles, basketes, sholvys, mattockes, a barrell of bere at the crosse, candyll all nyght ther, pytche, rosen, tallowe, ropys, wood /*nullus*/ [*f. 304*] ffor fyers in the market, caryeng a dede horse out of the market, with many other charges in the day and nyght, whose particlers it was not possybyll to wright nor to remembyr, as the tyme requeryd: xxxiij*s*

Item for a newe rope for the parcolas of Bestrete gates to Walter Feere: iij*s* vj*d*

Item to Thomas Poye for fechyng therof & settyng on: iiij*d*

/*My Lord of Warwicke*/ **Item** payd in the tyme of my lord of Warwykes beyng in the cite[11] these parcelles folowyng:

In primis payd for lede ij C iij quarteres xj *libr'* delyuered the fyrst nyght to the masters of the ordnaunce to make gon shotte, for so moche as the shot of dyuers peces war takyn by the rebelles the fyrst nyght, at vs C: xiiij*s* iij*d*

Item to ij men that sought for fremasons and joyners to make mowldes: viij*d*

Item for ffreston wherof was made mowldes & shote: xij*d*; for wood & astyll to melt ther lede: xij*d*; and to Stephyn Screvener for howse romythe: xij*d* – iij*s*

---

9 Raynbald is here referring to Robert Kett's celebrated 'Oak of Reformation' on Mousehold Heath, before which popular justice was dispensed and order maintained: Wood, 'Kett's Rebellion', pp. 280-1. Although the extent of looting was undoubtedly exaggerated, the homes of some prominent figures were, indeed, targeted: Moreton, 'A Break-In at Norwich', pp. 387-98.

10 William Parr (d. 1571), marquis of Northampton, reached Norwich with a royal army of 1,500 men on 31 July, but following a series of unexpectedly violent confrontations with the rebels on 1 August, when Lord Sheffield was killed, he rapidly withdrew: Wood, 'Kettt's Rebellion', pp. 280–1, 287–91, 298.

11 John Dudley (d. 1553), earl of Warwick, arrived outside Norwich with a force of as many as 6,500 men, including foreign mercenaries and local gentry, on 23 August, and on the following day sent his herald on an abortive attempt to negotiate with the rebels. Three days and nights of 'vicious street fighting' ensued, during which the rebels torched the south east of the city, but the arrival of reinforcements enabled Warwick to crush the uprising with great brutality. He remained in the city until about 9 September: Wood, *The 1549 Rebellions*, pp. 67–9, 72.

Item for xvj *libr'* candyll brent abought the crosse in the market the iiij^or fyrst nyghtes: ij*s* iiij*d*

Item for a pece of tymbyr & makyng of a payer of gallows at the crosse: viij*d*

Item to ij men that caryed the cyte crome[12] to the comon stathe whan yt was on ffyer: iiij*d*

Item payd to Bery Cartes for ij barrelles bere dronke at the crosse in the market amonges the soldyers *as* they came home out of the feld after that ys [*sic*] was wonne: xij*s*[13]

[*f. 304*] **Item** payd for the chargis of beryeng of xlix men that war hangyd at the crosse in the market, for makyng pyttes and caryeng to them: iij*s* ix*d*[14]

Item for mendyng of a leddyr that was broken at the crosse with hangyng of men: iij*d*

/*Rewardes*/ **Item** to a man that gatherd to guether ten *di'* C wightes & caryed them to an howse, whiche war scaterd & caryed awaye out of the crane howse at the comon stathe whan yt was brent: iiij*d*

Item to other ij men that getherd to guether & caryed to the guyldhalle certen yron worke that was fownde at the comon stathe & at dyuers gates of the cyte that war brent: viij*d*

Item gaffe in rewarde to Master Norry harwaurd at armys with my lord the erle of Warwicke: iij *li* vj*s* viij*d*[15]

Item to Master Blewmantyll harward: xl*s*[16]

Item to ij trompeters that same tyme: iiij *li*

Item payd to Henry Wodrof, laborer, attendyng vpon the accomptant xiiij days whyle my lord of Warwike was in the cyte, ronnyng of erandes, helpyng to melte the gon shote, caryeng of wood, moche tendyng to the masters of the ordynaunce, with moche turmoylyng worke, bothe nyght & day, at vj*d*: vij*s*

Item payd for fechyng of an yron gon to the guyldhalle whiche the accomptant fownde /*nullus*/ [*f. 305*] in the barly without Seynt Awstens gates the next day after the feld,[17] whiche in the nyght after he causyd to be conveyd in to a berne tyll after Myhelmes, & for howse rome & paynes ther payd: xij*d*

---

12 The crome would have been used to pull down burning buildings and create a firebreak.

13 That is the pitched battle at Dussindale, to the south of Mousehold Heath on 27 August, between the rebels and the earl of Warwick's troops: A. Carter, 'The Site of Dussindale', *NA*, 39 (1987), pp. 54–62.

14 The hangings took place on Warwick's entry into Norwich on 24 August: Wood, *The 1549 Rebellions*, pp. 67–8.

15 Sir Gilbert Dethick (d. 1584), Norroy and Ulster king of arms, was sent by Warwick to negotiate with the rebels on 24 August, but was humiliatingly rebuffed: *ODNB*, xv, pp. 922–3; Wood, 'Kett's Rebellion', pp. 281–3.

16 Edmund Atkinson (d. 1570), Bluemantle pursuivant: Godfrey and Wagner, *College of Arms*, p. 155.

17 See Appendix III.

/After my lord departid the cite/ **Item** payd to Henry Wodrof & Andrewe Robynson, laborers, makyng clene the market place after my lord was gon, yche of them xxiiij days; & to John Angell, laborer, xij days makyng clene & lodyng of cartes, at v*d* a day euery of them: xxv*s*

Item to Robert Rogers, laborer, makyng clene vyrounde the guyldalle without and also all the ledes, chambers & prysons, whiche war very sore noyed, xj days at v*d* a day: iiij*s* vij*d*

Item to Andrewe Robynson sonne helpyng hym & the other laborers xiiij days at iiij*d*: iiij*s* vij*d*

Item to John Cadbye for caryeng of lxij lodes mucke out of the market place at ij*d* *ob'* a lode: xij*s* xj*d*

Item to yong Ketryngam for xxiiij lodes: v*s*

Item to old Ketryngam for fourty lodes: viij*s* iiij*d*

Item to Henry Carter for xxij lodes: iiij*s* vij*d*

Item to William Thrower for xxxiiij lodes: vij*s* j*d*

Item to Edmond Hubbard for lxvj lodes: xiij*s* ix*d*[18]

Item more to hym for xxiiij lodes that came out of the guyldhall & prysons and from a bought that place without: v*s*

Item payd to dyuers men for sholvys, mattockes, baskettes, bolles, treys, wode, candyll, */nullus/* [*f. 305ᵛ*] drynke, brede, mete, cariages, ropys, nayles, menys labores & an C leke thynges not possybyll to be wryten particlerly, spent at my lord of Warwikes & my lorde Marqweys comyng for ramperyng of gates, stretes, lanys, dyekes, and abought stanching of the fyer in Conysford, with many other chargis requerid at dyuers menys hondes after the departing of the forsayd from the cyte ij lordes [*sic*]: iiij *li* iiij*s* ij*d*

Item to Sander Clarke & other laborers makyng clene the comon halle, howses & cloyster, whiche war wonderfully sore noyed with horse mucke, & makyng clene all the comon halle lane, layeng part of the mucke in the cloyster yarde and part caryed in to the strete, in all chargis at that place: xxij*s* v*d*[19]

Item to Cadby for caryeng of ten lodes of mucke out of the lane ther: ij*s* j*d*

/At Myhelmes/ **Item** payd to Pynchyns wyf for brede, drynke, frute & other thynges for Master Mayer, his brothern & others in the cownsell howse the xxᵗⁱ day of July last past: ij*s* iiij*d*[20]

---

18 In the right-hand margin, the number of loads has been added up in Arabic numerals, giving a total of 240.

19 In an earlier part of the account, Raynbald claimed 6*s* 8*d* spent on the removal of 38 loads of muck from streets and cockeys to the north of the river (where there had been heavy fighting) and around the common hall, which had been 'sore noysed with the kynges provision ther'. He effected other minor repairs and allocated 64*s* in compensation to one of the tenants who had made good further damage: NCR, 18A/7, ff. 292ᵛ, 295–5ᵛ.

20 Russell, *Kett's Rebellion*, p. 74, suggests that this entry should be dated 21 July, when York herald confronted the rebels, but the mayor (Thomas Codde) and aldermen may well have met on his arrival, the day before.

Item more to hyr for brede, drynke, mete, wyne, frute & other thynges for my lord Marqwes in the cownsell chambyr immedyatly after his entrans in to the cyte: iiij*s* viij*d*

Item to Norman for suger j *libr'* spent ther: xiiij*d*

[*f. 306*] **Item** to Master Wardeyn for iij menys labours that he payd on Mary Magdalen evyn for caryeng of erthe at Byshopps gates: xij*d*

Item for byrchyn bromys occupyed in the market place, comon halle & comon stathe whan they war made clene: vj*d*

Item to Gabryell, the peynter, for newe refresshyng of a tabyll of the kynges armys & newe peyntyng & guyldyng an other tabyll with the kynges armys that before hade Seynt Georges armys & for settyng vp the raggyd staffe[21] in syluer paper at all the gates of the cyte: vij*s*

Item for settyng vp the forsayd ij tabylles at Westwike & Seynt Stephyns gates: viij*d*

Item to Master Awsten Steward, alderman, vpon a byll for stoppyng of certen holes in the town walles nere Pokethorpe gates & Magdalen gates: iiij*s* j*d*

> **Summa xxxvj *li* xs vij*d***

[*Raynbald went on to claim an additional £175 in expenses arising from the 'commocon'. They included repairs to the guildhall, to many of the city gates and stretches of the walls, and to communal property outside the walls (notably the Town Close); £89 spent on Augustine Steward's suit for confirmation of the royal charter; £24 on attendant travel to London; and various miscellaneous outgoings, such as the payment of a surgeon for treating soldiers wounded in the skirmish in Bishopsgate on 1 August.*][22]

---

21 The arms of the earl of Warwick were a bear with a ragged staff, which the aldermen also displayed prominently over their doors as a sign that 'the forces of order had returned': Wood, *The 1549 Rebellions*, p. 71.

22 See Russell, *Kett's Rebellion*, pp. 184–96.

Appendix III
Inventory of moveables
belonging to the commonalty, 1552

[*NCR, 18A/7, f. 345*] *Memorandum* that here after folowithe an inuentory of all the movabylles bylongyng to the comialtie of the cyte of Norwiche made at Myhelmes in the iiij[th] yere of the reygn of owur soueraign lord Kyng Edward the sexte [*1552*] by Robert Raynbald, late chamberleyn of the sayd cyte, & *cetera*:

In the guyldhalle vowte[1]

In primis certen sawen sparrys, ffurryn sparrys, okyn postes and other tymbyr fytte for a bothe and for a wrostlyng place to be inclosed with rayles therto bylongyng

Item a sygne of a castyll sometyme bylongyng to the common inne

Item a gret tymbyr beame with a payer of yron chekes

Item ij whelys sometyme bylongyng to a gonne cald a slyng

Item oon whele bylongyng to the cokestole

In the halle

Item a cokestole without whelys

Item an howse crome of yron with a ffurryn shafte

Item a pece of tymbyr bownde with yron at the gret ende, whiche sometyme dyd bylong to an yron slyng

In the clynke

Item oon old tabyll with iiij feete and ij old ffourmys, the oon loose and the other nayled fast

Item an hambyr, a ponche, an eye and a blocke with a scythe, whiche parcelles ar delyuerd yerely to the shrevys by indenture

In the next howse

Item an yron gonne cald a slyng, whiche gonne Robert Raynbald fownde in the barly without Sent Awstens gates after the commocon and gaf yt to the comialte

---

1 For the layout of the guildhall, see I. Dunn and H. Sutermeister, *The Norwich Guildhall: A History and Guide* (Norwich, n.d.).

[*f. 345ᵛ*] In the chappell

Item a payer of chales parcell guylt with a patent conteynyng xij oz *di'*

Item a booke cald the Booke of Comon Prayer[2]

Item a newe Bybyll of the gyft of Sir Robert Dowe, chaplen ther[3]

Item ij alter clothis of dyaper & oon of course canvas, all iij very sore worn

Item a sleyvd surples

Item a cope of rede worsted imbrodryd with wrytynges

Item ij stolys to leane vpon & an old chest

Item a lytyll sacry belle

Item a belle hangyng in a frame without the chappell doore

In the sembly chambyr

Item a chekyr at the ovyr ende

Item iiij newe ffourmys ouerwharte the howse

Item ij newe long fourmys on the ij sydes

Item ij newe shorte fourmys, the oon stondyng next the old cownsell howse & the other next the newe cownsell howse dore

Item an old hutche ageynst the wyndowe

Item iij fframys that sometyme dyd bylong to iij potgonnys

In the old cownsell howse

Item certen bookes of recordes, inrolmentes, accomptes an[*d*] suche other leke thynges

In the newe cownsell howse

Item a grene clothe lynyd with canvas lyeng ouer the chekyr

Item a blacke coffer lectorn facon

Item a newe fourme stondyng next the dore

[*f. 346*] **Item** dyuerse bookes of the kynges statutes, of the statutes of the cyte, of the lybertes, <reuewe> revenews, rentes, recordes & other matters

Item a yarde wonde of brasse

In the chambyr ouer the sembly chambyr

Item an old chest bownde with yron and old hutche

Item ij trowes made to cary in fyshe

Item an old tabyll with ij old trustylles

Item a cresset with a ffurren shaft

In the chambyr ouer the old cownsell howse

Item a dobyll poley of yron with a bolt

Item ij brondes, oon with Seynt Georges crosse the other with a letter N

Item an old lache panne

---

2 Its use was made compulsory in March 1549: MacCulloch, *Thomas Cranmer*, chapter ten.

3 For Dowe, see *MFS*, pp. 220, 238, 302 note 94.

Item a lytyll yron beame with a payer of tymbyr scales

Item an old chest bownde with yron & therin certen evydences bylongyng to the comon halle

Item certen brasse wyghtes, that ys to saye oon *di'* C, oon quarter, oon vij *li*, oon iij *li*, oon ij *li* & oon flatte ponder conteynyng viij *li*, all havyng the kynges armys vpon them

Item certen sholvys in the same howse

In the menys pryson

Item a payer of stockes fastyd with a gret cheane

Item a brasse potte and a tryvet of yron

In the womens pryson

Item a payer of stockes

Item an other payer of stockes without the dore of the same pryson

In the vowte vnder the menys pryson

[*f. 346ᵛ*] **Item** a gret blocke with an yron stapyll and a cheane to <tr> tye prysoners vnto

In the custody of the chamberleyns

In primis a seale of syluer bylongyng to ther office

Item a payer of waffer yrons

Item a cope of <glothe> clothe of goold wrowght vpon whyte

Item an hopper to ffye greyne wythe

Item a boxe with certen indentures: and fyrst an indenture with an oblygacon of a lease grauntyd to Thomas Warner of the newe mylles & Heyham [*Heigham*] mylles

Item an indenture with an oblygacon of a lease grauntyd to Johnn Bronde of a kylyard in Southe Conysford

Item an indenture with an oblygacon of a lease grauntyd to Wylliam Waller of Seynt Maryes churche

Item an indenture of a lease grauntyd to John Derne of parcell of the same churche yarde

Item an indenture with an oblygacon of Richard Flecher, alderman, for a lease grauntyd hym of the clothe halle

Item an indenture of a lease grauntyd to Master Nycholas Sywhat, alderman, for a certen grownd, water and ffyshynges

Item an indenture of a lease grauntyd to William Haste, alderman, of a tenement in the kynges hondes in Cougate strete

Item an indenture of a lease grauntyd to Hewe Coplond of a tenement in Coblerrowe

Item an indenture with an oblygacon of a lease grauntyd to Bryan Doront of an other tenement in the same rowe

[*f. 347*] **Item** an indenture of a lease grauntyd to John Thurston of a tenement cald the Murage Loft

Item an indenture of a lease grauntyd to John Lynne of a pece of comon grownde next Helle gates

Item an indenture of a lease grauntyd to Wylliam Alman of a pece of grounde nowe newe buyldyd ouer the comon halle gate

Item an indenture of a lease grauntyd to John Clarke of a pece of grounde late parcell of the prechyng yarde ther

Item an indenture of a lease grauntyd to Robert Foxe of an entry at the est ende of the comon halle chappell

Item an indenture of a lease grauntyd to John Quashe of parcell of the gret gardeyn byonde the water

Item an indenture of a lease grauntyd to Wylliam Morront of an other parcell of the same gardeyn

Item an indenture of a lease grauntyd to Master Edmond Wood, alderman, of an other parcell of the same gardeyn

Item an indenture of a lease grauntyd to Wylliam Marche of an other parcell of the same gardeyn

Item an indenture of a lease grauntyd to John Byrche of an other parcell of the same gardeyn

Item ij indentures of a lease grauntyd to Henry Bakon, alderman, and Thomas Querles of a chappell & a tenement ther, parcell of the same

Item an indenture of a lease grauntyd to John Baker and his wyff of an other parcell of the same gardeyn and of a tenement next the river, parcell of the comon halle

In the handes of George Harryson, cowper
Item a bushell off brasse – to syse by[4]
Item a gallon off brasse – to syse by

[*f. 347*^v] In the custody of master mayer
In primis an hatte of crymsyn velvet for the sword berer
Item <with the hyltes and pomell> a sworde, the hyltes and pomell syluer and dobyll guylt
Item an other sworde, the hyltes & pomell syluer swage guylt
Item a scaberd of riche clothe of goold set with perles with a gret chape of syluer dobyll guylte
Item a scaberd of clothe of goold chekerd with a lytyll chape of syluer guylt
Item a scaberd of purpyll velvet with ij letters of H dobyll crownyd & a chape, all syluer dobyll guylte
Item a scaberd of crymsyn velvet with ij letters of H dobyll crownyd & a chape, all syluer dobyll guylt
Item a joynyd boxe of waynscote to kepe in the sayd scaberdes

---

4 That is to determine that all measures used commercially in the city adhered to the correct legal specifications, and did not defraud the public. The capacity of the bushel, gallon and quarter was fixed by act of parliament: Connor, *Weights and Measures*, pp. 155–9.

Item a mace of armys of syluer and dobyll guylt wrought vpon crystall and set with stonys

Item an other lesser mace of syluer dobyll guylt

Necessaryes bylongyng to the ryver
Item a mucke boote in fferme of Richard Walpoole
Item a payer of newe sheres for the ryver cuttyng with an hede & forelockes & other thynges therto bylongyng
Item an other leke payer of sherys in the custody of the myller of the newe mylles

Necessaryes for workmen
[*f. 348*] **Item** a ffurryn leddyr of xx^{ti} stavys lyeng at the comon halle
Item a bosse to drawe vp morter inne
Item a cage to swepe the comon halle wythe
Item a rabytyng stoole
Item iij ffurryn mastes wherof ij be at the pales

Vtensylles at the comon inne
In primis ij newe benchys in the halle, ij spyers and trustylles set in the grownde wherevpon the tabylles lye
Item oon lope of yron in the glasse wyndowe in the sayd halle
Item shelvys vyrownde the buttry
Item ij benchys in the parlowur and a closse spyer
Item v lopys of yron in the glasse wyndows in the chambyrs
Item loopys to euery wyndowe in the place that is not glasyd
Item dore loopys to all the dores in the place
Item a locke to the strete gate, a locke to the strete dore and a locke to the halle dore, a locke to the gret howse next Seynt Gregoryes, a locke to the dore of the same howse in to the strete and a locke to the chambyr ouer that howse

At the comon stathe
In primis a cheane of yron ovyr the ryvyr
Item a capstayn to drawyt yt vp with all thynges therto bylongyng
Item a lede hangyng in a furnace
Item at the key syde a crane with brasses and gogeons and all other thynges longyng to the same
Item hempyng rope to the same crane newe made
[*f. 348ᵛ*] **Item** a gret beame of yron with an old payer of scalys with yron chenys
Item ix half C wightes clade in brasse and oon halff C wight of yron: *summa* v C

At the tenements late lord suffrigantes
In primis in the fyrst tenement at the corner next Tomlond ij benchis that be movabyll, that ys to saye in the halle oon & in the parlour oon
Item in the second tenement toward Conysford oon benche
Item at the welle seruyng the sayd ij tenementes a pulley with chekes of yron and ij stoppys with <chekes> cheanys & hoopys of yron

Item in the ij^{de} tenement oon benche

Item in the iiij^{te} tenement oon benche

Item in the v^{te} tenement oon benche

Item at the welle seruyng the sayd iij tenementes a pulley with chekes of yron and ij stoppys with hoopys & chenys of yron

Item at the vj^{te} tenement no benche

Item at the vij^{te} tenement oon benche

Item in the viij^{te} tenement, whiche ys the corner house next the late Gray Fryers ij benchis, that is to saye in the halle & parlowur

Item at the ix^{te} tenement oon benche

Item in the x^{te} tenement oon benche

Item at the welle servyng the sayd v tenementes a pulley with chekys of yron, oone stoppe with hoopis & chenys of yron

Item at the tenement next Seynt Maryes churche, late Arnoldes, to the welle ther oon stoppe with hoopys & a chene of yron

At the newe mylles

[*f. 349*] *In primis* at the fyrst mylle cald the northe mylle ij stonys; at the second mylle cald the myddyll mylle ij stonys; at the iij^{de} mylle cald the southe mylle ij stonys, whose thyknes and brede are expressyd in the indentures of the lease grauntyd to Thomas Warner

Item vpon the ij brode dores of the mylle howses iiij gret yron stapelles and ij barrys of tymbyr therto bylongyng

Item on the dam brydge dore a locke

Item in the parlowur of the same place ij benchys & a closse spyer

Item in the wyndows of the same parlowur xv lyghtes of glasse

Item in the halle ij benches, a syngyll spyer and vij lyghtes of glasse in the same howse

Item a lede hangyng in the brew howse

Item a locke on the parlowur dore, a locke on the buttry dore, a locke on the chambyr dore, a locke on the halle dore, a locke on the brew howse dore

In the chappell at the comon halle

/*Comon Halle*/ *In primis* iiij deskys ffyxid above the steppys

Item ij long deskys bynethe the steppis not fyxid

Item ij dobyll stoolys bynethe them not fyxid

Item oon old long fourme and ij short fourmys

Item a coffer with iiij feete stondyng in the mydde chappell

Item ij long lectorns and ij turnyng lectorns

Item a beame that the roode sometyme stoode on

Item ij long plankes that war the crosse that the roode was nayled on

Item a lampe of latten with a wight of lede in the rof of the chappell

[*f. 349^v*] **Item** a stole of yron for oon to syt on

Item a payer of organs stondyng vpon a scaffold ffyxid at the chappelles ende next the stepyll

Item a newe fourme stondyng by the organs
Item a payer of joynyd stayers to go vp to the organs

In the vestry ther
Item ij alter clothys of dyaper
Item a corparas casse of whyte damaske with a clothe in yt
Item a vestment of grene velvet with an awbe therto
Item a vestment of blewe wachet with flowers of goold and lynyd with sylke and an awbe therto
Item a coberd ffyxed and an old benche
Item iij peces of hangynges of blacke worsted imbrodred with dede bodys rysyng out of gravis
Item a booke cald the Booke of Comen Prayers
Item a newe Bybylle

In the stepyll ther
Item ij belles hangyng in fframys with ij ropys longyng to them
Item a pulpet of waynscotte newe, whiche ys nowe at Seynt Stephyns churche

In the halle ther
Item an alter stondyng in the nether ende of the sayd halle in the stede of a cubbard
[*f. 350*] **Item** benchys betwixt all the pyllers ffyxyd
Item vij tabylles of popyll plankes joynyd
Item ij ashyn plankes for tabylles
Item xxx trustylles for x tabylles
Item x ffourmys for x tabylles
Item a coberd of waynscotte viij square
Item ij joynyd tabylles of ffurre for the ouer part
Item vj hye trustylles for the same tabylles
Item ij long ffourmys for the same tabylles
Item ij long footebankes for the benchys ther
Item iiij thycke popyll plankes for heynyng of the benchis
Item a coberd of popyll bourde for plate
Item rayless with tenter hookes for hangynges fyxid vyrownde the halle
Item a scaffold at the west dore with certen loose tymbyr lyeng vpon the same for the wayghtes to stond on
Item a locke on the dore betwyxt the halle & the stepyll
Item a long barre of tymbyr stondyng in a stapylle with a bolt and a forlocke of yron
Item a locke vpon the dore in to the prechyng yarde
Item a locke vpon the dore goyng out of the halle in to the entry next the kechyn

In the pantry
Item ij gret brede hutchis with couers
Item a planke to chyppe brede on
Item a ffurryn sparre to hang on towelles & napkyns

Item shelvys vyrounde the same howse
[*f. 350ᵛ*] **Item** ij lattyses at the ij wyndows
Item a locke to the same dore & a barre of yron on the insyde

In the buttry
Item a gret beryng stole for bere
Item a lesser beryng stole for ale
Item shelvys vyrounde the same howse of okyn plankes
Item iij lattyses at the wyndows
Item a cubbard set in the corner next the buttrace
Item a locke on the <barr> dore & a barre of yron on the insyde
Item on the dore out of the sayd buttry vpon the gret chambyr ij flatte barrys of yron

In the kechyn
Item a gret dresser in the mydde howse
Item an other gret dresser vnder the wyndowe
Item ij gret popyll plankes to laye on trustylles for dressers yf nede shall requere at any tyme
Item a dresser loope with hespys of yron
Item a gret choppyng stocke
Item a gret ston morter
Item ij lattyses at the ij wyndows, a locke on the dore

In the scaldyng howse
Item ij ledes hangyng in ij furnaces
Item a systern of lede
[*f. 351*] **Item** a gret okyn planke to dresse mete on
Item shelvys vyrownde the same howse
Item a dresser loope in to the entry with an hespe of yron
Item the wyndowe ys lattysed with wyer

In the dresser
Item a dresser ffyxyd & made of popyll plankes
Item a choppyng bourde of popyll
Item shelvys vyrounde the same howse
Item a locke on the gret dore next the dresser

In the pastry or backhowse
Item a gret trowe of oke with a couer of popyll
Item an other gret trowe made of popyll plankes and a couer of popyll to the same
Item iij plankes to mowld on aboughte the howse
Item a lattyse to the wyndowe

Item in the bultyng howse
Item a locke on the sayd bultyng howse dore

At the welle ther
Item ij stoppys with hoopys and chenys of yron
Item a pulley with chekys of yron & a bolt to the same
Item a condyte couerd with lede

In the wete larder
Item rayles with xxij fleshe hookes
[*f. 351ᵛ*] **Item** shelvys vyrownd the same howse
Item iij lattyses byfore the wyndows
Item a locke vpon the same dore

In the dry larder
Item iij course of shelvys vyrownd the same howse
Item ij lattyses byfore the wyndows
Item a locke on the same dore

In the cloyster
Item a newe wyndowe stalle with a loope with hookes, hengylles and stapylles, whiche late stode in the ende of Thomas Peckes shoppe, whiche is nowe a cowntyng howse
Item an old wyndowe with barrys of yron

In the tenement next the ij elmys
Item at the welle in the vowte vnder the kechyn a pulley with chekes of yron & ij stoppys with chenys & hoopis of yron
Item a ffayer closse spyer or portall in the parlowur
Item shelvys vyrownd the buttry
Item a lokke on the strete dore
Item a payer of myddyll gates
Item a joynyd seate fframyd without the strete dore
Item a locke on the closset dore cost iij*s* iiij*d*
Item a locke on the buttry dore
Item shelvys vyrownd the kechyn
Item <on> a locke on the dore that go out ouer the cloyster

[*f. 352*] At the crosse in the market
Item ij halff bushelles, an old and a newe
Item a lytyll belle hangyng in oon of the wyndows
Item certen ffreston within the howse ther

In a chambyr at the guyldhalle
Item a gret barre of yron for the carte gate at the comon stathe, whiche is v or vj foote long by estymacon
Item oon gret anker of yron & ij lesser ankers
Item certen hengylles and other yron worke gatherd vp in the same place after the ffyer

Item certen yron that came of the parcolas of Seynt Awstens gates and of Seynt Stephyns gates

Item a brokyn chambyr of a gret gon

Item iij gon stonys and other brokyn yron

Item at Master Sywhates berne certen yron that came of Fybryge gates

General glossary and word list

Works consulted: V. Chinnery, *Names for Things: A Description of Household Stuff, Furniture and Interiors 1500–1700* (Wetherby, 2016); R. Forby, *The Vocabulary of East Anglia* (2 vols, 1830; reprinted Newton Abbot, 1970); H. Kurath and S.M. Kuhn, eds, *Middle English Dictionary* (26 vols, Ann Arbor, Michigan, 1952–2001); L.F. Salzman, *Building in England Down to 1540* (Oxford, 1952); J.A. Simpson and E.S.C. Weiner, eds, *Oxford English Dictionary* (20 vols, Oxford, 1933; revised 1989); D. Starkey, ed., *The Inventory of King Henry VIII* (1998); D. Yaxley, *A Researcher's Glossary of Words Found in Historical Documents of East Anglia* (Dereham, 2003)

Words are here listed alphabetically in the form that appears in the text (as, for example, 'chean' rather than the modern spelling 'chain'), along with their most common variants. Thus, 'y' is often used in the place of 'i' and sometimes 'g' ('yeldehall' as well as 'guyldhalle'); and 'i' and 'j' and 'u' and 'v' are also interchangeable.

abatyng reducing the price

advyson an advowson or the right of presentation to a church or benefice

agenst, ageynst *either* in preparation for (hence **agenst the prest guyld** or in preparation for the feast day of the priests' guild) *or* near

agret, a gret, in grett a term applied to contracts whereby a fixed price is agreed in advance for everything, including materials, labour and workmanship

aldryng poles poles made of alder wood, widely used for scaffolding (*see also* **standerdes**)

Almayn halberdes long spears fitted with axe-heads in the German (**Almayn**) style

Almayn ryvettes a type of light and flexible body armour for infantry, made of overlapping plates that slid on rivets, named after the German armourers who developed it

almery an aumbry or cupboard with a door that could be used as a locker for food

alter, awlter an altar (hence the linen **awlter clothis** used as coverings)

anelyd annealled or tempered in a furnace (hence the **nelyng** or firing of a newly-built oven)

angell a gold coin bearing an image of St Michael and the dragon on the reverse, first minted in 1465 as a new issue of the noble; it was then worth 6s 8d, but its street value had risen to 8s by 1544 (*see also* **nobylle**)

anker, ankyr *either* an anchorite (hence **anker howse** or anchorhold) *or* an iron anchor or plate used to support heavy masonry, such as the hoods or mantels of fireplaces or pieces of timber

anno regni regis Henrici in the year of the reign of King Henry

annuyte a fee or pension paid annually, usually according to the terms of a contract

antycke work carvings or engravings in either the classical style or of ornamental grotesques

antycypacon the name given to a royal commission of June 1545 for the levy in advance, or in anticipation, of the parliamentary subsidy due in February 1546

apuruns ornamental aprons, as worn by the large-scale models of Samson and Hercules carried in civic processions (*see also* **gyantes**)

aras pece a sizeable piece of supporting timber of triangular shape in cross section, often placed diagonally so as to present a sharp edge (arris), which in mills and quays faced the water

armerer an armourer

armyn cotes canvas jackets worn under armour

arreragis arrears or money still owed by the accountant(s), carried over from the end of one account to the beginning of the next

ashyn made of wood from the ash tree (hence **ashyn plankes**)

ashyn shydes shides or strips of ash used to make hook nails

assyse *see* **rente off assis** *and* **syse**

astylles pieces of wood cut or split for use as firewood, thin boards, laths or hooks (*see also* **byllettes**)

augmentacionz, court of augmentacions a court established by the Crown in 1535 to deal with the administrative, financial and legal issues arising from the dissolution of monastic property

aumoner a monastic almoner

aventur a purchase made on sight, as the opportunity arose (hence paving stone bought at Carrow **at aventur as yt laye**)

awbes, awbys albs or long ecclesiastical vestments with sleeves

ayle barrell a barrel used to store ale, having a capacity of about 32 gallons

ayse yard an enclosed place or plot where osiers or willow trees grow (*see also* **oser grounde**)

backhowse *either* a lean-to, room or dwelling at the rear of a property *or* a bake house with an oven for cooking

backsyde the back or rear of a property

badryke a leather strap from which the clapper of a bell hangs

balffrey, barffrey a substantial piece of building timber

balkes baulks or large pieces of timber, sometimes used as tie-beams

bank a long seat or bench

bankettes civic banquets or feasts

barbowur a barber or barber-surgeon

barffrey *see* **balffrey**

barrough, barrowe, borough a wheelbarrow (hence **barowhele** or the wheel of a wheelbarrow and **barrowe spyndylle** to which the wheel is attached)

bast *either* fibrous material, such as hemp, flax or the inner bark of the lime tree, used to make rope *or* the rope itself (*see also* **hempyng rope**)

batorn, batron, batten a square cut plank or smaller piece of squared timber used in flooring and for the reinforcement of heavy doors or gates

battylment, batylment ornamental woodwork in the crenelated style, designed to look like a battlement, as, for example, on the top of a screen

bedde weuers specialist weavers of bedspreads, curtains and hangings made of heavy fabric

bedell a beadle or civic official responsible for keeping order and escorting the mayor

beleft, byleft remaining or left over

bellman, belman town crier

benevolens a personal contribution towards national or local projects (such as converting the Norwich Blackfriars for civic use) made on what was theoretically a voluntary basis, but which often involved an element of coercion

bereres wooden shelves

beryng stole a receptacle with two upright handles through which a long pole could be slotted for carrying ale or beer

best chepe the lowest or cheapest price available

blacke hede ston knapped flint, the cut surface of which appears black (hence a **blacke walle** made of the same material)

blacke plates thin sheets of iron for use in bath houses, where cold water was poured over them once they were red hot to produce steam (*see also* **stewe**)

Black Freres, Fryers the Dominican friary complex on both the south and north banks of the river Wensum, acquired by the city in 1540

blanket white, undyed woollen cloth

blewe cappys blue caps worn by the Norwich military levies as cushioning under their metal skull caps (*see also* **skulles**)

bochers butchers (hence **contry** or **countre bochers**, who came from the surrounding countryside, and **cyte bochers**, who were residents of Norwich and belonged to the Butchers' guild)

bochers pryckes skewers

Bochery the area in the market immediately south of the guildhall where meat was sold by city and country butchers

bochyng mending or making good

bolles bowls

bolsters long stuffed pillows or cushions

boltell, bowtell convex moulding

bonches *see* **sweyes**

bondes iron bands used, for example, to repair broken wheels

bosse a plasterer's tray or hod for carrying mortar

bote *either* a boat *or* a booth, such as those erected for the staging of wrestling matches

botewrite, botewright a boat-wright or maker of boats

bothyn tymbyr timber kept by the chamberlains to build market stalls and temporary, collapsible booths for wrestling and other entertainments

bourde *either* wooden boards *or* the provision of food and sometimes accommodation for workmen, perhaps as part of their contracts (hence **bourdyng hym selff** or paying for his own upkeep)

bower, bowyer a maker of longbows

boylyng howse, office a place where tallow is processed to make soap or candles

bracys, brases, roff brasys pieces of wood inserted diagonally in timber roofs to strengthen the frame; one end of the brace would be morticed into the under surface of the tie-beam (*see* **entertyse**) and the other into a supporting post or 'pendant', resting on a corbel (*see also* **pendons**)

bradde, brade, brodde a thin, long, flat-headed and tapering nail

brasers bracers or leather guards worn by archers to protect the arm

brasyng covering with brass

brayen stocke a block of wood used for beating or crushing, as, for example, when extracting the fibre from hemp

brede *either* the paxbred, a piece of wood carved with a crucifix set under glass that was kissed by persons taking an oath in the guildhall *or* breadth or width (hence **the brede of that howse**)

brede hutchis wooden receptacles or bins for the storage of bread

brekyng ston knapped flint (*see also* **blacke hede ston**)

brenne brine

brent burnt or baked (hence **well brent brycke** or brick baked for longer than usual in the kiln)

broches thatcher's broaches or sharpened lengths of hazel twisted into the shape of a hairpin or fork that were used with sways to secure bunches of straw or reed in place on roofs (*see also* **prykwondes** *and* **sweyes**)

brokely broken reeds, the detritus left behind by reeders and thatchers

bronde an iron brand, such as that bearing the letter 'N' used to mark civic property

bryklyng the process of 'brittening' or trimming and hewing trees immediately after felling

buckram a fine cotton or linen fabric (only later being stiffened with size)

buckyng pruning a quickset hedge to the height of two or three feet to encourage growth (hence to **bucke the fense**)

bultyng howse a place for the sifting or sieving of flour for use in bread or pastry

Burgony glasse high-quality coloured or white glass imported from the Rhine lands of Burgundy

bushell, busshell *either* a bushel or measure for dry goods equivalent in capacity to eight gallons *or* a basket of that size for measuring corn

busshop, busshopp a bishop (hence the **lord busshop** of Norwich)

butment an abutment or the solid part of a wall which supports the lateral pressure of an arch or some other structure (hence a **butment of freston** or freestone)

butte a pack or bundle (hence a **butte of lethyr**)

Buttelerhilles, Buttyr Hylles elevated ground, also known as **Butler** or **Boteleres Hills**, running between the Ber Street and Conesford gates, on the brow of which stood the southern part of the city walls

buttrace, buttrase a buttress

buttry a buttery or place for the storage of ale, bread, butter and cheese

bylle a halberd, comprising a broad, hooked blade with spikes at the top and back mounted on a pole about six feet long (hence **stavyng bylles** or replacing the poles)

byllettes pieces of wood cut or split for use as firewood, hooked nails, laths or the staves of ladders (hence **ashyn byllettes** made of ash)

byndynges, bynys lengths of rope or twine used to secure the thatch at the edge of a roof to prevent it from being detached by the wind

byrchyn bromys brooms made of birch twigs

C, centum *either* one hundred which, when dealing with some commodities, such as nails, might comprise a 'long hundred' of 120, *or* a hundredweight of 112 pounds

cadge, cage the wooden cage next to the guildhall where convicted offenders were put on show

calenderer a worker responsible for smoothing and pressing finished cloth

callough, collough hookes hooks used with hinges for hanging doors (*see* **hengille**)

cancred corroded or eaten away (hence **rustie & cancred harness** or rusty and corroded armour)

canspere of furre a long, angled pole made of deal (wood from the fir tree) used as a shaft for the **howse crome**

cantes sloping, obtrusive surfaces

capper a maker of caps and hoods

cappis metal studs

capstayn a revolving barrel-shaped piece of solid timber that can be set in motion by pushing the horizontal bars attached in order to wind or release a rope or chain (*see also* **cheane**)

caraways sweetmeats or confections containing caraway seeds (hence a box of **caraways & byskettes** or biscuits)

carsey a type of coarse hard-wearing cloth named after the village of Kersey in Suffolk, where it was originally produced

caryar a carter or carrier

casses quivers for arrows (hence **cassyng** or providing quivers)

castill, castyll dyche the massive ditch (39 feet deep and 88 feet wide) constructed across the south bailey of Norwich castle mound in the thirteenth century for defensive purposes, but used in the sixteenth as a site for stalls and booths during public festivities

castill, castyll ffee an area around the castle, previously under royal jurisdiction, the tenements here being charged with a fixed rent (also known as 'the castle fee') payable to the civic authorities from *c.* 1345 onward

castyng the process of removing dirt and other blockages from a cistern, dyke, gutter, road, or stream

casualtie an accident (hence **by casualtie off sodden ffyer** or by accident of sudden fire)

cawusey a causeway

certen, certeyn an annual mass for the dead, the time, place and cost of which, along with the names of the deceased, were determined in advance and therefore 'certain'

chalder a measure of capacity equivalent to 256 gallons, subject to local variations

chales a chalice

chape, chepe, japy *either* the part of a buckle by which it is fastened to a strap (hence **buckill & chepe**) *or* ornamental metal plates or mountings on swords and scabbards, sometimes bearing a heraldic image

Chapel Feldes, Chappell of Feld crofte land belonging to the city next to the college of St Mary in the Fields, to the south west of Norwich

chapter howse the designated meeting place where a monastic community assembled to hear readings from scripture and discuss business

chauntery prest a priest or chaplain paid to celebrate commemorative masses on a regular basis on behalf of a named individual or individuals

cheane the chain that spanned the Wensum at, or just below, the new common staithe and which could be raised or lowered by a capstan to control access to and from the city by boat

cheeffes sheaves or bundles (hence **cheeffes of thakke** or sheaves of thatching material)

cheke either of the outer pieces of a block which enclose a pulley

chekyr the chequered board or cloth (the exchequer) on which accounts were audited in the assembly chamber of the guildhall

chiste a chest

choppyng bourde, stocke a chopping board

Christe Churche the name accorded from 1538 to the former Benedictine cathedral (also sometimes known as **the college** and by its medieval name of **Holy Trynyte**)

chymney an umbrella term used in the sixteenth century to describe a fireplace, mantelpiece and hearth, as well as the chimney proper

cicle *see* **sicle**

civitatis Norwici the city of Norwich

claryfyeng clearing or cleansing (*see also* **fyeng**)

clarystorye a clerestory or the upper storey of the nave walls of a church pierced by windows

clave a vice or holder

clayman a worker in clay employed in the building trade to make floors and walls (*see also* **daubyng**)

clere dette the final sum outstanding in an account after all allowances and expenses have been deducted

clete a cleat or wedge

clothe halle one of the public buildings in the common inn immediately to the north of the market place, where cloth was inspected and sealed

clows cloves

clowtes cloths

clowtyng reinforcing a piece of timber with clouts or nails with short stems and large, flat heads

cloyster a cloister or four-sided covered walkway in a religious institution, having an open arcade or colonnade on the inside

clycke the latch of a gate that can be locked with a key

clynke a cell or room for detaining prisoners

clynke nayles rivets

clyppyd money gold or silver coinage that has been illegally 'clipped' or shaved at the edges and is thus worth less than its supposed value

coffer *either* a chest or container that might be used, for example, to store ecclesiastical vestments *or* an arrangement of sunken panels in a ceiling or vault

cogge whele a cogwheel or toothed wheel used in the mechanism of a mill

cokestole, cooke stole, cookstole a ducking stool erected by the river Wensum at Fyebridge for the punishment of scolds and other female offenders

cokey the name given in Norwich to the city's many streams, which ran along stone-lined, sometimes culverted gutters

colder, coldyr small pieces of stone or rubble (hence **coldryng** or stone-breaking)

coler, coller a 'U' shaped piece of iron used to fasten a gate by hooking over one of the posts

collrake *either* a coal rake, used for raking through the ashes of a dead fire to remove any unburnt pieces of fuel for re-use *or* a rake for spreading grain to prevent it from growing mouldy

comb a measure for dry goods, especially grain, equivalent in capacity to 32 gallons

comialtie the citizenry or freemen of Norwich, who acquired their status by patrimony, apprenticeship or purchase

comon to communicate or discuss matters (hence **to comon with the dukes grace**)

comon closse an enclosed plot of land in civic ownership outside St Stephen's gate, later known as Town Close

comon halle the name given to the nave of the former church (but sometimes the entire southern precinct) of the Blackfriars from 1543, after it had been taken over and refurbished by the city

comon inne a large building complex to the north of the market where foreign merchants could stay and where construction materials were stored by the chamberlains

comon stathes landing stages owned and maintained by the city on the Wensum in Conesford, the 'old', more northerly one, having been acquired in January 1379 and the 'new' just seven months later

comon store facilities for the storage of building materials (**comon stuffe**), new and recycled, in various places for use in civic projects

comyners commoners or the sixty elected members of the common council of the city (*see also* **counsel** *and* **sembly**)

condicte, condyte *either* a wooden track along which a gun carriage could be moved *or* a conduit or aqueduct

condyte money conduct money or cash given to soldiers to defray their expenses when travelling to or from a mobilisation point

contry the county of Norfolk

copyll sparrys *either* a pair of common rafters *or*, more specifically, of principal rafters in a timber framed roof, whose position corresponds to the division of space below into bays (*see also* **pryncypalls**)

corn powdur gunpowder processed into small grains suitable for priming

corporas casse a small chest used for storing the linen cloths (corporals) placed under the consecrated host and wine during the mass

corse a silk band or ribbon, often embroidered with silver or gold, attached to the scabbard of a ceremonial sword

coryer a cordwainer or worker in fine leather, generally for shoes

counsell, cownsell chambyr, howse the room in the guildhall where the mayor's court and members of the assembly met

couper, cowper a cooper or maker of barrels, buckets and water butts

courbyll a corbel

covys curved iron plates used to direct smoke into the flue of a fireplace or oven

cownsell a legal adviser (hence being **reteynyd a cownsell** or hired at an annual fee to act in this capacity for the city)

cownter nayle nails used in the process of counter lathing (*see also* **lathyng**)

cowntyng howse a room or office used for keeping accounts and conducting business in general

coyne a quoin or wedge-shaped block of wood used to raise or lower the breech of a gun

coyte an iron quoit-shaped ring for fastening a gate

cradelyng providing a supporting framework, such as wooden ribs, for a roof

crampette a cramp-iron or small metal bar with the ends bent in order to hold two pieces of timber, such as beams or principals, together

cranage the charge imposed for the use of a mechanical crane

cranys cranes, given as presents, often along with swans, as delicacies for the table (hence **cranet** and **pyper crane** for a young bird)

cravys crayfish

crepar a grapnel or device with a multiple hook at one end that can be used with a rope to secure a boat to its mooring

crepyll a low roof attached to that of an adjacent building

cresset an iron basket in which combustible material could be carried or hung to provide light

croft an enclosed area of land or ground

crome (pl. **cromis**, **cromys**) *either* the iron hook on a simple hinge *or* a long-shafted device, like a rake, with sharp metal prongs projecting at right-angles for removing weeds and rubbish or, in the case of a **howse crome**, for pulling down burning buildings during fires

crosse howse a room or workshop at the intersection or crossing of two wings of a building (hence a **crosse stabyll** or stable in this position)

crosse in the market the large ornamental cross, rebuilt in the early sixteenth-century, on the east side if the market, in the lower chamber of which building materials were stored

crown a coin worth 5s

cruettes small vessels for the storage of wine or water for use on the altar during the celebration of mass

crustes planks cut from the outer part of the tree (hence **okyn crustes** made of the less solid part of the oak)

cryckes creeks or rivulets

cryspyng cresting or coping the top of a wall to throw off rain and protect against frost

Crystchurche *see* **Christe Churche**

culler colour

cuttyng, kyttyng the rever the annual exercise of removing weeds, reeds and undergrowth from the Wensum south of Norwich to improve navigation and prevent flooding

damaske water rosewater, traditionally distilled from Damask roses

dandy pratte a dandiprat or small coin theoretically worth three-halfpence but often less because of debasement

daubyng, dawbyng the application of earth, clay or plaster mixed with straw or hair to laths or wattle to make walls (hence a **dawber** or workman skilled in this exercise)

declyneng to leaning against, next to

dedimus, dedymus potestatem (we have given the power) a royal writ authorising a named individual to assume judicial powers, as acquired by every mayor of Norwich on taking office

deffende to keep away from (hence to **deffende cartes from the walle** or prevent carts from damaging a wall)

deke, dyeke a dyke or ditch

dennyng a cavity or space (hence raising the **dennyng off the bote** or filling the bottom of the boat to keep the cargo out of bilge water)

denysen a foreign-born individual who has been granted specific rights of residence, usually by royal letters patent

dependyng vpon due from or charged to

determinacon settlement of an account or debt

deys *either* a dais (*see also* **hyhe desse**) *or* a base or platform for securing a piece of metal work, such as a weather vane or cross

di', dimidia half

didalle, dydalle *either* a spade with a sharp triangular blade *or* a long pole with a metal scoop or net (**didalle nette**) at the end, both used for dredging watercourses (hence the verb **to dydalle** or dredge) from a special boat (a **didall boote**)

discharge of homage release by the Crown from swearing fealty on the purchase or inheritance of property in royal hands, often in return for a fee

doblette a doublet or close-fitting garment (with or without sleeves) worn by men on the upper body, those made for the Norwich military levies having **Ytalyan wastes** or tight waists in the Italian fashion

dolages the dowels or wooden pegs known as duledges which connect the felloes of a wheel (*see also* **fellows**)

doles boundary markers, generally of stone

dore stalle a door frame or posts

dormantes horizontal beams extending between the principal posts of a timber-framed house to carry cross-beams and flooring

dorter, dortowur a monastic dormitory

dossen a dozen

dowes *either* doves *or* birds in general

drafte, draught *either* a draft or copy of a document *or* the flue leading from a fireplace

dresser a large open cupboard for the display of plate and other valuables

dresser howse a place for dressing meat

drome a drum

dry bourde boards of seasoned wood

dyaper fine linen fabric imported from Flanders woven with a diamond pattern

dyce hede nayle large iron nails with faceted heads, shaped like dice, often used for decoration

dyeke *see* **deke**

dystreynabyll liable for distraint or the confiscation of goods by process of law, usually for an unpaid debt

Dyvlyn grotes Dublin groats, a groat being a small silver coin theoretically worth four pence, but often less because of debasement

easement, iusment a right of way, right of access to water or similar entitlement enjoyed by a person or persons on the property of another

eeres, eerys the handles (ears) of a jug, basket or other container

ell, elle a measure of cloth equivalent in length to 45 inches

elmys elm trees

elys eels (*see also* **rostyng ele**)

entertyse a tie-beam or main horizontal transverse roof timber which carries the feet of the principal rafters at wall-plate level

erantes errands (hence **went of erantes** or went on errands)

ernest an initial payment, often of a token sum, made on the signing of a contract as an earnest or guarantee of future payment (*see also* **Godes peny**)

eschekyr *either* the royal exchequer *or* the exchequer board or cloth used in the Norwich guildhall for auditing accounts

eschetery the office occupied by an escheator

eschetour, excheter an escheator or official appointed to enforce the crown's right to any property and services that reverted to it as feudal lord (hence **londes eschetid**), and who in Norwich was from 1404 onward the mayor

espyn ladder a ladder made of aspen or poplar wood

evyn the day before a saint's day or festival (hence **Corpus Christi evyn**)

evysbordes, evys bourdes triangular-cut wooden boards placed at the edge of a roof to give the tiles a tilt so that rainwater can drain off more easily

ewen bowes longbows made of yew

extylltree, exyltre(y) an axletree or bar placed across the underpart of a wagon or gun carriage that has rounded ends on which the wheels revolve

faconette a falconet or piece of light ordnance of the culverin type, with a two-inch calibre

fadam *either* a measure of length equivalent to six feet *or* a quantity of reeds, comprising six bundles each one foot in diameter

fagottes bundles of sticks, twigs or small branches generally used for fuel, but when made of gorse (**brome**) for drying off workmen who had got wet

fane a weather vane

farmer *see* **fermour**

fatte a vat or, when connected to a gutter, a sink for the collection of water

fayers the two annual fairs held outside the walls of the city on Whit Sunday and Trinity Sunday

fee ferme a sum of money paid annually to the Crown by the citizens in return for specific franchises and liberties awarded by royal charter

fellows the felloes or individual curved sections that together make up the exterior rim of a wooden wheel

fenestralles window frames or lattices (*see also* **lattys**)

ferkyn *either* a small barrel *or* a unit of measurement (firkin) equivalent to nine gallons

ferme a lease

fermery the infirmary of a monastic house

fermour, farmer a lessee

fetnyght a fortnight

fisheng, fishing, fissherig a fishery or place for fishing

flagges turves

flecher, flecher a fletcher or maker of arrows

flekyn rede reeds that were used instead of laths, being laid across rafters, attached to them by other reeds and then covered in plaster

fleshe hooke a long-handled hook with curved prongs for hanging large cuts of meat or removing them from a cauldron

flew a flue or smoke-duct, generally in the form of a hood made of wooden boards (**flewborde, flueborde**) over an open fire, sometimes dressed with clay or plaster to render it less combustible

florthes, florthis flooring, usually of clay or earth, although carpenters might lay a **florthe of joystes** (joists) to carry floor boards

flyxe the flux, a generic name for enteric diseases such as dysentery or diarrhoea

fodder, fother, fudder a measure of lead, usually of about a ton, being sufficient to cover 160 square feet

foote bankes foot rests on benches or forms or under trestle tables

forelocke, forlocke an iron wedge driven through a bolt to keep it in place or, in the case of artillery, to secure the cap-square on a gun carriage

foren receptes miscellaneous sums received by the chamberlains from sources not routinely charged in their accounts (hence the **foren receyuour** who collected these sums)

fourmes, fourmys forms or benches

frame, framyng erecting the wooden frame of a timber-built house

framestodes *see* **stodes**

francensence frankincense, an aromatic gum used to fumigate and perfume rooms

fraye to frighten or intimidate

fraytour the refectory of a monastic house

freeres, freres friars, usually with reference to the precinct of the Blackfriars

frendys fringes

freston freestone or fine-grained stone of excellent quality that can be easily worked

Fryer Awstens the Augustinian friary in Conesford

fudder *see* **fodder**

furbusshing polishing, burnishing, removing rust

furre fir or spruce (hence a **furryn laddyr** or ladder made of fir)

furryng sparrys, furrynges of sparrys strips of timber or narrow battens laid across the grain of neighbouring planks to provide a level surface for the attachment of panelling on walls

fustyan fustian or a coarse cloth made of flax

fyeng cleansing or dredging (*see also* **claryfyeng**)

fylletes narrow strips or bands, usually of metal (hence **fylletes of lede** or lead)

fynyall a finial or ornament placed upon the apex of a roof or gable

gabyll a gable or area of wall (generally triangular in shape) at the end of a double-pitched roof (*see also* **peke wall**)

gage a pledge or surety

gallon, galon a measure of liquid equivalent to eight pints

gardyd trimmed or ornamented (hence **blewe cotes gardyd with rede** or blue jackets trimmed with red)

garlementes clothes or garments

garner a granary or store for grain

Gascoyn wyne wine from Gascony in south-west France

gate stalle the wooden posts or supports of a gate

gauday a festival or day of rejoicing

geamys jambs or side posts supporting a lintel, or, in the case of a fireplace, a mantelpiece

gemew, gemewe, gemou, gemow *see* **jemewe**

ger gear or equipment

gildestokkes deposits of money and valuables retained by members of the religious guilds that had been dissolved by the Crown and which, by a ruling of the assembly in July 1539, were appropriated for civic use

glaser, glasewright a glasier or glass-worker

glasse barrys iron bars for the protection of glazed windows

glouer, glovyr a maker of leather gloves

glouers shredes shreds of leather supplied by glove-makers to produce the size that was mixed with chalk dust to make whitewash (*see also* **syse for whytyng**) or with other colours for staining timber

Godes peny a token sum of one or two pence given as an earnest of future payment, usually on the sealing of a contract (*see also* **ernest**)

gogeon a metal socket used for hanging a door or gate by the 'har', or Roman, method by slotting it over a spindle inserted in the threshold

gold fyner an artisan responsible for refining or purifying gold, ready for work by a goldsmith, and for assaying (**tryeng**) metal

gonner a gunsmith or maker of artillery

gorgette a gorget or piece of armour designed to protect the throat

gother, goter a gutter or drain

gravour, gravyr an engraver, carver or sculptor

grene kendall a green woollen cloth originally produced in Kendal in Cumbria

gren, green nettes hyde the hide of a young heifer or bullock

gresynges steps or stairs

Grey Fryers the precinct of the Franciscan friars just south of the cathedral

greyne grain, usually wheat

grey salte inferior quality salt imported from the Bay of Bourgneuf in Brittany

grosse a gross or unit of quantity equal to twelve dozen (144)

grownselle, grownsylle *either* large balks of timber morticed together at the corners to form the rectangular base of a timber-framed building *or* the timber frame of a door or gate (hence **groundsilling, grownsellyng** or the process of making and inserting them)

grutchyd expressed reluctance, complained about

gryndyng sharpening or honing

grynt, bakers grynt a variable levy payable by Norwich bakers on each comb or quarter of wheat that they had ground at the city's mills, part going to the miller and the residue to civic funds

gullid worn away through the action of water

guylday the day set aside every year by each city guild for its feast and celebratory mass (as in **Seynt Georges guylday** on 23 April, the feast day of the patron saint)

guyldhalle, yeldehall, yeldhalde the guildhall, erected at the northern end of the market in 1411–14 on the site of a former tollhouse

guyrdlyng attaching belts or girdles to quivers of arrows for the use of archers

guyrdyns principal beams or girders

gyantes large models of the heroes Samson and Hercules that were carried in civic processions (*see also* **Mary Gorgeyn**)

hake an adjustable hook with a ratchet suspended above an open hearth from which cooking pots could be hung

hambyr, hamper the hanaper or repository for cash and other valuables kept in the guildhall

hance, hanse the lintel or horizontal beam over a door or window (hence **gravyng of hansys** or carving a pattern or image on a lintel)

harnes, harneys *either* a generic term for armour (hence **harneys nayle** or specialist nails used in the construction of metal or leather armour) *or* a verb meaning to clothe in armour

harte lath superior quality laths made from the inner heart of the oak as opposed to the exterior 'sappy' part, which were about half the price

haspe, hespe a hinged metal plate that formed part of a locking device on a door, gate, grating or pair of stocks, usually by fitting over a 'U' shaped piece of metal (*see also* **stapeller**)

hedeburghs capital pledges or reputable householders elected to serve on juries of presentment in the city's leet courts

hede mese, hede place principal messuage or dwelling place

heire, heyer to air a room, usually with fumigants

helve the handle of a weapon or tool, such as a pickaxe

hempyng rope a rope made of hemp

hengille, hengyll an iron hinge with eye-holes used for hanging a door

here hair used as a binding agent in the mixing of plaster (hence **here for selyng** or filling in cracks)

herse a hearse or triangular frame designed to carry lighted candles or to support the pall over the coffin of an important person

hespe *see* **haspe**

hetche a hatch

hewyng and sqwaryng the fashioning of timber by a sawyer into planks and rectangular blocks ready for use by joiners and carpenters

heye hay (hence **heye howse** or a place for storing hay and straw), which could be combined with mortar (**myxt with morter**) as a binding agent in the construction of walls

heygoday a haggaday or ring forming the handle by which a latch is raised

heynyng raising the height of ground with rubble or similar material, or of walls with masonry

hoke, hook nayles long nails whose point or tip can be bent into a hook

Holy Trynyte *see* **Christe Churche**

homlockes hemlock

hopper a receptacle shaped like an inverted cone through which grain is passed for the removal of impurities before being milled (hence a **Danske hopper** based on a Danish model)

hopyng encircling with hoops (hence **hopyng off tubes** or renewing the hoops around tubs or barrels)

hordas, hurdas a hurdis, bulwark, fence or partition originally made of wicker or hurdles

horsemete fodder for horses

hospitall, hospytall of Saynt Gyle the hospital of St Giles in Bishopgate, acquired by the city in 1547, when it became known first as God's House and later as the Great Hospital

howse a room, workshop or place set aside for a specific activity (*see*, for example, **scaldyng howse**)

hutche a wooden cage or container used for storage

hye bourde high table

hyhe desse a raised dais for civic dignitaries, such as that at the common hall

impechement of wast impeachment of waste or the liability of a tenant to be prosecuted for damage to property, which might be waived to allow for building improvements

inbatyd a window where batements, reducing the length of upper lights, have been adopted

inbostyng carving or moulding in relief

inbowyng *either* cutting or bending wood into the shape of an arch *or*, more generally, shaping or trimming the projecting end of a piece of timber, often with mouldings

indenter, indenture a document recording a transaction, two (or even three) copies of which would be written head to head on the same sheet of paper or parchment and then separated by jagged (indented) incisions; the parts could be matched for proof of authenticity

ingrossyng writing up a fair copy

inkennelld kennelled like dogs, a derogatory term used to describe Kett's rebels in their camp on Mousehold Heath

in primis first of all

interlude a light or humorous play or entertainment, albeit with a moral or didactic theme, traditionally performed during an interval between longer plays or courses in a banquet

ipocras, ipocrast *see* **ypocras**

iusment *see* **easement**

jacke a quilted doublet, usually interlined with metal or horn plates

jakes a privy (hence **jakes bourde** for the seat or seats)

jalmys, jeamys jambs or vertical wooden door or window frames or the stone supports of a fireplace

japys *see* **chape**

jemewe a hinge comprising a pin-plate and hanging-plate of identical size

jerkyn a close-fitting jacket

jolle the jole or head and upper part of a large fish, such as a salmon or a sturgeon

joppe, jowpece, jowpy a cornice extending between the main principals of a roof, supporting the lesser principals (*see also* **pryncypalls**)

jorneyman a craftsman or artisan who has served an apprenticeship

just weyght a precisely measured rather than approximate weight

kalender *see* **calenderer**

kechyn a kitchen

kele a keel or boat with a shallow draught used for transporting freight, often on rivers (hence **keleman**, the owner or skipper of such a vessel)

kendalle woollen cloth, usually green in colour, named after Kendal in Cumbria where it was produced

kille, kylle a kiln, usually in Norwich for the production of lime or malt (hence

kylle ston for building kilns or ovens; and **kylleyarde, kylyarde** a yard or enclosed space containing a kiln)

knottes small quantities or lumps of lead

knyllyng nailing

kynges awdyte an audit held by the Crown in various places for the payment of rents due to and from royal property

kynges taske a tax or financial contribution demanded by the Crown

kytlyngs whelps or cubs, a derogatory term used alliteratively to describe Kett's rebels

kyttyng *see* **cuttyng**

lache pan a dripping pan placed beneath a spit

lachys latches of doors, gates or windows

ladylles ladles attached to long poles for charging guns with loose powder

langable, langoll landgable, a modest annual ground rent payable to the civic authorities on many properties within the walls of Norwich

laten, latten an alloy or combination of more than one metal, such as brass (hence **laten wyer** or fine wire made of base metal)

lathe nayle a small-headed short nail for nailing laths to rafters

lathyng the placement of wooden laths, whose length was regulated by an assize of 1528, to carry roofing materials or to support the plaster on walls (hence **cownter lathyng** or the placing of strips of wood at right-angles)

lattys lattice made of thin wooden rods or wire set diagonally in a frame either to protect window glass or wells, or to cover unglazed windows, as in outhouses or belfries (*see also* **fenestralles**)

lawer a layer or shoot or twig that is bent over to take root and make a hedge

lectorn a lectern or reading stand in a church

leddyr stavys the rungs of ladders

lede lathe, lathys strong wooden laths for supporting a lead roof

ledes *either* leaden roofing and gutters *or* vats, tanks or cisterns made of lead

ledyng covering with lead

lees a lease

lernyd man a lawyer or person with legal training

lete *either* one of the city's ten leet courts, which dealt with local nuisances and misdemeanours, *or* the geographical area under its jurisdiction *or* the residents living there

lettyd *either* prevented *or* wasted (hence **lettyd ther tyme** or wasted their time)

leuer a lever or latch

leves, levys *either* the shutters of a window *or* the two sides of a double gate *or* the upper and lower parts of a hatched, stable-type door

leyeng providing a metal edge, reinforcement or component (hence **leyeng of a mattok** or replacing the iron pick of a mattock; *see also* **shoyng**)

leyser free time or leisure

li', libra a pound sterling, worth 20*s*

libr', libra a weight equivalent to 16 ounces

lifferey, lyuery a livery or uniform allocated annually to certain civic employees, such as the waits

loope, loopys, lopis *either* openings or frames for doors or windows *or* the structures, such as doors, louvers or shutters, made to cover or close them

Louelles stathe a landing stathe on the Wensum, south of the cathedral precinct, which marked the limit of the medieval prior's fee

luse *see* **pyeke**

lyghtes glass panes in a window

lyme brenner a lime burner

lymers limbers or shafts used on gun-carriages

lynpyn a linchpin or pin placed transversely through an axel to keep a wheel in position

lyntell, lyntelle a horizontal beam or piece of masonry over a doorway

maltyng howse, offyce a place for the production or storage of malt

malvesey malmsey or a sweet wine shipped from Greece

manchette the finest kind of wheaten bread

mantyltree a beam or lintel placed across the top of a fire-place to bear the weight of the masonry above

mark two-thirds of a pound sterling, worth 13*s* 4*d*

marle marl or clay containing an element of carbonate of lime, excavated in Norwich from pits

martyngales, martyngalys the straps attached to men's hose that fasten at the back, as worn by the Norwich military levies, allegedly after the style of Martigues in Provence

Mary Gorgeyn an image of a gorgon that was carried in civic processions alongside the two heroes, Samson and Hercules (*see also* **gyantes**)

Mastres Mistress, a courtesy title extended to the wives or widows of aldermen and other senior civic officers

matchis hemp cord impregnated with saltpetre and lime for igniting gunpowder

mawnde a maund or large wicker basket with handles (hence a **closse mawnde** or basket with a lid or cover for carrying fruit)

medilmote, mydyll mote, myddylmote middlemost, the middle one of three, usually with reference to the transoms of a window

mele sackes sacks for holding meal or grain

mener, men[o]ur manure or dung

menstrelles minstrels or musicians (hence the **kynges menstrelles**, who toured Norfolk in 1544)

merchantes ventrers the London Company of Merchant Adventurers, which invested in continental trade and maintained links with affiliated groups of merchants in provincial cities, such as Norwich

mese a messuage or plot of land with a dwelling house and outbuildings on it

meser, mesyr a measure (hence a **bare** or minimal measure and an **ode** or uneven measure)

mesers mercers or dealers in textiles and fine cloth

midiltre, myddyll tre a central post, such as that in a gate or pillory

m¹, *millena* a thousand or, in the case of some commodities, such as nails, a 'long thousand' of 1,200

milles, mylles *see* **newe milles**

minute expences miscellaneous expenses, such as gifts, that cannot be readily itemised under other headings in an account

Moder Mother, a style of address for a low status widow, such as **Moder Keddell**

money makyng counterfeiting

mortes a mortice or slot (usually rectangular in shape) cut into timber or stone to secure a matching piece of projecting wood or masonry

mote a moat

mouable, movabill, movabyll stalles temporary stalls in Norwich market, usually occupied by butchers on a short-term basis, that could be moved from one place to another rather than being fixed in a single spot

mowld a mould for casting metal

mucke bote, muk boote a large boat used to remove dung and household waste from Norwich for disposal lower down the Wensum, the farmer of which was paid for his services by residents

Murage Loft a sizeable building in the middle row of the marketplace, constructed in *c.*1294 for the collection of tolls, and subsequently used as the headquarters of the sergeant of the market, the ground floor being let out as wool shops

muscadell, muskadele of Gene muscatel, a strong sweet wine made from Muscat grapes, shipped from Genoa

musters *either* the military levies raised by the city of Norwich to fight for the Crown *or* the act of assembling these men for selection or review

mynder a miner or specialist in demolition

napery table linen or altar cloths

navys naves or the hubs of wooden wheels, generally made of elm

nelyng *see* **anelyd**

netterd a neatherd, who looks after cattle or oxen (**nettes**)

newe milles, mylles the water mills constructed in the early fifteenth century on the river Wensum where it entered the city near Hell gate from the suburb of Heigham

nobylle a noble or gold coin first minted by Edward III with a face value of 6s 8d, of which the **angell** was a later re-issue

nulla, nullus no, none. *Nullus* is often written at the bottom of a page where an entry runs over onto a new one to indicate that there is no charge on the first page, and to prevent the insertion of one

ob', obolus a halfpenny

oblygacon an obligation or legally binding written agreement, whereby one party undertakes to honour a debt or commitment of some kind to another, or to guarantee the readiness of a third party to do so (hence **wryting obligatory**)

obyte landes property set aside to fund the celebration of anniversary masses for the benefit of the soul of a named individual

occupyed used or employed for a specific piece of work

ode *see* **meser**

okyn made of oak

okyr ochre, used for staining timber

onch an inch

oon one

oores, orys oars

ordynance[s] equipment

oser grounde a place where osiers or willow trees grow (hence **oyseyarde, osyer yarde**)

ouerwharte across or at right angles

outrydynges journeys out of Norwich on official business

packthrede, pakthrede packthread or thick twine, used for binding or as a mason's plumb line or level

pale *either* an enclosed plot of land *or* a fence

paleys, pallace the bishop of Norwich's palace, to the north west of the cathedral precinct

palme a measure equivalent to either the length or breadth of the human hand

parclose, parclosse a partition or screen

parcolas, parcoles a portcullis

pare up to heap up or sweep into a pile

parfume panne a shallow metal pan for burning fumigants to cleanse the air

parlowur a parlour or small, private room

pastry howse a place for the making and storage of pastry and comestibles such as pies, tarts and pasties

patent royal letters patent issued from Chancery *or* a paten

pathyn *either* stone paving *or* the laying of it by a mason or paviour

pecke a peck or measure for dry goods equivalent in capacity to a quarter of a bushel or two gallons

peddes wicker baskets or panniers, usually carried as a pair, often with lids

peeres pears (hence **fryers peers** which presumably came from one of the city's former friaries)

peke wall a 'peaked' or gable wall at the end of a building (*see also* **gabyll**)

pekyng robbing or thieving

pelffer stolen goods or booty

pendons pendants or vertical posts used in conjunction with diagonal roof braces to support a tie beam (*see also* **entertyse**) or pentice roof; one end rests on a corbel and the other on the beam, while the brace is morticed into both the beam and pendon (*see also* **bracys**)

pentyse *either* a shed or lean-to attached to a building (hence a **pentyce stalle** erected against the west wall of the guildhall) *or* a sloping pentice roof over a window, gate or wall designed to offer protection against the weather

perk a loft, as erected in churches for the placement of organs

pety custome, petye custom *parva custuma*, or duty charged on goods coming to market from outside the city

pewterer a maker of pewter utensils (an alloy of tin and lead widely used for bowls, jugs and plates)

pixte, pyxt a pyx or box used to store the consecrated sacrament during the celebration of mass

plancher, plauncher *either* an entire wooden floor *or* planks for use as floor-boards (hence **plauncheryng** or the laying of floor boards)

plaster of palleys plaster of Paris, a fine type of plaster made from gypsum

platte a map or plan

plomer a plumber or specialist lead-worker employed in making gutters and laying or removing lead roofs

ponche *either* a punch or striking tool with a reinforced metal tip used, for example, to remove shackles (hence **newe stelyng of the ponche for the jaylour** or renewing the steel on the gaoler's punch) *or* part of the fastening mechanism of a gate

popill, popylle a poplar tree (hence the soft **poplyn** wood from it, used for low quality **popleborde** or boards and planks)

portall a panelled partition, sometimes with an inner door

potell *either* a pottle or measure equivalent to half a gallon *or* a vessel of roughly this capacity

potgonn a mortar or short cannon with a large bore

powderyng, powdryng sprinkling or scattering material to create a pattern, usually on walls (hence **brycke for powderyng**)

poyntes *see* **thredyn poyntes**

poyntyng filling the gaps in brickwork or stonework with mortar (hence **newe poyntyng the Ropery**)

prebendes prebendaries or members of a cathedral chapter

prechyng yarde the outdoor space on the south front of the former Blackfriars used for the delivery of public sermons

prentice, prentyse an apprentice (hence **bonde of a prentis** or indentures of apprenticeship)

proffer a provisional payment of estimated dues into the Exchequer

promoter a professional informer who was paid to denounce offenders against the law

prykettes spikes, such as those used in the base of candlesticks to keep candles upright

prykwondes, prykwoondes lengths of hazel used to make thatchers' broaches (*see also* **broches**)

pryncypalls, pryncypals a pair of inclined lateral roof timbers which rest at each end of a horizontal tie-beam and meet at the apex, supporting common rafters and purlins (*see also* **copyll sparrys** *and* **pyrlynges**)

pullery howse a place for keeping poultry (**pultre, pultrye**)

Pultrye market the poultry market, which originally lay on the south side of the church of St Peter Mancroft, but had moved to the north, near the butchery, by the early fifteenth century

purpose a porpoise, known in the sixteenth-century as a *porcus piscis* or 'hog-fish' (hence **purpose pygge**) and often presented as a gift to important individuals

pursevant, pursyvaunt a pursuivant, being either a herald or, less specifically, any official royal messenger

pyeke *either* a pike (hence a **pyeke cald a luse** from its Latin name *lucius*, denoting a young fish) *or* a weapon comprising a spearhead attached to a long pole (hence **morres pyekes** which were Moorish in appearance)

pykerell a pickerel or young pike, often presented as a gift

pykexe, pyxexe a pickaxe (hence **layeng a pykexe** or renewing the iron part of the implement)

pyles piles or large wooden stakes pointed at one end so that they could be driven into the river bed to shore up the bank or provide support for piers or jetties

pyller a mullion or vertical member between the panes of a window

pyllery a pillory for the public punishment of offenders, which in Norwich stood near the guildhall

pyllettes pellets of lead for gunshot

pynnyng attaching pieces of timber or planks together with wooden pegs or to other building materials (hence a **pynner** or carpenter employed for this purpose, or for pinning tiles to laths)

pyrlynges purlins or horizontal beams running along the length of a roof, usually resting on the principal rafters and supporting the common rafters

quantes long poles with prongs at the end employed to propel a boat through the water

qu', quartarium *either* a farthing or quarter of a penny *or* a quarter of a hundred-weight (28 pounds)

quarter fferme *either* a lease extending for a quarter of a year *or* the rent due for that period

quayer a quire or measure of paper derived from the French *quaier*, being four sheets of paper folded in half to provide sixteen pages

quere, qwere the chancel of a church occupied by the choir (hence **mydquere** or the middle of the chancel)

quietus est a release or formal acquittance (**quytans**) from debt

quylles cylindrical containers filled with gunpowder

quytans an acquittance

qwinces quinces, a type of fruit given as gifts to important people

rabytyng stoole a rabbeting stool or bench used by plasterers when mixing their mortar

racke stavys slender pieces of wood employed in stables to make mangers or racks to hold fodder

rage a flood or torrential downpour, notably that recorded in August 1542

rampere to build ramps to the top of walls or gates for defensive purposes

ransakyng searching or dredging (hence **cuttyng and ransakyng** the Wensum)

rapheman a raffman or dealer in general goods, particularly timber and tallow

rawe, rowe lede raw lead, not yet cast into sheets (*see also* **shet lede**)

recorder a lawyer retained to provide the city with professional advice and to ensure that court records were properly kept

rectorwryes parish registers

rede bedde thick matting made of reeds or rushes used during wrestling matches

redempcions payments made to the authorities by persons wishing to be discharged or temporarily excused from the obligation to hold civic office or to provide a guild feast

redemyng recovering an article upon payment of a sum of money

reders roofers working with reed (**rede**) and other types of thatch, such as straw and rushes ·

reffyn roofing

rente off assis, assyse fixed or assise rents charged in perpetuity upon specific properties often because of encroachments on waste or common ground

rente resolute fixed rent

replevye a writ of replevin or the legal remedy sought by a person whose goods have been wrongfully seized (hence a **sewte of a repleve** or action to recover confiscated property)

respectes sums of money 'respited' or allowed to the chamberlains at the end of their account

returne walle a wall built at a right-angle from the front of a building or running along its side

rodde, rode a rod or measure of length technically equal to 16.5 feet but open to negotiation when contracts were drawn up (being, for example, set at 21 feet by the chamberlain in 1545: NRO, NCR 18A/7, f. 170)

roffe tree the main beam or ridge-pole of a roof

roffys, roves tiles used as roofing along the tops of walls so that water can run off

rolle of matche a length of wick designed to burn steadily when lit at one end for firing a gun

rolles round balks of wood placed side-by-side as rollers under heavy objects to facilitate movement

romyth room or storage space (hence **howse romyth** or house room)

ronde a large piece of fish, such as sturgeon

Ropary, Ropery the row of stalls assigned to rope-sellers in the market, immediately north of the **Murage Loft** and east of the **Bochery**

rosen resin

rostyng ele an eel for roasting

rowcastyng rough-casting or plastering a wall (usually of lath or wattle) with clay or loam (*see also* **smothecastyng**)

rowe lede unworked lead that has yet to be cast by a plumber into sheets (*see also* **shete lede**)

rowe oke *either* a recently felled and unhewn oak tree *or* unseasoned timber from an oak

row mason a rough mason who positions unworked stone (**rowe ston**) ready for the attention of a free mason (**fremason**)

rowndelle a round pane of glass often decorated with heraldic imagery

rubbe a rounded piece of abrasive stone used for sharpening scythes and other tools

rybbys applied or embossed ribs bordering the edge of a piece of armour with the purpose of deflecting an opponent's weapon

rydyng in post riding at great speed, often with relays of horses

Rynye wine from the Rhineland, more commonly known as 'Rynnysh'

rystes lumps or uneven surfaces (hence removing **rystes & craneys** or chinks from walls)

ryve *either* to split wood along the grain to make laths or thin strips *or* to damage (as in **ryven ashyn sparrys** or damaged beams made of ash)

sacke *see* **wyne sacke**

sacry belle a sacring bell, rung in church to mark the consecration of the sacrament

sadlers nayle small round-headed nails used by saddlers to attach leather to wood

sakerment the sacrament or consecrated host, as carried in Corpus Christi processions

sallette a sallet or light helmet, with or without a visor and with a curved back to protect the neck, worn by foot soldiers

sappy timber that is still full of sap (hence **sappy sparrys** or unseasoned beams)

satten *reuersa* satin that has been trimmed or lined with another luxury fabric

sawyn pytte a saw-pit, where large pieces of timber are cut into required lengths (*see also* **stocke**)

scaffold, scafold a stage, usually erected for visiting players (*see also* **stagyng**)

scaldyng howse a place where the carcasses of animals are prepared for butchery through immersion in boiling water to remove hair, bristles and entrails (hence a **scaldyng lede** or the vat employed for this purpose)

scantling, skantlyn a scantling or agreed measure for the size and quantity of building materials, including nails, timber and stone (hence the **grettest** or largest scantling and a **meane** or average scantling)

scolys the scales hanging on iron chains at the common stathe

scope, skopet a scoop for use with a **dydalle** when dredging a watercourse

scoryng scouring, polishing or otherwise removing dirt

Scottyshe cappis caps or bonnets made in the Scottish fashion as worn by the city's archers

screnys screens

scryptorye a *scriptorium* or place set aside for book production, in either a monastic or commercial context

scyle, sylle the sill or ledge at the bottom of a window (hence **nether scyle** or outer sill and **ouer sylle** or upper sill)

seale & wrytynges a fair copy of a lease of communal property bearing the city's seal

segge sedge, a type of rush used for roofing

selerer a monastic cellarer

selyng *either* the process of panelling a room with wood (hence **selyng nayle** or small nails with tinned heads employed for attaching panels) *or* of filling in gaps in plasterwork, roofing or masonry (hence the purchase of **hey for selyng** or hay to use as infill)

sembly the Norwich assembly, comprising twenty-four aldermen, sixty common councillors and other leading civic officers who met in the **sembly chambyr** of the guildhall, rebuilt in the 1530s

sergeantes, seriauntes law-enforcement officers (hence the **sergeante at the mace**, who was responsible for arresting malefactors and collecting rents, and the **sergeant of the market**, who policed the market)

serpentyn powder fine gunpowder for use with a gun known as a serpentine

sesment, sessment a special assessment or rate, such as those levied on the residents of Norwich to pay for the cost of sending troops to Scotland and France

sessions quarterly meetings of the justices of the peace

sewtes, sutes lawsuits

sheeffes thakke sheaves of thatch for roofing

sheffe a sheaf of arrows, usually twenty-four in number

sheffe, shrofe a measure of glass, roughly equivalent to about six pounds in weight

sherman a shearman or artisan who shaves the nap from woollen cloth to create a smooth, faultless finish

shete, shotte lede lead that has been cast into sheets or webs (hence **shetyng lede**, the process of casting molten lead over a bed of sand by a plumber to make sheets)

shetylles part of a locking mechanism, referring either to bolts or the sockets into which they fit

shirehouse the meeting place of the county court in the south bailey of Norwich castle

sholdes sandbanks or areas of raised ground in the river

sholvys wooden shovels (hence **sholvys shodde** or strengthened with iron or steel rims and **bare sholvys**, which were not shod)

shordes shreds, fragments or scraps

shortyng shortening or making smaller

shotyng glovys protective gloves worn by archers when shooting arrows

shoyng *either* shoeing horses *or* the process of reinforcing wooden wheels or implements, such as shovels, spades and pickaxes, with iron (*see also* **leyeng**)

shreves sheriffs, two of whom were elected annually (hence **shrevalte** or the office of sheriff)

shruff rubbish or discarded items (hence **shruff of metall** or the unwanted pieces of base metal collected in Norwich for casting into guns)

shud, shudde a shed or outbuilding for storage

sicle, sykill, sykkyll a sickle, principally used for cutting weeds and reeds in and beside the Wensum

sistern, systern a cistern or large tank often sited at the mouth of a stream or cokey to collect dung and rubbish before it entered the river, and thus subject to frequent cleansing

size *see* **syse**

skeip, skepp, skop a large, deep basket used for carrying clay and removing rubbish

skewe on the slant or set at an angle (hence a seat **with a skewe**)

skulles protective metal skull-caps worn by infantrymen

slevyd syrples a surplice or loose ecclesiastical vestment with sleeves

slyng a sling or breech-loaded long iron gun used to fire scatter-shot, such a lead pellets

slyt, slytte damage or wear and tear, usually to equipment hired or borrowed by the chamberlains (hence **slytyn** ropes, ladders and pickaxes)

small bere weak beer of the kind given to workmen in hot weather

smothecastyng plastering a wall so that the surface appears smooth and even (*see also* **rowcastyng**)

snecke, snek a latch

sonde sand, which could be of different types, such as **morter sonde** for making mortar and **pathyn sonde** for use in paving

soo a large wooden tub, hooped like a barrel, for carrying water

sope howse a workshop for making soap from tallow

sowde[r] solder, usually made of tin or pewter

Spanyshe barrys, yron high quality iron imported from Spain

sparres, sparrys *either* beams or planks of wood *or*, more specifically, rafters, generally to be found in pairs (*see also* **copyll sparrys** and **furryng sparrys**)

sparres ffete, sparrys feete the feet of rafters, which rested upon beams known as wall-plates

spekynges, spykynges a generic type of iron nail, often quite large (**gret**), for heavy duty

spendill, spyndyll(e) a spindle or rod, usually of iron, serving as the axis upon which the wheel of a wheelbarrow turns

spent used

sperde shut or closed, *either* in the context of derelict buildings (hence **speryng vp** or closing) *or* the fastening of a breastplate to the shoulders of a jacket

spicebrede, spycebrede a rich bread or cake flavoured with spices, often consumed on important civic occasions or presented as a gift

splentes splints or pairs of small overlapping metal plates worn as armour to protect the elbow and arm, in some cases extending by means of rivets to cover the hand (*see also* **Almayn ryvettes**)

splent yarne string or yarn used to tie the splints, laths or wattle used in the construction of walls

sprygges small, slender and tapering nails or tacks, generally without heads, used for fixing glass in place in a window frame

spurne, spurnys props or stays made of timber

spyer a fixed wooden screen intended to exclude draughts

stagyng scaffolding (hence **stagyng hyrdylles** and **stagyng tymbyr** or the wooden hurdles and planks used for this purpose)

stalle *see* **dore stalle**

stamyn stamin, a type of coarse worsted cloth for which Norfolk was noted

standerdes substantial upright posts or pillars (hence **aldryng standerds** made of alder wood)

stapeller, stapille, stapylle *either* a piece of timber for framing the side of a window or grate *or* a 'U' shaped piece of iron driven into a gate post, door frame, grating or other structure to hold a bolt or hook

stapyll, stepill a tower (or, in the case of Blackfriars, a steeple)

stathe a landing stage or wharf

statute merchant a legally binding commercial contract generally entered before the mayor of a staple town, such as Newcastle-upon-Tyne or Bristol

stavys usually the staves of a ladder, *but see also* **bylle**

stayers, steyers stairs

stewe an enclosed space where hot water or steam baths could be taken for hygienic, medical and recreational purposes

stewynges windfalls used for hedging

steyes supports or props

steyng halting or bringing to an end (hence **steyng of certen procez** or halting legal proceedings)

stocke *either* the trunk of a tree that has been squared off into long rectangular balks (hence **base stokes** from the lower part) *or* the part of a gun carriage which rests upon the axel trees (hence **stockyng** a canon) *or* stocks for confinement

stock locke the locking mechanism for the stocks kept in the women's prison

stodes, stothis, stothys vertical timber posts known as 'studs' used to construct the walls of timber-framed houses, being tenoned into the wall-plates above (hence **fframe stodes**); they were also used to make door and window frames

stoles, stolys of the chappell stalls for the chapel at the former Blackfriars

ston a stone, which weighs 14 pounds

stondes large open tubs or barrels for removing dung and refuse

stoopys, stopes, stopps, stoppys water buckets on ropes or chains for use in wells and at watering places

strake the iron rim of a wheel

strangers *either* outsiders to Norwich (hence **a strange bocher** or butcher) *or*, in an ecclesiastical context, chaplains not employed by the civic authorities

stryke a strickle or straight piece of wood used to level the top of a measure full of grain by removing any surplus, as required by statute law before purchase

stulpys substantial wooden posts used as principal supports in paling fences or to restrict access to thoroughfares

subsidy a tax voted by parliament

suffrigan, suffrygant a suffragan bishop, who assists the diocesan bishop (hence **tenementes late lord suffrigan** or tenements leased to the city by John Underwood, former suffragan of Norwich)

summa sum

summa receptorum forensecorum the sum of foreign receipts

summa totalis omnium receptorum the sum total of all receipts

summa totalis omnium solucionum, allocacionum et respectorum the sum total of all payments, allowances and respites (allowances)

summa totalis omnium solucionum communis aule, awle the sum total of all payments on the common hall

summa totalis receptorum onerata the sum total of all receipts charged

survey, survey howse a servery or place from which meals are served and where eating utensils are kept

swage ornamental grooving or moulding on a metal object, such as the pommel of a sword

swaype a lever, handle or bolt (hence **swayptre** or a bed in which a bolt rests or runs)

swete sweet-smelling, fragrant

sweyes, sweys sways or long, pliable laths used in roofing, being purchased in bunches (**bonches**) and placed longitudinally across rafters to support layers of thatch

swordberer the civic official who carries the sword of office before the mayor on ceremonial occasions

sygnettes, synettes cygnets or young swans, often given as presents to important persons

sykkyll *see* **sicle**

synke a conduit, drain or other receptacle for removing or storing sewage

synters wooden scaffolding known as centerings, used by masons to support the arch of a vault until the mortar had set the stones or bricks in place

syse *either* to assess *or* the assizes

syse for whytyng a gelatinous fixative or size for use in the production of whitewash

syse peces cuisses or pieces of armour designed to protect the thigh

syse tyme the time of the Norwich assizes, which took place in July

sythe a scythe

tabernacle a small canopied receptacle used in churches to house the reserved sacrament or a holy relic

tabylle the water table or top course of the plinth of a wall, often made of special bricks

taillous pageont the play or pageant mounted annually by the Norwich tailors

tale a complete tally, sum or reckoning

tankerd a large tub-like vessel, bound with iron hoops, for carrying water

taske a tax, rate or levy (hence **kynges taske**, which was demanded by the Crown)

teke *either* a ticking case or cover for feather bedding *or* the fabric used to make one

tellttes, teltes tilts or awnings made of canvas or other coarse cloth for use as tents or to cover carts

tenter hookes hooked or right-angled nails used to support rails or hangings

tenth, x^th *either* the tithe payable from the dissolved Blackfriars to the Crown *or* part of the **tenth and fifteenth**, a tax on movables levied by the civic authorities

terre tar

tevell *either* a pipe, tube or the flue of a chimney *or* a board used with paper and line as a target at archery butts, perhaps bearing an image of the devil

thacke bourdes small boards nailed over rafters to carry **thackyng** (roofing material) of reed, tile or lead

thacke tyle, thaktyle roof tiles, generally made of brick (hence **brikke tyle**), whose manufacture and size were regulated by an act of parliament of 1477

thak a general term for reed, rushes or straw used for thatching

thredyn poyntes leather laces or cords used to attach one item of clothing to another, especially hose to a doublet, or, in the case of **armyn poyntes**, pieces of armour to each other

Tomlond, Tumlond Tombland, a large open space to the west of the cathedral close, the site of an early market place

tonne a ton or unit of weight equivalent to 2,240 pounds

tores structures or buildings

touche powder a fine type of priming powder or gunpowder placed in the pan over the touch hole in a gun

transposyng converting a building or room from one use to another

tresan a transom or horizontal piece of timber or stone between the panes of a window, or between the top of a door and a window

trivmphs, tryvmphis triumphs or civic celebrations to mark English victories and other important national events, generally with bonfires, gunfire and processions

trows troughs

trusse lyne rope or line used when erecting a truss or framework of timber

trustille, trustylle a trestle or 'A' shaped framework comprising a horizontal piece of wood, supported at each end by splayed legs, on which a table top or work surface might be placed

tryce a mobile crane or lifting gear

tryeng testing or assaying (hence **tryeng of certen metall** to establish its purity)

tryvet a trivet or three-footed stand on which pans are placed in an open hearth

turne the tourn, a special session of the hundred court held biannually at Easter and Michaelmas under the direction of one of the city's two sheriffs

twyes twice

tyle pynnys wooden pins, commonly of oak, used to attach roof tiles to the laths beneath

tyme of assyse (*see* **syse tyme**)

tynnyd covered in tin (hence **tynnyd hede nayles** or iron nails whose heads have been covered in tin to whiten them and prevent rusting)

typler a tapster or seller of ale

tyters tares or weeds growing in wheat

vnde super whence upon, a phrase used to denote those who still owed money at the end of an account

videlicet that is to say, namely

vorell *either* a ferrule or metal ring or cap placed over a length of wood to prevent it from splitting *or* a metal eye on the end of a hinge

voult, vowlt, vowte *either* a vault or arched ceiling of stone (hence **vowltyng** or vaulting) *or* a cellar with an arched roof

vyce a spiral or winding staircase

vyce of yron an iron vice, such as that employed to hold the city's seal

vyrownd around and about

vytallyng howses places selling food on a commercial basis (hence **vytallyng bothes** or temporary booths set up in public places, such as the castle ditch, to sell food)

wachet cloth of a light or sky-blue colour

wafers, waffers, light, thin, crispy confections, usually consumed with wine, sometimes as **wafer cake**, and often presented as gifts (hence the **waffer yrons** used to make them)

wallplate a beam laid horizontally along the top of a wall to support the feet of the rafters above; in a timber-framed house the posts and studs below are tenoned into it (*see also* **stodes**)

warde the inner or outer circuit of an enclosed space (hence **cloyster warde** and **yarde warde**)

wardysmen leading householders chosen to represent the residents of the city's four great wards or twelve sub-wards

warfage wharfage or the charge made for the use of storage space on a stathe or wharf

washyng stathis jetties on the Wensum set aside for the washing of clothes in the river

waster booke rough notes kept by the chamberlain for recording income and expenditure in detail on a daily basis

water bally, baly the officer or bailiff with jurisdiction over Norwich's waterways

waterbordes long boards of a triangular shape in cross-section used as weather-boarding or horizontal cladding for the walls of mills and other buildings beside streams and rivers

water shutte watertight

wateryngs, wateryng places designated places along the Wensum giving access to the river for the watering of horses and other animals

wayghtes, waytes waits or professional musicians, usually four in number, who were paid an annual fee to perform at civic entertainments and ceremonies

waynscote, waynsvotte wainscot or fine quality oak imported from the Baltic (hence **waynscot bourdes** or oak boards used for panelling)

webbe a sheet or *tela* of lead of various weights

wete larder a larder for the storage of fresh ('wet') meat and poultry, as opposed to a larder where dry and salted foodstuffs were kept

wey a long pole, usually placed across the shoulders, for carrying buckets

weyght, wight, wyght a weight for measuring (hence **C wyghtes clade in brasse** or hundredweight weights covered in brass)

weyng *either* weighing *or* raising from water (hence **weyng of an old mucke boote**)

whelewright a maker or repairer of wheels

whypcord thin, tough cord made of hemp

Whyte Fryers the Carmelite friary to the north of the river Wensum

whyte hede nayle nails with highly polished heads, used for decoration in upholstery work

whytyng *either* whitewash *or* the application of whitewash

woldes *either* bindings of strong twine *or* clamps made of iron (hence **woldes for stagynges** for use in the erection of scaffolding)

wolman a dealer in wool or wool merchant

workehowse a workshop or place for making things

worsted cloth woven from closely twisted yarn originally produced in the Worstead area of Norfolk and a major component of Norwich's economy (hence **worsted weuers** or weavers specialising in its production)

wose mud, sediment or slime (hence **wose brycke** or thick tiles or bricks for use in the bottom of wells and deep gutters)

wracke, wrecke weeds

wrestlyng, wrostlyn place a booth or temporary structure set up annually at Whitsuntide for public wrestling matches

wryte a wright or skilled craftsman, such as a mason or carpenter

wullen weuers weavers of woollen cloth, as opposed to **worsted**

wyndbemys wind-beams or cross-beams connecting and supporting the principal rafters in a roof (*see also* **copyll sparrys**)

wyndowe stalles window frames

wyne sacke dry white wine, usually from Spain

x^th *see* **tenth**

yarde wonde a measuring rod (usually of brass) one yard long

yche each

yeldehall *see* **guyldhalle**

yerde an enclosed area or yard

yle the aisle of a church

ylle money counterfeit or debased coinage

ypocras a restorative cordial of wine and spices named after the Greek physician, Hippocrates

yrons shackles used to restrain prisoners

yron stonys cannon balls

Ytalyon wastes *see* **doblette**

Saints' days, festivals and other dates

Annuncyacon the Annunciation of the Blessed Virgin Mary, 25 March

Assencon, Assenssyon weke the week in which Ascension Day (the Thursday 40 days after Easter) fell

Bartylmewtyde the feast of St Bartholomew (Seynt Bartylmewe), 24 August, and the days before and after

Candylmes Candlemas, 2 February

Clene Lent *Quadragesima pura*, the forty days of Lent as reckoned from Ash Wednesday

Clensyng weke the week before the start of Lent, in which sins were confessed

Corpus Christi the Thursday after Trinity Sunday and a major feast in the liturgical year

Crouchemaes Chrouchmas, 14 September

Dome weke the week before Easter

Ester evyn the Saturday immediately before Easter Sunday

Estern Easter Sunday

Estern term the law term beginning seventeen days after Easter Sunday and ending on, or before, the day after Ascension

Ester weke the week after Easter

Hallowmes, Halomes Day Hallowmas or All Saints, 1 November

Hillary term the Hilary law term beginning on 20 January and ending before the start of Lent

Imber weke byfore Crystmes the week containing the Wednesday, Thursday and Saturday after St Lucy (13 December), these being the Ember Days of Advent

Lames, Lammes Lammas Day, 1 August

Mandy Thursday Maundy Thursday, the Thursday before Easter

Mary Magdalen the feast of St Mary Magdalen, 22 July

Mydlent Sonday the fourth Sunday in Lent

Mydlent weke the week in the middle of Lent

Mydsomer Midsummer Day, 24 June, and the days around it

Mydsomer terme more commonly Trinity term, the law term beginning on the octave of Trinity (and from 1541 a week earlier) and ending on 8 July

Myhelmes, Mighelmes Michaelmas, 29 September

Myhelmes terme the law term beginning on 6 October and ending on 25 November

Owur Lady, Owur Lady Day unless otherwise noted the Annunciation, 25 March

Owur Lady Assumpcon the Assumption of the Blessed Virgin Mary, 15 August

Owur Lady Natiuite the birth of the Blessed Virgin Mary, 8 September

Owur Ladys quarter the Annunciation, 25 March, one of the four quarter-days on which rents were often due

Palme Sonday weke and **Passyon weke** contrary to Cheney (*Handbook of Dates for Students of English History*, p. 58), Passion week is treated as the week *after* Passion Sunday (the fifth Sunday in Lent), followed by Palm Sunday week (the week before Easter)

Pencost Pentecost (see **Whyte Sonday**)

Puryfycacon of Owur Lady the Purification of the Blessed Virgin Mary, 2 February

Relycke Sonday the third Sunday after Midsummer Day

Rogacon weke the week in which the Rogation Days, the Monday, Tuesday and Wednesday before Ascension Day, fall

Seynt Andrew St Andrew, 30 November

Seynt Faythe St Faith, 6 October

Seynt George St George, 23 April, a major festival in Norwich

Seynt Jamys St James, 25 July

Seynt Luke St Luke, 18 October

Seynt Nicholas, Nycholas St Nicholas, 6 December

Seynt Peter in Norwich the feast of St Peter *ad vincula*, 1 August, rather than *in cathedra in Antiochia*, 22 February

Seynt Stephyn St Stephen, 26 December

Seynt Symond St Simon, 28 October

Shroft Monday Shrove Monday, the day before Shrove Tuesday and thus the last Monday before the start of Lent

Shroftyde the Sunday, Monday and Tuesday before Ash Wednesday, when sins were confessed before Lent

Sonday in lxx Septuagesima Sunday, the third Sunday before Ash Wednesday

Trynyte evyn the Saturday immediately before Trinity Sunday

Trynyte Sonday the Sunday next after Whit-Sunday (Pentecost)

Twelthe the twelfth day after Christmas, the feast of the Epiphany, 6 January

Whyte Sonday Whit-Sunday (Pentecost), the seventh Sunday after Easter

Wytsontyde Whitsuntide, the period comprising Whit-Sunday, -Monday and -Tuesday

Wytson weke the week following Whit-Sunday

Bibliography

A. Manuscript sources

The National Archives (TNA) Kew
PC2/1; PROB 11/11/565, 11/16/551, 11/24/3, 11/26/282, 11/30/434, 11/32/288, 11/38/85; SP1/72, 136, 137, 150

The Norfolk Record Office (NRO)
Boileau Collection (BOI): 154/1, extent of Robert Raynbald's holdings in Ketteringham, etc, 1558
Dean and Chapter of Norwich (DCN): 69/2, register of wills and administrations, 1461–1559
Gillingham estate papers (GIL): 1/183, 184, conveyances of land in Toft Monks, 1535, 1537
Norwich City Records (NCR): 4A/12/54–5, deeds of the parish of St Vedast, 1550; 5A/1, sheriff's tourn, Wymer, 1541; 5D/2, sheriff's tourn, Conesford, 1550; 7A/1–43, treasurers' account rolls, 1293–1436; 7A/44–76, chamberlains' account rolls, 1457–1524; 7 I/18, alien subsidy return, 1540; 8G/10, William Clarke's notes on St George's guild, 1731; 8K/7(b), receipt for the purchase of Blackfriars, 1540; 9E/4–5, litigation over the city's water mills, 1481–2; 9G/7, draft composition in the city's dispute with the cathedral priory, 1524; 9H/11, 12, material relating to litigation over Trowse Milgate, 1544–53; 11G/1/1, foreign receiver's account, n.d.; 15F/7, indenture tripartite regarding the chamberlains' duties, 1449; 16A/3–5, mayors' court books, 1534–49; 16C/2, assembly minute book, 1510–50; 16D/1, 2, assembly proceedings, 1484–91, 1491–1553; 17B/3, *Liber Albus*, 1194–1638; 17D/1, First Book of Apprenticeship Registers, 1447–58; 18A/1, treasurers' account book, 1384–1448; 18A/2–8, chamberlains' account books, 1470–1567; 18D/13, clavors' accounts, 1550–1601; 24A/23, Great Hospital account roll, 1549–50; 24C/20/7, 9, accounts of the bailiffs of Barnham Hawkins, 1543–1645, and of expenses sustained in a lawsuit there, 1545
Norwich Consistory Court (NCC): probate registers Cawston, Corant, Goldingham, Hyll, Mingaye, Popy, Spyltymber, Veysye, Walpole
Townshend and other papers (BRA): 926/109, conveyance of property in Thwaite, 1525

B. Primary printed sources

Bird, W.H.B., ed., *The Black Book of Winchester* (Winchester, 1925)

Brewer, J.S., and others, eds, *Calendar of Letters and Papers Foreign and Domestic for the Reign of Henry VIII* (21 vols, and 2 vols of *Addenda*, 1862–1932)

Calendar of Charter Rolls, V, 1341–1417 (1916)

Calendar of Charter Rolls, VI, 1427–1516 (1927)

Corder, J., ed., *The Visitation of Suffolk 1561 Made by William Hervy* (2 parts, Harleian Society, new series, 2 and 3, 1981, 1984)

Cronne, H.A., ed., *Bristol Charters 1378–1499* (Bristol Record Society, xi, 1946)

Dashwood, G.H., ed., *Visitation of Norfolk in the Year 1563* (2 vols, Norwich, 1878, 1895)

Dobson, R.B., ed., *York City Chamberlains' Account Rolls 1396–1500* (Surtees Society, cxcii, 1978–9)

Fay, I., ed., 'The Norwich River and Street Accounts, 1557–61 and 1570–80', in E. Phillips and I. Fay, eds, *Health and Hygiene in Early-Modern Norwich* (NRS, lxxvii, 2013)

Fraser, C.M., ed., *The Accounts of the Chamberlains of Newcastle upon Tyne 1508–1511* (Society of Antiquaries of Newcastle upon Tyne, records series, iii, 1987)

Fox, F.F., ed., *Adams's Chronicle of Bristol* (Bristol, 1910)

Galloway, D., ed., *Records of Early English Drama: Norwich 1540–1642* (Toronto, 1984)

Grace, M., ed., *Records of the Gild of St George in Norwich, 1389–1547* (NRS, ix, 1937)

Harrington, D., and Hyde, P., eds, *The Early Town Books of Faversham c. 1251–1581* (Chippenham, 2008)

Howlett, R., ed., 'A Fabric Roll of the Norwich Guildhall', *NA*, 15 (1904), pp. 164–89

Hudson, W.H., and Tingey, J.C., eds, *Records of the City of Norwich* (2 vols, Norwich, 1906, 1910)

Hughes, P.L., and Larkin, J.F., eds, *Tudor Royal Proclamations: Volume 1, The Early Tudors (1485–1553)* (New Haven and London, 1964)

Johnson, C., ed. and trans., *Dialogus de scaccario: The Course of the Exchequer*, revised by F.E.L. Carter and D.E. Greenway (Oxford, 1983)

Johnson, G., ed., 'Chronological Memoranda Touching the City of Norwich', *NA*, 1 (1847), pp. 140–66

Latham, R.C., ed., *Bristol Charters 1509–1899* (Bristol Record Society, xii, 1947)

Livock, D.M., ed., *City Chamberlains' Accounts in the Sixteenth and Seventeenth Centuries* (Bristol Record Society, xxiv, 1966)

Luders, A., and others, eds, *Statutes of the Realm* (11 vols, 1812–28)

Masters, B.R., ed., *Chamber Accounts of the Sixteenth Century* (London Record Society, x, 1984)

Millican, P., ed., *The Musters Returns for Divers Hundreds in the County of Norfolk, 1569, 1572, 1574 and 1577, II* (NRS, vi, 1936)

Raine, A., ed., *York Civic Records, I* (Yorkshire Archaeological Society, Record Series, xcviii, 1939)

—, ed., *York Civic Records, IV* (Yorkshire Archaeological Society, Records Series, cviii, 1945)

Rodgers, M., and Wallace, M., eds, *Norwich Landgable Assessment 1568–70* (NRS, lxiii, 1999)

Rye, W., ed., *Calendar of the Freemen of Norwich from 1317 to 1603* (1888)

Sharpe, R.R., ed., *Calendar of Letter-Books of the City of London: Letter-Book A* (1899)

—, *Calendar of Letter-Books of the City of London: Letter-Book L* (1912)

Stevenson, W.H., ed., *Records of the Borough of Nottingham, III, 1485–1547* (1885)

Watkin, A., ed., *Inventory of Church Goods temp. Edward III* (2 parts, NRS, xix, 1947–8)

Vowell, *alias* Hooker, John, *The Description of the Citie of Excester, III*, ed. W. J. Harte and others (Devon and Cornwall Record Society, xiv, 1919)

C. Secondary printed sources

Ayers, B., 'Post-Medieval Archaeology in Norwich: A Review', *Post-Medieval Archaeology*, 25 (1991), pp. 1–23

—, *Norwich: Archaeology of a Fine City* (Cirencester, 2009)

—, 'Status, Power and Values: Archaeological Approaches to Understanding the Medieval Urban Community', in A. Falk, U. Müller and M. Schneider eds, *Lübeck und der Hanseraum: Beiträge zu Archäologie und Kulturgeschichte* (Lübeck, 2014)

Baker, J., *The Men of Court 1440 to 1550: A Prosopography of the Inns of Court and Chancery and the Courts of Law* (2 vols, Selden Society, supplementary series, 18, 2012)

Barringer, C., 'The Changing Face of Norwich', in C. Rawcliffe and R. Wilson, eds, *Norwich since 1550* (2004)

Barron, C., *London in the Later Middle Ages; Government and People 1200–1500* (Oxford, 2004)

Bindoff, S.T., ed., *History of Parliament: The Commons, 1509–1558* (3 vols, 1982)

Blomefield, F., *An Essay towards a Topographical History of the County of Norfolk* (11 vols, 1805–10)

Bowden, P., 'Agricultural Prices, Farm Profits, and Rents', in J. Thirsk, ed., *The Agrarian History of England and Wales, IV, 1500–1640* (Cambridge, 1967)

Brigstocke Sheppard, J., 'The Records of the City of Canterbury', *Historical Manuscripts Commission, IX, Part 1* (1883)

Brooks, F.W., 'York – 1066 to Present Day', in A.L. Stacpoole, ed., *The Noble City of York* (York, 1972)

Campbell, J., *Historic Towns: Norwich* (1975)

Carter, A., 'The Site of Dussindale', *NA*, 39 (1987), pp. 54–62

Challis, C.E., *The Tudor Coinage* (Manchester, 1978)

Cheney, C.R., revised Jones, M., *A Handbook of Dates for Students of British History* (Cambridge, 2000)

Clark, L., ed., *The History of Parliament: The Commons 1422–1461* (7 vols, Cambridge, 2019)

Connor, R.D., *The Weights and Measures of England* (1987)

Danbury, E., 'The Decoration and Illumination of Royal Charters in England, 1250–1509: An Introduction', in M. Jones and M. Vale, eds, *England and her Neighbours 1066–1453: Essays in Honour of Pierre Chaplais* (1989)

Dietz, F., *English Public Finance 1485–1558* (Urbana, Illinois, 1920)

Duffy, E., *The Stripping of the Altars: Traditional Religion in England 1400–1580* (New Haven and London, 1992)

Dunn, I., and Sutermeister, H., *The Norwich Guildhall: A History and Guide* (Norwich, n.d.)

Dunn, P., 'Trade', in C. Rawcliffe and R. Wilson, eds, *Medieval Norwich* (2004)

Erler, M., *Women, Reading, and Piety in Late Medieval England* (Cambridge, 2002)

Faye, I., *Health and the City: Disease, Environment and the Government of Norwich, 1200–1575* (Woodbridge, 2015)

Ffoulkes, C., *The Gun-Founders of England* (Cambridge, 1937)

Godfrey, W.H., and Wagner, A., *The College of Arms, Queen Victoria Street* (1963)

Grace, M., 'The Chamberlains and Treasurers of the City of Norwich, 1293–1835', *NA*, 25 (1935), pp. 181–201

Greatrex, J., *Biographical Register of the English Cathedral Priories of the Province of Canterbury c. 1066–1540* (Oxford, 1997)

Green, C., 'Becket's Chapel, Norwich', *NA*, 33 (1965), pp. 298–309

Griffiths, P., 'Bodies and Souls in Norwich: Punishing Petty Crime, 1540–1700', in P. Griffiths and S. Devereaux, eds, *Penal Practice and Culture 1500–1900* (Basingstoke, 2003)

Gunn, S., *Henry VII's New Men and the Making of Tudor England* (Oxford, 2016)

Harries, R., Cattermole, P., and Mackintosh, P., *A History of Norwich School* (Norwich, 1991)

Harrison, C.J., 'Grain Price Analysis and Harvest Qualities, 1465–1634', *Agricultural History Review*, 19 (1971), pp. 135–55

Hawes, T., ed., *An Index to Norwich City Officers* (NRS, lii, 1986)

Hawkyard, A., *The House of Commons 1509–1558: Personnel, Procedure, Precedent and Change* (Oxford, 2016)

Head, D.M., *The Ebbs and Flows of Fortune: The Life of Thomas Howard, Third Duke of Norfolk* (1995)

Hildred, A., '"Brass" Guns', in *eadem*, ed., *Weapons of Warre: The Armaments of The Mary Rose* (The Archaeology of the Mary Rose, 3, Portsmouth, 2011)

Horn, J.M., ed., *Fasti ecclesiae Anglicanae 1541–1857, VII* (1992)

Hoskins, W.G., 'Provincial Towns in the Early Sixteenth Century', *Transactions of the Royal Historical Society*, fifth series, 6 (1956), pp. 1–19

Houlbrooke, R., 'Refoundation and Reformation, 1538–1628', in I. Atherton and others, eds, *Norwich Cathedral: Church, City and Diocese, 1096–1996* (1996)

Howard, M., 'Recycling the Monastic Fabric: Beyond the Act of Dissolution', in D. Gaimster and R. Gilchrist, eds, *The Archaeology of Reformation 1480–1580* (Leeds, 2003)

Hoyle, R., 'War and Public Finance', in D. MacCulloch, ed., *The Reign of Henry VIII: Politics, Policy and Piety* (1995)

Hudson, W., and Tingey, J.C., *Revised Catalogue of the Records of the City of Norwich* (Norwich, 1898)

James, S.E., *Kateryn Parr; The Making of a Queen* (Aldershot, 1999)

Jones, W.R.D., *The Tudor Commonwealth 1529–1559* (1970)

Kermode, J.I., 'Urban Decline? The Flight from Office in Late Medieval York', *Economic History Review*, new series, 35 (1982), pp. 179–98

King, C., 'The Interpretation of Urban Buildings: People, Meaning and Appropriation in Norwich Merchants' Houses, c. 1400–1660', *World Archaeology*, 41 (2009), pp. 471–88

Kirkpatrick, J., *The Streets and Lanes of the City of Norwich*, ed. W. Hudson (Norwich, 1889)

Knoop, D., and Jones, G.P., *The Mediaeval Mason* (Manchester, third edn, 1967)

Kumler, A., 'From Sacrament to Street Food', *Cabinet: A Quarterly of Art and Culture*, 58 (2016), pp. 63–71

Liddy, C.D., *Contesting the City: The Politics of Citizenship in English Towns 1250–1530* (Oxford, 2017)

Maddern, P., 'Order and Disorder', in C. Rawcliffe and R. Wilson, eds, *Medieval Norwich* (2004)

Masters, B.R., *The Chamberlain of the City of London 1237–1987* (1988)

MacCulloch, D., 'Kett's Rebellion in Context', *Past & Present*, 84 (1979), pp. 36–59

—, *Suffolk and the Tudors* (Oxford, 1986)

—, 'A Reformation in the Balance: Power Struggles in the Diocese of Norwich, 1533–1553', in C. Rawcliffe, R. Virgoe and R. Wilson, eds, *Counties and Communities: Essays on East Anglian History Presented to Hassell Smith* (Norwich, 1996)

—, *Thomas Cranmer* (1996)

—, *Thomas Cromwell: A Life* (2018)

McClendon, M.C., *The Quiet Reformation: Magistrates and the Emergence of Protestantism in Tudor Norwich* (Stanford, CA, 1999)

McRee, B.R., 'Peace-Making and its Limits in Medieval Norwich', *English Historical Review*, 109 (1994), pp. 831–66

—, 'The Mayor's Body', in L.E. Mitchell, K.L. French and D.L. Biggs, eds, *The Ties that Bind: Essays in Medieval British History in Honor of Barbara Hanawalt* (Farnham, 2011)

Matthew, H.C.G., ed., *The Oxford Dictionary of National Biography* (60 vols and index, Oxford, 2004)

Merriman, M.H., *The Rough Wooings: Mary Queen of Scots 1542–1551* (East Linton, 2000)

Moreton, C.E., *The Townshends and their World: Gentry, Law, and Land in Norfolk c. 1450–1551* (Oxford, 1992)

—, 'Mid-Tudor Trespass: A Break-In at Norwich', *English Historical Review*, 108 (1993), pp. 387–98

Nelson, A., *The Medieval English Stage: Corpus Christi Pageants and Plays* (Chicago, 1974)

Page, W., ed., *The Victoria History of the County of Norfolk, II* (1906; reprinted 1975)

—, *The Victoria History of the County of Suffolk, II* (1907; reprinted 1975)

Pelling, M., 'Health and Sanitation', in C. Rawcliffe and R. Wilson, *Norwich since 1550* (2004)

Pound, J., 'The Social and Trade Structure of Norwich, 1525–1575', *Past & Present*, 34 (1966), pp. 49–69

—, *Tudor and Stuart Norwich* (Chichester, 1988)

Priestley, U., *The Great Market: A Survey of Nine Hundred Years of Norwich Provision Market* (Norwich, 1987)

Rawcliffe, C., *The Hospitals of Medieval Norwich* (Norwich, 1995)

—, *Medicine for the Soul: The Life, Death and Resurrection of an English Medieval Hospital* (Stroud, 1999)

—, *Urban Bodies: Communal Health in Late Medieval English Towns and Cities* (Woodbridge, 2013)

Richardson, W.C., *History of the Court of Augmentations* (Baton Rouge, Louisiana, 1961)

Rodgers, M., *The River and Staithes of Tudor Norwich* (Norwich, 1996)

Russell, F.W., *Kett's Rebellion in Norfolk* (1859)

Rutledge, E., 'Introduction', in M. Rodgers and M. Wallace, eds, *Norwich Landgable Assessment 1568–70* (NRS, lxiii, 1999)

—, 'The Documentary Evidence', in P.A. Emery, ed., *Norwich Greyfrairs: Pre-Conquest Town and Medieval Friary* (East Anglian Archaeology, 120, 2007)

—, 'An Urban Environment: Norwich in the Fifteenth Century', *The Fifteenth Century*, 12 (2013), pp. 79–93

Rye, W., and Tillett, E.A., *An Account and Description of Carrow Abbey, Norwich* (Norwich, 1884)

Salzman, L.F., *Building in England down to 1540: A Documentary History* (Oxford, 1967)

Samuel, M.W., 'The Fifteenth-Century Garner at Leadenhall, London', *Antiquaries Journal*, 69 (1989), pp. 119–53

Scarisbrick, J.J., *Henry VIII* (1968)

Schofield, R., *Taxation under the Early Tudors 1485–1547* (Oxford, 2004)

Shepherd Popescu, E., *Norwich Castle: Excavations and Historical Survey, 1987–98, Part II: c. 1345 to Modern* (East Anglian Archaeology, 132, 2009)

Slack, P., *The Impact of Plague in Tudor and Stuart England* (1989)

Stephens, G.A., 'The Waits of the City of Norwich through Four Centuries to 1790', *NA*, 25 (1935), pp. 1–70

Sutermeister, H., *The Norwich Blackfriars* (Norwich, 1977)

Tanner, N., *The Church in Late Medieval Norwich* (Toronto, 1984)

Tillyard, M., 'The Acquisition by the Norwich Blackfriars of the Site for their Church c. 1310–1325', in U.M. Priestley, ed., *Men of Property: An Analysis of the Norwich Enrolled Deeds 1285–1311* (Norwich, 1983)

Tittler, R., 'For the "Re-Edification of Townes": The Rebuilding Statutes of Henry VIII', *Albion*, 22 (1990), pp. 591–605

—, 'Reformation, Resources and Authority in English Towns: An Overview', in P. Collinson and J. Craig, eds, *The Reformation in English Towns 1500–1640* (Basingstoke, 1998)

—, *The Reformation and the Towns in England: Politics and Political Culture c. 1540–1640* (Oxford, 1998)

Venn, J., and Venn, J.A., *Alumni Cantabrigiensis I* (4 vols, 1922–7)

Virgoe, R., 'The Earlier Knyvetts: The Rise of a Norfolk Gentry Family', *NA*, 41 (1990–93), pp. 249–78

Wood, A., 'Kett's Rebellion', in C. Rawcliffe and R. Wilson, eds, *Medieval Norwich* (2004)

—, *The 1549 Rebellion and the Making of Early Modern England* (Cambridge, 2007)

Yaxley, D., *A Researcher's Glossary of Words Found in Historical Documents of East Anglia* (Dereham, 2003)

D. Unpublished theses

Jansssen, C.A., 'The Waytes of Norwich in Medieval and Renaissance Pageantry' (University of New Brunswick, PhD thesis, 1977)

King, A., 'The Merchant Class and Borough Finances of Late Medieval Norwich' (2 vols, Oxford University D.Phil. thesis, 1989)

Index

Only the most common variants of names are given here; many more appear in the text.

Civic offices held in Norwich are indicated as follows: (A) alderman; (Au) auditor; (CC) common clerk; (CH) chamberlain; (CS) common sergeant; (FR) foreign receiver; (M) mayor; (R) recorder; (S) sheriff; (St) steward; (T) treasurer. Individuals who discharged several offices during their careers are identified by the one with which they are *first* associated in this volume. Further details of official appointments may be found in T. Hawes, *An Index to Norwich City Officers 1453–1835* (NRS, lii, 1986)

The designation 'tenant' indicates a lessee of civic property.

Places in Norfolk are designated (N); all places in the city of Norwich and adjacent to the walls are listed under 'Norwich: places', apart from the Blackfriars complex.